AF361256

TRANSFORMATION ON
THE SOUTHERN UKRAINIAN STEPPE

Letters and Papers of Johann Cornies

TRANSFORMATION ON THE SOUTHERN UKRAINIAN STEPPE

Letters and Papers of Johann Cornies

VOLUME III: 1843–1848

Translated by Ingrid I. Epp
Edited by Harvey L. Dyck, Ingrid I. Epp, and John R. Staples

UNIVERSITY OF TORONTO PRESS
Toronto Buffalo London

ISBN 978-1-4875-5881-9 (cloth)   ISBN 978-1-4875-5883-3 (EPUB)
ISBN 978-1-4875-5882-6 (PDF)

Tsarist and Soviet Mennonite Studies

Library and Archives Canada Cataloguing in Publication

Title: Transformation on the Southern Ukrainian steppe : letters and papers of Johann
Cornies / translated by Ingrid I. Epp ;
edited by Harvey L. Dyck, Ingrid I. Epp, and John R. Staples.
Names: Dyck, Harvey L. (Harvey Leonard), editor. | Staples, John Roy,
1961– editor. | Epp, Ingrid I. (Ingrid Ilse), translator, editor. |
Container of (work): Cornies, Johann, 1789–1848. Works. Selections. English.
Series: Tsarist and Soviet Mennonite studies.
Description: Series statement: Tsarist and Soviet Mennonite Studies |
Includes bibliographical references and indexes. | Contents: v. 3. 1843–1848. |
Translations from the German.
Identifiers: Canadiana (print) 20159035791 | Canadiana (ebook) 20250130912 |
ISBN 9781487558819 (v. 3 ; bound) | ISBN 9781487558826 (v. 3 ; EPUB) |
ISBN 9781487558833 (v. 3 ; PDF)
Subjects: LCSH: Cornies, Johann, 1789–1848. | LCSH: Cornies, Johann,
1789–1848—Correspondence. | LCSH: Germans—Ukraine, Southern—
Correspondence. | LCSH: Mennonites—Ukraine, Southern—Correspondence. |
LCSH: Germans—Ukraine, Southern—History—19th century. | LCSH: Mennonites—
Ukraine, Southern—History—19th century.
Classification: LCC DK508.425.G47 T73 2015 | DDC 940.2—dc23

Cover design: Val Cooke
Cover image: Henry B. Pauls, "The Suitor." Courtesy
of Anne Konrad and Harvey L. Dyck.

We wish to acknowledge the land on which the University of Toronto Press
operates. This land is the traditional territory of the Wendat, the Anishnaabeg, the
Haudenosaunee, the Métis, and the Mississaugas of the Credit First Nation.

This book has been published with the help of a grant from the Federation for the
Humanities and Social Sciences, through the Awards to Scholarly Publications Program,
using funds provided by the Social Sciences and Humanities Research Council of Canada.

University of Toronto Press acknowledges the financial support of the Government of
Canada, the Canada Council for the Arts, and the Ontario Arts Council, an agency of
the Government of Ontario, for its publishing activities.

Contents

List of Maps — vii

Preface — ix

Acknowledgments — xv

Translator's Note — xvii

Introduction — xxi

Correspondence

1843 — 3

1844 — 151

1845 — 237

1846 — 321

1847 — 425

1848 — 547

Appendix I: Genealogy of Johann Cornies's Immediate Family — 587

Appendix II: List of Correspondents — 589

Appendix III: Glossary — 595

Bibliography — 597

Index — 607

Maps

Map 1   Mennonite Settlements in New Russia   xviii

Map 2   The Molochnaia Mennonite Settlement   xix

Preface

The eighteenth and nineteenth centuries saw the grasslands of the world open to agricultural settlement. In places as diverse as Argentina, the United States, Canada, South Africa, and Russia, people travelled to "promised lands" dreaming of peace, plenty, and escape from their overcrowded homes. They came with the urging and support of governments that viewed the grasslands as both a ground-spring of national wealth and a tabula rasa upon which to create new moral orders and shape new national identities. This age of settler colonialism brought devastation to the Indigenous populations that occupied the supposed tabula rasa.

Russia's expansion east to Siberia and south onto the steppe was born of this vision, but in the south – "New Russia" as Catherine the Great named it – the Russian imperial project intersected with geopolitical realities that gave it unique shape. Beyond New Russia lay the Ottoman Empire, a powerful competitor with its own imperial ambitions. Expansion towards the Black Sea and Balkans meant certain conflict between the two great powers.

Geopolitics shaped the contours of Russia's colonial project, and southward expansion was a carefully managed affair, constrained by the need to create communities that could support the Russian military. The clearest examples were the "military colonies" of peasant conscripts, relocated with their families to the New Russian frontier and ordered to build their own villages and grow their own food, all under harsh military discipline.

The Russian administrative ideal was cameralism, a theory of centralized planning and tight control, administered through an obedient and well-trained bureaucracy. It relied in part upon providing models of "proper" behaviour to the Russian and Ukrainian peasants who moved to the empire's new territories. Russia actively recruited settlers from the German states as "model colonists" who could teach their progressive agricultural methods by example. Prussian Mennonites, renowned for their hard work and agricultural successes, became a central target for such recruitment.

The Mennonites who immigrated to the Russian Empire in the late eighteenth and early nineteenth centuries brought little with them beyond a deep-rooted Christian Anabaptist faith and a tradition of hard work. Settled in New Russia, they built villages, ploughed the rich prairie, and established model farmsteads. They built farm machinery, milled grain, and manufactured cloth, creating a bustling, prosperous community, that in the late nineteenth century led the way in Russia's nascent industrial revolution.

By 1914, Mennonites were also the target of Russian nationalist resentment, singled out for their German language, their unorthodox religious beliefs, and their prosperity. The First World War, and then the Revolution, brought confiscations and persecution. Those who could, fled; those who remained were impoverished and – when they clung to their faith – harried, imprisoned, and killed. By 1991, the Mennonites had become a "blank page" in Russian and Soviet history, unknown even to the people who occupied the homes they had once built. The surviving remnants in Siberia and Central Asia well knew to keep their beliefs to themselves.

The Russian Mennonite story remained alive in the émigré communities that had left Russia in successive waves beginning in the 1870s and continuing into the 1940s. They settled in Canada, the United States, and South America, built new villages, and transplanted their Russian successes – and religious disputes – to their new homelands.

The story that these Mennonites preserved was mainly one of faith and suffering. Filtered through their late Russian and Soviet experiences, it stressed their religious values and sense of community. It ignored (or did not understand) their role in the larger Russian story of colonization and economic development. This was true even in the work of secular historians, who were almost exclusively dependent on in-group Mennonite accounts.

This document collection addresses the first period of Mennonite settlement. It reveals the foundations of Russian Mennonite prosperity in their hard work, self-discipline, and entrepreneurial spirit. It likewise reveals the fermentation of religious beliefs in their community.

Significantly, it depicts a sometimes contentious, sometimes cooperative, constantly evolving relationship to surrounding peoples and the Russian state.

The collection unveils the Russian colonial world through the eyes of Johann Cornies and his many correspondents. Cornies was the leading figure in his community – an ambitious, entrepreneurial, and energetic reformer. He accrued great wealth and power, and he devoted himself to transforming New Russia. In Moscow, St. Petersburg, and the West, his keen mind and tremendous work ethic brought him acclaim. In the Mennonite community, it brought respect, but also deep hostility, as his reform plans – and his imperious manner – created controversy.

Johann Cornies's correspondence and studies offer a rich and varied feast. They depict a Russian colonial world where colonists could play a key role in shaping their own fate, and even gain influence in the highest levels of imperial power. They reveal a Mennonite community in which money and political connections sometimes competed, but sometimes worked hand in hand with tradition and religious authority. Not least, they open a window onto the personal life of a remarkable man.

This Volume

The selection, translation, and editing of Johann Cornies's papers has posed a series of significant challenges. Copies of Cornies's personal and business correspondence, along with the correspondence of the Molochnaia Forestry Society and Agricultural Society, are preserved in the Ukrainian State Archive of the Odesa Region, intermingled with other Mennonite records. Originally gathered by the Molochnaia Mennonite Peter J. Braun, the collection was seized by the Soviet government in 1929 and then disappeared. It was rediscovered in 1990, microfilmed, and distributed as the Peter J. Braun Russian Mennonite Archive to selected Western depositories in the mid-1990s by the University of Toronto's Research Program in Tsarist and Soviet Mennonite Studies.[1] Between the time of the Soviet seizure of the documents and their rediscovery, some documents disappeared (primarily during Germany's Second World War occupation of Ukraine), some were damaged beyond repair, and some were destroyed. Although what remains is not a complete collection, the tens of thousands of surviving pages provide a remarkable and coherent record of Mennonite life. In this published collection the material of the Braun archive has been supplemented with documents from other archives and collections in the former Soviet Union and elsewhere.

The vast majority of the documents are written in German gothic script, often as copies of originals hurriedly recorded by Cornies's various secretaries, but sometimes in Cornies's own crabbed hand. The handful of Russian-language documents are accompanied by German translations, while the German-language correspondence to Russian officials is usually accompanied by Russian translations. Reading the documents is sometimes difficult and occasionally almost impossible; their translation represents more than a decade of painstaking work by Ingrid I. Epp, whose knowledge of the contents of the collection (and of nineteenth-century Mennonite German orthography) was unequalled.

Not everything that Cornies wrote is insightful, interesting, or revealing, and not all of it merits publication. The editors have tried to select documents that reveal:

- administrative policies and practices of Cornies, and of local, regional, and central governments and organizations;
- religious beliefs and practices of Cornies himself, of Molochnaia Mennonites, and of their neighbours and contacts at home and abroad;
- influences on Cornies, whether religious, philosophical, administrative, or practical, and Cornies's religious, philosophical, administrative, and practical influence on people and organizations he came into contact with; and
- Cornies's personal life, including his interactions with friends and family.

Frequently Cornies wrote what amounted to form letters reporting on his activities and offering advice and recommendations to his friends and superiors. For example, Cornies's letters to Samuel Contenius and Andrei Fadeev are often very repetitive. One of the major tasks of the editors has been to select for publication what they regard as the most informative or clearest versions of such letters.

A second major challenge has been to select and include representative examples from the correspondence of the Forestry and Agricultural Societies, of which only a small percentage survives. Cornies chaired and actively administered these societies, and their correspondence clearly represents his activities and attitudes, so there can be no question that they belong in this collection. However, they are often highly repetitive, sometimes, for example, consisting of identical letters sent to each village in the Molochnaia settlement. The editors have selected representative samples of this correspondence that elucidate important society policies and initiatives, and document significant events.

The documents selected for inclusion in the collection have been rigorously edited. The editors' first principle has been to retain the literal meaning of the documents at all costs. Beyond this, significant editing has been necessary. German syntax does not translate easily into English, and nineteenth-century Mennonite syntax – sometimes constructed by writers with little formal education – is often tortuous. Consequently, long sentences have been shortened and confusing syntax has been simplified in the interests of clear communication. One of the greatest challenges has been to retain the documents' original tone. Cornies was painfully aware of the social and political hierarchies within which he operated, and his correspondence with those whom he recognized as his superiors is frequently couched in terms of fawning obeisance. This is particularly apparent in the paragraph-long salutations that begin many of Cornies's letters, and their length and repetitively formulaic nature have led us to sharply abbreviate them, while retaining titles and attempting to replicate the signifiers of rank and status that appear in the body of the letters. Those readers for whom such signifiers are essential will have to turn to the originals.

The division of the collection into three volumes is necessitated by its sheer size. The dividing points are based on the quantity of correspondence, but they are not otherwise arbitrary. Volume 1 ends in February 1836, on the eve of the creation of the Molochnaia Mennonite Agricultural Society. Volume 2 ends in 1842 with Cornies's report on the Mennonite community's progress at the end of a tumultuous year of internal disputes climaxing in the Warkentin Affair. The last of the four ethnographic studies published in Volume 1 is undated, but was certainly written after May 1836. It is included in Volume 1 in order to keep Cornies's major ethnographic writings together.

NOTE

1 Harvey L. Dyck and Ingrid I. Epp, *The Peter J. Braun Russian Mennonite Archive, 1803–1920: A Research Guide* (Toronto: University of Toronto Press, 1996).

Acknowledgments

This project was made possible by the 1990 opening to scholarly study of previously secret collections in Soviet archives. One such collection in the Ukrainian State Archive of the Odesa Region, entitled "Mennonite Society in the County of Berdiansk," contained a rich collection of letters and papers of Johann Cornies, a leader in the settlement and transformation of the New Russia frontier (today southern Ukraine). A selection from this and other sources constitutes the basis for the three volumes of this project.

We are deeply grateful to Vladimir Malchenko, then director of the Odesa Archive, and Olga Konovalova, his associate, for drawing to our attention the existence of these sources, for guiding us through their intricacies and organization, and for agreeing to and overseeing their microfilming.

For their encouragement and assistance at every stage of our work, and for providing space, we thank Carol Moore, past chief librarian, University of Toronto Libraries, and her colleagues: Larry Langford, head of access and information; Karen Turko, head of microtext; and Jim Ingram, microtext specialist. Richard Ratzlaff, our then editor at the University of Toronto Press, cheerfully oversaw the creation of the first volume, while editor Stephen Shapiro has overseen the creation of the second and third volumes.

Translator's Note

The source of most of the Johann Cornies correspondence and other documents is the Peter J. Braun Russian Mennonite Archive housed in the State Archive of the Odesa Region in Ukraine. They were gleaned by checking the microfilm of the somewhat disorganized files of the first half of the Braun Archive, and cover the years 1812 to 1848, the period of Cornies's activity.

All of the German documents are written in the German Gothic script then in use, many of them in a careful, regular hand. Others were obviously dashed off or written by someone with limited practice in writing. The documents themselves show many personal styles and personalities and it is regrettable that these cannot be conveyed adequately without turning the translations into quaint documents. Russian-language documents in Cornies's papers are always accompanied by German translations, and the German versions have been used throughout this collection.

Transliteration methods have been as direct as possible. The spelling of German names has not been changed but Russian names have been spelled in the Library of Congress style of transliteration from Russian into English. The reference for the spelling of Mennonite village names is the map reproduced in Franz Issac's *Die Molotschnaer Mennoniten*. Names of organizations have been translated into English, for example, "Agricultural Society" for "*Wirtschaftlicher Verein*." Titles of German publications are given in German with the literal English translation following in parentheses. Sometimes translations could not be found for individual terms – often either terms of local application, or terms transferred from Russian – and in these cases the translator has made an attempt to convey the sense of the sentence, sometimes including the term in the document in square brackets.

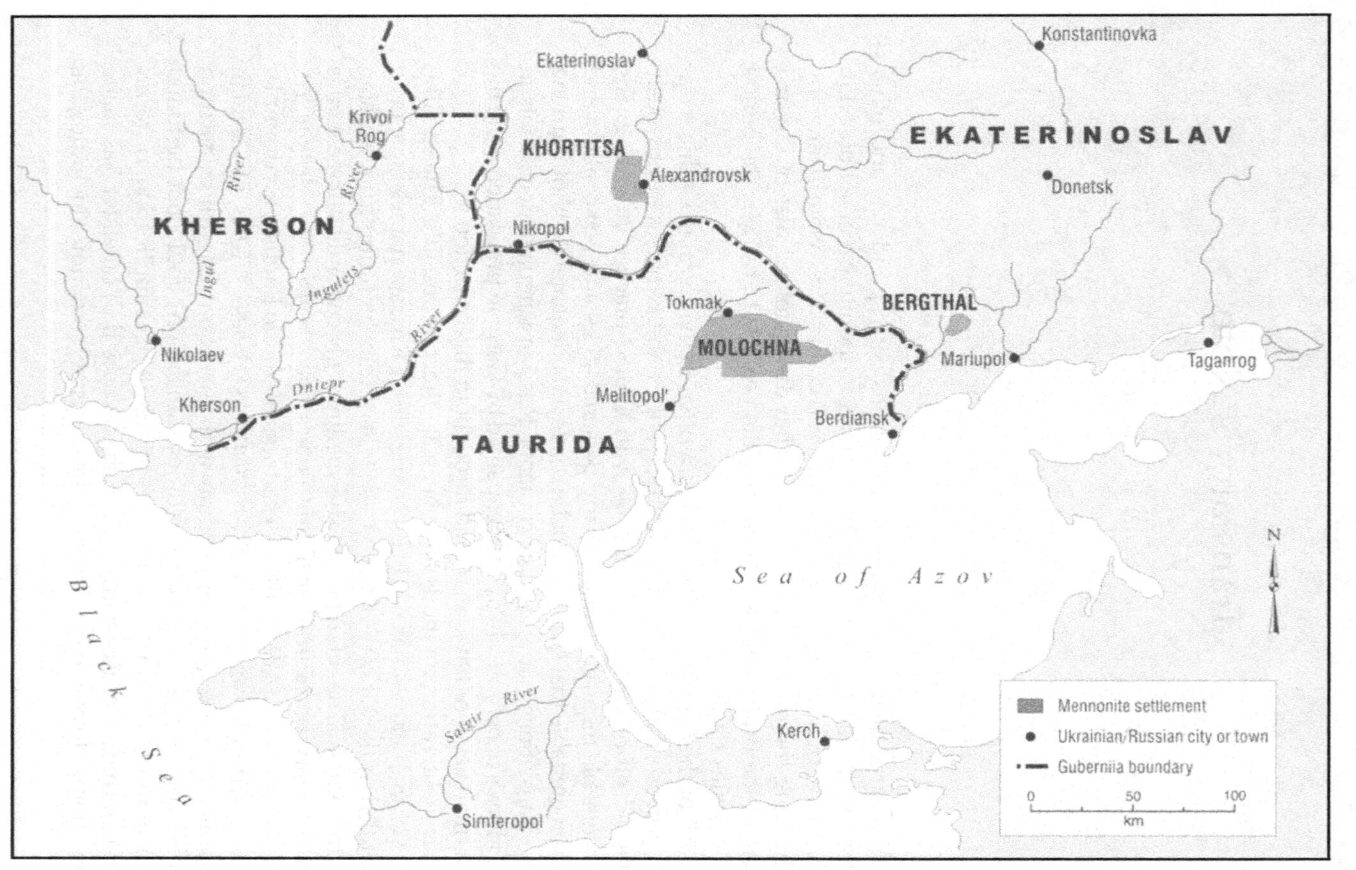

Map 1. Mennonite Settlements in New Russia. Harvey L. Dyck, trans. and ed., *A Mennonite in Russia: The Diaries of Jacob D. Epp, 1851–1880* (Toronto: University of Toronto Press, 1991).

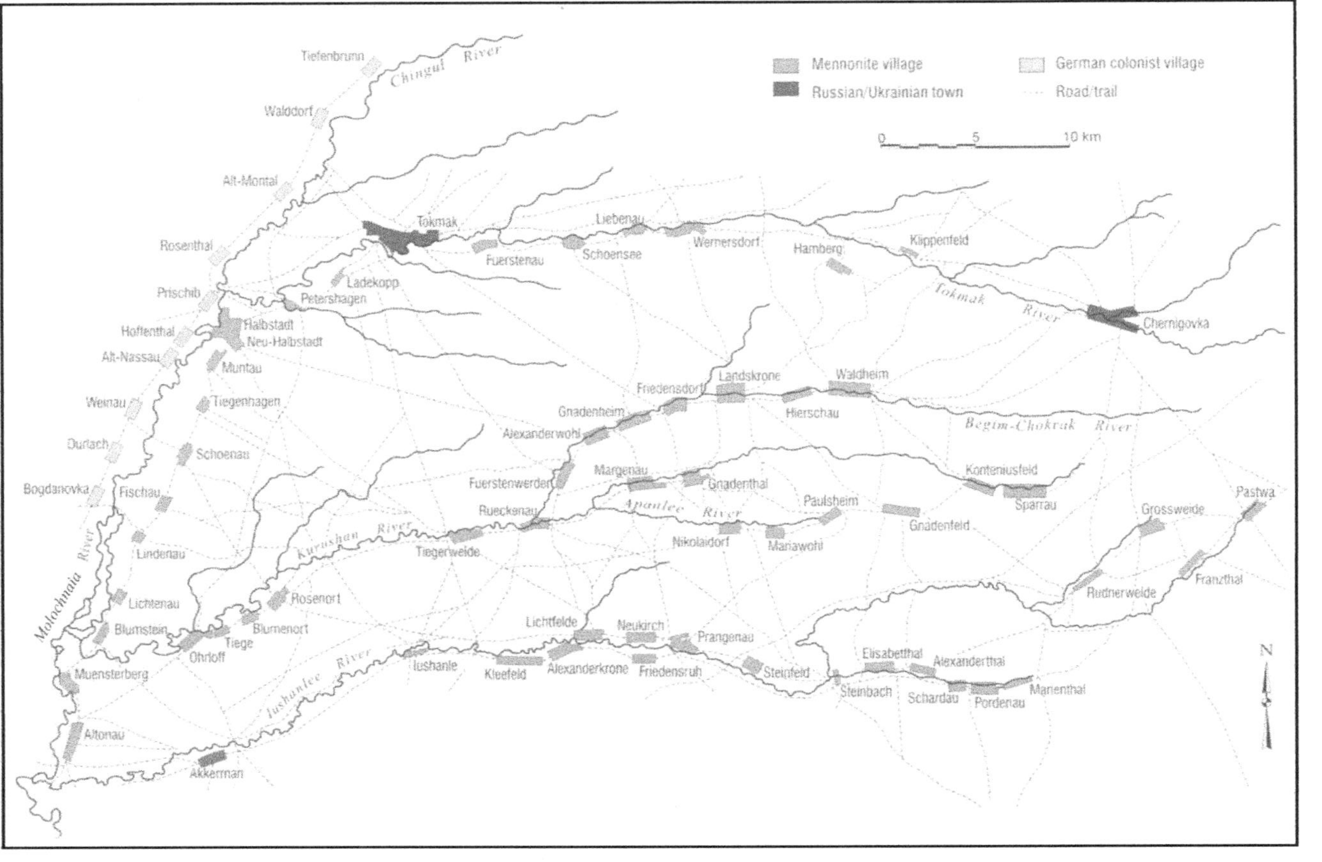

Map 2. The Molochnaia Mennonite Settlement. William Schroeder and Helmut Huebert, eds., *Mennonite Historical Atlas*, 2nd ed. (Winnipeg: Springfield Publishers, 1996). Used with permission.

Introduction

John R. Staples

Johann Cornies played a central role in the Mennonite community that settled along the Molochnaia River in southern Ukraine beginning in 1804. He used his keen understanding of the economic and environmental conditions of his region, his wealth, and his broad contacts in the Russian administration to help his community survive and flourish in times of internal strife, administrative shifts, and harvest failures. His extensive correspondence and studies provide a unique window into both the Mennonite community and the administrative world of the Russian colonial periphery in the first half of the nineteenth century.

Volume 1 of this three-volume document collection traces Cornies's rise to prominence in his community and the formation of his broad network of official and unofficial contacts in Russia and abroad in the years 1811 to 1836. Volume 2 covers the period from the creation of the Molochnaia Mennonite Agricultural Society in 1836 through the Warkentin Affair in 1842, which rocked the Mennonite settlement and pushed it to the precipice of a potential religious and political catastrophe. Cornies's complete political victory in 1842 left him free to pursue his most ambitious reforms, which are documented in Volume 3.

Cornies's power and influence faced no serious challenges after 1842. He expanded the authority of the Agricultural Society, reaching well beyond its official purview. In 1846 the society took control of education in both the Molochnaia and Khortitsa settlements, and in 1847 Cornies began overseeing the Khortitsa Mennonite Agricultural Society.[1] At the same time he increasingly acted as an agent of the Ministry of State Domains, supervising and advising on state projects that extended beyond his own Molochnaia community. These included apprenticeship programs for state peasants, a large-scale effort to promote potatoes in state peasant villages, and experimentation with a range of crops on behalf of the Ministry. In 1842 the Guardianship Committee asked Cornies to take over supervision of the Mennonite's Bergthal settlement near Mariupol, a daughter settlement of the Khortitsa settlement.[2] In 1843 the Committee asked him to step in and help resolve problems in the Württemberg settlement, a German colonist settlement just east of the Molochnaia.[3] In one of his last official roles, in 1846–7 he closely consulted on a project to create the so-called *Judenplan* villages, mixed Mennonite and Jewish villages that were established beginning in 1847.[4]

The demands on Cornies's time exhausted him, and by late 1847 his health was failing. He died at the age of 56, in March 1848. He left an important legacy of reform that helped place the Mennonites at the forefront of Russian modernization by the mid-nineteenth century. This justified the Mennonites' privileged status at a time when the state was circumscribing the rights of other ethnocultural and ethno-religious minorities. But Cornies's legacy was also one of controversies and deep divisions within the Mennonite community, as he increasingly became an agent of the state, intervening in Mennonite religious disputes and imposing his own sense of order on an often-disgruntled community.

By the time of his death Cornies was powerful, influential, and widely known in Russia. He met Tsar Alexander I and Tsar Nicholas I. Grand Prince Alexander, the future tsar, dined at his home in 1837. Pavel Kiselev, Nicholas's powerful Minister of State Domains, visited Cornies and corresponded with him about regional and empire-wide issues. Nikolai Miliutin, the most important architect of Russia's Great Reforms in the 1860s, visited and consulted with Cornies about peasant affairs. August von Haxthausen, author of a hugely influential nineteenth-century account of Russian peasant life, stayed at Cornies's home and described him as "one of the most influential men in Southern Russia."[5]

It is Cornies's integration into these broad and varied networks that makes him such a valuable window onto the Russian imperial project in the first half of the nineteenth century. Russian imperial policy is conventionally portrayed as contingent, constantly adapting to the remarkable diversity of the empire, cutting deals with local elites, and seeking little more than security, stability, and revenues. Willard Sunderland, in his influential study of Russian settlement of the steppe, shows that from the perspective of the imperial metropole the occupation of New Russia was at most ambiguously "colonial," and that in practical terms

Russian leaders often perceived the region as an extension of the Russian metropole.[6] Kelly O'Neill, writing of Russia's absorption of the Crimea, echoes Sunderland, suggesting that the southern part of the empire was not "the product of a binary relationship ... but ... an arrangement of interrelationships – a topology capable of stretching and bending, growing compact or attenuating, defined by connection rather than rupture."[7] John LeDonne labels the process an expansion of the Russian core.[8] Cornies, observing from a small corner of the periphery, shows one extreme of this ambiguous situation, for the use of the Mennonite settlement as a laboratory of modernity was emphatically colonial, and by the second quarter of the nineteenth century it reveals a hardening of the lines of demarcation between metropole and periphery.[9]

One of the particular values of the Mennonite case is that it *permits* such a deeper look at the evolution of imperial policy in the first half of the nineteenth century. Russia's interaction with its colonial subjects is largely written from the perspective of the imperial centre, often the only source of documentary evidence. In contrast, Cornies kept voluminous records, both of his correspondence with imperial bureaucrats and of his workaday administrative activities. Through his eyes we gain a unique view, from the periphery, of the central policies that evolved over the reigns of Alexander I and Nicholas I. These policies began as local and contingent but beginning in Alexander's last years and increasingly under Nicholas they coalesced into a national vision.

Volume 1: Before 1836

The introduction to Volume 1 of this series provides a full overview of Cornies's life and times, while the introduction to Volume 2 provides a more detailed overview of the period from 1836–42; the present introduction briefly summarizes the period covered by these first two volumes. Cornies, his brothers Peter and David, and his sister Katherina (1800–8) immigrated to New Russia with their parents, Johann Sr. and Aganetha, in 1805; a fourth brother, Heinrich, was born shortly after their arrival. The family settled in the Molochnaia Mennonite settlement along the Molochnaia River just south of present-day Melitopol.[10] The Molochnaia, a semi-arid steppe region with rich black soil, was on Russia's colonial frontier. It was peopled by semi-nomadic Nogai Tatars and by other peasant newcomers, including Lutherans and Catholics from the German states and Ukrainian and Russian peasants from the Russian empire's interior provinces.

The Mennonites were exceptional agriculturalists, recruited by Russia because of their reputation as hard-working and progressive subjects. They were fleeing the Prussian state's increasingly intrusive demands. The pacifist Mennonites feared that Prussia would impose military obligations on them that were incompatible with their religious beliefs. They negotiated a *Privilegium* with the tsar that carefully defined their rights to land and religious freedoms, including an exemption from military service, in exchange for their obligation to serve as a model for other colonists in the region.[11] This was a good bargain for both parties – within fifteen years the Molochnaia Mennonite settlement had gained the reputation of an "oasis on the steppe" where grain fields, orchards, and herds of cattle and sheep flourished in an otherwise apparently barren region.[12]

The Cornies family acquired a fullholding – a sixty-five-*desiatina* land allotment – in the village of Ohrloff on the southern edge of the settlement. Johann, the eldest son, soon went to work at the village flour mill, and then became a small trader carting butter and cheese to markets in Crimea. In 1811 he took advantage of a government program to encourage sheep-breeding and leased a swathe of pasture just east of Ohrloff along the Iushanle River. With his profits from sheep he partnered with his friend Wilhelm Martens to buy the regional brandy monopoly, which gave them control of the distribution of all spirits in the region. By 1817 he owned one of the largest sheep herds in the region, had purchased his own fullholding in Ohrloff, and was moderately wealthy.[13]

Along with Cornies's economic success came community respect, reflected in his 1817 appointment as the settlement's land surveyor. This was an important position, for beginning in 1818 a second wave of immigrants began to arrive from Prussia. The Mennonites appointed Cornies to the Settlement Commission, where he played a key role in choosing new village sites. This marked the beginning of his engagement with community affairs and led to his first contact with officials on the Guardianship Committee.[14]

The new immigrants brought with them from Prussia new experiences and ideas, including a Pietist sensibility that was controversial in the religiously conservative Molochnaia.[15] Cornies, who had close contact with the new immigrants due to his role on the Settlement Commission, welcomed their more worldly attitudes. This was reflected in his expanding role in the community: in 1820 he was one of the founding members of the Christian School Society, and in 1821 he helped form a

Molochnaia chapter of the Russian Bible Society, an offshoot of the British and Foreign Bible Society.

Conservative Mennonites viewed these new organizations as dangerous innovations, and their creation helped spark a deep division in the settlement. Conservatives believed that the original Mennonite congregation – the Flemish congregation – was too accommodating to the Pietist newcomers, and in 1824 they formed the Large Flemish Congregation under the leadership of Jacob Warkentin. More than half the Molochnaia Mennonites joined the new congregation.[16]

Warkentin now became a powerful figure both religiously and politically, and he and Cornies became bitter enemies. Warkentin used his position to influence elections for positions in the *Gebietsamt* (the elected settlement administration) and resisted religious innovation.[17] In particular he was an implacable opponent of the School Society, which he saw as a beachhead for secularism.

In 1823 the Guardianship Committee appointed Cornies Chairman of a newly created Wool Improvement Society – commonly called the Sheep Society – as part of its effort to promote economic reforms in the region. Usually Russian agricultural societies were voluntary organizations that linked the government and private sectors and were intended to promote economic modernization.[18] However, in the Molochnaia most Mennonites came to see them as direct agents of state authority. Cornies's work with the Committee in the Wool Improvement Society and later with the Forestry and Agricultural Societies (discussed below) heightened the tensions between him and Warkentin, who believed that Mennonites ought to take no role in the state's administrative apparatus.

The conflict between Cornies and Warkentin experienced its first crisis in 1826, when the Guardianship Committee asked the Mennonite Gebietsamt to send Cornies to Saxony to buy pure-bred merino sheep. The Committee expected the Mennonites to pay for the trip and the sheep from community funds, arguing that the improved wool from the sheep would soon pay for the expenses. To the dismay of both the Committee and Cornies, the Gebietsamt flatly refused. A furious and embarrassed Cornies resigned his position as land surveyor and went to Saxony on his own. This conflict marked the end of Cornies's attempt to work for change through the Gebietsamt as well as the beginning of nearly a decade of Warkentin's dominance in the Molochnaia.

Cornies returned to the Molochnaia in October 1827 and soon after fell seriously ill. The trip and his illness and convalescence removed him from community affairs for almost a year. When he returned to health in mid-1828 he focused his attention on his own business affairs. He remained chair of the Sheep Society and secretary of the School Society, but for a time he steered clear of settlement politics.

Warkentin's victory in Molochnaia Mennonite politics had potential consequences beyond the settlement. Tsar Nicholas I's ascension to the Russian throne in 1825 was met by the Decembrist Revolt, and while the revolt quickly fizzled, his reign was marked from the outset by repression of the "Western" ideas he associated with the rebels.[19] In the short term this did not mean much for Mennonites or other foreign colonists, for Nicholas's fears were focused on elites. For Russian officialdom, on the other hand, there was a danger that the new broom might sweep clean. Nicholas ascended the throne determined to get a grip on the internal administration of the empire, which his predecessor Alexander I had neglected. Officials – ambitious ones especially – would need to demonstrate their loyalty and value to the new tsar.

Andrei Fadeev, the director of the regional office of the Guardianship Committee that oversaw the Mennonites, was ambitious, and he saw the Mennonites as his ticket to higher office.[20] He needed a progressive ally in the community, and Cornies, who had worked closely with the Guardianship Committee since the early 1820s, was the obvious choice. The Ministry of Internal Affairs provided Fadeev with an agenda in 1828 when it announced a new afforestation initiative.[21] In 1830 Fadeev sent a draft afforestation program to Cornies. It proposed bypassing the Gebietsamt and creating a Forestry Society funded by the Guardianship Committee and headquartered on Cornies's estate at Iushanle. Cornies was to be the new society's Chairman, and its other members would be his hand-picked allies.

Fadeev issued a charter creating the Molochnaia Mennonite Forestry Society in 1831.[22] It charged Cornies with creating a systematic afforestation program throughout the Molochnaia settlement. The Forestry Society became the success story that Fadeev needed in order to advance his career, and within a few years trees had become one of the Molochnaia settlement's signature achievements. The Forestry Society also launched Cornies back into Molochnaia politics and put him on a collision course with Warkentin.

The key political issue in the settlement was whether the Mennonites were to be an active or a passive model for other colonists. The Privilegium was ambiguous on this front. Russia recruited Mennonites to New Russia because they were already model agriculturalists, and their early successes consisted mainly of recreating their prosperous Prussian agricultural villages in Russia. When travellers raved about a Molochnaia "oasis on the steppe," it was this achievement they were praising. Warkentin and his supporters – the majority of Molochnaia fullholders (owners of a sixty-five-desiatina land allotment) in the 1830s – argued that Mennonites had fulfilled their bargain with the state. Their reward, defined by the Privilegium, was religious freedom, which they interpreted as the right to be left alone as a self-administered quietist religious community. The problem for Warkentin and his supporters was that Nicholas I did not share their interpretation of the Privilegium. He wanted more from his foreign colonists, and at the local level the creation of the Forestry Society foreshadowed the greater demands to come.

In December 1834 Nicholas appointed General Pavel Kiselev to his Secret Committee on Peasant Affairs, charging him with developing a plan to reform the state peasantry, a broad category that included the Mennonites. In 1836 the Secret Committee evolved into the Fifth Department of the Tsar's Own Chancellery, and in 1838 it became the Ministry of State Domains. Kiselev served as the Minister of State Domains until Nicholas's death in 1854. Under his leadership the Ministry played a critical role in paving the way for the emancipation of the serfs in 1861.[23]

The appointment of Kiselev was a sign of Nicholas's determination to become more actively involved in the lives of his state peasants. Far away on the Molochnaia River no one could possibly know what the appointment portended, but within the state administration the implications quickly became clear: ambitious officials would need to show results. Fadeev's future rode on the success of the Mennonites, and particularly on that of his chief Mennonite ally, Cornies. For Fadeev, Warkentin's conservative vision of the Mennonite model was unacceptable.

In 1834 Fadeev and Cornies began talking about extending the Forestry Society model by creating an Agricultural Society that would place all Mennonite economic activity under Cornies's control. That year Cornies cautioned against moving too quickly – the Great Drought of 1833–4 had dealt a severe blow to the settlement, and he knew this was not the time to push so hard.[24] Instead he concentrated on Forestry Society projects.

In 1833 the Forestry Society had carried out a detailed inspection of the entire settlement, and in the process they unearthed the issue that would take centre stage in the political struggles of 1836–42: the widespread, unauthorized sale of fullholdings.[25] Landowning – the possession of a fullholding – was central to Molochnaia Mennonite economic and political life. The Russian economy was almost entirely agricultural, and there were few ways to make a living in the Molochnaia that were not based on owning land. Politically, only fullholders had the right to vote in Gebietsamt and village elections. The settlement had a finite amount of good agricultural land, and almost all of it had been distributed by the mid-1820s. As a consequence, by the 1830s there was a large landless population that relied on agricultural labour and small crafts for survival.[26]

The 1833 inspections revealed that at least one hundred fullholdings had changed hands without formal approval in the previous year alone.[27] These unauthorized sales provided Cornies with leverage for his reform plans. Some Mennonite fullholders dragged their feet in implementing the Forestry Society's plans, particularly during and immediately after the Great Drought of 1833–4, and the society's only means to enforce punishment was to ask the Gebietsamt to intervene. Warkentin dominated the Gebietsamt, and the Forestry Society's reforms were exactly the kind of external interference in the settlement that he opposed. Cornies alerted Fadeev to the illegal land sales and proposed that in future all purchasers be required to sign a formal contract that obliged them to adhere to Forestry Society tree-planting regulations, along with a variety of other requirements for the maintenance of their fullholdings. Fadeev approved, and ordered that the Gebietsamt introduce the contracts. Cornies now had the leverage he needed to force Molochnaia fullholders to follow Forestry Society orders. This arrogated to Cornies significant administrative authority, and accounts of fullholder defiance describe an impatient and authoritarian Cornies imperiously demanding compliance with society policies.[28]

By 1836 Cornies was beginning to expand his authority beyond what was envisioned in the Forestry Society charter. In February 1836, only a few months before the creation of the Agricultural Society, an inspection trip revealed concerns about twenty-two fullholders, most of whom the society said were beyond recovery.[29] The Forestry Society's solutions to these problems went far past the letter of the society's charter: it urged that the Gebietsamt force the landowners to give up their fullholdings.

The Forestry Society did not have the authority to compel fullholders to sell their property; it could only pressure village offices to take action. When the village offices failed to do so, the society pressed them to refer matters to the Gebietsamt. Notably missing from this process was the congregational leadership, and this portended the political battle that was looming. The Forestry Society could neither compel the transfer of fullholdings through civil authority nor bring pressure from the church to bear. It would need to expand its authority further to do more, and that expansion was going to be controversial.

As Cornies's authority grew, a second factor loomed in Molochnaia politics: the declining power of the Guardianship Committee. The first indication came in 1834, when the Committee closed its Ekatrinoslav office and transferred Fadeev to Odesa.[30] In late 1835 word of a far more momentous change reached the Mennonites: Fadeev was to be transferred to Astrakhan as guardian of the Kalmyk Tatars.[31] Cornies recognized the significance of these changes. He relied upon the power of the state to push through his plans, and that power was rooted in his personal relationship with Fadeev. Cornies scrambled to lay the basis for a transfer of allegiance, asking Fadeev to do all he could to ensure that Cornies would still have the ear of the authorities in Odesa. At the same time, he rushed to push through one last major project: he wrote to Fadeev urging the creation of the Molochnaia Agricultural Society.[32]

Volume 2: 1836–1842

On Fadeev's recommendation I.N. Inzov, Director of the Guardianship Committee, approved the creation of the Molochnaia Mennonite Agricultural Society in March 1836; it began activities in May 1836.[33] Its creation shows Cornies's growing authority, for the Agricultural Society had much more power than the Forestry Society and would eventually govern all the economic activities of Molochnaia Mennonites. Inzov granted Cornies virtually free reign in defining the new society's authority in internal Mennonite economic affairs.[34]

Fadeev's parting gift made Cornies stronger, but Fadeev's actual departure had the opposite effect. Inzov, now sixty-eight years old, was losing interest in colonial affairs. The era of large-scale colonization in New Russia was over, and along with it much of the justification for the Guardianship Committee's existence. Tsar Nicholas was focused on state peasant reforms, and his preference was to treat all of his state peasants, foreign colonists included, as a common problem. With the creation of the Fifth Department in 1836 there was every reason to expect that the Guardianship Committee would soon be disbanded. For the time being there was a power vacuum, and this set the stage for the coming Molochnaia Mennonite political battle, which focused on the interference of the Agricultural Society in the affairs of fullholders, particularly regarding the allocation and use of land.

Both Warkentin and Cornies identified the Privilegium as central to the dispute. For Mennonites it had a quasi-constitutional character, as a legal document that defined their relationship to the Russian state. Cornies used the Privilegium's requirement that Mennonites act as models to justify his reforms, while Warkentin used it to insist that Mennonites could reject innovations that they regarded as incompatible with their religious beliefs. Both saw the Privilegium as the basis of a negotiated relationship between the Mennonites and the state, and they fought over the right to be the Mennonite representative in the negotiation.

In 1837 Cornies gained an important political ally in the imperial capital of St. Petersburg: a senior state official named Peter Keppen. Keppen would become the head of the Ministry of State Domains' Learned Committee at its foundation in 1838, where he helped collect and publish studies of the Russian peasantry that influenced the Great Reforms of the 1860s. The St. Petersburg academician visited the Molochnaia in 1837, and Cornies made such a strong impression on Keppen that when the latter returned to St. Petersburg in 1838 he recruited Cornies as a corresponding member of the Learned Committee.[35] For Cornies, Keppen's arrival could not have come at a better moment, for in 1837 he badly needed a new patron to replace Fadeev. It helped that, with the Guardianship Committee in decline, he found his new patron in the influential Ministry of State Domains.

By the end of 1837 Cornies had marshalled allies at every level of the administration to back his reform plans. Warkentin had no such friends in high places, but he did continue to enjoy support in the Mennonite settlement, and it was there that a key contest was played out in the Gebietsamt elections of 1838. The energy that Cornies and Warkentin invested in these elections serves as a reminder of how important local administrative offices were on the Russian frontier. Regardless of the autocratic authority of the tsar and his officials, in the Molochnaia elected Gebietsamt officials were essential agents of Russian authority without whom no real reform was possible.

There was little that Cornies and Warkentin agreed on, but they both wanted to retain the distinct status granted Mennonites under the Privilegium. This is what made the Privilegium central to Molochnaia politics. What Warkentin and his supporters failed to recognize, and what Cornies recognized very clearly, was that the Nicholaevan state was increasingly unhappy with exceptions like the ones granted the Mennonites. The entire bureaucratic thrust of Nicholas's peasant reforms was to impose uniformity.[36] If Mennonites were going to keep their privileges they were going to have to earn them.

In April 1838 Cornies told Fadeev that Warkentin was employing "underhanded means" to oust District Mayor Johann Regier and his Senior Deputy Abram Toews, both stalwart Cornies supporters, and replace them with Warkentin's "close relative" and loyal supporter, the current Second Deputy Mayor Driedger.[37] Cornies asked Fadeev to use his influence to have the Guardianship Committee cancel the elections and reappoint Regier and Toews for another three years. At Fadeev's urging, Cornies asked Inzov to cancel the elections and reappoint Regier and Toews.[38]

Inzov issued a stern letter to the leaders of the five Molochnaia congregations reminding them of their duties. He did not cancel the elections, but he did give a strong indication of the results he expected, and in the end the settlement re-elected Regier and Toews with large majorities.[39] With the election over and Cornies's candidates in office, by the end of 1838 Cornies returned to the aggressive pursuit of his reform agenda.

Reforms, 1838–42

The 1838 election victory launched a flurry of activity on every front. Cornies pressed forward with a transformation to market-oriented crop agriculture and experimented with a wide variety of new crops. At the same time, Cornies expanded his emphasis on education, overseeing the opening of several new schools. Beyond the Molochnaia he promoted the interests of what he called the "Radishchev Mennonites" – the struggling Ukrainian Hutterite community – arranging their move to the Molochnaia. Cornies also became the state's local watchdog over events in the soon-to-be-exiled Molochnaia Doukhobor and Molokan communities, trying unsuccessfully to act as an intermediary with the state. He continued to work to "civilize" his Nogai neighbours, promoting policies that reflected the racist and Islamophobic attitudes of state policy and his own understanding, and at the same time he offered his expert advice to Fadeev on efforts to reform the Kalmyk Tatars. Still further afield, he began a regular correspondence with the Moravian Brethren community at Sarepta on the Volga River, offering advice and aid for its floundering economy.

By the late 1830s the Molochnaia settlement's viable reserve land was almost exhausted and sixty per cent of Molochnaia Mennonite families were landless. Providing employment for the landless became one of Cornies's top priorities.[40] His solution was to promote trades and commerce as alternative employment for the landless. In 1836 Cornies proposed the creation of a craftsman's village beside Halbstadt, the administrative centre of the settlement. With the support of Kiselev, the Minister of State Domains, in the summer of 1842 Neu-Halbstadt sprang into existence. It became the commercial hub of the settlement and ultimately of the entire region.

Cornies viewed craftsmen as vital servants to the Molochnaia agricultural economy, but as always, agriculture remained his central concern. Cornies had made his money raising sheep, but by the late 1830s he saw crop agriculture as the future. The harsh winter of 1825 and the Great Drought of 1833–4 had decimated livestock in the region, and Cornies thought that crop agriculture would be a more reliable source of income. He was keenly aware of international markets, where wool prices were falling due to rising production in Australia, New Zealand, and North America. A third concern was the growing population in New Russia, which was making pastureland scarcer and more expensive. He recognized that for most Mennonite fullholders, grain was the future.

A key factor in this conclusion was the opening of a port at nearby Berdiansk in 1836, which made grain exports viable. After the port opened, grain-growing rapidly came to dominate Mennonite agricultural activities.[41] Commercial grain-growing demanded new methods and new discipline, and the Agricultural Society was ready and willing to provide both. The society's most significant innovation was the introduction of a four-field crop rotation, which led to rapid increases in agricultural production.[42]

As a result of these reforms, by 1842 the Molochnaia Mennonites were among the most productive farmers in the empire. A secondary benefit was that the sale and transportation of grain provided jobs. In August 1838 several Molochnaia Mennonite families built homes and warehouses in Berdiansk, where they became grain merchants. Abram Wiebe of Rudnerweide emerged as the leading Berdiansk merchant, establishing a trading firm that supplied the Molochnaia Mennonite community with luxuries from abroad and that exported Mennonite wool and grain directly to international markets.[43]

Cornies's activities by the early 1840s have an ad hoc character; administrative officials in Odesa, Simferopol, and St. Petersburg bombarded him with requests for advice, and he did his best to help all of them. Underlying all of this was a clear vision for the development of the Mennonite settlement and its role within the empire. Mennonites were to be the standard-bearers of modern economic practices, from systematic field rotations, to mechanized agricultural implements, to trade and industry.

The Warkentin Affair, 1841–2

As Cornies's power and activities grew, Warkentin's opposition likewise grew. The outcome of the 1837 elections – a clear victory for Cornies's candidate Johann Regier – suggests a shift in the balance of power within the settlement. His reforms ushered in a period of great prosperity for Mennonite fullholders. While many Mennonites were religiously conservative, in terms of their agricultural practices they were progressives. If they did not like Cornies's manner, they surely liked his results.

Warkentin's opposition to Cornies centred on the contention that Cornies was impinging on congregational authority. The dispute also had a significant dimension solely within the religious realm. The tensions between Cornies and Warkentin originated in the 1820s with the creation of the Christian School Society and the Molochnaia branch of the Russian Bible Society. At that time it was a conflict between Mennonite quietism and Pietism. Cornies put religion at the centre of his 1842 account of the conflict, writing that "Warkentin's basic beliefs are contrary both to the Bible and to Mennonite beliefs."[44]

The Molochnaia settlement's fall 1841 district and village elections provided the setting for the Warkentin Affair.[45] As in 1837, Warkentin attempted to use the elections to reassert his own authority. His candidate was Peter Toews from the village of Tiege. Cornies's candidate was his old friend Jacob Penner, former Mayor of the Khortitsa settlement and former Chairman of the Khortitsa Agricultural Society.

The election was bitter and divisive, and in the end Peter Toews won with just 395 votes, or roughly 40 per cent of the voters.[46] However, Cornies asserted his authority as Agricultural Society Chairman to refuse to ratify the results. On 17 December the Guardianship Committee took Cornies's advice and blocked Toews's appointment, and in January it ordered a new election, which probably took place in late April or early May 1842.

The second election was even more bitter than the first, and Cornies alienated many Mennonites by circulating a sharp denunciation of his enemies. Cornies had gone too far, and Warkentin's candidate Peter Toews won a landslide victory. Warkentin seemed to have gained full control of the community, and rumours spread the Cornies might be exiled to Siberia. What saved Cornies was the appointment of Evgenii von Hahn as Deputy Chairman of the Guardianship Committee. Young, smart, and energetic, Hahn was sent to Odesa to straighten out the problems in the Committee and get the New Russian colonial experiment back on its feet. He was Inzov's deputy in name only; in practice he now oversaw all Guardianship Committee affairs. Appointed in January 1842, he made his first visit to the Molochnaia in May, just after the second election.[47]

Hahn recognized that if the Mennonites were going to continue to play a leading role in New Russian development he would need Cornies at the helm. He threw out the election results and, in a move that shocked the entire settlement, dissolved the Large Flemish Congregation, ordering Cornies to oversee the creation of three smaller congregations in its place.[48] He forbade Warkentin from playing any role in the new congregations. The controversies surrounding this resolution of the Warkentin Affair would ripple through the Molochnaia settlement for years to come. Dirk Thun, the Mayor of Muensterberg, continued to campaign against Cornies until Hahn ordered him flogged during a return visit in September. Such aftershocks left deep scars in the settlement, but in practice, by the end of May 1842 Warkentin's role in Molochnaia politics was ended and Cornies reigned supreme.

Volume 3: Consolidation, 1843–1848

After Fadeev's departure in 1836 the Guardianship Committee became distant and disengaged from Molochnaia affairs and the Ministry of State Domains eclipsed its influence. While Cornies continued to actively pursue his Mennonite modernization agenda through the Agricultural Society, many of his initiatives served the broader state peasant goals of the new Ministry. Cornies's political victory in 1842 positioned him as an agent of the state and opened a floodgate of new demands on his time and energy.

At the same time, Hahn's appointment revitalized the Guardianship Committee, and under his leadership the Committee powerfully reasserted its role in the New Russian colonial world. By Hahn's own admission he did not know much about agriculture, and he leaned heavily on Cornies's knowledge. While the Guardianship Committee was part of the Ministry of State Domains, the two institutions had clearly defined areas of authority and did not compete with one another. However, they did compete for Cornies's time and energy. A Russian peasant proverb holds that "God is high above and the tsar is far away." It means that local demands always come first, and for Cornies, this meant that Hahn and the Guardianship Committee would have to take precedence. Still, the demands of the Ministry could not simply be ignored.

Redefining Priorities

After the Warkentin Affair Cornies tried to pull back from his obligations to the Ministry of State Domains. Most notably, he began to disengage from Nogai affairs. "Civilizing" the Nogais was one of Cornies's first causes, and his successes had helped to cement his reputation with Russian officialdom.[49] Cornies used his Nogai projects to demonstrate to the Committee the success of the Mennonite model. Yet the Nogais are also one of the most important examples of the failure of the Mennonite model. For all that Cornies had promoted his successes, he had achieved little meaningful change among the Nogais and there was serious resistance to Cornies's reform program. As demands on Cornies's time grew in the 1840s, he backed away from his direct involvement with the Nogais, instead delegating the work to other Mennonites.

Forestry was an ongoing focus of Cornies's efforts, but here too he backed away from direct involvement, instead hiring other Mennonites to fill supervisory roles. In 1844 the Ministry of State Domains asked Cornies to oversee the creation of a model forestry planation near Berdiansk.[50] The Ministry envisioned a school to teach forestry to Nogais and other state peasants. Cornies took up the task but convinced the Ministry to hire two Mennonites as direct supervisors. In this project Cornies mainly served as a liaison to the Ministry. He was the local authority charged with ensuring that the plantation got off the ground, but he did his best to distance himself from its day-to-day operations.

In the 1840s Cornies also limited his role in the state's efforts to promote potatoes among state peasants. In March 1841 he accepted the task of "direction and leadership in the introduction of potato cultivation among state peasants," but he hired Heinrich Balzer to oversee the program, while other Mennonites provided instruction and supervision.[51] Apart from reporting on the results and occasionally interceding in problems he devoted little more attention to it.

Refocusing on Mennonite Projects

Increasingly Cornies tailored his activities on behalf of the Ministry of State Domains in ways that more narrowly served the Mennonites. In particular, he continued to carry out experiments with crops ranging from tobacco to oil radishes, each experiment carefully documented and reported back to the Ministry. Such experiments had broad benefits for Russia, but they also had the potential to benefit the Mennonites, and Cornies constantly had this in mind.

From a Mennonite perspective one of the most important of Cornies's projects was promoting the manufacture and sale of Mennonite agricultural machinery. The growing number of landless in the settlement needed employment, and he was keenly aware that there was not enough land to permit them all to farm; the Mennonite economy needed to diversify. He promoted Mennonite agricultural equipment and its inventors, sending model machines off to Simferopol and Odesa to demonstrate their value. In 1839 he bragged to Fadeev that the shift to crop agriculture in the Molochnaia had stimulated the production and improvement of agricultural implements; horse-powered threshing machines and three-tined ploughs were changing the face of agriculture in the Molochnaia, and they were also providing work for the landless.[52] This transition to machine agriculture placed Mennonites at the leading edge of agricultural modernization in the Russian empire. In the 1840s this industry was still in its infancy; it was not until the 1870s that it became a mainstay of the regional economy. It is evidence, however, of Cornies's careful attention to the issue of landlessness and the need to diversify the economy. It also shows how Cornies made use of his Ministry contacts to address internal Mennonite issues. Where the Ministry's plans had a direct local benefit, he was happy to give it his full attention.

A Resurgent Guardianship Committee

Cornies's efforts to back away from Ministry of State Domains' demands came as the demands of the Guardianship Committee grew. With Fadeev's departure in 1836 the Committee had neither asked much of Cornies, nor offered him much support, and he had necessarily realigned himself with the Ministry, but Hahn's appointment in December 1841 changed things dramatically.

Hahn's first steps in the Molochnaia reflected an assertive manner and considerable unfamiliarity with conditions in the region. He soon realized that Cornies was an essential ally, and a friendship between the two men developed.[53] He looked to Cornies to become his advisor, and he also pushed Cornies to take an active role in the administration of all foreign colonists in the region. This expanded Cornies's authority, but it also made him more directly subservient to the Guardianship Committee, at times almost functioning as an unofficial and unpaid state employee.

One consequence of this new relationship is that after 1842, the authority of the Agricultural Society and Cornies's personal authority blurred. Between 1836 and 1842, when the Guardianship Committee was weak and ineffective, Cornies relied upon the other members of the Agricultural Society to help promote his reform plans in the Mennonite community. After 1842 the Agricultural Society continued to exist and was the official agency through which Cornies's authority was asserted, but in practice Cornies relied less and less on other members of the society and more and more on his own personal authority, strongly backed by Hahn.

Cornies's increased power gave him a chance to take up a project that he had first proposed in 1835: the relocation of the Hutterites to the Molochnaia. Hutterites, like Mennonites, are Anabaptists, though they have distinct religious doctrines including community of goods. In the early sixteenth century, Anabaptists from various German states fled to Moravia to escape persecution. Jakob Huter united the fugitives into one congregation. Forced out of Moravia during the Thirty Years War, the Hutterites spent time in Upper Hungary and Transylvania before immigrating to the Russian Empire in the 1760s, where they established a community at Radishchev in Chernigov *Guberniia*, north-east of Kyiv. There they faced religious and economic challenges similar to those faced by the Mennonites.[54]

The Hutterites were a small community – a single village – so they did not have the large mutual support network that the Mennonites enjoyed. They struggled economically as well as religiously, and in 1818 a split in the community almost destroyed it. The Hutterite story was well known in Mennonite circles. Cornies saw the Hutterites as backward and impoverished Mennonites (he usually called them either the Radishchev Mennonites or the Hutterite Mennonites). He described them as "good, healthy, and industrious people," but while he believed that "their Christian morality has not deteriorated much," he fretted that "externally, in dress and economic arrangements, they are almost Russian peasants."[55] He made their rescue a personal project.

In late 1835 Cornies had asked for permission for the Hutterites to move to the Molochnaia.[56] This plan fell victim to the general Guardianship Committee malaise after Fadeev's transfer, but Cornies never abandoned the idea, and in 1841 he raised it directly with Kiselev. In February 1842 Cornies received assurances that approval for the move was imminent, and he wrote to the Hutterite leaders telling them to make preparations.[57] The first Hutterite families arrived in June 1842, sent ahead to mow hay as winter feed for their community's livestock. Cornies gave the newcomers hay and the use of ploughed land on his estate to plant winter rye.[58] They were issued seed grain that came from community reserves, and the Mennonite families who billeted them over their first winter in the Molochnaia provided them with food, to be repaid the following year from community reserves. Cornies arranged for the Hutterites to borrow money from Mennonite community reserves, which he personally guaranteed. He selected the new Hutterite village site and ensured that the village was laid out in an orderly fashion. He named the village Hutterthal.

From the outset the relationship of the Hutterites to the Molochnaia Mennonite settlement was ill-defined. Clearly it was Cornies's intention that they be integrated into the settlement. However, they did not live on settlement land, they were poor, and they spoke a Tyrolian German dialect that clearly marked them as outsiders. At first Cornies saw them almost as his personal wards. He endorsed candidates for the Hutterite Village Mayor and Deputy Mayors, men he believed to serve the Hutterites' best interests as he saw them.

According to historian Astrid von Schlachta, Cornies's long-term impact on the Hutterites had both positive and negative aspects.[59] The Radishchev community seemed on the verge of total collapse, and it may not be hyperbole to say that Cornies rescued the Hutterites from extinction. Yet at the same time, he introduced fundamental challenges to their core beliefs. Internal disputes echoed those of the larger Molochnaia settlement, and there was deep concern among some Hutterites about the intrusion of Russian civil authority into the community.[60] Support for community of goods, which Cornies controversially insisted on ending when the community moved to the Molochnaia, resumed in the 1850s.[61] Schlachta concludes that the turmoil that struck the Hutterites in the later nineteenth century had some seeds in Cornies's policies.

As for the Hutterites' impact on Cornies, they blended in with his broader concerns in the 1840s, as one more project to exhaust and exasperate him. They reveal, however, that Cornies recognized in Hahn's arrival an opportunity to take up the cause of this desperately poor and struggling population. They also reveal that his goals were shaped not only by state policies, but by an enduring dedication to the welfare of the Mennonites. For him, the Hutterite project was a matter of principle and morality.

The Bergthal Mennonite Daughter Settlement

Hahn's arrival placed heavy new burdens on Cornies. Among these was Hahn's order that he come to the aid of the Bergthal Mennonite settlement sixty kilometres east of the Molochnaia. Bergthal was the first Mennonite daughter settlement, created to provide an outlet for landless Mennonites from the overcrowded Khortitsa mother settlement. It consisted of four villages: Bergthal (est. 1836), Schönfeld (1837), Schönthal (1838), and Heubuden (1839). A fifth village, Friedrichstal, would follow in 1852.[62]

In June 1842 Hahn ordered Cornies to take over supervision of Bergthal economic affairs. While Hahn appointed a colonial inspector as the official voice of the Guardianship Committee in the region, it was clear that Cornies was to be the real driving force.[63]

On 28 October 1842 Cornies issued a brusque seventeen-point memorandum to the Bergthal Gebietsamt, defining his expectations for them to reform the new settlement.[64] This memorandum suggests how little had been done in the settlement over the preceding six years. Many of the fullholders had still not properly laid out their hearth-sites, and they were living in homes built of rough-hewn logs and stone. Cornies ordered that the villages properly demarcate hearth-sites and construct regulation homes and outbuildings of brick or stone. He also insisted that the Bergthalers begin to lay out forest and orchard tree lots according to Forestry Society guidelines and ordered the proper regulation of pasturage and watering holes.

In the following years Cornies inspected the Bergthal settlement annually and closely managed the progress of its villages. Bergthal soon conformed to the orderly pattern of development of the Molochnaia settlement, its rich agricultural land adding to Mennonite grain exports from regional ports. Cornies's intervention won him no friends in the Khortitsa settlement, upon which he laid most of the blame for Bergthal's troubles, but it further built his reputation with Hahn.

The Württemberg Settlement

Beginning in 1843 Cornies took a close interest in the affairs of a colonist settlement that lay between the Molochnaia and Bergthal settlements. Sometimes known as the Brüdergemeinde Colony, and usually referred to by Cornies as the Württemberg Colony, the Pietist settlement consisted of four villages founded between 1816 and 1819.[65]

Cornies became directly involved in the community in the 1840s as the result of religious disputes. Some Württembergers, disgruntled with their church leadership, sought to leave their Pietist congregation and join the Lutheran Church, and Friedrich Prinz, the settlement's District Mayor, asked Cornies for advice. Prinz told Cornies that the breakaway settlers were questioning Hahn's authority, and he asked Cornies to review a petition he had drafted for Hahn.[66] This began a regular correspondence between Cornies and Prinz, who routinely asked his powerful neighbour for advice and assistance.

Cornies helped organize the Württemberg settlement's agricultural economy and worked with its Agricultural Society in his normally efficient manner, but the more interesting problem that the community faced was the recruitment of a new minister for the congregation. The previous minister had resigned, leaving the community without a spiritual leader. Prinz asked Cornies for advice, and Cornies did his best to help.[67] After over a year of uncertainty, on 11 October 1845 a delighted Prinz sent a letter to Cornies to let him know that the settlement had finally found their new minister: Eduard Hugo Otto Wüst.[68] Though Prinz could not have known it, in Wüst he had found a dynamic and transformative figure who would profoundly affect both the Württemberg settlement and the broader New Russian religious world. By the 1850s Wüst's revival meetings and ecumenical Pietist appeals attracted huge audiences, including some Mennonites who were discontented with their conservative, quietist communities. Wüst had a central influence on the creation of the Mennonite Brethren in 1860, and consequently he had a deep impact on modern Mennonite beliefs and practices. He was equally influential in the growth of the Ukrainian Baptist movement.[69]

The Professionalization of Education

Cornies's last significant initiative in the Molochnaia, and one of his most important long-term contributions to the Mennonites, was the professionalization of the Mennonite educational system. On 10 July

1843 the Guardianship Committee ordered the Agricultural Society to take control of all schools in the Mennonite settlement. Cornies was to take responsibility for every aspect of schooling, from the condition of schoolhouses to the quality of teaching. As for religion, the directive allowed that "the church preachers should carefully supervise the schools to ensure that no lessons injurious to the Mennonite confession of faith are taught."[70]

In the 1840s Cornies frequently delegated the supervision of major projects to trusted associates, but the school reforms were close to his heart and he gave them his personal attention. He made it his first priority to improve and standardize the quality of instruction in all village schools. In April 1845 Cornies wrote and distributed to the schools what amounted to a pedagogical primer for teachers.[71] In fall 1845 the Agricultural Society expanded its efforts at school reform when it ordered that the forty-four schools in the settlement be divided into six school districts. The teachers in each district were instructed to meet and discuss best teaching practices and to establish a standardized school curriculum. They were to report the results to the society by the end of December.[72] The outcome of this exercise was the "General Rules on the Instruction and Treatment of Schoolchildren: A Manual for Teachers in Molochnaia School Districts."[73]

Cornies's educational reforms and their centrepiece "General Rules" constituted a critical juncture in the professionalization of Mennonite education. The outcome would be realized in future generations as Mennonites led the way in Ukrainian economic development in the latter half of the nineteenth century. But the "General Rules" offer something more: they are a window onto Cornies's broader world view at the height of – and near the end of – his power. They are an important reminder of why education was so contentious for Mennonites, for they express values and beliefs that go well beyond mere pedagogy. The "General Rules" were not secular, for they insisted that "religious principles must underlie all other principles," and they held up Jesus as the ultimate model of a teacher, the "one who is most worthy of love and emulation."[74] But if the "General Rules" stressed God as creator, it was God's creation – the natural world – that was to be the real subject in Molochnaia schools.

The "General Rules" told teachers that "all knowledge and understanding is the result of our observation of nature.... Human knowledge always begins with observation, proceeds from there to understanding and finally to judgments and conclusions." Cornies told Mennonite teachers to focus their lessons on the natural world and the creative role of humans within it, inculcating "a love of order and meaningful activity."[75] This defined Cornies's own world view succinctly: he had dedicated his life to reshaping the world in orderly, productive ways, and he now sought to educate a new generation of Mennonites to follow this example.

Expanding Authority: Khortitsa

In 1845 Hahn consulted Cornies on problems in the Khortitsa Central School, and this led to the direct extension of Cornies's authority into the Khortitsa settlement.[76] Following a June 1845 inspection Hahn fired the Khortitsa schoolteacher, Heinrich Heese, and asked for Cornies's advice about a replacement.[77] Cornies suggested Heinrich Franz, the former teacher in Gnadenfeld, who in 1845 was teaching at the Mennonite school in Ekaterinoslav while he studied Russian.[78] Hahn endorsed the selection, and in the summer of 1846 Franz replaced Heese. He went on to have a distinguished career in Khortitsa.[79]

Cornies's intrusion into the Khortitsa school system foreshadowed a significant expansion of his authority. From 28 July to 7 August 1846, Cornies toured the Khortitsa settlement with Hahn, and he returned to Khortitsa on 14 August and spent the rest of the month conducting a detailed survey in preparation for a visit by Kiselev. Kiselev arrived in Khortitsa on 1 September, and Cornies travelled with him through the district.[80] Three months later, on 5 December, Hahn placed Cornies in charge of the Khortitsa settlement's Agricultural Society.[81] Johann Siemens continued as chair, but he now took orders from Cornies.

The expansion of Cornies's authority to Khortitsa was controversial in the Khortitsa settlement, but it came too late in his life to have a major impact. By the end of 1847 Cornies's active public role was waning. His most significant and effective reforms had always relied on his direct supervision, and without strong allies in Khortitsa he had little direct impact on the settlement's economic life. By comparison, his educational reforms, which were backed by a strong state reform program, had far more impact on Khortitsa.

The educational reforms were one of Cornies's last significant projects to reshape the Molochnaia settlement. His description in the "General Rules" of punishment as the product of failure reflects an increasingly discouraged tone that penetrated his correspondence in the last years of his life. It was implicitly a reflection on his own failings. It was not, however, an admission of defeat, for he remained engaged in other projects.

The Judenplan

The last major demand that the state made of Cornies was for advice on a plan to create mixed Jewish-Mennonite agricultural villages in New Russia. The so-called Judenplan was part of the Russian state's anti-Semitic attempt to solve the "Jewish question" by convincing Jews to adopt the economic practices and administrative arrangements of state peasants. It is evidence of how Nicholas I's policies increasingly characterized non-Slavic, non-Orthodox communities as occupying lower rungs on the scale of social evolution, and likewise of how the imperial state was moving towards seeking a single, unifying policy for its diverse subjects.[82] It provides a final glimpse of Cornies's reform vision at the end of his life.

In March 1846 Hahn approached Cornies for advice on Kiselev's proposal to establish Judenplan villages in Ekaterinoslav, Kherson, and Tavrida Guberniias.[83] Hahn hoped that the Mennonites would take the lead. The plan was to place ten Mennonite families in each village, where they would serve as models to the fifty or so Jewish families that made up the bulk of the population. A salaried Mennonite supervisor would oversee each village. The Jewish families were drawn from the poor landless Jewish population of the overcrowded shtetls in the Pale of Settlement, and the state's hope was that, by teaching this population to farm, it could make them "useful" peasants.[84]

Cornies's role was to advise on the project and promote it to the Mennonites, and he dutifully obliged, but the project never occupied much of his time. It does, however, provide an important insight into Cornies's view of the value of the Mennonite model and his larger understanding of the Mennonites' place in Russia. In the last years of his life, he finally firmly rejected the very idea of Mennonites as model colonists.

Hahn was sceptical of the project, but Cornies, as ever convinced that good leadership could transform people, assured him that the plan could work. However, he told Hahn that it was unlikely any Mennonites would agree to move to such villages. Instead, it would be better to situate the villages close to the Molochnaia and provide each with a salaried Mennonite supervisor who would live in the village, farm his own fullholding, and teach the Jewish population. The villages could be built by Mennonites, who would at the same time teach their trades to the new Jewish inhabitants. The Jewish settlers, supervised by Mennonites, over time would adopt their ways.[85]

In asking for Cornies's help, Hahn pointed to the Nogai success story, but by 1846 Cornies had given up on the Nogais. In his response to Hahn he offered a highly qualified assessment of the value of the Mennonite model, writing that even the Mennonite impact on neighbouring Slavic peasant villages was "barely perceptible." While he allowed that there was some small change, he said that the Russian peasants "see the establishments of the [Mennonites] as too perfect and claim they are themselves too clumsy to ever achieve anything similar." If the Judenplan project was going to succeed, what was required was "special supervision combined with firm, step-by-step leadership."[86]

Leadership, rather than a model, was the most important thing that Mennonites could provide. This had been part of Cornies's vision dating back to his 1826 observations about the Nogais, but by 1846 supervision almost wholly replaced modelling in his view of how Mennonites could best serve the state and thereby justify their privileges. He had already implemented this new vision twice in the 1840s, using Mennonite supervisors to oversee Russian and Nogai potato growing, and to direct the model forestry plantation.

The relationship that Cornies was now proposing between the Mennonites and the state blurred the old, hard demarcation that distinguished the Mennonites from other Russian subjects, for it would make the Mennonite supervisors direct employees of the state. Mennonite potato and forestry supervisors already received state salaries, but the money passed through Cornies's hands and he oversaw the projects. He envisioned the same arrangement with the Judenplan villages, but the state rejected his proposal to place the villages in the Molochnaia and give them just a single Mennonite supervisor. Instead, it proceeded with the original plan of locating the villages in Kherson and populating them with contingents of Mennonite families as well as Mennonite village supervisors. Cornies accepted the final decision.

The Judenplan confronted Cornies with the fundamental problem of the Mennonite Privilegium and the model paradigm that justified it. Through his efforts at Iushanle, Akkerman, and elsewhere, Cornies had succeeded in satisfying the state that the Mennonites were earning the continuation of their privileges, but as he acknowledged, the model had very limited utility. Sooner or later the state would see what he already knew – while the Mennonites were thriving, their neighbours were realizing almost no benefits from the model. Cornies remained committed to preserving Mennonite privileges, and his arguments against the original conception of the Judenplan explicitly objected to the danger it posed to Mennonites: "Separated from their own brethren," he wrote, "they could not possibly assure themselves and their descendants of an untroubled future."[87]

Cornies now saw direct service, rather than passive modelling, as the solution to this conundrum. What he did not clearly articulate, though he seemed to sense, was that this, too, held enormous dangers. After all, every Russian subject was bound in service to the tsar, so the obligation to serve was a questionable justification for special privileges. He was fumbling towards an argument that Mennonites were particularly suited to serve by virtue of their membership in their distinctive community. Mennonites could supervise local projects – potatoes, forestry, Jewish settlements – while living in the Mennonite settlement, but Mennonites who separated from the settlement were in danger of losing their value to serve. At first he held to this view when he proposed establishing the Judenplan villages in the Molochnaia, but when he lent his support to the Kherson plan he opened the door to the wholesale challenges to Mennonite privileges that emerged during the great reforms of the 1860s and 1870s. He justified this change on the grounds that the Judenplan villages would have large enough contingents of Mennonites to retain their community values, but when Mennonites entered direct state employment as supervisors of Jewish villagers, they crossed a significant threshold in their relationship to the state.

Death and Legacy

In his final years, Cornies often complained that his administrative responsibilities were exhausting him. Beginning in 1845 a series of deaths took an additional toll. On 11 June 1845 his oldest friend Wilhelm Martens committed suicide. Eleven months later, on 15 May 1846, his daughter-in-law Justina died a week after giving birth to a daughter named Justina. Aganetha, his beloved wife, died on 30 March 1847 after a long illness. His brother Peter died on 10 September 1847.

By February 1848 Cornies's own energy and abilities were flagging.[88] His correspondence shortened to brief letters, a few sentences of questions and orders, with little sign of the attention to detail that had always been his hallmark. On 29 February Cornies fell ill. Two weeks later, on 13 March, he died. He was buried on 16 March at the Ohrloff cemetery.[89]

In October 1848 the German-language Odesa newspaper *Unterhaltungsblatt für deutsche Ansiedler im südlichen Rußland* published a long obituary. A Russian translation followed in the *Journal of the Ministry of State Domains*.[90] This obituary provided the foundations for much of what was written about Cornies by Mennonite historians in the late nineteenth and early twentieth centuries, but as historian Harvey Dyck points out, there are grounds for believing that in 1848 many in the settlement were not so laudatory. That fall, at the Ministry of State Domains' direction, the settlement compiled village histories, and most of them were pointedly silent about Cornies.[91] In the 1848 settlement elections David Friesen became Gebietsamt Mayor, marking the beginning of a conservative reaction that returned the Warkentin Party (sans Warkentin) to power. Conservative fullholders would dominate the settlement into the 1860s. That September Hahn left the Guardianship Committee, promoted to Director of the First Department of the Ministry of State Domains.[92] With both Cornies and Hahn gone, the power of the Agricultural Society waned.

If the power of the Agricultural Society did not survive, its reforms were more durable. The Molochnaia Mennonite settlement was at the cutting edge of Russian economic development in 1848, and while a plethora of events, conditions, and individuals had influenced its transformation, Cornies was undoubtedly instrumental. The spread of sheep rearing, the development of field agriculture and forestry, and the growth of the nascent manufacturing sector were all important parts of his legacy.

Most of the economic reforms were initiated by the state through the Guardianship Committee and the Ministry of State Domains, so we cannot credit Cornies alone for their conception. Still, the state promoted these reforms across New Russia and sometimes the entire empire, yet it was in Cornies's hands that they achieved their signal success. Afforestation is a case in point: planting trees on the steppe was a government priority from 1825 when Tsar Alexander I exhorted the Mennonites to expand their efforts, and in 1828 Tsar Nicholas I decreed the creation of forestry societies throughout New Russia. Despite this, in 1848 many New Russian travellers still encountered the steppe as a desert, with the Molochnaia settlement its astonishing oasis. Fadeev wrote the charter for the Molochnaia Mennonite Forestry Society, and the state provided thousands of rubles and hundreds of thousands of saplings and seeds, but it was Cornies who doggedly drove Mennonites to plant and nurture them. At the height of his power and influence in 1844 he wrote that "in my imagination, I see myself transported to a time when small forests, here and there, will shoot up and grow towards the sky on high steppe ridges. They will provide pleasure for travellers, draw in the air's moisture, increase the fruitfulness of the soils, and break the back of this region's damaging hurricanes."[93]

This passion extended into all of Cornies's reform efforts and helps to account for the remarkable role of the Molochnaia settlement in Russian economic development. Historian Natalia Venger shows that the Mennonites, a tiny minority, were "one of the critical factors in south Russian industrialisation" and served as a "gateway to innovation" for the entire empire.[94] Their agricultural accomplishments were no less impressive; by the end of the nineteenth century Mennonites were among the most modern, productive, and profitable farmers in the empire.[95]

Some scholars have characterized Cornies as a secular and secularizing figure who undermined the authority of the Mennonite congregational Elders and served as a fifth column for the modernizing state. James Urry, whose seminal *None But Saints* labels Cornies the "prophet of progress," argues that for Cornies, "the interests of the government appear to have taken precedence over religious scruples," and that Cornies functioned as a surrogate of the state's modernizing agenda.[96] There is considerable truth in this portrayal. In the early decades of the nineteenth century the Mennonites enjoyed significant independence from state interference in their religious, economic, and community life, and whatever Cornies's justifications, it is undoubtedly true that his reforms helped to reduce that autonomy, while his arbitrary and authoritarian manner deeply divided his community and attacked important traditional Mennonite values.

Still, it is worth asking what the alternative was. An implicit assumption of such criticism is that there was a pathway to avoid state infringement on Mennonite rights, but close attention to the broader history of the Russian Empire suggests that this is not true. Under Nicholas I, Russia was intent upon changing its relationship to all of its subjects, and those who refused to cooperate would suffer. Throughout his life Cornies consistently maintained that his reforms were intended to preserve Mennonite privileges, and he helped ensure that Mennonites would retain far more control of their community than other colonists in New Russia in the second half of the nineteenth century.

Conclusion

Volume 3 of *Transformation on the Southern Ukrainian Steppe* shows Cornies at the height of his powers. Cornies did not implement dramatic new reforms in this period; instead, 1842–8 saw him turn his reform efforts outward to the surrounding community, promoting afforestation and agricultural improvements in Slavic and Nogai villages. He also extended his power into the Khortitsa and Bergthal Mennonite settlements.

Cornies's role in the 1840s reflects the Russian state's movement away from accommodations with its diverse population, and towards the policy of Russification that would fully take hold in the last half of the nineteenth century. The Mennonites continued to function as colonial agents, but policies they implemented were more and more directly defined by the state. Their own agency, which had been so critical to their early successes in New Russia, was now tolerated rather than promoted as a model, and as Hahn made clear during the Warkentin Affair, that tolerance had strict limits.

As Cornies's authority and responsibilities expanded, his understanding of the relationship of Mennonites to the state evolved one last time. In the end he wholly rejected the idea of the Mennonites as model colonists, acknowledging that there was little sign that the model had produced meaningful impact on neighbouring communities. He now argued that Mennonites needed to play a direct supervisory role over other Russian subjects, as educated, progressive agents of reform. He himself was the shining example of this vision of the new Mennonite citizen. Cornies implicitly argued that this was the only basis for preserving the Mennonite Privilegium.

NOTES

1 The Guardianship Committee for Foreign Settlers in New Russia was
  the state agency that directly oversaw Mennonites and other foreign
  colonists. It answered to the Ministry of Internal Affairs until 1838, and
  to the Ministry of State Domains after its creation in that year. Regarding
  Cornies's expanding authority, see Cornies to Hahn, 24 October 1845,
  Transformation on the Southern Ukrainian Steppe (hereafter *TSUS*), vol. 3,
  doc. 502. The date that Cornies took charge of the Khortitsa school system
  is unknown. See Cornies's undated notes regarding a memorandum from

the Guardianship Committee to the Khortitsa Gebietsamt, n.d. [1846], *TSUS*, vol. 3, doc. 631. It occurred no later than August 1846, when Cornies began corresponding with Khortitsa teacher Heinrich Franz about school reforms in Khortitsa. Cornies to Franz, August 1846, *TSUS*, vol. 3, doc. 646.

2 The 4 June 1842 order is not extant; Cornies refers to it in Cornies to Hahn, 4 November 1842, *TSUS*, vol. 2, doc. 679, pp. 570–2.

3 Cornies to Hahn, 14 July 1843, *TSUS*, vol. 2, doc. 116.

4 Hahn to Cornies, 20 March 1846, *TSUS*, vol. 3, doc. 579. For an overview of the Judenplan, see Harvey L. Dyck, "Landlessness in the Old Colony: The *Judenplan* Experiment 1850–1880," in *Mennonites in Russia, 1788–1988: Essays in Honour of Gerhard Lohrenz*, ed. John Friesen (Winnipeg: CMBC Publications, 1989), 183–202.

5 August von Haxthausen, *Studien über die innern Zustände, das Volksleben und insbesondere die ländlichen Einrichtungen Rußlands*, 2:430.

6 Willard Sunderland, *Taming the Wild Field: Colonization and Empire on the Russian Steppe* (Ithaca, NY: Cornell University Press, 2004). On the historiography, see Valerie A. Kivelson and Ronald Grigor Suny, *Russia's Empires* (Oxford: Oxford University Press, 2017), 116–39.

7 Kelly O'Neill, *Claiming Crimea: A History of Catherine the Great's Southern Empire* (New Haven: Yale University Press, 2017), 4–5, https://doi.org/10.12987/yale/9780300218299.001.0001.

8 John P. LeDonne, *Forging a Unitary State: Russia's Management of the Eurasian Space, 1650–1850* (Toronto: University of Toronto Press, 2020), 6–10, https://doi.org/10.3138/9781487533311.

9 The concept of a colonial laboratory of modernity originated from Frederick Cooper and Ann Laura Stoler, "Between Metropole and Colony: Rethinking a Research Agenda," in *Tensions of Empire: Colonial Cultures in a Bourgeois World*, ed. Frederick Cooper and Ann Laura Stoler (Berkeley: University of California Press, 1997), 5, https://doi.org/10.1525/9780520918085. Robert J.C. Young provides a useful recent overview of the concept and its application in *Empire, Colony, Post-Colony* (New York: Wiley, 2015), 38–41. In a similar vein, Alexander M. Martin calls New Russia a "space of social experimentation" – Martin, *From the Holy Roman Empire to the Land of the Tsars: One Family's Odyssey, 1768–1870* (Oxford: Oxford University Press, 2022), 258, https://doi.org/10.1093/oso/9780192844378.001.0001. I develop the idea more fully in John R. Staples, *Johann Cornies, the Mennonites, and Russian Colonialism in Southern Ukraine* (Toronto: University of Toronto Press, 2023), https://doi.org/10.3138/9781487549183.

10 Regarding the family and its migration to Ukraine, see Staples, *Johann Cornies*, 5–7 and 24–6.

11 The *Privilegium* was a document promised to the first immigrants by Catherine in 1787 and granted by Tsar Paul I in 1800. Mennonites regarded the Privilegium as a fundamental, God-willed guarantee of their rights and privileges. It granted Mennonites "the liberty to practise their religion according to their tenets and customs," and a complete exemption from military service. It extended each family temporary tax exemptions and "incontestable and perpetually inheritable possession" of a sixty-five-desiatina (seventy-one hectare) land allotment, the right to build factories, to enter trade guilds, and to engage in commercial activities. The Privilegium is reproduced in translation in James Urry, *None but Saints: The Transformation of Mennonite Life in Russia 1789–1889* (Winnipeg: Hyperion Press, 1990), 282–4. Its role in Mennonite society is detailed in John R. Staples, "Religion, Politics, and the Mennonite Privilegium: Reconsidering the Warkentin Affair," *Journal of Mennonite Studies* 21 (2003): 71–88. On the larger history of Privilegiums, see James Urry, *Mennonites, Politics, and Peoplehood: Europe-Russia-Canada 1525 to 1980* (Winnipeg: University of Manitoba Press, 2006), https://doi.org/10.1515/9780887553448.

12 For an overview of Mennonite immigration to Russia and the early years of settlement, see Leonard G. Friesen, *Mennonites in the Russian Empire and the Soviet Union: Through Much Tribulation* (Toronto: Toronto University Press, 2022), 69–85, https://doi.org/10.3138/9781487505677. Throughout the nineteenth century visitors to the Molochnaia settlement called it an "oasis." See Staples, *Johann Cornies*, 43–5.

13 Staples, *Johann Cornies*, 29–35; 41–3. "Brandy" refers to all spirits.

14 Staples, *Johann Cornies*, 50–4.

15 Pietism emphasizes inner spiritual regeneration and evangelical activities; it emerged as a significant force in Prussia and the other German states in the eighteenth century. Originating as a reform movement within the Lutheran Church, Pietism promoted the cultivation of personal piety through an individual exploration of faith, and it consequently challenged the authority of the established Church. At the same time, because of the centrality of Bible-reading to this individual exploration, Pietism promoted literacy and education. Regarding the impact of Pietism on Mennonites in the Russian empire, see Friesen, *Mennonites*, 86–104.

16 Staples, *Johann Cornies*, 61–3; Friesen, *Mennonites*, 92–3.

17 Russia required Mennonites to adopt the district (*volost*) administrative system created by Paul I in 1797, of elected village mayors (*sels'skii vybornyi*) and ten-men (*desiatskie*). The Mennonite equivalent of a volost

was the *Gebiet*, and just as Ukrainian and Russian state peasants had an elected volost mayor (*volost'noi golova*), the Mennonites had an elected Gebiet Mayor (*Oberschulz*). The Mayor and his Deputies were collectively referred to as the District Administration (*Gebietsamt*).

18 On the general phenomenon, see Susan Smith-Peter, "Sweet Development: The Sugar Beet Industry, Agricultural Societies and Agrarian Transformations in the Russian Empire, 1818–1913," *Cahiers du monde russe* 57, no. 1 (2016): 101–24, https://doi.org/10.4000/monderusse.8334. For an extensive account of the Mennonite societies, see Staples, *Johann Cornies*.

19 The standard work on the Decembrists is Marc Raeff, *The Decembrist Movement* (Upper Saddle River, NJ: Prentice-Hall, 1966). The literature on the Decembrists and Nicholas's response is summarized in Kivelson and Suny, *Russia's Empires*, 154–61.

20 Fadeev, who had a distinguished career as a provincial bureaucrat, was also the father of novelist Elena Andreevna Gan, and grandfather of both Russia's future Prime Minister Sergei Witte, and the famous spiritualist Helena Blavatskaya. On his relationship to the Mennonites, see Staples, *Johann Cornies*.

21 *Polnoe Sobranie Zakonov*, ser. 2, vol. 3, 1828, no. 2280.

22 Fadeev to Cornies, 13 July 1831, *TSUS*, vol. 1, doc. 224, pp. 227–35.

23 On Kiselev, and historiographic debates about his impact, see David Moon, *The Abolition of Serfdom in Russia, 1762–1907* (Abingdon, UK: Routledge, 2002), 46–7; Carol Scott Leonard, *Agrarian Reform in Russia: The Road from Serfdom* (Cambridge: Cambridge University Press, 2010), 28–30, https://doi.org/10.1017/CBO9780511780639; Edward C. Thaden, *Russia's Western Borderlands, 1710–1870* (Princeton, NJ: Princeton University Press, 1985), 133–5, https://doi.org/10.1515/9781400854950. Volume 1 of this series incorrectly dates the creation of the Ministry of State Domains to 1836. However, the distinction between the Fifth Department and the Ministry had little practical significance for the Mennonites.

24 There is no record of this proposal in the 1834 correspondence, but Cornies refers to it in his 26 February 1836 letter to Fadeev, *TSUS*, vol. 2, doc. 1, pp. 3–4.

25 Cornies to Fadeev, 10 March 1833, *TSUS*, vol. 1, doc. 348, p. 315.

26 On landlessness in the first four decades of settlement, see John R. Staples, *Cross-Cultural Encounters on the Ukrainian Steppe: Settling the Molochna Basin, 1783–1861* (Toronto: University of Toronto Press, 2002),75–84, https://doi.org/10.3138/9781442673625.

27 Cornies to Fadeev, 10 March 1833, *TSUS*, vol. 1, doc. 348, p. 315.

28 Staples, *Johann Cornies*, 147–9.

29 Forestry Society records from February 1836, *TSUS*, vol. 1, doc. 536, p. 444.

30 Cornies to Fadeev, 13 September 1833, *TSUS*, vol. 1, doc. 385, pp. 338–9.

31 Cornies to Fadeev, December 1835, *TSUS*, vol. 1, doc. 519, p. 429.

32 Cornies to Fadeev, 26 February 1836, *TSUS*, vol. 2, doc. 1, pp. 3–4.

33 Inzov approved the society on 21 March (Inzov to Cornies, 21 March 1836, *TSUS*, vol. 2, doc. 10, pp. 10–11). It was created on 1 May 1836 (Forestry Society to Inzov, 12 May 1836, *TSUS*, vol. 2, doc. 13, pp. 12–13).

34 On the role of these societies, see *TSUS*, vol. 1, xliii–xliv.

35 On Keppen, see Staples, *Johann Cornies*, 157–9.

36 On Nicholas's policies and their impact on Mennonites, see Staples, *Johann Cornies*, 108–11. On the conflicting forces of integration and differentiation under Nicholas, see Kivelson and Suny, *Russia's Empires*, 175. The standard study of Official Nationality is Nicholas V. Riasanovsky, *Nicholas I and Official Nationality in Russia, 1825–1855* (Berkeley: University of California Press, 1969). For a recent summary in the context of imperial policy, see Kivelson and Suny, *Russia's Empires*, 157–61.

37 Cornies to Fadeev, 26 April 1838, *TSUS*, vol. 2, doc. 148, pp. 120–3.

38 Fadeev's response is not extant, but in a 15 August 1838 letter Cornies thanked him for the advice and support (Cornies to Fadeev, 15 August 1838, *TSUS*, vol. 2, doc. 162, pp. 133–5).

39 Regier received 563 of the 955 votes cast. Khariton Pelekh to General Inzov, 17 November 1838, State Archive of the Odesa Region, *fond* 6, *opis* 1, *delo* 4850.

40 Regarding landlessness in the 1820s–40s, see Staples, *Cross-Cultural Encounters*, 77. On the landlessness crisis of the 1860s, see Friesen, *Mennonites*, 114–19.

41 Regarding Berdiansk's effect on the Molochnaia economy, see Staples, *Cross-Cultural Encounters*, 123–4.

42 Cornies, Report for 1838, 1 January 1839, *TSUS*, vol. 2, doc. 185, pp. 151–6.

43 See, for example, Cornies's purchase of a barrel of wine, Cornies to Steven, 22 January 1842, *TSUS*, vol. 2, doc. 535, pp. 454–5. Regarding international export of wool, see Wiebe to Cornies, 1 March 1844, *TSUS*, vol. 3, doc. 280.

44 Cornies, Description of the Warkentin Affair, undated, between 10 September and 18 October 1842, *TSUS*, vol. 2, doc. 669, pp. 555–64.

45 The date and detailed results of these elections is unknown. For a full account of the Warkentin Affair, see Staples, *Johann Cornies*, 187–216.

46 Neufeld's account says 400 votes; Cornies said 395. Heinrich Neufeld, "A Further Examination of the Molotschna Conflict," trans. Ben Hoeppner

and Delbert Plett, *Preservings* 24 (December 2004), 21; and Cornies, Description of the Warkentin Affair, undated, between 10 September and 18 October 1842, *TSUS*, vol. 2, doc. 669, pp. 555–64.

47 On Hahn see Staples, *Johann Cornies*, 193.

48 Neufeld, "A Further Examination of the Molotschna Conflict."

49 Staples, *Johann Cornies*, 218–22, and John R. Staples, "'On Civilizing the Nogais': Mennonite-Nogai Economic Relations, 1825–1860," *Mennonite Quarterly Review* 74, no. 2 (April 2000): 229–56.

50 Rosen's original 6 March 1844 proposal for the project is not extant, but Cornies refers to it in Cornies to Rosen, 12 May 1845, *TSUS*, vol. 3, doc. 453. On the model forestry, see Staples, *Johann Cornies*, 219–20; and John R. Staples, "Iogann Kornis i osnovanie Berdianskogo Lesnichestvo," *Voprosy Germanskoi Istorii* (2017): 18–21.

51 Cornies to Rosen, 20 March 1841, *TSUS*, vol. 2, doc. 430, pp. 341–2.

52 Staples, *Johann Cornies*, 222–4. On the Mennonite role in the production of agricultural equipment in Russia, see Natalia Venger, *Mennonitskoe predprinimatel'stvo v usloviiakh modernizatsii iuga Rossii: Mezhdu kongregatsiei i Rossiskim obshchestvom (1789–1920)* (Dnipro: Dnipropetrovsk National University, 2009), 252–7; 298–307.

53 Hahn to Cornies, 16 June 1842, *TSUS*, vol. 2, doc. 601, p. 508.

54 On Hutterite history, see Astrid von Schlachta, *From the Tyrol to North America: The Hutterite Story Through the Centuries*, trans. Werner O. Packull and Karin Packull (Waterloo, ON: Pandora Press, 2008). For a more detailed account of the Hutterite move to the Molochnaia, see Staples, *Johann Cornies*, 225–9.

55 Cornies to Blueher, 4 August 1843, *TSUS*, vol. 3, doc. 132.

56 Fadeev to Cornies, 17 December 1835, *TSUS*, vol. 1, pp. 430–1.

57 Cornies to the Radishchev Village Administration, 16 February 1842, *TSUS*, vol. 2, p. 475.

58 Cornies to Hahn, 17 August 1842, *TSUS*, vol. 2, pp. 527–8.

59 Schlachta, *From the Tyrol to North America*, 149–51.

60 Astrid von Schlachta, "The Hutterian Brethren in the Molochna, 1842–74," *Preservings* 24 (December 2004), 39.

61 Schlachta, "The Hutterian Brethren," 40.

62 Cornelius Krahn, "Bergthal Mennonite Settlement (Zaporizhia Oblast, Ukraine)," Global Anabaptist Mennonite Encyclopedia Online, 1953, http://gameo.org/index.php?title=Bergthal_Mennonite_Settlement _(Zaporizhia_Oblast,_Ukraine)&oldid=144812. For a broader assessment of the Bergthal settlement, see William Schroeder, *The Bergthal Colony*, rev. ed. (Winnipeg: CMBC Publications, 1986).

63 The 4 June 1842 order is not extant; Cornies refers to it in a letter to the Guardianship Committee, 4 November 1842, *TSUS*, vol. 2, p. 572.

64 Cornies to Bergthal Settlement Administrators, 28 October 1842, *TSUS*, vol, 2, p. 568–70.

65 Staples, *Johann Cornies*, 231.

66 Prinz to Cornies, 21 June 1843, *TSUS*, vol. 3, doc. 108.

67 Ibid.

68 Prinz to Cornies, 11 October 1845, *TSUS*, vol. 3, doc. 508.

69 For Wüst's impact on the Mennonites, see Friesen, *Mennonites*, 109–13; Urry, *None but Saints*, 172–6; and Harold Jantz, "A Pietist Pastor and the Russian Mennonites: The Legacy of Eduard Wuest," *Direction* 36, no. 2 (Fall 2007): 232–46. For Wüst's broader impact, see Albert W. Wardin, *On the Edge: Baptists and Other Free Church Evangelicals in Tsarist Russia, 1855–1917* (Eugene, OR: Wipf and Stock, 2013), 57–64; and Sergei I. Zhuk, *Russia's Lost Reformation: Peasants, Millennialism, and Radical Sects in Southern Russia and Ukraine, 1830–1917* (Baltimore: Johns Hopkins University Press, 2004), 157–61.

70 Hahn to Agricultural Society, 10 July 1843, *TSUS*, vol. 3, doc. 117. Cornies's education reforms were drawn from contemporary Prussian pedagogy associated with Johann Heinrich Pestalozzi and Friedrich Froebel. For a more detailed analysis, see Staples, *Johann Cornies*, 233–8.

71 Cornies to Village Offices, 6 April 1845, *TSUS*, vol. 3, doc. 440. The instructions had two sections: "In the School in A," and "In the School in X." These are reproduced in Franz Isaac, *Die Molotschnaer Mennoniten. Ein Beitrag zur Geschichte derselben. Aus Akten älterer und neuerer Zeit, wie auch auf Grund eigener Erlebnisse und Erfahrungen dargestellt* (Halbstadt: H.J. Braun, 1908), 278–80, and translated in Epp, *Johann Cornies*, 60–2. Isaac and Epp dated the two documents a year later ("In the School of X" to 5 March 1846 and "In the School of A" to 6 April 1846), perhaps because they were using later copies.

72 Agricultural Society to schoolteachers, 28 November 1845, *TSUS*, vol. 3, doc. 534.

73 There is no extant original copy. Isaac reproduces it, identifying Cornies as the author (Isaac, *Die Molotschnaer Mennoniten*, 280–9). For an English translation see Epp, *Johann Cornies*, 53–60. The document's date is unknown; it came after the creation of the school districts in January 1846, and apparently grew out of the teachers' conferences in December 1845.

74 Epp, *Johann Cornies*, 53–60.

75 Ibid.

76 Cornies to Hahn, 24 October 1845, *TSUS*, vol. 3, doc. 502. The date that Cornies took charge of the Khortitsa school system is unknown. See Cornies's undated notes regarding a memorandum from the Guardianship Committee to the Khortitsa Gebietsamt, n.d. [1846], *TSUS*, vol. 3, doc. 631. It occurred no later than August 1846, when Cornies began corresponding with Khortitsa teacher Heinrich Franz about school reforms in Khortitsa. Cornies to Franz, August 1846, *TSUS*, vol. 3, doc. 646.

77 Cornies to Hahn, 24 October 1845, *TSUS*, vol. 3, doc. 502.

78 Ibid.

79 Agricultural Society to Heinrich Franz, 26 April 1846, *TSUS*, vol. 3, doc. 593. On Franz's distinguished career, see Peter M. Friesen, *The Mennonite Brotherhood in Russia, 1789–1910*, trans. John B. Toews et al. (Fresno, CA: Conference of Mennonite Brethren Churches, 1980), 709–13.

80 *TSUS*, vol. 3, doc. 659.

81 Johann Siemens to Cornies, 1 January 1847, *TSUS*, vol. 3, doc. 723.

82 Harvey L. Dyck, "Landlessness in the Old Colony: The Judenplan Experiment 1850–1880," in *Mennonites in Russia, 1788–1988: Essays in Honour of Gerhard Lohrenz*, ed. John Friesen (Winnipeg: CMBC Publications, 1989), 183–202; John W. Slocum, "Who, and When, Were the *Inorodtsy*? The Evolution of the Category of 'Aliens' in Imperial Russia," *Russian Review* 57, no. 2 (April 1998), 175, https://doi.org/10.1111/0036 -0341.00017; Kivelson and Suny, *Russia's Empires*, 166–7.

83 Hahn to Cornies, 20 March 1846, *TSUS*, vol. 3, doc. 579. On the Judenplan, see Dyck, "Landlessness in the Old Colony."

84 Hahn to Cornies, 20 March 1846, *TSUS*, vol. 3, doc. 579.

85 Cornies to Hahn, 6 April 1846, *TSUS*, vol. 3, doc. 590.

86 Ibid.

87 Ibid.

88 Epp, *Johann Cornies*, 130.

89 In April David Cornies wrote Traugott Blueher that Cornies was buried on the 17th, but all other accounts say the 16th. David Cornies to Blueher, 18 April 1848, *TSUS*, vol. 3, doc. 980.

90 For an English translation, see Gavel, "Agronomist Gavel's Biography of Johann Cornies (1789–1848)," trans. Harvey L. Dyck, *Journal of Mennonite Studies* 2 (1984): 29–41.

91 Dyck provides an excellent analysis of the Gavel obituary as well as the changing attitudes towards Cornies over the following 128 years in "Russian Servitor and Mennonite Hero: Light and Shadow in Images of Johann Cornies," *Journal of Mennonite Studies* 2 (1984), 9–28.

92 V.M. Karev et al., s.v. "Gann, Evgenii Fedorovich," *Nemtsy Rossii Entsiklopediia* (Moscow, 1999–2006).
93 Cornies to Peterson, 29 November 1844, *TSUS*, vol. 3, doc. 377.
94 Venger, *Mennonitskoe predprinimatel'stvo*, 7, 88.
95 See V.E. Postnikov, *IUzhno-russkoe krest'ianskoe khoziaistvo* (Moscow, 1891).
96 Urry, *None But Saints*, 119, 143.

CORRESPONDENCE

1843

**1. Johann Cornies to Christian Steven. 4 January 1843.
SAOR 89-1-925/2.**

Inspector for Agriculture v. Steven,

If manure is available, almost all fields designated as fallow in our local villages are fertilized. Potatoes are also planted on manured fields but we do not have special fields for potato cultivation. We likely have more manure available here than we can use. Manure must be suitable for the type of soil in question and be added to the same depth as the topsoil has been turned. Thorough mixing of soil and manure is essential to achieving a good harvest. Forty to fifty *fuder* (fifty *puds* each) of well-rotted manure per desiatina is considered about right for keeping the soil moist. Still one must take care because the sun's scorching rays may burn plant roots in light, dry soil fertilized with manure and full of insufficiently rotted straw.

Haymeadows are also fertilized by scattering manure evenly on them in fall. When frost has turned the soil spongy, harrows are used to break it into small bits during a thaw and to spread it evenly over the whole meadow. This treatment gives the soil a covering that prevents it from drying out. Such protection significantly promotes the growth of grass.

Grainfields can also be fertilized with ashes before seeding. Twelve carts of ashes are considered to be sufficient for one desiatina of land. Fertilizing with ashes occurs more often on haymeadows but neither ashes nor manure are sufficient in our area to fertilize all fields on a regular basis.

As far as I know, none of the other [colonist] settlements fertilize their agricultural fields, nor do nobles or Russian peasants.

2. Johann Cornies to Dedato Milinovich. 4 January 1843. SAOR 89-1-925/3.[1]

Merchant Milinovich in Berdiansk,

When I received your letter of 24 December, I immediately notified the local District Office and encouraged Johann Regier, Rudnerweide village Mennonite, to pay off his debt to you without delay. I am sure that he will repay his debt fully by 15 January. You are a humane man who would not, I am sure, do anything before then to cause Regier distress. Regier was quite without money when he visited me, nor could he get a loan to cover his debt. I hope that compassion towards a fellow citizen might guide you in this matter.

I also hope that our mutually beneficial relations might remain intact. They lift up the general well-being of our area and are of great value to our community.

Mr. Martens is presently in Kherson. Once he returns, I will let you know about the subject you raise.

With the greatest esteem, Johann Cornies.

3. Gerhard Klaassen to Johann Cornies. 5 January 1843. SAOR 89-1-911/1.[2]

Worthy Mr. Johann Cornies,

When you extended the term of my loan until the New Year, I gave you my word that I would repay you on the specified date. But now I find myself unable to carry out my side of the bargain and this causes me much pain. Do not be angry because the matter is not my fault. The money was promised and I am sure I will get it, but only sometime this month. Therefore, please be patient for another month when I will repay you with great thanks.

Counting on your kindness, I remain your obedient Gerhard Klaassen.

Lindenau, 5 January 1843.

---

1 Regarding Regier's debt, see *TSUS*, vol. 3, docs. 2, 7, 31.

2 Regarding Cornies's role as moneylender, see John R. Staples, *Johann Cornies, the Mennonites, and Russian Colonialism in Southern Ukraine* (Toronto: University of Toronto Press, 2023), 114–18. For a more general account of moneylending in nineteenth-century Russia, see Sergei Antonov, *Bankrupts and Usurers of Imperial Russia: Debt, Property, and the Law in the Age of Dostoevsky and Tolstoy* (Cambridge, MA: Harvard University Press, 2016), https://doi.org/10.4159/9780674972599.

4. Traugott Blueher to Johann Cornies. 6 January 1843.
SAOR 89-1-911/4.[3]

Mr. Johann Cornies, Ohrloff, Beloved Friend,

We have ended an old year that we survived with God's mercy, and I remember my treasured friends with great fondness. We share general convictions and the foundation on which we stand. I wish you and your dear family a blessed New Year. May the peace of God accompany you in all your undertakings.

Thank you for your valued letter of 15 October 1842. It confirms that you have received my remittance in good order.

Several buyers have offered last year's prices for your stored Spanish wool despite containing more of the fine variety than did the rest. For now, I have put off selling your wool.

You suggested that you buy Spanish wool for me earlier than last year. I'm happy to oblige. Please buy one thousand puds of washed Spanish wool this winter provided the price does not exceed twenty rubles per pud for medium-quality wool. Also, please examine the strength of the wool. May our loving Heavenly Father bless this undertaking.

You will have received samples of rapeseed and information about its use. I assume that if this branch of our economy is to succeed the seeds will need to be stored.

With friendly greetings for you and your family, I commend myself to your loving remembrance and remain, as before, your faithful friend, Traugott Blueher.

P.S. Couldn't you use English sheep-washing methods?

Answer 18 February 1843.

5. Johann Cornies to Evgenii F. Hahn. 7 [or 17] January 1843.
SAOR 89-1-925/4.

State Counsellor Hahn, Yr. Excellency,

I couldn't manage to do what you asked of me on 12 November 1842 any earlier. Please forgive the delay. I had a lot of business to do and there were other problems. "Man proposes, God disposes." All this causes me much pain.

---

3   Blueher was Cornies's Moscow business agent and a close personal friend. On the importance of their friendship for Mennonite economic development, see Staples, *Johann Cornies*, 74–5.

I will send Yr. Excellency an essay based on my own practical experience with the next mail. It is about guidance and instruction for the establishment of forest-tree plantations and their cultivation in Southern Russian villages. I then plan to tear myself away from my work and set out for Odesa.

With sincere trust and genuine esteem, I sign myself as Yr. Excellency's devoted servant, J. Cornies.

6. Johann Klaassen to Johann Cornies. 9 January 1843.
   SAOR 89-1-911/6.[4]

Mr. Johann Cornies, valued friend,

I enclose several samples of cloth in progress. To judge by the black, brown, green, and olive green [samples], Mr. Pefler should be a dyer. But the blues are not right. They have not been dyed properly and thoroughly and tend towards white or grey. I gave him six weeks to experiment but he has failed in this effort and used up three hundred rubles of testing materials in the process. I will have to let him go.

I feel sorry for Pefler. He is a man of good character, I am sure, but I cannot praise him for doing something for which he has not been properly trained. When I questioned him about his expertise, he gave me his word that Lehmann, a dyer in Novocherkask, could certainly accomplish it.

The samples are not meant to suggest the quality of the cloth, only its colour. The latter, including the best pieces, are not up to standard in regard to the colour.

I commend myself to you and sign myself as your friend, Johann Klaassen, Halbstadt, 9 January 1843.

7. Johann Cornies to Benjamin Ratzlaff. 11 January 1843.
   SAOR 89-1-877/70.

[Draft:] From Chairman of Agricultural Society, to Honourable Elder Benjamin Ratzlaff,

General Governor Count Vorontsov has personally asked me to help find an amicable settlement of a matter in dispute between the merchant Milinovich and Johann Regier, Mennonite from the village

---

4   Regarding Klaassen and his cloth mill, see Staples, *Johann Cornies*, 117, 168–9.

of Rudnerweide. His Excellency is afraid that the matter might bring shame upon all Mennonites. I myself have tried to have the matter thoroughly investigated in Berdiansk. The accounts there show that Regier owes the merchant Milinovich 5,776 rubles, 70 kopeks. Regier has accepted this figure as correct in a signed document to the merchant.

Inspector Pelekh tells me that, according to law, if the matter is not settled by 15 January and Regier is unable to defend himself, he would have to arrest him. The Inspector would have to submit a formal action. This would result in a judgment based on the documents submitted to the District Court for its decision.

Since such a thing should never happen according to the teachings of our faith, Regier would have acted unfaithfully in regard to his confession of faith. Since Regier has already admitted his debt with his signature, please, honourable Elder, get Regier to settle the matter quickly. If the law were to find Regier guilty the result would certainly bring dishonour to all of our Mennonites.

8. Johann Cornies to [Fedor F. Rosen]. 11 January 1843. SAOR 89-1-925/5.

Baron [Rosen],

I have it on good authority that potatoes stored in rooms in several villages have not been properly looked after because the stoves had not been adequately fired. The result is that potatoes that were frozen are beginning to rot. There may well be a lot of damage unless stern measures are taken. I would therefore ask Yr. Honour to instruct Mr. Andreevskii personally to inspect potatoes in all villages without delay. He should also order that storage rooms be kept warm, but not hot, and that potatoes not be stored right next to the stoves. Mr. Andreevskii should report his findings directly to you and inform me accordingly. Johann Cornies.

9. District Office notes to Johann Cornies. 12 January 1843. SAOR 89-1-906/30 & 34.

Notes from the District Office at Halbstadt for Chairman Johann Cornies, to be submitted to the Guardianship Committee for Foreign Settlers.

1. Construct special buildings for village offices because the number of fullholders in villages is too small.

2. Restrict the dispersal of rams from the community sheepfarm among villages. Specifically, only two or three rams should be released to each village community that should have chosen a special flock for them to service.

Also, ploughland agriculture and tree plantings at the community sheepfarm should be expanded. The sheepfarm's income is, however, insufficient to cover costs. Cost estimates for 1843 indicate that expenses will exceed income.

3. Order the necessary village seals.

4. Determine boundaries of crown land in this district by surveyor Tushchevskii. A third of all unusable land should be considered as usable. Since Tushchevskii has been occupied with this task for two years, should the work not be accelerated to save costs?

5. Construct a furnace facility [Brandhaus] in Halbstadt with an apparatus for steam.

6. Apprentice secretary Gerhard Neufeldt has expressed a desire to join the evangelical religion. When he returns after training with the Committee, he naturally cannot remain in his position any longer and must also repay his training costs. How can this be arranged?

7. Reports about the administration of the Halbstadt manufacturing village should be changed to make it annual and not monthly.

**10. District Office to Johann Cornies. [12 January 1843.]
    SAOR 89-1-906/32.**

Notes:
    1. Free years for the Radishchev Mennonites [Hutterites].
    2. Establishment of Chumak road on land assigned for it.[5]
    3. Communal buildings and bridge left standing in Radishchev.
    4. Community well to be dug for Radishchev Mennonites.
    5. Mariupul Mennonite land should be surveyed before the coming autumn by the Committee's surveyor.
    6. About two thousand and four thousand desiatinas of land in [illegible] District.
    7. Secretary Penner, now in Khortitsa District Office, to go to Mariupol District.

---

5   Chumaks were carters who transported goods primarily in Ukraine.

8. Beverage leases to Jews in the Mariupol Mennonite District.

9. Arrangement of hearth-sites in Berdiansk Colonist District.

10. About Mariupol colonist Christian Klaassen.

11. Fewer breeding rams at the Molochnaia Mennonite community sheepfarm to be dispersed among the villages.

12. Estimates of expenses for 1843 anticipate a spending increase of eight hundred silver rubles.

13. Boundaries of land in the Molochnaia Mennonite District to be determined by the Committee's surveyor.

14. Construction of the furnace facility.

15. Change the monthly reporting system for the craftsman's village.

16. Put village schools under the Society's direction.

17. Village office buildings.

18. Stallions on community accounts.

19. Protective plantings at four villages, Pastwa, Grossweide, Rudnerweide and Gnadenfeld.

20. Inspector ill and might be given an assistant for two months.

21. Construction of houses for the poor in the Molochnaia Mennonite District.

22. Ordering of craftsmen skilled in silk production from the Rhine for the Molochnaia Mennonite District.

[23.] Iushanle land.

11. [No heading – apparently Cornies's notes regarding document 10.] [12 January 1843.] SAOR 89-1-906/31.

1. Provided here.

2. To be considered on site in spring with surveyor.

3. Submission to be made about which buildings and bridges, by name, were left unsold.

4. Remains as submitted.

5. A surveyor will be sent to the Mariupol [Bergthal] Mennonites on my submission.

6. Money from the lease of the two thousand desiatinas goes to the crown treasury. I will make a submission as to who could settle on the other four thousand as model settlers.

7. The Committee will inquire whether the District Secretary is willing to do this.

8. The Committee will make inquiries and will not give permission.

9. Sketch of hearth-sites will be sent to the Berdiansk District Office.

10. Steps will be taken about Christian Klassen.

11–12. Submission will be made about breeding rams and about sheepfarm arrangements.

13. Submission will be made about when surveyor is needed.

14. Will be confirmed according to the agreement made between the community and those leasing it.

15. Inspector to make a submission about annual reporting.

16. The Society to develop a draft about the way in which the Committee should dispense directives on this matter.

17. To begin, special rooms could be arranged.

18. May be purchased.

19. Submission to be made.

20. About the Inspector – he is to be relieved.

21. Is recognized as being useful and beneficial.

22. Write to Prussia about hiring.

12. Johann Fast to Johann Cornies. 12 January 1843. SAOR 89-1-911/12.

Most esteemed Mr. Cornies,

To my very great sorrow, the honourable District Office in Halbstadt has informed me today regarding a communication from the Society telling me that I will be removed from my service [as teacher] in the Petershagen school. When I accepted this position I was not deceitful in any way.

It is impossible for me to sustain myself without a position. Now that I am losing my teaching position in the Petershagen church on the advice of the honourable District Chairman Toews, I would request that you, most esteemed Mr. Cornies, kindly help me to find another position to support my family.

I am convinced that you will do so. If you could assist me, I would try to carry out your instructions conscientiously, as far as I am able. You should have no doubts but that I will do so and not indulge myself in my previous life of dissipation. I have been punished enough for my misdeeds, and, after confessing my remorse, was reconciled with my congregation.

Because of my great need, I would again ask you to pity me and not hold my past misdeeds against me. Please help me find a position where I can support myself and my family. It is impossible for me to do heavy physical work because of my crippled feet. For the past year I have been able to look after myself only miserably.

An early resolution of this matter is requested by your obedient Johann Fast.

Halbstadt, 12 January 1843.

13. Johann Cornies to Christian Steven. 14 January 1843. SAOR 89-1-925/5v.

To the Inspector for Agriculture Mr. v. Steven,

On 2 January, two peasant youths from Ekaterinoslav Guberniia, Prokofii Uslich from Novomoskov District, and Semen Petrenko from Aleksandrov District were sent to me as apprentices to learn practical agriculture. I sent the latter back immediately because of his poor health. Then on 12 January, from the same village, the peasant youth Ivan Timoshnichenko (also known as Badak) came to take his place.

I now have nine youths and four girls from Tavrida Guberniia and four youths from Ekaterinoslav Guberniia learning practical agriculture with me. Johann Cornies.

14. Johann Cornies to Fedor F. Rosen. 14 January 1843. SAOR 89-1-925/6.[6]

His Honour, Baron Rosen,

The dates set for Nogais buying Spanish sheep on loan from Mennonites has passed, yet only a few Nogais have paid off their creditors as they had obligated themselves to do. Please have suitable people seriously urge the Nogais to satisfy their creditors as they had legally promised they would do. Only in this way would they pay off their debts for items given them, keep their word, and sustain and improve their economic establishments.

I have no doubt that my humble request will be carried out and remain, with the most exceptional esteem, Yr. Honour's respectful servant, Johann Cornies.

---

6 Regarding Nogai sharecropping of Mennonite sheep, see John R. Staples, "'On Civilizing the Nogais': Mennonite-Nogai Economic Relations, 1825–1860," *Mennonite Quarterly Review* 74, no. 2 (April 2000): 229–56.

15. Johann Cornies to Peter Keppen. 14 January 1843. SAOR 89-1-925/6v.

His Honour, State Counsellor v. Keppen,

I write in response to your commission of 1839 to open additional grave mounds in this region at the expense of the Imperial Academy and to send you the results.[7] In October and November 1842, I had six grave mounds opened and excavated. A description of the dig and the items recovered were sent to you with the kind assistance of State Counsellor von Steven. Enclosed is a detailed account of the costs incurred. I would note that six silver rubles, forty-four and two-seventh kopeks remain for further undertakings of this kind. In spring, I will open further mounds and report the results.

At this time, I humbly request that you, Mr. State Counsellor, kindly correct an inaccuracy that crept into the *Journal of the Ministry of State Domains* for 1842, volume 6, page 262. I would mention specifically that earthen dams are not heaped up with wagons, but with a specialized implement without wheels that we call an earth-sledge. This sledge resembles a flat, roomy box lacking one sidewall with the other walls as depicted in the enclosed drawing [not extant]. The work is done by two persons with two horses or oxen. One person controls the harnessed team, the other the sledge using an attached hand lever or haft. By means of the lever, the operator lifts the back of the sledge to such a height that the front tongue penetrates the ploughed earth and scoops up a full load of soil. Then, again using the lever, the front of the sledge is raised level to the ground and the sledge towed to the spot where the soil is needed. The operator then uses the lever to lift the back of the earth-filled sledge high again, tilting it forward. He then grasps the rope attached to the lever and uses it to pull the empty, tilted sledge back. It is then filled again according to the description above. This work continues without pause and is much easier for people and working livestock than the use of wagons. The machine also transports far more soil.

Since State Counsellor v. Hahn took over the direction of foreign settlements in Southern Russia, affairs have become much more active. All branches of agriculture and trades in the Molochnaia Mennonite villages seem to be at the start of a new and progressive advance. Despite this year's failed harvest and money shortages, many houses have been

---

7   Regarding Cornies's archaeological digs for Keppen, see *TSUS*, vol. 2, 603–40.

built of fired brick and roofed with Dutch roof tiles. Our villages are similarly, year by year, becoming more beautiful and tree plantations continue to spread. Field cultivation continues its remarkable growth. Sericulture will soon be so widely practised as to leave its mark on the household industry of families. On the next mail day I will send State Counsellor v. Steven a complete report about the advances that have been made in the Molochnaia Mennonite District in 1842.

I especially commend myself to your friendly remembrance and remain, with love and unchanging esteem and regard, Yr. Honour's humble servant, Johann Cornies.

Accounts for the cost of paying workmen to open six grave mounds:

The workmen supplied their own meals and implements and were paid thirty silver kopeks per day.

Grave mound			Rubles, kopeks, silver	
No. 1	8 days	7 men	16.	80.
" 2	7	6	12.	60.
" 3	7	5	10.	50.
" 4	2 1/2	6	4.	50.
" 5	3	6	5.	40
" 6	1/2	6		90.
Total				50.70

Fifty-seven rubles, fourteen and two-seventh kopeks were received from the Academy for this purpose. Consequently there are six rubles, forty-four and two-seventh kopeks in cash remaining for further excavations.

16. Johann Cornies to Christian Steven. 14 January 1843.
SAOR 89-1-925/9.

Inspector for Agriculture, State Counsellor v. Steven,

I have the honour to report that, in response to Yr. Honour's communication of 4 January I have persuaded three of our most exceptional agriculturalists to accept crown apprentices to learn practical agriculture on the same terms as those laid out in my own agreements. They are the Mennonites Peter Cornies and Cornelius Wiens of Ohrloff and Johann Sukkau of Blumenort. Under my supervision, each one is prepared to take on an apprentice for this purpose.

I would humbly request that you arrange for well-built youths with qualities essential to the attainment of the desired purpose to fill these positions. To ensure that no time is wasted in their education, those chosen should not be under sixteen years of age, seventeen if possible, and eighteen at most. Johann Cornies.

17. Johann Cornies to Fedor F. Rosen. 14 January 1843.
 SAOR 89-1-925/10v.

Baron v. Rosen,

I have not received the two sacks marked a. and b. that were sent along with Yr. Honour's communication No. 658 of 18 December 1842. Nor can they be found at Orekhov. The communication that originated in Orekhov was sent to me through Colonial Inspector Pelekh. Several times in the past like shipments have gone missing. To prevent similar losses at post offices in future, I would humbly request that Yr. Honour order a serious investigation of the matter.

18. Johann Cornies to District Chairman. [14] January 1843.
 SAOR 89-1-925/10v.

Dear District Chairman,

I find it necessary to monitor the proceedings surrounding the sale of Guenter's half-holding in Fischau. I have learned that people in Fischau are trying to prevent the sale of this half-holding to anyone who does not now live in Fischau. This is done to prevent someone from outside introducing innovations into the village that might disturb its old and humdrum ways.

Please give this matter your attention. I note that among those interested in the property is a certain Derksen, a foreigner.

19. Johann Cornies to Guardianship Committee. 22 January 1843.
 SAOR 89-1-1002/46.

[Draft:] To the Guardianship Committee,

I have the honour to humbly submit the enclosed eight sketches of forest-tree plantations projected for the Berdiansk settlers and for the Mariupol Mennonite District, with the request that they be graciously confirmed and returned to the appropriate District Offices and to the Society. Were the Committee to give these sketches the status of orders I

would be guaranteed that my directives for the establishment of plantations would in fact be carried out in accordance with the sketches made
on site and that related operations would be promptly realized. Might
the Guardianship Committee please inform me about the disposition
of this matter.

20. Johann Cornies to Guardianship Committee.
24 January 1843. SAOR 89-1-1002/48.

Chairman of the Molochnaia Mennonite Society for the Advancement of Agriculture and Trades

To the Guardianship Committee for Foreign Settlers in Southern Russia,

The Guardianship Committee for Foreign Settlers in Southern Russia
gave me the honoured commission to accomplish the resettlement of
the Radishchev Mennonites [Hutterites] transferred from Chernigov
Guberniia in a manner that would be most advantageous for them and
in accordance with my best insights. To fulfil this obligation I submit
the following report to the Guardianship Committee. Already greatly
restricted in their previous location by a serious shortage of land, the
situation of this group became almost calamitous as a result of their
transfer last year.

Specifically, they had to sell their dwellings, household fittings, field
implements, livestock, and all items they could not possibly take along for
low prices, or simply discard them. Considerable costs were incurred in
their journey to the Molochnaia. Now they are almost totally bereft, trusting in the willingness of their humane government to undertake whatever
is needed to promote their future existence on land graciously consigned
for their use. I am confident that they will demonstrate the needed industry to improve their situation significantly over the next few years.

I feel obligated in this regard to humbly ask the Guardianship Committee to take whatever steps are needed to grant the Radishchev Mennonites a six-year exemption from all taxes. This would help them to
make rapid progress on their new settlement site. Since the growth and
prosperity of the settlement is desirable, it is necessary, if they are not to
become dejected, to buoy up their spirits. These poor people are grateful for the monetary advances already received that will surely have
the desired effect. The wood and other building materials necessary
to establish the projected village with thirty fullholders will be bought
under my supervision and be to the greatest possible advantage of
these people.

But outside of this advance, the Radishchev Mennonites have few other means to fund their establishments and even fewer should they have to pay taxes from the start. They must buy everything for cash, draught animals and milk cows, field implements and various absolutely necessary items for day-to-day living. For most, the only sources of income are their own trades.

21. Johann Cornies to Guardianship Committee. 25 January 1843. SAOR 89-1-1002/51.

[Draft:] From Chairman to Guardianship Committee,

With the verbal agreement of His Excellency, the Acting Chief Curator, the Molochnaia Mennonite village community of Conteniusfeld decided that the following five neglectful fullholders be asked to transfer their fullholdings to better, more capable fullholders: David Enns, Jacob Fast with assistant Andreas Voth, Ludwig Dahlke with assistant Peter Dik, Abraham Cornelsen, and Johann Epp.

Except for Johann Epp, the above-mentioned fullholders submitted petitions to the Society, urgently requesting that the Society have patience with them for two years. During this time they promised to make every effort to improve all branches of their fullholdings to the complete satisfaction of the high authorities. The Society has urged the village of Conteniusfeld to provide the necessary security for these four fullholders in support of their stated promise that everything will be completed as demanded within two years.

I have the honour to include a formal community declaration in this regard sent to the Society in order that it might be graciously examined and approved by the Guardianship Committee. When so approved it should be returned to the Molochnaia Mennonite District Office and to the Society in order that the two, acting in tandem, might exercise firm supervision over the prompt realization of its terms. An order might also be given to the village community authorizing it to give the fullholding belonging to the fifth fullholder, Johann Epp, to another person should the community fail to provide security for him.

22. Johann Cornies to David Epp. 27 January 1843. SAOR 89-1-925/11.

Esteemed David Epp in Heubuden, beloved friend,

I have been here in Odesa for the past eight days trying among other things to influence the government to pay for the costs of getting two silk manufacturers of Mennonite confession and their families from the areas of Krefeld or Elberfeld in the Prussian provinces on the Rhine to join us here on the Molochnaia. Should a proposal for the Molochnaia Mennonite community in this regard be approved, I would ask for your kindly cooperation, dear friend, in making inquiries of Elders or other teachers in Krefeld or in one of the other cities in that area. Would there be several Mennonite families willing to join our community who know their craft and its basics well, are of good ethical and moral conduct, and are industrious and diligent? They would have to be willing to move to the Mennonite community in Russia at the government's expense, to bring along the needed equipment for their craft of silk weaving, and to establish themselves here permanently. All possible efforts will be made to facilitate their move. They would also receive a monetary advance to establish and accommodate themselves here. They must be Mennonites, otherwise they cannot be registered here.

The production of silk is spreading in our settlements and we need people who can instruct us in ways of improving what we produce, although they would naturally only manufacture a small part of this production themselves. Their position here would be advantageous for them, even if they are only able to provide ordinary but sound craftsmanship for products that will sell quickly and to their benefit.

I repeat again that even if they have limited means, these families must be of good conduct and show diligence. As said, they can only be Mennonites.

To accomplish this matter in an orderly fashion, I request that you give my address to the acquaintance with whom you are corresponding, and ask him to kindly exchange letters directly with me. These letters, in their original, should be in a form suitable for transmission to the Minister, should that be necessary. Please give me your opinion of this matter as quickly as you can.

I hope you will treat this proposal as a Christian who has the improvement of his brother's well-being at heart. With greetings to you and your dear family, I remain with constant love, your honest and obliging friend and brother, Johann Cornies.

23. Johann Cornies to Guardianship Committee. 28 January 1843. SAOR 89-1-1002/52.

[Draft:] From Chairman to the Guardianship Committee,

The Society and the Molochnaia Mennonite District Office have, for several years, shown great patience with Heinrich Teichgrew, a fullholder in Margenau village. Through neglect, his fullholding has deteriorated badly. As a result it has been decided to take the property from Teichgrew and give it to a more capable and energetic fullholder who will manage it properly. This matter was presented verbally to His Excellency, the Acting Chief Curator during his esteemed presence in the district.

Heinrich Teichgrew has been given the opportunity to voluntarily give his fullholding to an acceptable fullholder by 2 February 1843. Should this not occur, his few household possessions and plantings will be appraised by four Mayors in the district and passed on to the highest bidder at a public auction.

I would dutifully request that, should the above-mentioned resolution be sanctioned, the Guardianship Committee quickly issue a directive to the Molochnaia Mennonite District Office and the Society in order that this matter might be duly accomplished.

24. Johann Cornies to Guardianship Committee.
28 January 1843. SAOR 89-1-1002/53.

[Draft:] From Chairman to the Guardianship Committee,

According to directives issued at the time of the establishment of the Molochnaia Mennonite Society for the Advancement and Dissemination of Forest-Trees and Orchards, Sericulture, and Viticulture, the Society was granted the right to receive free postal correspondence via Orekhov. A post office was later built in the crown village of Novoaleksandrovka [now Melitopol] that is a convenient location for the Society. Free postal service, however, is still limited to Orekhov. This arrangement seriously impedes the speedy forwarding of mail to us because of the considerable distance involved.

I would ask that the Guardianship Committee for Foreign Settlers in Southern Russia graciously approve free postal service through Novoaleksandrovka for the Molochnaia Mennonite Society for the Advancement and Dissemination of Forest-Trees and Orchards, Sericulture, and Viticulture and the Society for the Improvement of Agriculture and Trade and to send the local post office a directive in this regard. We would ask that a suitable directive in this connection be sent to the Society as well.

25. Johann Cornies to Guardianship Committee. [January 1843.]
SAOR 89-1-1005/8.

[Undated draft] To the Guardianship Committee from the Society,

In response to the Society's submission regarding cultivated land for planting in Ohrloff village, it received directive No. 62387 in October 1842 and dutifully reports the following. In fall, seventy-one desiatinas of cultivated land assigned for this purpose were measured, divided, marked, [and distributed] equally among the twenty-one fullholders.

The prescribed enclosure [of these lands] by ditches should proceed unhindered this year, 1843. Two fullholders, David and Peter Cornies, have each already prepared a number of setting trenches for future plantings.

26. Agricultural Society to District Office. [February 1843.] SAOR 89-1-1002/44.

[Undated draft]: District Office from the Society,

Doerksen, a foreigner staying in Fischau village, appeared at the Society's office today ostensibly to request that he be permitted to lease half of David Guenther's fullholding in Fischau. We are in possession of information that this Doerksen had already purchased the above-mentioned half-holding from Guenther for 2,400 or 2,500 rubles. Unbeknownst to the Society, Guenther circulated an announcement in the villages about a public auction of his inventory. It follows that Doerksen secretly intended to effect the illegal transfer of the fullholding with the agreement of the Village Mayor. Such an action must be called sternly to account, especially if a legitimate Mayor was unfaithful in the exercise to his duty, agreeing to an illegal transfer or perhaps involving himself personally in the matter.

The Society therefore requests that the District Office investigate the matter:

1. From whom, by name, did the foreigner Doerksen receive authorization to buy the half-holding from Guenther and who counselled him to make the ostensible request for a lease even though the Society Chairman had expressly explained to him that he could not own or lease land until he had taken the oath of allegiance as a Russian subject and been entered into the revision lists?

2. Who told Guenther that he could circulate a publication in the district, using the system of rotating duties [Zechen] to auction his inventory without the District Office's prior knowledge?

3. Was the Village Mayor involved in these illegal matters? Did he give advice or know about them?

The Society requests that the District Office inform it about the disposition of this matter.

27. Agricultural Society to Cornelius Wall. 3 February 1843. SAOR 89-1-1002/45.

[Draft:] From Society for the Advancement, etc.

To Cornelius Wall, Manager of the Kurushan Community Sheepfarm,

Information received from the Society in 1842 indicates that you have harvested four *chetvert* of Chinese oil radish seeds. Since the Society is trying to increase considerably the planting of this seed in our local district, you are hereby asked to store all of this seed. We have heard from Berdiansk that this seed is now selling for eighteen rubles per chetvert.

Please inform the Society immediately about the quantity and price of this oil radish seed available for planting. The Society will send out notices to the villages in this regard encouraging village offices to increase the seeding of this plant in their villages during the current year.

28. Johann Cornies to Christian Steven. [4 February 1843.] SAOR 89-1-925/14.

His Honour, State Counsellor v. Steven,

Two copies of the booklet regarding silk reeling by Terrier were given to the Mennonites Enns and Wiebe, local silk-reelers, as gifts at the time of local inspections. The clear, thorough, and practical instructions have given Enns and Wiebe great pleasure. They intend to follow these instructions on how to reel local silk more profitably.

Two existing reeling machines are insufficient to reel all of the cocoons at the appropriate time. At least one additional machine will come into operation this year. Several more copies of the above-mentioned instructions will be needed for this purpose. I humbly request that you, Mr. State Counsellor, have five more copies of the instructions for the correct reeling of silk sent to me as soon as possible. I will not neglect to make the required payment.

With unchanging esteem, Yr. Honour's respectful servant, Johann Cornies.

29. Johann Cornies to Fedor F. Rosen. 8 February 1843.
SAOR 89-1-925/15.

Baron Rosen,

On 7 May 1842, the Gnadenfeld Village Office reported to the Agricultural Society that Filon Somarskii and Peter Gulich, two Andreev settlers serving with Peter Wiebe, had left the latter's service on the night of 6 May. The Society immediately applied to the Andreev village administration to have them handed over. One of them, Filon Somarskii, actually returned to service [of his own accord]. The other man failed to appear and the Society requested that Mr. Kalonichenko, assistant to the District Chief, take whatever actions are needed to effect this end.

There was no response to this request and no action was taken. The Society then sent request No. 203 on 4 October 1842 to the Melitopol District Administration to have the runaway Andreev settler Peter Gulich returned by appropriate means to the Gnadenfeld Village Office where his annual registration pass is held, in order that he might complete his term of service of one year. Although the Society was notified that the District Administration would make suitable arrangements in this regard, nothing has in fact happened. On 14 December, the Society again wrote to the District Administration in regard to this matter and now reports that the situation in the Andreev village administration has been submitted for investigation, as is shown by the enclosed copy.

Consequently, I find it necessary to ask you, Yr. Honour, to direct the Melitopol District Administration to order that Peter Gulich, the above-mentioned Andreev settler, be handed over immediately in order that he perform his service unfailingly for the time of his absence, especially since he still owes money [to his employer]. Irregularities of this kind encourage other servants to run away from their service to the great disadvantage of their employers. Gulich should, if possible, as an example to others, be punished for his offence.

30. Johann Cornies to Fedor F. Rosen. 8 February 1843.
SAOR 89-1-925/16.

Baron Rosen,

In response to Yr. Honour's communication No. 18 of 14 January, I have the honour to notify you that in several days' time we expect an opportunity to transport the potato mounders to Poltava and Chernigov. I would ask Yr. Honour to communicate immediately with the board, requesting the bill of lading. Should the mounders be shipped from here in two or three days' time, the cartage people, when they arrive, would be able to receive the money owed them. As soon as I find out about this matter, I will immediately inform Yr. Honour.

31. Johann Cornies to Traugott Blueher. 8 February 1843. SAOR 89-1-925/18v.

Esteemed Mr. Blueher,

Thank you for your valued communications of 2 October 1842 and 8 January 1843. I much appreciate your information about madder and the results of tests done on it. We lacked sufficient information about preparing the dye plant appropriately for this purpose and about finding good markets for it.

I have finally loaded the remainder of my last year's wool production onto carts. It consists of 506 puds, one-half *funt* in forty-seven balls, loaded on fifteen carts that were sent to you in Moscow on 5 February. Its quality is better than the wool I sent to you in summer, as buyers can judge. I enclose the contract with the carters, and a copy of the bill of lading that I gave them. When the delivery arrives the carters are owed 1,319 rubles, twenty kopeks. Please put this amount on my account.

It would give me great pleasure to buy some one thousand puds of wool for you. Over the last few years the number of sheep in our region has dropped considerably. I do not think I am mistaken in saying that it has been cut by half, especially among estate owners and other private Russian individuals. In the Molochnaia Mennonite District, for example, there were 170,000 sheep in 1838, 150,000 in 1841 and around 100,000 head last fall. The demand for wool has accordingly risen and I doubt that I could purchase wool for you at twenty rubles per pud, regardless of how hard I try. What should I do if the price of wool goes up by several rubles? I too have experienced a shortage of money and would be grateful if you could send me twenty thousand rubles for this purchase, specifically ten thousand directly to me and ten thousand to Baron v. Rosen, Director of the Tavrida Bureau of State Domains.

There is little winter weather here, and the days are as warm as in May. While grass and flowers grow luxuriantly on our fields, people plough and seed.

With many greetings to you and your family I remain your loving friend and servant, [signature crossed out, looks like Herm. Wurms, possibly Cornies's secretary].

32. Johann Cornies to Dedato Milinovich. 8 February 1843. SAOR 89-1-925/16v.[8]

Mr. Dedato Milinovich in Berdiansk,

I write to inform you that, even during my absence in Odesa, efforts have been made to ensure that the money owed you by Regier is repaid. Payment was not made on 15 January, however, because several repayments which Regier himself counted on had not yet been made.

Please be patient because all possible measures are being taken to expedite this matter to your satisfaction. I am always concerned, as is the District Office, that a good understanding be maintained between Berdiansk and our local community. This is endangered by disagreements of this sort.

Your most respectful Johann Cornies.

33. Johann Cornies to Fedor F. Rosen. 15 February 1843. SAOR 89-1-925/17.[9]

Baron Rosen,

According to the enclosed sketch, the mosque to be built in the model colony of Akkerman should be five *faden* wide, seven faden long, and two faden, one *arshin* high. The Nogais, however, object that they do not have the resources to construct a mosque of such dimensions. They wish to build it as they had decided earlier, three and one-half faden wide, five faden long, and one faden, two arshins high. Narrower and shorter mosques must be proportionately lower.

According to their plan, the roof is intended to rise only two arshins above the wall. Yet the plan to roof the mosque with Dutch roof tiles demands a height of three and one-half arshins, and this would be better. Otherwise, the plan is in accordance with the wishes of the Nogai Elders and, in my opinion, requires no changes. I humbly request that Yr. Honour confirm this plan, according to the wishes of the Nogais, as soon as possible.

---

8   Regarding Regier's debt, see *TSUS*, vol. 3, docs. 2, 7, 31.

9   Regarding the Nogai model village of Akkerman, see John R. Staples, *Cross-Cultural Encounters on the Ukrainian Steppe: Settling the Molochna Basin, 1783–1861* (Toronto: University of Toronto Press, 2002), 112–14.

34. Johann Cornies to Huebner. 15 February 1843.
   SAOR 89-1-925/17v.

His Honour, Mr. Huebner,

I write in response to your esteemed communication to let you know that eight hundred to one thousand two- and three-year-old fruit trees, as well as older ones, are available for sale from my tree nurseries. The price remains what it was, thirteen kopeks silver apiece regardless of the age of the trees. I will speak with Wilke about the varieties and act in accordance with your wishes. I will proceed similarly in regard to the varieties of bushes suitable for hedges. I should also mention that I do not have any improved cherry trees or "Reine Claude" [plums] for sale at the present time.

At least two carts will be needed to transport the trees, at from thirty to forty rubles apiece. I will see to it that the lifting and packing of the trees is done as well as is possible. I will entrust this task to Wilke, as you had wished, if he can get away for a long enough time from his work at my other estate some forty verstas away.

With all esteem, I remain, your respectful servant, Johann Cornies.

35. Johann Cornies to District Office. 16 February 1843.
   SAOR 89-1-925/23.

Molochnaia Mennonite District Office,

Dirk Esau, Mennonite from Schoensee village, has owed me seven hundred rubles since 22 September 1841. He promised to pay off his debt several times, but to no avail. I would therefore respectfully ask that the honoured District Office take measures to ensure that Esau will unfailingly appear to pay off his debt to me by 1 March 1843.

The honoured District Office's respectful Johann Cornies.

36. Johann Cornies to Fedor F. Rosen. 18 February 1843.
   SAOR 89-1-915/20.

Director Baron v. Rosen,

In response to Yr. Honour's commission, I am honoured to submit the enclosed record of potato yields for 1842 on thirty-nine desiatinas in Melitopol District and eight desiatinas in Dneprov District. Enclosed are receipts from village Elders for the delivery of implements used in the cultivation of potatoes, as well as records of assistant supervisors and apprentices occupied in the cultivation of potatoes in each village community.

Also enclosed is a signed statement of the outlay of 1,900 rubles for the hiring of Mennonites involved in the cultivation of potatoes, which I would respectfully request be remitted soon.

I have prepared a separate record of assistant supervisors who have distinguished themselves in their work, divided into four classes. I would recommend that they be suitably recompensed to encourage their efforts. Specifically I would first propose that fifteen silver rubles be given to Fedor Savchenko, assistant supervisor in the Dneprov District, and eight silver rubles to Kokei Trembetov, assistant supervisor in Melitopol District. Both are deserving of recognition for their exemplary work. Additionally, assistant supervisors in the first class in Melitopol District should be given five silver rubles, in the second class, three silver rubles, and in the third class, two silver rubles, for a total of 138 silver rubles. Should Yr. Honour kindly approve this proposal, I would most obediently request permission to take appropriate action.

37. Johann Cornies to Fedor F. Rosen. 18 February 1843. SAOR 89-1-925/22.

Yr. Honour, Baron Rosen,

When you last visited my Iushanle estate, Yr. Honour kindly promised to secure for me grafting shoots from superior fruit trees on Mr. Muehlhausen's plantation near Simferopol. They are intended for my fruit orchard. I especially desire varieties of good cherries that are well known for their excellence in the Crimea. I now take the liberty to ask that Yr. Excellency obtain for me, if possible, the desired grafting shoots from Mr. Muehlhausen's garden. Mail them to me via Novoaleksandrovka.

I hope that Yr. Honour will soon receive the promised ten thousand rubles directly from the Sarepta trading company in Moscow.

I have ordered five potato mounders, five markers, and five lifters for estate owners in your area. They will, in any case, be ready as indicated.

38. Johann Cornies to Evgenii F. Hahn. 19 February 1843. SAOR 89-1-925/21.

State Counsellor v. Hahn, Yr. Excellency,

The bearer of this, my friend Abraham Wiebe from Rudnerweide, is travelling to Odesa for commercial purposes. I take the liberty to humbly request that Yr. Excellency use this opportunity to obtain a funt of silkworm eggs from Mr. Norman to be sent to our local community. Also, would Yr. Excellency kindly send me some seeds of the pseudo-platanus which grows widely around Odesa?

Mr. Stempel, Inspector for the Mariupol Settlement District, has just arrived here.

With great esteem, your most respectful servant, Johann Cornies.

39. Johann Cornies to Evgenii F. Hahn. [19 February 1843.] SAOR 89-1-925/21v.

Mr. v. Hahn, Yr. Excellency,

Jacob Wiebe, the young Mennonite bearing this letter, has dedicated himself to the teaching profession, as Yr. Excellency knows. To improve his skills he has taken a position with Pastor Fletnitzer, as a substitute for the Mennonite Riediger.[10] The Pastor and I personally agreed on the essentials of this appointment.

I commend him to Yr. Excellency's benevolent supervision, and remain, with the deepest esteem, Yr. Excellency's most respectful servant, Johann Cornies.

40. Andrei M. Fadeev to Johann Cornies. 21 February 1843. SAOR 89-1-661/11.

My dear Cornies,

I have received no news from you for many months. Do write to me about your health and how business matters are progressing, both privately and for your community and your beloved brethren. I, my wife, children, and grandchildren continue as before. My wife warmly remembers the friendly reception you gave her last year.

---

10 Karl Fletnitzer was the pastor of the Odesa Lutheran congregation. A graduate of the Basel Missionary Society, he came to Russia in 1825 intending to do missionary work in the Caucasus, but after a brief stint in Karrass he ended up in Odesa, first as the director of the school, and then also as pastor of St. Paul's. He also played a leading role in Protestant Bible Society activities in the region. His school provided the best German-language education in New Russia, offering its students training in religion, German, Russian, French, arithmetic, geography, calligraphy, drawing, singing, and basic bookkeeping. See E.G. Plesskaia-Zebold, *Odesskie nemtsy 1803–1920* (Odesa: Institut germanskikh i vostochnoevropeiskikh issledovanii Gettingen, 1999), 179–85.

Winter has been mild and the prices for grain and other commodities have been moderate.

Keep your word and visit us this year, but please let me know in advance. I may travel to St. Petersburg in spring but hope to be home by the end of July.

May you fare well and in good health. Give my greetings to all my old acquaintances. How is our Martens doing?

Always and completely your respectful friend, Fadeev, Saratov.

Received 20 March 1843; answered 28 February 1844.

41. Johann Cornies to Fedor F. Rosen. 22 February 1843. SAOR 89-1-925/23v.

Baron v. Rosen,

I find it painful to keep bringing unpleasant matters to the attention to Yr. Honour, but I feel that I must when district officials continue to take uncaring and inappropriate actions that damage the well-being of the peasants and cause their decline.

Since I've not been notified of the sale of any potatoes in the districts, I must conclude that abuses are taking place. I have seen nothing of Mr. Andreevskii for two months and this entire branch of agriculture seems to have been neglected. When I travelled through Kiltshik from Odesa, I called on the Elder to inquire about the condition of potatoes in local pits, but he could tell me nothing and said dismissively that he had received no orders in this regard. Today an official from Mustapoi informed me that he had found rotted potatoes on his monthly trip around the Kiltshik District. I wrote to him today, noting that every Elder would be held responsible for rotting potatoes under his authority and would have to pay two silver rubles for every chetvert found.

I do not like to harbour the idea that district officials, from top to bottom, are involved in tricks in order that they might use these fields for their own purposes. I had hoped to do something useful for crown peasants at least in Melitopol District, but the present District Administration forces me to abandon even this hope.

For thirty-five years I have, in hope and generosity, sacrificed a large part of my life for the Nogais. Now that I am starting to get old and grey I had been looking forward to a little rest. Anyone who is not indifferent to his fellow man, loves others, and has Christian feelings, can judge how hard it is for me to entertain such thoughts. These words are animated by a zealous striving on my part to faithfully carry out all duties incumbent on me. It remains my holy assurance that service to my fellow man remains the greatest joy of my life. With faithfulness to this goal I remain Yr. Honour's respectful servant, Johann Cornies.

42. Johann Cornies to Evgenii F. Hahn. 22 February 1843. SAOR 89-1-925/25.

Mr. Hahn, Yr. Excellency, Gracious Sir,

During my last visit to Odesa, Yr. Excellency expressed benevolent kindness by graciously offering to intercede on my behalf in a matter that would allow me to gain possession and inheritance rights for the land I have leased since 1811. I enclose an accurate map of this land. My hope is that I might receive gracious permission from the Imperial government to own these five hundred desiatinas of usable land in perpetuity. This would permit me to improve further and extend my already established plantations and economic arrangements as models and examples [to the surrounding area].

As noted on the map, the Chumak roads are not actually two verstas wide. As the pencilled line shows, the width is only eight hundred faden as determined in 1810. Should the width be two verstas, the land between the Chumak road and my Imperial grant of land would consist of 459 desiatinas, 816 faden. According to the eight-hundred-faden width shown by the pencilled line, somewhat more than one hundred desiatinas of usable and unusable land would be added. Similarly, the other two pieces of land between the Chumak roads would be different if the road is eight hundred faden wide, as it is actually now. Pasture is available in abundance and sufficient for Chumak oxen travelling through the area.

I would dutifully request that Yr. Excellency favour me with your influential intervention. I, for my part, will show my gratitude for your benevolence and trust by fulfilling to the letter all obligations incumbent upon me.

In striving to make myself worthy of your favour, I remain Yr. Excellency's respectful servant, Johann Cornies.

43. Johann Cornies to Fedor F. Rosen. 25 February 1843. SAOR 89-1-925/27.

Baron Rosen,

I obligated myself to Yr. Honour to direct operations involved in introducing potato cultivation among state peasants in Melitopol and

Dneprov Districts for three consecutive years. Two years have now passed and the third will soon begin. In addition to the potatoes needed for seeding, I estimate that there must still be a considerable number of chetverts of potatoes in Melitopol District approved for sale or other purposes.

Spring is approaching rapidly and it is time to make decisions about potato seeding. I respectfully request that Yr. Honour inform me about the manner in which these arrangements should be made. Would you permit me, or find it appropriate, to hire a Mennonite as the main supervisor, at least in the Dneprov District? How many districts would he supervise and which ones, specifically? Should the first desiatina in Melitopol *volost* already prepared in each district be again planted with potatoes? Who will supervise this directly? Stern orders to volosts and districts to cooperate in this work must be issued as well. District chiefs and their assistants should also be firmly encouraged, since their neglectful behaviour with respect to potato cultivation has lulled the state peasants into a deep sleep.

Expecting your early resolution of this matter, I remain Yr. Honour's respectful servant, Johann Cornies.

44. Agricultural Society to Fuerstenau Village Office. Undated draft, March 1843. SAOR 89-1-960/6.

To the Fuerstenau Village Office,

The Society received and confirmed report No. 26, dated 14 [March?] about supervision of the lease of fullholding No. 17. The Society also orders the Office to estimate the jobs likely needed, according to general directives, to complete improvements to the above-mentioned hearth-site in 1843, specifically:

1. To repair fences and build new fences.
2. To improve ditches where necessary.
3. To repair and maintain buildings. To clean up the hearth-site.
4. To complete the planting of fruit trees according to the directives and new orders. Setting trenches should be prepared for the coming year.
5. To ensure regular progress in the planting of forest trees. Etc.

This program, with Village Office signatures, is to be submitted for confirmation to the Society by [?] March.

45. Notes of Agricultural Society inspection tour. [March] 1843. SAOR 89-1-973/4.

[Draft, with line through many items]

1. Road from Fuerstenau to Schoensee to be moved to a better location.
2. All bridges and dams in district should be assigned to a community for upkeep.
3. For meeting:

- Certification needed for Franz, son of Franz Isaac, Marienthal.
- Mikh. Regier and Isaac Klaasen have been in state of disagreement since they took over their hearth-site. Since this cannot continue, they must sell it voluntarily.
- Conteniusfeld elected – ;
- Wernersdorf, Bold, and Mayor to be ordered to meeting; Conteniusfeld, Bargen has four grown boys at home.
- Beer and brandy

46. Untitled list. N.d. SAOR 89-1-973/5.

1. Fuerstenau & Ladekopp to provide a ditch to fence off the entire length of their boundaries with Tokmak land.
2. Johann Bold from Wernersdorf disobeyed the Mayor's orders and must be called to account.
3. Liebenau, Heinrich Neufeld to build a stone fence in spring at all points where there is no fence around the rocks.
4. Ladekopp, Mayor's Office to be directed to order Bestvater to give up his fullholding, since matters cannot continue in this way. The cottager in the old schoolhouse must keep his children in better order and punish them for smoking tobacco in the barn. He must also put his front yard in order. Otherwise he will be required to rebuild an improperly built house and to make better arrangements.
5. Fuerstenwerder householder who fenced his orchard so badly that calves got in will be fined fifteen kopeks.
6. In Waldheim, ditches around hearth-sites have not been dug during this time when there was little work to be done. A regulation ditch must now be made. Manure must be hauled away from areas where trees are to be planted and fields ploughed to a depth of three or four *vershok*, according to regulations.
7. The Landskrone Mayor must keep a watch on Tehrmann, to ensure he builds a masonry chimney and keeps better order and cleanliness in

his house. He should be prohibited from making any unnecessary visits and from driving around.

47. Jacob Sineib to Johann Cornies. 6 March 1843. SAOR 89-1-955/12.

Esteemed Mr. Cornies,

I hasten to respond to your honoured communication of 9 February informing you that [German] colonist Joseph Pernitzky[11] from Neuhoff told me he had surveyed the land in eight villages (Russian and Greek) according to the number of souls. I checked this and am not aware of any complaints about the survey at this time.

Granted, Pernitzky encountered resistance to the survey from Bereslav community but no formal decision has yet been made in this matter. I cannot definitely confirm that the above-mentioned Pernitzky is completely up to this task. Such assurance involves an examination which I do not feel capable of administering.

Respectfully, Jacob [name illegible]

48. Johann Cornies to Fedor F. Rosen. 8 March 1843. SAOR 89-1-925/29.

Baron Rosen,

I just learned that the selection of village administrations in the Nogai District has been completed. It was done among the Nogais in Mr. Andreevskii's presence. In all other village communities in the district, selections were made by the head [*golova*] in each volost. I do not know whether abuses took place in Iugabkamgale and Ulkanbeskele volost selections.

However, I cannot avoid informing Yr. Honour about abuses that took place in Shuiut Dzhuret and especially in Burkut village community. When you visited here last autumn, Yr. Honour commissioned me to tell the Nogais to select Ali Berdilatov for a new term, and also Bultrak Modalov as Elder in Burkut. I carried out this assignment faithfully and understood that the Nogais would make this selection. However, when Mr. Andreevskii started the selection in Iugabkamgale volost, a rumour spread in Shuiut Dzhuret volost that Mr. Andreevskii would

---

11 Pernitzky's name is sometimes spelled Panitzky in the document. Here it has been standardized as Pernitzky.

not allow Bultrak Modalov to be selected as Elder. I explained my commission from you to Mr. Andreevskii and your wishes to have Ali and Bultrak selected again for their offices. I noticed that Mr. Andreevskii was not inclined to have Bultrak as Elder because he unfairly blamed Bultrak for several mistakes made when he was in office.

When Mr. Andreevskii arrived in Shuiut Dzharet volost he permitted the selection of Bekbulut, the young man in his service, as Elder for Bauerdak. Then he sent this man to persuade the Nogais not to select Bultrak but a certain Tulemishov from Bauerdak as Elder for Burkut. Bultrak thus got no votes. I know nothing about Tulemishov except that he is a young and wealthy man engaged in trade. Andreevskii allowed the selection of a certain Mulbali, a real rascal, as Elder in Burkut.

I request that Yr. Honour absolutely not allow these selections to stand in the Burkut District and that steps be taken to make a second selection without Mr. Andreevskii or any other official present. When this matter is conducted, the law must be followed under the administration of the District Elders.

49. Forestry Society to Heinrich Wiens. March 1843. SAOR 89-1-960/8.

[Draft:] Honoured Church Elder H. Wiens in Gnadenheim,

To beautify the area around community buildings, the Society has an obligation to require the planting there of various useful trees. The area along the street in front of churches should be planted according to our directives, as should the yard, or wagon area situated behind the churches.

The Society hereby requests that you, honoured Elder, ensure that the administrative directives for the churches belonging to your congregation are carried out this year. Strong, durable fences should be built if they do not exist and gates provided for entrances.

50. Johann Cornies to Carl Stempel. 27 March 1843. SAOR 89-1-925/36v.[12]

Mr. Stempel, Honoured Inspector,

Kindly forgive me for not carrying out my earlier promise. Only now am I able to send you the report about agricultural progress in the Molochnaia Mennonite District. I had intended to visit you and travel through

---

12 Stempel was the Colonial Inspector for the Bergthal and Würtemburg settlements.

your villages in March but this was frustrated by the unanticipated and overwhelming amount of work my business affairs required. I can still not determine the date in April when I will have the pleasure of seeing you.

The messenger bringing you this letter is a master mason. Working with fifty associates over the last ten years, he constructed the best and most excellent structures here in the Molochnaia Mennonite and [German] Colonist Districts, to the satisfaction of the people for whom they were built. He heard that a church was to be built in Grunau and is coming to make inquiries about taking over the construction of the church. He is in a position to provide the required security for this.

I heartily commend myself to your friendship and remain, with esteem, your friend and servant, Johann Cornies.

51. Johann Cornies to Fedor F. Rosen. 29 March 1843. SAOR 89-1-925/32v.

Baron v. Rosen,

I am honoured to report that, on 25 March, I made all arrangements for planting crown potatoes in thirty-nine village communities in Melitopol District. The job has been divided among twenty-three peasants trained for the work. Sixteen village communities in Dneprov District, specifically Great and Upper Belovka, Vesploi, Vadiana, Mustapoi, Kiltshik, Elisagash Iuskuiu, Sarebulat, Tashkishken, Karakuia, Rogatshik, Ivanovka, Dneproloka, Great Snamenka, and Lower Serogosa are under the supervision of the Mennonite Peter Ediger. To assist him in this task he has chosen three Russian peasants and one Nogai from Melitopol District, all trained for this purpose. It is my hope that if my arrangements are supported by District administrative officials in accordance with my instructions, everything, at least to some extent, will proceed quickly and with the desired orderliness, and the state peasants will be encouraged in their cultivation of potatoes.

52. Johann Cornies to Traugott Blueher. 29 March 1843. SAOR 89-1-925/33.

Esteemed Mr. Blueher,

Accompanying your valued communication of 1 March, I received five thousand rubles at the Novoaleksankrovka post office on 20 March. Deposits of seventeen rubles per pud have been made for approximately two hundred puds of Spanish wool still on the sheep. Little more can be done for the time being. The Berdiansk merchants are everywhere, paying advances for wool and making deposits wherever producers are in need of money. Producers who do not need money immediately are holding out for higher prices. As always, I will make every effort to seek your best interests in this purchase.

Even though I would have preferred to have it done differently, I thank you for your information that the sum of ten thousand rubles was not sent to Baron v. Rosen. I can now make other arrangements to pay this money from here in March, as promised. Otherwise, I would have been in a great dilemma. There is now no great hurry to have my money sent. It remains at your discretion whether you send me the whole sum requested earlier or after the purchase has been completed, as in previous years.

How are things going in Sarepta? I have received no news from my dear friend Doehring for more than a year. Is he still alive? Please tell him about my inquiries and give our heartfelt greetings to all of the dear ones there. My wife often suffers from a severe cough, but God be praised we are all still healthy.

We send sincerest greetings to you and your dear family, and remain, as always, your devoted friend and servant, Johann Cornies.

53. Johann Cornies to Fedor F. Rosen. 29 March 1843. SAOR 89-1-925/34.

Baron v. Rosen,

In response to your communication No. 122 of 8 March, I have the privilege to report that forest-tree seeds sent by the Ministry office arrived too late to be seeded this spring. All of the seeds or a portion of them will soon be forwarded to our Forestry Society for appropriate storage so that they retain their ability to germinate. This is with the exception of the oak and "barbaris" seeds. These seeds will be urgently needed in our villages next autumn and are accepted with thanks.

54. Johann Cornies to David Epp. 29 March 1843. SAOR 89-1-925/35.[13]

David Epp, Heubuden.
Very dear friend,

---

13   In 1843 letters from Abraham Regier, Elder of the conservative Heubuden congregation in Prussia, and other Prussian Mennonites, protested the treatment of Jacob Warkentin and the dissolution of the three Warkentin congregations in 1842. Cornies responded harshly to the letters from Prussia. See Staples, *Johann Cornies*, 208–9.

Our local community split twenty years ago because of the evil insinuations of several Prussian Elders and teachers. This disunity has increased to the point where it has been necessary to punish several people. Written submissions from here state that Elders and preachers from your area carry considerable responsibility for this state of affairs. Their communications over the last twenty years reveal their evil intentions to keep our community divided. In response to a summons of 5 September 1842, sent out by Elder Abraham Regier of Heubuden, new and highly damaging papers have again been received that are most harmful for our community. Persons involved have disavowed these papers as evidenced in a letter to Elder Regier. I enclose an exact copy of the letter from Neufeldt and Huebert with a request that Elder Regier be seriously questioned as to whether he has received a letter with the same contents. This matter is considered serious here. Elder Regier must explain his purpose and objective in challenging congregations to report to him about the details of recent dissensions here. His letter does say that the five Elders did not report anything.

Such an explanation must reach me by 15 June or Regier should expect other demands. Once you have presented this subject to Elder Regier, please write to me immediately in order that I might know what attitude has been take in this matter.

I also enclose a copy of a petition submitted to me from three Elders and four teachers [preachers], to give you some idea of the difficulties Ohm Regier's challenge has caused us here. With shame, I take note of the fact that the Elders are supposed to be messengers of peace. They should not seek to introduce dissension, even misfortune, into our communities, or take pleasure in hearing bad accounts of superiors.

With a friendly greeting, I remain your friend who loves you, Johann Cornies.

55. Johann Cornies to Doctor Herr. 7 April 1843. SAOR 89-1-925/37v.

Doctor Herr,

Membet, the messenger bearing this, is a Nogai in my service. For the past few weeks, he has suffered from a severe cough. I send him to you with a request that you kindly prescribe the most useful medicine for his use. This evil renders him incapable of adequately performing his service. With constant esteem, I remain your thankful servant, Johann Cornies.

56. Johann Cornies to Huebner. 7 April 1843. SAOR 89-1-925/38.

Highly honoured Mr. Huebner,

Immediately after the holidays, for approximately ten days, I intend to visit the Berdiansk and Mariupol Colonist Districts. I urgently need to speak with the Baron when he passes through and ask you, esteemed sir, to kindly inform me of the approximate time when the Baron expects to arrive here. This would enable me to arrange my departure accordingly.

With the regulations that I have instituted, potato planting is proceeding quickly, although the District Chief is maliciously trying to create difficulties. I find it impossible to achieve anything positive through Mr. Andreevksii, who has coarsely expressed his passionate opposition [to the potato project] in a sullen rage.

Nothing more has arisen in the case of the girl dismissed by the Mennonite Franz in Gnadenfeld except that Mr. Andreevskii has sent me a notice from the Tokmak village Elder, of which I enclose a copy. From this you can gather that even spiritual leaders forget their duty if there is no official in the district whom they respect.

With the most exceptional esteem, I remain your respectful friend and servant, Johann Cornies.

**57. Traugott Blueher to Johann Cornies. 9 April 1843.
     SAOR 89-1-911/26.**

Mr. Johann Cornies, Ohrloff village. Highly treasured friend,

With respect to my communication of 2 April, I hasten to report that the remaining thirteen balls of Spanish wool were delivered yesterday. All of the sacks are very wet and partly covered with a finger-thick layer of mud. I examined the worst sacks and found that the wool does not seem to have suffered. With nothing further today, my friendly greetings, Traugott Blueher.

**58. Isaak Fast to Johann Cornies. 16 April 1843.
     SAOR 89-1-911/31.**

To Mr. Johann Cornies in Ohrloff,

On my journey from Prussia in 1836, I had to leave books at the Polish-Prussian border and applied to our District Office in this regard. In 1839 the Ministry of State Domains sent me permission to import these books. Since then, few people going to Prussia have travelled through Mlava where I left these books. Moreover, the person authorized to bring me the books did not travel that route and I still do not have them.

I would like to have these books as soon as possible but am in no position to get them myself. Might this matter be submitted to His Excellency, State Counsellor von Hahn? I really do not know what might be the best course for me to take and would like your opinion.

Should you be willing to help me, please let me know when I might drop by. Because you have the well-being of every single person in our villages at heart, I flatter myself to think that you will fulfil my request. Isaak Fast.

Liebenau, 16 April 1843

59. Carl Stempel to Johann Cornies. 17 April 1843.
SAOR 89-1-911/37.

Esteemed Mr. Cornies,

Heartfelt thanks for kindly sending me a portion of your report concerning the progress made in all branches of agriculture in your area. It will, from now on, serve me as a guideline.

Although I would enjoy seeing you here, and the sooner the better, I am happy that you did not come in March. Having travelled to Odesa on official business, I might not have been at home. The State Counsellor was pleased to hear that you had tentatively, providing your schedule so permits, promised me to inspect locations for our forest plantations. I hope this matter comes to fruition. Until then I will not start anything.

I was unable to speak with the master mason in my absence, but your recommendation is enough for me to proceed with the building of a church. The State Counsellor told me the construction could begin this year, including a dwelling for me.

Hoping to see you soon, I commend myself to your friendship and remain, with true attachment, your friend, Carl Stempel.

P.S. Please thank Mr. Wiebe for the flower seeds. I would like him to send me the names of the various varieties of flowers. When they were seeded in my absence, the gardener was very careless. Not only did he fail to mark the little bags in which they came, he threw the bags away. Forgive me for bothering you with such small matters.

60. Johann Cornies to Fedor F. Rosen. 19 April 1843.
   SAOR 89-1-925/40v.

Baron v. Rosen,

   When I had the stock of [seed] potatoes in five village communities in Dneprov District examined by Peter Ediger, the supervisor I appointed, it was revealed that a further thirty chetvert of potatoes were needed for this year's seeding, estimating six chetvert for each of sixteen village communities. My arrangements for the distribution of crown potatoes for personal seeding by peasants in Melitopol District had already been made. To this end, I bought the above-mentioned thirty chetvert from local Mennonites at seven rubles per chetvert, for a total sum of 210 rubles, or sixty silver rubles.

   I request that provisions be graciously made to have the above-mentioned sum of money sent to me in order that these producers can soon be repaid.

61. Johann Cornies to Christian Steven. 19 April 1843.
   SAOR 89-1-925/41.

State Counsellor v. Steven,

   On 25 January 1843 I was sent two apprentices to learn practical agriculture, Demian Gordenenko and Ivan Schuneev, from Ekaterinoslav Guberniia, Bakhmut District. On 2 March 1843 the peasant's son, Semen Strakhov, from the same guberniia, Aleksandrov District, replaced the apprentice Semen Petrenko, who had left because of poor health, as stated in report No. 4 of 14 January to Yr. Honour. This apprentice showed limited powers of understanding and within a few weeks I sent him back.

   I now have nine apprentices and four girls from Tavrida Guberniia and six apprentices from Ekaterinoslav.

   As I am obliged, I have the honour of informing Yr. Honour in this regard.

62. Johann Cornies to Fedor F. Rosen. 19 April 1843.
   SAOR 89-1-925/42.

Baron Rosen,

   Yr. Honour will kindly forgive me for taking the liberty of mailing you the enclosed request from the Nikolaiev peasant Naum A. Lisovik.

This peasant's situation is such that speedy assistance and justice for him is urgent. I do so because I know how much Yr. Honour is sincerely inclined to provide support for anyone who is oppressed and to see that justice is done.

With sincere esteem, I remain Yr. Honour's devoted servant, Johann Cornies.

63. Johann Cornies to Cornelius Janzen. 19 April 1843. SAOR 89-1-925/42v.

Dear friend Cornelius Janzen,

I received your letter and thank you for the information. If old Novitzkii is well and with his children, please ask him kindly to come to my Iushanle estate to make good cheese and also to teach this skill to my administrator. I will not only thank him but pay him.

Have him hire a cart straight to Iushanle on my account if no transport is otherwise available. Since it is now time to make cheese, it should like to get him here as soon as possible.

In the hope that this is possible, I remain, with love and a friendly greeting your honest friend, Johann Cornies.

64. Carl Stempel to Johann Cornies. 22 April 1843. SAOR 89-1-911/51.

Esteemed Mr. Cornies,

I am again turning to you with a request. Although our community plantation contains more than sixty thousand trees, including original trees, improved trees, and unimproved trees, there is no order in what we do and the different varieties of fruit trees have not been [properly] organized. We do not even have a running account book as a record of the number of each variety or the total number of trees we have in our plantation. Since I am still a beginner and have no experience with this activity, I turn to you for help. Please give me brief, quick advice about how to manage this matter, but do not lose too much time over it. So far, the plantation is divided into sections with no running account book of the trees planted.

Since we have had a similar inquiry from the Ministry of State Domains, kindly inform me about agreements with Russian girls who are learning dairying in your area.

I commend myself to you most kindly, expect your arrival as soon as possible, and remain your honest friend, Carl Stempel.

Grunau, 22 April 1843. Answer 11 May 1843.

65. Bernhard Epp et al. to Johann Cornies. Sent Tiegenhagen, West Prussia, 23 April 1843. SAOR 89-1-917/3.

Mr. Johann Cornies in Ohrloff, Esteemed friend,

In response to a communication from friend Peter Siemens about a new settlement in Vitebsk and Mogilev Guberniias, we held a gathering on 13 April in Marienburg where deputies from all West Prussian Mennonite congregations were present. They carefully considered the subject in question and finally decided to communicate directly with you. Out of love for your Prussian brethren, please help us in this matter. We would be grateful if you, together with Peter Siemens (who is willing to return to Prussia this year), investigated the situation, including the quality of soil in these guberniias. Siemens would then return home.

Please do not think, esteemed friend, that we make this suggestion without first having considered the matter seriously. It is, on the contrary, of great importance to us. We would like to place the matter in the hands of the man best able to guide us surely and quickly. If you think it right for us to send a deputation from Prussia, we would be glad to do so. We would choose several men who would like to settle there. We therefore make the following proposal. Please let us know if you are prepared to go to the above-mentioned guberniias personally. When and where might you arrive? Could you select a time that would enable two of our men to meet you at this location? Under your good leadership, necessary matters could then be worked out. Should you consider this proposal unacceptable, however, and find it better or necessary to have these men come straight to you, would you then be willing to travel with them to the planned area? In that case, kindly set a time when these men should arrive in your area.

Treasured friend, we ask a great deal in approaching you with our proposal that you personally make this journey to the above-mentioned guberniias. Your generally well-known willingness to act, combined with your own abilities that are essential to the carrying out of these steps, prompt this request and give us the hope that we are not mistaken in making this request.

When you have received information regarding taxes and other constitutional matters for the new settlement, kindly send them to us.

Signed, in the name of all of the Deputies: Bernhard Epp, Johann Rahn, Jacob Froese, Peter Regier, Johann Wall, Peter Rahn, Peter Kroeker, and Peter Froese.

Received 6 May 1843; Communication to Baron v. Rosen 24 May.

66. Johann Cornies to Jacob Martens. 24 April 1843. SAOR 89-1-925/44.

To respected Jacob Martens in Tiegenhagen,

I hereby send you one funt, eight lot of madia seed with the request that you cultivate it. It is an exceptionally productive plant, rich in oil. Please let me know by autumn how things have progressed and regarding its yield. This would permit me to report the results to my superiors. I leave it to your discretion to share this seed with other good agriculturalists.

I include brief instructions for seeding and harvesting, with the remark that the plants were planted three vershok apart on my land last year, with good results.

67. Johann Cornies to Novitzkii. 24 April 1843. SAOR 89-1-925/44v.

Dear Novitzkii,

A few weeks ago I wrote to Cornelius Janzen, Schoenwiese, asking him to talk to you about coming to my Iushanle estate to teach my administrator how to prepare good cheeses. I have absolutely received no news from C. Janzen in this regard, and now doubt that Janzen received my letter. This gives me an opportunity to write directly to you. Please, if you can, come to my Iushanle estate to prepare good cheeses should your circumstances permit.

I will pay you thankfully for your effort and for teaching the art of preparing cheese. Please hire transport directly to Iushanle on my account. The sooner you come, the better it will be. Otherwise the best time will have passed.

With greetings, your friend Johann Cornies.

68. Carl Stempel to Johann Cornies. 29 April 1843. SAOR 89-1-911/41.

Esteemed Mr. Cornies,

When I got the pleasant news that you had arrived yesterday in Bergthal, I had wanted to visit you immediately even though I had to take a sweat-bath because of a cold. Then the rain got worse, the wagon I had planned to use was not in the village, and I had to postpone my journey to Bergthal until today.

Should your affairs allow, I would be pleased to see you today, although this may not be possible because of the damp weather. Still, you might come in any case. I commend myself to your friendship and remain, with respect, your honest friend, C. Stempel.

29 April, Grunau.

69. Johann Cornies to Evgenii F. Hahn. [Undated, after 23 March 1843.] SAOR 89-1-811/18.

His Excellency, Deputy General Guardian,
From Chairman

I find it necessary to send you this explanation in response to a presentation of the Khortitsa District Office to the Guardianship Committee on 23 March [1843].

1. Some Khortitsa Mennonite settlers admitted for settlement in the Mariupol [Bergthal] Mennonite District were not actually owners of the funds the authorities demanded of them. They only received funds their guarantor had pledged. One must therefore conclude that many did not have the funds required for settlement.

2. The guarantors think they did not guarantee the construction of side buildings, although estimates were for at least 2,500 rubles. The rules state that the money required to be deposited in the District Office is meant to pay for dwellings and side buildings. These are specifically understood as one dwelling, one livestock barn, and one threshing floor. A dwelling is estimated to cost from 1,200 to 1,500 rubles. The 2,500 rubles includes the side buildings and is part of the guarantee.

3. The guarantors even claim not to know about the difficulties faced by the Mariupol settlers. This is obviously contrary to the truth. The new settlers are children of the guarantors and directly connected with their mother settlement. Their situation could not have been unknown to them.

4. Negligence by local administrators is blamed for the settlement's poverty-stricken situation. I must say frankly that the Khortitsa District Office permitted the settlement of persons already known for their unreliable conduct, people who did not answer to the government's wishes. In so doing, the District Office showed how little it is motivated by concerns for the settlement's progress or its desire to accomplish the government's goals.

5. It is absolutely necessary that the guarantors indicate to the settlers how much of the 21,268 rubles advanced has been paid to each one, and

how much is still owed. This would enable each settler to assess his position on his fullholding and undertake the measures necessary on his site.

6. The guarantors admit that their guarantees may extend to the necessary fencing. I agree with Yr. Excellency's opinion that if it should not be possible to force the guarantors to pay at least half of the sum for fences, they must at least be encouraged to have all hearth-sites in the new settlement properly fenced this year. Many settlers do not have the means to do this and can only do so with the help of their guarantors.

It follows that the above submission from the Khortitsa District Office demonstrates that the directives and rules were entirely ignored in settling the Mariupol Mennonite settlement. On the whole, the [Khortitsa] District Office and the guarantors have made little effort to assist the settlers in their undertakings. They have no grounds to refute this conclusion and should not have used such unfounded excuses.

70. Carl Stempel to Johann Cornies. 1 May 1843. SAOR 89-1-911/43.

Esteemed Mr. Cornies,
I urgently request that you, upon your arrival, send the master mason to me at once. I would like to report this to the Committee as soon as possible. Also, kindly send me the rough plantation plan you drew up for me. I forgot to take along the official paper. Moreover, the estimates for the Grunau plantation were on its other side. Esteemed Mr. Cornies, I also request that you inform me when the State Counsellor arrives at your place, and what route he will then take. Will he travel to Bergthal first, or to one of the other villages? I would like to know where he expects to meet me and would find it awkward not to have met him.

Wishing you a safe return, I commend myself to your friendship, and remain with constant respect, your honest friend, C. Stempel.

Grunau, 1 May 1843.

71. Abram Wiebe to Johann Cornies. Sent from Rudnerweide, 4 May 1843. SAOR 89-1-911/49.[14]

Mr. Johann Cornies in Ohrloff,
Because of the complete stagnation in wheat sales, I am reduced to a situation in which I not only appeal to you for patience with the debts

---

14 Wiebe, one of Cornies's most important allies, was a leading figure in the Berdiansk grain trade, as well as in silk production. See Staples, *Johann Cornies*, 171.

I now owe but request an additional loan of ten to fifteen thousand rubles, with interest, for a term of three months. I might soon be able to sell some wheat or linseed that I am making available at a selling price below my purchase price, that is to say, at a small loss. However, I would rather not pass up the wool trade completely. I know of no one else who might give me enough money to make it worthwhile and so I turn to you as my old creditor.

I would like to get five to ten thousand rubles from you with this messenger, whatever you can manage to send me. Kindly inform me whether I can count on the rest of the amount within a period of fourteen days. Hoping that you will grant my request, I sign myself with love and respect as your friend, Abram Wiebe.

72. Traugott Blueher to Johann Cornies. 7 May 1843. SAOR 89-1-911/67.

Mr. Johann Cornies, Ohrloff village.

Highly valued friend,

It is with pleasure that I read your letter of 29 March with its news that Spanish wool purchases had begun. I await your further communications in this regard.

I am sorry that I did not understand your intentions in making the remittance to Baron v. Rosen since I had, on 7 February, informed your secretary that there was no special hurry about the matter.

Only small supplies of good varieties of washed Spanish wool are in storage here and I have therefore undertaken the following steps with the two shipments from you:

1. Sixty-seven balls sold yesterday at thirty-six rubles per pud, payment to be received by 25 May at the latest.

2. Twenty balls sent for sorting and washing, particularly the fifteen balls received last, which looked terrible.

3. I have kept back another fifty puds to retain a sufficient quantity of the various varieties. I did so principally because I wanted to know the extent to which opinions as to quality are affected by wool soiled by fodder.

[Paragraph illegible]

Should no unexpected events arise to increase the price of wool, the next test in regard to prices would probably come after the annual market at Nizhnii Novgorod, should the business at hand there end well. Owners who sent wool to Holland and England were forced to sell at prices much lower than those here, and they will venture no undertakings of this kind in future. Prices of all varieties of wool abroad are generally low, and there are no prospects of them rising soon.

Mr. Doering in Sarepta is well. I will send him your greetings the next time I write. A disease ravaged their horned cattle last summer. Except for a few cows, the whole herd they got from you was destroyed, with damage to their income. There are few markets for Sarepta's finished products. Its trades limp along, even at lower prices.

If I am successful, I will shortly send your dear wife an electuary especially for coughs. I ordered it from the Orphanage in Halle, and it helped my wife greatly.

We have not heard about your children for a long time, but we remember them fondly, especially also because various of your son's drawings hang in our living rooms. My wife asks about news from Agnes. Give both of them our heartiest greetings. We wish them the best of everything, spiritually and physically.

I send most sincere greetings to you and your esteemed wife, and remain your faithful friend and servant, Traugott Blueher, Moscow.

Received 26 May 1843; Answer and receipt 4 August 1843.

73. Johann Cornies to [Fedor F. Rosen]. 9 May 1843.
SAOR 89-1-925/48v.

His Honour, Baron Rosen,

I received your esteemed communication of 30 April. Although I am genuinely inclined to advance you the 3,200 rubles you request, I cannot do so when you travel through, even with the best of intentions. Should you need this loan when you pass through Moscow, however, I would be happy to give it to you then. Against my credit and property there, you could obtain this sum promptly with a certificate from me. You can count on this.

In March, I asked that ten thousand rubles be sent to you from Moscow, as I had promised, but this did not happen because my communication failed to include a clear-enough address. My circumstances now are such that I lack money and cannot produce the 3,200 rubles here on site.

I have still not found out if the railings have arrived in Berdiansk. There has been no response to any of my messages to Berdiansk about this matter. I hope to get reliable information by the time you arrive.

74. David Epp to Johann Cornies. Sent from Heubuden, 9 May 1843. SAOR 89-1-911/91.

Beloved friend,

On 27 April I received your communication of 29 March with two copied items, showing that the spirit of dissension is active in your community. On 17 April, the second day of Easter, our Elder told several brethren who hold office that he had received a letter with similar contents from Hiebert and Neufeld. For this reason, I did not feel free to make inquiries about the second question, but I do want to speak to Elder Regier personally. However, I did ask about the information that we have been receiving here because it varies so much. For example, I asked District Secretary Reimer if someone had really swindled the District treasury (as is repeated here). I wanted to know whether the news reaching us was true. Our Elder also asked persons and officials from the community for information about events there. I find nothing evil in such questions, even though I know that opponents of the Bible Society and the School have supported opinions opposing these ventures. All this is sad and destructive and I can say so without first speaking to Elder Regier. I do not consider it necessary to visit him first. The quarrel that has been going on for twenty years must end. It is sad that there are now two churches in Petershagen, one of them a monument to dissension.

According to our general publications, Russia is no longer so respectful of Germans as it once was, requiring that they respect the country's expectations and carry out its purposes as model agriculturalists.

I read the communication that Bonellas brought personally. The messenger, who spent the night here, showed it to me. I looked through everything but did not find as much evil in it as did the senders. The contents suggest that Elder Warkentin would not grant that his members could be punished, that he wanted to do two days of punitive work himself, and that a communication written to the [Guardianship] Committee on his advice resulted in a two-day increase in the punishment. No government (as far as I know) will stand for such nonsense, contrary to the law. This is evidence against the complainants.

Secondly, a communication from Elder Friesen of the Kleine Gemeinde to Elder Neufeld was included, admonishing the Warkentin brotherhood. He backs up his arguments with many Bible verses.[15] The opinion that this communication is evil obviously tells against them. You can easily convince yourself of this, since Elder Friesen will gladly show you a copy of it. Any effort to prevent this letter from seeing the light of day bears comparison with my communication of 30 June 1822, in which I listed [the merits] of the Bible Society. An opponent of the Bible Society wrote to me using Galatians 6, verse 10: "Let us do good to every man, but especially towards one's fellow believers." We cannot demand too much of people. Much will be demanded from those to whom much is given and from those who are given command. Luke 12.

Why should we not share our grievances with others, even if they are unjust? In secrecy, we strengthen our own sense of injustice, instead of correcting it. I am surprised at you! Why do you pay attention to such petty details? I consider this to be unmanly. You have more important matters to attend to.

You must have received my communication containing the letter from Brother Tauchnitz in Leipzig. It reported that your letter asking about silk workers was forwarded to Rev. Molenar who grew up in Crefeld.

May the God of peace give us.... Many loving greetings to you and your family, David Epp.

Treasured friend, enclosed, you will receive some things from Br. Tauchnitz and from C. Beindorf about silk fabrication. Should you want to order other items in this regard from the latter through me, I am at your service ... After I wrote the above letter I spoke with several brethren in office about your letter of 29 March. It is felt that it would be better to send these documents back to you, since they contain nothing that is well-founded about the dissension with Warkentin. God knows who is at fault .... [bits of further advice have been cross-written but are unclear]

Received 26 June 1843. Answered 15 July 1843.

75. Traugott Blueher to Johann Cornies. Sent from Moscow, 10 May 1843. SAOR 89-1-911/75.

Highly valued friend,

The fact that the purchaser of sixty-seven balls of wool actually made his payment before the specified date is an event as unusual as is this

---

15 This letter is reproduced in English translation in Delbert F. Plett, *The Golden Years: The Mennonite Kleine Gemeinde in Russia, 1812–1849* (Steinbach, MB: D.F.P. Publications, 1985).

year's comet crossing the firmament.[16] I am already in a position to send you the enclosed sum of 22,050 rubles. Kindly notify me of its receipt.

In six days' time I will get the twenty balls of wool that were sent to be sorted and washed, and not neglect to send you a detailed report.

Our local cloth manufacturers are disheartened by the last postal delivery from Kiakhta. There at the market, the Chinese offered such low prices for local cloth that sellers refused to sell and trade has remained small. I think my assumption is right that Spanish wool prices will not firm up soon unless something unusual occurs.

In the last few days we finally got warmer weather after a long wait.

I send my greetings with friendship and love, Traugott Blueher.

P.S. I wonder whether it would be in your interest if I sent this remittance in interest-bearing certificates. Since I do not know your circumstances and I can get these certificates at only a premium of eight-tenths of a per cent, I have been holding back with this idea. Please give me your opinion so that I might, in future, be better able to act on behalf of your interests.

Received 5 June 1843. Answered 12 June 1843.

76. Johann Cornies to Evgenii F. Hahn. 10 May 1843. SAOR 89-1-925/45.

Mr. Hahn, Yr. Excellency, Gracious Sir,

Because of the good weather we have finished our spring seeding. The seeds are growing quickly, much to the joy of our husbandmen. Hopes for a good crop are so high that our villagers are competing to finish the Society's proposed improvements to their fullholdings as soon as possible. Society members use this time to travel through the villages. They encourage and provide directions in order that the greatest number of improvements might be made before haying time. The Society would like to complete all spring directives by Pentecost, 30 May. Moreover, all Hutterite Mennonite families should by then be in their huts on their assigned sites in the projected Hutterthal village, and will be building their houses. Should I be permitted to suggest the time of your arrival, as Yr. Excellency mentioned to the Mennonite Riediger, I would propose that Yr. Excellency arrive at my estate of Tashchenak

---

16   The Great Comet of 1843. Its formal designation is C/1843 D1.

on the first Saturday after Pentecost, if possible. That would be 5 June. I will be there, waiting for you.

Please forgive this suggestion that reflects the simple sincerity of a man of the land. It is given in the hope that it will provide you with some small pleasure in observing the progressive improvements that have been made in our villages.

I look forward to your arrival and am Yr. Excellency's most humble and respectful servant, Johann Cornies.

77. Johann Cornies to Nikolai Schmidt. 10 May 1843. SAOR 89-1-925/47.

Dear friend,

I cannot give you any money because I am entirely without funds myself. They are stuck in all of the places from which I should be receiving money, even in Moscow itself. No funds have arrived from any of the places from which I would normally expect them. Please tell your father-in-law that he should not, for this reason, count on a loan from me.

With a friendly greeting, I remain your friend, Johann Cornies

78. Johann Cornies to Bureau of State Domains. 10 May 1843. SAOR 89-1-925/47v.

To the Tavrida Guberniia Bureau of State Domains,

In reply to communication No. 2851 of 17 April 1843 from the Tavrida Bureau of State Domains, I asked the former Mennonite supervisor, Abraham Huebert, about rotten potatoes in Kiltshik in spring. On 6 May he reported in writing that, according to S.35 of the instructions I distributed (of which I enclose a copy here), he gave the Elder in Kiltshik the same firm instructions that he had given to all others to check the navel-like openings on the wheel attached to the post standing in the middle of each pit. They were to be checked twice each week for bad smells coming out of the pit. When such odours occurred, the potatoes were to be lifted out and all of the rotten potatoes removed.

During my posting stop on the journey from Odesa, I ordered the Elder to examine the potatoes and, as I reported earlier, he answered casually that he had no orders to check on potatoes.

In other village communities such as Veseloi, for example, the Elder carried out Huebert's orders fairly promptly and fewer than half of the potatoes were lost. This is hard evidence that, with attentive supervision, potatoes will not spoil. Spoilage should be simply ascribed to an Elder's neglect.

79. Fedor F. Rosen to Johann Cornies. 11 May 1843. SAOR 89-1-955/26.

From the Director of the Tavrida State Domains Bureau, State Counsellor Baron Rosen,

To corresponding member of the Learned Committee in the Ministry of State Domains, Mr. Johann Cornies,

On 18 November 1840 you sent me a submission that I forwarded to the Minister of State Domains. My communication No. 577 of 20 September 1841 informed you about the answer I received to this submission. It referred to a watermill your brother Heinrich was going to build in the village of Konshegale on the Abitochna River that was to be developed as a model plantation. I also requested an early answer to several points the Minister mentioned. The Minister hoped your brother Heinrich would have no difficulty in explaining them.

I can find no answer to the above-mentioned item of 20 September 1841 in the documents here. I would ask that you, Mr. Cornies, kindly send your brother Heinrich guidance in regard to this undertaking without delay. Director B. v. Rosen.

80. Johann Cornies to Carl Stempel. 11 May 1843. SAOR 89-1-925/49.

Mr. Stempel, Honoured Sir,

In response to your esteemed communication of 22 April, I have the honour to inform you about guarantors for Mariupol Mennonites from the Khortitsa District. The messenger bringing the information is Master Mason Larion Dmitriev. The State Counsellor sent these declarations of the Khortitsa District Office to me, with a request that I give His Excellency my opinion about them. You, Mr. Inspector, need take no action in their regard.

Enclosed, I send you a copy of the terms under which youths and girls are sent to me to learn practical agriculture. I am also sending you a sketch of how a householder might arrange his hearth-site most advantageously. I draw attention to the rule, shown by dots, that the straight line of the buildings not be obscured from the garden area by straw or haystacks, manure, ashes, or similar objects. This renders the view from the street more attractive and ensures that such objects are not too close to the tree plantations. However, where back-buildings are built at an angle, they fall twelve *fut* [two faden] behind the house line. Naturally, when the locations of hearth-sites are determined, the situation at some locations may well make it necessary to diverge from this format in one way or another.

Yr. Honour is aware that cottager Franz Sawatzky will build his house beside the Bergthal plantation. I consider it of considerable importance that a properly proportioned and durable house be constructed as an example for others. Consequently, please suggest to Sawatzky that, should he build an attractive house as required, he might well be recognized as eligible for the specified three hundred rubles [subsidy].

The State Counsellor will probably arrive on 5 June at my Tashchenak estate. I will not neglect to inform you of the details of his route as soon as he arrives.

With the most complete esteem, I have the honour to remain Yr. Honour's respectful servant, Johann Cornies.

81. Carl Stempel to Johann Cornies. 14 May 1843. SAOR 89-1-911/58.

Esteemed Mr. Cornies,

Heartiest thanks for kindly sending the master mason to me and for the enclosure in your valued letter. The mason gave me precise information about the quality of building materials required, as based on the sketches for the church. I hasten to submit this to the Committee to ensure that the State Counsellor receives it before he leaves this area. It will not be a stone church, as stated in the estimates, but should be built of fired brick. I must have a brick kiln set up here. I ask that you, valued Mr. Cornies, inform the master mason when the State Counsellor arrives at your estate. This would enable him to come here when the State Counsellor arrives. All aspects involved can then be discussed in detail and agreed upon.

I intend to drive to Mariupol in a few days. Should I have the opportunity, I will inform Sawatzky that he will get three hundred rubles more if he builds a really attractive house according to the plan he decided on. Of course, it will also depend on how things are settled by the State Counsellor. He is justified in expecting more in return for his years of investigation, fear, and inconvenience.

I will be much indebted to you if you let me know when the State Counsellor arrives and what his travel route will be.

Commending myself to your friendship and kindness, I constantly remain with true respect, your friend Carl Stempel.

Grunau, 14 May 1843. Received 20 May 1843.

82. Johann Cornies to Hutterthal Village Office. 15 May 1843. SAOR 89-1-811/16.

[Draft:] Hutterthal Village Office,

I have been told that Jacob Walter and Paul Hofer put two head of cattle each onto the [village] pasture without the permission of the community. Walter accepted for pasturage two head of cattle from Alexanderwohl, the latter from Isaac Wiens in Altona, where Hofer had been quartered. This moved the Village Office to issue a public order prohibiting anyone from putting livestock on the pasture without the community's permission. No firm rule in this regard has yet been established in Hutterthal, but this will eventually have to be done following rules that exist generally in the Molochnaia Mennonite villages.

Walter and Hofer can therefore not be punished for their arbitrary action, but this incident should serve as a warning that anyone acting in such an arbitrary fashion will, from now on, be punished. The Village Office must report to me on what terms Walter and Hofer took the above-mentioned livestock onto the pasture.

83. M. Riesen to Johann Cornies. 20 May 1843. SAOR 89-1-911/95.

Highly esteemed Mr. Cornies,

Please excuse me for taking the liberty of sending you a few lines that express my gratitude to you for the friendship and friendly reception you have shown my son, Herrmann Sukkau, on his arrival in Russia. I was very pleased to be so informed in letters from him. It is a great comfort to know that my son was not abandoned in a strange country and that he also had the pleasure of enjoying the interest that you have taken in him. I would urgently ask you to continue to help him and to give him your kind advice. This will surely assist him in making some progress in Russia. It would likewise make me very happy to count on your sensible advice and generous help that is a great boon to so many.

Could you perhaps, until he has acquired property himself, provide my son with a position within the larger circle of your own activities? Perhaps a rural occupation would be best for him. Please advise and assist him in this regard. His stay will surely be of great value for him, all the more so if he is employed, a condition always best for young people.

I look forward to your help and commend my son to your further generosity. Greetings to you and your highly valued family, from me, my husband and my father, with esteem and appreciation, your devoted M. van Riesen, née Conwentz.

Elbing, 20 May 1843. Received 26 June 1843.

84. Johann Cornies to Fedor F. Rosen. 24 May 1843.
SAOR 89-1-925/52.

Baron v. Rosen,

In response to high governmental arrangements and Yr. Honour's communication regarding the settlement of Prussian Mennonites in Vitebsk and Mohilev Guberniias, I can report that I have approached the Mennonite communities in question and received their written reply. I enclose the original of this letter, signed on behalf of all Deputies from the West Prussian Mennonite communities. I would add my most humble request that you kindly assist in having this particular piece of land in Vitebsk and Mogilev Guberniias specifically assigned for settlement during the course of this year. I would further request an early reply as to the part of this land that could be provided for settlement by Prussian Mennonites. What decisions need still to be made in this regard that would put me in a position to inform the elected Prussian Deputies accordingly and, in general, to offer them more specific help?

85. Johann Cornies to Fedor F. Rosen. 24 May 1843.
SAOR 89-1-925/53.

Baron v. Rosen,

Despite admonitions and orders from Yr. Honour that urge Nogais to promptly repay the first half of the money that they owe the Mennonites for sheep they purchased with a guarantee from them, they have still made only a few, sporadic payments. Many are still quite unconcerned despite the fact that half a year has passed since the repayment date. Nor have their creditors given them any extensions.

The time is fast approaching when the Nogais will sell the wool shorn from these sheep and receive money for it. Livestock will also be sold. I would therefore repeat my most humble request that Yr. Honour issue stern orders compelling the Nogais to pay the first half [of the money] still owed to the Mennonites for their sheep.

86. Johann Cornies Jr. to Phillip Wiebe. 24 May 1843. SAOR 89-1-911/62.

Esteemed Wiebe,

Kindly write a letter on behalf of our oxen herdsman. I think he wants fifty rubles that you may give him. Also, please find out when I can send for the master carpenter who will bring along several items from there. Will money be sent along to pay the shearers, or am I supposed to send someone to fetch it? Let me know.

Your friend, Johann Cornies Jr.

Tashchenak, 24 May 1843. Sent May 30.

87. Daniel Janzen to Johann Cornies. 25 May 1843. SAOR 89-1-911/63.

Esteemed friend,

On behalf of our community, I am happy to let you know that we have collected some donations for the Hutterite brethren. These include approximately ten chetvert of grain. I am not exactly sure about the other contributions.

How should these collected items be made available to these brethren? Will they fetch them themselves or should we deliver them? Please reply as soon as you can.

Steinbach, 25 May 1843. Daniel Janzen.

88. Jacob Riediger and Gerhard Neufeld to Johann Cornies. 25 May 1843. SAOR 89-1-911/69.[17]

Esteemed Mr. Cornies,

When you left Odesa, we promised to let you know about our situation by 1 May. We would gladly have stuck to our promise if our studies had not kept us from doing so. Sometimes we get so much work that we hardly know where to begin. Granted, it should have been our first duty to provide you with the promised information at the time agreed

---

17 Student teachers training with Fletnitzer.

upon and not to make empty promises. Although we failed in not writing to you earlier, we hope that a good-natured gentleman like yourself would not be so exact with a pair of poor students, loaded down as we are with so many studies.

First of all let us give you our hearty thanks for the help you have given us for our journey and here in this place. We are healthy and are completing our work with much joy. Our work, moreover, is being crowned with God's blessing. We are finding Russian much easier than before, but we still have a long way to go. Should God grant us good health, we hope to overcome the last difficulties and consolidate our knowledge of Russian completely.

With a polite greeting, we express our hope that you will forgive us our negligence. Your willing servants, Jacob Riediger and Gerhard Neufeld.

Odesa, 25 May 1843

89. Benjamin Ratzlaff to Johann Cornies. 26 May 1843. SAOR 89-1-911/65.

Dear friend and brother Johann Cornies,

We have collected some small support, bread grains, and a few other foodstuffs, for the Radishchev [Hutterite] community settled at the Tashchenak. We have about ten chetvert of grain and some other things. We do not know whether they could pick them up from us. We have not had an opportunity to inform them of this gift. I would therefore ask you for your advice. I authorized the respected Daniel Janzen to report to you about this matter, but I do not know if you have received his report. I also hope that this small gift will help them at the present time, if we can only get it to them. If it seems to you that they cannot fetch it, we will deliver it ourselves. Please be so kind as to organize this matter. My dear wife and I send you and your dear wife loving greetings, and also your whole family. May God preserve all of us and conduct us to an eternal, blessed life.

Should it be possible, please visit us again. Any time is fine for us. May the Lord bless our souls during the present celebration of Pentecost. Amen. I sign myself as a weak fellow pilgrim on the way towards eternity, Benjamin Ratzlaff.

Rudnerweide, 25 May 1843.

N.B. My wife is still sick. In this way, the Lord seeks to prepare us for whatever He wills for us. If only He might be successful. Benjamin Ratzlaff. Answered 29 May.

90. Johann Cornies to Fedor F. Rosen. 28 May 1843.
SAOR 89-1-925/54.

Baron v. Rosen,

I write in response to your letter regarding the totally rotten potatoes found in Bolshaia Bielosenka. I have the honour to give you the following information. When potatoes received no rain in early summer there was little hope for even a moderate harvest. Several rains towards autumn moistened the soil and some potatoes sprouted new tubers, but these failed to ripen because it was too late. When harvested these potatoes were placed into pits in two states of ripeness. The unripe ones rotted and spoiled the others as well. All this could have been avoided only with the greatest vigilance on the part of the Elder.

91. Johann Cornies to Benjamin Ratzlaff. 29 May 1843.
SAOR 89-1-925/55v.

Esteemed Ratzlaff, Rudnerweide,

In the name of the Hutterthal community I send my warmest thanks to you and all brethren who, by contributing grain and other items to the poor Hutterthal Mennonites, have followed your good example in work pleasing to God. Because I am avidly concerned to help these poor brethren to prosper I am also well informed about their circumstances and can easily imagine how they will treasure your generosity.

At the same time, kindly forgive me if I ask you to forward your loving gifts directly to Christian Waldner, Hutterthal Mayor. The Hutterites are now occupied in constructing their houses, and their draft animals are weak.

Convinced of the well-known benevolent inclinations evident in your own community, I think that you will find my request quite in order.

In repeating my thanks, I remain, with heartfelt love, your faithfully obligated friend and servant, Johann Cornies.

92. Johann Cornies to [Daniel] Janzen. 29 May 1843.
SAOR 89-1-925/56v.

Esteemed Janzen,

With the greatest joy, I acknowledge the progressive striving of your congregation in support of our brethren. I have already replied to the esteemed Elder's most recent letter informing me of the donations your community has collected in support of the Hutterthal community for the donations collected. I am much in your debt.

Because the horses of these poor settlers have recently been put under great strain, I have asked Ohm Ratzlaff to consider delivering the contributions directly to the Hutterite community, to Christian Waldner, Hutterthal Mayor.

93. Johann Cornies to Mariupol & Berdiansk. 29 May 1843. SAOR 89-1-972/1.

[Draft:] From Chairman,
[No.] 205. Mariupol Mennonite District Office & [No.] 206. Berdiansk

Once you have received this communication, the District Office should immediately have every Village Office prepare a neat, accurate, and dependable overview following the enclosed format. It should be prepared on white paper and signed by the village Elders. With this document in hand, each Village Mayor and both Deputies are required to be prepared for the impending arrival of the Acting Head of the Guardianship Committee. They should receive him at the entrance to every village, dressed and in their Sunday jackets.

Meanwhile, the District Office should inspect all gardens and yards to ensure that everything has been put into the best of order. The District Office will receive definite information from me about the time of His Excellency's arrival.

94. Johann Cornies to District Offices. N.d. [Probably June 1843.] SAOR 89-1-972/7.

[Undated draft]: From Chairman to District Offices,
Before the General Guardian arrives, I find it necessary to instruct every village that their inhabitants behave politely and decently to distinguished visitors when they make their inspections. They should, when they face them, uncover their heads and not casually sit or hang about on the fences. Nor should they hide in corners, but stand freely and in an orderly fashion at the side of the street. Mayors must emphasize this to householders, who will accordingly inform their children in order that this directive might be carried out.

95. Johann Cornies to Fedor F. Rosen. 1 June 1843.
SAOR 89-1-925/54v.

Baron v. Rosen,

I humbly respond to Yr. Honour's inquiry No. 201 of 20 April 1843 asking if Mennonites from Prussia might be willing to settle in Russia in groups of four to six families on state model farms. I can quite reliably predict that no Prussian Mennonite agriculturalists would choose to do so. Wherever they reside, Mennonites form connections and a community and individual families choose not to settle separately for different reasons, including the education of their children and their own spiritual communion. Also standing in the way of such settlement is the Prussian Mennonites' inadequate knowledge of the Russian language and their particular customs brought along from their homeland.

I believe, similarly, no model agriculturalists in our local villages would agree to the government's [otherwise] most acceptable proposals. Given their spiritual state of mind, Mennonites quite correctly prefer to live in communities where they are able to thrive.

96. Johann Cornies to Christian Steven. [5] June 1843.
SAOR 89-1-925/58.

Inspector for Agriculture, State Counsellor v. Steven,

In carrying out Yr. Honour's communication No. 401 of 22 April 1843, I am honoured to remit the terms signed by Peter Cornies and Cornelius Wiens, Mennonites of Ohrloff village and by Johann Sukkau, Blumenort, who have agreed to accept one state peasant youth each to learn practical agriculture. I request that you specify that the youths in question be capable and physically strong. They should, according to these same terms, come provided with clothes for one year. They might be sent to me as soon as possible and I will pass them on to the above-mentioned Mennonites.

97. Phillip Wiebe for Johann Cornies to Traugott Blueher. 11 June 1843. SAOR 89-1-925/59.

Esteemed Mr. Blueher,

In my employer's absence, I dutifully inform you that your last remittance of 22,050 rubles was received in proper order from Novoaleksandrovka on 5 June.

I would also request that you kindly take this year's wool production of 998 puds, eight funt on consignment. The wool was sent off today, 11 June, on thirty-four carts. Enclosed is the original of the contract with the carters and a copy of the bill of lading. I would note that balls marked "#" contain lambswool. Due to an oversight, this was not marked on the bill of lading when the third variety was loaded at Tashchenak, but the balls are marked in this way.

Kindly pay the remainder, 1,194 rubles, twenty-four kopeks, owed the carters after appropriate receipt of the wool and put it on Mr. Cornies's account.

I would also request that, when you have received them, you send copies of Bible stories, church stories, nature stories, and geographies ordered earlier as soon as transport becomes available. We have a considerable number of requests that keep arriving.

The quantity of wool [that you requested be] bought on your account has almost been reached. Mr. Cornies will send you more detailed news in this regard later on. On site here, the price of a pud averages something over twenty rubles. Your most respectful Phillip Wiebe.

98. Johann Cornies to Christian Steven. 13 June 1843.
SAOR 89-1-925/60v.

Inspector for Southern Russian Agriculture, v. Steven,

I have the honour to report that on 8 June the state peasant youth Anisim Labodasho, from the village of Sherebetz, Aleksandrov District, Ekaterinoslav Guberniia, was sent to me to learn practical agriculture. The number of apprentices agreed upon, sixteen youths and four girls, has thus been reached. Enclosed, to inform Yr. Honour, is a list of their names.

99. Peter Neufeld to Johann Cornies. 14 June 1843.
SAOR 89-1-911/79.

Honoured Mr. Cornies,

I have been given much support by the local community. Otherwise I would likely be in a much poorer spiritual condition. I realize that the generosity I have received also obligates me to become useful to my community in future. Strong impulses have been aroused in me to improve my God-given powers through useful work.

I can, however, only worthily fulfil my duty to the community once I have properly learned the Russian language. My personal situation, however, does not allow me to do so on my own. Second only to God, I place my hopes in your kind assistance. I can assure you in advance that I am prepared to gratefully accept any course that you suggest. I joined the body of the Christian congregation this year through holy baptism, and this too encourages me to serve the well-being of our brethren. I am convinced that you are in sympathy with this goal and that I can put my trust in you to kindly help me out. Your respectful servant, Peter Neufeld.

Halbstadt, 14 June 1843. Received 16 June 1843.

100. Carl Stempel to Johann Cornies. 15 June 1843.
SAOR 89-1-911/76.

Highly valued Mr. Cornies,

Having just returned from your journey, I again take the liberty to inconvenience you with a request. The State Counsellor sent me an order to establish a community brick-firing kiln, as you will see from the enclosed papers. Please be so kind as to assist us in this task. Without you, we will not make progress. Help us with your advice and actions, and provide us with the brickmaker whom you kindly mentioned. Most immediately I need an estimate based on this order for submission to the State Counsellor. It would be gratifying to produce several thousand bricks as early as this winter.

Moreover, should it not be too burdensome, I would be grateful if you could provide me with a small sketch of a dwelling house. Otherwise it can perhaps wait until next year. Stones for the foundation will, in any case, need to be obtained this fall.

Also please inform me of the prices of our wool. You might also send us a merchant [to buy up our wool].

Thanking you heartily for your goodwill, continued support and advice for this young beginner, I remain constantly and with high respect, Your honest friend, C. Stempel.

15 June 1843. Grunau colony. Answer 20 June 1843.

5 July 1843 answer about the brick kiln.

101. Johann Cornies to Georg von Bradke. 18 June 1843.
SAOR 89-1-925/60v.[18]

Mr. v. Bradke, Yr. Excellency, Gracious Sir,

With the greatest concern, I have been doing everything that I can to resettle the deeply impoverished Radishchev Mennonites [Hutterites] from Chernigov Guberniia in our area. I am presently deeply concerned about a decree that would deny the above-mentioned Mennonites a year free of taxes. What I fear is that, despite my efforts, these poor yet highly moral people, who are deeply apprehensive about their future, will entirely lose their courage.

It is out of this concern that I direct a humble request to His Excellency, the Minister. He is the one who continues to be the most generous promoter of all that is desirable and useful [in Russia].

Please forgive me for my boldness in enclosing the above-mentioned request with this letter for the Minister. I place my complete trust in you, our worthy and esteemed benefactor, and live in the hope that Yr. Excellency's intercession will gain the Minister's support for the well-being of these poor settlers.

Striving to become ever more worthy of your esteemed generosity, I remain, with deepest respect, Yr. Excellency's humble servant, Johann Cornies.

102. Johann Cornies to Pavel D. Kiselev. 18 June 1843.
SAOR 89-1-925/62.

To Count Kiselev, Yr. Highness, Gracious Count,

Authorized by the Guardianship Committee for Foreign Settlers in Southern Russia to oversee the resettlement of the Radichshev Mennonites [Hutterites] from Chernigov Guberniia last year, I am keen to do what I can to improve their difficult circumstances in keeping with the wishes of our humane government. To my great joy, I can say that my convictions about these Mennonites have been positively affirmed. I can assure Yr. Highness that the Radishchev Mennonites are industrious, virtuous, orderly, clean, quiet, and obedient despite their current extreme poverty. Under purposeful leadership, something they have hitherto lacked, they will thrive as a result of their resettlement.

---

18   Georg von Bradke, a senior official in the Ministry of State Domains.

Upon my intercession with the Guardianship Committee for Foreign Settlers in Southern Russian, the new settlers were given a credit of fifteen thousand rubles to build their houses. This generosity touched their thankful hearts. Coupled with their own great exertions, this has made it possible for the settlers to build Hutterthal village in an orderly manner. Without exception, the Hutterians were forced to leave all their buildings in Chernigov Guberniia with virtually no compensation. Added to the considerable expenses and difficulties of their long journey, this meant that the small amount of money they brought with them, even when handled in a parsimonious manner, was soon used up and that they had to borrow more. This debt they have repaid out of their own earnings.

In the light of these circumstances, I ventured to make a humble application to the Guardianship Committee for a grant of three or four tax-free years to assist the settlers. I have a reply rejecting this request on the grounds that the above-mentioned Mennonites, in an Imperial order of 22 May 1801, had been refused such tax-free years during a similar resettlement. The same logic, it was said, prevailed now, especially given the fact that they had already received an advance of fifteen thousand rubles.

Please excuse my frankness in daring to suggest that the earlier resettlement was over a distance of only twelve verstas and cannot be compared to the present move of over five hundred verstas. As already mentioned, the generous advance of money is the only means by which they can construct their houses. These Mennonites have absolutely no money and an imposition of taxes would only subject them to coercion because they can in no way raise additional funds. At the same time, their brethren in faith, the Molochnaia Mennonites, cannot justifiably be asked to pay taxes for the new settlers because the Radishchev Mennonites have not yet really become part of their community.

When inspecting our villages this month, State Counsellor v. Hahn, Acting General Guardian for the Colonists, was persuaded of their extreme poverty as well as of their goodwill as reflected in the progress they had made in such a short period of time. All of this gives me the courage to appeal to the mercy of Yr. Highness, our greatest benefactor, and to make the dutiful request that the pressing situation of the Radishchev Mennonites at their new settlement be kindly considered and that three or four tax-free years be graciously granted them. I can assure Yr. Highness that these people will show their worth in only a few years.

Putting my unlimited trust in Yr. Highness's previous generosity towards my poor brethren, I flatter myself in the pleasant hope that my submission of this matter in so forceful a way will not have been in vain.

I plead from the bottom of my soul that God might long preserve Yr. Highness's blessed life on behalf of the general well-being and remain, with the most subjective esteem, Yr. Highness's most respectful servant, Johann Cornies.

103. Heinrich Heese to Johann Cornies. 19 June 1843. SAOR 89-1-911/82.[19]

Valued Friend,

My son-in-law Fast has informed me that one of the Nogai householders who is leasing my sheep does not want to continue this business but would like to buy the sheep on credit. I would gladly accept such a sale if friend Stobbe, my curator, were willing to oversee the transaction and gave me an assessment of the Nogai with respect to terms of payment. Please ask friend Stobbe to tell me about his decision soon. Once I am again a private citizen, after successfully completing my teaching four years from now, I very much doubt that I will be able to support myself on my present sheep income.

I can no longer travel because of my work and an incurable illness. The slightest infection is dangerous and threatens my life. This recently occurred in the presence of an eminent guest when my illness, quite unexpectedly, erupted with a serious haemorrhage that caused me to faint.

My second concern is the future of my Heinrich. I think he is best qualified to do agriculture. This I would like him to pursue if he could manage to do so without saddling me with enormous expenses. During his second journey to Moscow over the holidays he should be able to qualify himself in Russian and in the study of money exchanges. He'll then have only a year of study left to complete my school.

In the expectation of your kind sympathy for my son, I have the honour to be your most respectful friend, H. Heese.

Khortitsa, 19 June 1843.

---

19   Heese had been the teacher at the Ohrloff school until his dismissal in 1841. See Staples, *Johann Cornies*, 122–3, 239.

104. Johann Cornies to [Carl Stempel]. 21 June 1843.
SAOR 89-1-925/67v.

Highly valued Sir,

I respond to your valued letter of 15 June to say that I have spoken to Jacob Esau, a local Mennonite wool purchaser from Halbstadt, about the sale of your wool. If you were willing to sell it for twenty-two rubles per pud, he would be prepared to make a suitable deposit. His price is the same as what he paid me a few days ago for the wool produced in partnership with the Nogais. The wool is much like yours in quality. Kindly let me know by return mail. Should I take a deposit now or wait until Esau arrives and inspects your wool?

In a few days' time, once I have talked to master brickmaker Sharstov about establishing a brickworks in Mariupol District, I will put the estimates together and let you know about the whole matter.

With honest esteem, I remain your respectful servant, Johann Cornies.

105. Friedrich Prinz to Johann Cornies. 21 June 1843.
SAOR 89-1-911/89.

Esteemed Mr. Johann Cornies,

I again ask you for information and assistance in connection with the General's visit. Preacher Hekel later told me that the visit had resulted in much conflict for him on the subject of his support. Earlier, three villages had promised him some wheat from every householder as well as some cultivated land and a haymeadow. Since the visit, however, they say that the land should again be surveyed, and are unwilling to give him anything. This has made his position quite impossible. Additionally, the villagers have become more offensive, claiming that the General has nothing to do with the matter, since [St.] Petersburg is in control. There seems to be little hope for any improvement.

Please, if you will, take pity on our community, as much as you can. In future, the community will be much more willing and obedient. It will thank you and your relatives and you will reap rewards both here and in heaven. Your most humble servant, Friedrich Prinz.

Neuhoffnung, 21 June 1843.

Please permit me another question about the enclosed sealed paper for the General. Should it be submitted? Who should sign it? Return it to me if you think that this is best. Otherwise, keep it with you.

The paper is entitled, "Report from the Berdiansk District Office, [to] His Excellency, Mr. Acting General Guardian for the Colonists in South Russia, State Counsellor von Hahn."

The District Office considers itself responsible and compelled to respond to your remarks on [Ends here]

106. Carl Stempel to Johann Cornies. 30 June 1843.
SAOR 89-1-911/97.

Most valued Mr. Cornies,

Many thanks for telling me about the wool. Please make a down payment on my behalf if you think that twenty-two rubles per pud is a good price. He must fetch the wool himself.

I have a special request to make in regards to your promise that you would give me an estimate for the construction of a brick kiln. Please send me a sketch for an inspector's house to be built during the coming year, designed according to your tastes. I would gladly seek your personal advice on this matter, but it would be costly to rent a cart at this time of year when all of the horses are hard at work. I know, in any case, that you will take all factors into account.

With honest respect, I have the honour to call myself your true friend,
C. Stempel.

Grunau, 30 June 1843.

107. Johann Cornies to Hutterthal Village Office. 2 July 1843.
SAOR 89-1-954/47.

From the Chairman of the Molochnaia Mennonite Society for the Advancement of Agriculture and Trades, Tashchenak estate, 2 July 1843,

To the Hutterthal Village Office,

The Village Office must report as to how many bricks each householder has produced for house construction:

- how many bricks, in total, had been previously prepared?
- how many bricks were made during the past week, that is by Saturday?

A record in response to these questions should be sent to me together with a report.

Village officers should be careful to ensure that the clay is worked well until very tacky and that the bricks are made neatly. They should give directions to ensure that clay pits are not located too close to areas where buildings will later be constructed or where gardens and the like will be situated. Johann Cornies.

Please prepare a record of good clay bricks that were made earlier by each householder in Hutterthal village and how many each householder completed between 4 and 10 July, the week just past.

108. Johann Cornies to Fedor F. Rosen. 3 July 1843. SAOR 89-1-881/3.

[Draft:] Yr. Honour, Mr. Rosen,

Your Honour knows that some inhabitants of the Akhil Chodgiga village community were dissatisfied with Elder Ramahan, and that Yr. Honour punished them with community work. The reason for the discontent is that Elder Ramahan tried to carry out directives from the authorities promptly, with no exceptions for anyone. The punishments have embittered and angered the disgruntled individuals even more. It would seem that they have intrigued against the District Chief. They want him removed from office. An investigation will be carried out.

Ramahan has sent me a letter (I enclose the original) requesting that I appeal to Yr. Honour to leave him in office until you have inspected the region personally and convinced yourself that there are no grounds for these odious charges. Please make the appropriate arrangements as soon as you can.

I take the liberty of enclosing a letter by Elder Bultrak describing the intentions of Nogais who are petitioning to move to the Caucasus Guberniia. He hopes that they will not be permitted to move, or that a move would be made more difficult for them. Otherwise, their restiveness will ruin them and lead to the destruction of their undertakings.

With the most sincere trust and genuine respect, I sign myself as Yr. Honour's respectful servant.

109. Johann Cornies to [Carl Stempel]. 5 July 1843. SAOR 89-1-925/70.

Most esteemed Inspector,

I have prepared cost estimates for the establishment of a brickworks in the Mariupol Settlement District in accordance with your wishes. I have the honour of sending them to you now, with the proviso that the prices specified are what they would be here. There may, as a result, be some discrepancies in prices that would need to be adjusted.

With complete esteem, I have the honour to remain your most respectful servant, Johann Cornies.

110. Johann Cornies to Traugott Blueher. 5 July 1843.
   SAOR 89-1-925/70v.

Most esteemed Mr. Blueher,

On 27 June, 1,010 puds, twenty-five and three-quarter funt of washed
Spanish wool bought on your account were shipped from here, packed
in ninety-eight sacks loaded onto thirty-two carts. Enclosed is the
original of the contract concluded with carter Ivan Gerasimov and his
associates and, for your information, a copy of the bill of lading given
him, as well as Mennonite Dirk Neufeld's accounts for purchasing the
wool, packing it, etc. After subtracting the ten thousand rubles already
received from you, the accounts show that I advanced you 13,494 rubles,
thirty kopeks, which sum you might kindly remit to me by mail as soon
as possible.

By buying early, we were able to get the wool somewhat more cheaply
than if we had bought it here on site at twenty-two to twenty-three
rubles. May the Lord's blessing rest on this venture.

On your advice, the carters were given the address in the village outside the city where they were to halt and notify you in order that the
wool might be forwarded directly to be washed. Sending last year's
twenty balls of wool to be washed was very rewarding for me. Many
thanks for your continued efforts on my behalf.

Raw silk at ten rubles, fifty kopeks is already being sold here on site.
Last year producers obtained as much as twelve and one-half rubles in
Kharkiv. I cannot imagine that we will send silk to Moscow for these
prices.

Interest-bearing certificates are of no benefit for me. I would therefore
ask you not to include any of them with money forwarded to me.

With the friendliest greetings to you and your family, I remain, with
love, your faithful friend and servant, Johann Cornies.

111. Traugott Blueher to Johann Cornies. 5 July 1843.
   SAOR 89-1-911/107.

Mr. Johann Cornies, Ohrloff village, most valued friend,

In response to your communication of 7 May, I enclose sales accounts
for eighty-seven balls of Spanish wool received from you in two

shipments. You are still owed 5,680 rubles that I enclose. Since the two thousand rubles paid to Baron v. Rosen in accordance with your commission are listed in the account, this transaction is closed.

I return my obliging thanks for the trust you have kindly given us. I would be pleased if my efforts might in future benefit your interests.

According to Mr. Phillip Wiebe's communication of 11 June, I am expecting ninety-four balls of washed Spanish wool. I am inclined to have the whole quantity sorted and washed without delay unless you are of a different mind. Please let me have your opinion in your next letter.

I firmly expect to receive the church and nature stories ordered as well as the geographies sometime this year. I still have a supply of Bible stories with small copperplate prints such as those sent to you previously. These can be sent to you as desired.

Our weather these past few weeks has been exceptional. We have had rain and warm temperatures and the plants have been growing tall with unusual speed. Should our Heavenly Father grant us a favourable harvest as well, our crops from garden and field would exceed what we have rarely seen before.

I commend myself to your further loving remembrance and send you friendly greetings as your constantly respectful friend, Traugott Blueher. Received 21 July 1843.

112. Traugott Blueher to Johann Cornies. 5 July 1843. SAOR 89-1-911/109.

Mr. Johann Cornies, Ohrloff village.

Most valued friend,

I am taking the liberty of approaching you with the following inquiry. Two years ago, a foreigner (a Saxon) delivered several hundred sheep to this region and started a small agricultural enterprise. He then married. Since he understands well that it will be difficult to maintain a good livelihood here, he is now hoping to find employment as an overseer for a nobleman with a large sheepfarm. Since I assume that you are familiar with noblemen in your locality, I would ask you to kindly inform me if there is any prospect of his finding such employment there.

Should there be no prospect in this regard, he would be willing to set up a small establishment in your region. Can he lease some land for a specific payment from a German settlement? Should this be possible, he would rather not become involved with a Russian nobleman. This man seems to be honest and principled, and I very much hope for his success.

In the expectation that you will grant my request, I send you friendly greetings as always. Traugott Blueher.

Received 24 July 1843.

113. Evgenii F. Hahn to Agricultural Society. 10 July 1843. SAOR 89-1-917/6.

Copy to the Molochnaia Mennonite Society for the Advancement of Agriculture,

My inspection tour of villages in the Molochnaia Mennonite District in 1842 convinced me that the level of teaching in village schools in your district is still far from that needed to provide children with an adequate education. In keeping with the esteemed Regulation from His Majesty, the Tsar, I have made the following decisions. The intention of the Regulation is to promote the founding of new institutions for the welfare of all inhabitants and to improve the school system. Only through the latter can people make rapid advances in their culture.

I have decided to make Mennonites on the Molochnaia a model for other foreign settlers in this area. I would therefore expressly commission the Society for the Advancement of Agriculture and Trades to take responsibility for all schools in the district. There should be no delay in regulating them for this purpose. The Society should, among other things, ensure that all local schoolhouses are suitable for their purpose and fitted with all possible useful features.

The Society should specifically and carefully supervise the hiring and release of schoolteachers from particular schools in order that they might be suitably tested in advance of their appointment. It is, in general, the Society's duty to ensure that morally upright, well-educated teachers, suitable for their purpose, are eventually appointed in all village schools, and that the whole system is raised to an orderly and useful level.

With respect to religion and in accordance with their duties under Section I, #5, the church teachers [preachers] should carefully supervise the schools to ensure that no lessons injurious to the Mennonite confession of faith are taught.

I will expect periodic, detailed, and careful reports about progress in schooling. In every instance where obstacles of any nature occur, I should be informed immediately in order that these might be eliminated.

Odesa, 10 July 1843.
Acting General Guardian of the Colonists in Southern Russia
State Counsellor v. Hahn.

114. Evgenii F. Hahn to church leaders. 10 July 1843.
   SAOR 89-1-917/5.

Copy: To the Church Elders and Church Teachers of the Molochnaia
Mennonite District,

To ensure that the school system in the Molochnaia Mennonite District is regulated to correspond with its purpose, I have commissioned the Society for the Advancement of Agriculture and Trades to ensure that all schoolhouses are appropriately organized, and that, in particular, they are provided with good teachers. The Society is required to pay careful attention to ensure that a schoolteacher is not hired for any school without a preliminary examination and that he is not released or accepted in another school without further examination.

In order that the schools can make progress in their tasks without allowing obstacles to hinder them, I am publicizing this directive to assist the Society in carrying out its commission. I request that all Church Elders and church teachers supervise the village schools carefully with respect to questions of morality and religion. They should ensure that no teachers are giving instruction damaging to basic Mennonite principles.

Odesa, 10 July 1843.

Acting General Guardian, State Counsellor v. Hahn.

115. Peter Siemens to Johann Cornies. 11 July 1843.
   SAOR 89-1-911/100.

To Mr. Johann Cornies in Ohrloff. Most valued friend,

I cannot neglect to report about several items and to note that, with many thanks to God, I have arrived in my fatherland safely and in good health. I visited the worthy Elder Peter Regier in Tiegenhagen to talk about the new settlement in Mogilev and Vitebsk. I told him that once you are able to negotiate the acceptance of a deputation, you will notify us or Elder Peter Regier in particular. This notification is awaited here.

I know of nothing further to report since I have only just arrived. I wish you good health and well-being. With a friendly greeting, I remain your honest friend and servant, Peter Siemens.

Blumenort [West Prussia]

N.B. Please be so kind as to forward the enclosed communication to the esteemed Peter Neufeld. Received 29 July 1843.

116. Carl Stempel to Johann Cornies. 12 July 1843.
SAOR 89-1-911/99.

Most valued Mr. Cornies,

I received your dear letter with the estimate today. I have not reached an agreement with the brickmaker about setting up a brick kiln in Grunau. The sand required will be obtained from the crown village. The crown villagers complain a great deal, however, that should the kiln be established there they will lose their best piece of haymeadow. The brickmaker is of the view that Grunau has better clay than does the crown village.

I will, by the first mail, forward the estimate for confirmation. Meanwhile, I have agreed with the brickmaker that he will be here over the next two weeks to ensure that we do not lose time with needless discussion. It can be assumed that whatever the State Counsellor says will definitely be confirmed. The kiln must be set up in a way that would allow several thousand bricks to be spread out and fired this year.

I would again request in a most friendly way that when time and circumstances allow, you have a plan made for the house, since no one will do it as well as you. With constant respect, I remain your honest friend C. Stempel.

Grunau settlement. 12 July 1843.

117. Johann Cornies to Evgenii F. Hahn. 14 July 1843.
SAOR 89-1-925/72.

State Counsellor v. Hahn,

As promised, I have the honour of sending Yr. Excellency a short description of hedge mustard (*erysimum*) and of the harm it does among plants growing on fields. I list means to eradicate mustard from cultivated fields and to destroy it and also couch grass (*triticum repens*) and other weeds that hold back the growth of field plants.

I take the liberty of sending you an original letter from a Mennonite merchant and silk manufacturer in the city of Crefeldt on the Rhine for Yr. Excellency's kind perusal. Please give me your view in this regard and then return the letter. The letter is a response to the communication I sent from Odesa to the Mennonite congregation in Crefeldt on 7 January 1843. I inquired if there might be local Mennonite silk weavers whose families would be willing to settle here on the Molochnaia and give us the benefit of their skills. I promised that we would make their journey more attractive by providing them with quarters. Money would also be advanced for their first settlement.

District Chairman Prinz from Neuhoffnung reported to me that Pietists who had transferred to the local Evangelical Lutheran Church were still troublesome and did not wish to relinquish some of the existing arrangements affecting Pietists in general. I informed Inspector Stempel about this matter when he visited me four days ago. He asked me to visit the Berdiansk settlement myself to find out why these breakaway members seemed unwilling to live peaceably despite all warnings. Mr. Stempel suggested that I might try to find out who was supporting these people in their delusions.

The grain harvest in our local villages will be completed this week. It has generally turned out very well. Only the Arnautka wheat suffered and has many empty ears. The locusts did no noticeable damage. They are not flying about in swarms, but only appearing individually. Heavy rains and cold nights have destroyed many of them. Trees are growing much faster this year than in most of the previous five years.

To my most sincere pleasure, I must remark that Mr. Stempel is now completely satisfied with his settlers. He is concerned about them in all possible ways and shows great zeal and generosity in support of their well-being. He works hard to establish order among them and promotes their happiness and prosperity in every way.

The Hutterites will complete their good harvest this week and have enough hay to fatten their livestock. Healthy, they are busy as ants, and intend to begin building their houses soon.

With the greatest esteem, I remain Yr. Excellency's respectful servant, Johann Cornies.

118. Daniel F. Doering to Johann Cornies. 14 July 1843.
SAOR 89-1-911/101.

Mr. Johann Cornies in Ohrloff, Valued Sir and Friend,
Since I am again in Taganrog for several days to purchase wines and similar items, I cannot deny myself the pleasure of sending you a few

lines from here. I am naturally greatly in your debt. Please forgive me for not writing to you sooner.

In Moscow Mr. Blueher informed me of your kindly inquiries about me. This pleased me greatly. I would gladly have written immediately but I thought I might visit you personally on this journey. I would like to do so now, should that be possible. I have a pleasant travelling companion who would like to see the many things that have been established in your villages. He is the bookkeeper and assistant to our director in Sarepta.

If everything proceeds as desired, we intend to leave on 20 or 21 July, travelling via post to Neuhoffnung. It would be most pleasant for me to meet you and your dear loved ones in the best of prosperity, and to be able to talk about many things personally with you. In the meantime, I send you and your dear ones hearty greetings and remain in friendship, your humble servant, Dan. F. [Doering]

Taganrog. Received 20 July 1843.

119. Phillip Wiebe on behalf of Johann Cornies to unidentified correspondent. 15 July 1843. SAOR 89-1-925/74v.

Highly valued friend,

In response to your communication dated Tiegenhagen, 23 April 1843, on behalf of the collected Deputies of all West Prussian Mennonite congregations, Mr. Cornies had the original of the letter sent to the Ministry of State Domains submitted to the Director of the Tavrida Bureau of State Domains, Baron v. Rosen as No. 70 to the Ministry of State Domains in St. Petersburg on 24 May 1843. It was accompanied by the request that the particular land in Vitebsk and Mogilev Guberniias, during the course of this year, be specifically designated for settlement by Prussian Mennonites.

Mr. Cornies requests that the Deputies Bernhard Epp, Johann Rahn, Jacob Froese, Peter Regier, Johann Wall, Peter Rahn, Peter Kroecker, and Peter Froese be duly informed. As soon as the specific designation arrives from St. Petersburg, Mr. Cornies will be sure to inform the Deputies of his decisions for the early promotion of this matter.

Please let Mr. Cornies know to which of the Deputies, by name, he should direct further correspondence. With esteem, your respectful Phillip Wiebe.

120. Phillip Wiebe on behalf of Johann Cornies to David Epp, Heubuden. 15 July 1843. SAOR 89-1-925/75v.

Highly valued friend,

On 26 June, Mr. Cornies received a letter from David Epp, Heubuden, in response to an earlier communication about Elder Regier's highly damaging support for the resistance in the former Warkentin congregation. Mr. Cornies thinks it better to leave the latter completely unanswered, above all because Mr. Epp seeks to excuse Elder Regier's impure influence. He does not try to understand the situation, or judges it superficially because of his ignorance of the matter.

Elder Regier's assertions in the communication handed to me and lying before me are as follows: "According to this information, Ohm Warkentin was removed from office and the congregation was to elect a different Elder, or to divide itself among the other congregations. Surely this is unheard of since freedom of religious practice has always been allowed in Prussia. The situation cannot be allowed to remain this way without the reinstatement of Warkentin." When the Elder's communication arrived, it prompted extreme turmoil in the minds of those who had been egged on by Warkentin and stern measures were needed to suppress the extreme unrest.

Every well-disposed inhabitant of our district will continue to strongly fault Elder Regier. Ill-intentioned, he used the opportunity to instil mistrust in Russia's high administration and its most wise enactments. He interfered in things that were of no concern to him. It is no small matter that Mr. Epp meant to blame Mr. Cornies, who holds the true well-being of our local Mennonites close to his heart, even though many in our area and some in Prussia lack the insight to understand his selfless endeavours.

When the State Counsellor visited this district, he spoke with Elder Wiens from Gnadenheim and told him that it was only because of Mr. Cornies's intercession that the highly detrimental matter involving Elder Regier's interference had not been considered at further levels. Views here appear to be changing for the better and the State Counsellor was himself able to take pleasure in inspecting our villages.

It would be highly desirable if Prussian church teachers [preachers] themselves, without exception, were prepared, as a consequence of this matter, to listen to better advice and not succumb to similar temptation [to meddle in Molochnaia affairs] in future. They can further inflame an evil matter here, unforgivably disturbing the peace, household happiness, and well-being of many hundreds. Authorized by Mr. Cornies, I write to ask that Mr. David Epp show Elder Regier this letter and respond soon to the communication of 29 March 1843. Please notify Mr. Cornies by mail of the Elder's intentions and purpose in encouraging the former Warkentin congregation to report details of the dissensions here. Also, please have the papers received from church teachers Neufeld and Huebert destroyed, as requested. They are generally known by the administration here. They have been sealed and preserved here. Obtaining them from Prussia is consequently not permitted.

Please notify Mr. Cornies about the results of all aspects of this commission as soon as possible.

Your most respectful, Phillip Wiebe.

121. Johann Cornies to Fedor F. Rosen. 15 July 1843. SAOR 89-1-925/75v.

Baron v. Rosen,

I sincerely hope that you, most estimable Baron, and your dear family, have successfully completed your journey to [St.] Petersburg and are enjoying good health in the company of your relatives and acquaintances. Please also remember kindly the inhabitants of Tavrida and occasionally those on the Molochnaia as well. I take the liberty of enclosing a copy of the petition directed by my bother David Cornies to the Minister, Count Kiselev, on your kind advice. It is about limiting the ploughed fields on the land he has leased, and will be sent with today's mail. My respectful request is that you use your benevolent influence with His Highness should the opportunity present itself.

Everything here is going well. I heard that the new District Chairman assumed his position several days ago.

The lattice railings received for Yr. Honour in Berdiansk were sent to Mr. Leidlitz's address in Simferopol on 30 June.

With the appropriate esteem, Yr. Honour's respectful servant, Johann Cornies.

122. Molochnaia District Office and Agricultural Society to Guardianship Committee. 20 July 1843. SAOR 89-1-812/18.

[Draft marked:] "thrown out"

Report to the Guardianship Committee for Foreign Settlers in South Russia,

From the Molochnaia Mennonite District Office and the Society for the Advancement of Agriculture and Trades,

The District Office and the Society find it necessary to provide guidance for Mennonites from our district now resident in the city of Berdiansk. Fifteen families now live there and this number will increase from year to year. A qualified director, selected from their midst by a majority of votes, should maintain suitable order and promote good moral conduct among them. To retain a direct connection to these Mennonites and to contribute to a useful Mennonite presence in Berdiansk, this person will be subordinate to the District Office and the Society.

The election took place in the presence of a District Deputy Chairman and a member of the Society. David Fast, a local Mennonite, was elected and recognized as qualified by the District Office and the Society. For the above-mentioned reasons, the Guardianship Committee for Foreign Settlers in South Russia is asked to graciously confirm in office as elected director, the Mennonite David Fast of the city of Berdiansk, for a period of two years. The Berdiansk city administration should likewise be informed in order that it might support him in matters included in his office, and to give him the necessary recognition as local director of the Mennonites resident in the city.

District Chairman, Abram Toews, Deputy David Braun, Deputy Johann Neufeld, Society Chairman Johann Cornies, Member Gerhard Enns, Member Jacob Martens. Society secretary Wiebe.

20 July 1843. Ohrloff

123. Evgenii F. Hahn to Johann Cornies. 26 July 1843. SAOR 89-1-911/119.

I received the directions that were sent to me on how to eradicate weeds, as well as the letter from the Crefeld silk manufacturer. I thank you heartily for the first item, which I will have printed shortly, with several forceful instructions.

As for the letter, it is incorrect on several points. Silk fabrication and sericulture are two entirely different matters. The evidence for this exists in Milan and in France, and also in Russia. Our silk manufacturers are located in Moscow, although sericulture cannot, of course, be carried on there. Sericulture can be carried on by agriculturalists, but not silk manufacture. It is obvious that sericulture can only thrive where there is the possibility of selling the silk to advantage. In our case, silk factories would be established for no purpose other than to provide an advantageous market for the silk cocoons of the agriculturalist. We must therefore extend and perfect sericulture itself among the agriculturalists.

It would be hard to establish a community silk factory. It would also not be useful. Private interests are mainly responsible for the success of such establishments. Who might undertake the risks of establishing a silk factory in the Molochnaia Mennonite District under present conditions of sericulture there?

Let us begin by extending and perfecting sericulture that is still in its infancy in the Molochnaia District. Judging by the letter, this could not be forced by bringing in immigrants from the Rhine. In the Bulgarian colony of Parttani, about one hundred verstas from Odesa, sericulture is carried out on a large scale by an Italian. Last year, Mr. v. Rayko displayed his silk in Odesa. There was no market for this silk in Moscow simply because it was too fine, too beautiful, and consequently too expensive. Mr. v. Rayko has decided, in future, to send exceptional silk to France.

In this way, I simply want to say that well-conducted sericulture can, without travelling to Milan or France, be learned here as well. It would have been of great value if several Mennonite families, skilled in sericulture and silk manufacturing, could have been settled in the Mennonite District. On the Rhine, however, only weavers and craftsmen seem to be available. The former are of little use to us and the latter can only be useful to us when sericulture has made greater progress.

These are my thoughts. If you do not share them, do give me your opinion. Please be assured that my one desire is to promote whatever is useful and to offer you my hand in this regard.

Enclosed, I return the Crefeld letter. I also send a sample of this year's silk from Mr. v. Rayko, to enable you to judge your own silk.

The quarrels in the Berdiansk District give me great concern, and I would be grateful to you if you could quell them. Otherwise, I will keep my promise and resettle the weakest party [in the dispute].

Please receive the assurance of my honest dedication. E. v. Hahn.

Odesa, 26 July 1843. Received 5 August 1843.

124. August Wilke to Johann Cornies. 28 July 1843.
SAOR 89-1-911/110.

Most valued Mr. Cornies,

Please forgive me for the letters with which I often burden you. My son-in-law Braun asks me to put in a good word for him and to kindly request a loan of two hundred rubles for a year. Should this be possible, I would repay the loan at the time specified with the greatest thanks. I would gladly have spoken with you personally, but you drove away so quickly that I could not do so. My son-in-law will give me no peace until I have written to you. He bought a house in Prishib for which he borrowed two hundred rubles from Haubt. Haubt, however, has bought a fullholding in Mariupol District and needs the money himself. My son-in-law has no money to repay him and so has asked me to request your favour on his behalf.

Please forgive me for writing to you so boldly. I remain with all respect your servant, A. Wilke.

Tashchenak, 29 July 1843.

125. Carl Stempel to Johann Cornies. 3 August 1843. SAOR 89-1-911/123.

Most valued Mr. Cornies,

Whenever you receive a letter from me you know, even before you start to read it, that it will contain a request, as this one does.

The State Counsellor sent me confirmation for the establishment of a brick kiln. In the same communication, he asks where I intend to obtain the funds to hire a brickmaker and to provide the materials necessary for the kiln. He wonders whether I have lost sight of this aspect. On the contrary, I had assumed that the General would designate a specific amount to build a house for the Inspector. Since the bricks to be fired this year were supposed to be used to build the house, I had intended to cover the costs for the kiln using this money. The bricks, thereafter, would be paid for by settlers wanting bricks.

I do not know if I should submit the matter to the General in this way. Kindly give me your advice on how I might proceed. I am enclosing the papers from the State Counsellor to assist you in determining what kind of a submission should be made. If you have a small plan prepared for the building itself, please send it to me with this messenger.

I would further ask that you give me your honest opinion about a report from the District Office relating to [compulsory] driving duties. People here find it difficult to carry out such services, but I also dislike the idea of collecting money for a driving fund from each householder. This might create much resentment that I think the State Counsellor would not like. Commending myself to your favour, I remain with constant respect, your honest friend C. Stempel.

Please let me know when we can expect the pleasure of seeing you in our region again. We hope this will happen soon.

Grunau, 3 August 1843.

126. Johann Cornies to Ministry of State Domains. 4 August 1843. SAOR 89-1-925/82.

To the Tavrida Bureau of State Domains,

In response to the Bureau of State Domains' communication No. 6279 of 29 July 1843, I have the honour to report that the Tatar, Labit Laleoglu from Feodosia District, arrived here on 10 July, two months later than the communication of 13 May that he brought along from his local District Chief. It seems he was told to fetch the implements on order whenever it suited him. His main purpose in travelling to this region was to trade tobacco, however. The covered wagon on which he travelled, harnessed to one horse, was equipped for that trade. It was only possible to load one of the required markers, one mounder, and two lifters onto it. The open cart that was harnessed to two oxen that were originally ordered, would easily have been able to carry all of the implements.

It is necessary to send a more suitable cart to this area to pick up the three markers, three mounders, and six lifters that are still needed. These were ordered in the director's communication No. 199 of 9 April 1843 and were to be sent to the District Chiefs in both the Feodosia and Simferopol Districts. The implements ordered for Simferopol were fetched long ago. Johann Cornies.

127. Johann Cornies to Peter Keppen. 4 August 1843. SAOR 89-1-925/83v.

Mr. v. Keppen. Yr. Honour, State Counsellor,

On 15 July, I received your valued letter of 28 June 1843 from Moscow. Many thanks for purchasing the well thermometer for me. Mr. Blueher will see to it that I receive it from Moscow in good condition, perhaps with carters who transported my wool to Moscow in June. With thanks, I send you the enclosed twelve rubles, twenty-five kopeks that I still owed on your account with the Fidler Apothecary in Kharkiv.

Too much time has passed since you received a letter from me. Please forgive me. My life is a constant tumult of varied activities. I am rarely at home. Improvements are progressing rapidly in all villages. My services are demanded in three different settlement districts.

I was unable to continue excavations this spring because of my involvement in the settlement of the Radishchev Mennonites, but I have decided to open several mounds in September. I had previously designated these mounds on the shores of the Sea of Azov. I have made the necessary provisions and will send you the results of these excavations as soon as they are done.

Our summer has not been hot but rain was lacking just when the grain needed it most. Still, the harvest turned out moderately well, even though Arnautka wheat in a number of areas produced long straw and ears without kernels. Our orchards will produce little fruit because late May frosts destroyed many blossoms. Here and there, we have foot-and-mouth disease among the cattle. We will have a large quantity of potatoes this year. Introduced among Nogais three years ago, the fields should produce an abundant crop of potatoes that should please the Nogais very much. There have been great changes in our villages since you last visited them in 1837. The improvements have been remarkable. Tree-planting has been much extended and there has been much house construction.

Please receive the assurance of my sincere esteem, with which I have the honour of being Yr. Honour's respectful servant, Johann Cornies.

128. Johann Cornies to Traugott Blueher. 4 August 1843. SAOR 89-1-925/85v.

Esteemed Mr. Blueher,

As I send you the enclosed receipt to conclude last year's wool business, I include my most sincere thanks for your efforts in carrying out my affairs to my advantage. Be assured that I am entirely satisfied with your actions and opinions.

First and foremost, I can report that on 23 July my family and I were surprised by a very welcome visit. Mr. Doehring, my bosom friend from Sarepta, arrived here, together with dear Mr. Meinecke. The letter you wrote to Sarepta, including a greeting from me to Mr. Doehring, must certainly have prompted this journey. The visitors stayed with me in Iushanle, Ohrloff, and Tashchenak until the first of the month. They travelled around several villages and acquainted themselves with our local agricultural practices. They asked me to send you their hearty greetings.

My wife sends many thanks for your kindness in ordering an electuary for her cough that continues to torture her.

My son lives in Tashchenak and Agnes is her mother's support in Ohrloff. They both think of you and remember you and your dear family frequently. The loving reception they enjoyed in the circle of your worthy family will never vanish from their hearts. They send heartfelt greetings to you, your dear wife, and children.

I was not at home when your wool was dispatched but it will most certainly have been sent in good order. I hope that God will give it his blessing. Please proceed as you think best in selling my wool this year. I will always be satisfied. Otherwise there is nothing else to mention in this respect, except to say that if the sale were to seem more promising on credit, please offer such terms. Money is not needed here too badly. Moreover, if you think it would be to my advantage to have the wool washed, please do so. In any case, I would very much like to know how the quality of the wool marked "T" turns out in comparison with the rest of the shipment.

With respect to your inquiry of 5 July, I can report that the administrator of an estate in the Crimea belonging to Count Vorontsov asked if I knew of someone who might be hired on as a supervisor for eight thousand Spanish sheep. He would need to be a morally dependable person with the required knowledge…. Should the foreigner you referred to be willing to take on this job in the Crimea, and agrees to the above conditions, he should correspond about details with the assistant administrator of the estate. This must, however, be done in Russian.

On the next post day, I will submit your request concerning the foreigner, as you have described him to me, to Count Vorontsov's assistant administrator. I will urge him, should he wish to see such a person hired as supervisor of the Count's sheep, to write directly to you in Moscow.

To my knowledge, there are no areas of land close to our settlements available for lease. The person in question might well pursue this matter personally on site.

When an opportunity presents itself, please send me one hundred copies of the Bible stories with small copper engravings such as the ones you sent me earlier.

So far, our summer has not been hot. The grain suffered from drought and several severe night frosts in May. The latter also damaged the fruit that was just emerging on the trees. Despite all, the harvest turned out to be moderately good, but there will be little fruit.

All of the Hutterite Brethren have moved to this area. You were undoubtedly informed about them by Mr. Wigand, who visited them during the last century at Vishchenka, near Krolevetz in Little Russia. The

government commissioned me to settle them in the vicinity of the Mennonite settlements, close to my estate Tashchenak. Their Christian morality
has not deteriorated much, but externally, in dress and economic arrangements, they are almost Russian peasants. They still speak Tyrolian, as in
the past. There are fifty-one core families and they are very poor.

I commend myself to you and your dear family and assure you that it
is the joy of my life to be able to sign myself as your faithful friend and
servant, Johann Cornies.

Receipt:

29,933 rubles, 50 kopeks, after expenses, for seventy-eight balls of
wool labelled "J.C." consisting of 916 puds, three and one-quarter funt
net weight of washed Spanish wool that was forwarded on 11 July 1842
and 5 February 1843 to Messrs. A.G. Soerensen and Company in the
Sarepta Merchant Firm in Moscow to be sold on consignment have been
correctly received. This sum is herewith receipted and the transaction
has been completed.

Ohrloff village, 4 August 1843. Johann Cornies.

129. August Haxthausen to Johann Cornies. 4 August 1843. SAOR 89-1-911/125.[20]

My esteemed friend,

With great thanks, I am returning to you the enclosed report about
the Molokans after making a copy of it. You may be convinced that
I will make only good use of it, as I will also of the report about the
Doukhobors.

If you wish to communicate with me, please write to me in Moscow,
addressed to the Prussian consul, Mr. Rosenstrauch. I will be there in
October. May you fare well.

In company with my travelling companions I commend myself to
you with greetings for all of your dear people. From your devoted
Haxthausen.

Redutkali in Berdiansk District, 4 [August] 1843.

---

20 Baron August von Haxthausen, a Prussian nobleman, toured Russia in 1843 and
wrote an influential legal and ethnographic study of the Empire. He visited Cornies
and called him "one of the most influential men in Southern Russia" (August von
Haxthausen, *Studien über die innern Zustände, das Volksleben und insbesondere die
ländlichen Einrichtungen Rußlands*, 2:430).

130. Johann Cornies to [Stempel]. 6 August 1843. SAOR 89-1-954/41.

[Draft:] Esteemed Inspector,

I am honoured to send you my views in regard to your letter of 3 August.

1. With respect to the outlay required to defray the costs of the brick kiln, I estimate that if the manufacture of 150,000 (15/m) bricks is considered at twelve rubles per one thousand (1/m), two thousand rubles are needed. You could propose that this come from the community's budget, guaranteed by the whole community. The local Mayor's Office should encourage the village community to issue a statement to this effect, even should the money be borrowed.

2. The suggestion from the Mariupol Mennonites that a wagon be provided [at no cost] cannot be accepted because the Committee would not approve. This matter might be handled in the same way as it is in the Molochnaia Mennonite District where a wagon for such uses is constantly maintained. A community statement in this regard would be needed, but I would first like to discuss this matter with you in person.

My friendly advice is that you leave this matter alone and return the report of the Mariupol Mennonite District Office to the sender. Deny the request firmly without further explanation that might well lead to unpleasantness.

The plan and estimates for your house cannot be sent to you yet. Please forgive the delay because I must first deal with too many other matters of business.

I return the enclosed papers and remain respectfully, as always, J. Cornies.

131. Johann Cornies to Ministry of State Domains. 9 August 1843. SAOR 89-1-925/89v.

To the Tavrida Bureau of State Domains,

In response to communication No. 5669 of 15 July 1843 from the Bureau of State Domains about the order for threshing stones, I can report that fourteen stones of the type used to best effect in the villages are now in preparation. They can be fetched by 1 October 1843. The price of each stone is eighteen rubles without the framework, and twenty-eight rubles, nineteen kopeks with.

It would be best to make clear what the best use of such stones would be for the designated state peasants when they fetch them. They can make the simple but necessary observations here on site.

The models of threshing stones ordered will be ready by next October. I should also mention that our local masters will, once the harvest is ended, begin to manufacture other implements for the Poltava, Kyiv, and Kherson Guberniias, and for the Konstantinograd Crown Orchard. I will report as soon as these orders have been completed.

132. Johann Cornies to Forestry Department, Ministry of State Domains. 10 August 1843. SAOR 89-1-925/90.

To the Forestry Department, Ministry of State Domains,

In response to communication No. 642 of 28 June 1843 from the Forestry Department in the Ministry of State Domains, I have the honour to say that I am prepared to use all of my powers to help in the promotion of the general interest. I am happy to agree to His Highness, the Minister's most gracious request that I accept apprentices to learn forest-tree cultivation on the steppes.

In order not to fail in the purpose of developing industrious, practical people for this work, I would request:

1. That apprentices be healthy, with all that this implies. They should be seventeen or eighteen years old and selected by competent persons to ensure that I do not have to send them back. Having to do so wastes a great deal of time.

2. Apprentices should be assigned to their apprenticeships for at least four years. The tasks involved in the cultivation of forest-tree plantations vary greatly from one year to the next, depending on weather conditions. Several years of continuous observation [and work] are required with various varieties of seeded trees, their growth and transplantation. Young persons in their first year, before the [formal] start of their apprenticeship, must generally acquaint themselves with a variety of subjects. Only a very few apprentices with exceptional intellectual abilities might be in a position to leave my plantations after three years and achieve the results demanded in future by the government.

3. Because of my own local circumstances, I must limit the number of apprentices I accept for service in this area to four. I can accept them

for service only on the same terms as those individuals who apprentice with me to learn agriculture.

4. Their number and times of their acceptance may vary.

Mr. Graff, the forester, has been instructed to visit our local plantations. It will give me great pleasure to acquaint him with everything that I have learned over the years in this field. I will assist him in every respect, to the best of my ability. Johann Cornies.

133. Carl Stempel to Johann Cornies. 10 August 1843.
SAOR 89-1-911/127v.

Most esteemed Mr. Cornies,

Many thanks for your dear letter of 6 August with its friendly advice that agrees completely with my own views.

I must also inform you that Braun and Rempel were again here with another request to lease the tavern. I directed them to you, telling them that you considered it better to leave the matter as it is now. At present the crown leaser is threatening to seal the tavern because it lacks a certificate. He wants to know whether an application has been made in this regard. I thought I would find the information I need in the instructions for Bergthal, but this subject is not mentioned there. When I met former District Secretary Krei at the annual fair in Berostova, I asked him about these matters. He assured me that in Molochnaia this certificate is always given out annually. The procedure was not followed in this instance, however, out of ignorance. This could easily have bad results. The local leaser is also enraged because he had the contract written as it was first requested, which is now not correct. All this strengthens him in his opinion that there is a secret brandy trade going on.

I do not know how brandy can be sold in Bergthal. How could anyone pay 2,800 rubles for the lease? The leaser would not estimate the amount of the lease according to the quality of the brandy dispensed in Bergthal, but rather according to the advantages he would derive from the fact that brandy was transported out of Bergthal to other villages in his lease area. Braun and Rempel would surely not do this and it could be difficult for them to raise the amount of the lease.

Commending myself to your faithful friendship, I remain your honest friend who is attached to you with true attachment, C. Stempel.

134. Johann Cornies to Aleksandria Crown Model Farm. 11 August 1843. SAOR 89-1-925/92.

To the administrator of the Aleksandria Crown Model Farm,

According to a receipt from the New Russian Steamboat Commission in Berdiansk, on 6 July 1843 it received a plough manufactured for the Aleksandria Crown Model Farm, with all accessories, and also a small box containing a model of a Dutch wheeled cultivator for transport to Odesa on the steamboat *Mitridat*. I write to notify the administration in this regard and ask that these items be fetched from the warehouse. Its location can be obtained from the Guardianship Committee for Foreign Settlers, together with a description of the wheeled cultivator.

My expenses for the plough are as follows: woodwork thirty and a half rubles, ironwork eighty-eight rubles, transportation for nine puds of weight, eighteen rubles, fifty-nine kopeks, for a total of 136 rubles, sixty-four kopeks. The administration will kindly send me this money by mail via Novoaleksandrovka.

135. Friedrich A. Meinecke to Johann Cornies. 12 August 1843. SAOR 89-1-911/129.

Highly esteemed and beloved Mr. Cornies,

With beautiful memories of an exceedingly pleasant stay, a witness to our friendship, I report our safe arrival in Sarepta. At the same time, I offer you sincere thanks for your heartfelt reception and many demonstrations of love. Soon after our painful parting at Mr. Lange's, this dear friend and his wife and son-in-law took us to Friend Schmidt in Steinbach, where we arrived at seven o'clock in the evening. In the circle of these dear friends we spent a most pleasant evening. Finally Friend Lange and his son-in-law drove back to Gnadenfeld. The welcoming moon had already softened the darkness of the night. His wife stayed back with the somewhat sickly Mrs. Schmidt. Early on 2 August, we took our leave of Friend Schmidt.

We passed through Rudnerweide where we said our goodbyes to Abraham Mathies and his wife and drove on to Rosenfeld. There we stopped off for coffee with the two old Oppenlanders. The Village Mayor took us to Neuhoffnung. There we picked up our wagons and effects and at eight proceeded to the nearby posting station. Since Friend Iamen did not have his horses at home, but wanting to show us his friendship, he took us to the posting station with a pair of beautiful white oxen. It amused us greatly to try to post on oxen.

Praise God that our journey continued safely and quickly, without interruption, day and night. You are entirely correct in saying that on your journey to Sarepta you crossed the river Akhtuba on a boat. However, since 1835 a wooden bridge has been built across this river.

I extended your greetings to our Chairman, Mr. Mory, and told him about your experiences in planting forest trees. He asked me to give you his best thanks and commends himself to your further friendship. Would you kindly send us forest-tree seeds? Mr. Mory would especially like to have the following varieties: ash, maple, linden, birch, alder, sand willow, sumac, white-flowered acacia, wild olive-tree, and cherry poplar. We believe these varieties would suit our local soil and climate best.

Since Friend Doering found no time to write to you today, he asked that I extend heartfelt greetings to you and your dear family on his behalf. I add my own heartfelt greetings to you and your dear family, and to all the dear individuals I got to know.

I remain, with esteem and honest love, your friend, Fried[rich] Adolph Meinecke.

Sarepta, 12 August 1843. Received 27 August.

136. District Office to Wilhelm Martens and Johann Cornies. 14 August 1843. SAOR 89-1-911/132.[21]

Invitation to the beverage trade leaseholders in the Molochnaia Mennonite villages, the esteemed Wilhelm Martens in Halbstadt and Johann Cornies in Ohrloff.

On 8 August 1842, the Guardianship Committee for Foreign Settlers confirmed terms for the granting of leaseholdings for the beverage trade in local villages. The seventh point states:

"Should the community wish to build a new brandy distillery during the current four-year lease from 1843 to 1847, or do so under the immediate direction of the leaseholder, the leaseholder is at liberty to produce brandy on his own accounts, at advantageous grain prices. A special agreement should be concluded for such a construction."

---

21 The brandy sales monopoly was an important part of Cornies's business empire. See Staples, *Johann Cornies*, 43–4, 113–14.

All applicants for the lease were clearly informed of this previously determined condition and signed it personally. This condition is also contained in the fifth point of the contract which the District Office concluded with you. It reads, "The community can build a brandy distillery during the coming four-year lease from 1843 to the year 1847, or leave this right to the leaseholders, etc."

On 18 January 1843, on this basis, a declaration about the building of a brandy distillery for the local community was agreed to by all of the village communities. This community pronouncement said: "According to our signatures below, we the Village Mayors, with the agreement of our neighbours, hereby declare that we wish to have a brandy distillery with a steam apparatus built for the local Mennonite brotherhood. We leave the administration and keeping of accounts for this enterprise to the District Office in Halbstadt. Since the community treasury has no cash balance at present, it is our honest desire that the brandy leaseholders construct this distillery at their own expense. After its completion a special, detailed account should be submitted to the District Office and the community."

It clearly follows from the above-mentioned document that there are no impediments to the construction of a brandy distillery with a steam apparatus for the local Mennonite brotherhood, and that the village communities wish to have the leaseholders for the local beverage trade make the investment of money required.

According to the seventh point of the terms of your lease, the only thing still required is that a special agreement to construct the brandy distillery be concluded without delay, to assign rights and set the time and manner in which the money spent must be repaid to the beverage leaseholder. The above-mentioned community pronouncement authorizes the District Office to do so. A detailed report about the above-mentioned agreement should be submitted to the Guardianship Committee for Foreign Settlers for its examination and confirmation. In the contrary case, there must be a detailed report about the conduct of this matter.

To conclude this transaction for the construction of a brandy distillery for the local Mennonite brotherhood as soon as possible, the District Office hereby invites both of you to a joint discussion in the District Office this Friday, 20 August, at nine o'clock in the morning. At that time, after a report about negotiations, the above-mentioned agreement can be concluded.

District Office at Halbstadt, 14 August 1843.

District Chairman Toews, Deputy Braun, Deputy Neufeld, District Secretary Peter Reimer.

137. Peter Stobbe to Johann Cornies. 17 August 1843. SAOR 89-1-911/136.

Reported to District Office 17 August 1843:

On 6 August, I drove to Tiege to see Wilhelm Loewen about my painful throat. I arrived at twelve midnight, awakened Loewen immediately, and asked him to help me. He examined my illness but told me that he preferred not to receive such a request since Cornies was always dissatisfied with the doctors.

He explained my illness to me. First, he said that my back had slipped down on one side, my lower jaw must be out of joint, and my nose was much affected. He began to stroke me, asking whether that was painful, and I answered with a loud "yes." He said, "Yes, yes" this would continue to happen. He tried to break open my mouth with a pair of pliers. This was more painful even than the stroking. I grasped his hands tightly and told him I could not bear it. He told me to break my jaw myself, because my mouth must be opened. He then asked me to lie down to sleep, sending me to his granary, where he told me to wrap up my head. Because my mouth was always full of water, I could not sleep. My pain did not subside and, first thing in the morning, I informed Loewen accordingly. "What will we do?" he asked. Then he thought for a while and said "we must spray out your mouth," but this did not help. He then told me that I would gradually get better. Peter Stobbe.

138. Philipp Matthias to Johann Cornies. Sent Berdiansk, 17 August 1843. SAOR 89-1-911/137.

Esteemed Mr. Cornies,

You again reminded me that I should repay my debt, but I cannot do so until late in the year. If I give you my last kopek, I won't be able to pay anyone else. If I can't make more purchases, my business will soon fail. I hope to be able to repay you a thousand rubles by St. Martin's Day, however.

I am sorry that I am unable to keep my promise, but it is not simply my fault. I had hoped that a three-thousand-ruble debt owed me would have been repaid by spring. I have not received a kopek of this sum.

I remain your honest friend, Philipp Matthias.

Berdiansk.

**139. Johann Cornies to Church Elders. 17 August 1843.
SAOR 89-1-925/93.**

Esteemed Church Elder Bernhard Fast in Halbstadt,

Dirk Warkentin, Petershagen,
Heinrich Wiens, Gnadenheim,
Heinrich Toews, Pordenau,
Abram Friesen, Blumstein,
Peter Schmidt, Waldheim,
Peter Wedel, Alexanderwohl,
Friedrich Wilhelm Lange, Gnadenfeld,
Benjamin Ratzlaff, Rudnerweide,

Our high authorities have directed me to conduct the affairs and resettlement of the Hutterthal Mennonites to their benefit. I am required to concern myself with their welfare and to provide support in all cases. In this way the terribly poor situation in which they find themselves might be improved in a way that would enable them to progress economically and achieve the level of success attained by model settlers among their brethren in faith.

I have also obligated myself to assist the Hutterthal Mennonites in their house-building for which all materials should have been purchased and made available. I submitted a petition asking for temporary assistance. The resulting fifteen thousand rubles' support graciously granted by the high Ministry to construct thirty houses, is only exactly enough to purchase the necessary wood. The wood must, however, be transported from Ivanenka using their own carts. This would have been possible had several of their draught animals not died over the summer. Since the Hutterites do not have funds to replace these animals it has been quite impossible for some to transport construction materials from Ivanenka.

In this predicament, Elder Jacob Walther and Preacher David Hofer asked that I might, in their name, ask the entire Molochnaia Mennonite community for brotherly help for those ruined by the death of their draught animals. A kindly Christian contribution of money would assist these unfortunates to transport a sufficient number of beams and spars on hired Russian carts.

Their hearts touched by the benevolence already lovingly offered them by our community, both leaders said that they would not have the audacity to place a burden on the Elders and congregations if they were not moved by the wretched losses experienced by some of their members.

Convinced by the miserable situation suffered by some Hutterthal Mennonites as a result of this loss of their livestock, I accepted the plea for the unfortunate Hutterthal Mennonites, pleased to beg all leaders in our local Mennonite District to ask their congregations for brotherly assistance in the form of voluntary contributions of money. I do so, conscious of the fact that God will not allow even the smallest gift contributed to needy brethren to go unrewarded, and that one must do good to everyone, but especially to one's brethren in faith. Supported by this godly command and promise, I remain convinced that you, most esteemed Elders, will not deem this request arrogant and ill conceived, but will, as far as possible, encourage the congregation entrusted to your care generously to provide support money for these Hutterthal Mennonites.

With these hopes, I expect the results of my request from you as soon as possible, by 8 September at the latest. Otherwise such brotherly gifts might arrive too late.

With the most honest feelings of love and esteem, I remain, with brotherly greetings, your respectful servant, Johann Cornies.

140. Johann Cornies to District Office. 17 August 1843. SAOR 89-1-925/98.

To the esteemed Molochnaia Mennonite District Office in Halbstadt,

I submit this notice on behalf of the Mennonite Peter Stobbe, who is in my service. On 6 August Stobbe was struck by a throat illness called "Bruene." After his throat and face were badly swollen, Stobbe sought the assistance of Wilhelm Loewen, Mennonite in the village of Tiege.

Loewen explained to him that his back had shifted, that his lower jawbone was out of joint, and that he had also come down with erysipelas. Loewen unmercifully pressed down on the swelling and stroked it. Then, using pliers, he tried to break open Stobbe's mouth. In his agony, Stobbe tore the pliers out of Loewen's hands, making it impossible for Loewen to complete this operation. Since it was night-time, Loewen suggested that Stobbe rest in his granary. By morning, the pain had naturally increased. Loewen pondered a little and then said that Stobbe's mouth should be sprayed. This simply inflamed the swelling. Finally, Loewen released Stobbe with the consolation that he would probably get better gradually.

On his journey home, Stobbe was fortunately advised by a man in Altona to rinse his mouth. This somewhat relieved Loewen's burning. Dire consequences might otherwise have resulted.

I notify the District Office of this matter, as it is my obligation to do. I would ask that Loewen receive the deserved reprimand, insisting that he, in future, not presume to accept patients with illnesses about which he knows nothing. I might also mention that Loewen, at the start, apparently tried to turn Stobbe away because the latter is in my service, and Loewen knows that I am always dissatisfied with our doctors. Johann Cornies.

141. Evgenii F. Hahn to Johann Cornies. 18 August 1843. SAOR 89-1-911/144.

The main factor in the dissensions that have originated in the Berdiansk District is probably the lack of a proper spiritual head. By writing abroad, the people hoped to obtain such a person. I am unfamiliar with the disposition of this matter.

One of our colonial Lutheran pastors has now broken with his church authorities. After first asking me not to mention his name, he told me he would like to relinquish his position and establish himself as a spiritual supervisor among the Pietists.

Since a formal inquiry could compromise this man, I would ask that you mention his situation privately to your acquaintances and friends in the Berdiansk District. It would be necessary to know:

1. Where the matter stands in obtaining a spiritual head, and if any hope exists that someone would come from abroad.

2. If there is no hope, would these people agree to obligate themselves to a former Evangelical Lutheran pastor as their spiritual leader?

3. What monetary support could be assured to the latter?

The pastor under discussion is supposed to be a very good preacher. He has very zealous friends, but he finds little favour with the majority of the congregation. Where the fault lies is something I will not mention. He now has the use of 120 desiatinas of land and a salary of six hundred rubles, a good parsonage, and other income.

Kindly make this proposal public. Perhaps the Pietists would be well served by a man with these qualities. Then other friends and preachers would no longer be able to interfere in Pietist affairs.

A short time ago I travelled around the Khortitsa District. The progress they are making shows their honest intentions. Church Elder Dyck is no longer interfering in civil affairs.

I am leaving for the Crimea today, but will return in approximately ten days. I will then send several groups of foreign settlers living in this area to the Molochnaia Mennonite District. This might convince them personally that they have fallen behind in every regard.

District Chairman Bartsch has a plan to establish a small breeding station in the Khortitsa District to supply the community with good stallions. I await his program and will probably inform you of it at the appropriate time.

Please receive the assurances of my continuing affection, E. v. Hahn.

Received 27 August, answered 6 October 1843.

142. Johann Cornies to Huebner. 22 August 1843. SAOR 89-1-925/99.

Highly valued Mr. Huebner,

Kindly forgive my thoughtlessness in leaving you in the dark about the Baron's latticework for so long. According to the address I was given and the receipt from Mr. Bekbulatov, it was received in Sevastopol on 30 June. The Baron was also notified on 15 July, and the matter has been concluded properly.

As for the trees that you have asked for, I will look after it as best I can and am leaving the choice completely to Gardener Wilke.

I want to share the good news that the Baron can soon be expected back to continue his work among us. This is a blessing for the well-being of our local inhabitants.

Remaining, with the greatest esteem, your faithful and respectful friend and servant, Johann Cornies.

143. F. Prinz to Johann Cornies. 23 August 1843. SAOR 89-1-911/150.

Highly esteemed Mr. Cornies,

I am sending you this booklet, accompanied by a short extract about our inheritance procedures. Please go through it. We have not yet worked it through ourselves. If you think it best, return it to me for improvement. We could then copy it and send it on to the General as quickly as possible. On the other hand, if you consider it best, send the booklet on to the Guardianship Committee and inform me accordingly.

Your most obedient servant, District Chairman Prinz.

23 August 1843, reply 28 August 1843.

144. Gerhard Penner to Johann Cornies. 23 August 1843. SAOR 89-1-911/153.

Most valued friend,

Last autumn you proposed that I take over the duties as Secretary in the Mariupol District Office. I feel I should let you know that I have finally decided to agree to the salary suggested, five hundred rubles with a free dwelling, heating, and light, and also pasturage and winter fodder for five head of livestock.

Previously I hesitated because my wife was uncertain about the matter. During my next visit, I will provide a detailed explanation of why I wanted to change my place of employment and why I was moved to request the release granted me.

In my present job, the concepts needed to manage the varied subjects and circumstances locally are missing and this makes it hard to work on the basis of respectable business practices. As a result, I am inevitably blamed for every mishap. I think I will not be similarly open to reproach in the Mariupol Mennonite District. There will be less official business and fewer difficult circumstances. Under your guidance and supervised locally by the Inspector, who is nearby, I will be able to carry out my work without assistants.

I do not know what His Excellency's, the General Guardian's, directives will be in regard to this change in service which he encouraged my brother Wilhelm to undertake last January. At the time the latter declined the offer, excusing himself on grounds that were partially valid. Yet when His Excellency visited recently, my brother declared that he was willing to accept the job. His Excellency retorted: "You must become a secretary whose responsibilities are not like those here, but the same as those in your former position. You can of course apply for the position because you are a free man. In that case, one of the Molochnaia secretaries, Ham or Reimer, would have to step into your position here. A very considerable sum of community money has been applied to their education." His Excellency doubted that the salary would be equal to that here, namely 450 rubles, but I told him that Mr. Cornies offered five hundred rubles for this service. I qualified this by saying that the offer was not to me, since my decision was still not quite certain. Then His Excellency said that he was still making his decision.

I have now decided to take on the above-mentioned post, even if the salary is three hundred rubles less than what I received here. I have persuaded officials here to manage with Wilhelm, the apprentice secretary, and Abram Klassen, who teaches in a private school. I would also want to ensure that the secretaries Ham or Reimer would not have to move. I would therefore ask that you make the arrangements necessary for me to assume the position in Mariupol, and that you have the necessary dwelling prepared for me, should that be lacking.

I am happy to prove how much I am, with true esteem and humility, your willing Gerhard Penner.

Khortitsa, 23 August 1843. Answered 30 August 1843.

145. Johann Cornies to Christian Steven. 25 August 1843.
SAOR 89-1-925/100.

His Honour, Inspector for the southern guberniias, State Counsellor and Knight v. Steven,

Three state apprentices from Kherson Guberniia arrived here on 24 July 1843 to be taught practical agriculture. They submitted documents from their local director. According to the terms of our agreement, I have distributed the three apprentices among three householders: Peter Negresko, Ananiev, to Peter Cornies in Ohrloff; Joseph Letvinenko, Kherson, to Johann Sukkau in Blumenort; and Matvei Batichkovskii from Tiraspol to Cornelius Wiens in Ohrloff. I am honoured to make this report.

146. Bernhard Fast to Johann Cornies. 26 August 1843.
SAOR 89-1-911/155.

Beloved friend and brother, Johann Cornies,

In reply to your communication of 24 August that reflected concerns about the investigation scheduled for Gnadenfeld tomorrow, Friday. I can report that this hearing has been cancelled or put off for a long time. It was not our intention to disturb the peace that had been established. Our endeavours were meant to ensure that their teachings are based on the [life] of the Saviour and His Apostles.

We cannot, however, allow ourselves to be neglectful in regard to the many requests and pleas from several members of the Gnadenfeld community. For this reason, I have notified Ohm Ratzlaff in Rudnerweide that I might come to Ohrloff on Saturday morning, 28 August, to talk to you and reach an agreement about the views we hold.

I would therefore ask you, beloved brother, that, despite your many important business affairs, you arrange to meet in your house towards evening on Saturday, or even Sunday afternoon, to discuss and agree on what can be done for the well-being and happiness of the Gnadenfeld community.

Most sincerely thankful for your honest love, and with special greetings, your brother who is bound to you in the Lord, Bernhard Fast, Elder.

Halbstadt, 26 August.

147. Johann Cornies to Friedrich Prinz. 28 August 1843.
   SAOR 89-1-925/95v.

District Chairman Prinz in Neuhoffnung,

I did not forward the inheritance ordinances you sent for my perusal to the Guardianship Committee, as you wished. Since they were only an excerpt from an inheritance ordinance, I found them to be incomplete and inadequate as measured by the Committee's requirements. I return them with the explanation that I am having a copy made of the booklet which contains the complete and practicable ordinances mentioned above. I will then evaluate each point. I consider it preferable to personally submit the copy of the booklet to the Committee afterwards.

148. Johann Cornies to Friedrich Prinz. 28 August 1843.
   SAOR 89-1-925/96.

District Chairman F. Prinz in Neuhoffnung,

A communication has just arrived, asking me to report if your community has obtained the spiritual leader you intended to request from abroad. If this is not the case, you should know that there is a Lutheran pastor in the foreign settlements who seems to have separated himself from his denominational administration. He wishes to keep his name quiet for the time being, until he resigns completely from his position as pastor. He expressed the desire to become a spiritual leader with the Pietists.

It is therefore necessary to know what progress you have made in requesting a spiritual leader from abroad, and whether there is the possibility that someone will actually come. Would your community be willing to agree to having a former Evangelical Lutheran pastor appointed as spiritual leader? What amount can be assured him for his upkeep?

The pastor under discussion is supposed to be an excellent preacher. He has zealous friends but most of the congregation has little affection for him. It is left unsaid where the fault lies. He now has the use of 120 desiatinas of land, a six-hundred-ruble salary, a good residence, and additional income as well.

I request that you discuss this matter with the community and report to me in detail, specifically since I know nothing about your circumstances in this respect.

With a greeting, I remain your willing, Johann Cornies.

Enclosure with above letter:

In my opinion, the spiritual leader of a Pietist congregation should not only be a good preacher, but also a man of solid character, possessing quiet, peaceable, and loving qualities. The desire simply to lead the congregation to Christ must be close to his heart, since this is the only means of creating good citizens for human society. He must accept Pietist principles out of pure conviction and not only for the sake of a salary and his own employment. In social dealings, he should not try to present himself as being too far above members of his congregation. As a cultured man, he should lead the congregation as an example in his daily conduct and in the way he lives at a higher level.

I am not really aware if all of this can be expected from an ordinary Lutheran pastor. I would, however, advise you that all of these matters be considered and examined before he is accepted, for it is written: "examine everything and select the best."

149. F. Gross to Johann Cornies. 30 August 1843.
SAOR 89-1-917/10.

Most highly honoured Mr. Cornies,

You may think that I have forgotten you and not given thought to the drawings I promised you so long ago. How could this be after I had enjoyed your loving and friendly reception? Could I really show so little gratitude? That is contrary to my principles. Please remember that much time was involved including work incorporated in the information on the drawings I had assembled on my journey. I also encountered other obstacles and was sometimes unhappy, since my spirit was critical of the drawings I had done for you. Then I had to draw by hand something else. You can see I am being honest in informing you about everything.

My parents were pleased when I told them of how benevolently and lovingly you had received me. In their gratitude they wanted to supervise the work that you had commissioned me to do. My "Herr Papa" and then my "Frau Mama" eagerly made inquiries and gave me well-meaning encouragement. Esteemed Mr. Cornies, not I alone, but also my parents think of you with love and thankfulness. Although you are not acquainted with them, they directed me to send greetings to you as a mark of their esteem.

I now send you two views of your Iushanle estate. Should they provide you with some pleasure, and should I have gained your approval, kindly let me know by means of a brief letter. It would please me greatly.

Commending myself to your honoured friendship and benevolence, with the purest esteem, your thankful and honest friend, F. Gross.

30 August 1843. Received 6 September 1843; Reported the receipt on 8 September 1843.

150. Johann Cornies to Gerhard Penner. 30 August 1843. SAOR 89-1-925/100v.

Dear Friend,

I can absolutely not remember proposing that you serve as secretary in the Mariupol [Bergthal] Mennonite District. I therefore find your communication of 23 August most remarkable. I find it especially remarkable because you know that the Mariupol Mennonites are presently not really in a financial position to employ a secretary and his family adequately and to pay a large salary. The hiring of a secretary also depends on the District Office where you are presently employed and it would certainly not agree to such a transfer.

You do, however, know, since I spoke to you about this matter personally, that I had the secretary's position in the Mariupol Mennonite District offered to your brother, Wilhelm Penner. The Mariupol District Chairman agrees that he should be hired. A salary of five hundred rubles would probably not be offered to anyone. This naturally does not depend on me personally. It is the local District Chairman's responsibility if your brother is prepared to accept the secretary's position.

I find it necessary to notify you about this matter in response to your communication of 23 August. I remain, with a greeting, your friend, Johann Cornies.

151. Bernhard Fast to Johann Cornies. 4 September 1843. SAOR 89-1-917/13.

Beloved friend and brother, Johann Cornies,

I am sending you a small gift we collected in our congregation for the poor Hutterthal people. I believe this flowed out of neighbourly love. It would give us all pleasure were you to show us your love by forwarding this sum to the needy or by using it to extend a helping hand that would help to satisfy their needs. The sum amounts to 163 rubles, twenty-five kopeks, which is enclosed.

May the Lord's blessing accompany this modest gift.

Your friend and brother in the Lord who wishes you His unfathomable blessing, Berhard Fast.

Halbstadt, 4 September 1843.

152. Friedrich Prinz to Johann Cornies. 5 September 1843. SAOR 89-1-917/18.

To Mr. Johann Cornies,

I received your worthy letter of 28 August and read with pleasure about a communication you had received from an unnamed pastor of the Evangelical Lutheran Church who wishes to be appointed as a spiritual leader in a Pietist congregation.

I am honoured to inform you that we contacted a spiritual leader from abroad and we also received a communication from a spiritual teacher (called Henke, who is located in the Bessarabian settlements). He has some interest in obtaining appointment as spiritual leader in the Neuhoffnung congregation. We expect a formal agreement or a refusal soon, either through a letter or through his personal appearance.

You asked whether the congregation would agree to allowing a former Evangelical Lutheran pastor as spiritual leader here. An evangelical, apostolic pastor from the Evangelical Lutheran Church can be appointed to our congregation, since there is no difference between our teachings and those of the Evangelical Church. The difference lies in the outward church constitution and naturally such a teacher would have to adjust to ours.

What support could we assure such a person? The established salary consists of six hundred rubles and four chetvert of wheat, four chetvert rye, sufficient fodder for two cows, free heating, and a comfortable free dwelling.

Charges include one ruble to baptize one child, two rubles for confirmation instructions and confirmation, two rubles for a marriage, and two rubles for a funeral sermon.

At the present time I cannot give you any more information, since the response from the teacher described has not yet arrived. I will report to you as soon as we receive it.

Your obedient servant who sends you his greetings, District Chairman Prinz.

Neuhoffnung, 5 September 1843.

153. Heinrich Toews to Johann Cornies. 6 September 1843. SAOR 89-1-917/16.

To the Chairman of the Society for the Advancement of Agriculture and Trades, Johann Cornies in Ohrloff,

In response to your request of 17 August 1843, I am sending you the money collected by our congregation for the Hutterthaler people, [illegible] rubles, ninety-seven kopeks. Nothing more has yet come in. Should more come in, I will send it along later.

With a heartfelt greeting, I sign myself, in esteem and love as your friend, Heinrich Toews.

Pordenau, 6 September 1843.

[Either thirty-seven or eighty-seven rubles.]

154. Agricultural Society to Schardau Village Office. 10 September 1843. SAOR 89-1-925/104v.

To Schardau,

At its meeting of 9 September, the Society decided to respond to a report of 4 September from the Schardau Village Office ordering that you report, at the appropriate time, the names of those intending to hire Peter, son of cottager Abraham Funk. The householders who intend to take them into their services must be investigated to see if they are in a position to give the above-mentioned two young persons the appropriate direction in every respect. Providing this direction is the Society's primary concern, and it must be reported to the Society before they have been hired permanently.

155. Wilhelm Martens to Johann Cornies. 12 September 1843. SAOR 89-1-917/20.

Best of friends,

I asked Friend Neufeld to request that you advance me six thousand to seven thousand rubles on loan. Phillip Wiebe wrote to Neufeld that only three thousand rubles had come in, which you were prepared to lend me. I am therefore sending over my son, Heinrich Willms, with the request that you give him six thousand rubles, if possible. If not, I would be very thankful for three thousand or as much as you can spare.

I wish to repay the sum, together with the interest, as soon as possible, specifically after the wool is delivered, which should happen this month.

With hearty greetings, I remain your honest friend, Wilhelm Martens. Halbstadt, 12 September 1843. Loan 12 September 1843.

156. Wilhelm Lange et al. to Johann Cornies. 13 September 1843. SAOR 89-1-917/22.

Highly esteemed and beloved Mr. Cornies, treasured Friend,

It was with great reluctance that I considered burdening you again by a visit. However, we believed that we owed you a report on how matters now stand in response to the friendship you have demonstrated in our complicated matter. We thought that it would be better to do so verbally in order also to receive your valued advice at the same time. However, we have not had the pleasure of finding you at home and so I have asked Mr. Riediger to allow me to write down several things at the school. I do so with the request that you kindly consider them favourably.

We wrote the enclosed letter to the Elders at the conference called in Alexanderwohl but heard nothing until the evening, when Elder B. Ratzlaff and Church Teacher [Preacher] Jakob Janz from Schardau reported these decisions to me:

1. The Elders decided that the departing members need not first obtain certification from the congregation accepting them.

2. The Elders declared the acceptance of Wilhelm Lange's wife in Waldheim as valid.

To my objection that they had previously declared this acceptance to be invalid, they responded that they still considered the action as invalid but felt that the further misuse of this action could be prevented if they now declare it to be valid.

We must admit that we find it difficult to understand that an action once declared invalid is now recognized to be valid, especially since they cooperated with the two punished members when they had themselves admitted [their guilt] to our congregation according to the first declaration. What can and should we do about this? We are in no position to hold back the stream that will burst the dam in our congregation. We must allow everyone to deal with the Langes as they wish. If we do not permit this, there will be too many persons to punish.

We can absolutely not recognize that the valid acceptance in Waldheim which you, dear Mr. Cornies, were active in working out with Balzer and Janz, has now again changed. Your questions to the Elders indicate clearly that you also believe the regulations in our churches are endangered by this situation. For this reason, we could not stay quiet and let it go. We wanted to report it to you. In hereby reporting this, we want to know if you could or would like to give us advice in the matter. We especially wish to prevent such action in response to a regulation from the Society, or the District Office, or even from the higher authorities, because we can do nothing against such infringements.

However, if you believe this cannot be upheld, that what is unjust cannot be valid, that our acceptance of Janz and Balzer and therefore of your advice has now become ridiculous with the declaration of a valid acceptance of Wilhelm Lange, then you are aware that we need further advice and help. You must now call for written reports or personal appearances. If you do not do this, we will have to let the matter go under these circumstances, requesting only that you kindly not blame us if further disorder occurs because our church discipline lacks its full strength.

I am dashing down on paper these essential points in a great hurry to present them to you. We would certainly have preferred to speak with you personally. Should you consider it worth the effort to take further action in this matter – and we hope that you do – we modestly request that you do this as soon as possible. We must present the Elders' conference decision to our congregation by the end of this week, at the latest. We would like to hear your beloved advice.

With hearty thanks for everything positive you have done for our congregation, we remain with love and esteem, your most devoted W. La[ange], Abr. Re[imer], Abr. Remp[el].

Ohrloff School, 13 September 1843.

157. Peter Siemens to Johann Cornies. 20 September 1843.
SAOR 89-1-933/31.

Valued Friend,

In response to a communication of 15 July from Phillip Wiebe, I can report that your future letters about the new settlement near Vitebsk and Mogilev can be forwarded to the Hon. Elder Peter Froese in Tiegerweide, Marienburg District.

I can also report that I visited Hon. Elder Abram Regehr in Heubuden and conveyed your communication to him in the presence of the Hon. David Epp, Heubuden. However, I would ask that, in future, you please spare me in this matter.

Illness prevented me from writing any earlier. With a friendly greeting, I remain your honest friend and servant, Peter Siemens.

P.S. I request that you kindly forward the enclosed communication to the Wiebe family in Lichtfelde.

Blumenort [West Prussia], 20 September 1843; Received 28 October 1843.

158. Bernhardt Baum to Johann Cornies. 20 September 1843.
SAOR 89-1-917/36.

To Chairman Cornies,

When you passed through here last spring, you honoured me by inspecting my few vines and promised to have some vines sent to me from your own plantings. I would now politely request that you provide me with three hundred Riesling and three hundred Gutedel vines. When it is time to dig out the trees, I will fetch both trees and vines. I will first expect to hear from you as to when I should come.

Your most humble friend, Bernhardt Baum.

Neuhoffnungsthal, 20 September 1843.

159. Andrei M. Fadeev to Johann Cornies. 21 September 1843.
SAOR 89-1-661/14.

While I recuperate from my journey, I am using some hours here in Sarepta to write to you, my dear and most valued Cornies. I found it most pleasant to hear from our good Doering that you are healthy, energetic, and active, and also that you have not forgotten me. I regret that circumstances did not permit you to visit our region this year, but

I hope you will do me this favour next year. The Minister, Count Kiselev, visited me recently, spending four days with me in Saratov. We then spent another four days travelling together along the Volga. We spoke about you as well. He regrets that there are not several men like Cornies among the German settlers in Russia. Among other directives, he asked me to supervise and direct the resettlement of local settlers onto lands apportioned for them. You must help me with this. Please write to me about the arrangements and methods used by Mennonites to move out of overcrowded villages into new places. What kind of help do they get from the community? What are the rules in laying out new villages, etc., etc.? I would like to introduce approximate models of your settlements as much as it is in my power to do so and make arrangements and regulations our local settlers could understand.

The harvest did not turn out to be as abundant as people had hoped in summer. Wheat suffered especially. Locusts are appearing and have done much damage in one area.

Tomorrow I will return to Saratov. May you fare well. Do not forget me. My wife sends hearty greetings. Your most sincere friend, A. Fadeev. Sarepta.

Received 12 October [1843].

160. Agricultural Society to Berdiansk Mennonite Village Office. [September 1843.] SAOR 89-1-954/11.

[September 1843]

[Undated draft:] To the Berdiansk Mennonite Village Office,

The election list of Molochnaia Mennonites resident in the city of Berdiansk has been prepared for the election of village officials. It was submitted to the Society and to the District Office to be used in establishing a Village Office. As a result, the Mennonite David Fast was selected as Mayor and Peter Rempel and Peter Balmann as his Deputies.

The Society and the District Office therefore install these persons in their functions until confirmation can follow from higher authorities. These three should undertake their obligations and duties in the Village Office according to the directives and observe promptly everything that serves the general order and well-being among Mennonites in Berdiansk. May peace and calm reign at all times. Good order and active endeavour that promotes the general well-being and the well-being of every individual should adorn every household.

161. Agricultural Society to Mennonites in Berdiansk. 21 September 1843. SAOR 89-1-954/4.

[Draft:] To the Mayor of Mennonites in the city of Berdiansk and his council,

At its meeting of 9 September, the Society reviewed the list of names of all Mennonite families living in Berdiansk and ordered these residents to hire a qualified schoolteacher to teach the not inconsiderable number of [Mennonite] school-aged children [in Berdiansk]. The purpose is to give these children an appropriate education for their future professions. Those children who are too old for schooling and can otherwise obtain no useful occupation with their parents or have fallen into indolence, should, on the other hand, be apprenticed to good tradesmen, or hired out to exemplary agriculturalists in the local district.

The Society directs you and your two Deputies to make the necessary arrangements to ensure the early establishment of purposeful school teaching, and also arrangements for any children who are past school age and are superfluous to their parents' needs. This should be done in a manner appropriate to the intended purpose and carried out to benefit your local inhabitants. You and your two Deputies must report the results of this work to the Society in a timely way.

162. Wilhelm Lange to Johann Cornies. 27 September 1843. SAOR 89-1-917/29.[22]

To the Chairman of several generally useful Societies, Mr. Johann Cornies in Ohrloff. Highly honoured and beloved Mr. Cornies,

I take the liberty of sending you the enclosed answer we received from Ohm Ratzlaff in response to our letter, which he returned to us at the same time. In his disconnected response, he takes refuge in saying that the decision is only the congregation's to make.

What can we do now? We will probably have to declare to the congregation that since the Wilhelm Langes have not yet returned to the fold as penitent and repentant, they must continue to be considered and treated as if they are under punishment, and anyone who acts contrary to this ruling should be punished. We see no other way out. Otherwise

---

22 Regarding the marital dispute between Henrietta Lange and Friedrich Wilhelm Lange, see Staples, *Johann Cornies*, 209–12.

the Elders will overthrow our whole congregation and its discipline. Granted, in looking ahead we can assume that large numbers of our congregation will act contrary to this ruling or join other congregations, which is more likely.

W. Lange has been behaving improperly since winter, acting as though all of our church teachers are worthy only of being tied to a millstone and thrown into the sea. He has treated the whole congregation worse than a secretive thief and written deceitful perjuries to Prussia. Yet, he is still a congregation member, although an unrepentant one. May God consider this behaviour.

You probably see no other way out of this dilemma than to commend the entire matter to God. Even if we wish to complain piously, this may not be useful in a larger context. It might be best to continue our suffering until such time as the Almighty decides to resolve it. It is not worthwhile to continue corresponding with the Elders, since they have sent our communication back to us. This answer is as appropriate as hitting us in the eye with their fists.

Should you find it worth the effort to send a few written or personal words my way, I would be very pleased and thankful. Your heartily loving friend and servant, W. Lange.

Gnadenfeld, 27 September 1843.

163. Johann Cornies to Forestry Department. 30 September 1843. SAOR 89-1-925/108v.

Forestry Department,

At all times and with all of my powers, I have tried to assist in promoting whatever is useful and to fulfil the wishes of the higher Ministry with zeal. However, despite my best intentions, I cannot change my decision No. 86 of 12 August 1843, about accepting [only] four state peasant apprentices to learn practical tree cultivation on the steppe. I must adhere to the specific reason I mentioned before, namely that within a limited period of time I cannot possibly turn peasant apprentices into individuals who are sufficiently appropriate to the purpose [of steppe afforestation]. Monetary compensation can contribute little. Even the limited length of time provided for is essential to teaching apprentices the basic processes and concepts in all aspects of forest-tree cultivation. No specific compensation for the work required can be considered.

I am compelled to humbly present this response to my communication No. 1217 of 6 September, and make the humble request that the liberty I am taking in openly explaining my reasons for doing so redound to my favour. Otherwise, by not being able to fulfil my promise, I would misuse the government's high trust and act contrary to my firmest principles.

164. Johann Cornies to Viktor Roslavets. 30 September 1843. SAOR 89-1-925/109v.

Governor Roslavets,

I respond to Mr. Gulkevich's esteemed commission from Yr. Excellency that I accept one young man and one girl to learn the practices of country housekeeping and dairy-keeping on my estate. I could not make an immediate decision for a variety of reasons, mainly because the purposes of their education had not been established. I promised to report to Yr. Excellency as soon as possible.

I now have the honour to say that I find it possible to accept the two above-mentioned individuals for the purpose described, specifically on the terms under which I now accept them from the crown, the young man for four years and the girl for three years. You must assign these young people especially for this purpose. To accomplish the purposes of the apprenticeships they must have strong physical constitutions, be in good health, and possess the necessary intelligence. They can begin forthwith and only bring along the clothes they need, appropriate to their class.

Since, as time progresses, they will compensate me through the work they do, I will assume the expenses of their maintenance during the entire time of their service. For my part, I will make every possible effort to educate and instruct these two young people as is desired, and make it my genuine pleasure to become useful to Yr. Excellency in this respect.

165. Agricultural Society to Franzthal Village Office. [September 1843.] SAOR 89-1-954/8.

[Undated draft]:

Your local fullholder Heinrich Hooge conducted an open auction of his fullholding to the highest bidding Mennonite and it went to Claas Wiebe from Conteniusfeld village.

The fullholding in question is in extremely bad condition. It is unworkable and the buildings are close to collapse. Can this fullholding be improved sufficiently by passing it on? The buildings should be rebuilt and Wiebe does not have sufficient funds to do everything required.

Your village community has taken these factors into consideration and intends to wait for a more capable householder with better means to take over the dilapidated fullholding. For these reasons, it made the decision not to accept Wiebe's purchase. According to regulations, the above-mentioned fullholding requires a zealous fullholder with means. It is desirable that eventually, when it has been appropriately established, it can serve as a model for other fullholders in Franzthal.

However, since the time for fullholding transfers has actually passed, the village community has made a further decision. If such a desired householder cannot be found shortly, the village community will undertake to put the house on the fullholding in the condition required by regulations until a capable, acceptable fullholder with funds is eventually found.

166. Forestry Society to Gnadenfeld Village Office. September 1843. SAOR 89-1-954/31.

[Draft:] To the Gnadenfeld Village Office,

To walk to church, the Gnadenfeld congregation uses a footpath between hearth-sites assigned for this purpose. The Society for the Advancement and Dissemination of Plantings orders the Village Office to make regular plantings along this walkway in Gnadenfeld to increase the existing but still insignificant plantings intended to beautify the village. Immediate preparations must be made for this purpose, making pits [for plantings] of regulation width and depth and two *sazhen* apart on both sides. The trees must be planted during the coming October. The Society has chosen elms as the most suitable variety of trees to be planted on both sides of the walkway. The Village Office should take care to check that the trees chosen for planting all have straight trunks and are not less than five feet high at their crowns. At the appropriate time, the Society will expect a report that this order was carried out.

Society for the Advancement and Dissemination of Plantings in Ohrloff.

167. Forestry Society to village offices. September 1843. SAOR 89-1-954/33.

[Draft:] To Village Offices,

On 25 September 1842, orders No. 339–44 were issued to all Village Offices in response to an order from the Guardianship Committee for Foreign Settlers in Southern Russia that greater zeal be shown in the planting of wild pear trees along village streets and in other suitable places.

The Society hereby repeats that order, with personal directives to Village Offices to proceed ardently in the planting of wild pear trees. It seeks, in particular, to extend these plantings along village streets this year. As is known, no other trees may be planted in these places. The inhabitants of every village must be duly informed.

At the appropriate time, the Society will require lists documenting the results achieved in response to this high directive from the authorities, and will verify these results.

Society for the Dissemination of Plantings in Ohrloff.

168. Forestry Society to Sparrau Village Office. September 1843. SAOR 89-1-954/35.

[Draft:] To the Sparrau Village Office,

The forest-tree plantation at Sparrau village must, as previously directed, be started this year. The Society orders the Village Office not to waste time in making the required soil preparations for this planting. The first line must be neatly drawn straight along the plantation's upper side, where planting places for all fullholders should be clearly marked off with staves. In this way excuses to delay this work are to be avoided and everyone will know how to govern himself in order that all further irregularities cease. Every fullholder not staying within this line should be warned that he will be compelled to transplant his trees. This notice must be observed.

Society for the Dissemination of Plantings at Ohrloff.

169. Forestry Society to Acting Curator [Evgenii von Hahn]. [September 1843.] SAOR 89-1-954/37.[23]

[Undated draft:] Humble submission from the Molochnaia Mennonite Society for the Advancement and Dissemination of Forest-Trees, Orchards, Sericulture, and Viticulture and for the Advancement of Agriculture and Trades.

---

23 Regarding David Reimer's Felstenthal estate, see Helmut T. Huebert, *Molotschna Historical Atlas* (Winnipeg: Springfield Publishers, 2003), 116–17.

To the Acting Curator,

In 1820, with the agreement of the Molochnaia Mennonite community, the local Mennonite David Reimer built a watermill on the Tokmak River on crown land assigned for Mennonite settlement. The mill is now located behind Wernersdorf village which was founded later. Because almost no similar establishments existed at the time because of a shortage of means and expert knowledge, the mill served the Mennonites of this district and neighbouring crown peasants well. David Reimer has operated the mill profitably until the present day.

Meanwhile Reimer also established an orderly fruit orchard beside the mill and his dwelling place. For this reason the Senior Member of the former Ekaterinoslav Bureau for Foreign Settlers, according to decision No. 403 of 19 November 1831, negotiated the perpetual use of four desiatinas of land by Reimer with His Excellency, the Chief Curator, General v. Inzov.

Since 1831, Reimer, in a most exemplary manner, has not only planted these four desiatinas to various fruit and forest trees, but another six desiatinas of leased crown lands as well. He has also established important nurseries which supply thousands of varied fruit and forest trees at moderate prices to many local inhabitants, crown peasants and people from the Crimea and Mariupol.

The Mennonite Reimer is likewise an experienced, meritorious, and prudent proprietor, as reflected in the details of his establishment, the Felstenthal estate.

Despite these significant achievements, the Mennonite Reimer has no hope of keeping his establishments as a continued personal possession or of receiving restitution should the creation of further settlements [in the surrounding area] force him to leave. With his advancing age he is thus not permitted to hope for a happy future for his descendants. For this reason and because he is so exceptional a model householder who puts ever more effort into his undertakings and is entitled to have sixty-five desiatinas of land assigned to him (as is every other Mennonite) the Society takes the liberty of submitting the following proposal to Yr. Excellency.

Considering Reimer's quite splendid efforts, might sixty-five desiatinas of usable land abutting upon his plantation be assigned to each of his three hopeful and already grown sons for their perpetual ownership? The site, it should be mentioned, is not suitable for the establishment of a village. The land would, moreover, eventually become part of still-to-be founded later settlements on the Begim-Chokrak streams, between the villages of Landskrone and Waldheim. These allotments might later on be incorporated into these villages. The soil on this land, it bears noting, is very average, and has no haymeadows.

In this way, the Mennonite Reimer would be in a position to [continue to] make exceptional efforts in field cultivation and other new branches of agriculture. The latter include the introduction of various new fodder and dye plants into the local region. Reimer's well-known perseverance would guarantee that considerable advantages would flow from such a development.

The Society awaits a gracious resolution of this matter.

170. Forestry Society to Evgenii F. Hahn. [September 1843.] SAOR 89-1-954/39.

[Undated draft:] His Excellency, Acting Chief Guardian for the Colonists of Southern Russia, State Counsellor and Knight, v. Hahn,

Humble submission from the Molochnaia Mennonite Society for the Advancement and Dissemination of Forest-Trees, Orchards, Sericulture, and Viticulture,

The cottager Stephan Kerber in Alexanderthal has an exemplary fruit and forest-tree plantation which is generally most useful for the Molochnaia Mennonite District. It is striking for the many thousands of trees he has himself raised from seed and the great variety of young trees he has planted with great diligence at an elevated spot on the steppe. These efforts have twice won him the praise and approbation of authorities. First, Kerber received a prize of fifty rubles from the community treasury. Later, Kerber received written thanks from the Guardianship Committee for Foreign Settlers in Southern Russia. These gestures have encouraged Kerber to become even more useful in his efforts. At present, he is about to extend his plantation considerably at a place granted him voluntarily by the village of Alexanderthal.

Because it borders on a cattle right of way, the new location must be enclosed within a durable fence. A weak fence could easily, as Kerber correctly fears, cause it to suffer much damage. The Society for the Advancement and Dissemination of Forest-Trees, Orchards, Sericulture, and Viticulture therefore ventures to approach Yr. Excellency with a humble proposal. To encourage Kerber's future endeavours, it dutifully requests that he be granted monetary support for the long-lasting protection of his new tree plantation, without being required to repay the outlay. According to a reliable estimate, a strong fence ninety-four sazhen long and built as economically as possible would cost forty-five silver rubles.

Such benevolence would spur Reimer on to more useful undertakings and make fellow inhabitants more alert to the recognition that every useful endeavour evokes.

The Society awaits an early resolution of this matter.

171. F. Gross to Johann Cornies. 1 October 1843. SAOR 89-1-933/5.

Highly esteemed Mr. Cornies,

Several weeks after I sent you the perspectives I had drawn of Iushanle, I received a letter which seemed suspicious because it was written in your proximity, but you had not actually signed it. The whole letter, which consisted of four lines, reads: "Commissioned by my employer, Mr. Cornies, I am to report to you that the two views of Iushanle were received with thanks.

Ohrloff, 8 September 1843. Secretary. P. Wiebe."

It is of course possible that the drawings fell into someone else's hands, and that they sent the letter in your name. These few lines, it seems, were written in so haughty a tone that I cannot find your loving and friendly character in them. Since the two drawings cost me several days of work (and because I knew for whom I was making them, I worked on them with pleasure and love), I cannot imagine that a man like you, gifted with your knowledge, insight, and noble inclinations, would ever be ungrateful and dispatch me with a few proud lines from the hands of another. I cannot believe you are capable of this.

Hoping for your answer, I remain, with genuine esteem,
Your humble servant F. Gross.
Received 4 October 1843; answered 28 October 1843.

172. Johann Cornies Jr. to Johann Cornies. 2 October 1843. SAOR 89-1-933/3.

Esteemed Father,

I gave the roof-tile maker twenty silver rubles from the treasury here to pay his people. According to his information, the bigger worker was owed fifteen silver rubles, the smaller five silver rubles. He wanted to pay them here. Since they had not kept accounts for themselves, however, these people did not know exactly how much they were owed. This was a matter they had left to the tile maker. Today (because they allegedly did not have their passes with them), I found out that the tile maker had intended to settle accounts with them in Ohrloff.

Palokay requests that he be allowed to ride home for the Bairan holiday this coming Friday, 8 October. If I am permitted to release him, please send me an appropriate document.

With childlike esteem, I am your devoted son Johann Cornies.
Tashchenak, 2 October 1843.

173. Johann Cornies to Evgenii F. Hahn. 6 October 1843. SAOR 89-1-925/111.

Mr. Hahn, Yr. Excellency, Gracious Sir,

In response to Yr. Excellency's esteemed commission of 18 August regarding the subject of the spiritual concerns of the Berdiansk Pietists, I can report as follows:

1. The Berdiansk Pietists themselves feel the absence of a proper spiritual director [pastor] and frankly admit that the discord among them originated because of this. The discord has not yet been completely eliminated.

For this reason, they have written abroad for such a spiritual leader but have not yet received a reply. Meanwhile, they are in communication with a missionary or preacher by the name of Henke who is presently resident in the Bessarabian settlements. They expect to receive a formal letter of acceptance or refusal from him shortly.

2. They are prepared to agree to the appointment of an apostolic pastor from the Evangelical Lutheran Church in their midst, since they are of the opinion that no differences exist in the teachings of their own congregation and those of the Evangelical Lutheran Church. Although the two are considered different only in regard to their external church constitutions, they would expect that a pastor who desires an appointment with them would naturally have to agree to their arrangements in this respect.

3. They have fixed the salary of a proper preacher as follows:

A definite annual cash salary of six hundred rubles, four chetvert wheat, four chetvert rye, sufficient fodder for two cows, free heating and a comfortable, free residence. Charges would be as follows: infant baptism, one ruble; confirmation classes and confirmation, two rubles; a marriage service, two rubles; a funeral sermon, two rubles.

It would be highly desirable and fortunate for these good people if they could reach an understanding with a spiritual leader who loves order and knows how to keep himself within appropriate bounds. With economical housekeeping and a rural lifestyle, the salary should be adequate for a family to maintain itself.

With honest esteem and regard, I remain Your Excellency's respectful servant, Johann Cornies.

174. Johann Cornies to Evgenii F. Hahn. 6 October 1843. SAOR 89-1-925/112v.

State Counsellor Hahn,

The Kleine Mennoniten Gemeinde Church Council has sent me a written request, dated 3 October, asking me to make a respectful submission to Yr. Excellency. According to Yr. Excellency's communication No. 4500 of 28 June, His Highness, the Minister of State Domains has decided that it is permissible to hold worship services in private houses until a church has been built. Yr. Excellency required that their church teachers [preachers] submit their opinions in regard to such a construction.

This congregation would be pleased to have its own comfortable church in which to hold their worship services, but feel that this would be unhelpful for the time being. Because the congregation's members reside in villages throughout the entire district, they could not visit the church regularly. It is for this reason that they humbly request that Yr. Excellency kindly deign to permit them to postpone making a decision to build a church until they have found a location appropriate to this purpose. Once this has been done, they will immediately, in reply to Yr. Excellency's communication, make their respectful submission.

Since you have, in so generous a manner, placed their future on a firm foundation it is not possible to describe in words the feelings and attitudes the above-mentioned congregation harbours for Yr. Excellency's person. The leaders would like to underline the heartfelt thanks of all of their members. Please spare me the dissatisfaction of trying to do so imperfectly, much as I would like to transmit the congregation's true feelings in all of their force. May Yr. Excellency be convinced of the genuinely respectful sentiments of the Kleine Gemeinde dedicated to you.

It is the joy of my life to be able to call myself in future as well, with the most respectful thanks, etc. etc.

175. August Haxthausen to Johann Cornies. Sent Odesa, 8 October 1843. SAOR 89-1-933/29.

My most esteemed friend,

I got back safely from the Caucasus, and am now here. Regrettably, I could not visit the Doukhobors on the road to Achalzik. I could not endure long rides on horseback, and the Doukhobors can only be reached by riding a horse along Cossack trails. None of the people accompanying me had been along the trail to visit them. Still, I assured them that an official would read the letter which had been entrusted to me.

I made the acquaintance of v. Hahn, director of foreign settlements, whom I liked a great deal. I told him that you had expressed a desire to get permission to construct a schoolhouse, using the 1,500 rubles offered to the Hutterite Brethren to look for water and to dig wells, money that is now not needed for this purpose. It was his opinion that, should you apply to him, this would not be a problem.

I will arrive in Moscow towards the end of this month, and hope that your assorted notes about the Doukhobors will have arrived by then.

May you fare well and may God protect you. Give my hearty greetings to your wife, daughter, son, brother and the good people there, from your devoted A. Haxthausen.

Odesa. Received 22 October.

176. Johann Cornies to Mariupol Mennonite District Office. 9 October [1843]. SAOR 89-1-900/6.

[Draft with 1843 items:] 9 October.

From the Chairman to the Mariupol Mennonite District Office and the Forestry Society,

Because I have received administrative authorization to begin with the planting of forest-tree plantations in Bergthal settlement, it is my decision to proceed this autumn, even if only one row of trees can be planted. I would therefore order the District Office and the Society to assume that the following directions must be applied. Specifically:

1. According to administrative regulations, it is stipulated that no fewer than one-third of all trees planted in each forest-tree plantation

must be mulberry trees. The other two-thirds should be forest trees. Specifically, the order is to plant mulberry trees separately, either at one end or on one side of the quarter sections and not mixed in with the forest trees.

2. Absolutely no varieties of fruit trees should be planted in these quarters, and also no varieties of poplars. Because the latter spread out their roots so widely, they are highly damaging to other trees. Should orchard fruit trees or poplars be found in quarter parts during an inspection, those planting them should expect an order to dig up these trees and plant other trees of all varieties of forest trees, according to the regulations. The intention is that many varieties of trees should be planted alternately and not only a few varieties.

3. All trees in quarter parts should definitely be planted in straight rows, with all trees less than a sazhen away from each other. A hedge consisting only of mulberry trees should form the border around each half desiatina quarter part, according to the enclosed diagram. This hedge must be planted thickly with an entrance one sazhen wide, exactly in the middle of each side and of each end of the half desiatina quarter, and exactly between the rows of trees. It has been decided to begin by planting a hedge only on two sides or two ends of the quarter part, because this makes it easier to clean the forest trees and to plant further trees.

The street down the middle of the Bergthal plantation should have forest trees planted along both of its sides, as indicated. They should be in a neat straight line one sazhen from the entrance in the mulberry hedge that will be laid out later. Each fullholder must comply with this requirement. Should he not carry it out, he will be required to replant them according to regulations.

4. Planting should not be done in a manner that would permit fullholders to simply claim that the trees have been planted, but in a fashion that would enable the plantings to grow and endure.

It is obvious that all the work and effort involved in planting is futile if the soil has not been well worked deeply enough to plant trees, since their roots usually spread further beneath the surface than the branches spread out in the air. It is therefore assumed that the soil will be made friable and light before planting is begun so that these beginnings can thrive and make enduring progress.

After investigating the area, it is my firm conviction that the soil in the Bergthal plantation is friable enough by nature to make the regulation deep-ploughing to three-quarter arshins superfluous. I therefore direct that there be no delay in the ploughing of both sides of the street in the middle of the plantation to a depth of one foot with an ordinary plough drawn by six horses. The area where the planting must begin this autumn should be smoothed with a harrow before trenches one arshin wide and deep are dug. The trenches are to be mounded after trees have been planted. Unplanted areas are to be used only for root crops such as potatoes.

5. If these forest-tree plantations are to thrive it is essential that fences surround them. The District Office and the Society should immediately make arrangements to fence the sides and ends of the Bergthal plantation neatly, to include a regulation ditch, and to erect passable gateways at the appropriate entrances.

177. Martin Riediger to School Society directors.
13 October 1843. SAOR 89-1-933/15.

To the Directors of the Society School in Ohrloff from the Society School teacher in Ohrloff,

In the past, it was decided to use *Tappes Grammatik* (Tappe's grammar) as the Russian reader for local Society School pupils. Because not all pupils own this grammar book and are in no position to obtain one, I have given the matter mature reflection and decided that a Russian-language translation of the New Testament is to be used as the reader. It would be most beneficial to use for the specific reason that, since the New Testament is already used as the German reader, the students are more familiar with it than with any other reader. Since the price is appreciably lower than it is for *Tappes Grammatik*, it is also more likely that parents will be able to buy such Testaments for their children.

I politely submit this instruction to the School Directors, and request that about one hundred copies of such Testaments be ordered as soon as possible. Since other persons wanting a copy will also be found, these New Testaments would not only be intended for use in this school. It would be best if the librarian of the Reading Association, Mr. Jacob Martens in Tiegenhagen, have these New Testaments purchased.

Kindly notify me about further decisions on this matter.

Teacher in the Society School, Mart[in] Riediger.

178. Viktor Roslavets to Johann Cornies. [13] October 1843. SAOR 89-1-933/17.

Dear Mr. Cornies,

I am sending you the boy and girl whom you have agreed to accept and teach in your agricultural establishment with the request that, if possible, you keep both of them for a period of three years.

I hope you can convince these two young people that they must, in their work, be motivated by economy, order, and honesty. In an enclosed document I authorize you to keep the above-mentioned boy and girl under your control. Having supplied them with everything that they need, I trust that you will do so. With this, I remain, Viktor Roslavets.

Received 18 October 1843; answered 28 October 1843.

179. Agricultural Society to Church Elders. 15 October 1843. SAOR 89-1-900/10.

[Draft:] From Society for the Advancement of Agriculture, etc.

To the Elders who, on 8 September 1843, reached a decision in Alexanderwohl about the banned married couple, the Wilhelm Langes who have now been accepted into the Waldheim congregation. On 11 October, the Gnadenfeld Church Assembly sent a formal document of complaint to the Society for the Advancement of Agriculture and Trades asking the Society for a decision in this case. In the event that the Society should find it impossible to reach a decision, this document should then be sent along [to higher authorities].

1. The Gnadenfeld Church Assembly complains that several Church Elders (including Elder Benjamin Ratzlaff who is named specifically), reached a decision at a conference in Alexanderwohl on 8 September to declare the reception of the Wilhelm Lange couple into the Waldheim congregation valid despite the fact that the Gnadenfelder congregation had banned them. This was done even though the Church Elders had earlier declared such actions to be unjust and invalid. Elder B. Ratzlaff informed the Gnadenfeld Church Assembly of this matter on the day that the decision was reached.

2. The Gnadenfeld Church Assembly considers this decision of 8 September to be contrary to our confession of faith and to church discipline and productive of evil consequences that are already coming to light within the congregation. In light of these developments the Gnadenfeld

Church Assembly on 17 September sent a protest (remonstrance) to Elders who had assembled in conference on 8 September, asking them either to cite the [biblical] text which formed the basis of their action and the legitimacy of the acceptance of the Wilhelm Langes into the Waldheim congregation, or to retract the decision of their conference.

3. The Gnadenfeld Church Assembly complains that these Elders sent the objection of 17 September back without answering the points raised in it. On 29 September, the Gnadenfeld Church Assembly again remitted the document to them, repeating its request for an answer by 5 October. Nothing has yet been returned. The Gnadenfeld congregation therefore fears for its existence should this illegal action be allowed to pass in such a manner. The discipline of all congregations could suffer similarly. Moreover the Elders assembled in conference offered no [biblical?] text in defence of their action which is contrary to their own retraction of their earlier decision and that of the last conference. Indeed, these Elders did not even consider it worthwhile to answer the Gnadenfeld Church Assembly.

4. The Gnadenfeld Church Assembly concludes that it has no choice but to request protection and a decision of the legal authorities. As a result of the repeated interference to which it has been subjected, the Gnadenfeld congregation has already suffered considerable losses in pursuing its agricultural activities. Discouragement and despair are setting in. Because of the conference decision in this matter the Gnadenfeld congregation thinks that a resolution of the matter is urgently necessary.

This is the extent of the grievances outlined to the Society that include all of the required written evidence. In presenting the Gnadenfeld Church Assembly's grievances to the esteemed Elders who made the decision of 8 September at the above-mentioned conference, the Society now asks you in friendship to consider the just claims for fairness and decency of the Gnadenfeld assembly and reply to its questions and documents that you have in hand. This is your duty. Please settle this issue promptly and reconcile yourselves. This should be done in a manner that would preclude this matter from reaching a point where it is necessary to submit it to the Guardianship Committee. The Society is not authorized to make decisions in such matters but is obligated to present them to higher authorities without delay.

If, within fourteen days, there is no evidence of a reconciliation between the conference of Elders and the Gnadenfeld Church Assembly, the Society would find it necessary to refer the matter to higher authorities. This it would do reluctantly, conscious of the fact that it would redound to the community's shame. Under the circumstances currently prevailing that have triggered extensive discouragement and despair in Gnadenfeld village, measures must be taken to avoid this.

The Gnadenfeld Church Assembly has been informed by the Society of this fourteen-day delay.

180. Evgenii F. Hahn to Johann Cornies. 21 October 1843.
SAOR 89-1-889/6.

Thank you for your communications regarding the spiritual situation among the Berdiansk Pietists.

Mr. Henke is a genuinely capable and qualified man who is presently negotiating his acceptance of a pastorate in Bessarabia. He told me he would be open to taking a position with the Pietists only if these negotiations were not to succeed.

It seems to me that the salary set for a spiritual teacher in this case is sufficient, but much lower than what a pastor would receive in church circles in our local settlements. This is true even though a spiritual minister teacher in the Separatist village of Hoffnungsthal near Odesa would be dealing with a single congregation.

Please be so kind as to inform me when Mr. Henke's answer arrives. He would be a very good acquisition for the Berdiansk Pietists, but I doubt that he will accept the post. [note in margin: reported 13 January 1844]. I share your desire to find a spiritual teacher for these good people as soon as possible. Reuoff, the people supporting him, and Pastor Holtfretter have sent a formal complaint to the Consistory in St. Petersburg. They seek to protect the oppressed Lutherans from District Chairman Prinz who has opened a letter (an old story) and to seek his punishment according to the law. I would like to prove to the Consistory that the other complaint is false by dealing with the complaint as one does with slanders. Mr. von Stempel has received orders to make his way to the Berdiansk Pietist District and there undertake a formal investigation. When we get his results we will know whether anyone deserves punishment.

The Minister would like to see the building of a church for the Kleine Gemeinde but does not insist that construction be started immediately. We can give this congregation time to discuss the matter. I will also report to the Minister that the Kleine Gemeinde is grateful for this permission. Please be assured of my respect, E. v. Hahn.

Odesa, 21 October 1843. Received 4 November 1843.

Communication to Kleine Gemeinde, 24 November 1843.

181. Johann Cornies Jr. to Johann Cornies. 21 October 1843.
SAOR 89-1-922/21.

Esteemed Father,

The German mason might finish the granary this week. The plasterers have completed plastering the house. If they are willing to work and the weather stays nice, should the pig barn be plastered as well? The plasterers will probably depart this week. What should I give these two men for beer? Workmen are roofing the pig barn now and will probably complete it tomorrow. I am thinking of ending our threshing since only the maize remains. The trees arrived in good condition.

With a hearty greeting I remain, your son Johann Cornies.

When the tin roofer has finished in Iushanle, he can finish the balcony here. The boards are being nailed today.

Tashchenak, 21 October 1843.

182. Johann Cornies to Christian Steven. 27 October 1843.
SAOR 89-1-925/123v.

State Counsellor v. Steven,

I take the liberty of sending you a chest containing the results of excavations done here this year, with the humble request that Yr. Honour might kindly send it on by mail to State Counsellor v. Keppen in St. Petersburg. You should also include the descriptions that accompany the chest.

Since your departure our weather has been beautiful, warm, sunny, and dry during the day. There have been two nights with five degrees of frost. Villagers have been able to thresh their harvest, but the kernels are soft, especially those of the wheat that cannot be sold. In Berdiansk, the price of wheat is fourteen to fifteen rubles [per pud], rye and barley here on the spot are three rubles. No one is buying oats. Potatoes are from two to three rubles and the head cabbage on offer is so large that one thousand (1/m) quite large heads were eventually sold for ten rubles. In Moscow my wool sold for forty-one and one-half rubles [per pud].

I would be thankful if you could perhaps send mulberry seeds for the use of the Berdiansk settlers and the Bergthaler Mennonites. I am curious to know how you liked the cheeses.

For the last three weeks we have been waiting for Baron v. Rosen to appear. He wrote that he had left Moscow on 1 October. Only God knows what might have befallen him on his journey. The Hutterthal people have completed the roofs on sixteen houses but will probably continue to live in *zemliankas* [sod huts] this winter that were built to stay warm. I intend to lend one thousand chetvert crown potatoes to the poor Nogais for one year, hoping that they will become better accustomed to them and plant more themselves.

With esteem, etc.

183. Johann Cornies to Mr. Gross. 28 October 1843.
SAOR 89-1-925/122v.

Mr. Gross,

Both drawings came to my hand in good condition. Your drawings please me very much and I am grateful for them, but the houses are not drawn quite accurately. The more distant view is better, more accurate than the closer one. I think that the light and shadow is beautiful.

Please forgive me for not writing personally immediately after receiving your drawings. I was just leaving to travel some distance from home when they arrived and, as I do on other such occasions, I authorized my secretary to notify you that the pictures had been received in good order. This is what occurred and made you dissatisfied. For this I am sorry. It is my fault.

You have not specifically listed your charges for the drawings. The value of fifteen silver rubles was marked on the envelope. I enclose this amount with the request that you accept it on the assumption that you will kindly report to me if it should be insufficient.

With constant esteem, J. Cornies.

184. Johann Cornies to [Viktor] Roslavets. 28 October 1843.
SAOR 89-1-925/123.

Governor Roslavets,

In accordance with Yr. Excellency's honoured communication, the youth, Fedor Shkabinov, and the girl, Anna Leshinskaia, arrived healthy and in good condition. Following Yr. Excellency's wish, I will do everything I can to educate and teach these two individuals about landholding and dairying. I cannot determine in advance whether they can attain the desired level of achievement in three years. This depends on their personal abilities and understanding.

Because I did not have any room to put them up at Iushanle, I have sent both to my estate on the Tashchenak, managed by my son. Johann Cornies.

**185. Johann Cornies to Fedor F. Rosen. 29 October 1843.
SAOR 89-1-925/120.**

[Draft:] Submitted to Baron Rosen:
I raised the enclosed tobacco leaves this year on my Iushanle estate. The seeds from the Governor General of New Russia, Count Vorontsov, were labelled "Albanian tobacco seed." The Count explained that the tobacco from this seed was of exceptional quality, had a good taste, was neither too strong nor too weak, and that the Great Sultan usually smoked it.

The plants adapted themselves well to our conditions and grew to an astonishing height of three to four arshins. They produced few side shoots and were only pruned once before the leaves were broken. The cultivation of these plants and their treatment until the leaves were ripe was done as with ordinary tobacco. On 240 square fathoms, I obtained ten puds, thirty funt of the first variety; five puds, eleven funt of the second variety; and four puds, thirty funt of the third variety; for a total of twenty puds, thirty-one funt.

**186. Johann Cornies to Molochnaia Mennonite Village Offices. 3
November 1843. SAOR 89-1-900/54.[24]**

To Village Offices,
Romahan Farlarov, Nogai from the village Farlar and bearer of this note, has permission to purchase sheep in the villages in this district, with a loan of eighty-five silver rubles. They are, however, not to be released to him until the purchase has been documented at the Society, according to regulations.
Society at Ohrloff, 3 November 1843.
Chairman of the Society. Johann Cornies.

**187. Johann Cornies to Fedor F. Rosen. 4 November 1843.
SAOR 89-1-925/124v.**

Baron v. Rosen,
In response to Yr. Honour's communication No. 1796 of April 1834, I have the honour to report about three funt of madder seed which were

---

24   This is one example of a series of similar permissions issued on the same day.

sent to me. I distributed it to various places for seeding by good agriculturalists. Overall, it produced only twelve lot in one spot. The seed did not come up at all in some places because of the dry spring, when moisture was lacking. In other spots the seed did come up but the plants soon died. On the whole, almost all the seedings failed. I will keep these twelve lot for seeding next spring when, with favourable weather, we will surely have greater success.

188. Johann Cornies to Third Department of the Ministry of State Domains. 4 November 1843. SAOR 89-1-925/125.

To the Third Department of the Ministry of State Domains,

After carrying out the Third Department's directive No. 2540 of 28 February 1843, I have the honour to dutifully present the enclosed record of the growth of the various grains and grass seeds received this year. I would observe that, as can be seen from the above-mentioned record, several of the varieties established good and excellent plants in the first year. Yet, it is not possible to immediately determine whether they will prove themselves in the long run for the local region, that is, whether each variety is suitable for the local climate. I will not neglect, at the appropriate time, to make my report in this regard.

189. Johann Cornies to Fedor F. Rosen. 4 November 1843. SAOR 89-1-925/128v.

Baron v. Rosen,

Of the summer rye accompanying Yr. Honour's communication No. 658 of 18 December 1842, one funt cleaned and one funt not cleaned was seeded on my Tashchenak estate on 20 March 1843. It came up well and grew admirably but later on rust spots appeared on its stalks and leaves. This hindered its progress. The ripened seed was far from perfect and suggests great doubt as to its future. Its ability to germinate has presumably suffered greatly, if not entirely.

190. Johann Cornies to Third Department, Ministry of State Domains. 4 November 1843. SAOR 89-1-925/129.

To the Third Department, Ministry of State Domains,

The clover seed received with directive No. 8840 of 23 July 1842, (*Domicuburea, trifolium hybridum*) was seeded on 20 March 1843 on my

Tashchenak estate. It came up very sparsely because of the long spring drought. I observed that this seed had been mixed with other varieties of clover. The plants that appeared grew very well and hold out promise for the future.

191. Evgenii F. Hahn to Johann Cornies. 9 November 1843. SAOR 89-1-889/8.

As the year nears its end I would respectfully ask that you send me short descriptions of the various kinds of progress that the Molochnaia Mennonite District has been able to evidence over the past year. Please do this as soon as possible during the first half of January. This information will appear as a supplement to my annual report, which must be reported for the Colonial Inspectors in a prescribed format that can contain only cold numbers. In my report I want to mention everything that is deserving of the Minister's approval and that could vouch for the achievements of your district.

With my complete affection, E. v. Hahn.

Odesa.

192. Evgenii F. Hahn to Johann Cornies. 10 November 1843. SAOR 89-1-889/9.

The Directive which serves as a guideline for your Society has revealed itself to be quite inadequate for like organizations in other settlements. Societies there exist as only a pretense. This makes it necessary to draw up a set of new instructions. I have done this on the basis of my own convictions and on orders from the Minister. I am required to submit this new Directive to [St.] Petersburg by the end of year. Because I would like you to examine it first, however, I have had it translated into German as well as is possible. I send it to you, enclosed, with a request that you perfect this work according to your own best insights, and send it back to me with your opinions.

This new Directive is not intended to be applied to you, but will apply only to other local settlements. Since it would be of great value to develop orderly working societies on the basis of this Directive it begins with an explanation of the characteristics, conditions, and duties of Society members. One cannot demand too much from people because they will, in that case, do nothing.

I hope that this Directive will benefit much from your examination and corrections. Do not judge it, however, against the standard of the way things are done in your area. The people here and their inclinations are different and hence require different rules.

Yours truly, E. v. Hahn.

Odesa. Received 19 November 1843. Answer 9 December 1843.

193. Evgenii F. Hahn to Johann Cornies. 17 November 1843. SAOR 89-1-889/52.

I received a small quantity of rice especially valued in China and thus called Imperial rice. I can make no better use of it than to send it to you, with the request that you report to me any results you might obtain. Short instructions on how to cultivate this rice are included, although I am convinced that you do not need them.

You will also receive the enclosed instructions for a new system of field cultivation by Hoelbling, which could be of interest to an expert like you.

I find it necessary to issue a special order regarding the transfer of fullholdings, since most unusual things are occurring in this area. With this order, I also intend to connect people more closely to their fullholdings and to prevent them from neglecting their holdings. We have many fullholders here who are paying crown debts of as much as two hundred silver rubles without possessing even twenty-five silver rubles themselves. There were also several individuals who owned nothing but the land. This they passed on for a considerable sum of money, together with the crown debts. This order has been sent out everywhere with the exception of the Mennonite Districts. Your fullholding transfers are conducted in another manner and it is perhaps not useful to change this. I am, however, sending you one copy of this order with the request that you notify me about the extent to which it might be applied in your district.

Please receive the assurance of my constant appreciation,

E. v. Hahn.

Odesa. Received 2 December 1843; half to Iushanle & half to Tashchenak.

Answered 20 December 1843 & Communication No. 64, 17 January 1845 [?].

194. Fedor F. Rosen to Johann Cornies. 17 November 1843. SAOR 89-1-955/58.

[Copy] From the Director of the Tavrida State Domains Bureau, Ministry of State Domains,

About Mennonite resettlement from Prussia.

To the Corresponding Member of the Learned Committee in the Ministry of State Domains, Mr. Cornies,

The Vice-Director of the Second Department notified me in communication No. 1549 of 12 October 1843, that he had submitted to his colleague, the Minister of State Domains, my presentation about Prussian Mennonites who wish to settle in the guberniias of Vitebsk and Mogilev and are requesting permission, if possible, to inspect the land that has been determined for them this year. Because of obstacles that have arisen in these guberniias to the desired separation of crown lands for this settlement, His Excellency has deigned to order that the Minister of State Domains purchase a piece of land on which to settle about three hundred souls along the shores of the well-known navigable Dvina and Dnieper rivers. Orders to identify the most useful sites for this purpose have gone out to the directors of the Domains Bureaus of the Vitebsk and Mogilev Guberniias. They are to begin negotiating with owners. Because reports about the results of these orders have not yet been received, it is still inappropriate to determine at what time the land to be purchased can be inspected. Once it is purchased, you will be notified as to when you and the Mennonites wishing to resettle from Prussia can inspect it, as well as the conditions under which this settlement can take place, assuming that they differ from those contained in the code of laws, volume twelve. There the rights and duties of new settlements are spelled out for persons settling in Russia, including their freedom of religious practice.

I have the honour to report this to you, dear sir.

The original was signed by State Counsellor and Knight, Baron v. Rosen.

195. Johann Cornies to Peter Schroeder et al. 30 November 1843. SAOR 89-1-1002/1.[25]

Notes made at Tashchenak, 30 November 1843

---

25 This is an excerpt from a long document providing similar authorizations for payments.

• Esteemed Peter Schroeder in Neuteich is requested to give the bearer, Zacharias Mueller from Hutterthal, an advance of forty rubles towards the wages of his daughter Justina, to purchase a horse. I, the undersigned, obligate myself for the punctual completion of service and working off of this money. Chairman, Johann Cornies.

• With Aron Peters, Altahir, Zacharias Walther forty rubles for his daughter Maria, for a horse.

• Heinrich Friesen, Rueckenau, to Joseph Waldner's brother-in-law Johann Hofer, forty-five rubles for a horse, with the agreement of the guardian Samuel Glanzen. 3 December 1843.

• David Schellenberg, Tiege. Fifty rubles to Dorius Stahl, Hutterthal, for his son Mathias, to purchase a horse.

196. Johann Cornies to Hutterthal Village Office. [November 1843.] SAOR 89-1-1002/3.

[Undated draft:] To the Hutterthal Village Office,

I direct the Village Office to promptly observe and carry out the following:

1. The Village Office is required to investigate sod huts. If the indoor air is found to be foul and dense and hence detrimental and damaging to health, it must insist that appropriate methods be sought to bring cleaner and healthier air into the rooms. For example, potato and cabbage barrels with trash and foul-smelling odours should be removed from rooms, stoves should be kept from smoking, and fat or other putrid substances should not be dumped into the stove pipes by negligent housekeepers. The Village Office is generally required to ensure that cleanliness prevails indoors and everywhere else. This is the primary measure to be taken to improve the quality of the air and to maintain a good state of health for inhabitants.

2. The Village Office is required to establish the office of nightwatchmen. Two men with rattles should be assigned in the following manner: Each watchman, equipped with a rattle, should appear punctually at ten o'clock in the evening at the Mayor's yard and give notice, with numerous rattling sounds, that the night watch has begun. Until daybreak, one watchman will keep watch over one half of the village up to the central street, and the second over the other half until daybreak. Every hour, each watchman must appear at the Mayor's yard and make many rattling sounds at each of two spots, yet to be determined, in his

half of the village. Too much or too little rattling will be considered offensive and should be punished. The night watch is assigned to fullholders and cottagers in rotation, with the exception of the Mayor and the Church Elder who are exempt from this duty.

Once the watch is completed in the morning, each nightwatchman must take the rattle to the watchman next in the rotation. He should hand the rattle to the man in question or to his wife, thus passing on the duty for the next night watch. Should no one be at home, he should place the rattle on the table in the home. A transfer of the rattle by wives, children, or servants is forbidden, nor should the rattle be left with children or servants. Should this regulation not be observed and the night watch missed, the guilty person will be required to pay fifty silver kopeks into the village treasury as a fine. A nightwatchman who does not discharge his watch in the prescribed rotation is likewise fined fifty silver kopeks.

Every nightwatchman will carry out the watch in his half of the village quietly, walking back and forth calmly, without singing or making a noise. Should he see anything around houses and yards that arouses his suspicion, he should immediately proceed to that place. Should he hear people shouting or wailing, or livestock bellowing or growling, he should immediately hurry to the spot in question. If help is needed, he should call for it as quickly as possible.

Every watchman must desist from lurking at windows or from disturbing anyone unnecessarily. Anyone so doing must be punished. Watchmen should conduct themselves with decency and civility towards travellers, especially lost travellers, and direct them along their way without expecting a reward. Should travellers desire shelter, they must be directed to one in the village.

3. The Village Office should seek to prevent its inhabitants from unnecessarily visiting settlers in Novoaleksandrovka or from travelling elsewhere. Such behaviour can result in a waste of time, an overstraining of horses, and disorderly housekeeping.

4. The Village Office must be alert to prevent families from dividing a fullholding into individual establishments. Only through common efforts and unity can a fullholding survive, progress, and advance. For this reason, the father, the oldest brother, or the most prudent person must be recognized and considered as the head of each fullholding and his advice and orders should be followed in all matters. All other members of the fullholding owe him their obedience. A fullholding will degenerate if all members seek to give orders and do not obey others

or if each person wants to work and use only his portion of the full-holding. Unable to achieve even moderate wealth, such families will remain poor and continue to drag themselves along miserably until the fullholding, to prevent its complete decline, is taken from them. It must then be turned over to better managers.

5. Beginning with the New Year, 1844, every inhabitant must keep accounts of income and expenditure in a book kept for this purpose. Every seeding and the result of each harvest should be recorded. Every sale of produce, livestock, and other goods should likewise, each time, be recorded, with the date. This record book will eventually be investigated to ensure compliance.

197. Johann Cornies to Hutterthal Village Office. 30 November 1843. SAOR 89-1-1002/5v.

[Draft:] To the Hutterthal Village Office,

1. When weather this autumn permits, hearth-sites must be neatly ploughed to a depth of not less than three vershok in order that they be ready for the planting of potatoes and other vegetables in spring. Grain may never be planted on the hearth-site.

2. Unless already dug or completely finished, ditches should be dug around all hearth-sites when the weather is mild. They must be completed to the width and depth ordered.

3. Stored wood must be recorded and piled up in appropriate places, so that it does not warp or become unusable for its intended purpose.

The Village Office should dutifully pay attention to these matters and report the results to me.

Tashchenak, 30 November 1843.

198. Johann Cornies to Christian Steven. 2 December 1843. SAOR 89-1-925/135v.

Inspector of Agriculture v. Steven,

In carrying out Yr. Honour's communication No. 223 of 25 February 1843, I am honoured to humbly report that seven of the eight varieties of tobacco seeds received grew very well, forming splendid shrub-like plants and reaching the appropriate maturity. The exception was No. 7, the Havana seed, which, for unknown reasons, produced few plants. The Maryland, Knaster, Brazilian, and Salonika tobaccos produced excellent tobacco. The Hungarian and American tobaccos were decidedly inferior and, because their small tobacco shoots branched out to the sides, required more than twice the work. I found that, when smoked, the last-named varieties had a strong narcotic effect.

I am sending two bunches of each of the seven varieties named, and one of the eighth (of which little was obtained), numbered as follows: No.1. Salonika, 2. Maryland, 3. great Hungarian, 4. Knaster, 5. Brazilian, 6. Hungarian, 7. Havana, 8. American.

199. Johann Cornies to Fedor F. Rosen. 2 December 1843. SAOR 89-1-925/136.

Director Baron v. Rosen,

In carrying out Yr. Honour's communication No. 129 of 11 March 1843, I am honoured to report that a total of 350 individual so-called ministerial potatoes received in spring for experimental seeding were distributed to four village communities in our local district and to a number of individual state peasants and local Mennonites. The total number returned to me was 9,942 potatoes, of which a few weighed as much as three funt each. Specifically, the average return was twenty-nine-fold, but it reached as high as eightyfold with some individual agriculturalists. Stored in village communities to await future disposition, a total of 4,115 potatoes were distributed as follows: in Great Tokmak 1,033; Chernigovka 500; Andreevka 1,202; Novoaleksandrovka 698; Mikhailov Volost 682. The remainder were left with the persons mentioned for future planting.

Although the potatoes produced were not very large, they provided remarkably good starch. Specifically, I obtained thirty-five funt from one chetvert. Since they have a strong, sharp flavour, and are considerably inferior in taste to local potatoes planted on the steppes, the potatoes were generally more suitable as livestock fodder than for human consumption. Considerable difficulty is involved with the so-called ministerial potatoes that must, if they are to grow successfully, be planted in low-lying areas. The tubers of local varieties multiply well on the high steppes, even in average years, and produce a rich harvest. Because they must be planted far apart, the ministerial potatoes require twice as much space to produce the same quantity of potatoes.

The principal consideration for a man of the land is probably that the varieties planted locally can be worked systematically, which spares him much labour. The ministerial potatoes, on the other hand, that need to be planted far apart, require much more work.

200. David Voth to Johann Cornies. 3 December 1843.
SAOR 89-1-923/44.

Valued and treasured Brother Cornies,

I have for long owed you a personal or written appearance, but have not done so because of my fear and anxiety at not having appeared at the repayment date for my loan. It was not inattention that made me stay away. I have been filled with distress and worry day and night, and can think of nothing but to again ask you, bowing deeply, to spare me. If you can, please forgive me and grant me another nine months of your patience. I want to repay everything. Please grant me this interval. I would have appeared before you personally, but was held back by fear. Yes, with tears, I would have begged you to spare me. I find it hard to name all the reasons why I have not made my payment, but I would rather remain silent in this regard. I make only the humble request that you spare me, for God's will, and grant me the mentioned time. As long as God grants me life and health I will repay everything. Finally, I again repeat my request. I can do nothing other than ask that to show me further patience. In my poverty I will later thank you especially for that. For your kindness, I am in your debt a thousand times. Greetings from your humble and very loving brother, David Voth.

Alexanderwohl, 3 December 1843.

201. Friedrich Prinz to Johann Cornies. 4 December 1843.
SAOR 89-1-923/9.

Most esteemed Mr. Cornies,

The General Guardian has now directed me to send him various pieces of information by 6 January 1844. Since I am doing this for the first time and lack experience, I enclose the directive and dutifully ask you to show me how to prepare this information. I also enclose a request I wrote to the General reporting that I would ask you to look over the report for me. Should something be missing or overdone, kindly make improvements and return it to me with this messenger. If anything directly in relation to me is still missing, please notify me so that I can include it in the very near future. Your respectful Friedrich Prinz.

I will be able to notify you shortly about the clergyman.

Neustuttgart, 4 December 1843. Answered 5 December.

202. Johann Cornies to [unknown]. December 1843 to Kerch.
SAOR 89-1-764/9.

[Draft without salutation:]

You have been so considerate as to write to us about two German wagons seized by local police in Kerch. Two owners from this district responded to the descriptions of the wagons. Franz Thiessen in Blumenort and Franz Baerg in Halbstadt reported wagons like this stolen from them last fall. They have failed to find any trace of them.

The messengers carrying this message are two Mennonites mentioned above, Thiessen and Baerg. In response to your communication, they travelled to Kerch with a legal order to recover their wagons. I respectfully request that you give these two men your assistance and benevolent advice. Please, if necessary, act as their advocate in places where they will need it. By doing so you will much oblige me. I remain your respectful....

203. Johann Cornies to Traugott Blueher. 6 December 1843.
SAOR 89-1-925/138.

Esteemed Mr. Blueher,

Upon receiving your communication of 20 October, I summoned the driver Gerasimov from Second Eregas, and questioned him in detail about his failure to deliver a crate he had accepted from you in Moscow for delivery to Mr. Johann Klaassen in Halbstadt. He gave me the enclosed explanation. Because he had received the items from driver Gerasimov in Kharkiv for delivery to Mr. Klaassen, I also summoned the other driver, Emelian Shablikin from Veseloi, for the same purpose. I questioned him as well and obtained an explanation.

It follows from both explanations that the crate was not delivered to the drivers by the employees responsible for it in your warehouse in Moscow. It may still be located there. I cannot find out anything more about this matter here. My inquiries demonstrate that both drivers are reputed to be people who conduct their lives in an honest and irreproachable manner. Their declarations deserve to be believed. They are both wealthy agriculturalists.

With the assurance of my honest sympathy, and with a friendly greeting, united in love, I remain your friend and servant, Johann Cornies.

204. Declarations of the two drivers. N.d. SAOR 89-1-925/140.

Ivan Gerasimov, from Second Eregas, declares that after he unloaded the wool and completed the accounts, he went to Mr. Blueher, who had earlier told him about items he was to pick up and deliver. Mr. Blueher brought the bill of lading from the warehouse and gave it to him without reading it to him first. He ordered that the items be delivered to Gerasimov. Gerasimov had earlier overheard the maid in Mr. Blueher's house call him Akimovich. Gerasimov asked Mr. Blueher how many puds the items weighed and Mr. Blueher's answer was twelve puds. He then went home. Two workers were involved in delivering these items, one of whom, as he carried the packs out of the store, asked Gerasimov for a tip of a silver ruble. Gerasimow refused the request.

Gerasimov received three packages weighing about six, three, and twelve puds. Evening had meanwhile fallen and Gerasimov hurried off to transport the packages to his inn, without having the bill of lading read to him first. He loaded the three packs onto his wagon and transported them to Kharkiv, where he passed them on to the driver, Emelian Shablikin. He has nothing further to declare.

Emelian Shablikin, from Veseloi, declares that he received three packages from Gerasimov in Kharkiv, but no crate. He asked Gerasimov their weight, and Gerasimov said twelve puds. He delivered the packages in Halbstadt as well as the bill of lading, which was never read to him.

Only in Halbstadt was it discovered, according to the bill of lading, that one crate had gone missing and he was docked thirty-one rubles, twelve kopeks. He knows nothing further.

205. Johann Cornies to Traugott Blueher. 6 December 1843. SAOR 89-1-925/139.

Esteemed Mr. Blueher,

State Counsellor v. Steven from Simferopol writes that almost a year ago he had a shipment of silk sent to Mr. Kritsch, a wine dealer in Moscow, by the latter's brother, a Simferopol merchant. It was intended for sale in Moscow. Recently he heard that it had still not been sold. He asks that you obtain this crate of silk from Kritsch, who has already been informed about the matter by his brother in Simferopol and asked to transfer it to you. I would therefore request that you have the silk picked up from Mr. Kritsch and kindly sell it as well as you can. Please inform

State Counsellor v. Steven accordingly. I enclose the note from State Counsellor v. Steven, on which the varieties of silk have been noted.

In hopes that my request will be granted, I send greetings to you and your dear family, and constantly remain, with honesty, your loving friend and servant, Johann Cornies.

206. Johann Cornies to Peter Keppen. 6 December 1843.
SAOR 89-1-925/141v.

State Counsellor v. Keppen,

On 27 October 1843, I asked State Counsellor v. Steven to send you the results of excavations I undertook this year in grave mounds on the Sea of Azov. To the degree that I can judge, I do not believe that any of these items originated in very early times, since partially decayed leather, silk cloth, and linen pieces, all still recognizable, were found with these corpses.

Driven by curiosity, Nogais from several surroundings villages turned up in large numbers at the excavations. They assured me that these graves were not made by Muslims because they did not lie in the direction prescribed by Muslim law for the arrangement of graves. Their traditions suggest to them that these regions have seen no nomads who did not belong to Muslim national groups for more than two hundred years. They claim that their holy man (Ahis), entombed in a vault in the village of Lasintogien, has, for more than two hundred years, demonstrated a singular healing power, especially for eye diseases. He must have been a Muslim and not of another nation and belief. Otherwise he could not have possessed such singular powers.

I humbly enclose an account of the expenses incurred in the opening of these mounds in the sum of sixteen silver rubles, seventy-five and five-seventh kopeks.

With complete esteem, I have the honour to be Yr. Honour's most respectful servant, Johann Cornies.

[Draft:] Account of expenses incurred in excavations in Melitopol District in the autumn of 1843:

Six workers for twelve days	15.64
Feeding the same	4.32
Implements used, e.g., spades, etc.	3.24
	23.20

6.44 2/7 remaining of the two hundred rubles earlier received from the Academy [of Science]. Outstanding debt to me is therefore: 16.75 5/7 silver

207. Johann Cornies to Peter Keppen. 6 December 1843.
   SAOR 89-1-925/144.

State Counsellor v. Keppen,

Your lovely letter from Nikolaievka, Izum District, dated 20 August, arrived only on 4 November. How pleasant it would have been for us if you, Mr. State Counsellor, had been able to honour us with a visit. Your friendly communication, while informing us that this was not possible, gives us the joyful hope that this might happen in future, perhaps even soon. On that occasion we will have the satisfaction of attending upon you personally, while showing you the progress that has been made in our villages since you were last here. I am sure you will note the marked progress and considerable improvements made in many areas, including our agricultural pursuits, in village beautification, and in house construction. Granted, you will also find much that might still be done better or more attractively. We must, however, not stride forward with giant steps if we intend to provide a foundation for something that is permanent and enduring. We must move ahead materially but also develop our intellectual strength.

Should your brother-in-law, Mr. v. Fiedler, do me the honour of a visit, I will neglect nothing to make his stay with me as comfortable as possible, show him everything he wishes to see, and provide him with whatever explanations he needs. You may count on this. I have not written to him yet, but will do so shortly. As much as I would like to, I am still uncertain whether I could arrange to accommodate one of Mr. v. Fiedler's men on one of my estates to learn the practical breeding of sheep and also wool sorting. I am overwhelmed by apprentices of this kind, but will do my utmost.

This year's harvest in our area was not very good. Arnautka wheat ears were either empty or the kernels very sparse. The other varieties of grain provided only an eightfold to tenfold return. Locusts did not appear in large numbers but we fear that they may appear in larger swarms next year. They are said to have laid eggs in Dneprov District. Although the cattle plague broke out in the villages of Edinokhta and Bauerdak, the police did not take even the most elementary measures to contain the evil.

Except for millet, the Nogais experienced crop failures this year with all varieties of grain. Since potato cultivation has been introduced generally and turned out well, potatoes will now have to meet their needs.

Respectfully commending myself to Yr. Valued Benevolence in future, I have the honour to be, with exceptional esteem and sincere honesty, Yr. Honour's respectful servant, Johann Cornies.

208. Johann Cornies to Evgenii v. Hahn. 9 December 1843. SAOR 89-1-925/147v.

State Counsellor v. Hahn,

It gave me pleasure to review the directives drawn up for the German settlements of Southern Russia. I read them through several times as Yr. Excellency had charged me to do. To the extent that I know the settlers in the area, and what my experience has honestly taught me about their well-being, I found that everything was applicable, desirable, and suitable to current conditions. I sincerely admit that I am not in a position to improve on any part of them or to make them more complete. Enclosed, I return them to Yr. Excellency.

In ten to twenty years, after settlers in the area have improved their circumstances or, as it were, have grown out of this directive, it will perhaps be necessary to change several points of this directive.

209. Abram Jantzen to Johann Cornies. 10 December 1843. SAOR 89-1-923/19.

Most esteemed Sir, J. Cornies,

Kindly excuse me for burdening you with the following request. My illness has prevented me from pursuing my business for sixteen weeks, a time during which I have earned nothing. I am completely dependent for my livelihood on the work of my hands. At the same time, I have had considerable expenses for medicine, and so on, and find that I must take advantage of your kindness, of which I am totally convinced.

Doctor Herr's treatment restored me to the point where I can again take care of my business, though always in pain. Still, to prevent a relapse I have to protect myself from the outside air. Finally, because I have to finish various jobs that require outlays and necessities in advance, I must ask you (since I am unable to help myself without your assistance) if you might, in your kindness, grant me a loan of thirty silver rubles for three months. Only thereafter can I count on an income. At that time the work ordered for you will also be ready.

Anticipating your kindness, I sign myself with exceptional respect, your obedient Abram Jantzen.

Tiege, 10 December 1843.

210. Evgenii F. Hahn to Johann Cornies. 13 December 1843. SAOR 89-1-889/11.

District Chairman Prinz was elected as District Chairman of Berdiansk District without opposition but requests his release from this position. Enclosed is his petition that I would ask you to send back to me with your opinion. Do you think that such a change in the District Office is desirable? Alternately, would it be better to keep Prinz in his position?

The Inspector has not complained about Prinz. He reports that there is no other candidate for the job and that his election should be confirmed according to the law. Yours truly, E. v. Hahn. Odesa.

Received 23 December 1843. Answered 24 December 1843.

211. F. Gross to Johann Cornies. 16 December 1843. SAOR 89-1-923/27.

Mr. Cornies, most worthy of esteem,

Kind Mr. Cornies, please forgive me for not thanking you earlier for your letter of 28 October with the enclosed fifty-nine rubles. Baron Rosen charged me to travel to the southern coast to inspect almost sixty villages. During that time the lamb pelts arrived at my parents' place.

I would have been satisfied with less. I have not mentioned the fifteen silver rubles which also arrived. Granted, I am not a rich man and live off my earnings, but I did not wish to insult you by asking an unreasonable sum for my efforts. However, I considered it unnecessary to set a price for someone like yourself, a person not lacking in means, insights, knowledge, or goodwill.

I received the fifty lamb pelts you kindly sent me. Since there was no price included, it seems as though you wanted to reward me equally. Since our financial positions are quite different and since I cannot reward you as you have rewarded me, please let me know what the cost of the pelts is in order that I might repay my debt.

Next spring I am supposed to travel into your region again. It would give me heartfelt pleasure to find you and yours in stable good health and constant well-being.

In the meantime, with the purest esteem, I remain your devoted friend and servant, F. Gross.

Simferopol.

212. Johann Cornies to Fedor F. Rosen. 16 December 1843.
    SAOR 89-1-925/146v.

Baron v. Rosen,

According to a statement made by Ali Berdibolotov, he is in a quandary because of various complaints made against him and submitted to the local police. This has compelled him to submit a petition to Yr. Honour to assist him, if possible, in his situation and to speed up the matter with the District Chief.

He is very discouraged and suffers a great deal. Please excuse me if I respectfully ask you to treat this matter involving the District Chief as best you can so that the police investigation might be as short as possible.

Please forgive me my boldness and the liberty I have taken in troubling you. With complete esteem and faithful devotion, I remain Yr. Honour's respectful servant, J.C.

213. R. Schmit to Johann Cornies. 18 December 1843.
    SAOR 89-1-923/28.

Highly esteemed and valued Mr. Cornies,

I am in a real bind and need your advice as director of schools. The time to rehire schoolteachers is fast approaching and I would gladly continue in my present position. I understand, however, that the majority of my neighbours are against my teaching methods and have started to look around for another teacher. I learned from pupils that Johann Woelcke and Gerhard Fast had approached the Marienthal teacher in this regard, but had not hired him.

Last Friday, members of the Village Office, Mayor Fast, Deputy Martens and Cornelius Janzen visited the school from early morning until noon. They looked through everything and observed how I taught my classes. After school, I asked them if they would let me stay on as teacher. They replied that this might be possible if I taught my classes as they wished. I asked what they expected of me. They proposed that I have the Halbstadt teacher, as the best teacher in the settlement, teach me how best to proceed and to provide direction. I was, at the same time, to stop handing out tracts to the children. Tracts, they said, were produced by people who did not believe in the resurrection, and were only catechisms. I promised to stop. Had they not asked for permission to take them home to read in the evening, I would not have handed them out. I was pleased because I thought it better for them to read in the evening than to gad about and become involved in all kinds of mischief. I also encouraged them to read the tracts eagerly on Sundays.

People often say false things about me. They ridicule me, especially if I am walking along the street where they hang out, laughing at me. Mayor Fast's son Abraham, who is still in school, told the other boys that I had erected a cross at school and forced them to kneel before it and cross themselves every day. This story spread to other villages. As a result, preachers Krueger and Tiessen and Elder Warkentin visited the Village Office members one afternoon. Preacher Friesen from Halbstadt was also there. They carefully reviewed my teaching methods and concluded that everything was fine, except that the children were somewhat behind other schools in their writing and arithmetic. They did not find anything else to say.

Nor did they mention anything about the cross that I would have been happy to explain. All that I had done was to erect a small support for the wall-primer on my desk where I had the little ones recite once a day. The story was invented to insult me. I went to see the Mayor and complained to Abraham's parents, the Fasts. Fast's wife said that the cross had been talked about in other villages as well, but it was her son who had first spread the story because I often punished him for his bad behaviour. As punishment, I had set up a square kneeling board that hurt a little more than kneeling on the ground. His parents may have disagreed with this approach, since their children usually got their own way with them.

In closing let me say, valued Mr. Cornies, that I very much hope to get the position in the Hutterite community. I would much rather teach humble folk. I am a humble person myself, and not comfortable among superior people, as they are here.

Your obedient servant, R. Schmit. Petershagen.

[List of pupils in school follows letter.]

**214. Friedrich Prinz to Johann Cornies. 18 December 1843.
SAOR 89-1-923/35.**

To Chairman Cornies of the Molochnaia Mennonite Society for the Advancement of Agriculture and Trades,

No. 1008. Report from Berdiansk District Office,

The spiritual office in Berdiansk District has informed this District Office that a meeting of church leaders was held at which all villages in the Berdiansk Pietist Congregation agreed to act in accordance with their religious freedom and support the preacher's position within the congregation.

They will therefore elect their own preachers from within their fellowship and maintain their own independent church organization. They do not request any learned clerics at this time.

The District Office has the honour to submit this report to you for further action. District Chairman Prinz, District Secretary [Pfifky].

Received 21 December 1843 and reported to State Counsellor on 10 January 1844.

215. Johann Cornies to Tavrida State Domains Bureau. 20 December 1843. SAOR 89-1-925/148.

To the Tavrida State Domains Bureau,

I write in response to the State Domains Bureau's communication No. 9742 of 30 October 1843 regarding the crown potatoes in Kiltshik. The local village administration explained that the potatoes had rotted not because an inspection had been neglected but because of the orders of Huebert, the Mennonite supervisor. I have the honour to humbly report that, in response to several questions put to Huebert, he stated that he had acted according to his directives, clearly ordering the Kiltshik Elder to use an inspection device set up above the pit twice weekly to check that the potatoes were not rotting. In cases where there was the smell of rot, the potatoes were to have been brought up out of storage and cleaned. I also questioned the assistant supervisor, Fedor Savchenko from Novogrigorievka. Asked about the same matter, he gave evidence recorded in the accompanying document. Savchenko also says that, shortly before Christmas, following my orders, he visited all districts in Dneprov District where potatoes were stored in pits and repeated the same orders.

In following my orders, Huebert forbade the complete opening of pits as long as there was no smell of rot. Since opening the pits could cause damage, it was necessary to prevent air from entering the pits. For this purpose, wheels were laid over the pits and provided with coverings in order that the condition of the potatoes could be checked by uncovering only the hole in the centre.

I believe that the Mennonite Huebert did not promise the Elder that he would return after he gave him the potatoes and received a receipt for them. It was absolutely not his assignment to take further action. When no further cases of this nature arose, Huebert was convinced that he would not need to make any further trips in this matter.

216. Johann Cornies to Evgenii F. Hahn. 20 December 1843. SAOR 89-1-925/149v.

State Counsellor v. Hahn,

I am honoured to respectfully respond to the order of 17 November circulated by Yr. Excellency about regulating future transfers of full-holdings in settlements. The essential contents of the directive faithfully achieve exactly what both the District Office and the Society consider best for the Molochnaia Mennonite District.

Though varying in several rules considered appropriate and acceptable here, the directive would be entirely applicable here as well. It is principally the fifth point regarding price estimates, however, that is not necessary in our local district. If there should be special crown debts involved in the transfer, transferring a fullholding is not permitted before specific pricing is applied. This also applies if obvious improvements have been made to the fullholding to be transferred, so that fullholdings are prevented from acquiring large debts.

With the most complete esteem and faithful respect, Yr. Excellency's respectful servant, Johann Cornies.

217. Johann Cornies to Evgenii F. Hahn. 24 December 1843. SAOR 89-1-925/152.

State Counsellor v. Hahn,

To best answer the questions contained in Yr. Excellency's esteemed communication of 13 December, I hasten to submit the following: To change the Berdiansk District Office by dismissing Chairman Prinz would be absolutely of no use. I think that his dismissal would have extremely serious consequences for the whole Pietist community. I am convinced that, with his leadership, much that is positive could still be done for these people over time, building on the achievements already made by him. He follows orders faithfully and seeks positive advantages for his community. For his zealous efforts, he has already won the settlers' respect.

I assume that an important reason for his desire to be released from his duties is the low Chairman's salary in the Berdiansk District. It may, at the very least, have contributed to his discouragement. He is forced to see his own fullholding suffer neglect despite his best efforts to be a model settler in every respect.

I submit my best and most honest opinion in this matter with respect and faithful obedience as measured against Yr. Excellency's best insights. Yr. Excellency's respectful servant, Johann Cornies.

218. Traugott Blueher to Johann Cornies. 24 December 1843. SAOR 89-1-923/36.

Mr. Johann Cornies,

I was pleased to note that Mr. Wiebe's notification of 20 October reports the arrival of the remittance of 1 October. I was not, however, informed as to whether my communication of 29 September had arrived. It may well not have come to your hand. I can, if necessary, send a copy.

Because the local post office does not accept the publication, I ordered one copy of the *Landwirtschaftliche Dorfzeitung* (Agricultural village newspaper) that you had ordered from a bookseller.

I was grateful for your communication of 6 December but regret that your helpful efforts in investigating local carters had no favourable results. The fact that the missing case was stolen from carters on the street, as happens often when only a peasant is left in charge of a wagon, is a warning that people of this kind are not to be trusted.

Mr. Kritsch sold the silk you mentioned a long time ago, at an average price of nine rubles, which is really a terrible price. The greatest contribution to the sharp drop in the price of nice native silk is that no appropriate arrangements have been made to have the silk reeled or twined according to foreign fashions. The thread machines ordinarily used here only produce a product equivalent to Greek silk at its best.

A silk mill set up here by a local official twines five different varieties very well, exactly according to foreign fashions. Samples already available here suggest that our native silk should attain its real value. Italian organza silk is regularly valued at twenty-five to thirty rubles locally, and several thousand puds are produced annually. Kindly inform Mr.

Steven in this regard. I would be pleased to give him what assistance I can locally, to the extent that this lies in my power. Since he commands a large quantity of silk, he would have made an incomparably better bargain by sending it abroad. This is not of course worthwhile for small quantities.

Mr. Leonard recently placed a notice in newspapers regarding the cultivation of Chinese rapeseed that you are promoting in settlements there. This could be highly important for Russia if the oil could be used in factories in place of olive oil. But where the oil is used only for local consumption its significance drops because transportation costs from your area would make the oil very expensive. In any case, I would be most interested in your views on this matter.

I have, through merchant Bigsev, sent you a small case of medicine from Halle for your dear wife. I hope it will have good results eventually. Please let me know since inhabitants of your settlement visit the market in Kharkiv.

We have again, through God's forbearance, patience, and benevolence, lived through another year and enter the New Year with trust in the Lord's further assistance. At this time of transition, we send you and your whole family our heartiest congratulations and sincerely wish you the greatest well-being, spiritually and physically.

I commend myself to your loving memory and remain your faithful, unchanging friend, Traugott Blueher.

Moscow, 24 December 1843. Answered 2 February 1844.

219. Isaac Conrad to Johann Cornies. 28 December 1843.
 SAOR 89-1-923/40.

Most valued Mr. Cornies,

We have a most important request to make of you. In September, our son was taken from us and put into service with Dirk Neufeld in Altona. Both of us find this to be a most difficult matter, but will try to accept it if we must.

However, we ask you from the bottom of our hearts that you take measures to ensure that our son is not treated too severely and is able to retain the use of his healthy limbs. Both of us have long lost our health. My wife already has two hernias. In my childhood I fell into a ditch with a horse that crushed my chest and the area between my shoulders. As a result, I often still have such excruciating pain that I can hardly speak.

We would therefore humbly request that you show us your kindness by ensuring that our child is not placed under too heavy a load and cruelly punished. He was often sick but as long as his body remains healthy, his work should not be too difficult for him later on as ours has become for us. The good Lord will not leave you unrewarded for any mercy you might show to us as poor individuals.

Full of hope that you will fulfil my request, Isaac Conrad. Margenau, 28 December 1843.

220. Johann Waldner to Johann Cornies. December 1843. SAOR 89-1-923/18.

To our Mr. Cornies,

Please do not be offended at this letter but need drives me to write to you. I cannot continue to carry on my handicraft without the means needed to purchase essential materials. I therefore respectfully request that you lend me twenty rubles for such purchases. If you cannot help me, I will be unable to earn anything this winter. Since you are our benefactor and father who takes care of us, I place my trust in your not denying my request. We will pay it back to you soon. Johann Waldner.

[In margin in Cornies's hand: "Lend him twenty silver rubles until 1 March 1844."]

221. Inspector to Johann Cornies. 31 December 1843. SAOR 89-1-1094/7.

Announcement from Inspector of Molochnaia and Berdiansk [colonist German] settlements to Johann Cornies, Mennonite in Ohrloff village,

In response to directive No. 86003 of 20 November from the Guardianship Committee for Foreign Settlers in Southern Russia, I hereby invite you to appear in my office on 11 or 12 January 1844 to accompany me to Heidelberg village. There we will inspect the recently built Roman Catholic church to ensure that the appropriate documents can be completed and forwarded to the Guardianship Committee. I also ask you to invite two other Mennonites knowledgeable in house construction to inspect the church with us.

31 December 1843. Inspections Secretary D. Branndler

222. Johann Cornies to [illegible]. Undated draft, 1843.
SAOR 89-1-811/31.

Since 1836, the Society has experimented by responding to requests from fullholders who, without a sufficient number of persons able to do the work required, are not capable or prudent enough to work their fullholdings sufficiently to improve it and make it more productive. [In such cases] we have provided a second, tested and capable young family [to work with them] on equal terms. The same was similarly done experimentally with fullholdings that had to be given over to others because of old age or death. In these instances two young, energetic families were permitted to take on cooperatively such a fullholding according to the following rules [not extant]. We now have eighty such fullholdings worked by two families in our district. The six years since these arrangements were made have demonstrated that the prosperity increased particularly quickly for the aforementioned householders, placing them in an advantageous position.

A rule for two families on one fullholding could be approved and confirmed according to, first…. [end of draft document]

223. Forestry Society to Village Offices from Altonau to Ladekopp. Undated draft, 1843. SAOR 89-1-901/29.

The combined meeting of the Society and the District Office on the 13th [month not given], decided that two more setting trenches should be dug and prepared this autumn between the trees already planted along the post road. The Society hereby requires that villages from Altonau to Ladekopp mark off the full length of the post road on both sides of their villages without delay, fixing the location for two setting trenches in a straight line between the trees already situated there, always keeping the trenches equidistant from each other. Markers of the required size must be cut into the grass so that workers ordered to do the digging are not delayed. Village Offices should report the results of such activities to the Society by the 25th without fail, so that the above-mentioned work can be inspected on site by one of its members.

224. Agricultural Society to District Office in Halbstadt. Undated draft [1843]. SAOR 89-1-901/29v.

The Blumstein Village Mayor made a submission about Johann Hoffer, a Hutterite Mennonite. Hoffer does not have enough space to pursue his trade in the accommodation he was given. The Society has therefore given three souls from Hoffer's and Tobias Walther's families quarters with the Blumstein cottager Abram Loewen in Blumstein. Loewen agreed to this proposal. The District Office is hereby informed.

225. Forestry Society to Jacob Martens. Undated draft [1843]. SAOR 89-1-901/28.

[Undated draft]: You are hereby informed about a report from the Lindenau Village Office that, during the night of the fifteenth of this month, seven of the best-growing trees along the post road between Lindenau and Lichtenau were intentionally broken off. You are to inspect this incident on site and investigate carefully if it might be possible to find the culprits. Results are to be reported at the appropriate time.

226. Agricultural Society to Village Offices. Undated draft [1843]. SAOR 89-1-954/25.

To all Village Offices,

Records listing householders in this district who keep accounts of their incomes and expenditures indicate that many are ignorant of what keeping accounts actually means. Village Offices do not explain or test the figures given them but without giving the matter any thought, enter them into categories suggested by the householders themselves. It must be understood that the keeping of accounts for income and expenditure means that each householder uses a specific sewn booklet into which he punctually enters all income on the first side of the page and every expenditure on the opposite side, noting the date of each entry. In this way, an accurate comparison can be made of income and expenditure at the end of each year, documenting the household's progress.

The Society hereby orders Village Offices to summon all householders who undertook to keep accounts to establish whether they have proceeded as mentioned above. They may also undertake such inspections with individuals in their homes. The results are to be reported to the Society by [blank], giving the names of those who actually kept accounts for income and expenditure in the appropriate manner. The Village Offices should not make superficial judgments but must work towards a thorough introduction of this system. This can be of great value for inhabitants.

227. Johann Cornies to Village Offices. Undated draft [1843].
   SAOR 89-1-954/46.

When I travelled around this district with His Excellency, the Acting General Guardian for the Colonists of Southern Russia, the latter expressed great dissatisfaction to me that many dwellings in our villages have only small, unsightly windows facing the street that are offensive to the eye. This gives our villages an unattractive appearance. His Excellency ordered that houses are absolutely not to be built in this way in future.

Accordingly, the Society has introduced a specific rule for Village Offices, ordering once and for all that from now on, whenever fullholders and cottagers build dwellings, no windows will be permitted on the street side which do not have regulation windowsills and two glass panes. It is the responsibility of Village Offices to publicize this directive immediately and properly, and to enter the required letter, J.S.B. in the journal.

228. Agricultural Society to Blumenort Village Office.
   Undated draft [1843]. SAOR 89-1-954/43.

[No.]587. To Blumenort,
   The Village Office is charged with questioning the local householder, Peter Willms, immediately about his motive in approaching Jacob, son of Peter Kroeker in Rueckenau and now in service with Johann Sukkau, and offering him 146 rubles for his service in the coming year. Does Willms not know with whom he must arrange the hiring of the above-mentioned Jacob, as was done when Sukkau hired him? The Office should report to the Society in detail by tomorrow, the 28th of the month.

229. Agricultural Society to Margenau Village Office. Undated draft
   [1843]. SAOR 89-1-954/43.

To Margenau,
   In accordance with the open agreement between Kroeker and Albrecht made at the Society meeting in spring, Kroeker is not expected to pay Albrecht anything for the hearth-site this year. The Society made no decisions about any other agreements between these two. Meanwhile, the Society directs the Village Office to order Kroeker not to delay construction and to point out to Albrecht that he should not presume to

make any demands on this hearth-site. Should he take contrary action, he will be called to account. This ruling must be observed.

230. Agricultural Society and District Office to Village Offices. Undated draft [1843]. SAOR 89-1-954/44.

To all Village Offices,

When His Excellency, the Acting General Guardian for the Colonists of Southern Russia, State Counsellor v. Hahn, toured villages in this district, he noted that several good householders had made improvements to their properties that offered praiseworthy examples of broad applicability. He gave explicit orders that all fences along streets and all gables on dwellings should now be painted. This would underline the advantageous distinction achieved by our Mennonite villages. Because of the special rights that Mennonites have received, it is His Excellency's opinion that it is proper for them to provide leadership for all other settlers, providing them with good examples to follow in every respect.

The Society for the Advancement of Agriculture and Trades and the District Office informs the Village Offices accordingly.

In accordance with His Excellency the Acting General Guardian's order, directions are given to carry out this order promptly. All inhabitants, fullholders and cottagers alike, should be adequately informed. Without losing time, provision should be made already this year, and no later than 1 June 1844, to paint all fences along streets that belong to fullholders, cottagers, and all community structures with gables on the street side as well. Owners are left to choose the colour according to their tastes. Oil is not necessarily required for this paint. Other mixtures can be used to good effect as well. These have been tested here and there in villages and have demonstrated their endurance.

From now on, Village Offices must immediately proceed to carry out the above-mentioned directive according to the wishes of the high authorities. This is for our own profit and to maintain our paternal government's benevolence for us.

231. Johann Cornies to church leaders. Undated draft [1843]. SAOR 89-1-954/12.

According to information I have received, the teachers [preachers] of Lichtenau, Margenau, and Pordenau unlawfully sent to Elders in

Heubuden, Prussia, written documents detrimental to the state. They paid a willing Mariupol settler to carry them out secretly. All of the documents sent to Prussia with the teachers' [preachers'] signatures have been confiscated and sealed here. In these documents our local teachers [preachers] refer to you, among others, as supposedly having said that they find the actions of State Counsellor v. Hahn against Warkentin unjust and that the State Counsellor is not authorized to dismiss him. I doubt that you made such declarations to these teachers. I am giving you friendly advance notice that would enable you to establish the truth of these matters before you are drawn into an investigation of these papers.

232. Johann Cornies to unknown Elder. Undated draft [1843].
   SAOR 89-1-954/17.

Honoured Elder,
   Please write briefly, officially, and without any further explanation to the Agricultural Society about what you told me verbally, specifically that the church teachers fulfilled their duty in investigating schoolteacher Heinrich Franz in regard to the shameful accusations made against him. Neither of the girls involved admitted these accusations in any way. Therefore, in accordance with the Mennonite confession of faith, the community cannot declare schoolteacher Franz guilty and he cannot be shunned by the community.
   Please send this to the Society as soon as possible, in friendship, your sincere ...

1844

233. Tobias Geyer to Johann Cornies. 3 January 1844.
SAOR 89-1-1094/8.

His Honour, Johann Cornies,

I have heard about your kindness in assisting me to regain the chest I lost or to obtain restitution for damages. I thank you and take the liberty of sending you a letter from our friend, Blueher, describing in detail the evidence given by two witnesses as to how the chest was received and forwarded. This makes the carter's lies obvious.

I would have taken the liberty of bringing Yr. Honour this letter personally, but my business affairs regrettably require me to stay at home. Please continue to support me with your advice and actions.

May our loving God reward you for the benefits you have granted me as a beginner. I remain, with esteem, your humble servant, Tobias Geyer, Bookbinder in Molochnaia.

Molochnaia, 3 January 1844. Answered 8 January 1844.

234. Julius Lange to Johann Cornies. 4 January 1844.
SAOR 89-1-1094/12.

Highly valued Mr. Cornies,

Today father passed on your admonition regarding my debt to you. I do not want to abuse your kind consideration and thought I would surely repay this debt by the due date. Circumstances have kept me from doing so. It is difficult for me not to keep my word or recognize your kindness. When the weather clears up, I plan to go to Berdiansk. Upon my return, I will gratefully repay my debt. Please be patient with me. You will find me to be a thankful debtor. Do not be angry with me. Julius Lange.

Gnadenfeld, 7 January 1844.

235. Evgenii F. Hahn to Johann Cornies.
6 January 1844. SAOR 89-1-889/12.

If it were enough, I would be inclined to negotiate a salary increase for District Chairman Prinz. Since the sole source for such a raise is the community treasury, it should first give its consent. But if Prinz has enemies, I could do nothing but write a recommendation on his behalf.

Please give your friends in the Berdiansk District a suggestion as to what they might do. They should get their community to raise District Chairman Prinz's salary for his many years of service, but with the proviso that this would benefit only Prinz. His successors would get the old salary. Should all four communities submit statements in this regard, we would confirm the increase. These statements should be clear about the amount of the increase.

I am now writing Prinz to tell him that I must turn down his plea to be released from his office.

Yours truly, E. v. Hahn.

Odesa, 6 January 1844. Received 20 January 1844.

236. Johann Cornies to Evgenii F. Hahn. 8 January 1844.
SAOR 89-1-1088/3.

State Counsellor v. Hahn,

On the occasion of this New Year, I would wish Yr. Excellency much happiness. May our gracious God protect you and bless you with good health, strength, and joy. May Yr. Honour enjoy continuing well-being and may Yr. deserving wife live to a ripe old age.

I will for my part, try to make myself ever more worthy of Yr. Excellency's favour. I consider it the joy of my life to continue to describe myself as Yr. Excellency's most respectful servant, Johann Cornies.

237. Copy of the State Counsellor v. Hahn's Directive No. 40 to
District Chairman Prinz. 8 January 1844. SAOR 89-1-1094/28.

I write in response to your request of 9 December 1843 to inform you that I find your work in the Berdiansk District indispensable to its future well-being. This is an important time in which agricultural improvements are being undertaken and surveying will be done. I can therefore not grant your request that you be released from service. It is my wish that you continue as you have before on behalf of the community's welfare.

Signed, Acting General Guardian of the Colonists of Southern Russian, State Counsellor v. Hahn.

238. Copy of State Counsellor v. Hahn's directive No. 39 to District Chairman Prinz. 8 January 1844. SAOR 89-1-1094/28.

I write in response to your submission No. 1025 of 28 December 1843 to inform you that when a complaint was lodged against settler Ruoff for an old misdemeanour, you should have called him to account with a severe punishment. On the other hand, his old age and otherwise good moral behaviour should not be ignored.

In consideration of these circumstances I order you to restrict yourself to imprisoning Ruoff in the District Office for a limited time, after which he should be freed. It should be impressed upon him that he must, in future, refrain from slandering his superiors. Signed State Counsellor von Hahn.

239. F. Martens to Johann Cornies. 10 January 1844. SAOR 89-1-1094/16.[1]

My father W. Martens has asked me to write to Mr. Forestier in Odesa. Please have him make inquiries with Tielov, who works in the merchandizing firm Radi Kanakens, about the main characteristics of the Presnitzer Baths in Silesia. Tielov was good enough to tell my father about the baths on a visit to Odesa in spring. Are the treatments likely to help Father's illnesses, hypochondria and abdominal hardening? I would be grateful if Mr. Forestier could get me dependable information

---

1 Wilhelm Martens's illness, which Cornies called "hypochondria," probably consisted of bouts of severe depression, accompanied by manic periods of irrational anger and indecision. See Susan Baur, *Hypochondria: Woeful Imaginings* (Berkeley: University of California Press, 1989), 21–8, https://doi.org/10.1525/978052035194. The earliest known manifestation of Martens's illness came in 1830, and a second attack followed in 1837. After 1837 Martens was frequently incapacitated, and on 11 June 1845 he hanged himself.

about the baths. Ask him for his help as soon as he can. Father needs the information before spring. F. Martens.

Tiegenhagen, 10 January 1844. Wrote to Forestier 12 January 1844.

240. Johann Cornies to Fedor F. Rosen. 10 January 1844.
SAOR 89-1-1088/2v.

Director Rosen,

Adding to my Report No. 1 of 5 January, I must say that the list of state peasants deserving of awards for potato cultivation should be extended. Two peasants in the village of Bolshoi Tokmak planted potatoes earlier in 1843, and have weeded them well. Karp Martchenko harvested eighty and one-half chetvert from eight and one-half chetvert of seed, and Grigori Schapovalenko harvested twenty-seven chetvert, five *chetveriki* from five chetvert, six chetveriki of seed.

In 1843 the Akkerman Nogai, Mitalip Tenbaiev, planted five hundred mulberry trees in his mulberry plantation. He is ready this year to plant the whole desiatina assigned to him for this purpose. The setting trenches have been prepared.

241. Johann Cornies to Evgenii F. Hahn. 10 January 1844.
SAOR 89-1-1088/4.

State Counsellor v. Hahn,

Communication No. 1008 of 18 December 1843 from the Berdiansk District Office reported that the Berdiansk Pietist Congregation had called together a gathering of church leaders. They decided to do what they had done before, choose preachers from their own ranks and preserve their independent church order. They do not think they need a learned cleric, wonder what kind of cleric they might otherwise get, and decided to stay with their own people. Because we have talked about these matters before, I thought I owed Yr. Excellency this information.

With exceptional esteem, I remain Yr. Excellency's respectful servant, Johann Cornies.

242. Johann Cornies to Evgenii F. Hahn. 10 January 1844.
SAOR 89-1-1088/5.

State Counsellor v. Hahn,

I have still not been told about my shipment of 6 July 1843 to Yr. Excellency's address. It consisted of a garden cultivator with one wheel, a German plough for the crown model farm of Aleksandria, and one small case. These items were shipped by steamboat from Berdiansk. I would ask Yr. Excellency to graciously inform me whether the above-mentioned implements have arrived. Johann Cornies.

243. Friedrich Prinz to Johann Cornies. 11 January 1844. SAOR 89-1-1094/17.

Highly esteemed Mr. Cornies,

A letter from a Pastor Henke eight days ago reported that a review of our church practices had recommended that we re-establish our old church order. Young men from among us would be selected to preach instead of a hired preacher who might not be suitable for our purposes. A small council was set up to oversee this matter and documents needed to this end have been gathered together. I will send you our constitution and directives about the reconstitution of our practices, with the request that you look them over to make sure they are ready to be submitted to the Guardianship Committee.

A majority of our community thinks that the burden of building a [new] house [of worship] and the remuneration needed [for an outside preacher] are too costly. Several members, however, think otherwise because we had earlier asked the administration and the General to give us their views about appointing someone from outside. Please tell us what you think so that we can conclude this matter. Also, please return the enclosed letter to me.

With greetings to you and your honoured family, I remain, with esteem, your dutiful Friedrich Prinz.

11 January 1844, Neufhoffnung Settlement. Response 20 January 1844.

244. Johann Cornies to Evgenii F. Hahn. 13 January 1844. SAOR 89-1-1088/5v.

State Counsellor v. Hahn,

In preparing my annual report about our local villages in 1843, I consulted the District Office's statistical overview, and was astonished to find that Mennonites had been found guilty of twenty-eight different violent crimes in the Mennonite District in 1843. This comes to approximately one offence for 475 settlers. I think that this rate is infrequently so high in our region, even among the Nogais.

Since I am conversant with every such case in the district, I concluded that the statistics seemed to be exaggerated and obtained an exact memorandum from the District Office to convince myself of their accuracy, as is my duty.

The District Office sent me the enclosed list of names of people who had been found guilty of misdemeanours. They had been included in the statistics submitted to the high authorities at the Inspector's request. I now realize that these misdemeanours are not of the type that should be included on this form. As a result, the whole community is in danger of losing the esteem of our high authorities despite the fact that the District Office and the Society is meticulous in severely prosecuting every immoral offence. Yr. Excellency might kindly investigate this matter and convince yourself that these persons labelled as criminals are subject only to penalties decided upon by their local administration and should not appear in the statistics.

To preserve the good name of our community, I feel compelled to obediently submit this matter to Yr. Excellency. The District Office insists that no changes in these statistics can be made here on the spot. The Inspector insists that each one must be recorded as a crime. He does so as though he were determined to prove that a large number of severe misdemeanours were recorded in settlements entrusted to his oversight. Members of the District Office fail to recognize the importance of this matter despite the fact that these statistics must be submitted to the Inspector in the Russian language.

Yr. Excellency might graciously forgive me for submitting my views about this matter, especially given the existence of a previous case that transpired in Odesa in January 1843 in which I was questioned about trivial events that had likewise been entered in the statistics as crimes. These were later changed.

Commending myself urgently to Yr. Excellency's further benevolence, Yr. most respectful servant, Johann Cornies.

245. Johann Cornies to Christian Steven. 13 January 1844. SAOR 89-1-1088/7v.

Mr. v. Steven,

I will shortly have the honour to submit the annual report about progress made in the Molochnaia Mennonite District in 1843.

I take the liberty of sending the enclosed small sample of silk that has been reeled in our district, in order that it might be assessed.

With constant esteem, Yr. Honour's humble servant, Johann Cornies.

246. Johann Cornies to Forestier. 13 January 1844.
SAOR 89-1-1088/7v.

Esteemed Mr. v. Forestier,

My friend, the merchant Wilhelm Martens of Halbstadt, urgently requests that I write to you with a request that you be so kind as to consult Tielov, employed in the trading firm Radi Kanakens, about the cold Presnitzer Baths in Silesia? Might they in fact be beneficial for the cure of this illness, hypochondria and abdominal hardening? The above-mentioned Tielov recommended the baths to Martens last spring. Furthermore, might it be possible to obtain more specific information about the above-mentioned baths directly from Silesia?

I heartily request that you, dear Sir, write in detail to Mr. Martens about this matter, and do what you consider necessary in this regard. If, with God's help, the Presnitzer Baths are suited to curing this physical suffering, Martens would like to make this journey in spring.

You would oblige him as well as me, if information about this matter might be received as soon as possible.

Commending myself to you, I remain, with esteem, your most respectful servant, Johann Cornies.

247. Johann Cornies to Friedrich Prinz. 20 January 1844.
SAOR 89-1-1088/8v.

District Chairman Prinz in Neuhoffnung,

I received your letter of 11 January and also read its enclosure from the preacher, Mr. Henke. I advise you to do nothing other than to continue the process you have started in arranging your own church affairs. Do not change with the weather. It is evident from Preacher Henke's letter that he would not be inclined to go to Neuhoffnung if he had been able to find a position with [a church] that had more members and income. He is naturally renewing the old offer because he now has no position. I do not blame him for this, since every person aspires to what he prefers and whatever will ensure his existence. Since no one can tell if Mr. Henke would bring you peace, it is my opinion that you should select your preachers from your midst, since they share your frailties, your views, and your other habits and so are acquainted with them. You must, however, begin to work towards educating several young, intelligent youths as church teachers, and I would gladly help you with this.

You have nothing to fear from the State Counsellor. I mentioned something about your church establishment after you reported to me. I expressed myself in a straightforward manner to him, telling him that you do not need a learned cleric in future, since your church now has a different basis and is more firmly grounded.

Please write to me if your request to be released from service has been approved, and what results will follow. Johann Cornies.

248. Johann Cornies to Christian Steven. 20 January 1844. SAOR 89-1-1088/10.

Mr. v. Steven,

Mr. Blueher, Head of the Sarepta Trading Firm in Moscow, wrote to me on 24 December 1843 that your silk was sold by Mr. Kritsch quite some time ago, at an average price of nine rubles, a terribly low price. Mr. Blueher said further that the greatest problem with our native silk, although it is very nice to a degree, is the total absence of an appropriate establishment to reel the silk, and to double it according to the foreign manner. This devalues it greatly. Only a very ordinary product is emerging from thread machines used until now and it can only be compared to Greek silk at best. An official in Moscow has now built a silk mill that throws off five different varieties very well, according to the foreign manner, and has already produced samples. This will result in native silk that can be sold at its real value. Italian organza silk is consistently selling in Moscow at twenty-five to thirty rubles per funt, and several thousand puds are being produced annually.

Mr. Blueher asked me to report this to you. He would be pleased to be useful to you in Moscow as far as it lies in his power. He thinks sending your silk abroad could possibly be more advantageous for your accounts, but not for smaller amounts.

Common spelt or winter spelt is not cultivated here. I regret that I have not yet found an opportunity to send you the cheeses you ordered.

We have a great deal of snow here now, one to two fut deep, and almost all communications are obstructed. Whenever tracks have been made, the wind immediately drifts them shut again. No one here can remember having had snow as deep as this. There are reports of frozen hands and feet and a few dead persons have been dug out of the snow. A sudden thaw would cause terrible floods and great damage in many villages. The temperature is tolerable, five to seven degrees below freezing, with eighteen degrees [below] one day.

With exceptional esteem, I endeavour to remain Yr. Honour's respectful servant, Johann Cornies.

249. Evgenii F. Hahn to Johann Cornies. 22 January 1844. SAOR 89-1-889/15.

The orchard weeder for the German colonies, the German plough, and also the small crate for Aleksandria all arrived in good order by steamboat at the appropriate time. I immediately sent the last item to Aleksandria. I intended to inform you about this when they were received and I cannot understand why this did not occur. I heartily regret that I neglected this, since I am otherwise personally punctual and my numerous business affairs and frequent travels are my only excuse. I feel assured that you will not be too offended with me.

I have been experiencing much sorrow and anxiety recently because my wife was ill and the son she gave me died after three weeks.

I will send your highly interesting overview of the Molochnaia Mennonite settlements for the year 1843 to [St.] Petersburg in the Russian language so that it can be printed in the Ministry's journal, as was last year's.

I would like to help the Hutterthal people to build a schoolhouse. One thousand silver rubles is likely not a great deal for this purpose. Despite my intercession, the Ministry does not want to do anything for these people and this indifference prevents me from attempting to assist Hutterthal again. However, it is better to receive a refusal than to do nothing, in case there was a chance that something could have been achieved. For this reason, I ask you to give me your suggestions for the use of funds that could assist Hutterthal. In my opinion, the only suitable funds are those targeted for well-digging. A loan would not be in Hutterthal's interest because a loan must be paid back, and Hutterthal is already in debt.

Rest assured that I have the best of intentions, and that I expect a suggestion from you to enable me to act properly. Yours truly, E. v. Hahn. Odesa, 22 January 1844.

Received 10 February 1844. Answered 12 February 1844.

250. Abram Toews to Johann Cornies. 22 January 1844. SAOR 89-1-1094/26.

Esteemed friend,

Inspector Pelekh wrote to the District Office on 14 January that Surveyor Tushchevskii has requested the administration's decision about completing a search for salt locations in this district so that these can be added to the third section of usable land. He insists that one of our District Elders should visit him in Mikhailovka to discuss this matter and to bring him the plans.

The Guardianship Committee assigned Mr. Fedorovich to deal with this business matter, and so it is necessary that we negotiate with you beforehand. Requesting that you share your well-disposed opinions with me, your honest friend, Abram Toews.

22 January 1844. District Office in Molochnaia (corrected)

251. Johann Cornies to Fedor F. Rosen. 24 January 1844. SAOR 89-1-1088/11v.

Director Baron Rosen,

In response to your communication No. 9471 of October 1843 and also No. 11435 of 22 December 1843, from the Tavrida Bureau of State Domains, I have the honour to report that implements ordered for Kursk Guberniia will be ready by 1 March 1844. Specifically they are: one plough at 102 rubles; one harrow at twelve rubles; one roller at thirty-seven rubles; one mounder at eleven rubles; one marker at three rubles; and one lifter at one ruble, eighty kopeks. The total of 167 rubles for the master craftsman should be sent to me.

There might be a good opportunity to transport these implements to Rostov, but no earlier than August, when carters travel from this region to fetch iron. Yr. Honour might kindly make a decision about this matter.

252. Johann Cornies to Fedor F. Rosen. 24 January 1844. SAOR 89-1-1088/12.

To the same [Rosen],

In response to communication No. 9146 of 15 October 1843, and No. 11424, dated 22 December from the Tavrida Bureau of State Domains, I report that threshing stones to be given to Melitopol state peasants Tarasenko and Pristupka have been ordered and should be ready by 1 June 1844 at a price of twenty-six rubles, forty kopeks apiece. I would like to receive the total of fifty-two rubles, eighty kopeks then as well.

The stones could be transported by peasant carts ordered from Melitopol.

253. Johann Cornies to Fedor F. Rosen. 24 January 1844.
SAOR 89-1-1088/12.

To the same [Rosen],

In response to Yr. Honour's communication No. 166 of 29 March 1843, the implements ordered for Kherson Guberniia, specifically fourteen markers at three rubles each; fourteen lifters at one ruble, eighty kopeks each; six rollers at thirty-eight rubles each; for a total of 227.25 rubles, will be ready to be picked up, as will the fourteen grain rollers for Poltava Guberniia. The total sum is therefore 824 rubles that will be forwarded to the master craftsmen.

The price for the grain rollers is higher than it was on the carefully calculated estimates at prices current in 1842. It was presented to the Ministry of State Domains in 1843 at a time when wood of the required thickness could not be obtained at the earlier price from the woodyards on the Dnieper, despite all of our efforts. Few such pieces could be floated down the river because of low water levels. This is generally the reason for the fluctuation of wood prices that are subject to constant change.

254. Friedrich Prinz to Johann Cornies. 27 January 1844.
SAOR 89-1-1094/27.

Most esteemed Mr. Cornies,

I would thank you for the helpful advice you provided us in your communication of January 1844. We accept it and will act accordingly. Since you requested information about my inquiry, I enclose an accurate copy of the State Counsellor's resolution as well as a copy of a directive regarding punishment of settler Ruoff. The latter seems most remarkable. I would further inform you that our Garden Society was quite unexpectedly strengthened by a new member. This was confirmed for an indeterminate time by District Deputy Meister in Rosenfeld.

The Neuhoffnung community has asked me to write to you about a breeding stallion. Please let me know soon whether you have one, his age, and price.

Several villagers wish to return to our congregation. They went to Pastor Holtfretter to apply for testimonials but he only gave them a certificate saying that no testimonials would be drawn up until the consistory makes a decision.

Another request – in autumn last year you ordered a potato plough for me that I could not fetch because of the bad weather. Please ask the man in question to store the plough for me until better weather, when I will call for it.

With hearty greetings to you and your esteemed family, I remain your obedient servant, District Chairman Prinz.

Neuhoffnung, 27 January 1844.

255. Johann Cornies to Christian Steven. 31 January 1844. SAOR 89-1-1088/13v.

State Counsellor v. Steven,

Kindly forgive me if I burden you with a matter that might have great importance for our local agriculturalists. In newspaper No. 8, I read of a new variety of linseed in the Crimea that reputedly thrives on steppe soil. I very much doubt this. How can a seed that is twice the size of an ordinary one require only one-quarter of the seed when sown. As a rule, the amount of seed sown is judged according to the size of the kernels. Too close or too sparse seeding does not promote an abundant growth, but is more likely to be harmful.

Nevertheless, in order to find out whether it would make sense to introduce this linseed into our villages, I would ask you for your view. How promising is this linseed and does it produce good flax?

Our snow is melting quickly, rivers overflow their banks, and haymeadows are being flooded. This makes communications very difficult. This week a few heavy frosts reduced the speedy thawing. Otherwise several villages would have been severely flooded. This is no longer to be feared.

With the most exceptional esteem, I am Yr. Honour's respectful servant, Johann Cornies.

256. Johann Cornies to Traugott Blueher. 2 February 1844. SAOR 89-1-1088/15.

Mr. Blueher in Moscow,

Please forgive my delay in answering your letter of 29 September 1843. During November, December, and a considerable part of January, the burden of my many business affairs took so much of my time that I was almost at my wit's end. Which task was I to do first? On top of that I was bothered by interruptions by gentlemen from [St.] Petersburg or Odesa [wanting to know this and that]. As a result things were forgotten or became confused and I almost lost my courage. All this was accompanied by severe illness in my family. Seven weeks ago my son fell ill and is only now starting to improve and to get back on his feet.

Things, thank God, are now quieter and brighter. Thank you for reminding me to answer your letter of 29 September. I was very pleased that you had my wool sorted and washed. The price I got owes everything to your energetic efforts. I was also informed about the wool's quality, knowledge that will help me to improve my wool next time around. I plan in future to separate the wool from my two sheepfarms, Iushanle and Tashchenak, on the understanding that you will continue kindly to accept it for washing and sale.

When I learned in December that seven to eight hundred puds of wool were for sale in Berdiansk, I sought out more accurate information. It turned out to be wool from pelts [*Fellwolle*], short and extremely dirty, that sold for ten rubles, fifty kopeks. I have been unable to turn up any wool for sale. To date, the wool trade here is still very quiet. The sheep have kept very well over the winter and with warm weather and rich pasture the wool should grow without pause, evenly and long and promising of an abundant shearing.

Since carts from the yearly market in Kharkiv have not yet arrived, I have received no Bible stories. Similarly, medications you kindly bought for my wife have not yet been received.

I just reported to Mr. v. Steven about the sale of his silk by Mr. Kritsch. I was most interested in your remarks about appropriate arrangements for reeling and doubling silk at a newly invented silkmill. I think someone from our community should be sent to Moscow to learn to reel and double correctly, and to purchase a silkmill and ship it to this region. The production of silk increases much from year to year. It amounted to more than fourteen puds this year and will likely almost double in the coming year. What do you think of our silk? Please give me your advice.

The Chinese oil radish you mention is cultivated here. Pressed cold, its taste and other properties make it a suitable substitute for olive oil in foods. I do not know whether it would provide the same substitute for olive oil in factories. Our local cloth manufacturer Klaassen doubts if it would be any good.

The winter this year was warm and without snow until the New Year. So much snow fell in January that no one can remember its like. It has now thawed. Because the soil had not frozen it was well moistened. This leads me to conclude that these regions will have a fruitful summer.

Hearty thanks for your well-meaning wishes for happiness for the New Year. I am convinced that they flow from a loving and benevolent heart. Please allow me and my family to wish you much happiness in the New Year. May our ever-gracious God protect and keep you and your dear family, and grant you good health, strength, and joy. May your lives be blessed with the most enduring well-being. With greetings to you and your dear family, I remain, as always, your obligated friend and servant, Johann Cornies.

257. Johann Cornies to Peter Froese. 2 February 1844. SAOR 89-1-1088/18.

Mr. Peter Froese in Tiegerweide, West Prussia. Valued Friend,

Enclosed is a copy of a preliminary decision of the Ministry for State Domains in St. Petersburg about a settlement in Vitebsk and Mogilev Guberniias. I should point out that the estimation of an immigration stream should not, at this time, be given any particular consideration. Anything more definite will only be possible once a deputation from Prussia has been convened and has inspected the designated land. I will inform you about this matter at the appropriate time.

Commending myself to you, your respectful friend, Johann Cornies.

258. Evgenii F. Hahn to Johann Cornies. 3 February 1844. SAOR 89-1-889/14.

The Imperial Agricultural Society in Odesa supports selected trainees in various agricultural establishments who are eventually to become practical estate managers. Since your trainee program is in the Society's opinion the finest, it expressed a desire to appoint an adult trainee to your ranks. Because I seem to remember that you are reluctant to accept such trainees I offered to make friendly overtures to you before doing anything officially. Are you inclined to accept this proposal from the Imperial Society?

The Society accepted a German called Pommer among its trainees and it is this young man the Society would like to send to you for a period of three years. The Society provides three hundred rubles annually in support of its trainees.

Please inform me of your opinion, openly and candidly. Yours truly, E. v. Hahn.

Odesa, 3 February 1844.

Received 18 February 1844. Answered 8 March 1844.

259. Johann Cornies to Evgenii F. Hahn. 7 February 1844. SAOR 89-1-1088/20.

State Counsellor v. Hahn,

When Mr. Stempel, Inspector of the Mariupol settlements, was here eight days ago, he told me that the Schoenthal village community refused to allow its former Village Mayor, Johann Doerksen, to continue in office. They insist that the recently selected fullholder must be confirmed in that position.

I am however convinced that Schoenthal cannot, at this time, have a more capable Mayor than Doerksen. He honestly keeps the well-being of these poor people close to his heart. My numerous trips around the villages in that settlement show that Doerksen is, to some extent, convinced that he should adopt forceful measures to promote the speedy improvement of Schoenthal.

I feel compelled to request that if Inspector Stempel should send Yr. Excellency a presentation regarding this matter, you might graciously reply with a directive to the Mariupol Mennonite District Office forcefully informing the Schoenthal village community that it is the will of the high authorities to have them re-elect the former Village Mayor Doerksen to the same office. This is the only way to convince the high authorities that the Schoenthal Mennonites are prepared to follow their own principles of obedience [to authority].

I am convinced that this matter is not really important to most Schoenthal residents. Only a few fullholders are behind this opinion and have persuaded some of their fellows to agree with them. I think this matter could have been resolved in advance if the District Chairman had taken the matter more vigorously in hand. I think a directive from Yr. Excellency would certainly have the desired effect.

With the most complete esteem, I remain Yr. Excellency's respectful servant, Johann Cornies.

260. Johann Cornies to [Fedor F. Rosen]. 7 February 1844. SAOR 89-1-1088/21v.

His Honour, State Counsellor,

In responding to Yr. Honour's inquiry of 31 January, kindly forgive me if I say that I cannot, under any circumstances, accept the award so honestly offered to me. I know that Yr. Honour wishes to award me in this way but my response to this gracious offer is to commend myself to your further benevolence.

My continuing enjoyment of the widespread recognition and appreciation of my accomplishments is honour enough. This encourages me to further efforts, as far as I can, to assist wherever possible in our humane state which so generously blesses me and my brethren with its many benefits.

Yr. Honour's thoughtful and noble heart will kindly excuse the candour with which I express my feelings, and bless me further with your honoured benevolence.

With respectful esteem, I will constantly remain Yr. Honour's most respectful servant, Johann Cornies.

261. Johann Cornies to Carl Stempel. 7 February 1844. SAOR 89-1-1088/22.

Yr. Honour Mr. v. Stempel,

The plan for your inspector's house has finally been completed. Please forgive the long delay. I think the cost estimates will be sufficient to build the house, even though the price of wood bought at the Dnieper is estimated without transportation. Other items such as lime alabaster and similar materials required are estimated in larger quantities than will be needed. I believe that the settlers can fetch the small amount of wood needed from the Dnieper without much difficulty, while the carpentry work will be cheaper. These decisions can be made after the estimate is finally approved.

As we agreed, I just wrote to State Counsellor v. Hahn about the Schoenthal Mayor. The stupid attitude in Schoenthal will undoubtedly be broken.

I was very concerned and fearful about your journey home after the snow thawed so suddenly. A few lines about your safe return home would reassure me. You are aware of my friendship and how much I value you. I do not need to repeat this assurance.

It is my pleasure to continue to show you my unchanging sympathy as I remain Yr. Honour's respectful servant, Johann Cornies.

262. Johann Cornies to Evgenii F. Hahn. 12 February 1844. SAOR 89-1-1088/23v.

Yr. Excellency [Hahn],

Following your kind advice, which compels me to admire Yr. Excellency's noble sympathy for the poor Hutterthal people even more, I have the honour to submit the enclosed proposal to obtain the money needed for their schoolhouse. I have tried to explain my reasons for this request. Yr. Excellency's enlightened insight might now be employed in carrying this matter forward as you find best.

Communications from the Third Department have informed me that no tax-free years will be granted the Hutterthal people. I will accordingly ensure that the payment is made this month without delay.

I offer Yr. Excellency my deepest sympathy on the sorrow in Yr. most valued family that you have had to overcome. May our dear God grant you His rich blessing now and forevermore.

Especially commending myself to your further benevolence with respect and esteem, I have the honour to remain Yr. Excellency's most respectful servant, Johann Cornies.

263. Johann Cornies to Christian Steven. 14 February 1844. SAOR 89-1-1088/24v.

Inspector for Agriculture, State Counsellor v. Steven,

In response to Yr. Honour's communication No. 45 of 13 January 1844, I can report that I have found five of the most exceptional fullholders in this district who are willing to accept apprentices and to teach them practical agriculture. The terms will be the same as they were for similar apprentices accepted earlier. By name, they are the Mennonites Peter Cornies in Ohrloff and Johann Sukkau in Blumenort, who will each take another apprentice in addition to those they already have. They have enough work on hand to occupy them adequately. The others are the Mennonites Isaac Wiens in Altonau, and Jacob and Peter Neumann in Muensterberg.

In notifying Yr. Honour about this matter, I humbly request that you have more copies of the German translation of the terms sent to me, since I have only one copy left. I will then return them to you, with the signatures of the above-mentioned fullholders. These five Mennonites request mentally capable apprentices with healthy, strong bodies and good characters. This I humbly request as well. Would you please take measures to move this matter along in order that the apprentices might take part in all agricultural operations starting in spring.

264. Evgenii F. Hahn to Johann Cornies. 17 February 1844. SAOR 89-1-889/18.

I regret that I cannot carry out your wishes in retaining Schoenthal Village Mayor Doerksen in office because Mr. Stempel recommended the newly elected Heinrich Bergen as a good proprietor, although he has doubts about his abilities. I ordered Mr. v. Stempel to appoint Bergen. If the improvements that have been introduced stall and it is revealed that he is at fault, submissions must be made immediately requesting Bergen's removal.

At the present time, several circumstances make it necessary for me to follow the letter of the law as much as possible. The law says that whichever good proprietor receives the most votes must be confirmed in office. I do not doubt that Doerksen is better than Bergen, but the latter's lack of ability must first be proven. The Inspector also has the right to put the new Mayor under his supervision and give Doerksen directives as before. I ask you to do this as well. I express the hope that you will again accompany me on my inspection tour this year. Also, please indicate to me at what time I should come? Yours truly, E. v. Hahn.

Odesa, 17 February 1844. Received 1 March 1844; answered 20 March.

265. Johann Cornies to Aleksandrov Model Establishment. 26 February 1844. SAOR 89-1-1088/27.

To the Aleksandrov Model Crown Establishment,

I have the honour to notify you that the Guardianship Committee for Foreign Settlers in Southern Russia in Odesa sent me 135 rubles for the German plough provided for the Aleksandrov Model Crown Establishment. According to the accounts submitted, one ruble, sixty-four kopeks is still owing.

266. Johann Cornies to Christian Steven. 28 February 1844. SAOR 89-1-1088/29.

Inspector for Agriculture v. Steven,

In communication No. 462 of 28 June 1843, from the forestry department, I was asked to accept several peasant youths to learn the raising of forest trees on the steppe for a limited time period of two years at the most. I responded on 10 August 1843 stating my honest opinion that a minimum period of four years was needed for such an apprenticeship. Only very few apprentices with quite exceptional capabilities would be competent to leave my establishment within three years.

The offer in question was urgently renewed by the forestry department and a monetary compensation [for the program] proposed if the apprentices could be taught sufficiently in two years' time. I countered this offer decisively by saying that I could not possibly turn peasant lads into useful subjects, effective for this purpose, in less than four years. A monetary remuneration would not change this. A longer apprenticeship was needed to enable apprentices to acquire specific, logical concepts of every aspect of forest-tree cultivation.

I heard nothing further about this proposition and thought the matter had been laid to rest. A few days ago, however, authorities in Ekaterinoslav Guberniia sent me four apprentices for the purpose mentioned above. I do not know under what conditions they have come, but dare humbly to request that Yr. Honour make inquiries in the appropriate places and kindly inform me of this matter as soon as possible.

267. Johann Cornies to Fedor F. Rosen. 28 February 1844. SAOR 89-1-1088/30v.

Director Baron v. Rosen,

I have received no specific, detailed information about potato planting, although the time to begin preparations is fast approaching. It is urgently necessary to organize the stored seed and to assign the selected desiatinas for potato planting to prevent the peasants from ploughing and seeding the best and most conveniently situated land for themselves. Also, the extent and specific names of workers involved in the expansion of potato planting in the Dneprov District must soon be decided. If, as Yr. Honour suggested during your last visit, a Mennonite should again be the main supervisor for potato planting in the Dneprov District, I would recommend last year's supervisor, Peter Ediger from Lindenau village, for the job at the same salary of two hundred silver rubles. I am also prepared to assume responsibility for a wider area myself.

To make general arrangements for this year's potato planting, it will be necessary for Yr. Honour to make an early decision as to whether Ediger should again be hired as supervisor. This would enable Ediger to make specific arrangements on site.

268. Johann Cornies to Andrei M. Fadeev. 28 February 1844.
SAOR 89-1-1088/31v.

Mr. Fadeev,

My delay in answering your valued and esteemed letters of 20 March 1843 and 23 September 1843 is not excusable. I feel chagrined at my negligence and seek redemption in this apology. With happy assurance, I am able to hope that Yr. Excellency's noble heart will forgive me.

I hasten to send Yr. Excellency the enclosed copy of the rules and methods for the founding of new settlements now in force:

1. the rules established by the Society, and confirmed by the Chief Curator;

2. an extract [from the rules] about the size of property deemed sufficient to permit families to settle;

3. a form for an undertaking of obligation to be signed by guarantors responsible for the settler's property;

4. a sketch of a yard, and how it is to be divided for a family;

5. a sketch of a second type of yard; and

6. a report about the initial founding of a village settled by Mennonites who had moved from Radishchev, in Chernigov Guberniia, in 1843. Founded on area No. 15, at the Tashchenak, it is called Hutterthal.

Should it be necessary to add further, more detailed information and explanations, I am ready to discuss these in more detail, to the extent that this is possible, as soon as Yr. Excellency asks for them. I believe that the second drawing according to which the Radishchev Mennonites are building Hutterthal village, could also be useful for the Saratov settlements.

Everything is progressing quickly here in our villages, as you will kindly notice from the annual report about the Molochnaia Mennonite District for 1843, that will be printed in the Ministry of State Domains journal.

The burden of my affairs bears down on me and I long for a respite. Should it be possible to tear myself away this coming summer, I plan to seek recuperation in the Volga regions and to return, refreshed and strengthened in body and spirit to again assume and carry on my daily work.

After so long a time, I have a great desire to see you personally, my honoured Sir, and to attend upon you. There is nothing further to add here except to express the hope that your kind disposition towards me might endure.

I am aware how much I owe you and I daily renew my intention to remain, with great and unfeigned esteem, Yr. Excellency's respectful servant, Johann Cornies.

269. Abram Wiebe to Johann Cornies. 1 March 1844. SAOR 89-1-1094/41.

Mr. Johann Cornies in Ohrloff. Treasured Friend,

With this messenger I send you eight thousand rubles to reduce my debt. Please put it on my account. I have not yet found it possible to repay you all that I owe, but I hope to visit you soon and repay more of this amount and also the remainder I have owed you for a long time.

Our foreign wool business turned out to my satisfaction and I intend to continue enlarging it somewhat this year. This coming summer we hope to send a shipment of wool directly from Berdiansk and to this end plan to take wool on consignment. Wool cannot be the only freight loaded onto a ship, however, and heavier commodities must be loaded below. For this purpose I will need credit again for some time. I would ask that you count on doing this for me, if possible. It would be in the second half of May and in the sum of fifteen to twenty thousand rubles for three, at the most four months.

When I visit you I will have other topics to discuss with you, including our wool business.

With heartiest greetings to you and your family, I remain your friend, Abram Wiebe.

Rudnerweide, [1] March 1844.

270. Traugott Blueher to Johann Cornies. 1 March 1844. SAOR 89-1-1094/44.

Mr. Johann Cornies, Ohrloff village. Highly treasured friend,

Your communication of 2 January made me deeply aware of the distressing situation you have been experiencing. Your further letters suggested that the worst has been overcome. Please give our warmest greetings to both of your dear children. We frequently remember them with great love.

I trust that you have received the medications I sent you. I added them to a case for Mr. Tobias Geyer, fearing that the small package might otherwise have been lost.

I will try to get information about the two manufactured materials. Since this business is still undeveloped here, it would not be advisable to take further steps at this time. Your facility will surely have made progress in the meantime. Since the money has already been invested, it should not be abandoned now.

The payment for wool sold on consignment is due next month. Since there is considerable advantage in remitting larger amounts, I will probably delay sending this money until I can send the whole amount.

Locally, most branches of business are depressed, principally because of large failures of credit within the merchant class. Where today can one find even a little honesty?

The time to think about this year's wool business is approaching. Please arrange to buy for me a thousand puds of clean, strongly grown, and well-washed Spanish wool. Ensure that as much of this wool as possible is bought from larger sheepfarms. My highest price for medium quality wool is up to twenty-three rubles per pud, relatively more for fine wool, and less for coarser wool. I know I can count on you to keep me abreast of things and to work in my interests. I am not ready to set a higher price at this time. To be frank, I hope that this purchase can be made at last year's price, since prospects for wool are certainly not encouraging.

I send you and your dear family greetings of honest friendship, and remain constantly your devoted, Traugott Blueher.

Moscow, 1 March 1844. Received 21 March 1844.

271. Friedrich Prinz to Johann Cornies. 6 March 1844. SAOR 89-1-1094/31.

Highly esteemed Mr. Cornies,

I gladly respond to your thoughtful communication, knowing that you are willing to take me under your wing. I am grateful for your love and will do what I can to accommodate your every wish as well as the wishes of the General. I await the decision about an increase in my salary, having specified an extra 150 rubles that would raise my total income to 100 silver rubles. I included a report explaining my reasons for requesting such an increase. Who knows whether it will be approved.

With hearty greetings to you and your esteemed family, I remain, with respect, your most humble servant, District Chairman Prinz. 6 March 1844.

272. Johann Cornies to Evgenii F. Hahn. 8 March 1844.
SAOR 89-1-1088/38.

State Counsellor v. Hahn,

Honoured as I am by the proposal of the Imperial Agricultural Society, I must explain that my establishment is not organized to provide a trainee the education desired by the Imperial Society. The level of agricultural cultivation in my establishment is barely a degree higher than among other agriculturalists in our local villages. It could hardly achieve what is desired in this case. Moreover, I do not have the time to realize this proposal because of the many projects demanding my attention. I must, in any case, remain true to my principles and not undertake anything that I might not be able to finish.

I am so bold as to submit this matter to Yr. Excellency's inquiry of 3 February 1844, with the sincere assurance that I will never cease to be, with constant esteem and devotion, Yr. Excellency's most respectful servant, Johann Cornies.

273. Andrei M. Fadeev to Johann Cornies. 12 March 1844.
SAOR 89-1-661/16.

You have forgotten me entirely, my dear, beloved Cornies! I have not received a single line from you for almost a year. That troubles me, especially when I know how punctual you really are. Are you well? Please write to me again since I take an interest in everything concerning you and your good brethren.

Your respectful A. Fadeev.

N.B. I had just finished writing this letter when I received yours of 27 February. What a relief. Please keep your word and come to Saratov this summer. I should be home except for a few small trips.

Saratov, 12 March 1844.

274. Friedrich A. Meinecke to Johann Cornies. 15 March 1844.
SAOR 89-1-1094/63.

Esteemed Mr. Cornies,

Although I have not heard from you personally, I feel a desire to send you my greetings. A local agriculturalist who knows about the Chinese turnip seed grown in your area from the *Handelszeitung* (Commercial newspaper), would like to plant it here this summer. Could you send him a *chetverik* or more of seeds? Because transporting it is difficult, he suggested you send him a small amount by mail. I will repay your expenses.

I thought you might be interested to know that I was married last fall. Your daughter, during her stay in Sarepta, got to know my present wife under the name Maria Vogel, a single sister. She sends her greetings.

With warm greetings to you and your family, I remain, respectfully, your devoted Friedrich A. Meinecke.

P.S. Please send me directions for cultivating the turnip seed, and preparing its oil. Will we really have the pleasure of seeing you here this summer? The above.

Sarepta, 15 March 1844. Answered in July.

275. Johann Cornies to Christian Steven. 18 March 1844.
SAOR 89-1-1088/41v.

State Counsellor v. Steven,

I have the honour to reply to Yr. Honour's esteemed letter No. 60 of 18 January 1844. A report from Mr. Abramovich to the Mariupul Mennonite District Chairman reports that the Armenians keep many foreign goats on leased crown land some forty verstas from the Bergthal settlement, Aleksandrov District. Abramovich's people do not know these goats, only that they had been sent across the sea and were fetched from Tiflis by Abramovich. The District Chairman has not personally seen them. They are now kept on Armenian land beyond Taganrog on the Zambek and had been driven there by an outbreak of disease. Some 250 out of 400 head have fallen.

The District Chairman does not know their name, only that the goats are spoken of as "crown goats." Mr. Abramovich has undertaken to provide the crown with five hundred goats in ten years' time. No one seems to know what their hair sells for. Some people had heard of one sort that was sold in Moscow to the crown at sixty rubles per pud, the best at one hundred and twenty rubles. The goats are said to produce two funt of hair per head. It is used to make cashmere. The enclosed sample is from a kid said to have been bred by a pure-bred ram and a common goat.

A certain Mr. Sherbakov is said to own a number of such goats on the steppe river Ilangtshik, twenty-five verstas beyond Kalmius, in the Don Cossack area. The District Chairman was unable to provide more detailed information.

With the most exceptional esteem, I remain Yr. Honour's respectful servant, Johann Cornies.

276. Johann Cornies to Christian Steven. 18 March 1844. SAOR 89-1-1088/43.

Mr. v. Steven,

I am honoured to enclose the signed conditions for the acceptance of five crown peasant apprentices to learn practical agriculture. These come from four fullholders in Mennonite District villages: Peter Cornies, Ohrloff; Isaac Wiens, Altonau; Jacob and Peter Neumann, Muensterberg; and Johann Sukkau, Blumenort. I humbly submit the signed originals so that arrangements can be made, as requested in my Report No. 23 of 14 February 1844.

277. Johann Cornies to Evgenii F. Hahn. 18 March 1844. SAOR 89-1-1088/43v.

Mr. Hahn in Odesa. Yr. Excellency,

A directive from the Guardianship Committee to the Molochnaia Mennonite District Office dated 19 October 1843 is in answer to representations made regarding the acceptance of new immigrants. It draws attention to special, legally established rules on this subject. I would ask what the situation might be for immigrants who manage their own establishments in Prussia and might equally, because of their proven qualifications, be of great use to new settlements in Russia. At present, eight such persons in the district have passed a two-year trial period with flying colours. They would like to remain in Russia permanently and can secure the needed acceptance from the village communities in which they live.

Professionals such as painters and others are not specified in the law. Coming from important cities, they are much needed because of their brisk involvement in the trades that increase rapidly in our flourishing villages. Whatever we need can be produced in our villages, to the advantage of professional tradesmen and agriculturalists. I would humbly ask you to let me know if there is any possibility of settling these useful Prussian Mennonite tradesmen and professionals in the Molochnaia Mennonite District?

Might Yr. Excellency kindly forgive my boldness in approaching you in this way. Convinced of your humane kindness, I remain Yr. Excellency's constant and obedient servant, Johann Cornies.

278. Johann Cornies to Evgenii F. Hahn. 18 March 1844.
SAOR 89-1-1088/45.

Mr. v. Hahn in Odesa. Yr. Excellency,

I am deeply honoured to be asked to accompany Yr. Excellency on your annual inspection tour of our settlements. I take the liberty, esteemed State Counsellor, to let you know that June would be the best time for such a tour. Many agricultural tasks would be done by then and open for inspection.

If you find this time suitable, I will expect to see you on my Tash-chenak estate on 5 June. I am ready and willing to be at your disposal.

With deep esteem and humility, I remain Yr. Excellency's most obedient servant, Johann Cornies.

279. Evgenii F. Hahn to Johann Cornies. 26 March 1844.
SAOR 89-1-889/19.

I respond to your inquiry regarding the acceptance of new immigrants [from Prussia]. Let me explain that the Ministry recently said that it would make no exceptions to the rule that only settlers conforming to the regulations would be accepted. This means blood relatives and craftsmen named in point 128 of part XII of the Codex. For this reason we drew those regulations in question to the attention of the District Office. I grant that in a presentation made last year I pointed out that such limitations would not be applied to Mennonites deemed important by the crown after a proper investigation. Since I have not yet received an answer to this statement, I am unsure if my opinion on this matter has been accepted.

It would in any case be better if only relatives were presented for acceptance. This should not be difficult for Mennonites since so many of them are related. Once an exception is confirmed by the Minister, further action can be taken. As you know, transfers from one settlement to another depend on us. Everyone must seek acceptance where he has relatives. Once accepted, he can transfer to where he would like to settle. Yours truly, E. v. Hahn.

Odesa, 26 March 1844. Received 23 April 1844.

280. J. Martens to Johann Cornies. 28 March 1844.
SAOR 89-1-1094/69.

To the Society Chairman J. Cornies in Ohrloff,

It is said that Abraham Enns was required to come back from Gerlitzke without delay, presumably at the instigation of Elder Heinrich Wiens, who now alleges that Abraham Enns was excluded from his congregation more than a year ago. This does not agree with past reports that Enns simply did not wish to attend church.

It is remarkable that Wiens is making this claim only now, presumably after he had to admit the real reason once the District Office insisted on him doing so. Should this be the case, why were the congregation and Enns not so informed earlier?

What about the reason for Enns's removal? Does the Elder really believe that it has been forgotten? The Society and the District Office are not the only parties who know why it occurred. Knowledge of it is worldwide. It happened only because Enns gave the Society, at its request, a written report in 1842 about an unjust action by Elder Heinrich Wiens involving the Margenau brotherhood. Is it contrary to scripture, or forbidden, to make declarations about unjust dealings by an Elder? Is there a commandment that an Elder shall be free of blame, etc.?

What are the facts of this case? Was the Elder blameless? My answer is that rebellion was involved. Unknown to the Society, the Elder's intended purpose was to work in opposition to local authorities and to the intent of the administration. Why must Abraham Enns be abused and disgraced for reporting this matter? In such a case not only Enns but the Society as well are guilty. The Society should not allow this matter to continue since the Society and every right-thinking person recognized his report to be valid. Why is it invalid now?

I fail to understand this matter. Either the Society or the Elder have been struck blind. For my part, I would like to be informed about this matter, or see that Abraham Enns is vindicated.

Above all else, I request that Abraham Enns not be forced to come here now. He is absolutely indispensable on the Gerlitzke estate owned by my father, Wilhelm Martens. I request that he be given a pass at least until September. Please negotiate this with the District Office, because it is said that the Office ordered Enns to come back or will soon do so.

I must also inform you that once Enns returns to the Molochnaia, which will definitely happen in September, he will look for a different congregation. J. Martens.

Tiegenhagen, 28 March 1844.

[Note in secretary hand:] Disregarded entirely.

281. Johann Cornies to Traugott Blueher. 1 April 1844.
SAOR 89-1-1088/50.

Esteemed Mr. Blueher,

I made an advance payment today of twenty-four rubles to a local sheepfarm owner for about five hundred puds of wool still on the sheep. His wool is eagerly purchased by buyers each year. This price exceeds your maximum price by one ruble. I do not believe this to be a risky deal since the quantity is large. On the contrary, I hope to have advanced your interests in this case since the wool is not of high quality but long and of a good average grade, on well-nourished and cleanly kept sheep.

Given this purchase I would ask you to remit ten to twelve thousand rubles in connection with this deal. This would enable me to make further purchases of wool in plenty of time. At present, I am unable to make a large outlay from my own accounts.

Commending myself to your valued and continuing friendship, I remain your friend and servant, Johann Cornies.

282. Johann Cornies to Fedor F. Rosen. 3 April 1844.
SAOR 89-1-1088/51v.[2]

Baron v. Rosen,

I write in response to your esteemed communication No. 189 of 3 March 1844 that deals with the possibility of me establishing a model tree plantation and accepting several peasant apprentices to learn practical forest-tree cultivation on it. I am still in doubt about this matter myself and can reach no firm conclusion. I would humbly request an opportunity to discuss this matter with Yr. Honour personally. Would adequate resources be made available to me to establish this proposed model plantation on a solid foundation that would answer to the high Ministry's expectations and involve the acceptance of peasant apprentices for an adequate education in this field? Such a conference would put me in a position to give a formal response to Yr. Honour's important proposal.

---

2   This is the first reference to a proposed Berdiansk model forestry plantation. The project is described in detail in Staples, *Johann Cornies*, 219–20, and John R. Staples, "Iogann Kornis i osnovanie Berdianskogo Lesnichestvo," *Voprosy Germanskoi Istorii* (2017): 18–21.

Should you, Honoured Baron, grant me this humble request, I would expect your honoured visit sometime this month. Its primary purpose would be personally to confer with you on the matters mentioned above.

Most urgently commending myself to your blessed benevolence, I remain, with esteem, Yr. Honour's most respectful servant, Johann Cornies.

283. Cornelius Eytzen to Johann Cornies. 6 April 1844. SAOR 89-1-1094/78.

To the Chairman of the Molochnaia Mennonite Society, Johann Cornies in Ohrloff, (Settlement of account)

Most valued Chairman,

It was requested that I come to see you. Please do not be offended when I tell you that this is impossible at the present time. I am down with a fever and otherwise sickly. I want nevertheless to report to you on how things stand with my accounts and how much has been paid to me. On 1 December, the first Nogai paid me sixty rubles; on 2 December four Nogais paid me 320 rubles; on 14 March three Nogais paid me 116 rubles; on 16 February, one Nogai made a second payment of thirty-one rubles, forty kopeks and a third payment on 22 March of forty-four rubles, eighty-eight kopeks. I received everything in banco, without interest, which they promised to pay properly. I came to an agreement with each Nogai about the amount of money still owing and gave a dated receipt for the amounts settled. The receipts show how much each still owes.

I very much request that you, most valued Chairman, urge the Nogais to pay me the remainder immediately, since I am not a man who can sell the excess from his wool business. I sold all my goods and chattels to build a mill to earn my living. I bought the wood in July for eight hundred rubles in cash. The millstones are waiting in Alexander. They cost 260 rubles or 250 rubles if I pay cash. I have already paid fifty rubles and I borrowed the rest. I have paid fifty rubles for stones to build the house. The carpenters were also contracted last year, and they received a hundred rubles in advance. None of this construction was done since my debts prevented me from having the wood transported. However, interest charges continue.

For this reason, I again request that you, most valued Chairman, might take this into consideration and allow me to obtain what is mine, according to the receipts. Money in small quantities will not help me.

I sign myself as your most dutiful servant, Cornelius v. Eytzen. Orekhov, 6 April 1844. Answered 18 April 1844.

284. Contract between Ohrloff village and Johann Cornies. 20 April 1844. SAOR 89-1-872/6.

In accordance with the verified map, the Ohrloff village community hands over to the local inhabitant, Johann Cornies, for his temporal use, two cottage plots on either side of the church, which are designated as "D" and "G" on the map. The area of the first is 2,348 square sazhen and of the latter one desiatina, 1,021 square sazhen. These plots are at present enclosed by ditches and fences. The purchase price is 171 silver rubles, forty-two kopeks, which was correctly paid at the conclusion of this contract. The purchaser, Johann Cornies, is further bound by an obligation to pay an annual ground tax of [blank] for both plots to the benefit of the village community.

In testimony thereof, signatures were given by the Ohrloff Village Office representing the village community, with impression of the village seal, and by the purchaser.

285. Traugott Blueher to Johann Cornies. 21 April 1844. SAOR 89-1-1094/99.

Mr. Johann Cornies. My sincerely beloved friend,

Honest, loving friends sincerely take an interest in the sufferings and afflictions we all encounter from time to time. I therefore turn to you, my good old friend, in a matter of great importance for us as parents. Might you be willing to find a position for my son Joseph in your own office, or elsewhere for good, upright people? He needs to be occupied full-time. Tedium cannot lead to anything good, especially for youth.

His writing is really excellent, as you can see from the accounts you receive from me. His Russian is perfect and his drawing is not unskilled. I make absolutely no demands with respect to salary. He might be paid enough to cover his needs, but should that be impossible, I would support him myself.

Should I one day appear before God's throne with concerns about his best interests, I must get him away from here. He is far too inclined towards youthful society. I need to put him in a place so isolated that he will be totally cut off from such company. I would naturally send him off to Sarepta if there were any prospects of that helping.

I would ask you to interest yourself in this matter. Send me if you can with the next mail, information about prospects for my son so that I might do what I can.

I remit to you with today's mail, and under the crown's seal, 3,500 silver rubles for the wool business.

In sending you and your dear family sincere and hearty greetings, I remain the friend you know, Traugott Blueher.

P.S. I also wrote to Switzerland about a position for Joseph, but it is probably best for now to accommodate him here in Russia, naturally in accordance with my wishes. There may be other ways of meeting his needs, but I must keep the future in mind more than the present.

Moscow, 21 April 1844. Received 13 May 1844, answered 22 May 1844.

286. Johann Cornies to Fedor F. Rosen. 26 April 1844.
SAOR 89-1-1088/64v.

Director Baron v. Rosen

In accordance with Yr. Honour's communication No. 292 of 29 March 1844, I can report that it would likely take 4,800 fired bricks and 4,600 Dutch roof tiles to complete the warehouse building projected for the city of Melitopol. It will be about eight sazhen long, four sazhen wide, and have a two-level foundation.

One thousand bricks are priced at twenty-five rubles and one thousand tiles at sixty rubles. Since I am still unable to determine my own requirements of bricks and tiles, I will not be able to provide them from Tashchenak. At these prices, bricks will be available in Altonau and tiles in Ohrloff.

I should point out that if the decision is made to build the warehouse of wood, it would still need a fired brick foundation. One thousand bricks would be needed for this purpose.

287. Gerhard Dyck to Johann Cornies. 27 April 1844.
SAOR 89-1-1094/104.

Esteemed and beloved friend,

My brother-in-law, H. Harder of Gnadenfeld, just passed on the contract for the construction of a furrow scraper according to the drawing I made. I immediately made a copy, signed my name to it, and placed it in a sealed envelope to prevent its being soiled by strangers' hands and pockets. When he was summoned to see you in Ohrloff, I gave it to my neighbour, treadmill owner B. Regier, to return to you. This, if I understood you correctly, was what you required.

As for the drawing I prepared and sent along, I must ask to be excused in two respects, first because I was in a hurry and secondly because I could not find better paper. The paper was loose and fibrous and tended to become quite woolly when rubbing out pencil marks. Moreover, I could not send along the accompanying description because that would have involved much time and you wanted the drawing as quickly as possible. When I started to prepare the drawing for transport the dispatch rider already stood beside me with his marching orders. I hope it will reach you in good shape.

Hoping for your continuing goodwill, I dutifully sign myself, with a friendly greeting, G. Dyck.

Rudnerweide, 27 April 1844.

N.B. Silkworm eggs were sent to me by Brother G. Ensz in Altonau but there was nothing else.

288. Agricultural Society to Village Offices. N.d. [Probably May 1844.] SAOR 89-1-872/15.

[Undated draft:] To Village Offices,

Once this is received, all Village Mayors must establish whether any fullholders and cottagers need to repaint their fences and buildings. In the past each village had a number of residents who had done the work superficially. They must be identified in the above-mentioned investigation and directed to do the required repainting by 25 May 1844, at the latest. The main concern is not beautification but preservation of the wood. Village Offices must give this matter greater attention and promptly report to the Society whether everything has been painted properly by 25 May.

289. Johann Cornies to Traugott Blueher. 8 May 1844. SAOR 89-1-1088/70.

Esteemed Mr. Blueher,

I have received 4,400 silver rubles and the accounts and enclose a receipt to conclude last year's wool business. What remains is to thank you warmly for the efforts you have made on my behalf. I would, at the same time, ask you to again assume responsibility for selling this year's wool on consignment.

Believing that you have not received my communication of 1 April 1844, I include a copy of it with this letter and request a response to the question it asks.

I have not yet received the medications, but I expect them at any time. Your valued communications of 1 and 31 March and 10 April were correctly received.

While sending you and your dear family best greetings, I commend myself further to your friendship, your respectful Johann Cornies.

I would request one funt of red fir (*pinus abies*) seeds and one funt of spruce (*pinus silvestis*) seeds. Send them to me by mail.

290. Johann Cornies to Fedor F. Rosen. 16 May 1844.
SAOR 89-1-1088/74v.

Director Baron v. Rosen,

Enclosed, I have the honour of respectfully sending Yr. Honour the records of potatoes seeded this spring in sixty-nine village communities in the Berdiansk, Melitopol, and Dneprov Districts. It must be noted that the difference in the quantity of potatoes seeded has to do with the varying sizes of potatoes. Fewer large potatoes make up a chetvert than small ones.

According to report No. 222 of 2 December 1843, 4,115 individual so-called ministerial potatoes were stored at four village communities. I had the supervisor divide them among good agriculturalists in all village communities in the older region of Melitopol District on the condition that each individual must return the same number of individual potatoes he had received for setting in fall. He could keep the rest.

291. District Office to Johann Cornies. 17 May 1844.
SAOR 89-1-1094/144.

To the leaseholder of unsettled crown lands in the Molochnaia Mennonite District, esteemed Johann Cornies in Ohrloff,

Under No. 2453, dated 8 April, the Guardianship Committee for Foreign Settlers has informed the District Office that His Excellency, the Minister of State Domains, has made the following decision with respect to the 260 desiatinas of land to be used by Mennonite David Reimer for his own establishment. Because the crown land on which Reimer built his Felstenthal estate is intended for the settlement of a growing number of Mennonite families, he will only be permitted the use of land now occupied by his establishment. The rest of the land now under his use cannot be used any further except for the payment of rental fee until such a time as the land is needed for settlement. The Guardianship Committee therefore orders that the above 260 desiatinas of land be fenced off for Reimer's use, that a rental fee be collected from him, and that arrangements in this regard be made with you.

To implement this decision, the above-mentioned 260 desiatinas should be fenced off for the use of the Mennonite, David Reimer, and a rental fee of four kopeks, silver, per desiatina should be collected beginning 1 January 1843. You are hereby informed of this decision.

Molochnaia Mennonite District Office in Halbstadt.

District Chairman Toews; District Secretary Peter Reimer.

No. 2404. 17 May 1844.

292. Evgenii F. Hahn to Johann Cornies. 20 May 1844.
SAOR 89-1-889/22.

In keeping with your invitation, I plan to arrive in Tashchenak on 4 or 5 June, when we will discuss the village inspections. Expecting to see you soon, Yours truly, E. v. Hahn.

Odesa, 20 May 1844

Kindly inform Messrs. Stempel and Pelekh, as well as the Molochnaia Mennonite and the Berdiansk District Offices. It is not necessary for Mr. Pelekh to meet me, but he should expect me in Prishib.

[Note added to above address label:] Teetotalism – abstention from all fermented beverages. Teetotalitarian Society.

293. Johann Cornies to Traugott Blueher. 22 May 1844.
SAOR 89-1-1088/75.

Esteemed Mr. Blueher,

To begin, I notify you of the correct receipt of 3,500 silver rubles on account for your wool business.

With respect to the transportation of this year's wool, which you would like to have done with ox carts, I must honestly say that I am always wary of entrusting wool to the Chumaks [carters], although the costs might well be markedly lower (specifically about 175 kopeks banco per pud, as Mr. Forchhammer has written to me). The wool is not really safe with these people. They are often slipshod in its handling. After your last letter, I hired the carters for three rubles per pud.

I have received the medications for my wife from Halle in good condition. Thank you, dear friend, for your sympathy and good management.

I will do everything I can for your dear son whom you have kindly entrusted to my care. In fact, this would give me great pleasure. Please, from the bottom of my heart, allow me, at least in part, to repay you for what you have done unassumingly, and in so many ways for me and particularly for the well-being of my dear children.

I think that putting him to work in my office is not a good idea. It would virtually imprison him. This might not bring about the purpose we desire for a young person who has been brought up in a noisy and populous city. It is therefore my opinion that it would be better to put him into a business. I have found such a position for him with the Mennonite merchant, Isaac Mathias, in Rudnerweide village. He has a retail shop and also does considerable business with butter, wool, and wood. He would be able to employ your son in addition to the two young Mennonites already working for him. This would be a suitable position for him within a righteous and active family that nurtures honest sympathy and Christian teaching. Their way of life is simple and rural, as behoves all Mennonites. Feel free to send your son to us at your convenience. He will find a warm welcome here. There is no need to decide on his exact remuneration as yet. It is a matter that we can be in touch about later on.

294. Johann Cornies to Forchhammer. 22 May 1844. SAOR 89-1-1088/77.

Esteemed Mr. Forchhammer,

I write in reply to your communication of 5 May to let you know that it will not be necessary to hire ox carts in Kharkiv for the transport of approximately two thousand [2m] puds of wool from the Molochnaia District to Mr. Blueher in Moscow. I had already hired carters for this purpose before your letter arrived and have informed Mr. Blueher accordingly with today's mail. Commending myself to your valued good-will, I am with esteem Yr. respectful servant, Johann Cornies.

295. Johann Cornies to Fedor F. Rosen. 29 May 1844. SAOR 89-1-1088/79v.

Baron v. Rosen,

In response to communication No. 228 of 9 May 1844, I am pleased to report that master tradesmen will charge one hundred silver rubles for an accurately constructed model of the locally used, horse-driven threshing machine. This is one hundred rubles banco more than what I mentioned in my report No. 51 of 8 October 1841. At that time, parts of the model intended to represent iron were to have been painted black. The present estimates are really for better construction. If a decision were to be made by next month, the machine would be ready by this coming October.

Our master tradesmen would not like to have the model sent by mail as they fear that its various parts might well be jolted out of their proper positions.

A complete horse-driven threshing machine can be built here for eight hundred to one thousand rubles. Our tradesmen will not, however, undertake to transport it to Stavropol. It is also not possible to know beforehand what such transportation would cost.

296. Evgenii F. Hahn to Johann Cornies. 1 June 1844.
SAOR 89-1-889/23.

Unexpected business forces me to postpone my departure to the Molochnaia villages and I cannot say when I will be able to come, although the sooner, the better! I very much regret that you have had to wait for me in vain, but our time does not belong to us alone. It is often necessary to sacrifice something pleasant to what is necessary.

Hoping to see you soon, yours truly, E. v. Hahn.

Odesa, 1 June 1844.

297. Johann Cornies to Fedor F. Rosen. June 1844.
SAOR 89-1-1088/80v.

Baron v. Rosen,

I waited in vain for the arrival of State Counsellor v. Hahn, although I had been notified in writing from Odesa three days ago that he planned to arrive in Tashchenak on 4 or 5 June. Something important must have happened for Mr. v. Hahn would otherwise have arrived at the set time.

If Mr. v. Hahn were to arrive here today or tomorrow, I would notify you immediately by special messenger. Please let me know the address to which I should address the message if you can no longer be reached in Melitopol. It would really be regrettable if Mr. v. Hahn were not able to speak to you here.

With constant esteem and honest devotion, I remain, as always, Yr. Honour's respectful servant, Johann Cornies.

298. Johann Cornies to Carl Stempel. 11 June 1844. SAOR 89-1-1088/81.

Most esteemed Mr. Inspector v. Stempel,

For eight days I waited fruitlessly in Tashchenak for the General's arrival and finally decided to return to Ohrloff. There I found His Excellency's letter notifying me that unanticipated business had forced him to postpone his departure for the Molochnaia and made it impossible for him to decide on a later visit. He also states that it would obviously be best if he could come soon. He will, in any case, notify you well before his arrival.

I think you should free your mind of worries about the matter. Once I hear more, I will let you know.

I think you are quite wrong in thinking that the words you spoke about the emigration to Georgia of several of the worst settlers displeased the State Counsellor. Doing what you did is surely politically wise and within the stiff rules of the law. As I know the General, he could not encourage such recruiting, but under other circumstances he would cooperate with all his power.

In my view, you can ease your mind completely. I know only too well that the State Counsellor lets no opportunity pass without acknowledging the value of your many efforts. I think that his late arrival had nothing to do with this. He remains your utterly dependable patron.

I presume that Acting State Counsellor Kaloshin will inspect the villages only superficially. His main purpose is to deal with the crown peasants. The Guardianship Committee is not devoting much attention to him and special preparations in the villages will not be necessary.

I am very pleased that Doerksen finally came to his senses and again accepted office. This will make it much easier to improve the Schoenthal settlement and your efforts will not go unrewarded.

Because I have been away from Iushanle, I do not know if the stallion colt you wrote about was delivered there.

Most heartily commending myself to your friendly understanding, I remain your most honest Johann Cornies.

299. Johann Cornies to Fedor F. Rosen. 15 June 1844.
SAOR 89-1-1088/83.

Director Baron v. Rosen,

In reply to Yr. Honour's inquiry No. 189 of 3 March 1844 about the acceptance of several crown apprentices to learn forest-tree cultivation, I make the following report. As things are at present, I can only accept six such apprentices at the beginning. The terms would be the same as those relating to crown apprentices in practical agriculture presently under my direction. I would repeat that the apprentices should be at least seventeen years of age, of good behaviour, physically strong, and armed with the intellectual abilities needed to produce useful subjects, as the government wishes.

300. Johann Cornies to Traugott Blueher. 15 June 1844.
SAOR 89-1-1088/84.

Esteemed Mr. Blueher,

On 13 June of this year, I again sent you in Moscow washed sheep's wool on consignment from both of my sheepfarms, Iushanle and Tashchenak. Carter Nikita Chenkashchin and his associates from Melitopol District were responsible for 1,144 puds, ten funt net. One hundred and twenty-eight balls marked "J.C." were loaded onto forty carts. The agreement is for freight charges of three rubles per pud, which makes a total of 3,432 rubles, seventy-five kopeks. Of this sum carter Chenkashchin has been advanced 2,300 rubles. Upon delivery of the wool kindly pay him the remainer, 1,132 rubles, seventy-five kopeks, on my account.

I know that you will act in my interests in selling this wool, and notify me of its arrival. As previously, the wool from Tashchenak is marked with "T." Please find out how the sales of the two parts compare.

The carters have been directed to stop in the village from which the straight street leads to the wool-washing station. As you prefer, they should report to you when they arrive in order to avoid the difficulties that would otherwise be involved in driving into the city.

For your information, I enclose the original of the contract with carter Nikita Cherkashin, and one copy of the bill of lading.

One thousand puds of wool on your account are already packed, and will be forwarded next week. I estimate the purchase price at about twenty-four rubles [per pud]. Despite every effort, it has not been possible to get a better price. The demand for wool here is generally very strong. With few exceptions, all the wool was quickly bought up by travelling merchants from various regions, especially from Odesa, and prices ranged from twenty-three to twenty-eight rubles per pud. An insignificant quantity will go to the wool market at Romen.

I received your letter of 25 May and the small case of seeds. I trust you have received my letter of 22 May about a position for your son. I anticipate his early arrival. We will welcome him warmly as the son of a highly valued friend.

After commending myself to your further friendly remembrance, and with greetings and love to you and your dear family from us, I remain your faithfully obligated friend and servant, Johann Cornies.

301. Travel journal for Johann Cornies. 15–20 June 1844. SAOR 89-1-1092/16.

June 15. Tomorrow, Friday, Pastwa must keep two posting horses and a driver in readiness to drive to Andreevskii.

[June] 16. Franzthal must report who, by name, seeded grain on several cottage lots and why this was allowed, or whether this was done without permission.

[Crossed out]: Note, Gnadenfeld about drainage of water; Grossweide poor progress in forest cultivation.

[June] 16. Mariupol Mennonite District Office. By tomorrow, Saturday, I must know the names of all persons in four villages of this district who do not have window shutters on their dwelling houses as well as the names of those who have not constructed fences along the street and from the street to the dwelling house and who did not paint their fences along the street.

In addition, there must be no delay in closing any holes still found in roofs. No exceptions are allowed. Chimney frames must be whitewashed neatly. The owner of the house will be fined one silver ruble for each hole in a roof if it is noticed during the inspection tour of the Acting General Guardian.

June 17. To the same,

Martin Siemens, Khortitsa inhabitant, proposes that when his son Franz Siemens's hearth-site is passed along to someone else, the sum of 420 rubles still owing should be collected. Martin Siemens still owes this to the Khortitsa Orphans' Administration and must repay it. I commission the District Office to charge the appropriate person the above-mentioned 420 rubles and to pay it directly to the Khortitsa Orphans' Administration.

June 17. To the Mariupol Mennonite District Office,

I hereby inform the District Office, in response to its 7 April report about transferring the Schönfeld village fullholding inhabited by Bernhard Friesen to the Heubuden cottager Abram Rempel, that the transfer was approved for the reason given at the local investigation.

[June 17] Society,

The Society is hereby sent the enclosed planting register approved and prepared for the Bergthal plantation. After the rules included in it have been thoroughly taken into account, it should be forwarded to the Bergthal Village Office for its correct use. This action must be taken promptly.

302. Johann Cornies to Benjamin Ratzlaff. 20 June 1844. SAOR 89-1-1088/86.

Worthy Elder Benjamin Ratzlaff in Rudnerweide,

Directed by the worthy Church Elder of the Bergthal congregation, Mariupol Mennonite District, I respectfully notify you that the Pastwa inhabitant, Aron Dick, was accepted back into his local congregation after he demonstrated his repentance and his honest desire to be part of the congregation.

303. Johann Cornies to Fedor F. Rosen. 22 June 1844. SAOR 89-1-1088/86.

Director Baron v. Rosen,

In addition to my presentation No. 210 of 15 June, I have the honour to most respectfully request that you, esteemed Baron, have two more peasant apprentices selected to educate them in practical forest-tree cultivation, in addition to the six apprentices I have [previously] decided to accept on my estate.

Mennonite David Reimer, owner of Felstenthal estate, expressed a desire to accept apprentices for this same purpose and on the same terms. He is definitely the man who should teach apprentices. His plantations are completely suitable for this purpose and they can be taught there just as well as by me. In accordance with my obligations, please send the apprentices to me in Ohrloff to be assigned to Reimer.

304. Johann Cornies to Tobias Geyer. 23 June 1844.
SAOR 89-1-1088/86v.

Dear Mr. Geyer,

I have finally received printer's ink from Simferopol which, in my opinion, it is still too thick. However, I do not know what should be used to thin printer's ink. I hope you can tell me specifically and obtain the materials. If suitable, I would like to take an imprint of the stone in the coming week. Please drop me a few lines so that I can make my own plans and preparations.

With respect, your friend Johann Cornies.

305. Johann Cornies to Carl Stempel. 27 June 1844.
SAOR 89-1-1088/88v.

Yr. Honour, Mr. v. Stempel,

I was just notified by State Counsellor v. Steven that Director Levshin of the Third Department of State Domains will, after visiting the Lugansk firm at Bakhmut and Mariupol, arrive at my residence on 20 July. Since I assume that Mr. Levshin is likely to pass through your settlements on his travels, I am informing you in this regard, so that his arrival will not come as a surprise for you.

With true esteem, I remain Yr. Honour's respectful servant, Johann Cornies.

306. Johann Cornies to Christian Steven. 27 June 1844.
SAOR 89-1-1088/88v.

Mr. Steven in Simferopol.

Yr. Excellency,

Many thanks for your kind intercession on my behalf and for graciously informing me about the arrival of State Counsellor Levshin, Director of the Third Department.

I would be indebted to Yr. Excellency if you might have two or three chetvert of winter barley purchased for me. As for the introduction of madder seed among local Mennonites, I very much doubt that they would have any interest in its cultivation. There is a shortage of labour here and a greater interest in orchard cultivation. On your advice, I had several small beds of madder planted on my land three years ago and offered to distribute it, but have found no interest in doing so.

I will certainly provide you with two or even four [wagons] of roof tiles as soon as possible.

The steer I slaughtered two years ago weighed 1,629 funt, with head and hide but without entrails. I have no doubt that it would have weighed fifty puds more if weighed when alive. I do not, however, know the weight of the wethers.

307. Johann Cornies to Christian Steven. 27 June 1844. SAOR 89-1-1088/89v.

Mr. v. Steven, Yr. Excellency,

Because the soil was deeply penetrated by moisture in winter and by heavy and continuing rainfall in April and May, grass has grown thickly, especially around the Molochnaia River, and we are able to cut hay even on the highest ridges of the steppes. Among fodder crops the yellow dwarf lucerne has grown exceptionally well. Two feet high and as thick as if it had been sown, it has grown to maturity on the steppe as far as the eye can see. Everyone has provided himself with hay for two or three years. Not nearly all of the grass was mowed because it is now grain-harvesting time, and it will remain as pasture. Except for oats, which suffered because of heavy rainfall and produced bifarious heads, all grains are growing very well. We began the barley harvest yesterday.

There are good prospects for an excellent fruit harvest. The spiral caterpillar was everywhere this year, but damaged few apple trees, and the crop was very good. Pears, plums, and cherries are undamaged and there will be many of them. Tree branches, especially on cherry trees, are so full that they may well break off.

Horse prices were good. Many were sold to the cavalry as mounts for prices up to 230 rubles per head, but there was little demand for horned cattle. Foot-and-mouth disease is spreading sporadically in our villages, and there is cattle plague in Melitopol, Edonovka, Semenovka, and fourteen Nogai villages.

At the start of the shearing, wool was selling at twenty-two to twenty-three rubles per pud, but later rose to twenty-eight and even thirty-three rubles for several good lots of washed wool. There is little demand for sheep and wethers.

As far as I can tell, sericulture is going well everywhere, but the final crop yield is still uncertain.

Forest trees in the plantations will yield a plentiful quantity of several varieties of seeds. It will, as a result, no longer be necessary to fill our requirements for a few ordinary varieties of forest trees from outside our villages.

Almost all varieties of vegetables are growing well and appearances suggest that the potato crop will be excellent.

The highest temperature in May was twenty-two degrees, and it has not yet risen above twenty-six degrees in June. Most days in May were cloudy.

Locusts are appearing only in a few places. Numbers are low and the vermin are quite small in size. We have little fear that they will do appreciable damage.

308. Johann Cornies to Traugott Blueher. 27 June 1844.
SAOR 89-1-1088/91v.

Esteemed Mr. Blueher,

In response to your instruction, I had 1,005 puds, twenty funt of washed Spanish wool bought for you here. It left for Moscow on 23 June with wool loaded on thirty-five horse carts. Enclosed are the original contract concluded with the carters and the bill of lading.

From the enclosed purchase account, you will see that purchases exceeded the price you specified by fifty-five and one-half kopeks. When shearing began, there were few buyers, which allowed me to purchase wool for twenty-one to twenty-three rubles per pud, at the highest price. Most sheep owners refused to sell at such [low] prices, however, and waited until after the yearly Pentecost market in Kharkiv. As soon as sales then began, Odesa and Berdiansk buyer rushed to our area and paid twenty-three to twenty-six rubles straightaway. Within a week, the prices had climbed to twenty-seven and twenty-eight rubles. Our community wool sold at even thirty-three rubles a pud. Not more than 1,500 puds of wool was shipped to the wool market in Romen and I think it would be difficult to find one hundred puds of unsold wool remaining in this region. I cannot remember when wool sales were completed as early as this year. It was of course your good fortune that I was able to buy wool for you so cheaply when compared with prices paid in the market here, although I paid twenty-three rubles for a few hundred puds. Most wool was sold for twenty-seven and twenty-eight rubles.

The balls marked "A" are wool from a good, well-known sheepfarm. I would like to know what it sells for after it has been washed.

According to the enclosed account, the overall total amount of wool [sold on my behalf] is 26,806 rubles, eighty-one and a quarter kopeks.

From this total I received 3,500 silver rubles, or 12,250 rubles banco on 25 May. Therefore, my advance is 14,556 rubles, eighty-one and a quarter kopeks. I request that you deduct my debts from this amount and then send me whatever is my due.

As I was about to seal this letter, I received your valued communication of 12 June, and see that your dear son Joseph will soon be arriving here. I trust that he will be able to accustom himself to the home of Mr. Isaac Mathias quickly. This is my sympathetic hope.

Our harvest is very abundant this year and the grass on the steppes is thicker and longer than we have ever seen it before. The general state of people's health leaves nothing to be desired.

I commend you and your family to God and trust that the Lord might bless this business matter. Friendly greetings to you and your family from your greatly obligated friend and servant, Johann Cornies.

309. Johann Cornies to Daniel Doering. 27 June 1844. SAOR 89-1-1088/93.

Esteemed Mr. Doering, most beloved friend,

I have received your letter and letters from Mr. Meinecke and Chairman Mory. My replies have been delayed because I had planned to visit you personally in July to both recuperate and to enjoy myself in the company of my dear friends in quiet Sarepta. That would have also given me an opportunity to discuss various matters with you. Regrettably, the pressure of business matters and the announcement of visits by illustrious persons from [St.] Petersburg in July force me to postpone my visit to the end of August or the beginning of September. Please do not read anything into the delay of my visit. I think you know of my situation and how it fetters me and give me the benefit of the doubt out of the goodness of your heart.

Our entire region has been much blessed this year. The grass has grown extraordinarily well. Vegetables, grain, and fruit are promising of the most splendid harvests. Wool prices went as high as twenty-eight rubles. Horses found a market and prices were good. Only horned cattle have found no buyers. Foot-and-mouth disease has spread into our villages and there was even cattle plague in Nogai villages.

We thank God that everything is going well here and are pleased to hear the same about your dear Sarepta.

Greetings from all of us to you, your dear wife, and children. Kindly give Mr. Meinecke, who has personally seen the Molochnaia region, my congratulations and wishes for a happy marriage. Please tell him that I would love to hear from him as often as he finds the leisure to do so.

The packed oil-radish seed has lain in storage here for some time. I will send it soon with an enclosure of instructions for its seeding and further treatment. This year, our local forest-tree plantations should produce an abundance of various forest-tree seeds. If you would like to receive seeds of some trees, let me know, specifying the varieties you need. My outlay for you, according to the enclosed account, does not have to be paid at once. Perhaps I will fetch the payment myself.

Since I value your true sympathy for the happiness of my family, I must report that my wife's health has been restored and she is better than she has been for years.

May you and your loved ones and all good acquaintances accept our loving greetings, with continuing friendship from your honestly loving friend and servant, Johann Cornies.

310. Johann Cornies to Peter Keppen. 10 July 1844. SAOR 89-1-1088/96v.

State Counsellor v. Keppen,

Despite my best intentions, I was unable to begin opening mounds any earlier. Willing workers are hard to find. This may well be, to a degree, because meals for workers on the open steppe are neither as good nor as complete as what workers are accustomed to getting in the villages. The work of opening burial mounds also demands selected, strong, solid, and tireless workers who can be found only during the period before haying when there is no other work to be found. It is a time when several thousand Russians from the newer guberniias come to work at haying. For these reasons, I request your kind consideration.

Yr. Honour has again put me under obligation by kindly sending me copies of the reports you made to the Imperial Academy about my excavations. I cannot thank you enough for these. I am greatly interested in your opinion that the mounds originated at the time of the snake cult and were constructed for purposes of religious sacrifice. Your opinion is confirmed by mounds of the first height which are found here in certain spots connected to each other by paved footpaths of stone or fired bricks. I have not yet visited any of these.

This year is richly fruitful in our region, especially in the Molochnaia villages. We are blessed with a bounty of grass, grain, and fruit quite beyond what our oldest inhabitants can remember. Even on the highest ridges of the steppe, where hay could never be made before, the grass was thick and luxuriant and almost half the height of a man. It was not possible to mow nearly all of it. Locusts appeared in a few spots, but will do no damage. Wool prices were good this year, up to thirty rubles per pud for washed wool. Horses also sold well. However, foot-and-mouth disease is prevalent among horned cattle in some villages and there is actual cattle plague in many neighbouring Russian and Nogai villages. Improvements begun in agriculture in our villages are making rapid strides, encouraged by prospects for a good harvest. There is naturally much left to do.

Should the journal, *Contributions to the Knowledge of the Russian Empire*, which you kindly mention in your letter and recommend to me, appear in the German language, I would request that you send me copies by mail, putting the costs on my account. They could also be sent through the Sarepta Merchant Company of G.G. Soerensen & Company in Moscow that would pay my costs.

Please accept my honest assurance that I will remain obligated to you for your friendly communications, and remain, with true esteem, your most humble servant, Johann Cornies.

311. Johann Cornies to Birkhan. 12 July 1844. SAOR 89-1-1088/99.

Mr. Birkhan in the Crimea.

Most esteemed sir,

I write with reference to your friendly order of 20 April for a so-called garden weeder/cleaner. I can report that the implement was immediately ordered from one of our local master tradesmen at a price of thirteen rubles. It has been ready for a long time. Regrettably, I have not yet found a good opportunity for forwarding it to you. This makes me very uncomfortable. I notified you of this matter in a communication sent to you through the Baron, but he may simply have forgotten it because of his many business affairs. I regret to have so burdened our good Baron. I will forward the implement to you as soon as an opportunity arises.

It is impossible that a person whom I value as much as I do you should ever vanish from my memory. Your valued stay in Iushanle and our hearty conversations about many matters will live on as a treasured memory. Please do not be angry with for my long delay in answering your letter. Please receive sincere greetings from myself and my family. Valuing you greatly, I remain, with respect, your Johann Cornies.

312. Johann Cornies to Fedor F. Rosen. 12 July 1844.
SAOR 89-1-1088/100v.

His Honour, Baron Rosen,

As much as I regret arousing your displeasure, valued and honoured Baron, I must do so for the sake of justice and your humane intentions. I write to inform you in confidence that, for his own purposes, District Supervisor Raiskii is seeking to provoke the Molokans into immigrating to Georgia.

He has again stayed in their midst for almost two weeks and listed all families that would like to move to Georgia, without regard to the number of their souls capable of working. This so dejects other Molokans who do not wish to move to Georgia that, with tears in their eyes, they complain to me about their grief. They also neglect their [agricultural] establishments. They do not know whom to believe, their esteemed Director or the District Supervisor. The latter says the opposite to what the director says to them, specifically that no one with more than two souls capable of working in their family will be allowed to go to Georgia. The District Supervisor is listing the names of everyone who pays him money and wants to move to Georgia, even if these are families with many more souls. I fear that, in this dilemma, the Molokans will explain these events to Director Levshin of the Third Department when he travels through. This compels me to faithfully inform you about this matter, with the humble request that you not consider these comments as slander. Instead, kindly accept them as a pure example of my feelings for the well-being of these people and because I esteem and value your noble actions for the happiness of many thousands. I flatter myself with the hope that you will not diminish your kind benevolence towards me on this account.

With the most exceptional esteem and feelings of honesty, I remain Yr. Honour's respectful servant, Johann Cornies.

313. Johann Cornies to Roslavets 12 July 1844.
SAOR 89-1-1088/103v.

Yr. Excellency, Tavrida Civil Governor, State Counsellor and Knight v. Roslavets,

There is an abundantly flowing spring near the hill in the middle of the village of Terpenie, in Melitopol District. The Doukhobor community has built an orphanage and a bathhouse beside it. Quite a large fruit orchard is also laid out at this location of small hills, bisected by ravines, with spring water gently flowing through it.

As soon as the Doukhobors have been resettled to the Transcaucasus, they will turn over their buildings and orchard to the government. Although the buildings are themselves of little value, the orchard and especially the spring are subjects that merit the greatest attention on these steppes, with their shortage of spring water. This encourages me to make a most respectful submission to Yr. Excellency regarding a development of Terpenie that would have local advantages for the German settlements.

The spring in Terpenie and the orchard would qualify as a hydropathic institution. The orchard's romantic location could be enlarged to more than double its present size and would provide amusement and walks for visitors taking a water cure. At the present time, the government may not be ready to agree to the expense of building houses and other arrangements for visitors taking a cure. The region is not sufficiently populated and private persons prepared to establish such an institution at their own expense may be difficult to find. However, the spring, the orchard, and the area around it could be left unassigned for other purposes until a future time when the government might itself decide to establish such a water-cure institution beside the spring at the cost of the crown. Alternatively, it might allow the development of such an establishment by private persons, who could surely be found in the course of time.

I would ask that Yr. Excellency graciously grant consideration to this, my most humble submission, and take measures so that the spring and the orchard with its appropriate surroundings are not immediately assigned for some other purpose. The orchard itself, now in an unmanageable condition, might be put under supervision and considered for a future water-cure institution.

314. Johann Cornies to Peter Keppen. 13 July 1844.
SAOR 89-1-1088/106.

State Counsellor v. Keppen,

I have the honour to send Yr. Honour the enclosed accounts for the costs of excavations I have undertaken and for impressions I have made of a stone as I reported in the last mail.

Sericulture is quickly spreading among local Mennonites. With last year's yield of almost fifteen puds, this branch of the economy will presumably be doubled because of our favourable weather conditions. Indeed, with the passage of time, sericulture may well be elevated to a noteworthy pursuit. If it does it would ensure a not inconsiderable additional income for many families, provide useful occupations, and promise to contribute much to a general increase in the well-being of the Mennonites.

Sericulture was established among the Mennonites in 1837, with a harvest of fifteen funt, two loth of silk. Because we lack a real understanding of how the cocoons should be unwound, however, the price we obtain for our silk is not what might be expected if it was handled with greater skill. [Better prices] would give us the best incentive.

With exceptional esteem, Yr. Honour's humble servant, Johann Cornies.

315. Evgenii F. Hahn to Johann Cornies. 13 July 1844. SAOR 89-1-889/26-7.

The Molochnaia Mennonite District Office is requested to deliver the enclosed communication to Mr. Cornies.

State Counsellor v. Hahn. Odesa, 13 July 1844

Should our dear Lord permit, I will leave Odesa on 15 July, visit several settlements along the way, and arrive in Tashchenak on Tuesday or Wednesday. If I do not find you there, which is quite possible, I will, because I want to talk to you first, immediately continue on to Prishib or to Halbstadt to await you. Yours truly, E. v. Hahn. Odesa, 13 July 1844.

316. Johann Cornies to Evgenii F. Hahn. 14 July 1844. SAOR 78-1-1088/106v.

Yr. Excellency, v. Hahn,

Industrious activity has dominated the life of the Molochnaia Mennonite District since spring. Considerable progress is noticeable in all branches of agriculture. Our villages and their fullholdings are improving at an increasing pace and have become excellent models [for others]. Grain and fruit promise an extremely good harvest and the hay harvest has been extraordinary. The village of Hutterthal has laid in for itself a three-year supply of good hay fodder. On average, their grain has grown astonishingly well and is the most exceptional in this entire region.

Last month I travelled around the Mariupol settlement villages. With appropriate directives and untiring activity, Mr. v. Stempel has transformed them into an admirable economic condition. I was astonished when I caught sight of the regularly divided fields, the cultivated fields, and the fallow. The locations for forest-tree plantations beside each village have been ploughed and enclosed within ditches on two sides. Fences along streets and the gables of houses have been generally painted. Much encouraged by Mr. v. Stempel, cleanliness and neatness have begun to improve around houses.

The settlers are fully occupied with their work. It is the one true means of establishing morality and decent behaviour that can lead to prosperity. By contrast, nothing has changed in the Molochnaia [German] Settlement District.

We greatly regret that the land surveyor Mr. Fedorovich fell ill immediately after his arrival and was unable to start work for a period of six weeks. We thank God that he has now recovered and is surveying Felstenthal.

All of us have found it difficult to forego Yr. Excellency's visit, but are consoled by the hope that you will soon bless us with the hope of the visit we have awaited with such longing. This would allow us to share with you our joy and permit us to vent our warm feelings towards your esteemed person. With the greatest esteem, I remain Yr. Excellency's respectful servant, Johann Cornies.

317. Johann Cornies to Carl Stempel. 14 July 1844.
SAOR 89-1-1088/108v.

Yr. Honour, Mr. v. Stempel,

Today I received your letter of 3 July and hasten to inform you that I have informed Master Mason Larion that one of his people is ill and that he should send you two people to expedite the work.

The General presumably did not arrive at the specified time because he wanted to allow Mr. Koloshin and Mr. Levshin to first travel through the area to avoid the appearance of his having prepared the settlements to make a good impression. People in power are generally very suspicious today, and this is natural since they are so often deceived. I have so concluded because the General Inspector for Agriculture wrote to me, "I wanted to visit you in June, but now I will let the gentlemen travel through first." There is probably no other reason for State Counsellor v. Hahn's failure to appear.

It is now eight days since the grain harvest began, and it is turning out to be most abundant this year.

I would ask you to report to the Bergthal District Chairman that land surveyor Fedorovich may arrive next week and that good lodgings should be arranged for him.

There is a further subject I would like to inform you of in confidence, with the request that you keep it secret. According to information I have received, the Tsar will travel through southern Russia in September and through several settlements as well.

With exceptional esteem, I remain Yr. Honour's respectful servant, Johann Cornies.

318. Johann Cornies to Fedor F. Rosen. 19 July 1844. SAOR 89-1-1088/111.

Director Baron v. Rosen,

Cattle plague is ravaging horned cattle in Russian and Nogai villages in this region with extraordinary force and gives me reason to send Yr. Honour the enclosed description. This terrible ailment carries off a massive portion of the state's wealth in an extraordinarily short time. Yet many investigations, experiences, and measures have by now accumulated without achieving the desired results.

My description deals with the prevention and extermination of cattle plague as carried out in 1833, when almost no locality in our guberniia was unaffected by great devastation. At that time it also broke out in my herd of 163 head. By observing and following the rules I include here [not extant] to the letter, I lost only eighteen head and was able to eradicate the disease from my stock of animals. Specifically, on 29 July 1839, when the plague was causing great devastation in Ekaterinoslav Guberniia, I sent this description to State Counsellor v. Keppen in the Learned Committee of the Ministry of State Domains, to have it tested and publicized. As far as I know, it was printed in the agricultural newspaper at that time because I was thanked by a number of estate owners in Ekaterinoslav Guberniia who handled their livestock according to these rules and kept them healthy or who suffered the loss of only a very few of them.

I presume that this thorough description of cattle plague and its prevention is unknown among the peasants, as are effective rules to prevent and eradicate it. I think it would be highly desirable and of general benefit, if the rules were immediately printed and publicized and accompanied by an extremely stern order from the Domains Bureau that they be strictly followed. The government could hardly do more for the peasantry than to adopt measures that would halt and completely eradicates cattle plague through rules and measures appropriate to the purpose.

319. Johann Cornies to Fedor F. Rosen. 29 July 1844.
SAOR 89-1-1088/112v.

His Honour Baron v. Rosen,

I write to you about a matter that is most embarrassing for me. I know in advance that it is not deserving of consideration, but I still feel that I must submit it to you.

When you last visited here, Staff-Doctor Kovalev in Orekhov approached me with a proposal that I make a request to you on his behalf that you graciously appoint him as District Chief when such a position becomes vacant in this guberniia. I absolutely object to such methods myself, but I felt compelled to comply because of his insistence. Indeed, I promised him that I would submit this matter to you when an opportunity presented itself. I was unable to speak to you at the time and so have not yet kept my promise. Mr. Kovalev now insists that I do.

Please help me out of this embarrassing situation with, perhaps, a few lines stating that no District Chief positions are vacant in this guberniia. Please excuse me for burdening Yr. Honour with so useless a letter when you are overwhelmed by so many more important matters of business.

With great esteem, I strive to remain Your Honour's respectful servant, Johann Cornies.

320. Johann Cornies to Reimer. 2 August 1844.
SAOR 89-1-1088/114.

Valued friend Reimer in Kronsgarten,

I sell two varieties of breeding rams, the first at one hundred rubles per head and the second at fifty rubles. Both are of pure Saxon descent. I usually have available only a few rams of the first variety. Most are of the second variety.

The buyers themselves select rams according to the ewes they each have. Mr. Levchenko would have to be at my estate promptly on 23

September. According to the accepted rules, rams cannot be made available even one day ahead of time. On that particular date, buyers would make their own first choices.

Assuring you of my honest respect, your Johann Cornies.

321. Johann Cornies to Traugott Blueher. 2 August 1844. SAOR 89-1-1088/114v.

Esteemed Mr. Blueher,

This year a considerable quantity of silk was produced in our villages. Some of it has already been reeled. I send the enclosed twenty-two lot sample with the request that you try to establish the price it might fetch. This would enable us to make appropriate decisions in advance. Discussions are underway about the possibility this fall of forwarding a considerable quantity of this year's silk production directly to Moscow.

A little more experienced than they were, our silk-reelers are now trying to produce better silk. If it is practicable, please sell this sample immediately as a way of establishing its quality. I would urgently ask that you inform me by mail of the expert opinions you have received and advise us as to how we might proceed.

Completely convinced that you will do what you can to advance the interests of our local Mennonites whose pursuit of sericulture is increasing considerably from year to year, I look forward to your early reply.

Heartily wishing you and your dear family all the best, I remain your ever honest friend and servant, Johann Cornies.

322. Johann Cornies to Fedor F. Rosen. 3 August 1844. SAOR 89-1-1088/115v.

Director Baron v. Rosen,

I acknowledge receipt of eighty-three silver rubles, twenty-eight kopeks that were enclosed with communication No. 7020 of 5 July 1844 from the Tavrida Domains Bureau as payment for the implements manufactured for Kherson Guberniia. The entire amount should have been eighty-four and one-third silver kopeks more. The difference was deducted by the post office. This the masters could naturally not have known. Please send me this difference and I will forward it to the masters in question.

323. Johann Cornies to Hutterthal Village Office.
6 August 1844. SAOR 89-1-1092/8.

[Draft:] To the Hutterthal Village Office,

Hutterthal villager Paul Tchetter appeared here today with a complaint relating to the construction of his house. After obtaining all of the building materials needed for construction except fired bricks, he had asked the Village Mayor for a certificate that would entitle him to receive the desired number of fired bricks in Tashchenak. Yet after making arrangements to have the bricks picked up, the Mayor refused to grant him the requested certificate except to say that Moses Stahl should begin building his house first (although he had not yet acquired any fired bricks himself).

I therefore order the Village Office to inform me by eight o'clock tomorrow morning at the latest why Tchetter was not given a certificate for bricks, and why Stahl is being preferred. Even if there exists a well-founded reason for giving Stahl preference, Tchetter should still be granted a certificate for the purchase of bricks, lest he become discouraged.

6 August 1844.

324. Evgenii F. Hahn to Johann Cornies. 8 August 1844.
SAOR 89-1-889/30.

I have been given specific information that might help Loewen in his efforts to obtain his medical papers. According to regulations confirmed at the highest level on 28 December 1838, such examinations are only conducted in academies for medical education, such as those in [St.] Petersburg and Moscow, or at universities. To avoid a long journey, Loewen would thus have to visit Kharkiv or Kyiv for this purpose. However, [the examinations are so difficult] that I genuinely doubt the possibility of his success.

To enter the profession of an ordinary doctor or medico, Loewen would have to pass examinations in sixteen different subjects including mineralogy, botany, zoology, physics, chemistry, anatomy, physiology, pathology, etc. It is difficult for even well-informed individuals to pass such examinations after serious preparation. How much more difficult would it be for Loewen.

Kindly communicate this to Loewen. Nothing can be done for him in Odesa and a visit would therefore be of no avail.

Yours truly, E. v. Hahn.

Odesa, 8 August 1844. Received 15 August 1844.

325. Johann Cornies to Christian Steven. 9 August 1844.
SAOR 89-1-1088/117.

Inspector for Agriculture in Southern Russia v. Steven,

In communication No. 912 of 20 May 1844, the Forestry Department agreed to send me four crown peasant apprentices to learn practical forest-tree cultivation on my plantations. The terms of the apprenticeships are the same as those for apprentices in agriculture. Since 4 August, I have a full complement of apprentices on my Iushanle estate. They are: Anton Kovtun and Semen Tarasenko from Bakhmut District, here since 22 February 1844; Samoilo Kichkin from Aleksandrov District, here since 16 February 1844; and Gavrilo Martenenko who arrived on 4 August.

I have the honour of obediently submitting this matter to Yr. Honour.

326. Johann Cornies to Christian Steven. 9 August 1844.
SAOR 89-1-1088/117v.

I have the honour of obediently reporting to Yr. Excellency that, according to an earlier agreement with five local Mennonite model agriculturalists, four crown apprentices have been provided by the Kherson District Administration. They are: Fedor Rabulo and Nikolai Dionditz, Village Handrabur; Ivan Didenko from Gvosdavkii; and Ivan Spulenko from Golm. The Kherson District Administration writes that a fifth, Samoilo Koshuchar from Handrabur village is ill and cannot be sent.

Meanwhile, ample time has elapsed. I would therefore request that the full complement of five apprentices be assigned for service to specific agriculturalists. To this end I would ask that Yr. Excellency graciously take measures to ensure the early arrival of the fifth apprentice.

327. Johann Cornies to Hutterthal Village Office. 11 August 1844.
SAOR 89-1-1092/6.

[Draft:] To the Hutterthal Village Office,

1. I would repeat that the Village Office should supervise horned cattle more strictly because cattle plague is widespread in the area and specifically in the crown village of Novonikolaievka. Carts drawn by oxen should not be allowed to leave the Chumak road and pass through

villages or the land of villages where cattle are pastured. The *Starshii* in Novonikolaievka should be notified that Hutterthal village will not allow ox carts to pass across its land.

2. Your shepherd must be kept under closer supervision to prevent his leaving the sheep in one spot all day long after putting them out to graze early in the morning, as has occurred. So long as it is cool in the morning and afternoon, he should wander abound, permitting the sheep to spread out and graze. Because lambs can be afflicted with the plague from the early growth after seeding, he should drive them off ploughed land before it germinates. He should regularly change the places where cattle graze.

3. Threshing wheat should be started next week and completed during that week. The laying of foundations for house construction should be started. Floors and similar carpentry work should begin next week. Carpenters for this work should be fetched on Sunday.

4. The Village Office should personally visit every hearth-site, and investigate and give orders to ensure that hay and grain stacks are set up in an orderly manner. Areas between and around the stacks should be kept clear and free of hay and straw.

It is not enough to simply be in possession of a quantity of grain. A good householder ensures that everything is set up in an orderly and clean manner in order that even the smallest amount of grain or hay fodder is used and not allowed to be trodden underfoot or left to rot. The Village Office must direct the *desiatnik* (ten-men) to inspect the stack areas twice a week in future and then report to the Village Office.

Most importantly, care should be taken to prevent fires. Anyone caught smoking tobacco or handling fire outdoors will be fined one silver ruble for the first offence. For the second offence, he will be sent to the Kurushan Community Sheepfarm to do community work. Anyone who sees a tobacco smoker or a person making fires and does not report him, will be punished in the same way.

The Village Office should conduct itself strictly and promptly with respect to all of these matters.

328. Johann Cornies to Hutterthal Village Office.
   15 August 1844. SAOR 89-1-1092/9.

To the Hutterthal Village Office,

Let me, in reply to the Village Office report of 15 August, inform you that I strongly support a design in which two one-paned windows

were installed in all gables, as illustrated in the accompanying sketch.
15 August 1844.

[Sketch has a triangle-shaped gable with two rectangular windows, evenly spaced.]

329. Johann Cornies to Gerhard Enns. 21 August 1844. SAOR 89-1-1088/120v.

Honoured School Director Gerhard Enns in Altona,

From the business manager for the Society School in Ohrloff,

I remit to the Ohrloff Society School's administration the enclosed contract concluded with teacher Martin Riediger, as approved and confirmed by me. I request that this contract be sent to the treasurer, honoured Peter Isaac in Tiege. Its terms should be followed in computing Riediger's salary.

330. Evgenii F. Hahn to Johann Cornies. 26 August 1844. SAOR 89-1-889/31.

I have had German directions for tobacco cultivation prepared. They have been copied from various compositions, mostly by Steven. Before they are printed to guide still-inexperienced settlers, I will have them revised and condensed. First, however, I send them to you for your comments. I would ask that these be kept in the margins. Yours truly, E. v. Hahn.

Odesa, 26 August 1844. Received 2 September 1844; answered 17 February 1845.

331. Guarantee from Johann Cornies. 1 September 1844. SAOR 89-1-1134/78.

Claas Penner and Aron Regier from Margenau, guardians of Heinrich Teichgrew of the same village, can borrow up to four hundred rubles a year for his upkeep. I guarantee this arrangement which is certified by my signature, in my own hand. Ohrloff, 1 September 1844. Johann Cornies.

[In margin:] Same guarantee given 15 October 1845.

332. Johann Cornies to Gerhard Enns. 1 September 1844. SAOR 89-1-1088/123v.

Dear friend, Mr. Gerhard Enns, Altona,

State Counsellor v. Hahn writes that Zamero, an Italian, will visit us because sericulture is being carried on significantly in our local district and he would like to see it. His purpose is to decide whether it might make sense for him to become more involved in our region, something that would require the agreement and assistance of the local community. Knowing how silk can be perfected, the State Counsellor has decided to send him here to help us obtain higher returns from our sericulture.

It seems to me that he would like either to buy up cocoons or have them reeled and sold under his direction. He would naturally have to be able to make a profit from this himself. I would ask that you discuss this matter with him and show him around. Please write to me because the Society may well have to judge this entire matter.

Fare well. Your friend Johann Cornies.

333. Johann Cornies to District Office. 2 September 1844. SAOR 89-1-1088/124.

To the Molochnaia Mennonite District Office in Halbstadt,

In following the directives stating that no foreign ox carts will be allowed to travel in this district outside of the Chumak road, Village Offices have also concluded that they are not permitted to admit my ox carts from the Iushanle estate.

The Iushanle estate is situated at the centre of the district and is completely enclosed in it. Interior communications have not been proscribed. I would humbly request that the District Office make arrangements to prevent our surrounding villages from halting or sending my oxcarts from the Iushanle estate away. Kindly inform me about your decision in regard to this matter.

334. Johann Cornies to District Office. 6 September 1844. SAOR 89-1-1088/125.

To the esteemed Molochnaia Mennonite District Office at Halbstadt,

On the night of Saturday, 2 September, two horses disappeared from my Iushanle estate. They are:

1. a thin, nineteen-year-old gelding of a light fox-colour, branded with an "h" on his left hind-shank;

2. a four-year-old black and brown gelding with a swelling on his back, but without any other markings.

The District Office is humbly asked to publicize this loss in our local villages in order that I might regain possession of them.

335. Johann Cornies to Fedor F. Rosen. 7 September 1844. SAOR 89-1-1088/126.

Director Baron v. Rosen,

To answer Yr. Honour's communication No. 679 of 23 August 1844, I have the honour to report that my verbal promise is firm. I will accept crown peasant apprentices for the purpose of learning practical forest-tree cultivation on the steppe for a period of four years. In that time period they can expect to be appropriately trained. I have given the Forestry Department the specific reasons for my position. On other terms, I would like it confirmed that they would be decided on terms similar to those for agricultural apprenticeships.

At the same time, I would ask that Yr. Honour not send me any Tatar boys for the above-mentioned purpose. I had to send one back as unsuitable from the Aritochin Volost. Little can be expected from such boys under conditions where they would first have to learn Russian before starting the forest-tree cultivation program.

I will await an early answer about Yr. Honour's decisions.

336. Johann Cornies to General Guardian. 7 September 1844. SAOR 89-1-1070/2.

[Draft:] General Guardian, from the Chairman,

The Radishchev Mennonites moved from Chernigov Guberniia and have been settled on tract No. 15 situated on the Tashchenak in Melitopol District in a village with thirty hearth-sites. Eighty-three Mennonite families with 456 souls of both genders have thus been settled on land designed for fifty-one families. The limited land set aside for their use may well allow them to live but is insufficient to promote their speedy progress. It is not large enough for them to found, establish, and build a second village at their own costs. The ploughed land for grain cultivation, in particular, is sufficient for thirty families, but there is no further ploughed land available without seriously limiting livestock pastures and haymeadows. Also, fallow land must definitely be set aside by 1846. This would remove a quarter of all ploughed land, further limiting the land for the new settlers, despite the fact that they would be richly compensated for their present loss in later years.

For these reasons, I feel I must promote the interests of the Hutterite Mennonites by requesting that when the current leases now held on land in tract No. 15 end, Yr. Excellency graciously allow all of this land to be distributed among the Hutterthal Mennonites for their settlement and use, with the requirement that they pay the legal land taxes.

One thousand, eight hundred and twenty-four desiatinas of this tract are still under lease, while the rest of the land, now apportioned for fifty-one families, is supporting all eighty-three families of Hutterthal Mennonites. It is doubtful the Hutterthal Mennonites could flourish on this limited amount of land, whether in one or in two villages.

Might Yr. Excellency benevolently consider the basis of my submission, and kindly provide me with a suitable directive as to what to do next as soon as possible.

337. Johann Cornies to brother. 13 September 1844. SAOR 89-1-1070/1.

Dear brother,

I was in Neukirch yesterday and spoke with Penner, who is building a mill for Peter Fast. He will not be finished at Fast's for at least five weeks. This means it is too late to have Penner build another mill this autumn. I asked Fast what he thought his mill would cost, and he said that it would be not much less than two thousand rubles. Your brother Johann Cornies.

Iushanle, 13 September 1844

338. Johann Cornies to [Aleksei] Levshin. 18 September 1844. SAOR 89-1-1088/128.

Director of the Third Department in the Ministry of State Domains v. Levshin. Yr. Excellency,

In response to Yr. Excellency's commission No. 103 of 26 August 1844, I would point out that the wealth of many landowners in West Prussia has been much reduced by the great floods of this past summer.

As a result, a significant number of Mennonite families with good agricultural skills might be prepared to immigrate to Russia. This was not true a year ago when landowners were flourishing.

Before the terms of such a move could be discussed, I would need to know what land, in what region, and of what quality the government might graciously set aside for a new Mennonite settlement. This would enable me to make a detailed, attractive presentation to my correspondents in West Prussia, encouraging them to accept the high Ministry's invitation. A formal invitation might be sent to Mennonite families who could then dispatch several deputies to inspect the land and conclude draft terms of a settlement with the government.

In my judgment, this would be the best method of reaching an early decision. I would propose that the high Ministry make me a concrete proposal soon. I am happy to promote the proposed immigration and will try to carry it out, using all of the powers at my command.

339. Johann Cornies to Cornelius Wiens. 21 September 1844. SAOR 89-1-1088/129v.

Esteemed Cornelius Wiens, Ohrloff,

From the corresponding member,

Acting State Counsellor Mr. v. Steven asks you to provide your crown apprentices with Sunday clothing of the usual style to give your crown apprentices an appropriate look, as is done for crown apprentices with me and with the esteemed Peter Cornies and Johann Sukkau.

340. Johann Cornies to Fedor F. Rosen. 21 September 1844. SAOR 89-1-1088/130.

Director Baron v. Rosen,

Forty-seven rubles, ninety and one-half kopeks in silver for agricultural implements to Kursk Guberniia were received with Yr. Honour's communication No. 598 of 19 July 1844.

To the same,

Fifteen rubles, eight kopeks silver [were received] with communication No. 8050 of 2 August 1844 from the Domains Bureau for threshing stones presented to crown peasants in the city of Melitopol.

To the same,

In response to Yr. Honour's communication No. 366 of 19 April 1844, local masters completed implements for Kursk Guberniia as follows: one plough, one harrow, one roller, one mounder, one marker, and one lifter. They were delivered to the Rostov Domains administration in good order on 1 September, according to the enclosed receipt. I paid nine rubles, eighty-five kopeks silver in cash to have these implements transported from here to Rostov, and request that Yr. Honour have this money repaid to me as soon as possible.

341. Johann Cornies to Hermann Klassen. 1 October 1844.
SAOR 89-1-1088/135v.

To Mr. Hermann Klassen in Prishib.

Esteemed friend,

You are most politely requested to answer the following questions:

1. Were you formally accepted into the Mennonite brotherhood through baptism? Did you partake of the Lord's Supper in a spirit of unity with this brotherhood? Where did this last occur?

2. Did you bring along a church attestation from Prussia to show that you really are a brother within the Mennonite community? From which Elders?

3. What is the name of the Elder here in the Molochnaia to whom you gave your attestation, or is it still in your possession?

4. Which congregation of Mennonite brethren did you join, assuming spiritual membership in it?

5. Did you leave the community of Mennonite brethren or do you intend to leave it?

Dear friend, I would like to have you clarify these questions, and urgently request that you reply as soon as possible. In this way we could forestall any unpleasantness.

With friendly greetings, I respectfully remain your well-meaning friend, Johann Cornies.

342. Johann Cornies to Christian Steven. 3 October 1844.
SAOR 89-1-1088/136v.

Inspector of Agriculture in Southern Russia v. Steven,

To carry out Yr. Excellency's communication No. 1843 of 10 November, I have the honour to report that the Chinese silkworm eggs you sent were given to good agriculturalists for incubation and raising, as you wished. It was observed that they fed in a much more sluggish fashion than did the usual worms and that they passed into the pupa stage much more slowly and irregularly. On average, their cocoons are larger, but also looser and weaker. One chetverik of Chinese cocoons produced three-quarter funt of reeled silk, while worms customarily kept here produce about a funt and a quarter of silk.

Four of these cocoons and one sample of reeled silk are enclosed for Yr. Excellency's closer examination and judgment. I would note that this variety of worms is being cultivated further in our villages to acclimatize them to our conditions and to enable us to judge them more accurately.

343. Johann Cornies to Christian Steven. 3 October 1844. SAOR 89-1-1088/137v.

Inspector of Agriculture v. Steven,

I have the honour to present an overview of the current stock of trees owned by Mitalip Tenbaiev, Nogai from Akkerman. His plantations are all the work of his own hands. This man's efforts to be generally useful have caught the eye of officials. I would propose that he be further encouraged with the award of a small medal to be worn in his buttonhole.

344. Johann Cornies to Carl Stempel. 3 October 1844. SAOR 89-1-1088/138.

Most esteemed Mr. v. Stempel, presently in Odesa,

A visit by the Mariupol Mennonite District Elders caused me to make arrangements to immediately have all documents removed from District Secretary Penner's possession because of his irrational behaviour and moved to Khortitsa without delay.

I obediently ask that you delay implementing the Schoenthal community's verdict, because the Strumer family agrees to submit to all demands in order that they might be allowed to remain here. The old man remains obstinate and demands passes to Turkey, but he is presently seriously ill and it is doubtful that he will recover.

I intend to leave here tomorrow, 4 October, to carry out the commission to work with the Swedes.

Commending myself to your friendly remembrance, I remain, with esteem, your humble servant Johann Cornies.

345. Johann Cornies to Zamero. 5 October 1844. SAOR 89-1-1088/139v.

Most esteemed Mr. Zamero,

Kindly forgive us for making you wait so long for an answer on a matter we initiated when we needed your advice for the improvement of our silk reeling.

The association formed for this purpose is encountering so many completely unexpected obstacles that we have serious doubts about carrying this matter to a conclusion. First of all, several points in your demands seem too burdensome for our association to bear. Secondly, it seems to us that while good quality silk is highly desirable in the long term, it is too early in this process to have the desired value for the community.

I hasten to inform you of these matters in order that the situation not be further delayed. For the reasons mentioned above, I regret to report that I doubt very much that any progress can be made in the realization of this project.

On the other hand, if you, esteemed Mr. Zamero, decided that our interest would be well served through the establishment of an organzine machine to produce organzine of a quality to equal that of Italian organzine, and also to train three young Mennonites thoroughly in the skill of doubling, I would do what I can to arouse local interest and persuade the association to strike an agreement that would accomplish this undertaking. Should this be the case, I would expect an early answer that would help me to understand what else is needed to expedite this matter.

With the most complete esteem, I remain your respectful servant, Johann Cornies.

346. Johann Cornies to Evgenii F. Hahn. 16 October 1844. SAOR 89-1-1088/143v.

Yr. Excellency, Mr. v. Hahn,

The Molochnaia Mennonite District is making constant efforts to advance and disseminate sericulture and to make it a more important part of our economy. Evidence shows that this can only be accomplished by raising the quality of our silk and by encouraging sales at higher prices. To promote the community's interest in this situation, our local Society proposes to establish a silk-reeling facility under its direct leadership and supervision. It is estimated that this would cost about three thousand silver rubles.

I write to ask whether Yr. Excellency would consider it possible that the authorities would permit us to build such a facility at the cost of the community treasury and permit the community to retain it as its own property. The building would be constructed and arranged for ten to forty reelers, adding to their numbers as they are gradually required.

The money would not all be needed at once, but would, in any case, be limited to three thousand silver rubles. The operating costs would be sought from private sources.

The Society hopes to promote the rapid growth of sericulture among Mennonites. I would obediently request that Yr. Excellency let us know whether a formal submission pertaining to this matter should be made.

347. Johann Cornies to Traugott Blueher. 28 October 1844. SAOR 89-1-1088/144v.

Most esteemed Mr. Blueher,

The sum of six thousand silver rubles sent earlier arrived in good order as did the five thousand rubles included with your communication of 4 October in payment for wool sold on my account.

I would further request that you make arrangements to forward 250 copies of Bible stories, and fifty copies each of biblical natural histories, geographies, and church histories at the time of the Kharkiv market, when a transport with local merchants might be available. If the above-mentioned quantities are not in supply, kindly order them on my account and have them sent to me as soon as possible.

With hearty greetings to you and your valued family, your faithful friend and servant, Johann Cornies.

348. Johann Cornies to Levshin. 1 November 1844. SAOR 89-1-1088/145.

Mr. v. Levshin, Yr. Excellency, Most gracious Sir,

In response to Yr. Excellency's honoured communication No. 132, I submit, by return mail, my honest opinion about the matter you have raised.

1. Most importantly, I fear that the Prussian Mennonites might well be drawing back from this intended group settlement because it involves such a small number of families. Specifically, a Mennonite brotherhood consisting only of forty families and settled at such a considerable distance from here will encounter various obstacles in the making of its internal arrangements.

2. The limited quantity of land that the high administration has set aside near St. Petersburg for the use of the Prussian Mennonites does not correspond to the expectations of those who might consider leaving

the agricultural properties they now farm in Prussia. If the purpose of this settlement is to be achieved, it is highly important that good agriculturalists in possession of their own properties be included. At present, such people are still farming more land than they have been offered here. They will only decide to emigrate if the land allocated for their settlement in Russia is larger and offered on advantageous terms.

These are my assumptions based on a knowledge of the matter. I strongly doubt that people can be found who are interested in emigrating to a settlement near St. Petersburg on such terms. Still, I am sending an urgent invitation to my correspondents in Prussia because the effects of flooding there may trigger decisions contrary to my assumptions. Once I hear back I will not hesitate to report to Yr. Excellency on the results of my queries.

With exceptional esteem and the deepest respect, I remain Yr. Excellency's most obedient servant, Johann Cornies.

349. Johann Cornies to Peter Froese. 1 November 1844.
SAOR 89-1-1088/148.

From the Corresponding Member, etc.

Honoured Elder Peter Froese in Tiegerweide, West Prussia,

When he travelled through our local region, His Excellency, Director of the Third Department v. Levshin wrote to me from Kharkiv to say that His Highness, the Minister of State Domains, had deigned to commission him to discuss with me a settlement of Prussian Mennonites near St. Petersburg and to inquire whether it might be possible to find interested persons in Prussia for this purpose.

I submitted my opinions to Mr. v. Levshin and inquired about the kind and quantity of land the government intended to set aside for the desired settlement. His Excellency responded with No. 132 on 7 October 1844 from St. Petersburg.

Under government administration, swamps have been dried out in the vicinity of St. Petersburg and assigned for Mennonite settlement. Four hundred desiatinas of arable land in two sections have presently been included in the plot. The government will add thirty-six desiatinas to this total to enlarge the settlement. An estimated ten to twelve desiatinas of this land will be allocated for the use of each family.

As directed by the Director, and according to the Minister of State Domains' wishes, I hereby inform you of this matter. I would humbly request that you arrange a meeting in this regard with all Deputies earlier chosen in the matter of a settlement in Mogilev and Vitebsk Guberniias. Following this meeting, please send me a detailed official report about opinions expressed and decisions made that would enable me to send the original copy of your report to the Ministry, should this be desired.

I must further explain that, while the land assigned for each family is relatively small, it is near St. Petersburg. If purposefully cultivated, it could yield good profits from crops that could be sold at high profits in the immediate vicinity. The settlers must naturally be exceptional agriculturalists with some means. They must know how to manage their property in ways that would attain the purposes of the highest authorities. Exceptional attention must be given to this issue. A failed settlement would generally damage the good reputation Mennonites have maintained till the present time.

Please note that settlement in Mogilev and Vitebsk Guberniias has not been suspended because of this newly initiated project. The only thing still missing is the Ministry's report on the quantity of land purchased for this purpose on the Minister's orders. As soon as I receive this information, I will inform you at once.

350. From Society Members to Zamero. 3 November 1844. SAOR 89-1-1088/150v.

Most esteemed Mr. Zamero,

In the absence of Society Chairman, Johann Cornies, we have the honour to respond to your valued communication of 9 October 1844 that expressed an interest in undertaking reforms in the reeling of our local silk. We agree completely that to increase the value of our silk, the twisting of threads, doubling, etc., all depend on the proper reeling of the silk thread.

Since it is quite impossible to obligate ourselves to provide you with fifty puds of silk needed, we cannot consider your proposal. Certainly the production of such a quantity cannot with certainty be expected next year. Unanticipated events may well transpire that create obstacles for our producers that might well undermine their undertakings completely or to a large degree.

For these reasons, we are in no position to enter into a discussion with you of your proposals. Please excuse us for the delay in answering your last communication.

With complete esteem, your respectful Society Members, Gerhard Enns and Jacob Martens.

351. Johann Cornies to Fedor F. Rosen. 12 November 1844. SAOR 89-1-1088/151v.

Director Baron v. Rosen,

I am honoured to submit to Yr. Honour the enclosed records of seeding and harvesting of crown potatoes in sixty-nine village communities in Berdiansk, Melitopol, and Dneprov Districts and of maize in forty-nine village communities in Berdiansk and Melitopol Districts. These should enable you to make further rulings in regard to this subject.

In several village communities little or absolutely no maize was obtained. The collared pratincole and also a specific maggot were noticed in the soil and they destroyed the seed as it sprouted in spring. Later, large quantities of small beetles caused much damage to the maize ears. In general, maize was completely spared in only a few places.

Yr. Honour will kindly obtain the necessary information about the quantity of maize produced at Novogrigorievka from the Berdiansk District Supervisor. It may well be unacceptable because of the local *Starshin*'s deceit when the required receipts were handed out. I gave it to the District Supervisor for investigation.

I will shortly have the honour of sending a supplementary record of the number of so-called ministerial potatoes still to be dealt with in the various village communities.

352. Johann Cornies to Fedor F. Rosen. 15 November 1844. SAOR 89-1-1088/152v.

Director Baron v. Rosen,

I am honoured to report on Yr. Honour's 31 January 1844 communication No. 63, to say that I divided the American summer rye sent to me and had it seeded in five separate places, specifically three funt in Mikhailovka, three funt in Kaikulak, and three funt in Andreevka, as well as three funt at my Iushanle estate and one funt in Tashchenak. Another two funt were missing from the supposed total quantity.

This variety of grain succeeded best in Andreevka, where twenty-seven funt were harvested, with nineteen and one-half funt in Mikhailovka, and nineteen funt in Kaikulak. It is stored in their village offices for further disposition. In contrast, observations on my Iushanle estate showed very mixed results, with only six and one-quarter funt of pure summer rye and two funt of "Hamalei" barley. On the whole, expectations that this grain will thrive and be useful in this region cannot be determined from this first seeding, especially because this year's summer was very unfavourable to summer grain.

353. Johann Cornies to Fedor F. Rosen. 15 November 1844. SAOR 89-1-1088/153.

Director v. Rosen,

Yr. Honour is humbly requested to kindly have a copy of the *Journal of the Ministry of State Domains* ordered for me and also for Mikhail Golubov, crown peasant from Novovasilievka village for the coming year, 1845. The required silver ruble is enclosed.

354. Johann Cornies to Fedor F. Rosen. 15 November 1844. SAOR 89-1-1088/153v.

Director Baron v. Rosen,

I must report to you, Honoured Baron, that I still have potato implements ordered for Tavrida Guberniia in storage here, namely thirteen mounders, one marker, and thirty-eight lifters, all paid for. I have another two markers not yet paid for, which were built for no particular destination.

Delivered to various places in Berdiansk District, in return for receipts, and now in use are twenty-one mounders, thirteen markers, and ten lifters. In Melitopol District, there are twelve mounders, seven markers, and four lifters and there are three lifters in the Dneprov area. Listed as broken were one mounder and one marker in Chernigov Volost, Berdiansk District.

355. Johann Cornies to Evgenii F. Hahn. 19 November 1844. SAOR 89-1-1088/156.

State Counsellor v. Hahn,

During the many years that the Pietist community has existed in this region, I have treasured its honest intentions and have the greatest sympathy for its welfare in all circumstances. I thus found it extremely gratifying to receive Yr. Excellency's trust in directing me to be helpful in raising the well-being of these good people. I had hoped that the desired fruits might be clearly visible in a few years' time. This would have given me great pleasure.

Since Mr. v. Stempel investigated the local matter in question, the Pietists have collectively drawn down upon themselves Inspector Pelekh's undeserved and irreconcilable hatred and my work among them suffers from a decided prejudice.[3] Because of his particular aversion, the Inspector tries to report certain not unknown facts about the Elders in the Berdiansk District to the [Guardianship] Committee, thus intimidating them. They lose courage in the struggle to carry out the obligations demanded by the agricultural improvements underway.

The District Office Elders were again extremely distressed because they were forced to give settler Bauer's fullholding in Neuhoffnungsthal to someone else. The specific reason cited was that the census change had not been observed, either inadvertently or out of ignorance. The Inspector should have alerted them to this fact. The fullholding went to settler Gakstaeter quite impartially, with the consent of the village community, and he promised to become a most excellent householder. Then the matter turned around and Gakstaeter suffered substantial losses and must now consider himself ruined. The District Office could be blamed for this. In their honest simplicity, the Office members know they are not to blame and are rapidly losing their courage. All of the improvements that I was striving to bring about with great effort are now threatening to come to a complete halt.

Although I try to console the people and encourage them, they seem to have lost any real trust in the Inspector. When the Inspector orders them to do this and that they immediately respond in such haste that I must remain quiet. For example, among other things, the District Chairman told me that he had informed the Inspector that basic principles prevented Pietists from undertaking unnecessary travels and business on Sundays and religious holidays when they are required to go to church or conduct devotions at home. The Inspector responded by saying that if the District Chairman allowed such limitations, he should be immediately arraigned before the courts, without first asking the Committee.

In another case, the District Chairman complained to the Inspector that the Neuhoffnungsthal community objected to every demand

---

3 Cornies's dispute with Khariton Pelekh seemed to centre on religious disputes in the Württemberg settlement. It ultimately resulted in Hahn transferring the Colonial Inspector to Odesa. See Staples, *Johann Cornies*, 228.

that tax payments among villagers should be based on the number of working adults. The Inspector is supposed to have said that they were really not required to pay on this basis. Each village community is required to make its own decision and follow its own preferences in distributing taxes. When the District Chairman showed him the Committee's statement, the Inspector admitted that he could not counter it.

In my opinion, the Inspector's actions are not helpful. Trust is lacking on both sides. The two regard one another as enemies who are trying to damage the other. For this reason, it would be preferable if the supervision of these settlements were soon entrusted to Inspector v. Stempel. The Pietists have complete trust in him.

May Yr. Excellency's noble heart and concern for the well-being of everyone allow you to judge fairly in this matter.

I yield to the pleasant hope that Yr. Honour might continue to consider me worthy of your grace. With lively feelings of esteem, I remain, Yr. Excellency's respectful servant, Johann Cornies.

356. Johann Cornies to Benjamin Ratzlaff and Peter Wedel. 22 November 1844. SAOR 89-1-1092/2.

No. 1288 [Draft scattered through file 89-1-1092]:

Esteemed Church Elders Benjamin Ratzlaff in Rudnerweide and Peter Wedel in Alexanderwohl,

On 20 November, the assembled Gnadenfeld congregation requested that a communication be sent on its behalf to this Society, presenting its complaint against fullholder Wilhelm Lange. The latter was excluded from his congregation eight months ago, on 1 July, because of his bad conduct, including deception and intrigues that involved him and others. He tried to damage the Gnadenfeld congregation and destroy its beneficial regulations based on our confession of faith. He was able to draw other Elders and congregations into his rebellious attitudes. Using all of his powers and illegal actions, he tried to make life difficult for the Gnadenfeld congregation.

Finally, during his most recent visit, His Excellency, Acting General Guardian, State Counsellor v. Hahn had taken forceful action in part because the Elders had submitted their own report to him. The Wilhelm Langes were deemed punishable and placed under the ban. No one was to have any further contact with them. The Gnadenfeld congregation hoped that this would end the disorder in the congregation and bring peace. They had also hoped that their disciplined members would be moved to return to the discipline of the congregation.

The church assembly expresses its regrets that it was disappointed in this hope. They say that the Elders paid no attention to the cause of Wilhelm Lange's situation, basing their actions on an illegal conference agreement of 8 September 1843. Congregational members who have been called to account for their contacts with the punished openly assert that it is not true that their Elders have appealed to the State Counsellor. They say that the fact that the Elders paid no attention to Elder Wilhelm Lange indicates this clearly, as does their failure to send a notice to their congregational members.

Various congregation members insist that only their own consciences guide their behaviour, allowing them to have contacts with the punished individuals as though they were not under the ban, to the annoyance, offence, and insult of other members of the congregation. Malice and stubbornness are increasing, making it increasingly difficult, yes almost impossible, to keep order within the congregation. The vital church ban has not only become ineffective, but even ridiculous. Wilhelm Lange boasts that he can go wherever he wishes in our villages and no one avoids him. Members of the Rudnerweide and the Alexanderwohl congregations are, in particular, doing the most obvious damage to our community.

The Gnadenfeld assembly has urgently asked the Society to deal with these complaints. It asserts that Elders and members who are dealing with the Wilhelm Langes, contrary to church regulations, should end this behaviour as soon as possible, and, in so doing end the disorder that is so damaging to the Gnadenfeld congregation.

In keeping with the declaration that the esteemed church teacher Johann Wiebe made personally, on behalf of the Elders, to the Acting General Guardian, State Counsellor v. Hahn in the presence of the Society Chairman, the Society sends the following friendly request to the esteemed Elders Ratzlaff and Wedel. Please consider the Wilhelm Langes to be persons put under the ban. In accordance with Mennonite teachings, no dealings may be conducted with them and no other congregation may accept them [as members]. The esteemed Elders should announce their decision to their congregations, notifying the Wilhelm Langes about it as soon as possible. Otherwise the Elders would draw down upon themselves just retribution for their neglect.

The Society expects that it will receive a report that this has been done.

357. Evgenii F. Hahn to Johann Cornies. 23 November 1844.
SAOR 90-1-889/33.

To the Chairman of the Molochnaia Mennonite Society for the Advancement of Agriculture and Trades,

Your communication of 26 October reveals the intention of the Agricultural Society to build a silk-reeling facility that would promote the development of the silk industry in the Molochnaia Mennonite District. It is estimated that this would cost circa three thousand silver rubles.

In my opinion, the requirements for building such a facility on the community's accounts are:

1. The community has sufficient means available to establish it.

2. The expenses involved in establishing it should be advantageously returned to the community through the use of the facility.

If the Society's submission makes it clear that these two conditions have been met, the colonial administration will not hesitate to approve the purpose in question.

In actual fact, however, the building of a community reeling facility has long seemed questionable to me so long as the community has no mulberry plantation. For the same reason, I doubt that it is possible to reach an agreement with the foreigner Zamero. A silk-reeling facility of the extent projected by the Society will require a huge number of cocoons that your community will have to purchase because it lacks a community mulberry plantation. As a result your reeling facility will have to work for nothing if your agriculturalists purchase such a large quantity of cocoons at a price of two silver rubles, fifty kopeks apiece. On an average, sixty measures of cocoons are required to produce one pud of silk. If these cocoons cost 150 silver rubles, it is obvious that the silk must be sold for at least two hundred silver rubles per pud. This is a very good price for silk, difficult to obtain unless the silk is excellent. It is impossible to produce only excellent silk and to obtain two hundred silver rubles for every pud. The Italian Zamero's excellent silk probably was appraised at three hundred silver rubles. However, not appraisals but sales are under discussion here and Zamero will be very happy if he is able to get 250 silver rubles for this particular silk.

These are only my impartial observations. My objective is first to encourage an awareness of the fact that you must do what you must to ensure that you can acquire the requisite quantity of cocoons cheaply before a community reeling facility can be established.

It will, in any case, be my pleasant duty to assist in the realization of this useful undertaking, and others like it.

Yours truly, State Counsellor v. Hahn.

Odesa, 23 November 1844. Answer 16 December 1844.

358. Johann Cornies to Christian Steven. 27 November 1844. SAOR 89-1-1088/161v.

Inspector for Agriculture v. Steven,

As a result of terms concluded on 6 March 1844 with Molochnaia Mennonites Peter Cornies, Ohrloff; Isaac Wiens, Altona; Jacob and Peter Neumann, Muensterberg; and Johann Sukkau, Blumenort, four crown peasant apprentices from Kherson Guberniia were received on my Iushanle estate 20 May 1844. On that date, Fedor Rabulo went to Isaac Wiens, Nikolai Dionditz to Johann Sukkau, Ivan Liubenko to Jacob Neumann and Ivan Didenko to Peter Cornies for the agreed-upon purpose of learning practical agricultural and household skills. The fifth apprentice who is still expected will go to Peter Neumann after his arrival on my estate. I will inform Yr. Honour of this development at that time.

359. Johann Cornies to Evgenii v. Hahn. 27 November 1844. SAOR 89-1-1088/162v.

State Counsellor v. Hahn, Yr. Excellency,

It causes me great pain to rob you of precious moments that you might otherwise devote to your heavy load of business, but circumstances are so urgent that I must fall back upon your generally well-known willingness to help the suffering.

I appeal on behalf of the family of Friedrich Wilhelm Lange, Church Elder in Gnadenfeld. About six years ago, he inherited a very considerable sum of money from Mrs. Lange's relatives in Prussia. With his wife of five years, Lange travelled to Prussia to attend to the matter of this inheritance, to take receipt of it, to bring it to Russia, and to deposit it in a banking establishment where it might collect interest.

Informed that his wife's relatives in Prussia intended to make the transfer of this money difficult, he did not venture to take all of his children along but left several of them behind as a precaution. His wife is vain and proud of her large fortune and her Prussian relatives might well seek to persuade her to divorce her husband and remain in Prussia forever. I am unsure of what miserable experiences Lange may have had with his wife in Prussia, no doubt at the instigation of her relatives and others. Something, however, made Mrs. Lange quite furious to judge by what she told me and the way she behaved towards her husband and children after her return from Prussia. In high dudgeon, she has done what she could to leave her husband and children and return to Prussia forever.

A capital sum of some ten thousand thaler Prussian currency is still in Prussia, lent out at low rates. Letters from Prussian representatives, not Mennonites, lead one to conclude that they are on Mrs. Lange's side. Instigated by a Gnadenfeld congregation member, Wilhelm Lange, they goad her into divorcing her husband. When Friedrich Wilhelm Lange was in Prussia, these agents lied in persuading him to sign a document declaring that she would have to co-sign every time he tried to withdraw money from the inheritance. Moreover, the District Office would have to confirm the validity of the signature and seal.

Friedrich Wilhelm Lange has now received a letter from these authorized representatives affirming that they paid money from the capital fund to relatives in Prussia at Mrs. Lange's request. Not only did her husband Lange not agree to this, but he did not even know about it. This woman's whole family is suffering because of her storming about and grumbling. She has so assailed them that her husband and children have been reduced to the greatest grief. For this reason and because of the abuse she has poured down upon her congregation, the latter barred her from their communion service. She is now obviously trying to have herself excommunicated and hopes to separate from her husband and travel to Prussia.

On behalf of this family's welfare, I would ask Yr. Excellency for your gracious advice as to how it might be possible to transfer this capital sum to Russia. Peace will not prevail until the money is transferred, intrigues in Prussia cease, and Mrs. Lange herself is satisfied.

I look forward to receiving Yr. Excellency's gracious advice in this troubled situation, and remain, with honest assurances of my esteem, etc.

360. Johann Cornies to Evgenii F. Hahn. 27 November 1844.
SAOR 89-1-1088/166.

Mr. v. Hahn,

Johann Siemens, Chairman of the Khortitsa Society, visited me yesterday. He wanted advice on various agricultural developments the

Society plans to establish. He related how these efforts sparked plenty of annoyance, despite intentions and efforts to reform economic arrangements and regulations following the example of what had been done on the Molochnaia.

Siemens explained, among other things, that Herod and Pilate had now become friends to thwart his directives. Specifically, Elder Jacob Dick and the District Chairman were in friendly communication with schoolteacher Heese, collaborating against Siemens [head of the Khortitsa Agricultural Society], despite the fact that they had been sworn enemies for the longest time. As proof, he related that, after Yr. Excellency had visited Khortitsa, Heese had drawn two sketches of the ridging plough. Although Heese had not asked to be recompensed for his work, a meeting of the Society decided to pay Heese twenty-five rubles for the drawings. Since the Society has no resources of its own, its Chairman asked the District Chairman to dip into its treasury for the outlay. The District Chairman said that he was not authorized to make such expenditures from community accounts. In order to stop all this vexation, Siemens simply took sixty rubles out of his own pocket and paid them out, as demanded.

Siemens is a simple householder who has to carefully count every kopek. He has encountered difficulties in his own family economy because of delays in his farming occasioned by the demands of his public office, for which he gets no recompense. Sixty rubles are therefore a considerable sum for him to lose.

Although it is painful for me to burden Yr. Excellency with such disagreeable episodes, the subject seems so important that, to salve my conscience and prevent such disturbances in future, I have no hesitation in exposing this oppressive situation that threatens the work of Chairman Siemens.

With constant devotion and esteem, I remain Yr. Excellency's respectful servant, Johann Cornies.

361. Johann Cornies to Acting General Guardian [Evgenii F. Hahn]. 27 November 1844. SAOR 89-1-1092/1.

[Draft:] Acting General Guardian,

In response to Yr. Excellency's Directive No. 8616 of 30 October 1844, I have the honour to report to you as follows regarding the possibility and utility of engaging in viticulture on the Molochnaia:

1. It is clear that the soil and climate of the Molochnaia are suitable for viticulture, as demonstrated by Count Orlov-Denisov's vineyards on the Abitochna, close to the Molochnaia. Experiments locally confirm this impression.

2. It would, however, be of no use to our inhabitants to introduce viticulture in the Molochnaia villages at the present time. To make sense, viticulture must depend on the labour of many workers. Under present conditions, our settlement does not have nearly enough workers to manage the demands of field cultivation and various other branches of agriculture. They must be hired from outside of our settlement.

3. The general introduction of viticulture at this unsuitable time would therefore withdraw a large proportion of inhabitants from other major occupations.

362. Johann Cornies to Carl Stempel. 27 November 1844. SAOR 89-1-1088/168v.

Most esteemed Mr. v. Stempel,

I find I cannot answer your honoured letter of 19 November asking about the number of rams and ewes your sheepfarm would need to improve significantly. I do not know the total number of sheep you have or what kind of sheep they are, whether rams, ewes, old or young. In our villages, sheep are priced at six to seven rubles, immediate cash payment. Russians and Nogais usually buy ten to thirty head wherever they can, depending on the surplus each agriculturalist is willing to sell.

I have sold no sheep this year. A year ago I sold my surplus at eight rubles per head. This year I want to sell six hundred head of good, young, fine ewes with a lot of wool and no defects, at ten rubles apiece, immediately after shearing which is about 1 June. Three lambs can be bought for the price of one sheep. I sell rams with their wool at various prices in April, or after 23 September, for four to six silver rubles per head. The rams that I sell for four to six silver rubles would markedly improve the quantity and fineness of your community flock's wool. Villages buy these rams to improve their flocks every year. Rams priced at fifteen silver rubles are needed only for specially selected flocks.

I do not agree that your area does not need to develop its wool to the same degree of fineness as mine. Once fineness, uniformity, thickness, and length of wool have been achieved, willing buyers will always be ready to pay a good price for them. Also, the annual surplus, as my experience proves, will find a ready market without causing you worry and grey hair.

If you are thinking of buying my sheep, you should have someone with expert knowledge inspect them. These are not rejects, generally understood to be bad, old, or weak. My surplus are sorted according to the quality of their wool, not according to their age or physical faults. They consist of two- to five-year-olds, with very few six years old. One hundred to two hundred sheep good enough to improve the fineness, thickness, uniformity, and length of wool could easily be chosen from this flock and, when bred with suitable rams, come to constitute a selected stock. This would provide an essential advantage for your flocks. Granted, rams priced at fifteen silver rubles should be used for such selected flocks. In such cases, only a few rams of the best quality would need to be bought each year thereafter.

I do not, however, know about the wethers you mention and the contribution they might make to the improvement of your flock. They might be intended for sale but the profit is usually small since butchers only buy fat-tailed wethers, leaving you with some that you cannot sell. In such cases they drag down your profit and cause it to disappear.

It is too late to find accommodations among Molochnaia Mennonites for the eight families from Hesse-Darmstadt, as the Committee suggests in its directive to you. This should have been done in September. Accommodations are now full and well-paying jobs are gone. It is too late in the season for these people to move. By the time they have made their arrangements, spring would be on its way and they would be preparing for their move to their assigned locations.

Master Mason Larion is presently not at home, but I will soon let you know what can be done.

With honest esteem, I remain Yr. Honour's respectful servant, Johann Cornies.

363. Johann Cornies to Peterson. 29 November 1844. SAOR 89-1-1088/171v.

Mr. v. Peterson, Yr. Honour,

It is high time that I thank Yr. Honour for the books you sent me, for which I am very grateful. You are very kind. I found so much in them to enlighten me and I have also learned so much that is useful for the work that I do.

I had hoped that I might see you in our region again this summer. State Counsellor v. Keppen had suggested as much this spring, but by late summer I suspected that your extensive business affairs would probably not let you get away from St. Petersburg.

Our tree plantations are making wonderful progress. As they grow and flourish they inspire even Russian and Nogai peasants close to our villages to believe that it is possible and reasonable to forest the steppes. In my imagination, I see myself transported to a time when small forests, here and there, will shoot up and grow towards the sky on high steppe ridges. They will provide pleasure for travellers, draw in the air's moisture, increase the fruitfulness of the soils, and break the back of this region's damaging hurricanes.

We already have examples of forest trees that grow well on the high steppes. I believe that many thousands of trees will grow and prosper in places where one hundred trees are growing now. It has been shown that this is possible. Yet, we still lack the perseverance and a responsible and enterprising spirit to give us courage when misfortune strikes, as it surely will, and disrupts our progress for a few years.

In early November I visited the forest-tree plantations founded by Mr. Graff in Aleksandrov District, and took pleasure in their good order and regular plantings. I was astonished and marvelled that it was possible for the estimable Graff to accomplish such order with the lazy, stupid, disorderly peasants of his region, and that he did not lose courage and allow the hair-splitting officials in the Domains Bureau to drive him mad.

His zeal and perseverance do him honour and give promise that these forest-plantations will be crowned with outstanding success. It would be only fair if the government encouraged and supported this young man directly from the Forestry Department. You know Graff, and fortunately I know your noble, philanthropic heart. This makes it unnecessary to write another line about this subject.

With the greatest respect, and constantly willing to be of service to Yr. Honour, Johann Cornies.

364. Johann Cornies to Fedor F. Rosen. 29 November 1844.
SAOR 89-1-1088/175v.

Director Baron v. Rosen,

Yr. Honour is respectfully requested to graciously agree, as you did in 1843, to a remuneration of five silver rubles per desiatina for the supervisors who promote and disseminate the cultivation of potatoes and maize. They need to be rewarded for the work and time required in supervising the planting of potatoes on sixty-nine desiatinas in Berdiansk, Melitopol, and Dneprov Districts. This would encourage them further.

Please provide me as soon as possible with the required sum of 345 silver rubles to distribute to the supervisors, each according to the potato fields under his supervision and to the success of their efforts.

365. Johann Cornies to Fedor F. Rosen. 29 November 1844. SAOR 89-1-1088/176.

Director Baron v. Rosen,

After our discussion, I made inquiries about fired bricks for the projected crown structures and found an oversupply at two locations. In Altonau, Isaac Wiens has forty-five thousand of the first variety and thirty-three thousand of the second variety, and in Rudnerweide, Jacob has fifty thousand of the first variety and thirty thousand of the second variety. They have been well fired and are of the size accepted here among our Mennonites. The average price in both places is twenty-two rubles per thousand.

If the above-mentioned bricks are to be purchased for the crown, I would respectfully ask Yr. Honour to notify me as soon as possible about making a deposit for them. Buyers anticipating construction next year are beginning to order them.

366. Johann Cornies to Fletnitzer. 29 November 1844. SAOR 89-1-1088/177v.

Very worthy Pastor Fletnitzer,

Your letter of 3 November gave me great pleasure, revealing as it does your loving sympathy for our village schools. Please accept my warmest thanks for supplying the wall-primers and the handheld primer and for your instructions as to their use. I hope that you would be equally willing, in future, to supply us with additional wall-primers, as needed.

I respectfully remit your one-hundred-ruble outlay and commend myself to your further kindness as your respectful servant, Johann Cornies.

367. Johann Cornies to Christian Steven. 29 November 1844. SAOR 89-1-1088/178.

Mr. v. Steven,

Many thanks for the trees that you sent me with Reimer. I will try as soon as I can to send you the cheese you ordered and to buy you a pair of good horses.

We have had dry frosts here constantly since 1 November and today the temperature fell to eighteen degrees. Yesterday, the first snow of any consequence fell, but there was almost no wind. About half a fut of snow covers the dry earth, but it is so light that it could drift away with the first wind. Sheep prices are rising, as are those for wheat. In Berdiansk they are again paying from ten to thirteen rubles [per pud]. The cattle plague continues to rage in Nogai and Russian villages, and pestilence has greatly reduced the Nogais.

Although we were unable to reach an agreement with Mr. Zamero, we think he has taught us enough about the better reeling of cocoons that we should be able to sell silk for at least two hundred rubles per pud. For this purpose, we intend to set up a facility with at least ten reelers this spring, etc.

368. Johann Cornies to [Fedor F. Rosen]. 29 November 1844. SAOR 89-1-1088/172.

[Draft:] Director,

Although I paid fifty-five rubles for sacks to transport seed potatoes from one village to another this spring, the sacks fell apart and are completely unusable. I would kindly ask Yr. Honour to repay me this money as well as the twenty-one rubles, eighty-five kopeks that I spent on postage and messenger fees relating to the cultivation of potatoes.

369. Johann Cornies to Fedor F. Rosen. 6 December 1844. SAOR 89-1-1088/183v.

Director Baron v. Rosen,

In carrying out Yr. Honour's communication No. 970 of 6 November 1844, I am honoured to submit the following report. During the summer I asked around and learned that several peasants, perhaps even many, were planting potatoes. Still, it seems to me that no one in the

Berdiansk, Melitopol, or Dneprov Districts has excelled sufficiently to be deserving of an award.

One person has distinguished himself in the cultivation of maize, the Nogai Begal Amangelov from Kanligare village. Specifically, he received two *garnitz* of maize seed and harvested one chetvert, one chetverik, and four garnitz of maize. I would bring this matter to Yr. Honour's attention, requesting that the reward be negotiated in the appropriate place as a means of encouraging him and other Nogais in their efforts.

370. Johann Cornies to Carl Stempel. 6 December 1844.
SAOR 89-1-1088/184v.

Mr. v. Stempel,

After our friendly leave-taking in Bergthal, I visited the Berdiansk Colonist District in November. I found that the Pietists were again discouraged after Inspector Pelekh and another official had stayed with the District Chairman for several days. None of my efforts to console and encourage had any effect and I was compelled to make a submission regarding this situation to the State Counsellor on 19 November. Yesterday, I received preliminary information from the State Counsellor regarding a decision of the Committee to place the Berdiansk villages under your administration once Inspector Pelekh has presented his annual statements for the current year, 1844. I wish you good fortune and congratulate you from the bottom of my heart that heaven's daughter, freedom of conscience, will finally enter this community and permit it to follow its own religious principles and decide on its economic arrangements. It has longed for this resolution for many years. I have no doubt but that outward prosperity will soon flourish of its own accord because of the simple way of life of these people.

With true esteem and happy respects, I am again Yr. Honour's respectful servant, Johann Cornies.

371. Johann Cornies to Friedrich Prinz. 6 December 1844.
SAOR 89-1-1088/185v.

Dear District Chairman,

I have encouraged Mr. Silvander, the candidate in theology, to see you. I judge him to be a calm, steadfast Christian and, to the extent that I know him, am convinced that he could well be able to direct your community spiritually, provided that he allows himself to be received into your community and share in it spiritually. His knowledge and experience in church matters gives me hope that he might be the man who is best suited to meeting your needs.

Judge yourself. You will speak with him to convince yourself of his views and suitability. Please treat Mr. Silvander's visit seriously and see it as a hint from God. Allow him to stay with you and in your midst for several weeks. Do not deny him permission to preach. In this way, the Lord's exalted Will might become clear to you.

You have endured much suffering. My hope now is that the joy of peace and of calm might come to dwell among you in the New Year. If you wish to build well you will have built upon God.

I remain, as always, your sympathetic and honest Johann Cornies.

372. Evgenii F. Hahn to Johann Cornies. 9 December 1844. SAOR 89-1-889/35.

To the Chairman of the Molochnaia Mennonite Society for the Advancement of Agriculture and Trades, Mr. Cornies,

To my honest regret, your communication of 27 November informed me that an inheritance in Prussia is causing dissension within the family of the esteemed Friedrich Wilhelm Lange in Gnadenfeld.

I would very much like to contribute to the restoration of this family's household peace, as you recommend. Regrettably, my cooperation could at most consist of making arrangements to have the inheritance forwarded from Prussia. Yet even here, according to your letter, the inheritance in question is too large to allow the Prussian government to send this amount to Russia without the wife's permission. According to our laws, it is impossible to restrict Fr. Lange's wife's rights of disposal over the capital she inherited. I very much doubt that this could be otherwise in Prussia.

If it is Mr. Lange's wish, I would be willing to apply to the Ministry and to the Prussian Embassy in St. Petersburg, but even this is doubtful. One cannot hope for any special success until Lange's wife gives preliminary approval to the transfer of the inheritance to Russia. It could then be quickly worked out officially.

Were Lange to have children who are still minors, this could prevent his wife from leaving the country and from divorcing him.

Yours truly, E. v. Hahn.

Odesa, 9 December 1844

[Marked]: Wrote to Lange, 16 December 1844

373. Johann Cornies to Carl Stempel. 12 December 1844.
SAOR 89-1-1088/187v.

Esteemed Mr. v. Stempel,

The letter you sent by messenger arrived yesterday, Monday, 11 December. I will be unable to get the sketch you asked for before Tuesday evening. I include it here. You will naturally change it and add to it as your heart desires, for no matter how gladly one person wishes to help another, he cannot enter into his inclinations, despite the greatest interest.

I hope you have received my reply to your letter of 30 November, which I received the day before yesterday.

Let me answer more fully in reply to your questions about the sheep I have for sale. The entire number consists of 580 head, of which 260 are two- year-olds, 170 are three-year-olds, and 150 are four and five years old. This total number is, on average, suitable for breeding purposes. I permit a purchaser to reject forty head according to his own choice. It is therefore necessary to take only 540 sheep. Should the community be interested in pursuing this matter it could send knowledgeable people to examine the sheep in January, since it is possible to make a reasonable judgment of their quality and wool growth at that time.

With feelings of true esteem, I remain at all times your willing servant, Johann Cornies.

374. Johann Cornies to Christian Steven. 13 December 1844.
SAOR 89-1-1088/188v.

State Counsellor v. Steven. Yr. Excellency,

I urgently need books to teach crown apprentices to write Russian, but none are available in the towns of this area. In this dilemma, I turn to Yr. Excellency with a request for several copies of good books in this regard that you might graciously obtain and send to me by mail. I will gratefully repay you.

With esteem, Yr. Excellency's respectful servant, Johann Cornies.

375. Johann Cornies to Traugott Blueher. 13 December 1844.
SAOR 89-1-1088/189.

Esteemed Mr. Blueher,

The pine seed that I obtained through your efforts was sown last autumn. It seemed to me that it was not of the desired variety and that much of it was incapable of sprouting. For these reasons, I make another request that you kindly obtain one pound of *pinus abies* seed (red pine, or ordinary pine) as soon as possible, and forward it to me by mail. I would like to seed it in February. In addition, I would be pleased if you could get me a detailed listing of current prices for all varieties of seeds available from merchants selling forest-tree seeds in your area. Such a listing would give me a standard against which to judge appropriate prices for several varieties of seeds that become available for sale from my plantation.

I received your valued communications of 28 and 30 October in good order. Please forgive me if I postpone answering them for a few more mail days because I am over my head in business dealings.

Heartily commending myself to you, and with a friendly greeting, your respectful servant, Johann Cornies.

376. Johann Cornies to Hutterthal Village Office. N.d. [1844?] SAOR 89-1-811/8.

To Hutterthal Village Office,

Because our high administration has directed me to concern myself with the Hutterthal community's well-being and to advance its morality and prosperity as quickly as possible, I consider it my duty to make the following order to the Village Office. From now on, no Hutterthal village inhabitants are free to hire out their children, siblings, or wards who are already in service in the Mennonite community or are being trained there. They are first required to obtain written permission from me. This should be done as follows: not the Hutterthal inhabitant but the Molochnaia Mennonite must obtain the permission from me. He should then provide your Village Office with the permission to hire one of the Hutterthal people for a year.

Anyone acting contrary to this order will find that the hiring is not valid and his disobedience will be punished. This must be observed punctually.

377. Agricultural Society to Fedor F. Rosen. N.d. [1844?] SAOR 89-1-811/12.

[Undated draft]

From Molochnaia Mennonite Society for the Advancement of Agriculture and Trades,

To His Honour, Director of the Tavrida Bureau of State Domains, State Counsellor and Knight, Baron v. Rosen,

Marina Zokurinkova, a crown peasant girl from Bolshoi Tokmak village, took a position with the Gnadenfeld schoolteacher Heinrich Franz with the permission of her guardians. She soon ran away, and was sent back to her employer with the help of the Bolshoi Tokmak village administration. Eventually she ran away three times and was always returned to her employer. Each time she declared that she would not serve. The Tokmak priest took her part in the dispute, asserting that she had not been allowed the appropriate food to keep her fasts. He appeared before the village administration and Mr. Andreevskii reported that he had behaved rudely to all of the officials, treating them disparagingly. Investigation in Gnadenfeld showed that the girl had not only received food to keep her fasts, but her employer had also encouraged her sternly to fast. She had not been mistreated, but did not like to keep the fast.

The third time she ran away and the investigation about fasting had been completed, the Society informed the Bolshoi Tokmak village administration that it would not permit the girl to get away with her obstinacy and urged that she be punished and returned to service. This was done, but as soon as the girl arrived, she again declared that she would not serve. The Bolshoi Tokmak village administration writes that she cannot be legally forced to serve, that accounts should be settled, and that she should be let go. The Gnadenfeld Village Office sternly refused to agree to this and the girl ran away again, for the fourth time.

The Society is therefore forced to apply to a higher level in regard to this matter and dares to politely request that you might graciously take stern measures to break the girl's obstinacy with serious punishment as a warning example to others, and to have her delivered back into service as soon as possible. If this matter is not settled now similar cases might well repeat themselves in future.

1845

**378. Agricultural Society to Ohrloff Village Office. N.d.
[January 1845?] SAOR 89-1-1224/5.**

The Society has reached a decision about the nasty description of school-teacher Unger written by the son of Cornelius Siemens. His punishment for his offensive behaviour must be six blows of the rod administered in the schoolroom, in the presence of the other pupils and of his father, Cornelius Siemens.

The Society orders teacher Unger to carry out this punishment without delay. It should be seriously impressed upon Siemens that he has duties as a stepfather and he must require his children to show proper, well-mannered behaviour towards teachers and all others. Taking care to ensure that the children entrusted to his training are not spoiled, he must personally act as a good example in educating them as good, useful people. Siemens should be made aware that acts of disobedience by his stepchildren can be ascribed to his own bad teaching, and that he will have to answer for them.

A report should be made immediately to the Society that this punishment has been carried out and that Siemens has been warned.

**379. Agricultural Society to Andreas Voth. January 1845.
SAOR 89-1-1205/n.p.**

[Draft:] Information for schoolteacher Andreas Voth in Pastwa,

Young people from our settlement are known to travel outside our villages to complete their education. Yet experience teaches us that those who attend outside institutions to learn Russian often return discontented with its necessarily simple endeavours. As a result, young people who had been thought of as among the best of our schoolteachers are no longer useful to the brotherhood to which they had belonged. Also, they are unhappy among their own people.

Although the Society is obliged to improve the school system, it does not think that this necessarily requires the introduction of Russian everywhere in our village schools. This must be done as needed by the times. Moreover, village teachers who wish to learn the fundamentals of the Russian language have opportunities in our settlement to do so at no great cost. The Society should, if needed, support them in this endeavour.

For these reasons, the Society rejects Schoolteacher Voth's wishes as inappropriate, and has decided not to release him from his current position.

380. Johann Cornies to Traugott Blueher. 5 January 1845. SAOR 89-1-1207/4.

Esteemed Mr. Blueher,

Please forgive me for not answering your valued letters of 28 August, 20 November, and 8 December any earlier.

First, thank you for your interesting explanation regarding silk sales. Your letter arrived at a time when a skilled Italian silk-reeler was eager to reach agreement with us about starting to reel our silk. Although we failed to reach an arrangement, he showed us the silk he had produced and reeled in the Bulgarian settlement of Parkani near Odesa. It was valued at three hundred silver rubles per pud in Odesa. Although secretive about his art, his stay was useful. It helped us avoid mistakes in reeling cocoons and in delivering better silk. We intend to set up a facility with ten reelers at first that will eventually be expanded to forty reelers. An association of local members has been formed for this purpose.

Most of last year's silk was sold at the Romen and Kharkiv markets at ten to twelve rubles per funt. Through Messrs Eiseler & Comp., I was only able to send you another thirty-eight funt, twenty-two lots of twelve-thread silk reeled in an improved manner, to be sold as you think best. Every producer here has been mixing his own cocoons, good and bad, and having them reeled himself. If our association buys up the cocoons and has them reeled in our facility, I hope the product will turn out to be evener and better and could perhaps be sent on its way earlier.

To the best of my knowledge, there are no sheepfarm owners in our locality with long-haired English sheep. Nor could I, hard as I tried, find out what it was selling for. If you want me to buy such wool in future, please name the producer.

In accordance with your letter of 20 November, I tried to find a man in our local villages who wanted to purchase two thousand puds of Zigay wool in Bessarabia on your account. For me, the region is unfamiliar and distant and I have no personal acquaintances there that might be counted on to purchase wool for you.

I am grateful to you for selling my wool at such a favourable price, and conclude this matter with the enclosed receipt.[1]

Local prices for wool are still going up and down. Since November, Odesa merchants have offered deposits of twenty-two to twenty-five rubles for wool on the sheep. Deposits have already been made on a large quantity of wool among Russians and Nogais. This did not, however, have much of an effect on wool prices in general. Only a few who needed money took such deposits. Nevertheless, early deposits suggest that almost everyone is assuming that wool prices will be even higher in spring. Still, I failed to find anyone with sheep approaching better quality who had the slightest interest in selling his wool or setting a price for it.

The owner of the sheepfarm from whom you bought the balls designated as Litt. "A." last year has not yet decided to set a price. I know his flock well and can report that the better parts of the fleece had not, as you suggested, been removed. I have never found anyone locally who would commit such an injustice. Moreover, the owner of this sheepfarm is wealthy and too much of an honest man to involve himself in something so base. The poor quality stemmed from the plague (*Raende*) that infected his herd last winter and could not be cured because of the cold weather. It affects mostly the thinnest spots and places where the wool is finest. It therefore ruins the most preferable parts of the fleece. Wool sorters must have noticed this and also the fact that the small diseased places still clung to the wool.

As I have done in the past, I will make the same conscientious efforts this year to have 1,200 puds of wool bought on your account, as you asked, and at the lowest possible prices.

---

1   The receipt for 52,349 rubles is located in SAOR *fond* 89, *opis* 1, *delo* 1207/18.

Some time ago, State Counsellor v. Steven, who is an estate owner in the Crimea, gave me the enclosed notice that his landed estate is up for sale. He asked me to send it on to you so that interested purchasers in Moscow might know.

I have still reported nothing about your dear son Joseph's stay with us. He seemed quite happy and cheerful when he spent the holidays at my house and in the circle of my family. He has not, however, developed a real liking for the simple, rural life, although he has yet to comment on the subject. Still, I am surprised that he has adjusted so well to our life. After all, a young man from the big city must think poorly of us when he is suddenly thrust into a small, monotonous, quiet village with customs and a lifestyle quite different from what he knows. He has, by now, shaken off the worst of such impressions and may, with time, become more accepting of our way of life. He is a healthy and vigorous young man who knows that he has a son's access to my home and family equal to that of his parental home. Everything else is in God's hand.

I cannot express strongly enough our feelings of gratitude for the support and sympathy you have given us this past year. Our hearts feel greatly blessed by the love you have shown us. Please commend us to your dear family.

I consider it a great joy to call myself your thankfully obligated, Johann Cornies.

381. Johann Cornies to Carl Stempel. 9 January 1845. SAOR 89-1-1207/20.

Highly esteemed Mr. v. Stempel,

I received your letter of 8 January from Berdiansk at seven this morning and am sorry to hear that you could not find the lodgings you need. Ali arrived here at three on Sunday afternoon. Your summons arrived when he was not at home, but in another village some twenty verstas away. I hope he managed to locate you in Berdiansk on 8 January with the carters, although even they were late. I also notified Abraham Mathies to meet you in Berdiansk on 10 January.

I wish you good health from the bottom of my heart. It is needed for your work. Please spare yourself and remain assured that no one is more sympathetic to the state of your health than your respectful and loyally interested servant, Johann Cornies.

382. Johann Cornies to Evgenii F. Hahn. 13 January 1845.
SAOR 89-1-1207/22.

Mr. v. Hahn, Yr. Excellency,

On 8 January, Mr. v. Stempel wrote me that he had come to Berdiansk to investigate the theft of wheat by the Nogai, Absaut Chelebi, from the Mennonite Abraham Mathies six years ago. The investigation, assigned to the Berdiansk judge Tolstonog, had not yet been completed. The latter was intentionally using his yearly accounts as an excuse to delay the investigation. He told Mr. v. Stempel that the Nogai Absaut was innocent in this matter. He had not stolen the wheat. This aroused in Mr. v. Stempel the suspicion that Absaut had bribed the judge. Raiskii, the District Chief, informs me that he agrees with Mr. v. Stempel's opinion, and feels that Tolstonog should be removed from the investigation. I grant that it is difficult to believe the Nogais, but many of them have reported that Absaut had boasted that he had recently given the judge one thousand rubles to take his side. There was therefore no need to be concerned. Had briberies not taken place, the judicial investigation would not have been neglected. The wheat had been stolen in broad daylight and there are witnesses to prove it. The theft had been reported in the proper place six years ago and a judicial investigation had been urged on several occasions. This injustice is too great to be allowed to pass in silence. I would urgently request Yr. Excellency's strong and early support for measures to halt this injustice in the Berdiansk lower courts. Attempts are being made to frighten the witnesses by charging them in court and the court is giving Absaut Chelebi every support in these efforts.

It is my opinion that Judge Tolstonog must be removed from this investigation quickly and the whole matter transferred to Eshen, the Melitopol judge.

With lively feelings of esteem, I am Yr. Excellency's respectful servant, Johann Cornies.

383. Johann Cornies to Carl Stempel. 14 January 1845.
SAOR 89-1-1207/33.

Highly esteemed Mr. v. Stempel,

Your valued communication from Neuhoffnung of 8 January hardly surprised me. I have never heard Mr. Tolstonog praised as a just judge. Still, I was pleased that he talked to you so candidly and that you have gotten to know him. In keeping with your wishes, I wrote to Mr. Rosen and Mr. Hahn. I hope that results will soon follow. This is a matter that we must pursue with great vigour. We must preserve a sense of justice and ensure its victory.

Ali arrived in Berdiansk on Tuesday after you left and talked to several people. He encouraged the Nogai witnesses to remain steadfast in their testimony despite every intrigue, and not permit themselves to say anything but the truth. He thinks that the investigation promises good results if it is transferred to Eshen. At the least, he hopes that Eshen will insist on Chelebi reaching an accord.

With genuine respect and esteem I remain, as always, Yr. Honour's honest servant, Johann Cornies.

384. Johann Cornies to Fedor F. Rosen. 15 January 1845. SAOR 89-1-1207/35.

To Director Baron v. Rosen,

Eight varieties of tobacco seed sent on 21 March 1844 with Yr. Honour's communication No. 275 were received on 2 April. This was far too late for seeding last year and will be used this year, 1845.

I am pleased to send you two bunches of each variety of tobacco harvested on my Iushanle estate. Their names are listed as follows: [sixteen numbered items listed].

385. Johann Cornies to Evgenii F. Hahn. 16 January 1845. SAOR 89-1-1207/37.

State Counsellor v. Hahn. Yr. Excellency,

Were it to benefit the Hutterthal community to assume the lease for the remaining 1,824-desiatina plot of land in section No. 15, Andreas Wollmann, a Hutterthal Mennonite, will appear before the Guardianship Committee, supported by my brother, David Cornies. Yr. Excellency made this proposal in your directive No. 8484 of 24 October 1844. Please support the Hutterites with your kind advice in order that the well-being of the Hutterthal community might be furthered. It would be preferable if the community were not required to pay the security in cash, but pay the appropriate interest on it.

Please forgive me for daring to burden you with this matter. Your sympathy for the progress of the poor Hutterthal Mennonites gives me hope that I have not made an error in my request.

With genuine respect and honest feelings of the greatest esteem, I have the honour to call myself Yr. Excellency's most respectful servant, Johann Cornies.

386. C.S. Eiseler company to Johann Cornies. 17 January 1845. SAOR 89-1-1132/6.

Mr. J. Cornies in Ohrloff,

In answer to your esteemed letter of 30 [December], we notify you that we have received the silk you sent to us to be forwarded to the Sarepta Trading Company in Moscow. We have passed it on to our local transport bureau. I will send it on as freight over the next few days for one ruble. The outlay for insurance is one ruble, which we received from the messenger bearing your letter.

Constantly ready to carry out your esteemed commissions, we commend ourselves, with respect and devotion, C.S. Eiseler & Co.

Kharkiv, 17 January 1845.

387. Johann Cornies to Fedor F. Rosen. 17 January 1845. SAOR 89-1-1207/39.

Baron v. Rosen,

Based on the enclosed letter from Mr. Sheremetev, I promised Heinrich Hildebrand, Mennonite from Muensterberg village, to lend Sheremetev the desired wagon until this year. When Hildebrand demanded payment I learned that Sheremetev had died. Yr. Honour will kindly forgive me for burdening you with this matter. I would urgently request that you collect the money for the wagon from the appropriate source. It amounts to 240 rubles. The interest for four months is nine rubles, sixty kopeks, making a total of 249 rubles, sixty kopeks, as agreed. Please have it sent to me by mail to satisfy the Mennonite Hildebrand.

Yr. Honour will graciously credit my boldness and be convinced that I remain at all times, with the greatest respect, Yr. Honour's most respectful servant, Johann Cornies.

388. Peter Froese, Prussia, to Johann Cornies. 17 January 1845. SAOR 89-1-1141/5.

Mr. Johann Cornies, Ohrloff. Honoured Friend,

Your agreeable communication of 1 November 1844 informs us that, to our pleasure, the Russian government intends to allow a village of

Prussian Mennonites to settle in the St. Petersburg area on four hundred desiatinas of land made suitable for cultivation. Applicants for this purpose are to be found in Prussia and you are to conduct the negotiations. We acknowledge this gracious offer from the high Russian government with grateful hearts, and take great pleasure in the prospect that, with the guiding hand of God our Father, our brethren in faith would find suitable conditions to support themselves and their families.

Yet as generous as this offer is, and although it gives us joy, the possibility of an early settlement in that place still involves many difficulties. The earlier possibility granted us by the Russian government for a settlement of Prussian Mennonites in Vitebsk and Mogilev Guberniias, has long dominated the attention of all brethren in faith interested in emigration. Every wish and desire favours that location. We assume that a model settlement could not properly be achieved on a small area as proposed for the St. Petersburg area. The vegetation in such a cold climate may well be less promising than in Vitebsk and Mogilev [Guberniias]. Moreover, the number of people interested in emigration is still too small to establish settlements in both locations at the same time. Most people living here are not yet inclined to emigrate although the prospect for future growth here is limited given the shortage of land available for easy purchase [in Prussia]. Even if the number of emigrating families is not especially large at first, it is certain that others willing to follow in their footsteps will be found from year to year.

Under these circumstances, we turn to you with a friendly request that you present a petition to the highest Russian government asking that the first settlement of Prussian Mennonites be made in the Vitebsk and Mogilev Guberniias. You, esteemed friend, will have the best insight into all aspects of this matter. Your honest love for our fellow believers is our guarantee that you will spare no effort in promoting this important concern. Once we have received your reports and summons we will gladly carry out whatever we can to further the success of this matter.

We still hope that the high Russian government will issue orders early this summer to have Deputies appear in Russia to inspect the land indicated for settlement and to agree to the conditions [of emigration]. We also hope that you will conduct this matter and join our Deputies personally at the location without asking them to first take a long detour to your place of residence. We are prepared to accommodate ourselves to your arrangements.

May God, the Almighty, direct everything to the advantage of our insignificant little group. May He especially pour his rich blessings out over you and give you good health and the strength needed to carry out this important matter. This is the wish of all Mennonite congregations in West Prussia, in whose name I most respectfully sign myself, your most humble friend, Peter Froese.

Tiegerweide, 17 January 1845. [Marked] Copy.

Received 4 February 1845. Report 7 February 1845, No. 21.

389. Johann Cornies to Friedrich Silvander. 24 January 1845. SAOR 89-1-1207/42.

Dear Mr. Silvander,

I was sorry to learn that intrigues by the District Secretary frustrated your visit to the Swedes. With today's mail, I requested that Inspector Kirschner act to put this matter back on track and to report to me, giving his reasons why your intentions were foiled.

Once you have received this letter, please see the Inspector in order that you might reach an agreement in this matter and secure your goal. I hope you will find the Inspector ready to do this. Please send me word about the results as soon as possible.

With esteem, your respectful Johann Cornies.

390. Evgenii F. Hahn to Johann Cornies. 28 January 1845. SAOR 89-1-889/37.

Wollmann leased the leftover land in area No. 15 for nine kopeks silver. He was not able to present an authorization from his community and therefore had to lease the land in his own name. This was the way the document was issued legally, but since the amount is so inconsequential, about thirty-three silver rubles, there would hardly be any use in charging interest.

Year after year you have sent such highly interesting letters about the circumstances and progress of the Molochnaia Mennonite District that I am now unwilling to forgo such reports for 1844. I still hope to receive them.

Several months ago I sent you instructions about the cultivation of tobacco. Did you receive them?

The pile-up of business matters has kept me from answering your letter of 16 December regarding sericulture. I have also been waiting for a report from His Excellency, Mr. Levshin in St. Petersburg. Mr. Levshin has turned his attention to sericulture and promises his cooperation in the development of this industry. It is his wish to have the Italian, Zamero, hired in the Molochnaia District. I have therefore informed Mr. Levshin about the fundamental reasons why his wish cannot be realized. I also explained to the government that, with its support, a large sericulture facility could be set up in the Molochnaia District without Zamero. I have not yet received an answer and will not wait for it any longer. Instead, I will use the first possible moment to discuss this subject further with you, since I cannot approve your viewpoint without first doing so. Yours truly, E. v. Hahn.

Odesa, 28 January 1845. Received 6 February 1845.

391. Traugott Blueher to Johann Cornies. 29 January 1845. SOAR 89-1-1132/72.

Mr. Johann Cornies, Ohrloff.

Dearly loved friend,

Many thanks for your two most recent communications. They gave me great pleasure, especially the rich contents of the latter and the feelings of friendship expressed.

One funt of fresh pine seed was sent by mail. I had to wait several weeks for it to arrive. My outlay was one and one-half silver rubles.

I enclose the current price list from one of the best local seed merchants. It must be understood that if you intend to sell to a merchant here, the prices you will receive will only equal 50 per cent of those listed. You could also attempt to sell your seeds through our stall. This would involve high costs since several advertisements in local newspapers would be absolutely necessary if buyers are to become familiar with your seeds.

I was interested to note that serious steps to improve your silk spinning are being taken in your villages. I await the arrival of the silk sent to me through Mr. Eiseler. This will give me a chance to orient myself in deciding how best to deal with it.

When this year's wool is purchased, please, if possible, consider the sheepfarm from which the balls marked with the [letter] "A" came. It is of good quality.

I made inquiries about long-haired wool and discovered that this particular flock had been sold and completely scattered. It was in Ekaterinoslav Guberniia.

Prospective purchasers could probably be found for the purchase of an estate in the Crimea. Mr. v. Steven should give the exact details and sign them personally. Publicizing this in the local newspapers will cost about five silver rubles.

I am frequently asked about supervisory positions on sheepfarms in your region. I would appreciate receiving whatever information you can give me in this regard.

Included in the case of 250 copies of Bible stories, I also sent price lists for several kinds of sheep shears. I would ask that you pass them on to a capable merchant. Freight charges must be added to the price.

Recognizing with sincere pleasure Joseph's stay with you over the holidays, we thank you for showing him your friendship. May he walk in the right path so that we might take joy in what he is doing.

I send you and your dear family greetings of sincere love, and remain your faithfully obligated friend, Traugott Blueher.

Moscow, 29 January 1845. Received 17 February 1845.

392. Peter Wedel to Johann Cornies. 29 January 1845.
SAOR 89-1-1132/21.

Most esteemed Mr. Cornies,

In response to your request I can tell you that today, 29 January, the esteemed Elders Bernhard Fast, Peter Wedel, and Heinrich Wiens and the preachers Sawatzky and Peters of Friedensdorf visited our local schoolhouse where they held a meeting of the brethren in our congregation. The congregation has long suffered disunity. But little hope emerged out of this meeting despite the fact that the churchmen were willing to help lead our restless congregation away from its mistaken path.

After a stirring sermon by Elder Bernhard Fast, several members reached an agreement with our preachers. This, in my opinion, was not because these members wanted to join us in love, but because they wanted to make their departure from our district somewhat easier.

Several restless members of the congregation were not ready to reach any agreement, but did not explain their reasons for refusing.

Waldheim, 29 January 1845. Village Mayor Wedel.

393. Johann Cornies to Evgenii F. Hahn. 31 January 1845.
SAOR 89-1-1207/45.

State Counsellor Hahn, Yr. Excellency,

Please forgive me for the delay in completing my short annual report about the agricultural progress made in the Molochnaia Mennonite District during the past year. It is enclosed. I had to find missing notes from scattered sources to finish it.

Included is accurate meteorological information gathered from here. I trust it will be of interest to Yr. Excellency.

I will soon submit reports about improvements in the Berdiansk villages, in the Mariupol [Bergthal] Mennonite District, and in the newly settled Hutterthal village.

With respect, commending myself to Yr. further benevolence, I remain Yr. Excellency's respectful servant, Johann Cornies.

394. August v. Haxthausen to Johann Cornies. 3 February 1845.
SAOR 89-1-1132/n.p.

Valued Mr. Cornies,

I trust that you will not have forgotten the traveller who visited his dear countrymen on the Molochnaia with a group of associates during the summer of 1843. The time I spent in your company in the Mennonite settlements was the most pleasant and informative of my entire trip to Russia.

You may recall that on the last day of my visit we dropped in on your neighbours, the Hutterite brethren. There I found three interesting books about their fortunes and teachings:

1. a volume of 586 folio pages, beginning with the creation of the world and continuing to the Reformation and the experiences of the Hutterite brethren, ending in the year 1665.

2. a book in quarto that contained an extract from the above volume plus the story of their community from 1725 to 1787.

3. letters and dispatches of the Elder, called the Epselbuch, dated 1565.

I stated at the time that these books contained a genuine treasure of church history, and that I would try to have the Royal Library in Berlin copy them. Since the originals might be lost in an unfortunate incident, fire, etc., such copies should also be of interest to the Hutterite Brethren. They could then rest more easily, knowing that copies existed and that another one could be made.

[illegible section]. Please send me a brief letter reporting that you have received this communication in good order. In the interests of security and caution, please address the letter to the Imperial Russian Ambassador Baron v. Meyerdorff in Berlin.

With greetings to you, your wife, children, brothers, and everyone I got to know, I pray that God might protect all of you.

Keeping you, more than anyone else, in friendly remembrance, your respectful, A. Baron v. Haxthausen.

Imperial Prussian Government Privy Counsellor.

Berlin, 3 February 1845. Received 11 March 1845.

Answered 30 June 1845.

395. Unknown to Guardianship Committee. N.d.
SAOR 89-1-1167/n.p.

[Undated draft]

Guardianship Committee President,

I have been honoured with a directive to have a copy made of the chronicles of the Hutterite Brethren. I would point out that the blessed Cornies made efforts to have this done as early as 1845 when Baron Haxthausen offered seventy silver rubles to have the copying done, if that were at all possible.

A careful examination of the manuscripts revealed that they had been written in a script of that time that was so different from a contemporary script that no one was capable of making an actual copy. The contents would need to be retrieved, letter by letter. To complete such a copy in a readable form would require unusual persistence and an enormous amount of time.

It is my judgment that, because many Hutterthal residents would strongly oppose any agreement to allow the chronicles to leave their hands, one could prepare a copy only if the government were to commission an especially qualified person to produce it on site.

396. Johann Cornies to Peter Froese. 7 February 1845.
SAOR 89-1-1207/48.

Mr. Peter Froese, Tiegerweide, West Prussia,

On 4 February, we received your valued communication of 17 January. With today's mail I am sending the original along to the high Ministry to enable them to take whatever action they deem right. As soon as possible, I will send you information regarding steps that the Ministry intends to undertake in this matter. Respectfully, J. Cornies.

397. Johann Cornies to Levshin. 7 February 1845.
SAOR 89-1-1207/49.

Director Levshin of the Third Department,

I can report that in response to Yr. Excellency's honoured directive of 7 October 1844 regarding the settlement of Prussian Mennonites near St. Petersburg, I wrote to my correspondent in West Prussia as mentioned in my report of 1 November 1844. I have now received an answer that, in the original, I hasten to submit to Yr. Excellency.

According to this information, the Prussian Mennonites are of one mind in their preference for the Vitebsk and Mogilev Guberniias [as settlement areas.] It is their desire to establish themselves in this area as proposed to them by His Highness, the Minister, through the Tavrida Domains Bureau on 11 August 1842. At the time, I tried to persuade them to accept this offer. Arrangements to carry out this project were made by the Vice-Director of the Second Department in the Tavrida Domains Bureau, in document No. 1549, dated 12 October 1843. The only thing left undone was to purchase the land necessary for this purpose.

Yr. Excellency may therefore proceed as you think best. Please let me know what further action I might take in regard to this matter.

398. Johann Cornies to Evgenii F. Hahn. 7 February 1845.
SAOR 89-1-1207/51.

State Counsellor Hahn, Yr. Excellency,

Mennonites Abraham and Hermann Sudermann, Prussian subjects who have lived here for a number of years, find it necessary to visit Prussia to look after some personal inheritance matters. They have decided to leave for Prussia this coming spring.

The aforesaid Abraham and Hermann Sudermann were accepted into our local Mennonite community according to Guardianship Committee directive No. 5174 of 6 July 1844. They are still waiting for the concluding decree to complete their acceptance as Russian subjects. I would therefore graciously ask Yr. Excellency for advice as to whether it would be possible for these two individuals to undertake this journey despite the fact that they cannot, at present, be considered as either Prussian or Russian subjects and cannot, as such, obtain passes.

In the firm assurance that Yr. Excellency will grant me Yr. benevolent advice, I remain with the deepest esteem, Yr. Excellency's respectful servant, Johann Cornies.

399. Johann Cornies to Evgenii F. Hahn. 7 February 1845. SAOR 89-1-1207/53.[2]

State Counsellor v. Hahn, Yr. Excellency,

Mennonites who moved from Volhynia to the Molochnaia with ministerial permission in 1832 settled in the village of Waldheim on forty fullholdings. There are now a total of ninety-four families living in the village. The Waldheim community insists that colonist status should be revoked for about thirty of the worst and least active of these families, and that they should return as free people to their brethren in faith in the region around Ostroga and Dubna.

These are unruly people who were never pleased with our area. The larger community has had many difficulties with their disruptive ways and they have become a mounting burden to the whole village. One assumes that peace will never come to Waldheim as long as these people are required to stay, nor will it establish a firm foundation for its future until they leave.

Might it be possible to obtain permission for these people, because of their unpredictable ways, to leave our locality and return to the place where they once lived? This is the only way for Waldheim to establish conditions that would permit the government to achieve its objectives [in the village]. The Waldheim community would certainly like to be rid of them. Nor are there obstacles locally to their departure. It would be desirable if this migration were to take place in early spring. It is with longing that our whole community looks forward to their departure.

Yr. Excellency might graciously let me know what further steps should be taken to facilitate this move.

With constant esteem and deepest devotion, I remain Yr. Excellency's most obedient servant, Johann Cornies.

---

2   The Molochnaia village of Waldheim was founded in 1836 by Mennonites who had originally settled in Volhynia. In this letter Cornies incorrectly dates the founding of the village to 1832. About half of the village residents returned to Volhynia in 1845. For a summary of the village and related sources, see Glenn Penner and Steve Fast, "Waldheim, Molotschna and Heinrichsdorf, Volhynia, 1833–1851," Russian Mennonite Genealogical Resource Page, Mennonite Genealogy, https://www.mennonitegenealogy.com/russia/Waldheim_and_Heinrichsdorf.pdf, 25 June 2016.

400. Johann Cornies to Fletnitzer. 9 February 1845.
SAOR 89-1-1207/58.

Pastor Fletnitzer,

Please forgive me for asking you to help us obtain another forty copies of the wall-primer, for which I enclose four hundred rubles. The primers are very useful and their introduction into our local village schools essential.

With the greatest respect for your benevolent interest in providing our young people with an education, it gives me pleasure to call myself your faithfully obligated friend and servant, Johann Cornies.

401. Johann Cornies to Evgenii F. Hahn. 14 February 1845.
SAOR 89-1-1207/60.

Mr. v. Hahn, Yr. Excellency,

Yr. Excellency must have doubts about my protracted, too protracted failure to write a single syllable to you regarding directions for the cultivation of tobacco that you wrote and asked me to look over and comment on more than half a year ago. When I received Yr. esteemed letter of 28 January, which reminded me of my duty, I was shocked at my own negligence. Think what you will, honoured State Counsellor, but not that I could cease to esteem, treasure, and love you.

Your directions for tobacco cultivation arrived as I was about to leave on an obligatory business trip through the villages. I read the letter quickly and the directions not at all, intending to do so when I could find time. It was the deed of a procrastinator who puts off till tomorrow what he could well do today, and after many todays and tomorrows has done nothing. Please forgive me, forget my lateness, and accept my promise that I will thoroughly mend my ways.

I will, of course, describe my own practical experiences with tobacco cultivation as well as the experiences of others, and submit them to you with the next mail. With genuine feelings of esteem, I remain Yr. Excellency's most respectful servant, Johann Cornies.

402. Johann Cornies to Fedor F. Rosen. 14 February 1845.
SAOR 89-1-1207/63.

Director Baron v. Rosen,

I hasten to respond to Yr. Honour's esteemed communication No. 79 of 7 February. I am very familiar with conditions in the Berdiansk settlements that are under my supervision. In my opinion they have no good professional craftsmen such as blacksmiths, wheelwrights, and carpenters that might take on apprentices from the Crimea with any promise of success. With particular reference to settler Abraham Janzen, who has offered to take on orchard apprentices from the crown, I must report that he is generally known as a slipshod fullholder and highly flighty person who cannot be trusted with any such undertaking.

I am grateful to Yr. Honour for this communication that might well prevent unpleasant consequences arising from Janzen's negligence.

403. Johann Cornies to Christian Steven. 14 February 1845. SAOR 89-1-1207/65.

Acting State Counsellor v. Steven,

Field cultivation is conducted on a four-field system in all villages in the Molochnaia Mennonite District and is pursued in this way. Three fields are sown with grain and the fourth is kept black and clear of weeds in summer by means of repeated ploughing. The following year barley, or possibly red wheat, is sown on the fallow field; in the second year wheat is sown; and in the third year rye or oats. In the fourth year the same field is again left fallow. In summary, after three seedings, the field is left fallow during the fourth year. Fertilizing insofar as one has sufficient manure for this purpose is done mostly for grain, less for potatoes, hardly ever for flax.

Winters here drag on and the steppe is coated with a crust of ice. At this date we have had to provide fodder for our livestock for fourteen weeks without interruption. Still, the frost is moderate, between seven and thirteen degrees. The price of wheat is eleven to twelve rubles [per pud], while sheep fetch seven or eight and even ten rubles, with quite a demand. Advance payments for wool are already being made at twenty-five to thirty rubles per pud.

I sent the notice about your steppe estate to Mr. Blueher in Moscow, as you wished, with the request that he might make an effort to find buyers for it.

We were not able to accomplish anything in trying to deal with Mr. Zamero, but we live in hope that we will be able to perfect our silk production without him. For this purpose, we are on the verge of establishing a silk-reeling facility, beginning with ten reels and eventually increasing it to forty.

With exceptional esteem, I have the honour to be Yr. Excellency's respectful servant, Johann Cornies.

404. Daniel Janzen to Johann Cornies. 14 February 1845.
   SAOR 89-1-1132/51.

Valued Friend,

I hereby send you the geography textbooks you ordered from me. However, only sixteen copies were left in Pordenau, not a full two dozen. There are more in Rudnerweide and I will try to send the rest from there. The price is twenty-five silver kopeks each.

With a greeting, your friend Daniel Janzen.

Steinbach, 14 February 1845.

405. Evgenii F. Hahn to Johann Cornies. 17 February 1845.
   SAOR 89-1-889/45.

In response to your submission of 7 February, I can inform you that, based on S.465 in the Directive for the Colonial System, colonists cannot transfer from one guberniia to another without first obtaining the advance agreement of the Ministry of State Domains.

The District Office must submit its case to the Guardianship Committee. This would enable it to make a submission to the Ministry permitting the transfer of thirty Waldheim settlers from their present location and to attest to the fact that the individuals in question wish themselves to be transferred. A list of the names of these persons, a document agreeing to their release from the Waldheim community, and an acceptance document issued by the new community must also be submitted. Information should further be presented about the disposition of the fullholdings owned by these thirty Waldheim families after they move.

Odesa, 17 February 1845. State Counsellor v. Hahn.

Received 2 March 1845.

406. Evgenii F. Hahn to Johann Cornies. 17 February 1845.
   SAOR 89-1-889/46.

In response to your submission of 7 February, I write to inform you that the Prussian subjects Abraham and Herrmann Sudermann can certainly be considered as colonists. They may not have been included in the relevant register because the District Office completed its census lists only last December. If the brothers Sudermann cannot wait until their admission is completed, they might take the following course of action. A document regarding their Russian citizenship should be drawn up that describes them as Mennonites resident in the village where they will be included in the census. Temporary passes as Mennonites in that village could be granted them once they provide guarantees promising to return from Prussia. With these temporary passes they must, one, appear in Odesa to obtain a pass to go abroad, or, two, the District Office must submit the temporary passes to the Guardianship Committee that will take the necessary steps to negotiate a pass for the Sudermanns.

Odesa, 17 February 1845. State Counsellor v. Hahn.

407. Johann Cornies to Carl Stempel. 17 February 1845. SAOR 89-1-1207/67.

Esteemed Mr. v. Stempel,

In response to your valued letter of 8 January from Neuhoffnung, I have the honour to report that Ali was not at home when you sent him a communication from Ohrloff that he received at daybreak twenty verstas from his home. He immediately came to Ohrloff. Since he was dressed in his everyday clothes, he went home, put on proper clothing, and arrived in Berdiansk only on Tuesday after you had already left.

He said little to the District Director. The witnesses stand rock-firm in their declarations. Ali is clever enough to keep Raiskii from charming words out of his mouth. He said that if it really became necessary he would also repeat what Absaut Chelebi had told him in the District Chairman's presence, in particular that he would come to see me to pay for the wheat, etc.

The Baron replied to my communication to the General and to Baron v. Rosen, asking that Judge Tolstonog be removed from the investigation and Judge Eshen put in his place. He explained that he could not take any official steps with the Governor for this purpose. He also suggested that a report be made to the Committee in an effort to have Eshen appointed to the investigation. This I have done. Two weeks ago I told Eshen that he would probably be appointed to the investigation of the stolen wheat. I was of the opinion that it would be best to undertake the investigation in some Nogai village, not in Berdiansk.

Eshen said that Absaut's complaint about the main witness was irrelevant because these quarrels had occurred after the declaration of the witness. Ali said he would testify under oath about everything that he knows and has heard and is surprised at Raiskii's opinion that he should not appear as a witness. It is his opinion that, since he has received his reward, he is even more obligated not to cover up any injustice. If it becomes necessary, he will also submit a petition. In the next few days, Ali is travelling through almost all of the Nogai villages on crown business. I directed him to act and gave him a formal order. He will also secretly explore Chelebi's activities.

I will be travelling to Tashchenak next week at the latest and will stop over in Melitopol to see Eshen. I will immediately inform you about what he has reported in this regard.

Although I do not at the present time plan to inspect the Berdiansk villages, I would gladly meet you there should you decide to do an inspection. I need to organize my business affairs in a timely way. Please let me know how matters stand about eight days before your expected arrival. I long to see you.

The General has asked me to write directions for the cultivation of tobacco that would be printed. I have finished them and will mail them to Odesa tomorrow.

Pleased with your well-being, I commend myself to your friendly remembrance and with sincere feelings of esteem, call myself Yr. Honour's respectful servant and friend, Johann Cornies.

408. Johann Cornies to Evgenii F. Hahn. 17 February 1845. SAOR 89-1-1207/73.

State Counsellor v. Hahn,

I have read through the instructions for tobacco cultivation that Yr. Excellency sent me and must say that they are generally not comprehensible enough for settlers. In places they have too much detail, especially with respect to the preparation of soil. I therefore decided to describe my own practical experience as simply as possible, including information from others as well. This is intended for the simple man of the land, who is generally against written instructions. He is especially suspicious of directions that would seem to demand even the slightest more work. He reads them with his own prejudices and rejects them, without recognizing their advantages. Even if he chooses to follow them, he does so neglectfully and without benefit to anyone.

I do not suggest that my instructions will be treated differently. My sole intention is to prevent anyone from using the idea that tobacco cultivation is too much work as an excuse for refusing to add it to other branches of his agricultural economy.

Yr. Excellency will know best how to extract from these instructions whatever is correct and most suitable to the purpose and will be able to take the most effective measures in this respect.

With the most complete esteem, I have the honour to be Yr. Excellency's most respectful servant, Johann Cornies.

409. Traugott Blueher to Johann Cornies. 19 February 1845.
SAOR 89-1-1132/68.

Johann Cornies, Ohrloff. Valued Friend,

We are again in a dilemma and turn to you in trust, as our old proven friend, asking for your kindly advice about our son's affairs. He continually pleads with us that we call him back home. We have written down our thoughts and opinions about this in the enclosed letter to him. I leave it unsealed for your perusal. As parents, we are quite unacquainted with his present situation and unable to embark on the correct path.

If he wants to travel to the Crimea and you think that this would be useful for him, please give him 150 rubles, which I will repay later. I would also ask you to give him a further one hundred rubles for the journey home.

The parcel of silk arrived a few days ago. I have not yet found time to work with it, but will shortly send you whatever information I can give you.

Greeting you and your dear family heartily from both of us, I remain your faithfully obligated friend, Traugott Blueher.

Moscow, 19 February 1845.

410. Abram Wiebe to Johann Cornies. 21 February 1845.
SAOR 89-1-1132/58.

Valued Friend,

I hereby pay my old debt, amounting to 3,142 rubles, seventy-five kopeks, according to the accounts received. Since I received this amount on 2 March 1844 at 1 per cent monthly, I ask you to calculate it at 8 rather than 12 per cent [these are the numbers Wiebe uses]. This would settle my account. However, do so only on the understanding that the action will not cause me to lose my credit with you. In that case, I would rather pay what is lacking.

Our wool trade for the last year has not yet been completed. Yesterday, I received the sales accounts for wool sent from here, but still have no news about wool we sent to Odesa to be sold there. It was only unloaded there at the beginning of January. This delay in our wool trade, combined with the many promised but unpaid responses to my demands from my own debtors, are the reasons why I could not keep my promise to pay off my debt before the New Year. I must ask you to forgive me.

With greetings of friendship to you and your valued family, I remain your humble friend, Abram Wiebe.

Berdiansk, 21 February 1845.

411. K. Fletnitzer to Johann Cornies. 23 February 1845. SAOR 89-1-1132/62.

Highly esteemed Mr. Cornies. Sincerely beloved friend,

I have the honour to humbly inform you that I have received your letter of 10 February in good order, with the enclosure of four hundred rubles to cover the costs of forty copies of the wall-primer. I can report that the desired copies are stored here, ready to be sent. The earliest secure opportunity to send them to you undamaged would be in several weeks' time. When I heard that our young friend Wiebe, who has been with us until now, was planning to return to Ohrloff soon I asked him to do me the favour of taking along these forty copies of the wall-primer, keeping them in good condition on the way. He responded in a friendly manner, saying that he would do so with great pleasure.

Your welcome letter truly pleased me, as did your comments about the undeniable advantages of this teaching method. It was introduced in my church school twenty years ago and has proven itself to be very practical for the dear little children. I am sincerely convinced that the words of our blessed Saviour, "Let the little children come to me and do not hinder them" applies in this case. It enables them to learn to read easily, quickly, and with pleasure. His precious Gospel, the words of our omnipotent, compassionate God and Saviour, can quickly be placed in their dear little hands. They can read the Acts of the Apostles and search in the Word themselves, making it possible for the treasured Word, "Jesus Christ came into this world to seek us poor lost sinners and to save us," to happen.

May our beloved Saviour, for His blessed purpose, richly bless the use of these wall-primers in all of your church schools. They can be considered as a good implement in the work of our schools, preparing the heart sooner and more thoroughly to receive the seed of God's Word.

May it sprout quickly, grow favourably, blossom, and be reproduced thirty, sixty, and one hundredfold.

With honest love and hearty greetings to you, your beloved family, all valued brethren and friends in the Lord, I remain, with true esteem, your faithfully united friend and servant, K. Fletnitzer.

Odesa, 23 February 1845. Received 11 March 1845.

412. Traugott Blueher to Johann Cornies. 26 February 1845. SAOR 89-1-1132/65.

Mr. Johann Cornies, Ohrloff. Valued friend,

Your communications of 7 and 10 February pleased me. The first letter included a detailed notice about State Counsellor v. Steven's estate. I will make it my business to carry out this friend's wishes, and send further information later. This is naturally not a matter that can be dealt with quickly.

My communication of 29 January informing you that sheep shears were sent probably arrived soon after you wrote your last letter.

There is not the remotest reason to think that the higher Spanish wool prices in your area can be maintained. Our local manufacturers are working without profit because of last year's prices. Cloth prices are still the same as they were in the past. Sales of medium and fine wool varieties are also extremely feeble. According to the latest news, wool sales are stagnant abroad as well and price reductions can definitely be expected.

It would be folly to join in fraud. I request medium varieties, in accordance with your earlier shipments, agreeing to prices not higher than twenty-eight rubles per pud. Since it produces a higher income, a higher price can be paid for finer and cleaner wool. In the past, wool in washed condition did not command a higher price but it does now if it is worked more carefully. Fine shipments, not soiled by a lot of fodder, are more valuable. I would therefore ask you to agree to a higher price at especially good sheepfarms, with a base price of twenty-eight rubles per pud for medium quality.

You would be showing me your great friendship if you were to continue to make these reports available to me. This would enable me to make arrangements elsewhere, should no purchase of wool be possible in your area.

Commending myself to your further friendly remembrance, I send you respectful greetings, obediently Traugott Blueher.

Moscow, 26 February 1845. Received 19 March 1845. Answered.

413. Johann Cornies to Carl Stempel. 26 February 1845.
SAOR 89-1-1207/76.

Most esteemed Mr. v. Stempel,

The reason your house must be limited in size is its sloped and uneven location. This makes anything larger impossible. Its design is meant specifically for that location and it should be built on a high foundation. Otherwise all its proportions will be wrong. The size of the interior space must take the future into account, since such a substantial house is intended to last for many years. If the inspector is a single person, he can be accommodated easily, but, as you say, an inspector with a large family could eventually occupy this same house. His office demands its own section, since the old building now housing the chancery cannot be expected to last for long. Still, the proposed dimensions of the building should still answer only to specific needs and provide for nothing else. It should be at least fifty-four fut (nine faden) long and at least thirty fut wide. Dwellings in the country for persons of any and all ranks should include living rooms and also storage rooms. They must all be economically planned, since it is necessary to obtain a year's supply of provisions that cannot be purchased fresh every day, as they can in the city.

The building should accordingly have the following sections:

1. Entrance halls at front and back, 2. chancery, 3. a general family room, 4. bedrooms, 5. cupboards, 6. rooms for servants, 7. a kitchen, 8. at least one food storage room and one cellar.

These are all reasons why one should not hesitate to approach the Committee and why I agree with your opinion that submissions should be made to the Committee about any limitations on this house. This is my response to your previous letter.

When you were away on 21 February, two local Mennonites Gerhard Bergen and Isbrand Friesen officially reported to your chancery about the horse thief Emelian Sviridenko in Kominka, requesting your kind action in this matter. On their return journey, these Mennonites found that the thief had arrived in Kisilovka at daybreak without the horse. He must have known where to dispose of it. One can thus assume that Sviridenko has connections to others. I have just received news in this regard and add my most respectful request that you graciously take strong steps to deal with this situation. Ensure that the horse is returned to these Mennonites and that the thief gets his just deserts.

Heartily commending myself to you, I respectfully remain Yr. Honour's most honest friend and servant, Johann Cornies.

414. Johann Cornies to District Office. 3 March 1845. SAOR 89-1-1207/81.

To the District Office in Halbstadt,

In response to an inquiry about debts owed by Jacob Tessmann of Landskrone, I have the honour to report that said Tessmann has owed me a capital sum of fifty rubles since 17 August 1840 for which the accumulated interest at one-half per cent per month amounts to thirteen rubles and sixty kopeks. Therefore my demands from Tessmann are sixty-three rubles, sixty kopeks.

415. Traugott Blueher to Johann Cornies. 9 March 1845. SAOR 89-1-1132/69.

Mr. Johann Cornies, Ohrloff. My highly valued friend,

I am now trying to work on State Counsellor v. Steven's business matter [the sale of his estate]. Every single discussion I have had ends with the question, "what annual income can be expected from this capital?" Our friend should therefore draw up an account for the proceeds of each of the last three years, and then deduct expenditures. Anyone interested in the purchase will naturally not buy the land without first inspecting it, nor will anyone interested in such a purchase travel from here to the Crimea without having first been given a clear overview.

Please give my son Joseph the two enclosed letters.

I send my friendly greetings of love to you and your dear family and remain your faithful friend, Traugott Blueher.

Moscow, 9 March 1845. Received 26 March 1845.

416. Johann Cornies to Fedor F. Rosen. 14 March 1845. SAOR 89-1-1207/90.

Director Baron v. Rosen,

In response to Yr. Honour's communication No. 153 of 1 March, I immediately assigned one of the most energetic overseers for potato cultivation, Kokoi Nembetov, Nogai from Moshkin village, to find a desiatina in each of six villages in Perekop District that would be suitable for potato growing and to have them prepared. I also appointed a second overseer, Abdir Akmambetov, Nogai from Ulkanbeskele village, a dependable apprentice, to accompany him. They will both depart from here on 17 March.

To prevent loss of time, I hasten to request that Yr. Honour kindly send direct orders by the first mail to the applicable authorities in Perekop District. This should be done in order that:

1. two able apprentices are selected and assigned in every village community;

2. seed potatoes are obtained, six chetvert per desiatina. If none can be delivered on site, they should be provided from here. The twelve carts needed should be ordered without delay;

3. implements are delivered to the overseers, or are shipped from here;

4. the overseers Kokoi and Abdir are given all possible help to implement all directives relating to this project. The *starshins* should be warned that they will be held responsible for damage done on the potato fields.

When the District Director is given his orders in this regard, he should be informed about all of the directives from the Domains Bureau. We must ensure that the overseers meet no delays in their work. They will not return until all potatoes have been planted and all directions for future care have been given.

417. Johann Cornies to Christian Steven. 14 March 1845. SAOR 89-1-1207/93.

Mr. v. Steven. Yr. Excellency,

Many thanks for Yr. great interest in the improvement of our silk production. Although we appreciate Yr. Honour's advice that we send several apprentices to learn from the Italian Zamero, we hope that you will appreciate that we are unable to follow Yr. benevolent advice immediately. Indeed we expect to take up valuable connections with him later on.

With faithful respect, I consider it to be my most pleasant good fortune to be able to call myself Yr. Excellency's most obedient servant, Johann Cornies.

418. Johann Cornies to Evgenii F. Hahn. 14 March 1845. SAOR 89-1-1207/95.

Mr. v. Hahn. Yr. Excellency,

I again write to ask about the current whereabouts of Aide-de-camp Mr. Lushin, as I know him. His agricultural enterprise in Voronezh

Guberniia has been in debt to me for six years. During that time, he also sent me an apprentice to learn practical sheep breeding. Since his certification expired three years ago, I would like to return this man to him.

I thought you might have Mr. Lushin's current address. I would kindly request it so that I might negotiate these matters with him.

With the most exceptional esteem, I respectfully remain Yr. Excellency's servant, Johann Cornies.

419. Johann Cornies to Chairman of the Khortitsa Agricultural Society Siemens. 17 March 1845. SAOR 89-1-1207/106.

Dear District Chairman Siemens,

Inspector v. Stempel writes that Johann Neufeld's daughter from Rosenberg was impregnated in Schönfeld by the Mennonite Jacob Schmalchinskii. A written deposition has been made to this effect. It was impressed with the Schönfeld Village Office seal. The Grunau pastor gave the Inspector a copy of the deposition and asked that the matter be dealt with according to the law.

The Inspector finds this matter very unpleasant, especially given the fact that the deposition was impressed with the Village Office seal, an absolutely unauthorized use. He would prefer that no further difficulties arise with this Mennonite.

In informing you of this matter, please try hard privately to have Schmalchinskii reach an early agreement with Neufeld. A monetary compensation would presumably be enough to satisfy Neufeld. A written agreement in this regard should then be given to the Inspector as soon as possible. We do not want this disagreeable matter to become widely known, to the shame of all Mennonites.

The Schönfeld Village Office should be sternly reprimanded. Please have a settlement concluded a soon as possible. Please report to me privately. I have also informed the Inspector about the matter.

With a greeting, your well-meaning Johann Cornies.

420. H. Sudermann to Johann Cornies. 17 March 1845. SAOR 89-1-1132.

Mr. Johann Cornies, Ohrloff,

Let me thank you on behalf of myself and Abraham Sudermann from Berdiansk for securing us passes for our Prussia trip despite the fact that we have not been enumerated [in Russia]. Please do not regard us as ingrates for having given up our journey. With your permission, I will save the excuses until we can discuss this matter with you personally.

My situation, which you know, remains as it was. Please do not forget me as I continue to search for accommodations here. My dear little mother wants to pay for my land and I may soon become a partner in a business.

Commending myself to your friendship, I am, with all love and respect, H. Sudermann.

Gnadenfeld, 17 March 1845. Received 24 March 1845.

421. Johann Cornies to Fedor F. Rosen. 19 March 1845.
SAOR 89-1-1207/108.

Director Baron v. Rosen,

In response to Yr. Honour's communication No. 1069 of 26 December 1844, I made sure that the 345 silver rubles enclosed were paid out to assistant overseers, state peasants in Berdiansk, Melitopol, and Dneprov Districts. Neglecting their own agriculture, they oversaw the crown potato fields. A receipt for each district was noted in a booklet, with the names of the overseers and the amounts they received. I have the honour to submit this record [not extant]. Let me say that to deal with this matter fairly, I had to make decisions about the remuneration of each overseer in keeping with local circumstances and the effort expended by each one.

422. David Cornies to Johann Cornies. 20 March 1845.
SAOR 89-1-1132/n.p.

Dear Brother,

Yesterday, 19 March, we arrived in Odesa at two in the afternoon where I talked to General v. Hahn of the [Guardianship] Committee. He asked me to see him at ten this morning. When I arrived, he asked me to examine Mr. Varishkin's stallion. Good and strong, he had, at the exhibition, pulled 250 puds of weight on a large wagon along a level street. He thinks the stallion would be a good acquisition for our villages and that I should buy it. It is really a beautiful horse, of good stature, and there do not seem to be any other bidders. I would have preferred to write you tomorrow, but the mail goes out at two o'clock today. Maybe I will write Friday, also a mail day. The General asks me to send you his greetings. I greet you, your wife, and children and remain your brother, David Cornies.

[P.S.] Please give my greetings to my wife. Tell her that we arrived safely on 19 March and are staying in No. 421 on the second floor of the inn owned by Mr. Ulkovits. I remain Yr. brother David Cornies.

20 March 1845, Odesa. Received 23 March 1845.

423. Johann Cornies to Fedor F. Rosen. 27 March 1845. SAOR 89-1-1207/111.

Yr. Honour Baron v. Rosen,

I have the honour to enclose the bill for items that were forwarded to Yr. Honour in Simferopol and transported by Shrakai Tulemissov, Nogai from Burkut village.

I would also request that you kindly assume responsibility for the two rubles, twenty-five kopeks still owed by Mr. Brailko for cartage charges and the thirteen rubles for the garden-weeder Mr. Birkhan received. I would ask that you enclose these sums in your payment of this bill.

Please forgive me for burdening you in this way. Be assured of my most sincere esteem, as I remain, from the bottom of my soul, Yr. Honour's respectful servant, Johann Cornies.

Bill for State Counsellor Baron v. Rosen for:

Twenty-five puds rye flour (at 150) 37.50; Five flour sacks (at 150) 7.50; Three puds groats (at 120) 3.60; One pud, thirty-five and a half funt cheese (at 40 per funt) 30.20; also, for Mr. Huebner, seventeen funt cheese (at 40 per funt) 6.80, and for Lagori sixteen funt cheese 6.40; cartage charges to the location 17.50; packaging costs for cheese 2.10: Total 111.60 rubles.

424. Traugott Blueher to Johann Cornies. 30 March 1845. SAOR 89-1-1132/70.

Mr. Johann Cornies, Ohrloff. My valued friend,

On 26 February I took the liberty of sharing with you my views regarding this year's purchase of Spanish wool on my behalf. Meanwhile, I have noticed that the price of wool is likely to rise considerably (granted, without any solid reason). Because of these changed circumstances, I would ask you, in purchasing wool for me, to proceed on the basis of your best insights, even if you have to exceed the price limits for the wool set at that time. I would also ask you to please pay particular attention to long-haired wool.

With nothing further for today, I send you greetings of honest, heart-felt love as your faithful friend, Traugott Blueher.

P.S. Please be so kind as to forward the enclosed as is convenient. The same. Moscow, 30 March 1845. Received 20 April 1845.

425. Agricultural Society to Gerhard Enns. April 1845. SAOR 89-1-1333/49.

To the esteemed Society member Gerhard Enns in Altonau,

Eager to inform inhabitants of our local district about progress in agriculture and its various new branches, the Society has ordered several copies of the *Landwirtschaftliche Dorfzeitung* (Agricultural village newspaper) for the attentive reading and benefit of our best agriculturalists.

You will, in addition to the enclosed three issues, receive subsequent issues as well. Using your own judgment, pass them on to good agriculturalists in Altonau and neighbouring villages. Have them sealed and forwarded with the first opportunity. The last participant should return the newspaper to you for safekeeping, again as opportunity allows. Please send the Society, from time to time, the names of readers who must have obtained your permission.

Society at Ohrloff, [blank] April 1845. The Chairman.

426. Agricultural Society to Guardianship Committee. 4 April 1845. SAOR 89-1-1145/1.

[Draft:] From Chairman of the Molochnaia Mennonite Society for the Advancement of Agriculture and Trades, Ohrloff.

[To] His Excellency the Acting General Guardian for Foreign Settlers in Southern Russia

In response to Yr. Excellency's gracious proposal for the introduction of hail insurance in this district, I have the honour to submit this [concrete] proposal, with the humble request that, following completion of your gracious examination, Yr. Excellency might provide assistance in its introduction [the report is not extant].

427. Johann Cornies to Village Offices. 6 April 1845. SAOR 89-1-1222/1.

To Village Offices,

Enclosed is the promised description of school "A." Notice should be taken of this different kind of school. Village Offices should have two correct copies of the description made by their schoolteachers. One copy should be included in the files of school documents to be preserved in perpetuity and the other added to papers kept in Village Offices. After copies have been made, the original is to be forwarded to the next address and returned to the Society from Schoenau. Chairman, Johann Cornies.

Society at Ohrloff, 6 April 1846.

428. Johann Cornies to Fedor F. Rosen. 7 April 1845. SAOR 89-1-1207/118.

His Honour Baron v. Rosen,

Some seventy to one hundred foreign families from Prussia live in villages in the Mariupol [German] Colonist District. Most of their passes have expired. Since they cannot obtain a certificate of residence [*Heimatscheine*] from their fatherland that would enable them to secure a certificate of protection [*Schutzschein*], they must either register as Russian subjects or obey government laws and cross the border into their fatherland. They absolutely do not want to return to Prussia. Too poor to journey themselves, and without prospects of supporting themselves once they arrive, they face a future of extreme misery.

Mr. v. Stempel, Inspector for these villages, informs me that these people have decided to have themselves registered as Russian subjects. He has applied to the Director of the Ekaterinoslav Bureau of State Domains in this regard. The latter promised they would be accepted as peasants and arrangements made for their registration once they had sent him a petition. Mr. v. Stempel, however, who stopped them from proceeding in this way, advised them to register in the peasant estate in Tavrida Guberniia if possible. He requested that I ask Yr. Honour whether these people might be accepted as the equals of Russian peasants and settled in this guberniia.

I would therefore ask Yr. Honour to kindly inform me whether, if these people submit a petition to Yr. Honour, they might be accepted as peasants in the former Doukhobor villages, with twenty or more families settled together in each village.

The families in question have been harshly oppressed. With his philanthropic outlook, Inspector v. Stempel is trying to be as helpful to them as he can. Trusting in Yr. Honour's noble heart, he is making every effort to bring these German immigrants under your jurisdiction.

Hoping for an early response, I remain with esteem and the deepest respect, Yr. Honour's respectful servant, Johann Cornies.

**429. Agricultural Society to Guardianship Committee. 10 April 1845.
SAOR 89-1-1145/3.**

[Draft:] From the Chairman of the Molochnaia Mennonite Society for
the Advancement of Agriculture and Trades, Ohrloff.

To the Guardianship Committee for Foreign Settlers in Southern
Russia,

I respond to report No. 190 of 5 April from the Berdiansk District
Office, asking that a site be designated for the planting of 150 forest
trees. According to Guardianship Committee decision No. 7871 of 29
September 1844, local Elders had been sentenced to plant these trees as
punishment for spending funds contrary to the law. I have chosen a site
near the District Office. The trees can be properly protected there and
will be of use in future as well.

I have the honour of obediently reporting this to the Committee.

**430. Agricultural Society to Village Offices. April 1845.
SAOR 89-1-1145/17.**

[Undated draft:] To Village Mayors in Gnadenfeld, Grossweide, and
Pastwa,

The Society ordered several issues of the *Landwirtschaftliche Dorfzeitung* (Agricultural village newspaper) to inform inhabitants of our
district about agricultural progress being made abroad and the development of many new branches of agriculture. If read diligently, the
newspaper can be useful to our best agriculturalists. Village Offices in
the above-mentioned villages of the newer settlement will receive one
copy for local reading. Village Offices should single out several good
fullholders and Mayors to participate in this activity. The sealed newspapers should be sent on to each person, as possible. From Pastwa they
should be returned to the Society.

Should other landholders express an interest in reading these newspapers,
they should be reported to the Society and included in the list of readers.

**431. Johann Cornies to Evgenii v. Hahn. 10 April 1845.
SAOR 89-1-1207/124.**

State Counsellor v. Hahn. Yr. Excellency,

My brother has told me of Yr. Excellency's plan to visit us this summer and of your request that I suggest the best time. I do so gladly,

mindful of Yr. Excellency's benevolence towards me and of my striving to make myself ever more worthy of Yr. kindness. I will await your arrival at my house at Tashchenak on 7 or 8 June, immediately after Pentecost as in the past, and attend upon you.

My brother bought the stallion from Mr. Boman for 560 rubles and brought it back with him. It is a good, strong horse, entirely suited to improving the breed of horses in our villages. Since the community stud-horse facility for the breeding of local mares is still being established, I have, for now, taken over the care of the stallion myself.

With quiet assurance and sincere longing, I look forward to Yr. Excellency's visit and am, with the most perfect esteem, Yr. Excellency's respectful servant, Johann Cornies.

432. Johann Cornies to Traugott Blueher. 10 April 1845. SAOR 89-1-1207/125.

Most esteemed Mr. Blueher,

According to a letter I have just received, State Counsellor v. Steven, who is unable to manage his estate any longer, is putting it up for sale. As a result his income is barely half of what it might otherwise have been. The enclosed estimates you asked about do not correctly reflect the real value of the property. Recently, Count Tolstoi bought several thousand desiatinas in the neighbourhood at twelve rubles per desiatina. This is the usual price for good steppe land there.

I cannot suggest a supervisor for sheepfarms in your region. As far as I know, there are few people here with the requisite knowledge for such a position, chiefly because most sheepfarm owners supervise their own operations.

The prices for wool in our area seem to have stagnated and intoxication with the subject may well have subsided. Matters are presently so confused that I can hardly determine the actual price myself. I will write again once I am able to be more specific.

Heartily commending myself to you and your dear family, I remain with respect, your truly devoted friend and servant, Johann Cornies.

433. Johann Cornies to Traugott Blueher. 18 April 1845. SAOR 89-1-1207/127.

Most esteemed Mr. Blueher,

It seems quite impossible this year to purchase wool for you at the prices specified. A few weeks ago it seemed that wool buyers had abandoned their heady speculation, but it has now started again. Recently Kharkiv merchants put down deposits of thirty-three to thirty-four rubles per pud for large quantities of wool. Yesterday an Italian merchant from Berdiansk told me he was ready to buy a large quantity of wool for shipment abroad, and was ready to pay high prices. Under present circumstances I am therefore unable to respond to your wishes. I doubt that I will be in a better position to do so later, after shearing time.

The best and most respected sheepfarm owners refuse to entangle themselves in transactions, no matter how many visits buyers make, and will only sell after shearing. I would conclude that, this year, you cannot count on making wool purchases here. Should prices after shearing be lower, however, I could purchase wool for you to the amount you have specified. Just as I was finishing this letter, my friend Neufeld from Altonau told me that we should not agree to prices now being paid anywhere.

Your son Joseph will leave for the Crimea 1 May and, on his return, will leave for Moscow in the second half of May. He visited us at Eastertime and seems brimming with life.

With heartiest greetings to you and your dear family, I remain your faithfully devoted friend and servant, Johann Cornies.

434. Johann Cornies to Fedor F. Rosen. 18 April 1845.
SAOR 89-1-1207/130.

His Honour Baron v. Rosen,

His Highness, the Minister, has graciously decided to permit my brother David Cornies to keep the lease on his land for a further twelve years after 1852. He suggested that, in return, forest trees should be planted on several desiatinas of this land. He will travel to Simferopol to conclude this contract. Several dates in May will be best for him, at which time he would gladly attend upon Yr. Honour. I would be grateful if Yr. Honour could drop me a few lines indicating whether my brother will find you in Simferopol at the above-mentioned time.

With complete esteem and deep respect, I remain Yr. Honour's most respectful servant, Johann Cornies.

435. Johann Cornies to Carl Stempel. 24 April 1845.
SAOR 89-1-1207/134.

Yr. Honour, Mr. v. Stempel,

I have read your draft several times and think that the essential contents do not require specific changes. You may nevertheless find that it is rejected right from the start. To ensure that this does not happen, I would recommend that you make the draft shorter and more straightforward. This you can do without leaving out any of its fundamental aspects.

Despite my best intentions, I cannot weigh up all the circumstances surrounding your situation and hence know what you might best do. What I have written is intended at best to introduce this subject.

I enclose something of a draft, but it is not yet completely sufficient or appropriate. Please insert whatever you find missing.

With this I remain, Yr. Honour's sympathetic servant, Johann Cornies.

P.S. I cannot yet decide how soon I will manage to get to Bergthal, but I think it will happen sometime this month.

436. Johann Cornies to Fedor F. Rosen. 28 April 1845. SAOR 89-1-1207/143.

Director Baron v. Rosen,

In response to Yr. Honour's communication No. 679 of 23 March 1844, I can report that only four youths have been sent to me to learn practical forest-tree cultivation (three from Melitopol District and one from Dneprov District). I would ask that, in order to avoid the waste of any more time, you send me another four youths to complete the number called for of eight apprentices for me and for the Felstenthal estate.

437. Johann Cornies to Fedor F. Rosen. 11 May 1845. SAOR 89-1-1207/148.

Director, Baron v. Rosen,

Seed potatoes have been bought for two village communities, Akimovka and Bolshoi Tashkishken, where there was virtually no harvest last year, and also for six village communities in Perekop District and for the village communities of Ulkanbeskele and Bulutmek. In the latter stored seed potatoes were frozen in the one village and burned in the other. The District Supervisor was notified accordingly. This makes a total of sixty chetvert of seed potatoes, at six chetvert per desiatina for ten village communities. Six chetvert were bought for five rubles per chetvert and fifty-four chetvert for six rubles. I request that the sum of 354 rubles or 101 silver rubles, fourteen and a quarter kopeks be remitted to me.

438. Johann Cornies to Traugott Blueher. 11 May 1845.
SAOR 89-1-1207/152.

Esteemed Mr. Blueher,

Having earned your valued confidence, I have kept the letter to your dear son in which you encouraged him to make an early return to Moscow in the near future. I thought this would be in his interests. I also thought that he should extend his stay here until the New Year, 1846, at the earliest. It seemed to me that, during this time, he could become more steadfast in his good resolutions and learn about many important matters.

I had just decided to send you a letter in this regard when your son appeared. He had said his farewell to Mr. Mathies without my knowledge, was quite ready to travel, and asked for my permission to return [to Moscow]. He said that his parents had already given their consent and would not oppose his return. He indicated that he had heard about your decision from someone in Moscow. I did not, however, give him my approval and also made no mention of your letters. Indeed, somewhat indignant, I admonished him, making him feel my displeasure at his haste. I sent him back with orders to remain in his present activities until the first of the month when he would leave for the Crimea.

As for your dear son's circumstances in Mr. Mathies's household, you can be assured that he lacks for nothing and has, according to local custom, been treated like a child of the house. The only thing he complained about was the unaccustomed quiet lifestyle in the country, and the limits placed on his youthful inclinations by Mr. Mathies who is too stern in this respect.

On 3 May, Joseph left for the Crimea on a German vehicle especially hired for this purpose. He took along the papers he would need there to cover expenses. I think he will come back to Ohrloff by 20 May and then return to his home as soon as he can. He is in good health. The Molochnaia seems to have agreed with him and he is quite cheerful about seeing the Crimea.

Wool prices here are up in price so much that they cannot be expected to fall soon. Hence I can see no prospect of making the wool purchases for you at the price you gave me as a maximum.

Commending myself to your valued friendship, I remain your faithfully devoted friend and servant, Johann Cornies.

439. Johann Cornies to Fedor F. Rosen. 12 May 1845. SAOR 89-1-1207/156.

Director Baron v. Rosen,

I respond to Yr. Honour's communication No. 170 of 6 March 1845 about the laying out of a model plantation in Berdiansk District and the cost estimates approved for this project. Hermann Sudermann, Mennonite from Gnadenfeld village, agreed to fill the position of gardener on this plantation and took up service on 1 May. Yr. Honour is respectfully requested to confirm Sudermann in this position as gardener and to make arrangements for his salary that will begin on the first of the month.

440. Johann Cornies to Fedor F. Rosen. 12 May 1845. SAOR 89-1-1207/157.

Director Baron v. Rosen,

I have found it necessary to alter several points in the conditions under which the sheep have been given over to the care of Nogais for one half share of the returns, and have the honour of submitting these points in improved form to Yr. Honour for examination. Once the terms have been confirmed, they should be sent on to ensure that the Nogais in Berdiansk District have been duly informed. If the situation should make it necessary to violate these conditions, village Elders should be able to grant my supervisor a hearing. Judgments could then be made and implemented without delay, according to village law.

441. Johann Cornies to Deubner. 16 May 1845. SAOR 89-1-1207/158.

Esteemed Mr. Deubner,

In response to your communication of 10 March 1845, I inform you that bookbinder Tobias Geyer does not live in the Mennonite District but is a foreigner, not under the direction of the Agricultural Society. Since you mention that Mr. Reimer, a member of the Mennonite community, recommended him to you, the Society has asked the latter to explain his recommendation and whether Geyer used it to obtain credit in Riga. To the extent that the Society knows Geyer, it has no reason to doubt his fidelity but his action would still be contrary to the principles of the Mennonite brotherhood.

In the accompanying letter of 11 May, Mr. Reimer has done what he was asked to do. The Society is sufficiently convinced that Reimer wishes the best for Mr. Geyer, as an honest man, but has no business connections with him and no impure motives of any kind.

With exceptional esteem, your respectful Johann Cornies.

442. Johann Cornies to Franz. 16 May 1845. SAOR 89-1-1207/160.

To Mr. Franz in Ekaterinoslav. Dear friend,

It is wrong to assume that, in future, no Molochnaia Mennonites, during the time they are learning Russian, would not be permitted to live outside this district. The only persons thus constrained would be those unable to carry out such an undertaking with honour for our brotherhood. They must, in other words, be stable enough to provide a foundation for their own good fortune.

Permission for you to study another year [outside of the settlement] will depend first of all on your community. You must personally seek their agreement and then submit it to the Society for judgment.

Your honestly well-meaning friend, Johann Cornies.

443. Johann Cornies to Christian Steven. 16 May 1845. SAOR 89-1-1207/161.

Mr. v. Steven, Yr. Excellency,

In the Ministry of State Domains' response to your presentation about a decision to introduce angora goats on the crown's model farms, His Highness, the Minister of the Third Department, ordered me to state my opinions and terms if, as suggested, I were to accept three male goats and ten she-goats of this variety in my establishment as an experiment. As I understand the situation, were I to agree to this proposal, the government would be prepared to purchase the goats and cover the initial costs of their accommodation.

Before deciding to proceed in this matter, I most respectfully request that Yr. Excellency kindly give me your opinion regarding the situation. What specific conditions might I expect? Or might it perhaps be better if I were to purchase several such goats at my own cost? This I would prefer.

I would be much in Yr. Excellency's debt if you were to give me your mature advice on this matter. Also, kindly let me know what the approximate price for angora goats from Mr. Papkov would be.

444. Evgenii F. Hahn to Johann Cornies. 17 May 1845. SAOR 89-1-889/40.

I would have liked to come to Tashchenak on 8 June, as you suggested, but flooding in the Ekaterinoslav and Khortitsa settlements made it necessary for me to take a different route. I now intend to leave Odesa for Ekaterinoslav on 1 June. I will visit the settlements that have suffered water damage first. Then I will travel on to the Molochnaia settlement via Orekhov and Tokmak. That could still happen around 8 June.

To save time, when I reach Prishib I will definitely notify you about my arrival. Instead of starting the visit in Tashchenak, we could end it there.

I very much look forward to seeing you soon and chatting about so many things. Yours truly,

E. v. Hahn. Odesa, 17 May.

[P.S.] I leave for the Crimea on the steamboat today but will be back in nine days.

Received 22 May 1845.

445. Johann Cornies to Christian Steven. 22 May 1845. SAOR 89-1-1207/165.

Inspector and Acting State Counsellor v. Steven,

The Guardianship Committee for Foreign Settlers has sent me a document informing me that the illustrious gold medal has been conferred upon me. I have the honour to respectfully notify Yr. Excellency in this regard.

446. Johann Cornies to Knoerzer. 22 May 1845. SAOR 89-1-1207/165.

Very valued Mr. Knoerzer,

The excellent wool prices here on the spot and guaranteed by some local, but mainly foreign merchants, had prompted me to consider selling a small part of my wool production, around 450 puds, locally this year. The wool is from a flock on one of my sheepfarms [whose wool] had picked up quite a bit of fodder from long barn feeding. The price being offered, fifty rubles per pud, exceeds anything I thought I could possibly get in Moscow.

When you speak of the favourable prospects that seem to be determining the market for sheeps' wool this year, I must say that I am reluctant to break off my connection of many years with Moscow. My interests there have been energetically pursued, thanks to Mr. Blueher. I have therefore decided to do what I have done for years and forward my entire wool production for sale to Moscow. Preparations in this regard have already been made.

Commending myself, I remain your respectful Johann Cornies.

447. Johann Cornies to Peter Keppen. 23 May 1845.
SAOR 89-1-1207/168.

Mr. v. Keppen,

Heartfelt thanks for sending me eight volumes of *Beitraege zur Kenntnis des russischen Reiches* (Contributions to the knowledge of the Russian Empire) and reports about the opening of tumuli in our area. I received the third volume in French, and request permission to return it in exchange for a copy in German.

Each year, all settlements in Southern Russia are making considerable progress in all branches of agriculture. Increasingly, the Molochnaia Mennonite villages have distinguished themselves as models, in advance of all others with their regular construction of new houses and agricultural buildings with tiled roofs. Through improved field cultivation and livestock breeding, and the introduction of new branches of agriculture and crafts, the Molochnaia Mennonites have similarly sought to increase their achievements beyond that of other settlements. Their advance in sericulture can be measured by the almost thirty puds of silk produced during the past year (weight is always measured in reeled silk and not in cocoons). Our hopes this year, however, fell when many thousands of silkworms starved after a heavy late frost on 20 and 21 April froze the buds on our mulberry trees. Sericulture also gained greater acceptance among the Molochnaia [German] colonists, about whom I know considerably less.

Over the last few years Mennonites have been planting good varieties of tobacco. Samples suggest considerable hope for the future. We had an abundant supply of fruit last year but this year's prospects are for a poor to moderate harvest. The demand for wool is high and the price has risen to forty rubles for washed wool. Trees planted in orchards, plantations, and along streets are thriving and travellers are amused to see tall trees growing on several elevations across the steppe.

There was little snow this past winter and the soil was very dry. Spring seeding was completed in beautiful weather. The seeds came up well and, although a late frost damaged the seedlings, especially barley and oats, hope for quite a good harvest was heralded by the arrival of rainy weather. May, generally cool, favours all forms of vegetation.

The last Doukhobors left the area this week. Only a few had accepted baptism. A number have returned from beyond the Caucasus and their descriptions of local conditions are extremely sad. Perhaps others will return in future. It seems that all the Doukhobors, despite cheerless descriptions, insist on seeing the site to which they have been banished. Russians from various guberniias, for the most part a poor and lazy rabble, are being accepted into the Doukhobor villages.

Every year a number of Molokans with their families move to Georgia and settle in the region between Lengkoran and Salian. These people indulge in an especially fraudulent fanaticism that drives them away from the well-being they had experienced locally.

Easy sales of wheat to Berdiansk have moved Nogais to increase their cultivation of wheat. At the same time, the excessive breeding of livestock is decreasing. Potato cultivation and Spanish sheep breeding have been introduced into every village.

It would give me great pleasure if I could repay you for the friendly sympathy Yr. Honour has shown me.

With the most complete esteem, I remain Yr. Honour's most respectful servant, Johann Cornies.

448. Agricultural Society to J. Martens. 23 May 1845. SAOR 89-1-1337/4.

[Draft:] From the Society,

To the esteemed J. Martens in Tiegenhagen, Chairman of the Molochnaia Mennonite Reading Association library,

The Society has inspected the catalogue for the circulating book collection of your Association. It believes that the efforts of your Association promote morality by making informative and instructional publications available to each member of the community at a low price.

The Society confirms the usefulness of your Association and promises to offer it its assistance wherever it can. It expects and encourages you to take care in strongly applying basic Mennonite principles in the selection of your books. We equally affirm your duty as Chairman to submit to the Society the introductory catalogue for recently added books semi-annually, on 1 July and 1 January.

449. Johann Cornies to Carl Stempel. 29 May 1845.
SAOR 89-1-1207/173.

Mr. v. Stempel,

Yesterday I had a conversation with the Waldheim Mayor about the costs of transportation to Ushtesheluk. When I learned that the carters insisted on charging four hundred rubles for the trip, I told the Mayor that they would not get a penny more than 350 rubles. Today I received their formal agreement which I have the honour to enclose. Please give me your opinion. If you are agreeable, set the time of departure and let me know.

With constant goodwill, I continue to be your willing servant, Johann Cornies.

450. Johann Cornies to Carl Stempel. 6 June 1845.
SAOR 89-1-1207/177.

Most esteemed Mr. Stempel,

Baron v. Rosen, Director of the Tavrida Domains Bureau, just responded to my inquiry whether seventy to a hundred [colonist German] families who have emigrated from Prussia could settle in Tavrida Guberniia, possibly on Doukhobor land. According to the enclosed paragraph No. 647, section nine of the book of laws, the families in question are to be permitted to settle on crown lands. If they wish to do so, they should submit a petition on sixty silver kopek–stamped paper to the Tavrida Domains Bureau.

Once this petition has been received, a suitable proposal should be made to the minister. We will then learn whether these families will receive approval to settle on the Doukhobor land or on other crown lands. With exceptional esteem, etc.

451. Johann Cornies to Carl Stempel. 11 June 1845.
SAOR 89-1-1207/181.

Most esteemed Mr. v. Stempel,

Yesterday evening, I received your gracious communication of 8 June 1845 from Berdiansk. I would assume that Pelekh instructed the Bengs brothers to obtain passes. District Chairman Toews told me that shortly before the holidays, Inspector Pelekh had informed the District Office that there should be an investigation in Gnadenfeld to establish whether the Bengs brothers were dangerous to the community and whether they were in the possession of passes. Otherwise, they should be sent to the Mariupol Colonist District in accordance with your demands.

The District Office did not, however, investigate this matter. In several reports to the Society, the Village Office reported that the community wished to get rid of the Bengs because they were of a destructive disposition. The communication from Mr. Pelekh remains at the District Office and has not been carried out. Mr. Pelekh has increasingly demonstrated where his [true] inclinations lie. He has completely destroyed my trust in him and that of the entire Molochnaia Mennonite community.

Please remain calm about the General's arrival. I will sound the trumpets once I hear about his arrival in Prishib. You can count on hearing about it in lots of time. I have heard from dependable sources that, although the Khortitsa District Chairman had requested permission to go to Odesa, he had been told that the General himself would find his way to Khortitsa on 15 June.

Wilhelm Martens met a sad fate in Halbstadt yesterday. He hanged himself in despair and will be buried tomorrow.

Farewell until we meet again. Meanwhile, remain assured that no one has greater sympathy for your joys and sufferings than Yr. Honour's thankful servant, Johann Cornies.

452. Johann Cornies to Peter Wedel. 12 June 1845.
SAOR 89-1-1207/185.

Esteemed Elder Peter Wedel in Alexanderwohl,

In doing what I promised you, I had a discussion with the District Chairman about exempting Peter Pankratz, preacher in your congregation, from Gnadenfeld's general rotation of duties. The District Chairman explained that it would be inappropriate to release him from this responsibility in response to the church council's declaration. He also added that this would apply as long as Pankratz lives in Gnadenfeld, among the members of the congregation that expelled him as preacher.

The District Chairman said the situation would be different if Pankratz were living in Alexanderwohl among his own congregation. Then his exemption from the rotation of duties could take place without it becoming a District Office responsibility.

With constant respect and friendly greetings, I remain your friend, Johann Cornies.

453. Johann Cornies to Carl Stempel. 16 June 1845.
SAOR 89-1-1207/189.

Most esteemed Mr. v. Stempel,

The General [Hahn] arrived in Prishib yesterday. His Excellency has notified me that he will be arriving in Halbstadt tomorrow, Sunday, where I will have the honour of welcoming him. The General will not arrive in Rosenfeld before Tuesday, 19 June. I can assure you that you will receive further details in due course. This year, in accordance with his wishes, I will also have the pleasure of accompanying His Excellency on his trip through the Berdiansk and Mariupol settlements. Please inform the Bergthal District Chairman about his imminent arrival.

Anticipating an early, happy reunion, I remain, with the highest esteem, Yr. Honour's humble servant, Johann Cornies.

454. Johann Cornies to Evgenii F. Hahn. 16 June 1845.
SAOR 89-1-1207/110.

State Counsellor v. Hahn, Yr. Excellency,

In response to your esteemed communication of 15 June, I will expect Yr. Excellency in Halbstadt tomorrow, Sunday. Should it still be agreeable to you, it would give me pleasure to then accompany you on your inspection tour through the villages along the Molochnaia as far as Altonau.

I would request that from Altonau you do me the honour of visiting my home in Ohrloff for the night. From there Yr. Excellency might graciously order further inspections of our villages.

With exceptional esteem, I respectfully remain Yr. Excellency's most obedient servant, Johann Cornies.

455. Johann Cornies to Traugott Blueher. 16 June 1845.
SAOR 89-1-1207/194.

Esteemed Mr. Blueher,

On 15 June, 126 balls of sheep's wool for the year, marked "J.C.," were packed and loaded on thirty-nine carts with a net weight of 1,139 puds, one-fortieth funt. They were sent to you in Moscow on consignment with the carter Nikita Chenkashchin and associates. The freight charges are three rubles per pud, for a total of 3,417 rubles, two kopeks. I paid down 2,278 rubles, two kopeks of this sum and would ask that you kindly pay Chenkashchin the remainder of 1,139 rubles once the carters have completed their delivery. The original of this contract and a copy of the bill of lading are enclosed.

The wool from Tashchenak has again been marked with "T." I had forty puds of the worst-affected wool removed during shearing. Most of the wool from Iushanle is mixed in with more fodder than is usual because of the long period of barn feeding. I would like to find out how the two lots compare.

Kindly inform me about the arrival of the wool. Convinced that at all times, and with the blessing of the Lord, you have made it your most urgent concern to act in my interest, I leave the details of sales to your further discretion.

On your account, I had the same quantity of wool purchased for you as you received last year. Five hundred puds, marked "A," were purchased at forty rubles per pud. The wool was washed clean and contains considerably less fodder [than in previous years]. These sheep in particular were cured of "Plague" and no wool was lost. Another batch of about forty puds of wool, finer on average but not quite as clean, was also purchased on your account for the same price. However, I cancelled all further purchases that did not seem to be to your advantage because forty and even forty-two rubles were being paid for very average, and much less clean wool. Your wool will be shipped shortly.

With a friendly greeting to you and your valued family, I commend myself to you as your constant, honest friend and servant, Johann Cornies.

456. Heinrich Cornies to Johann Cornies. 19 June 1845.
SAOR 89-1-1132/2.

Mr. Johann Cornies in Ohrloff,

State peasant Mikhail Petrov from the village of Sherebetz in Ekaterinoslav Guberniia, Aleksandrov District, was hired to herd oxen from 23 April 1845 until 14 November 1845 for seventy-eight rubles. He was permitted to go home for three days on 2 June. At different times he had already received twenty-eight rubles, two kopeks of his wages.

I would assume from his failure to return to the estate that he is not inclined to resume his service. For this reason, action might be taken to have him sent back soon. Heinrich Cornies.

Iushanle Estate, 19 June 1845.

[Marked]: 30 June 1845, wrote to Sherebetz District Chairman.

457. Johann Siemens to Johann Cornies. 21 June 1845.
SAOR 89-1-1132/n.p.

Highly valued friend,

I am grateful to you for letting me know about the arrival of the Acting General Guardian. It permitted me to make arrangements for the exact time of His Excellency's visit. The honoured visitor arrived in Khortitsa on 13 June and inspected the damage done in our local villages by the Dnieper River when it overflowed its banks. He left on the evening of 14 June and should, in the meanwhile, have visited you.

I was counting on your visit when the State Counsellor arrived. I would have been pleased to receive both of you at the same time. If you are unable to drop by because of your many business affairs, I would plan to come to your area late in July, should you be at home. I have nothing worthwhile to report about any special changes here.

With friendly greetings I remain your obligated friend, Johann Siemens.

Khortitsa village, 21 June 1845.

[Marked]: Invited to come here end of July.

458. Johann Cornies to Traugott Blueher. June 1845.
SAOR 89-1-1207/199.

Esteemed Mr. Blueher,

Because of the circumstances of which I informed you, I was unable to complete your wool business as would have been desired. I have therefore limited my purchases for you for the two lots I wrote about, one marked "A," the other one marked "H." Even though the price of forty rubles per pud exceeds that specified in your instructions, I am still confident that the purchase will be to your advantage. This is my honest desire. May the Lord give you his blessing.

On 21 June, sixty-nine balls of wool, a total of 549 puds, five and a half funt, departed for Moscow on twenty carts. Enclosed is the original contract and a copy of the bill of lading, with the request that you pay the rest of the freight charges owing, 549 rubles to carter Mikhail Semenov.

According to the enclosed purchase account, I have advanced the sum of 24,019 rubles, eighteen and a half kopeks. Please be so kind as to attend to the remittance of this money as soon as possible.

The twenty dozen sheep shears were all sold except for twenty-one shears of the third variety, which are difficult to sell. Please deduct the proceeds from the accounts. If you should send me more shears next year, please, because of the difficulty of selling them, send me mostly variety No. 1, fewer of No. 2, and absolutely none of No. 3. Some No. 3 shears were sold this year simply because no other sheep shears were available.

Your dear son will by now have arrived home. My outlay for him was 303 rubles, ten kopeks according to the enclosed account, which you might be so kind as to settle.

With hearty greetings, Johann Cornies.

Accounts of cash advances made for Mr. Joseph Blueher

• With Is. Mathies in Rudnerweide, for various things, 90.48 and cash obtained, 45.50. Total, 136.

• Paid for service with Mr. Mathies 70.

Therefore, my outlay	66.
Journey to Crimea	104.7 1/2
Journey to Kharkiv	57.7 1/2
1 ride to Rudnerwiede & back	5.
Transport charges to Kharkiv	70.
Postage for letters sent home	3.95
Total	303.10

459. Johann Cornies to August, Freiherr v. Haxthausen. 30 June 1845. SAOR 89-1-1207/203.

To the Prussian Imperial Privy Counsellor, Baron v. Haxthausen.

Honoured Baron,

I feel highly honoured to have remained in your esteemed memory. It is highly unlikely that I would ever forget your visit, which was warmly received by me and by all of us.

I received your treasured letter of 3/14 February letter on 29 February/11 March. I immediately made efforts to find a qualified copyist for the three Hutterite books you mentioned. I must, however, regretfully say that I cannot find anyone able to undertake this commission for the seventy silver rubles you mention, or for even double that amount. Your interest in these [Hutterian] books has had a huge impact locally and they are now being closely scrutinized. Their script is, in many respects, quite different from the one currently in use. For this reason, a copyist would need unusual perseverance and much time to complete the translation with the required accuracy.

I am deeply moved and grateful for your trust in me. Even if that trust is not well placed, as in this case, it would still give me great pleasure to provide you with any other type of assistance that you might require. Commending myself to your further treasured benevolence, I remain, with the greatest respect, Yr. Honoured Baron's most respectful servant, Johann Cornies.

460. Agricultural Society to Village Offices. July 1845. SAOR 89-1-1220/58.

[Draft:] To Village Offices,

Measures have been taken by higher authorities and applicable Russian administrators have been emphatically informed that they are required to [obtain and] return all state peasant passes and tickets of any duration to their appropriate places as soon as they are no longer valid. A definite monetary penalty will be levied on state peasants who neglect to do so.

Many Russians of both genders are constantly in service in our villages. The Society has been informed that some local inhabitants do not return passes to their servants when they are discharged and also that they have been careless, losing passes or not retaining them. For these reasons, the Society orders Village Offices as follows:

1. According to the directive, passes for Russian servants must be carefully and punctually preserved, unsoiled, in the Village Office.

2. When the term of work for any servant ends and they are released, their pass must immediately be given back to them.

[note added]:

If a person leaving service is still indebted to his householder, or if there is some other reason why the pass might be withheld from him, the pass must absolutely be submitted to the Society without delay and with the submission of an adequate explanation.

[originally signed at Ohrloff, July 1845]

461. Johann Cornies to Eiseler & Co. 4 July 1845. SAOR 89-1-1207/209.

Eiseler & Co., in Kharkiv,

I think it inadvisable to buy the cows you wanted here for forwarding to Kharkiv, at least not now, when the animal plague is raging in many places in our locality. As is known, very good cows are often driven from here for sale in Kharkiv. In my opinion, your friends who are thinking of purchasing cows might prefer to buy them on site there where they can make the selection themselves. They could, in any case, be purchased more cheaply that way since the transportation costs per animal are much higher if only three head are forwarded than when a larger number of livestock are involved.

462. Johann Cornies to Fedor F. Rosen. 4 July 1845. SAOR 89-1-1207/210.

Director Baron v. Rosen,

I write in response to Yr. Honour's communication No. 124 of 20 June 1845 in regard to apprentices who have be sent to learn practical steppe forest-tree cultivation [with me]. I have the honour to submit a list of names of those who are presently here. I would note that I found the Nogai apprentice sent from Berdiansk District incapable of learning this skill and have therefore asked the District Supervisor to return him [to his place of origin]. The administration of the Domains Bureau has been asked to select and send a Russian apprentice in his place.

463. Johann Cornies to Christian Steven. 4 July 1845. SAOR 89-1-1207/211.

Inspector of Agriculture v. Steven,

In response to Yr. Excellency's inquiry No. 453 of 7 May 1845, I hasten to inform you that the fruit harvest in our local villages will not even cover local household needs, not to speak of having anything extra for sale. Late frosts at blossom time destroyed our hopes for a good fruit harvest. For this reason, I do not think it necessary to send Yr. Excellency the requested samples.

Last year dried fruit sold here in large quantities for sixteen rubles per pud, but none was delivered to Moscow.

464. Johann Cornies to Evgenii F. Hahn. 7 July 1845. SAOR 89-1-1207/212.

State Counsellor v. Hahn, Yr. Excellency,

On 4 July, Judge Tovstanog from Berdiansk visited me with an order from the Tavrida Guberniia requiring the preparation of an official travel route for His Imperial Highness, Archduke Konstantin Nikolaivich, beginning at Berdiansk on 10 August and passing through the Molochnaia Mennonite villages to Melitopol. It was to have been submitted to the governor. The Judge asked for my advice in this respect and I outlined a route along the road from Berdiansk through the villages of Andreevka, Chernigovka, to Great Tokmak. The one through the Nogai villages above Steinbach is somewhat shorter, but many of the Nogai villages H.I.H. would pass through have been burned down and new fires are constantly occurring. This road would therefore provide H.I.H. with very depressing sights. It seems to me that the first route described is the most suitable.

From Great Tokmak, H.I.H. would find the best route through Muensterberg village, or Altonau, and from there through Ohrloff, Blumenort, Iushanle, to Melitopol. Previous experience makes me doubt whether the desired travel route I have outlined would be accepted, although it would be the best. I would nevertheless respectfully request that you use your influence to ensure that the road I outlined might be selected for this trip. Since all of our Mennonites would try to make the passage for H.I.H as pleasant as possible, our trusting and obedient request is that Yr. Excellency might graciously be present in the Mennonite villages at the time of this exalted visit, to give H.I.H. the necessary explanations about us. I would be grateful if Yr. Excellency would reply to me before H.I.H.'s visit.

With the greatest esteem and the deepest respect, I have the honour to remain Yr. Excellency's obedient servant, Johann Cornies.

465. Johann Cornies to Christian Steven. 9 July 1845. SAOR 89-1-1207/216.

Acting State Counsellor v. Steven, Yr. Excellency,

Mr. Blueher, head of the Sarepta Trading Company in Moscow, wrote to me on 15 June 1845 to say that he has tried repeatedly to find a bidder for Yr. Excellency's estate. These efforts seem to have been in vain, at least for now. Other buyers may well try to be in touch with you through the mails given that the sale was publicized in local newspapers distributed in all parts of Russia.

Mr. Blueher's costs for publicizing this sale are thirteen silver rubles. He asks that you be so kind as to forward this amount to me. I have the honour of informing Yr. Excellency about this matter.

With exceptional esteem, I remain Yr. Excellency's respectful servant, Johann Cornies.

466. Franz Dueck to Johann Cornies. 8 or 9 July 1845.
SAOR 89-1-1132/n.p.

Valued Chairman,

The point of this report is mainly to provide you with information about the attitude and disposition of pupil Jacob Doerksen from Rudnerweide, whom you mentioned. He is ready, once agreement has been reached with his parents and guardians, to enter your service at any time.

If you wish to approach me about this matter in any way, you should know that I am preparing to leave on a long journey of four weeks' duration.

Wishing you much success I commend myself respectfully to your further friendship, Franz Dueck.

8 or 9 July 1845, Steinbach.

467. Jacob Isaac to Johann Cornies. 10 July 1845.
SAOR 89-1-1132/n.p.

Highly valued sir,

I understand that you would like to employ Jacob Doerksen, the stepson of our local resident Gerhard Neufeld, as one of your secretaries. I have spoken to him about the matter and found him prepared and willing to enter your service. Nor do his parents and his other guardian have any objections. Since a few matters with respect to his clothes and linen still need to be arranged before he begins his service, his parents ask for a delay of fourteen days. You can pick him up from here on 24 July.

With respect, I have the honour to call myself your obedient Jacob Isaac.

Rudnerweide, 10 July 1845.

468. District Office to Johann Cornies. 11 July 1845.
SAOR 89-1-1132/n.p.

To the esteemed Johann Cornies in Ohrloff,

You are hereby requested to appear at the District Office at ten on the morning of 25 July in regard to your demands of Cornelius Wedel, junior, in Waldheim.

District Office in Halbstadt, 11 July 1845. District Deputy Neufeld.

[Marked]: Johann Neufeld, Halbstadt, commissioned on 17 July 1845.

469. Johann Cornies to Fedor F. Rosen. 11 July 1845.
SAOR 89-1-1207/221.

Yr. Honour, Baron [v. Rosen],

I am sending Yr. Honour a communication I have received from Temir Tenbaiev, the Schuiut Dzhuret District Chairman. You will kindly note that Begitir Assanov, the current *Starosta* of Akkerman, has resigned his post. This may well lead to turmoil. I would ask that, since Assanov is really not capable of holding the position of Starosta, Yr. Honour confirm the local Nogai, Esale Bokushiliev, in his place. This could be of great benefit to the village community of Akkerman since the latter seems to be more enterprising and a better manager than the former.

As a warning and an example to his fellows, Assanov should, however, in all fairness be punished for the considerable damage he has done through his carelessness, the neglect of ditches around building sites, agricultural arrangements in general, and the commission of various arbitrary acts. Johann Cornies.

470. H. Franz to Johann Cornies. 13 July 1845. SAOR 89-1-1132/n.p.

Valued Mr. Cornies,

I would like to spend another year in Ekaterinoslav learning the Russian language, and have asked the Gnadenfeld community for their permission to do so. This I have received as the enclosed certificate demonstrates.

I would ask you to help me get the required permission in a timely fashion from the Agricultural Society in Ohrloff, as well as the required certification from the District Office in Halbstadt.

In submitting this request to your kind guardianship, I am pleased to be your obedient H. Franz.

Gnadenfeld, 13 July 1845.

471. District Office to Johann Cornies. 17 July 1845.
SAOR 89-1-1132/n.p.

To the esteemed Johann Cornies in Ohrloff,

As you know, our brethren in the Khortitsa villages have suffered much from flooding along the Dnieper [River]. Many have been totally ruined and a considerable number have been left without resources. At a meeting of all Village Mayors, the District Office decided to take up a voluntary collection in all villages of our district in support of Khortitsa brethren in faith who have become poor through no fault of their own.

The District Office requests that you also arrange such a collection on your estates, inviting inhabitants to make charitable contributions. These should be sent to this office by 1 August, with a list of donors. The District Office hopes that the people on your estates will provide much loving support for our brethren in faith who have been accidentally robbed of their resources.

District Office at Halbstadt, 17 July 1845. District Chairman Toews.

[Marked]: Contributions sent on 28 July 1845.

472. From Waldheim Village Office. 17 July 1845.
SAOR 89-1-1220/48.

Declaration:

The Waldheim Village Office has been informed that, on 1 July, Johann Neufeld, previously of Kuchtin but now of Orekhov, picked up a large cogwheel built for him. While loading the wheel and with others on the street later that evening, he made various evil and offensive comments about our authorities.

This resulted in the circulation of false rumours. Neufeld, among other things, referred to an earlier crown investigation and the dismissal from office of this settlement's administrators. He suggested that the local district would soon receive considerable relief from its oppression and that different and better arrangements would then follow. He further claimed that on his way to Waldheim he had visited Inspector Pelekh. The latter, in confidence, had told him that he had received a communication from Odesa favouring Pelekh in relation to accusations levelled against him and the conduct of his office. He also said that if the General Guardian v. Hahn did not settle the matter satisfactorily, he could not be considered a fair judge but a stupid fool. He circulated many similar rumours insulting to the administration.

Waldheim, 17 July 1845.

473. Johann Cornies to Fedor F. Rosen. 20 July 1845.
SAOR 89-1-1207/223.

Director Baron v. Rosen,

As a result of Yr. Honour's communication No. 660 of 17 August 1844, I have the honour to report that seven grain rollers ordered for Tavrida Guberniia will be ready to be picked up by 20 August 1845.

Please have the money for these rollers sent to me to pay the master tradesmen. It comes to thirty-seven rubles, eighty-seven and a half kopeks each, for a total of seventy-five silver rubles, seventy-five kopeks.

474. Johann Cornies to Fedor F. Rosen. 20 July 1845. SAOR 89-1-1207/224.

To the above,

Following my submission No. 115 of 12 May 1845, I am pleased to report that I have found a second Mennonite family that is ready to take over a position in the administration of the Crown Model Plantation near Tambovka. Peter Fast from Blumstein village is interested in gardening, which he prefers, while Hermann Sudermann might, in my opinion, be more qualified as overseer. I would propose that the Mennonite Sudermann be confirmed as overseer and Fast as gardener. I propose that the latter's term of service be counted from 1 August 1845.

475. Johann Siemens to Johann Cornies. 27 July 1845. SAOR 89-1-1132/n.p.

Treasured friend,

My father's severe illness has kept me from visiting you. I am sorry about this because I wanted to discuss a few matters with you. Might I drop by in early September?

Recently a nobleman, Ponrovskii, asked if you might be willing to sell him about twenty breeding ewes and a good ram this fall. Since I could naturally not give him the requested information, I would ask you to inform me accordingly.

I respectfully remain your very obedient Johann Siemens.

Khortitsa, 27 July 1845.

[Marked:] Ewes not under ten rubles, rams not under fifty rubles, paid immediately.

476. Johann Neufeld to Johann Cornies. 28 July 1845. SAOR 89-1-1132/n.p.

To the respected Johann Cornies in Ohrloff,

On 22 May and 17 July, I appeared in the District Office on your behalf in regard to demands for the repayment of several debts. I would inform you that:

1. The property of Abraham Enns in Neukirch has been taken over by the Village Office and will, at the first opportunity, be sold. Outstanding demands on it will be collected by the District Office.

2. It has been made public that the movable and immovable property of Cornelius Wedel Jr., in Waldheim, has been noted on his account. He is not to receive further credit. His property, until further action, has been placed under the supervision of the Waldheim Village Office.

3. Eduard Janzen has almost no property. The fact that he should receive no further credit has been made public.

Halbstadt, 28 July 1845. Johann Neufeld.

477. District Office to Johann Cornies. 28 July 1845. SAOR 89-1-1132/n.p.

On 28 July 1845, the respected Johann Cornies of Ohrloff turned over to the District Office donations in the sum of 250 rubles, six kopeks for Khortitsa inhabitants left destitute by the flood.
District Chairman Toews.

478. Johann Cornies to Christian Steven. 30 July 1845. SAOR 89-1-1207/229.

Inspector for Agriculture v. Steven,
A communication of 24 September 1842 from the Tavrida Bureau of State Domains, a department of the Ministry of State Domains, states that peasant apprentices from Tavrida Guberniia appointed to learn practical agriculture or forest-tree and orchard cultivation with me are to be freed from crown taxes during their apprenticeship and until their return home. Money collected for them in 1841, and later, should be remitted to their parents.

Apprentices with me and other Mennonites come not only from the Tavrida Guberniia but also from the Ekaterinoslav and Kherson Guberniias. Their relatives have asked to be relieved of the above-mentioned taxes as well. I would respectfully request that Yr. Excellency petition for the appropriate authority to resolve this matter and ensure that all peasant apprentices enjoy the same rights in this regard. Appropriate authorities should receive orders specifying that the money already contributed is returned and that no further taxes are levied.

I await Yr. Excellency's resolution and decision regarding this issue.

479. Johann Cornies to Fedor F. Rosen. 29 August 1845. SAOR 89-1-1207/240.

Director Baron v. Rosen,

Although the time to plant forest-tree seeds is fast approaching, I do not know whether I will receive seeds from anywhere. I also do not know to whom I can turn in this respect. I would respectfully request that Yr. Honour make timely arrangements throughout Crimea and institute special efforts to collect good seeds of all varieties of deciduous forest trees and bushes. As many seeds as possible should be gathered. Beech tree seeds are especially desired, and others as well. I urgently ask that seeds be gathered quickly and sent on by mail.

The surveyor has marked out the Crown Model Plantation. I will make every effort to promote this matter once I have recovered somewhat from the illness that has kept me bedridden for the past five weeks.

480. Johann Cornies to Hutterthal Village Office. 3 September 1845. SAOR 89-1-1134/2.

[Draft:] No. 1196. Hutterthal,

It is shameful for the whole community that I must report that records submitted to me about this year's wheat harvest in Hutterthal plainly show that several fullholders have acted deceitfully. This is something that I will absolutely not tolerate. I therefore sternly order the Village Office to act, without losing any time. It must immediately assume responsibility for measuring each villager's Arnautka and Hirka wheat. The results should be presented to me personally at Tashchenak with records, including names.

His Excellency, Acting General Guardian for the Colonists in Southern Russia, State Counsellor v. Hahn has directed me to make every effort to collect as much of the money advanced to the Hutterthal community by the crown as soon as possible. To receive these repayments, as I have been directed to do, I will stay over in Tashchenak for some time. This will enable me to devise arrangements that would set limits to what dishonest inhabitants of Hutterthal can do to prevent them from falsely reporting this year's wheat harvest.

481. Johann Cornies to Hutterthal Village Office.
3 September 1845. SAOR 89-1-1134/3.

[Draft:] No. 1197, Hutterthal,

I herewith pass on to the Village Office the completed account for the construction of thirty houses in Hutterthal village. According to this account, the total paid for construction was short thirty rubles, seventy-three and a quarter kopeks of what was needed. I have advanced this amount. It should be collected equally from all thirty fullholders, and sent in without delay.

According to the accounts, every house cost 593 rubles, fifty-eight kopeks. I have prepared a receipt book in this amount for each owner. Every payment, as it is made, should be accurately entered into the book. Receipts for payments must each time be signed by the Village Mayor. He should also do this for monies already paid and entered into the books. These receipt books are to be handed out to fullholders, by number, with the stipulation that they should be stored away, unsoiled, and brought along to the Village Office whenever a payment on the debt is made.

482. Johann Cornies to Fedor F. Rosen. 5 September 1845.
SAOR 89-1-1207/243.

Director Baron v. Rosen,

I hasten to make my report in response to Yr. honoured communication No. 597 of 25 August 1845. It has not been possible to begin the construction of houses at the location selected for the model plantation because the wood needed to build such structures is unavailable. At present, however, I am communicating with the builders in this regard. It is my intention to ensure that at least a properly built house adequate for the Mennonite families is constructed this autumn, weather permitting. If the roof is completed, it can be made liveable early in spring and the families can move in. On the other hand, the little house for the watchman can be completed immediately. This would enable him to stay over winter and keep a watchful eye on the building site and the materials already delivered.

The two desiatinas of land for the first planting could not be ploughed because severe drought has made the ground too hard for ploughing. Although this could not be adequately accomplished this autumn, next year no obstacles should stand in the way because of arrangements that have already been made.

To provide needed water a well must be dug as soon as the masonry work begins. This should require little effort since it is to be located on the lowland and not on a hill.

I intend to have the implements made in our villages over the winter, a favourable time for the masters, so that they will be ready to be used in spring when the planting starts.

The severe illness I have overcome still leaves me very weak. It has generally caused me much delay in the round of my activities. Now, for this reason, I must summon all of my strength to make up for lost time. I will also not spare any effort to establish the plantation. As soon as I am in need of money to start digging, I will ask for it in writing.

483. Johann Cornies to Hutterthal Village Office. 6 September 1845. SAOR 89-1-1174/11.

[Draft:] To the Hutterthal Village Office,

Calculations have been made to determine the exact quantity of wheat, Arnautka and Hirka, needed to repay the advance the government graciously made for house construction. I hereby order the Village Office to inform the community that every fullholder is required to deliver the quantity of wheat specified on the enclosed list. There must be no objections. Specifically, the whole community is required to transport a total of 644 chetvert, four chetverik of wheat to Berdiansk as soon as possible. It will there be sold at the highest possible price.

This should serve as a warning to individuals who do not want to deliver the specified quantity of wheat, that they will be held accountable.

The Village Office should keep watch to ensure that the delivered wheat is clean and dry and report the results to me. This must be observed.

Tashchenak, 6 September 1845.

484. Agricultural Society to Village Offices. September 1845. SAOR 89-1-1174/n.p.

[Draft:] To Village Offices,

Villages in this district differ in their requirements for school attendance by children. Many villages do not stick to the general norm for the schooling of our young people, specifically between the ages of six and fourteen. Some villages consider this term to be from age seven to age thirteen, others from age six to age twelve.

The Society is hereby compelled to order Village Offices to inform their inhabitants that they should follow the ages for school attendance specified and this requirement should be emphasized especially in villages that do not follow the norm. The time for schooling begins no earlier than the sixth year of age and ends when the individual turns fifteen. In dealing with the school attendance of their children, everyone, and especially Village Offices and schoolteachers, must govern themselves accordingly. Ignorance of this rule will not be accepted as an excuse for not following it.

485. Johann Cornies to Christian Steven. 22 September 1845. SAOR 89-1-1207/251.

Inspector for Agriculture,
I intend to release the three crown apprentice girls in my household with certificates for their excellent deportment and good progress in household management. They are Evdokia Dudkina from Mikhailovka, Marfa Bishtek from Melitopol, and Matrona Skelechina from Dneprovka. I send Yr. Excellency my most respectful request that you graciously take measures to have them fetched from my estate by 11 November 1845, and taken to their villages for further instructions. I will then have to hire other servants to prevent my household from suffering.

In accordance with the terms of their program, all three girls deserve to receive the monetary reward established for their zeal in the program. I would, at the same time, inform Yr. Excellency that, for a variety of reasons, I will not accept further girls from the crown to learn housekeeping. I have sent a communication with this same content to the Director of the Tavrida Domains Bureau.

In response to the esteemed communication No. 541 of 20 August 1845, I will mail the records and required information regarding all crown apprentices and girls with me and other Mennonites as soon as possible.

486. Johann Cornies to Fedor F. Rosen. 22 September 1845. SAOR 89-1-1207/253.

Director Baron v. Rosen,
The potato harvest in crown villages has been partially completed and the results, on average, are regrettably poor because of the severe

drought. Everywhere, the third variety of potatoes and, in places, also the second variety of potatoes cannot be kept in storage because they are sprouting. The sooner they are sold, the better.

For this reason, I would request that Yr. Honour graciously take measures to sell all potatoes unsuitable for further seeding immediately, as I advise. Kindly inform me of your response and about the price you would determine for each variety. In our villages only parts of the potato crop turned out well. Potatoes are selling at ten to twelve rubles per chetvert for the best ones.

487. Johann Cornies to Fedor F. Rosen. 28 September 1845. SAOR 89-1-1207/258.

Director Baron v. Rosen,

I have hired a soldier discharged in Kherson in 1840 to act as watchman in the crown's model plantation. Called Mikhail Seliutshka and a resident of Bolshoi Tokmak, he is fifty years old and has worked for me regularly in my plantations since his discharge [from military service]. He has consistently distinguished himself by his exemplary behaviour. We have agreed on a wage of sixty silver rubles. His service will be calculated from 1 October 1845.

In informing Yr. Honour about this matter, I most obediently request that Seliutshka be confirmed in this position, with the agreement that his salary will begin on 1 October 1845. The watchman's house will be constructed next week. He will have to move in as soon as it has been sufficiently completed for him to make his arrangements for the winter.

I await notice of an early decision.

488. Johann Cornies to Fedor F. Rosen. 28 September 1845. SAOR 89-1-1207/260.

Director Baron v. Rosen,

In response to Yr. Honour's inquiry No. 622 of 12 September 1845, I have the honour to report that the plough for Kursk Guberniia shipped via Rostov did not have a shaft. This is the general practice with Mennonite masters here because ploughing is always done with horses and the craftsman thought he did not have to take this into consideration at all. He provides a chain instead of a wooden shaft for local agriculturalists or lets them use their own devices.

489. Johann Cornies to Hutterthal Village Office. 28 September 1845. SAOR 89-1-1134/51.

[Draft:] Hutterthal,

An election has been ordered for Mayors and Deputies in all villages in the Molochnaia Mennonite District, including Hutterthal. I find it necessary to point out that as the Hutterthal village community makes its preparations for a new selection, it should not be oblivious to the need to keep in office at least its present Mayor, Chr. Waldner and its Deputy Mayor, And. Wollmann. This is needed so long as some accounts are still missing and individual economic establishments have not been completed. No other selection can be made without creating difficulties in the regulation of village affairs. This the community should definitely keep in mind.

In the case of the other Deputy, P. Hofer, whose situation with a sick wife should be taken into account, an energetic fullholder should be elected in his place. Every election not carefully undertaken according to the law will trigger another, etc.

This must be observed punctually and the results reported.

490. Johann Cornies's notes for Agricultural Society business. N.d. SAOR 89-1-1134/61.

1. Household account books kept in households should be checked from time to time.

2. The planting of *Kruschki* along streets must be completed wherever they are still missing.

3. Fallow fields should be inspected occasionally.

4. Are cemeteries properly enclosed and the entrances provided with strong gates? Also, has planting been completed? Special attention should be paid to these matters.

5. In Tiege, the cottager house belonging to the late Abram Kroeker was supposed to have been dismantled last spring.

6. Keep the enclosing of plantations under observation.

7. Have all directives and wall-primers in the village schools actually been posted? Are there Bible stories for the children in all schools?

8. Require fullholder Peter Baur in Landskrone to plough the regulated fallow, and punish him for his disobedience.

9. If No. 6 in Pastwa has not yet removed the cherry trees, he should be ordered to do so and be punished.

10. Similarly for fullholder Wall in Prangenau.

11. Neukirch likewise.

12. The same for Margenau, where owners of weedy plantation plots are to be punished according to the rules.

13. In Schoensee or Tiegenhagen some boards of the wall-primers are still missing. These should be sent.

14. Check whether wall-primers in Rudnerweide are of the right kind.

15. Similar orders about the wall-primer in Gnadenfeld.

16. Have the two hearth-sites in Conteniusfeld been put in order as they should be and according to the cost estimates? Jacob Fast's full-holding in Conteniusfeld should be inspected to see whether he can continue to maintain it or, alternately, if it must be passed on in the same way as the other two.

491. Johann Cornies to Khortitsa District Office. 6 October 1845. SAOR 89-1-1207/269.

To the Khortitsa District Office,

Gerhard Penner from Einlage and former District Secretary in the Mariupol Mennonite District, obtained a loan of two hundred rubles from me, according to the enclosed signed certificate. On 26 September 1845, I received 102 rubles, four kopeks towards the repayment of the debt from the Mariupol District Office, which the office owed Penner for items sold.

In notifying the Khortitsa District Office about this matter, I am sending my respectful request that this certificate be passed on to Penner, with the explanation that I am content with 102 rubles, four kopeks and will never demand the rest.

492. Prinz to Johann Cornies. 11 October 1845. SAOR 89-1-1132.[3]

Most esteemed Mr. Cornies,

The moment we have long yearned for has arrived and the Almighty God has heard our pleas by again granting us a spiritual leader to lift us up out of our confusions and to keep us upright in our walk. We can

---

3 Regarding Wüst, see James Urry, *None but Saints: The Transformation of Mennonite Life in Russia 1789–1889* (Winnipeg: Hyperion, 1990), 172–6; and Harold Jantz, "A Pietist Pastor and the Russian Mennonites: The Legacy of Eduard Wuest," *Direction* 36, no. 2 (Fall 2007): 232–46.

give him our complete trust to be used wisely in praising the Lord. We have found this leader in an immigrant from the Kingdom of Württemberg called Eduard Hugo Otto Wüst. In a few months' time he has earned the appreciation of persons on all sides.

It would please us greatly if we could honour him by receiving a visit from you. This would undoubtedly confirm our decisions about him.

I have decided to proceed differently in the matter of planting. Because of this year's exceptional drought, the trees will not, if they are dug up now and replanted, obtain sufficient strength for the winter. I humbly ask your opinion about this matter.

I had seriously intended to visit you when I was at Iushanle during His Imperial Majesty's journey through the area. I would otherwise have come myself but did not want to burden you when you were so ill. I am, in any case, firmly convinced that you have long known about my honest respect for you. It is therefore not necessary for me to make further excuses. It is my most heartfelt wish that the dear Lord might grant you complete health and a long life.

With hearty greetings to you and yours, I am constantly your humble District Chairman Prinz.

Neuhoffnung, 11 October 1845; Answer 16 October 1845.

493. Johann Cornies to Berdiansk District Office. October 1845. SAOR 89-1-1220/73.

To the Berdiansk District Office,

The subject of this communication is directive No. 6500 of 25 September 1845 from the Guardianship Committee regarding the matter of the church teacher requested from abroad by the village of Neuhoffnung. It informs the District Office that the Ministry in question made a decision in a similar case a few months ago. Separatists also exist in other Tavrida settlements, but have, thus far, been satisfied to choose leaders from their own midst. It is thus not considered inevitable that a foreign church leader should be called for one individual village, Neuhoffnung. This decision can consequently not be approved.

Moreover, in accordance with the will of the highest authorities, foreign preachers in purely Lutheran settlements cannot be appointed until they have become Russian subjects. Because he is not a Russian subject, the theologian Wüst, the candidate who was called [by the Neuhoffnung church] from abroad, is therefore not permitted to occupy the office of church leader or spiritual shepherd.

**494. Agricultural Society to Diedrich Warkentin. 12 October 1845.
SAOR 89-1-1134/67.**

[Draft:] To Church Elder Diedrich Warkentin in Petershagen,

The Fischau Village Office has submitted a report to the Society that its village community has not agreed to accept the newly introduced wall-primers and school directives into their school, despite the fact that they have been accepted by the authorities and ordered by the Society. They maintain that wish to stay with their old teachings and not admit anything new.

These wall-primers and school directives for schools are, however, desirable since they advance teaching in the schools and are, in the Society's opinion, in no way contrary to our Mennonite principles. To advance teaching in the schools of our district, the Society therefore finds it necessary to submit the insubordination of the Fischau village community for judgment to the higher authorities.

For this reason you, esteemed Elder, are hereby requested, in the carrying out of your obligations, to inform this Society as soon as possible and no later than 24 October, as to whether the contents of these wall-primers and the school directives already introduced everywhere in our village schools, are contrary to the principles of the Mennonite confession of faith and to the Holy Scriptures. [Your communication] will be presented to the higher authorities with the Society's report.

**495. District Office to Johann Cornies. 13 October 1845.
SAOR 89-1-1132/n.p.**

To respected Johann Cornies in Ohrloff,

Abraham Enns, inhabitant of Neukirch village, gave the District Office a declaration that you are prepared to leave the debt he owes you standing. Therefore, your presence in the District Office next Wednesday, 17 October, is politely requested, so that the matter dealing with the sale of his house can be completed.

District Office in Halbstadt, 13 October 1845. District Deputy Braun.

[Note:] 16 October. Nothing more to add if District Office accepts this decision and the creditors can also come to an agreement.

**496. Agricultural Society to Guardianship Committee.
October 1845. SAOR 89-1-1134/98.**

[Draft:] From Society,

To the Guardianship Committee for Foreign Settlers in Southern Russia,

This Society encouraged the Altonau village community to follow the exemplary precedent set by Ohrloff village and it has agreed to do so. According to the enclosed plan, it will, in order to form a windbreak, systematically plant trees and mulberry hedges on one hundred desiatinas, or an area of twelve thousand fut of its cultivated land, beside its forest-tree plantation.

With this in view, the following essential operations have been ordered:

1. Immediately in the spring of 1846 two sides and the upper end [of the area] should be enclosed within ditches five fut wide and four fut deep.

2. Preparation of the regulation setting trenches, two sazhen apart, should be completed during the course of the summer.

3. Planting trees selected especially for this purpose, with trunks at least four fut high to the crown, should be completed immediately in autumn of the first year. Elms have been selected as most appropriate for this purpose.

4. In the early spring of 1847, mulberry hedges should be planted throughout the rows of trees, the stems one foot apart.

The Society obediently requests that the Guardianship Committee graciously confirm this plan, as described. Further, it is requested that the necessary directive be provided when the confirmed plan is remitted.

497. Johann Cornies to Christian Steven. 13 October 1845. SAOR 89-1-1207/273.

Inspector for Agriculture v. Steven,

In response to Yr. Excellency's communication No. 577 of 20 August 1845, it should be noted that records were prepared for all crown apprentices, boys and girls, who are with me and with other local Mennonites, including required notations about those who are lazy and those who have completed their apprenticeships.

On the matter of designating apprentices for release, I am also moved to emphasize what I have said earlier. Specifically, in order to achieve our goal completely, the apprentices should [upon the completion of their apprenticeship] be settled together in one village. In my view, I would suggest Terpenie in Melitopol District for the Russians, and the village of Edinokhta in Berdiansk District for the Nogais. In this way these young people would not be separated from one another, but live together in the same vicinity. I would also be close by, available to give them advice when needed.

I am happy to give the best of all possible recommendations regarding the apprentices who are ready to be released. The high authorities should not be in any doubt about providing each of them the two hundred rubles designated for this purpose. I must at the same time note that this amount, the clear limit of their reward, is quite inadequate for them to establish even the smallest model establishment. All, without exception, lack even the smallest of properties or funds of their own. They possess neither houses, livestock, nor field implements. The Nogai apprentices in particular must also buy their wives and pay dearly for them.

In order not to fail in the government's goals in this regard, I would stress that it is absolutely necessary to assign at least 150 silver rubles [each] as their reward for the setting up of their first households. This money would help them to build houses and to purchase the necessary field implements. Only in this way might they be able to achieve what they have been designated to become. Moreover, with appropriate leadership and increased obligations of the government, their desire to become disciplined model agriculturalists would be much increased.

In my opinion, the creation of such a village might also be the only way to awaken and give life to the desires of peasants to learn these new ways in future. On the other hand, it would surely have detrimental effects on the apprentices and might even arouse their distrust, if they were forced to scrape along without the least assistance. Such support would only be needed for the best model apprentices, such as these now being released, and not for those coming later.

I am prepared to take on the requisite number of new apprentices to replace those now chosen for release. I would, however, urgently request that the new apprentices be old enough, at least sixteen years of age, and have the needed mental and physical powers and good behaviour to ensure that no time would be wasted in returning unqualified apprentices [to their home villages].

498. Johann Cornies to Department of Agriculture of the Ministry of State Domains. 13 October 1845. SAOR 89-1-1207/277.

13 October 1845

To the Department of Agriculture, Ministry of State Domains,

This is a response to proposal No. 690 from the Minister of State Domains. In April 1845 His Highness proposed that I accept a number of angora goats on my estates on special terms to assist in the still very limited raising of angora goats in Southern Russia.

After having overcome a severe and lengthy illness, I write to say that I am now ready to buy a number of angora goats suitable for this project. I agree to His Highness's wishes that the descendants of the goats be sold at very low prices in our local regions.

To this end, I approached the Inspector of Agriculture for Southern Russia and other estate owners in Tavrida, Ekaterinoslav, and Poltava Guberniias. The goal was to find out where genuine angora goats were for sale. I have now made arrangements for knowledgeable people to inspect goats at all of these locations.

In due course I will report on the results of my purchases, the raising of goats, and their propagation.

499. Johann Neufeld to Johann Cornies. 16 October 1845. SAOR 89-1-1132/n.p.

Dear Brother-in-law,

I send you a summary of smugglers active in our district:

1. Jacob Warkentin, Conteniusfeld, has transported brandy six times from noble estates for a total of thirty-one pails, seven quarts. He sold eight pails to Abraham Duek, Pordenau, two pails to Abraham Reimer, Wernersdorf, one pail to Elias Regier, Sparrau, two quarts to Franz Loewen, Gnadenfeld, three quarts to Tailor Klassen, Gnadenfeld, and gin to various others. However, most of the brandy was sold to Russians.

In the case of Warkentin the District Office has decided to order the Conteniusfeld Village Office to remove Warkentin's horses and wagon from his care, and to sell them at an open auction on 20 October.

2. Franz Wall in Alexanderthal, together with Heinrich Nachtigal, Waldheim, fetched four pails of brandy from Konske, which they sold in Wernersdorf.

3. Peter Martens, Waldheim, and Heinrich Nachtigal, Waldheim, brought four pails of brandy from Konske. Most they sold to Russians and local residents.

4. Johann Martens, Peter Martens, David Nachtigal, and Jacob Richert each brought one pail of brandy from Karloie for their own use.

5. Franz Kroeker, Conteniusfeld, and Peter Wiebe, Conteniusfeld, each brought two pails of brandy from Konske. Kroeker sold small

portions of his to various persons, mostly Russians. Peter Wiebe sold his to a Russian. When they were caught, Kroeker and Wiebe immediately confessed their guilt, although Kroeker admitted to no more than we already know.

All of the above were caught with Peter Wiebe's help.

Since the number of people to be punished is so large, please give me your views as to how this matter should be handled. Does the person who brought the brandy into our villages bear the same guilt as the one who sold it?

I think that persons with no brandy in their possession should be punished to a lesser degree. In Warkentin's case, since we found one and a half pails of his smuggled brandy in Wernersdorf, we can do nothing but report him to the authorities.

We will find others who also obtained brandy. The investigation is likely to take some time.

With further questioning more smugglers will be found. But since we plan to begin handing out punishments next week, please give me your views as soon as possible.

With a greeting, your brother-in-law Johann Neufeld.

Halbstadt, 16 October 1845.

500. Johann Cornies to Peter Froese. 17 October 1845. SAOR 89-1-1207/279.

Mr. Peter Froese in Tiegerweide [West Prussia].

Esteemed friend,

I agree entirely with the decision you informed me of on 17 January 1845, namely that a Mennonite settlement would be unable to maintain its character as a model village on a small area the size of that allotted near St. Petersburg. I was pleased to submit to the high authorities this sensible viewpoint as expressed in writing by the Prussian Mennonites.

Yesterday, however, I received the following news from His Excellency, Director for Agriculture in the Domains Department. I enclose a correct translation. In July 1845, two Prussian Mennonites, Berg and Dik, arrived in St. Petersburg asking about land and making demands that do not in any way correspond to the intentions of the Russian government. Since there is no sense in settling two Mennonite families [on their own] they were thus not accepted for this purpose. The documents of the above-mentioned Mennonites, Berg and Dik, were returned to me for forwarding.

I am now sending you the enclosed three certificates to be passed on as appropriate. I request a receipt. I cannot, at the same time, refrain from criticizing Berg and Dik for their actions and especially also the Elbing Church Elder. The latter undoubtedly had knowledge of the exchange of letters being carried on about this subject. Before providing them with certificates for such an undertaking, he should have been able to give more careful and mature thought to the aims of the Russian government and to the highly thoughtless undertaking by these two Mennonites, Berg and Dik. The certificate is not at all in keeping with the obligations of a Church Elder. Instead of confining itself to religious subjects, the certificate's main intention is to confirm the certification received from the Office of the Elbing District Magistrate.

As for the settlement [of Prussian Mennonites] in the Vitebsk and Mogilev Guberniias, I find it necessary to note that your original letter of 17 January was sent to the Third Department. The Director of the same department informed me on 13 March that the Second Department was notified because the matter involves intentions to purchase the necessary land. Nothing further has meanwhile happened.

I think you could speed up this whole matter if you were to repeat your written approach. This would allow me to refer to your communication in another submission to the Department.

501. Johann Cornies to Fedor F. Rosen. 20 October 1845.
SAOR 89-1-1207/283.

Director Baron v. Rosen,

All materials for the buildings to be constructed on the Berdiansk model plantation have already been transported to the site. The watchman's house is almost completed, and work is proceeding on the main building. I would therefore ask you to have the estimated money needed for these structures, 1,075 silver rubles, paid out in full. Also, the wages owing to the employees now providing services might be remitted.

502. Johann Cornies to Evgenii v. Hahn. 24 October 1845.
SAOR 89-1-1207/284.

Yr. Excellency,

When I had the honour to attend upon Yr. Excellency in June on my Iushanle estate, you expressed dissatisfaction with the Khortitsa schoolteacher Heese and asked me if I knew of a better one. Should I find one, you directed me to report his name to you. I now take the liberty of proposing that the Mennonite Heinrich Franz, former schoolteacher in Gnadenfeld village, be asked to fill Heese's position.[4] For the past two years, while perfecting his Russian, he was able to obtain excellent results as a teacher in an institution in Ekaterinoslav. This young man was educated as a teacher in Prussia. For several years in Gnadenfeld he demonstrated his perseverance and abilities as a teacher. Coupled with his sound principles in the teaching profession, he would, I think, make an entirely dependable teacher in the Khortitsa school. His teaching in Ekaterinoslav ends when the holidays begin. Should the Molochnaia Mennonite community release him for this purpose, something he would first have to request, he would gladly accept this position for an annual salary of eight hundred rubles. Boarding costs for the pupils would also be lower. Above all, however, the pupils would make much greater progress than they have with Heese.

Although it would like to be rid of Heese, would the Khortitsa community accept Franz as their teacher despite the fact that he comes from the Molochnaia? I think that emphatic orders from Yr. Excellency would, in this regard, be needed. In any case, however, hiring a different and better teacher to replace Heese would in every respect be an act of goodwill for the Khortitsa school.

503. Evgenii v. Hahn to Johann Cornies. 26 October 1845. SAOR 89-1-889/51.

I have received your silk and will send you an official communication once an appraisal has been made. In the meantime I can tell you that knowledgeable people here have found it to be excellent and valued it at three hundred silver rubles per pud. I will send the silk to Moscow to discover its true price in that market.

But do not feel badly, beloved friend, if I tell you honestly that in my opinion this estimate seems overly optimistic and that the Ministry will not agree to pay the amount demanded. It is also only fair to have Wiebe and the two reelers remunerated, but standards must be set for such payment. The people needed for the silk business would naturally have

---

4   On Heinrich Franz's distinguished teaching career, see Peter M. Friesen, *The Mennonite Brotherhood in Russia, 1789–1910*, trans. John B. Toews et al. (Fresno, CA: Conference of Mennonite Brethren Churches, 1980), 709–13.

learned a profession useful for their own purposes, but they should not expect exceptional money payments in return. The salary paid to the world-famous scholar and botanist Professor Nordmann is not even ten rubles daily and the daily wage of the most skilful reeler here is barely thirty kopeks silver. What right does Wiebe have to demand ten rubles per day and three rubles for each reeler, days of rest included?

I am sending you the enclosed account, with the request that you look it through and shorten it wherever possible.

My opinion is as follows:

1. Wiebe should be paid one silver ruble per day and the reelers fifty kopeks silver for the time and effort involved.

2. Meals should be charged at cost.

3. The same for the room and the blower [*Blaskassten*].

4. Carters should receive the usual charge for the horses there and back. The distance from Halbstadt to Odesa and back is about 950 verstas. This means seventy silver rubles for the horses and possibly another ten to fifteen silver rubles for transporting the reeling machines.

I believe that this pay scale would ensure that everyone would receive what he deserves in abundance. I will leave the matter to your more precise insight as long as the estimates you submit are decreased. What is proposed will seem excessive to the Minister, even as it has greatly exceeded my expectations.

I would again ask that you not react badly to what I am honestly saying, but realize that I am demonstrating my genuine friendly feelings towards you.

Yours truly, E. v. Hahn

Odesa, 26 October 1845

[Marked:] Another estimate submitted [1] December 1845.

504. Johann Cornies to Christian Steven. 30 October 1845.
SAOR 89-1-1207/289.

Inspector for Agriculture in Southern Russia, His Excellency,

To answer Yr. Excellency's esteemed communication No. 686 of 15 October, I respectfully report that the fourth female crown apprentice, Evdokia Onkianikova, cannot be released at the same time as the [other] girls. She married crown apprentice Pavel Schkurko, and he has not yet served the period needed to complete his thorough training. It is still doubtful that the apprentices now being released might be inclined to marry the girl crown apprentices also being released, as might be desirable. I am still uncertain about saying anything definite in regard to this matter just yet.

Since none of the three girls being released have living parents, they would like to receive the following transportation: Evdokia Dudkina to her uncle Akim Lushenko in Mikhailovka, Marfa Bishtek to her aunt Anna Dolbinskaia in Spasskoie, and Matrona Shelechina to her sister's husband, Vassily Balin in Dneprovka.

505. Johann Cornies to Fedor F. Rosen. 30 October 1845. SAOR 89-1-1207/290.

Director Baron v. Rosen,

In carrying out Yr. commission of 30 September 1845 contained in communication No. 646, I have the honour to report that, after taking local conditions into consideration, I have assigned the same prices for crown potatoes in all locations, as follows, specifically two silver rubles for the first variety, one ruble, fifteen kopeks for the second, and seventy-five kopeks for the third.

I have also informed the area supervisor about potatoes that must necessarily be sold immediately and also about their quantity.

506. Johann Cornies to Fedor F. Rosen. 31 October 1845. SAOR 89-1-1207/292.

Director Baron v. Rosen,

I am honoured to submit to Yr. Honour the enclosed record of this year's seeding and harvesting of crown potatoes and maize in four districts, Berdiansk, Melitopol, Dneprov, and Perekop. The area supervisors have each been sent their respective records.

Because of the early summer drought and the late arrival of rain that finally permitted the potatoes to multiply, the results are very limited. Since they could not fully ripen, many of the potatoes are useless for proper storage. For this reason, measures have already been taken to sell the third variety immediately and the second variety in some places. It is also necessary to maintain careful supervision in all districts so that, while a few potatoes are sold here and there, the potatoes mainly needed for next year's seeding are stored in roomy places or in cellars, but not in pits.

At the same time, I should note that four markers and eight mounders were delivered to Dneprov District this year. They were taken from the supply of implements that were in storage with me last year. Also four mounders went as rewards from the higher authorities to local peasants, three to the Melitopol District Supervisor and one to the supervisor in Berdiansk District. Consequently, my supply now contains one mounder, one marker, and thirty-eight lifters that, after being used in Dneprov District, were collected here.

507. Johann Cornies to Fedor F. Rosen. 31 October 1845. SAOR 89-1-1207/294.

To the above,

Yr. Honour is respectfully asked to provide me with the wages for Peter Ediger, Mennonite from Lindenau village, the head supervisor for crown potato and maize cultivation on thirty-two desiatinas in Melitopol and Dneprov Districts in order that he can be paid the two hundred silver rubles owing him.

508. Johann Cornies to Fedor F. Rosen. 31 October 1845. SAOR 89-1-1207/294.

To the above,

Yr. Honour will kindly take measures to have five rubles, ten kopeks silver remitted to me. This is the amount I spent this year on postage and messengers on behalf of crown potato and maize cultivation.

509. Agricultural Society to Village Offices. November 1845. SAOR 89-1-1134/32.

To Village Offices,

Quite some time ago it was drawn to the Society's attention that several villages in this district hold full-fledged festivities in the Village Office on the occasion of [year-end] accounting sessions. It has become a custom for all neighbours, even their wives, to gather in the Village Office. Not infrequently, people reproach one another because of past disappointments. This can lead to further irritations and resentments. Since it is forbidden to cover the expenses of partying out of the funds of community treasury, the Society remains ignorant of the source of such money. For the above reasons, the Society absolutely orders that Village Offices where the custom of festive meals has sunk root discontinue this practice. In accordance with orderly practice, the usual meeting must be held in the Village Office without festivities.

Every Village Mayor who deviates from the purpose of such accounting sessions will be fined three silver rubles.

From the meeting of the Society for the Advancement of Agriculture and Trades, on [blank] November 1845.

510. Johann Cornies to Evgenii v. Hahn. 4 November 1845. SAOR 89-1-1207/297.

Yr. Excellency,

The Society has to a degree already been entrusted with the task of organizing a local silk-reeling facility. Since it is so important for the community, the Society would like to complete this matter as best possible. To do so I would make the following request of Yr. Excellency. In Odesa there are undoubtedly men who are acquainted with such facilities abroad and may have a closer knowledge of them. Could you graciously obtain a simple sketch of the layout of the interior of such a facility and have it sent to me. There may also be a book with relevant drawings. My purpose is to acquire a drawing of the best design for such a structure.

Yr. Excellency's obedient servant, Johann Cornies.

511. Johann Cornies to Fedor F. Rosen. 6 November 1845. SAOR 89-1-1207/300.

Director Baron v. Rosen,

In response to Yr. Honour's communication No. 664 of 8 October 1845, I had a test done with the garden weeder invented by Larion Voroshchishev, Molokan from Novovasilievka village. The test demonstrated that the weeder answers fully to its desired purpose, and is simple in design. This implement harnessed to one horse can clear two desiatinas of garden land of weeds in one day. It can also, at one time, cut through a strip of soil three-quarters of an arshin wide.

512. Johann Cornies to Evgenii v. Hahn. 7 November 1845. SAOR 89-1-1207/300.

Yr. Excellency,

After hearing from you about the high costs of hiring silk-reelers, I prepared a new estimate based on Yr. calculations. I personally believe that this estimate would provide each reeler with an adequate income. I would remind Yr. Excellency that on the occasion of your visit while I was ill, you commented that this venture would be very costly. At the time, I failed to realize how long I would have to wait for silk-reelers and for an agreement with the carters.

With the most exceptional esteem, Yr. Excellency's most obedient servant [Johann Cornies]

513. Evgenii F. Hahn to Johann Cornies. 21 November 1845. SAOR 89-1-889/57.

Troubled by the dissatisfaction that Inspector Pelekh's behaviour has aroused, it is my greatest desire to put an end to this matter as soon as possible. It is not, however, fitting to suddenly remove a man from his position after so many years of service. Nor do I have another position to offer him. I am expecting a new decree from day to day, and that things will then change. Meanwhile, I would ask you to show a little more patience, especially since it would be difficult to replace Mr. Pelekh according to your wishes. It would be hard to find a second Mr. von Stempel for the job and I assume that the comparison with him has most damaged Mr. Pelekh's reputation. Otherwise he really does possess some good qualities.

As unpleasant as the incident in Hutterthal was, it cannot be the occasion for a legal complaint against Mr. Pelekh. It was his duty to hold a formal investigation into any suspicions he had of the Hutterthal Mennonite. I can therefore not direct an official inquiry into this matter.

I again request patience. I will try to end Mr. Pelekh's influence over the Mennonite District as soon as I can.

How is your own health? I hope that it has been restored and that you are not suffering any after-effects.

I approached you with an inquiry into the possibility of establishing a hospital, believing that it might be possible to persuade the Martens heirs to make a donation that would further the district's well-being. His Excellency also asked me about such a hospital when he was last here, expressing his concern that none yet existed among the Mennonites. Most sincerely yours, E. v. Hahn.

Odesa, 21 November 1845. Received 26 November 1845.

514. Johann Cornies to Traugott Blueher. 24 November 1845.
SAOR 89-1-1207/304.

Esteemed Mr. Blueher,

My wool business turned out to my complete satisfaction again this year, for which I thank God. It is finished and I thank you very much, treasured friend, for your efforts on my behalf. I should also mention that all items sent by mail via Kharkiv have been received as sent. I would note that a book dealer in Riga has been directed to subscribe to the *Landwirtschaftliche Dorfzeitung* (Agricultural village newspaper) in future. It can be obtained more economically in this way.

The past summer was difficult for me, involving obstacles and hardships. I eventually fell ill and had to spend five weeks in bed. Another five weeks were needed to regain my strength. I am now again strong, vigorous, and healthy.

Travelling wool speculators are still making the rounds and recently a merchant from Moscow bought a quantity of very poor wool for forty rubles per pud. In response to rising wool prices, the sheep are increasing in numbers. The beautiful fall weather gives me hope for an abundant shearing. Should you like to purchase a quantity of wool on your account again, this should probably not be authorized until late in April. If you did it earlier, producers would insist on high prices and be reluctant to conclude agreements. Last year, they got used to high demand and high prices. It might not, on reflection, be a bad thing if you were able to make up your mind earlier. It is really hard to tell when things might change and what might be done to your advantage.

I have heard nothing from Sarepta for a long time. Perhaps it is my own fault. I promised to travel there, but could not manage it. I've not yet given up on a trip but do not know when it might proceed.

Esteemed friend, you have been generous with your kind and obliging efforts for many years. Please accept our honest feelings of thanks and commend us to your dear wife and treasured family.

May you long remain the loving friend of one who considers it his most pleasant joy to call himself your thankful friend and servant, Johann Cornies.

515. Johann Cornies to Evgenii F. Hahn. 28 November 1845.
SAOR 89-1-1207/308.

Yr. Excellency,

Yr. Excellency's special favour bestowed on me during the time that I have been honoured to work under your leadership, make it my duty and pleasure to report that after an illness of five weeks, during which I was bedridden, I needed another five weeks to recuperate. I am now, thank God, entirely healthy, and so strong that I do not feel even the slightest weakness of the kind that often lingers on among people of my age. I can continue my business matters as in the past, without suffering physically.

As for the establishment of a hospital, etc., for the local district, I will give you the opinions of the District Office and the Society for your judgment in the next mail. I will soon write to the Martens heirs, with a request that they make a contribution to the construction of a hospital.

When Yr. Excellency's directive No. 8014 arrived, the Society, under the supervision of member Jacob Martens, made arrangements to obtain a new reeling machine of the type Mr. Nordmann desires. The purpose would be to conduct tests and assess results. I will, at the appropriate time, submit the results of our activities to Yr. Excellency.

I obediently request assurance of your treasured benevolence and commend myself anew to your protection. With the liveliest feelings of esteem, I will continue to count it the joy of my life to call myself, with the deepest esteem, Yr. Excellency's faithfully disposed servant, Johann Cornies.

516. Agricultural Society to schoolteachers. 28 November 1845. SAOR 89-1-1205/n.p.

To the schoolteachers in villages in the first district,

None of the six school districts submitted a reply to the Society's circular of 29 [October] 1845 asking about the assistance that teachers in our schools need to create an environment to best teach children within the divisions of the school classroom and occupy them purposefully.

Instead of proposing an [appropriate] method, as the above-mentioned circular directed, they have merely submitted timetables without further explanation. There were only a few exceptions in the fourth district. The Society is forced to conclude that these schoolteachers have no idea of a so-called "method."

The responses and timetables we have received (which do not even list the subjects of instruction) show that no purposeful school teaching for small children can be carried on without greater leadership. The Society hereby directs the schoolteachers in the first district to select a committee of two of their most capable men. The names of these two teachers are to be submitted to the Society before 15 January 1846 in a report signed by all of the other teachers. Further steps will then be taken to obtain more of the detailed knowledge needed to pursue this matter.

517. Agricultural Society to Altonau Village Office. 28 November 1845. SAOR 89-1-1205/n.p.

Altonau,

This Society orders the Village Office to dismiss the present schoolteacher, Hildebrand, from his position at the end of the current school year. It has become obvious that he is incapable of teaching children destined for an agricultural life. The Village Office should try to find a more capable schoolteacher and present him to the Society for its required appraisal. This must be done promptly.

The Village Office should further note that the Society will do what it can to find a capable member of the teaching profession, to improve the Altonau village school.

518. Agricultural Society to schoolteachers. 29 November 1845. SAOR 89-1-1205/n.p.

To schoolteachers of the first district in the villages of Ohrloff, Tiege, Blumenort, Rosenort, Tiegerweide, Rueckenau, Margenau, Lichtfelde, and Neukirch,

It can definitely be assumed that we have few school classrooms where all pupils can be placed in one division [grade], or in which all pupils are at the same level and can be taught at the same time. In mixed classes it therefore often occurs that only one grade, usually the first, is taught regularly while all other pupils are taught only now and then, when opportunity allows. This leads to an indescribable disadvantage for the other grades. Not only do they fail to learn anything useful but lapse into thoughtlessness and tedium. This neglect is inexcusable.

It is common knowledge that many schoolteachers in our local district [fail to] follow real methods and use inappropriate approaches to encourage good order, punctuality, and care and also for the stern regulations required for even-handed activity. This prompts the Society responsible for the supervision of the school system in the Molochnaia Mennonite District to provide uniform leadership for all teachers in village schools, and to inform them of "how a teacher in our elementary schools might best teach the various grades of a school class at the same time, and occupy them in a useful manner." [quotation marks in original]

To move this purpose along, today's meeting of the Society decided to divide the forty-four schoolteachers in the local district into six school divisions. All of [the teachers in these divisions] have been given the special assignment of enlightening one another [about teaching] out of their own varied experiences. [Once the teachers have reached] an appropriate agreement [as to curriculum], the subjects of instruction should be consistently scheduled for the five school days of each week. All teachers, without exception, should try to identify useful approaches out of this assignment without expecting [to try] anything new or unusual.

The Society therefore directs village schoolteachers of the first division to design a method of instruction appropriate for instruction in our local villages. A plan should be made in accordance with the above-mentioned ideas that have been considered repeatedly and in great detail, as appropriate. The plan, signed by all teachers, should be submitted to the Society by 23 December 1845 in order that it might be thoroughly reviewed and final results drawn from it.

The first gathering for this purpose must have been held by early December 1845 and a preliminary report sent to the Society to ensure that all schoolteachers of the first division, without exception, were in fact assembled to introduce this subject and to hold pertinent discussions about it.

This must be observed punctually.

From the Society meeting of [blank] November 1845.

519. Ohrloff School Society to Gerhard Enns. [November] 1845. SAOR 89-1-1220/29.

[Undated draft:] To the school director of the Ohrloff Society School, esteemed Gerhard Enns, Altonau,

In response to a report of 11 [November] from the school directors, you are requested to appear at the Society school together with school director Gerhard Fast on Saturday, 15 [November] to meet teacher Riediger and to investigate complaints brought forward against him by Thomas Wiens, father of Johann Wiens. He complains that attendance at school is of no value for children because the teacher's indifferent instruction prevents them from making any progress in their studies. He also objects that the rooms occupied by the children are raw and cold and unheated. The results of this investigation are to be reported to the Society.

520. Johann Cornies to Fedor F. Rosen. 10 December 1845. SAOR 89-1-1207/312.

Director Baron v. Rosen,

In carrying out Yr. Honour's communication No. 144 of 27 February 1845, I ensured that the Syrian tobacco seeds sent to me from Latana and Dshebel were sown. Although the wind did much damage to all varieties of tobacco, these produced good leaves. The ones from Dshebel were especially good and much preferable to the ones from Latana. I am sending Yr. Honour two bunches of each variety as samples. The one from Dshebel is No. 2, the one from Latana No. 3.

521. Johann Cornies to Ministry of State Domains. 13 December 1845. SAOR 89-1-1207/319.

To the Department of Agriculture in the Ministry of State Domains,

I have the honour to respectfully report about the progress made with carrot seed sent to me with communication No. 2413 of January 1845. It was sown this year and the harvest was very satisfactory. The crop is unquestionably an excellent livestock fodder. Still, the effort required to cultivate this plant in large quantities in our region is hardly worthwhile given the fact that cheap supplies of hay and fodder can be gathered here with little effort. Given our shortage of labour, the cost of cultivating carrots would unquestionably exceed the cost of obtaining the usual fodder from here.

522. Johann Cornies to Fedor F. Rosen. 18 December 1845. SAOR 89-1-1207/322.

Director Baron v. Rosen,

The crown apprentice Gavril Kulinskii from Voianekh, Melitopol District, sent to me to learn forest-tree cultivation, is unsuited as a worker in this field because he is stupid and exceptionally lazy. I am entirely convinced of this. According to the agreement, I am sending him back to his village administration.

In reporting this matter to Yr. Honour, I would ask you to be so kind as to select and send me another more capable youth, who must definitely not be too young.

523. Johann Cornies to Levshin. 22 December 1845.
SAOR 89-1-1207/325.

Yr. Excellency v. Levshin,

I take the opportunity of your honoured communication No. 4261 of 31 December 1844 to express my heartfelt thanks to Yr. Excellency, my high patron, for your support in the granting to me of this high distinction.[5] To the extent of my limited powers, I will try to make myself ever more worthy of it.

May our loving God preserve you, to the joy of many, including my brethren, and, over a long life, bless Yr. Honour for the generosity of your many useful undertakings.

With honest and heartfelt thanks I will forever remember your paternal favour, and humbly remain Yr. Excellency's most obedient servant, Johann Cornies.

524. Johann Cornies to Christian Steven. 22 December 1845.
SAOR 89-1-1207/326.

Yr. Excellency v. Steven,

Your great kindness and support over many years fill me with true respect. On this occasion when the all-highest distinction has been granted to me on the strength of Yr. recommendation, I feel deeply the need to demonstrate my honest feelings of sincere thanks.

Always remembering Yr. many benevolent deeds, I remain, with the greatest esteem, Yr. Excellency's most respectful servant, Johann Cornies.

525. Johann Cornies to Fedor F. Rosen. 27 December 1845.
SAOR 89-1-1207/328.

Director Baron v. Rosen,

As is my duty, I respectfully present several state peasants to Yr. Honour as deserving of awards. They are, to a degree, models of enterprise in the systematic cultivation of potatoes and maize.

---

5   Cornies was probably referring to the award of a gold medal for his services to the Guardianship Committee. See *TSUS*, vol. 3, doc. 445.

1. In Berdiansk District:

a) Stepan Dsenko, of Saltishinsk village, seeded three chetvert potatoes and three garnitz maize. He harvested eleven and a half chetvert of potatoes and one and a half chetvert of maize. For these efforts, and especially also for his zealous efforts in spreading these crops among domain peasants, he deserves the first prize of twenty-five silver rubles.

b) Trofim Verkhovskii, from the same village, seeded three chetvert and harvested eleven and a half chetvert of potatoes. He is deserving of a prize of fifteen silver rubles.

c) Pavel Deriaven, of Orekhov city, seeded one garnitz maize and harvested fifty-six-fold, which comes to seven chetverik. He deserves a prize of fifteen silver rubles.

d) Mrat Ramakanov, in Ulkanbeskele, seeded four garnitz maize, and harvested four chetverik. He deserves a prize of fifteen silver rubles.

2. In Melitopol District:

In the village of Terpenie, four state peasants each seeded four garnitz maize.

In my opinion it would be worthwhile to publicize this award in the Domains Bureau's circular in order that it might become general knowledge.

3. I could not find one single peasant in the Dneprov District who was exceptional and should be acknowledged in this way.

4. One person in Perekop undertook potato cultivation this year, as he has done in the past. Finally, two Tatars from the village Ahs made small attempts, but the supervisor could not give me their names.

526. Peter Stobbe to Johann Cornies. 27 December 1845. SAOR 89-1-1132.

Esteemed Sir,

Several local villagers have been very dissatisfied with me because the sheep they got back from the Nogais were not all free of plague. As you know, the Nogais should have received money to cauterize the sheep with "Plague," but this was never done. I was sick at the time when the sheep [of the Mennonites and the Nogais] were divided between them. Mikhail Jantzen from Silberfeld has spread the rumour that I had not been ill at the time, but simply did not want to become involved. Jacob Reimer Jr. specifically told Mambet that, because no supervisor had been present, the sheep under my supervision should be returned without payment.

It will cause me much difficulty if this rumour continues, and I cannot remain calm about it since I have had to borrow to buy the medicine. I did not take over the sheep with any stipulation as to their being returned to me in the same clean condition. Plague is far too common among Nogai herds. Furthermore, I can hardly expect to physically force sheep owners to cauterize their sheep in order that they might be free of plague.

You were informed that I purchased bad medicine against plague. This should be investigated. The medicine I obtained can still be checked with the respective merchants and with the Nogai sheepfarms now free of plague.

Please do not deny me your opinion, advice and judgment, since I wish to collect the above-mentioned money now. I would, at the same time, kindly ask you to release me from this entire business.

Peter Stobbe.

Tashchenak, 27 December 1845.

527. Memorandum to Tashchenak employees. N.d. [1845?] SAOR 89-1-1160/n.p.

1. Count by kind on 15 April and 15 October of each year. Horses and horned cattle, owned or belonging to others, must be carefully counted by kind.

2. Keep accounts of horses and horned cattle removed.

3. Note number of loads of hay left over from the winter in Iushanle and on the Arap.

4. Keep draft notes as to the provisions given workmen firing bricks, specifically by kind.

5. Count the number of days each mason works in summer, listing the places of his work.

6. Same for carpenters.

7. How many bricks were hauled in for the planned construction, by kind?

8. On 15 April and 15 October of each year, make detailed inventory of agricultural implements [in my possession], such as wagons, ploughs, harrows, yokes, pitchforks, rakes, etc.

9. Once seeding is completed, enter into draft notes amount of grain seeded in spring and in fall.

10. Maintain special monthly account of the number of trees sold. When accounts are closed, the income generated from the sale of trees is to be entered into the cash accounts.

11. Enter expenses for the maintenance of crown apprentices and girls monthly into the account book for apprentice youth and girls.

12. Money can be withdrawn from the cash box only with the permission of the administrator Cornies. Each time he will record the details of the dispersal. He will each time provide a note in this regard as to the sum involved, the recipient, and the purpose for which the money is dispersed. This note is to be preserved.

1846

528. Agricultural Society to Fuerstenwerder Village Office. January 1846. SAOR 89-1-1334/75.

[Draft:] To the Village Office in Fuerstenwerder,

According to well-known directives for Russian servants and maids, discretion is not permitted with respect to their observance of legal fast days. Inhabitants are absolutely expected to ensure that specific fasts are observed punctually. Your local fullholder Abraham Wiebe did not carry out this rule in the case of the runaway servant, Hordli Krivoruchenko of Novogrigorievka. For this reason, the Society cannot assist in supervising the latter's return.

Russian village authorities are generally justified in relying on our villagers to encourage their servants to observe fasts ordered by the Orthodox Church. No inhabitant should make himself guilty of neglecting this duty.

This must be observed and care taken to ensure that, in future, this directive is carried out better.

529. Forestry Society to Guardianship Committee. January 1846. SAOR 89-1-1229/56.

[Draft:] From Molochnaia Mennonite Society for the Dissemination of Forest-Tree and Orchard Cultivation, Sericulture, and Viticulture,

To the Guardianship Committee for Foreign Settlers in Southern Russia,

The Society most obediently submits the Society's running account book for its income and expenditures in 1845 to the Guardianship

Committee for gracious audit. At this time a newly bound account book to record Society monies [received and expended] for 1846 is presented for confirmation. It most respectfully requests that, after audit and confirmation, they be returned to the above.

The Society submits for examination cost estimates for expenditures that will presumably occur this year, 1846. It remarks that, according to the running account book for 1845, the amount of 121 silver rubles, eighteen and a quarter kopeks estimated for this year was still available on 1 January 1846. No payment from the community treasury will thus be necessary for the current year.

530. Johann Cornies to Fedor F. Rosen. 9 January 1846. SAOR 89-1-1170/3.

Yr. Honour, Baron,

I have been informed that when an Elder in the Iamberkekli village community was selected, the former Elder, Mrak Bamasanov received eighty-three votes while another man, Kuvadik Chenaleev, received sixty-five votes. The local supervisor is acting to have the latter presented for confirmation. In the interest of the well-being of the Nogais in the above-mentioned village community, I respectfully submit that the present Elder, Mrak Bamasanov, be acknowledged as a good agriculturalist and qualified person. He is much to be preferred over Kuvadik Chenaleev, from whom nothing good can be expected. It is desirable that Bamasanov be again confirmed as Elder.

Most respectfully and with the highest esteem, I remain Yr. Honour's respectful servant, Johann Cornies.

531. Conteniusfeld Village Office to Agricultural Society. 10 January 1846. SAOR 89-1-1334/26.

Report to the Society in Ohrloff,

In response to the Society's communication No. 21 of 8 January asking for an explanation as to why Abraham Koop and Franz Quiring did not appear when ordered to, we submit the following report.

When we received order No. 1677 of 22 December on the evening of 23 December, both individuals were immediately called to the Village Office and ordered to appear at the Society's Office on 24 December at 10:00 a.m.

Abraham Koop set out at once. Upon reaching Tiegerweide he lost control of his horses and was unable to continue. It was by then late in the afternoon and, assuming that he would be unable to reach Ohrloff that day, Koop returned home.

After the Mayor ordered Franz Quiring to go to Ohrloff, he rose early in the morning and travelled to Chernigovka.

Mayor Wall, Deputy Kroeker, Deputy Reimer.

532. Johann Cornies to Fedor F. Rosen. 11 January 1846.
SAOR 89-1-1170/5.

Director Baron v. Rosen,

Seventy-five silver rubles, seventy-five kopeks were received with communication No. 14589 of 10 December 1845 from the Domains Bureau for the grain rollers to be used in Tavrida Guberniia.

The roller is an excellent field implement, especially in the local region. Once seeding has been done and the field is well harrowed, the weight of the roller is used to press down the topsoil. This puts the seeds closer to the particles of earth, favouring faster sprouting and stronger plant growth.

When seed is spread out on a cultivated field in dry weather, the field should be well rolled diagonally at least once, preferably twice. The soil can then not dry out as easily even during a drought that may well follow. Yet whatever the conditions when seeding is done, rolling is always useful, even where potatoes have been planted. Nor should fields be too wet when they are rolled.

533. Molochnaia Mennonite Bible Society to Main Evangelical Bible Committee in St. Petersburg. 12 January 1846.
SAOR 89-1-1247/3.

To the highly worthy and honoured Main Evangelical Bible Committee in St. Petersburg,

Report from the Molochnaia Mennonite Section Committee,

The Molochnaia Section of the Committee respectfully informs the Main Bible Committee that the Director of this Section, Church Elder Peter Wedel of Alexanderwohl, who is now aged, will be replaced. His former secretary, teacher Peter Neufeld of Ohrloff, has been elected in his place. According to statutes approved at the highest level, this action is presented to the esteemed Main Bible Committee for its gracious approval.

To the above,
The Molochnaia Section Bible Committee obediently submits its accounts for the sale of copies of Holy Scripture for 1845 to the Main Bible Committee. Moved by honest feelings in regard to this highly important matter, it respectfully forwards the proceeds of sales and contributions received. They consist of a total of 260 silver rubles.

534. Molochnaia Mennonite Bible Society to Gerhard Fast.
12 January 1846. SAOR 89-1-1247/4.

Esteemed Gerhard Fast in Ohrloff,
In accordance with the statutes of the Evangelical Bible Association in Russia, approved at the highest level, the Molochnaia Mennonite Section of the Bible Committee writes to inform you that you have been elected as its secretary to replace teacher Peter Neufeld. In informing you of this matter, the Section Committee demonstrates its confidence that you will be a zealous co-worker in this highly significant work of disseminating Bibles.

535. Molochnaia Mennonite Bible Society to Isaac Mathies.
12 January 1846. SAOR 89-1-1247/4.

Mr. Isaac Mathies, Rudnerweide,
The local Bible Committee requests that you inform it regarding your willingness to accept copies of the Bible and the New Testament for sale, as you have in the past. This would make it possible for you to better supply our brethren with Bibles who live at a considerable distance from Ohrloff.

536. Phillip Wiebe to Traugott Blueher. 18 January 1846.
SAOR 89-1-1170/7.

Esteemed Mr. Blueher,
Directed by my employer, Mr. Cornies, I would respectfully ask that you kindly forward to him as soon as you can three hundred [copies of] Bible stories, fifty geographies, fifty nature stories, and fifty church histories. We have received these books from you in the past. Please leave the charges for later payment and send the books to us as soon as you can.
With esteem, Yr. respectful Ph. Wiebe.

537. Johann Georg Rueckel to Johann Cornies. 18 January 1846. SAOR 89-1-1230/17.

Highly honourable Mr. Cornies,

I send you one hundred rubles as payment on my debt along with your brother-in-law Mr. Neufeld. You have had patience with me for long and have not pressured me in this regard. I trust, with assurance, that with your noble generosity you will continue to be mindful of my difficult circumstances and show forbearance until I have obtained the remainder of the money through the sale of my house in Grunau. Although I am poor, I do not wish to be thought of as a scoundrel nor found unthankful for the benevolence I have received.

Your upright debtor, Johann Georg Rueckel.

With one hundred rubles to be passed on.

538. Johann Cornies to Ohrloff Village Office. After 22 January 1846. SAOR 89-1-1224/21.

[Draft:] To the Ohrloff Village Office,

In response to schoolteacher Unger's request of 19 January, the Society sent directive No. 93 of 20 January requiring an investigation of complaints made against him. This was done, according to the Mayor's report No. 8 of 22 January. Investigation proved that the students' dissatisfaction with the teacher's methods was without foundation. Moreover, the monthly attendance records make it abundantly clear that a number of family fathers have been very neglectful in sending their children to school on a regular basis.

To their shame, there are some people who seek to insult the teacher with their idle gossip, and try to make him hated in the village community and among the children. Out of a sense of fairness and in support of his children's welfare, every upright family father should resist such talk and try to instil [in his children] respect for the teacher. How much can a child learn in school if, in his parents' home, he hears nothing but contempt for the teacher? Parents of this kind make the teacher's position extremely difficult and do damage to their own children.

Fullholder Peter Penner spread falsehoods and gossip in the village. He accused the schoolteacher of barbaric acts, and tried to arouse anger of disgruntled individuals against the overall instruction given in the school. For this he will not escape punishment. The incident demonstrates that there are other people like Penner in his village community. Claas Siemens's son would not have dared lampoon his teacher if his parents had admonished him to obedience and shown respect for the teacher. The Society holds Siemens responsible for this situation and will ensure that his son Claas is punished with blows of the rod, for his own improvement and as a warning to others.

The Society encloses an extract from the three-month school attendance record ordering all family fathers named on it to visit the Village Office and explain what obstacles prevented their children from attending school on at least half the school days. The Society further underlines the Mayor's major responsibility for remedying this situation. The Mayor should immediately send the results of his inquiries to the Society.

To repeat, the Mayor's bounden duty is to insist that the fathers of families send their children to school on a regular basis. The schoolteacher must include reports in this regard every month.

The Mayor is obligated to visit the school often, to reprove the teacher for negligence on his part, or to report him for such negligence to the Society. The Mayor should, at the same time, protect the teacher from harassment by his pupils. The purpose is to ensure that the class proceed calmly, without disturbance, and in an orderly way. The Mayor must finally see to it that fathers inform the teacher as to the reasons for the absence of their children from school. These reasons must be spelled out in his monthly attendance records.

To conclude, this memorandum stresses the Mayor's major responsibility for ensuring that pupils attend school on a regular basis and that villagers and the teacher play key roles in providing a peaceful and quiet atmosphere in the school in general. He must emphatically investigate all slander and unjust complaints from either side. He must punish transgressions against these rules himself or report them to the Society that supervises the entire school system.

539. Johann Cornies to Evgenii F. Hahn. 26 January 1846. SAOR 89-1-1224/16.

[Draft:] His Excellency President of the Guardianship Committee for Foreign Settlers in Southern Russia, State Counsellor and Knight, v. Hahn,

From the Chairman of the Molochnaia Mennonite Society for the Advancement of Agriculture and Trades,

When I received Yr. Excellency's directive No. 8014 of 15 November 1845 that accompanied a copy of a document from Director Nordmann, our new silk-reeling machine was operating under the direct supervision of Society member Martens. We observed the machine carefully to judge its specific advantages and disadvantages and concluded that the machine is preferable to the simple reeling customarily done here.

We were unable to realize our hopes, however, because of various obstacles that stood in our way. Our damp, cloudy winter weather is considered to be the first obstacle and the building where the machine had to be located is still new and had a damaging effect on the working of the machine and on persons occupied in this task. It was especially noticeable that, contrary to expectations, the machine turned much more tightly and therefore more slowly, greatly limiting the production of reeled silk. A second obstacle, no less important, was the necessity to use the few bad cocoons left over from the trial last year because of a shortage of better cocoons.

For these reasons, I have cancelled all further trials in order that we might begin anew next summer with more favourable weather and fresher, better cocoons. It can, however, be safely assumed that with these factors and other trials made earlier, the estimated production promises only one funt of organza silk. This is true, even if it were possible to work the machine for eight summer days with three workers. Should it be possible to produce twice as much, that is two funt of the most beautiful silk in eight days, which the Graff machine can unquestionably do, it can be assumed that this machine, because of the time and costs involved, can provide no substantial benefit for our silk production, no matter how good the prices are.

Were we permitted to do so, we believe that a similar machine might be fabricated here. This would require several alterations and improvements in its design, using spools that can store at least eight times as much silk. A redesigned machine should also be able to separate the operations of reeling and twisting. In this way, one could daily produce eight times as much silk with the labour of only twice as many workers. The cost would be only a quarter of what present arrangements require and the effort would be correspondingly rewarding. At the moment, I do not wish to pursue this latter point. Once we have conducted a second trial, we could send you a fuller appraisal.

In response to Director Nordmann's wishes, I enclose a quantity of silk butterfly eggs.

540. Johann Cornies to Carl Stempel. 26 January 1846.
SAOR 89-1-1224/18.

Inspector v. Stempel,

According to report No. 31 of 19 January from the Mariupol Bergthal Mennonite District Office, Christoph Striemer, fullholder in Schoenthal village, could not be persuaded to sign the contract releasing his fullholding, even though he had been offered another one free. I would therefore respectfully request that Yr. Honour proceed to take away Striemer's fullholding from him legally, as you had earlier proposed. In that case, his signature is not necessary. The justice of such an action is clear, since Striemer is the most negligent and worst manager [of his fullholding] in every respect. Because of his poor management and rough and nasty character he is probably unworthy of further efforts on his behalf.

I have notified the Mariupol Mennonite District Office accordingly[1]

541. Johann Cornies to Carl Stempel. 26 January 1846.
SAOR 89-1-1170/8.

His Honour Mr. v. Stempel,

It is high time to send you a letter. I delayed answering your worthy letters and commissions because I hoped that I would be able to attend upon you personally in my home. I regret that your health does not permit you to travel. With sympathy, I wish you an early return to good health.

In reply to your letter of 14 December, I have taken the liberty to make some changes in the draft addressed to the General Superintendent. Please receive it in a kindly spirit. I assume that your letter to the Superintendent will not fail in its purpose. I would confidently advise you to send it.

Please remain calm regarding the construction of your house until I can talk to you and give you my views and advice. I will keep the drawings and estimates until you visit me. I hope everything can be proposed in a way that will satisfy the General and not burden you in any way.

---

1 This notification is located in SAOR *fond* 89, *opis* 1, *delo* 1224/28.

From the bottom of my heart and with honest love, I offer you my sincerest wishes for a happy New Year. I regard the happiness and contentment that might fill your life as though they were my own. Man proposes, God disposes. We can achieve nothing [on our own], despite efforts, grief, and worry. We must accommodate ourselves to what is essential. Be patient. Tomorrow is another day. It will give us new life and joy. I am so completely convinced of the General's esteem and appreciation for you, that I need not say another word in this regard. Time will, I am sure, convince you of the truth of what I say.

I was aware of the enquiry regarding the Separatists that you received from the Governor more than a month ago. I informed District Chairman Prinz about the letter in order to prepare him for the questions you would undoubtedly have. In law, the people separated from the Lutheran Church are called Separatists. To my knowledge, they receive no preference over other settlers, other than the right to follow their own religious practices spelled out in the Church's constitution and legally to utter a "yes" and "no" instead of making an oath.

I think they will give you detailed explanations if you ask them to. Although I do not know the purpose of these questions, I know the results will not be injurious for them since the whole constitution of the Pietists has been confirmed in law. I would, however, like to run my eyes over the Pietists' explanations before they are sent on.

I have many things that I need to discuss with you at some length, but I will limit myself this time to what is most necessary in the hope of an early personal conversation. God be praised, my health is again good and stable. I wish you calm as well. May you soon be restored to good health and recover your energy to serve the settlements under your care.

With true esteem and honesty, I remain Yr. Honour's etc.

542. Johann Cornies to Fedor F. Rosen. 27 January 1846. SAOR 89-1-1170/12.

His Honour, Baron,

The enclosed letter from Pavel Komalenko, Schuiut Dzhuret District Secretary, urgently requests permission to remain in his current position until spring. He has already made all of his household arrangements for the winter, and would be forced to take a great loss by moving to Ulkanbeskele.

It is not in my competence to accede to the above-mentioned Komalenko's repeated pleas despite the fact that he has at all times, as far as I know, taken care of his business in an orderly manner. Since delay is difficult, I present this matter for Yr. Honour's better judgment as to whether something can be done for the petitioner. My motives arise from the purest Christian charity. Do not accept them unkindly.

With the appropriate esteem, I will constantly remain Yr. Honour's respectful servant.

543. Andrei Fadeev to Johann Cornies. 28 January 1846. SAOR 89-1-661/17.

My dear and good friend, I have not heard from you for a very long time and am probably to blame for this. Difficult matters arising from my service have kept me from carrying on a regular personal correspondence with good acquaintances. For almost five years I have had to bear a heavy load with many difficulties in my position as Governor of Saratov Guberniia. Over fifty-five years I have never encountered so many annoyances and difficulties. Thank God that I have now been freed of these burdens. Though I am poor and my family and I will likely have to deny ourselves many of life's comforts, I have a clear conscience and calm spirit, and think I will be much happier than before.

I am now off to Saratov to relinquish my position and to make decisions with my family as to where and how we will now live. My wife strongly feels that we should live simply on our small estate near Odesa. However, I still wonder whether the difficulties of that long journey, and especially the separation from our daughter who has married in Saratov, will keep us from realizing this plan. I still receive suggestions as to further service, but I doubt that I will accept any. I am thoroughly disgusted with the way service matters are now being dealt with.

Accustomed as I have been to loving and valuing you for thirty years, I will now have time to discuss many matters with you in writing. I would be happy to take up our correspondence again. Please, my good friend, let me know whether you are still healthy. How are things going in our dear Mennonite settlements, etc., etc.? News of this kind will always be of great interest to me.

I am leaving here today and intend to be in Saratov within eight days. I will remain there, in any case, until May.

Farewell. Give my greetings to all your family and, I repeat, do not forget your sincere friend, A. Fadeev.

Moscow, 28 January 1846.

544. Peter Neufeld to Johann Cornies. 28 January 1846.
SAOR 89-1-1230/18.

Esteemed Chairman,

What we had hoped for has come to pass. I happened to meet Teacher Andreas Voth of Pastwa here in Gnadenfeld last Sunday and was able to carry out the commission you had kindly given me. He has not yet concluded a contract with the Pastwa village community, although both sides had declared their inclination to do so. I was not able to get a single word out of him on the question of accepting the Halbstadt school position. Nevertheless, I firmly think that, after he comes to see you in Ohrloff this Sunday and hears your reasons, he will decide to do so.

With esteem, your respectful Peter Neufeld.

545. Johann Cornies to Fedor F. Rosen. 29 January 1846.
SAOR 89-1-1170/13.

Director Baron v. Rosen,

In my view, the first task in establishing the Crown Model Plantation will be to cut a road suitable for this location along a straight line from the post road. The first operation should be to plant trees along both sides of the road as soon as possible. However, a small corner of land belonging to the Burkut village community is situated along the post road and along my projection for this new road. Because trees are required along the road, the Nogais will not be able to use the land as they wish. Yet if they were given the same quantity of land in another spot, the above-mentioned village community could give up this small corner to the advantage of the plantation.

Accordingly, enclosed for Yr. Honour's consideration and judgment is the Burkut village community's statement and a sketch of the above-mentioned land. I most respectfully request that, if possible, this small piece of land measuring six desiatinas, 111 sazhen, land that is of no use to Burkut, be made part of the Crown Plantation in time for the beginning of spring work.

Perhaps hill No. 2 could be added to this plot. It would make the plantation more attractive. As can be seen on the enclosed drawing, it lies hard by the boundary indicated, along the Burkut side. The boundary could be drawn about twelve to fifteen sazhen further out.

I await Yr. Honour's early decision and resolution.

546. Johann Cornies to Fedor F. Rosen. 30 January 1846.
SAOR 89-1-1170/15.

Director Baron v. Rosen,

The dwelling for Mennonite families on the Crown Model Plantation was almost completed last autumn. However, despite the greatest
thrift, the total of one thousand silver rubles provided for this task was
not enough. I am therefore submitting the sketch of this same house
to Yr. Honour with an exact estimate of all materials necessary for its
construction, including workmen's wages. I would ask that a decision
be kindly made to forward 313 silver rubles, twenty-five kopeks, the
money still outstanding.

547. Johann Cornies to Fedor F. Rosen. 30 January 1846.
SAOR 89-2-1170/16.

To the above,

I have the honour to respectfully submit the enclosed sketch and
exact cost estimate for 545 silver rubles, seventeen and a quarter kopeks
for the construction of a building projected for the Crown Model Plantation. It is intended to provide storage for the various tools and implements necessary for the plantation, with an adjoining wagon shed and
accommodations for several head of livestock. I request that the above
be graciously examined and that I be informed about the decision in
time to take further measures.

548. Johann Cornies to Evgenii F. Hahn. 1 February 1846.
SAOR 89-1-1170/17.

Yr. Excellency,

Yr. Excellency will kindly forgive me if I presume to request information about a certain situation. Specifically, several Prussian citizens
are living and earning their livelihood in our local Mennonite District.
When such people arrive, they send their birthplace certificates [*Heimatscheine*] they have brought with them to St. Petersburg in order that
they might receive safe-conduct permits [*Schutzscheine*] from the Prussian ambassador. I have the honour to submit the enclosed document
belonging to a workman called Tietz.

I would like to know if Tietz or other Prussians are permitted to stay
in our settlements or if they have to obtain special passes from the head

of the appropriate guberniias. This would involve heavy expenses because of the distance involved.

Anticipating early information, I respectfully remain Yr. Excellency's servant, Johann Cornies.

549. Evgenii F. Hahn to Johann Cornies. 1 February 1846.
SAOR 89-1-889/90.

Best of friends, I am officially sending you notice regarding the publication of an *Unterhaltungsblatt für deutsche Ansiedler im südlichen Rußland* (Newspaper for German settlers in Southern Russia). I also think it my duty to turn to you privately in this regard. I can think of no one who could offer greater help in the publication of this newspaper than you. Please supply us with as many interesting articles as you can.

Let me start with a specific request. Appearing in the first issue of this publication will be an enclosure with directions for the cultivation of tobacco. In the first issue of the paper, the newspaper will contain only a special invitation suggesting settlers turn their attention to tobacco cultivation and its advantages. I need the following information. How many puds of tobacco can a half or a quarter desiatina of land produce over a number of years? What is the average price at which good tobacco can be sold? Please be so kind as to send me this information, based on your own experience. I would also like to receive a complete description of circumstances in this regard at Felstenthal and other Mennonite estates and also of their operations.

I thank God that your health is good again. This makes me very happy. Won't you visit us when Toews does? The young people from your settlement are clever and I would very much like to keep them for another few years. This would also be useful for the young people in question. Could they perhaps go home for their baptism and then return to us?

We are now working on the basis of our new budget, but it is regrettably so limited that I do not know how we will manage. I had decided to give Inspector Pelekh a new position, but the new budget has so reduced the number of officials in question that I have no other position to offer him. It would be easier to dismiss him entirely. Please give me your view as to whether it is possible to dismiss him without being unjust. Yours truly, E. v. Hahn.

550. Johann Cornies to Mrs. Wilhelm Martens and family. 1 February 1846. SAOR 89-1-1170/18.

Statement of thanks to the esteemed Widow, Mrs. Wilhelm Martens, and heirs in Halbstadt.

In response to a kindly initiative taken by the President of the Guardianship Committee for Foreign Settlers in Southern Russia, I have taken the liberty to approach you, esteemed lady and heirs, to request that you willingly sacrifice some of the rich blessings that have come to you in so exceptional a way, and that exceed those of so many of our brethren, by providing some generally useful institution for our community.

To judge by an appreciable sum that you have donated for this purpose, my expectations have been met. This benefaction will be remembered by our distant descendants. On behalf of the whole community, I send you, honoured lady and all esteemed heirs, my heartfelt thanks for this generous contribution. I would also note that His Excellency, State Counsellor v. Hahn, has been notified of this gift.

With respect, I remain, your Johann Cornies.

551. Johann Cornies to [unknown]. 1 February 1846. SAOR 89-1-1167/n.p.

For my part, I have nothing further to add to the agreement between the Martens heirs and the Peter Schmidt heirs except that, according to section three of the contract with the Guardianship Committee, the leaseholders are only permitted to pursue field cultivation for their own household needs. The Martens heirs must carefully observe this stipulation as well as all other points of the legal contract, and not permit themselves any contrary demands of leaseholder Schmidt that he could later turn to his advantage.

552. Johann Cornies to Evgenii F. Hahn. 1 February 1846. SAOR 89-1-1170/20.

Yr. Excellency,

Taking the opportunity Yr. Excellency gave me with a suggestion that the Martens heirs might perhaps be moved to sacrifice something for the general welfare, I immediately sent an urgent communication to his widow, Mrs. Martens, and all the heirs suggesting that, in view of the rich blessings they had enjoyed in the community in so exceptional a way, they might show their benevolent intentions by making a contribution of money to a good cause.

The above-mentioned heirs have now donated 2,450 rubles for the projected medical establishment in Halbstadt, and two thousand rubles for the Ohrloff Society School's new building. Additional contributions have been made for the latter cause by persons who owe their own education to this institution. I respectfully inform Yr. Excellency in this regard, with a further comment that the two thousand rubles has been granted the Society school only as long as it remains an educational institution for our local youth. If, on the other hand, the building is given over to a private person for other purposes, the gift of money must remain as a perpetual community asset. It must be repaid in full and applied in some other way useful to the community.

With genuine esteem, I have the honour to remain Yr. Excellency's most respectful [Johann Cornies].

553. Johann Cornies to Deubner. 8 February 1846.
SAOR 89-1-1170/21.

Esteemed Mr. Deubner,

The St. Petersburg academic newspaper praises Julius Loenenberg's geographic primer of countries, recently published in Berlin, as being highly interesting and useful. It is said to be most useful in familiarizing small children in country schools with the basic principles of geography. I most respectfully request that you obtain five copies of the book for examination and send them to me by mail via Melitopol. If they should turn out to be well suited to our local schools and not too expensive, it should be possible to order a considerable number of such primers in future, as needed.

In the hope that my request might soon be filled, I sign myself with esteem as your respectful servant, Johann Cornies.

554. Evgenii F. Hahn to Johann Cornies. 11 February 1846.
SAOR 89-1-889/60.

In response to your communication of 1 February I must inform you that, according to law, no foreigner may live in Russia without a formal residence permit from the guberniia government. Since such documents are not sufficient, the local colonial officials can therefore not grant the Prussian subject Tietz, whose safe-conduct permit [*Schutzschein*] you have presented, nor any other foreigner with such a permit, the right to remain in our villages without being subject to legal punishment.

The foreigner Tietz's safe-conduct permit is enclosed.

Yours truly, E. v. Hahn

555. Johann Cornies to Evgenii F. Hahn. 13 February 1846. SAOR 89-1-1170/23.

Yr. Excellency v. Hahn,

Yr. Excellency's esteemed letter of 1 February just arrived and I hasten to respond. It will give me great pleasure to contribute positively to the *Unterhaltungsblatt*, to the extent of my abilities and knowledge. Enclosed, for the first issue, is information about the usefulness of tobacco cultivation, based on my own experience.

With a moderate amount of cultivation, one can always expect to get an average of twenty-eight puds of good tobacco annually from a quarter desiatina of land. The yield will seldom be less than this and frequently more, especially if the planter sees to it that appropriate cultivation precedes the sowing. The average price of tobacco is estimated to be eighteen rubles per pud and can easily be sold for this at all times, without exception. These calculations are based on several years of cultivation of tobacco varieties most suitable here: Albanian, Chebel, Goldleaf, Maryland, Brazilian, Salonika, Virginia, and Havana with narrow leaves (Havana with wide leaves produces little).

As desirable as it might seem for me and Toews to appear before you in Odesa and to visit the Swedes, I can still not leave home at this time. The varied agricultural activities must be introduced for the coming year, and these give me no leisure. Furthermore, the oversight of the school system would suffer as a result. Presently, the latter demands my full attention and it is necessary to frequently confer with the schoolteachers themselves. Please forgive me for speaking so freely. No subject of less importance would be able to keep me away.

I will discuss our young people in Odesa with the District Chairman and the efforts they have made to deserve Yr. Excellency's favour, something that gives me great pleasure. The Chairman will personally have the honour of reporting our decision to you.

The soil here retained much moisture this winter. At present, all steppe rivers are full of water, and the meadows have been flooded despite the fact that the steppes are still completely covered with snow and ice. Such a winter is very encouraging for the agriculturalist and permits great hopes for a good harvest.

Enclosed, Yr. Excellency will receive several short essays for inclusion in the *Unterhaltungsblatt* should they be deemed suitable.

With esteem, I remain Yr. Excellency's most respectful servant, Johann Cornies.

556. F. Martens to Johann Cornies. 14 February 1846. SAOR 89-1-1229/29.

Mr. J. Cornies in Ohrloff,

Bookbinder Wolf is beginning to effect miraculous water cures here. We already have a number of examples in which our esteemed doctors were unable to provide help, despite their many learned arts. Wolf succeeded in eliminating many [health] problems. I think we should try to find him a place nearby, perhaps in Terpenie, where there are springs of water beside the hill.

It seems to me that the man has practical experience in these matters and is familiar with many illnesses and their causes. Most important, perhaps, is that he is a sober, upright, honest, and Christian man, who has sympathy for human suffering. He is eager to remove all sufferings more cheaply and easily than has been done in the past. He is a man for our time. I am greatly disposed in his favour and feel moved to make this declaration to you. Perhaps he might be assisted in providing such help to sufferers in our midst.

It would be a pity to allow Wolf to move away to Berdiansk. If he were hired on as a water-cure doctor close by, he could provide great advantages for our whole area, especially in a place such as Terpenie. The latter might, in time, become a very busy village.

I do not doubt this for a moment, even though there are still few believers in cold-water cures among us. It would be best for everyone if the results of fresh-water therapy were demonstrated and became increasingly well known. More experience would confirm this fact.

F. Martens, Tiegenhagen, 14 February 1846.

557. Johann Cornies to Fedor F. Rosen. 19 February 1846. SAOR 89-1-1170/27.

Director Baron v. Rosen,

In response to Yr. Honour's communication No. 770 of 19 November 1845, I am pleased to send the enclosed receipts for payments made by

1 January 1846 to the individuals hired for the Crown Model Plantation, supervisor Sudermann, gardener Fast, and watchman Kliuchko. I would, at the same time, respectfully request that, if possible, Yr. Honour have January salaries for these particular persons remitted to me in order that I might pay them. They urgently need this money in their new workplace on the site of the plantation.

I would also like to know at what time these salaries will be paid in future, whether in advance for each term, or afterwards. I could then govern myself accordingly and inform the interested parties about this matter.

558. Johann Cornies to Fedor F. Rosen. 19 February 1846. SAOR 89-1-1170/28.

To the above,

With feelings of gratitude, I acknowledge the Economic Department's readiness to provide the best markets for my tobacco products. I had the pleasure of reading this in Yr. Honour's esteemed communication No. 942 of 29 December 1845. The prices of seven to ten silver rubles per pud advertised by manufacturer Bogosov are certainly worthy of note. I find the appraisals listing the changing prices for different varieties very useful. When I plant tobacco in future I will use this information to my own considerable advantage.

I cannot, however, allow myself to depend on this information for now, since the quantity of tobacco produced here is still too small for such a distant market. But within a few years, good prices will spread tobacco cultivation considerably in our settlements. I will then take the liberty of asking for new information in this regard.

The largest part of last year's tobacco went to a cigar manufacturer in Berdiansk who works it best and pays six to eight silver rubles per pud.

559. Johann Cornies to Christian Steven. 20 February 1846. SAOR 89-1-1170/30.

Yr. Excellency,

Young mulberry plants are no longer quite as necessary in our local villages as before, and it would be far too expensive at present to send a special cart to pick them up. I would therefore urgently request that a quantity of mulberry seeds be sent by mail for the settlements at Mariupol and on the Berda.

Because of the great efforts we have made to promote sericulture, I find that silkworms have become so scarce that we are unable to sell any, or even a few. Though I would like to fill your request, it is not possible to do so.

With esteem, I remain Yr. Excellency's respectful servant, Johann Cornies.

560. Johann Cornies to Christian Steven. 20 February 1846. SAOR 89-1-1170/31.

Yr. Excellency v. Steven,

Given our shortage of small, good cheeses, that we sold out long ago, I am sending Yr. Excellency a large cheese of the same variety and of the best quality. It weighs twenty-six and a half funt. I know you will be satisfied with it. Should you want another cheese of the same variety, please write to me immediately.

I will also, as soon as possible, send you several funt of my own good butter. Your order came as a surprise and I had little on hand. Please pay me later. There will be no charges for the transportation.

Most thankfully, I am finally returning the agricultural newspaper for 1843, wrapped in oil cloth. I apologize for the delay.

We have had fine winter weather, and the thermometer has not dropped below thirteen degrees. There is much moisture from falling snow and rain on our local steppes, and I look forward to an abundance of grain and hay. The steppe streams are full of water and our meadows are flooded. Frost has virtually left the soil and only a few nice days are needed to bring out the ploughmen. Winter grain has suffered no damage. Even the winter barley that came up extremely well in fall seems to have suffered little frost damage over the winter.

There is shortage of fodder in places, especially among the Nogais. The steppes were overgrazed, especially last fall, and the good weather will not be able to make up this shortfall until much later. Grain is priced at eighteen rubles per chetvert for wheat, eight for rye, ten for barley, and nine for oats. Spanish sheep are being sold for eight rubles, but there is presently no demand for horses and horned livestock.

Urgently commending myself to your further benevolence, I have the honour to remain, with greatest esteem, Yr. Excellency's respectful servant.

Account: 26 1/2 funt cheese at forty kopeks per funt: 1,060 plus crate forty;

15.22 funt butter at thirty-five kopeks. 2 small barrels 1.5. Total 27.27 rubles

561. Johann Cornies to Peter Keppen. 20 February 1846.
SAOR 89-1-1170/34.

His Honour, State Counsellor v. Keppen,

I received the two volumes (volumes one and nine) of the *Beitraege zur Kenntnis des russischen Reiches* (Contributions to the knowledge of the Russian Empire) that accompanied your honoured communication of 14 October 1845. Thank you for the continuation of this work. It finally gives me a closer familiarity with Russia.

I will not neglect your request that I examine mounds of considerable height that are connected to one another by paths paved with stone or fired bricks. They do exist here. I will investigate them as soon as I can, once spring arrives, and send you detailed information without delay.

I have further received your equally welcome second letter of 9 November, together with a published text describing conditions in areas between the lower Dnieper and the Sea of Azov. I am obliged and grateful. I have also received another volume of the *Beitraege* with your valued note of 10 January 1846.

With heartfelt wishes for happiness in the New Year and a request that you remember me kindly in future, I remain Yr. Honour's most honestly respectful and obedient servant, Johann Cornies.

562. Evgenii F. Hahn to Johann Cornies. 21 February 1846.
SAOR 89-1-889/61.

I hasten to send you, best of friends, the enclosed German-language communication I received from the Department of Agriculture. You will see that the Department plans to appoint an expert on tobacco-growing to instruct our planters through appropriate instructions. Please give me your opinion. I think tobacco cultivation is not yet widespread enough in our settlements to warrant the efforts of an expert at a cost of four hundred silver rubles. Till now, only a few individuals have occupied themselves with the cultivation of tobacco and they are spread all over New Russia. A teacher cannot be everywhere at once.

I will await your answer before I advise the Department on this subject.
Yours truly, E. v. Hahn.

563. Johann Cornies to Fedor F. Rosen. 23 February 1846.
SAOR 89-1-1170/36.

Director Baron v. Rosen,

I have already assigned three of the most skilled of our previous supervisors to oversee the cultivation of potato and maize fields among the crown peasants of the Berdiansk, Melitopol, and Aleshai Districts this year. They are specifically Trofim Klimenko from Kaikudek for Berdiansk District, Ivan Kholodnoi from Veseloi for Melitopol, and Ivan Beloi from Terpenie for Dneprov. I hurry to inform Yr. Honour about this matter and respectfully ask that the necessary orders be sent to me for these three persons and for myself, in order that harnessed horses might be provided for us to travel to our assigned areas. I would also ask that in a timely fashion you send appropriate directives to local authorities that would encourage the cultivation of potato and maize among crown peasants.

564. Johann Cornies to Fedor F. Rosen. 25 February 1846.
SAOR 89-1-1170/37.

To the above,

Moved by the enclosed papers provided to me by Village Mayor Timev Tenbine, I would request, on behalf of the Nogais, that justice be accorded the Shuet village community by confirming the current and newly re-elected Elder, Dschungase Nasargulov, in office. Though he is the more capable candidate, efforts are afoot to force Bekube Batirov on the community. The latter should be excluded according to law. He has no wife or agricultural establishment and does not have the slightest qualification for such a post. I believe that he is already familiar to Yr. Honour as a good-for-nothing.

I would add that Bolat Chaikbaiev from the village of Shuet, a young man and a good agriculturalist, is by far the most capable person to fill the other office in question.

Aware of your kind heart, I would ask you to excuse my insistence. My purpose is purely and simply the well-being of my fellow man.

Commending myself to your further goodwill, I remain with respect, Johann Cornies.

565. Johann Cornies to Fedor F. Rosen. 27 February 1846.
SAOR 89-1-1170/40.

Director, Baron v. Rosen,

To realize Yr. Honour's directive No. 1896 of 21 December 1845, I have the honour to submit the enclosed booklet with accounts of the money dispersed to the supervisors of the crown potato and maize fields, a total 337 silver rubles. I distributed it among the supervisors in greater and lesser amounts depending on their work.

566. Traugott Blueher to Johann Cornies. 1 March 1846.
SAOR 89-1-1230/40.

My valued Friend,

In carrying out your request, I have sent the two arithmetic books you ordered, and debited your account for one ruble, twenty kopeks silver. Although the 1833 edition is no longer available, I found that an earlier edition was identical in content. I also ordered 150 copies of Bible geographies, natural histories, and church histories from abroad that you should receive by fall.

The time to decide on whether to buy Spanish wool is fast approaching, and I am still uncertain as to what I should do. The prospects for this business are still quite risky. Please let me know by return mail about local prices and whether a number of larger sales have already been concluded.

I hope that you and your dear loved ones are healthy and well, which is the case here, thank God. In closing, I send our heartfelt love and greetings to you and your dear family.

Commending myself to your further friendly remembrance, I remain your faithful friend, Traug. Blueher.

567. Johann Cornies to Evgenii F. Hahn. 2 March 1846.
SAOR 89-1-1170/42.

Yr. Excellency,

Yr. Excellency is quite correct in your opinion that an expert with the Department of Agriculture who is to assist in teaching about the cultivation of tobacco in settlements, cannot be everywhere in New Russia to instruct growers. Such an appointment is also senseless given the fact that an ordinary agriculturalist is quite unwilling to accept an improvement pressed upon him from outside. As we know, he will agree to grow tobacco only when he witnesses successful examples of innovations by his peers. And how could it be otherwise? It is quite unfair to blame an agriculturalist for opposing improvements that might well disrupt the pursuit of inherited branches of his economy.

The inhabitants of our local villages confirm this broad statement. Specifically, during the last four years I have annually harvested the most exceptional tobacco leaves on my estate. They are recognized for their distinction far and wide and bought up quickly at good prices. Several villagers have tried to grow tobacco, but without positive results. Why? Prejudice prevents them from recognizing the value of growing tobacco. Yet this obstacle has suddenly vanished completely, as though people were awakening from a deep sleep. This year, tobacco cultivation will gain a firm footing in our villages. A zeal for tobacco cultivation has emerged among some inhabitants of the Molochnaia Mennonite District.

There can be no doubt that when other settlers are similarly encouraged, they will eventually follow this example. And only when tobacco cultivation has become general should thought be given to improving tobacco cultivation through appropriate instruction. Until such time, special efforts by hired experts, etc., for the above reasons, can do more harm than good.

This is my opinion, which Yr. Excellency encouraged me to give and which I am pleased to submit.

With the greatest esteem, I remain Yr. Excellency's most respectful servant, Johann Cornies.

568. Evgenii F. Hahn to Johann Cornies. 3 March 1846.
SAOR 89-1-889/62.

Enclosed are instructions for the cultivation of potatoes from seed and a small quantity of seed. Should you undertake a small test with these seeds, kindly notify me of the results.

Hahn. 3 March 1846.

569. Evgenii F. Hahn to Johann Cornies. 5 March 1846.
SAOR 89-1-889/66.

Best of friends,

Along with my new proposals on the subject of a silk-reeling facility, I am sending you a letter, at Mr. Royko's request, with a copy of his work in this field.

Mr. Royko would really like to visit the Molochnaia Mennonite villages this summer and I would be very pleased if he did. He has studied the subject of sericulture thoroughly and could be very useful in discussing the construction of a silk-reeling facility with you.

For someone who has not seen anything similar built on such a large scale, the creation of such a facility is not something to be taken lightly. For this reason, it is my opinion that twenty reelers should be used at the start. Expenses will be considerably lower and the facility much better once it has been established for several years.

Yours truly, E. v. Hahn.

570. Johann Cornies to unidentified. 5 March 1846.
SAOR 89-1-1170/47.

Valued friend,

Much as I would like to, I cannot presently be of service to you in the purchase of a year-old pure-bred breeding bull. Ours have all been sold. Should you, however, wish to buy a nice three-year breeding animal of this type, such a specimen could be made available to you at a price of fifty silver rubles. Since I would need definite information in this regard, I await your early reply.

With greetings, your friend Johann Cornies.

571. Johann Cornies to Fedor F. Rosen. 5 March 1846.
SAOR 89-1-1170/48.

Director Baron v. Rosen,

To supervise the potato fields in Perekop District, I would again suggest the previous supervisor, Kokoi Trembetov, Nogai from Mashmir village. I would respectfully request that Yr. Honour have suitable arrangements made in order that Trembetov could make on-site inspections of the seed potatoes still remaining and have the assigned fields prepared.

572. Johann Cornies to Fedor F. Rosen. 5 March 1846.
SAOR 89-1-1170/48.

To the above,

Although planting time is upon us and preparations could soon begin at the Crown Plantation, I have not yet received any decisions in this regard from the Domains Bureau, or about the hiring of workmen the Bureau has decided it will need. I therefore urgently ask Yr. Honour to institute suitable measures in this matter.

Plantings cannot thrive unless they have been sufficiently enclosed. Even if such measures could not be completed beforehand, I think it necessary to begin digging these ditches at the same time as the planting is done. Since peasants have not yet begun to plough their fields, it would be best to do this at the present time.

While the ditch work is beginning, a decision should be made about the suggestion that a piece of land be obtained for the plantation from the Burkut village community.

573. Johann Cornies to Deubner. 8 March 1846. SAOR 89-1-1170/51.

Esteemed Mr. Deubner,
Please obtain two copies of the newest, most complete foreign-language dictionary, edited by Dr. J.H. Kaltschmidt and published by Brockhaus in Leipzig. I also need the Russian-German and German-Russian dictionary that you consider to be best. Have the books sent to me here, via Melitopol. Kindly include the bill so that your charges can be paid without delay.

With esteem, your respectful Johann Cornies.

574. Johann Cornies to Fedor F. Rosen. 9 March 1846. SAOR 89-1-1170/51.

Director Baron v. Rosen,
Seeding time is upon us and there are still stored potatoes in various places in the crown villages of Berdiansk, Melitopol, and Dneprov Districts. I would respectfully propose that, without delay, Yr. Honour take steps to sell any potatoes not needed for seeding in Kherson District. Given the great shortage of seed potatoes everywhere, and because seed potatoes are already being sold for as much as ten rubles banco and higher in our villages, the price could be set at two and a half silver rubles per chetvert.

575. Johann Cornies to Fedor F. Rosen. 9 March 1846. SAOR 89-1-1170/52.

To the above,
It was Yr. Honour's decision that twenty thousand fired bricks needed for the plantation be obtained from Novovasilievka. I have been notified by Master Mason Larion Dmitriev that these bricks are quite

suitable for the erection of interior walls in the plantation house because they need only to be constructed to a width of one brick.

I would respectfully request that Yr. Honour have the above-mentioned twenty thousand bricks delivered to us from Terpenie Brick-works for a price of fifteen rubles per thousand.

576. Heinrich Cornies to Johann Cornies. 10 March 1846. SAOR 89-1-1230/46.

Dear brother,

Because he would like to buy trees, I showed Mr. Horn the nursery. He likes the large apple trees and thinks that the pear trees are good, though small. There are few apricot trees. We cannot sell him more than seven hundred trees: four hundred apple trees (most are large trees), three hundred pear trees, and twenty apricot trees.

Everything on the estate is going well, but I am still very weak. I had to stop several times while writing these few lines, but I hope that with God's help I will soon be better.

A heartfelt greeting to you, your friend, H. Cornies.

Iushanle, 10 March 1846.

[In margin:] If Mr. Horn is sending carts, have him send at least four large ones.

577. Johann Cornies to Christian Steven. 13 March 1846. SAOR 89-1-1170/53.

Yr. Excellency,

I have found suitable transportation and therefore take the liberty of sending Yr. Excellency a three-year-old Dutch cheese from my own production. Please have the cheese tasted to determine whether it keeps well once it has been cut open. Does mould appear, as it did with cheeses obtained from me earlier?

I send Yr. Honour this cheese to demonstrate that I will never cease to remain, with the most perfect respect and deeply felt thanks Yr. Excellency's most respectful servant, Johann Cornies.

578. Johann Cornies to Fedor F. Rosen. 19 March 1846. SAOR 89-1-1170/56.

His Honour, Baron,

Herman Wolf, a foreigner from the city of Koenigsberg, Prussia, who has lived in the Molochnaia since immigrating last autumn, has a very good, practical knowledge of hydropathy. He has already given remarkable help to invalids with water alone, even where patients had been treated otherwise and in vain. He strongly desires to use the beautiful water spring in the crown village of Terpenie for a small hydropathy institution, such as the one in Prinsnitz, Silesia. This is the only well in our local region that is suitable for the development of such an institution.

I know that Wolf is an upright man with good principles. He has a family and belongs to the evangelical confession. He is fifty years old and seems to be fully capable of undertaking what has been described. The institution under discussion would at the same time add life to the village of Terpenie and to the entire region and could serve in tandem with the crown healing institution established for the peasants.

I am ignorant of how such institutions in Russia can receive permission to function. Graciously give me more detailed information about these matters. How can a man like Wolf establish such an undertaking legally?

I remain, with deeply felt esteem and trust in your kindness, Yr. Honour's most respectful servant, Johann Cornies.

579. Evgenii F. Hahn to Johann Cornies. 20 March 1846. SAOR 89-1-889/67.[2]

The government is very interested in establishing agricultural settlements for Hebrews and intends to found such settlements in Kherson, Ekaterinoslav, and Tavrida Guberniias. The Minister thinks that the best way of achieving this purpose is to entrust such settlements directly to the leadership of orderly German fullholders, especially Mennonites.

Enclosed is a German translation of a communication directed to me by His Excellency [Kiselev]. I would politely request that you send me your opinion about these arrangements.

It is probably very difficult to turn Hebrews into agricultural people. However, your success in reforming the Nogais makes it possible to hope that this can also be done with the Hebrews, especially if their

---

2 Regarding these mixed Jewish-Mennonite villages, called the "Judenplan," see Staples, *Johann Cornies*, 240–3; and Harvey L. Dyck, "Landlessness in the Old Colony: The Judenplan Experiment 1850–1880," in *Mennonites in Russia, 1788–1988: Essays in Honour of Gerhard Lohrenz*, ed. John Friesen (Winnipeg: CMBC Publications, 1989), 183–202.

villages were established in close proximity to good Mennonite villages and if these people were provided with everything needed to establish their existence. The biggest question remaining, however, is whether good Mennonite fullholders would be willing to settle with the Hebrews, as the Minister wishes.

Yours truly, E. v. Hahn.

580. Johann Cornies to [Wilhelm] Baumann. 20 March 1846. SAOR 89-1-1170/58.[3]

Esteemed Mr. Baumann,

I am happy to report that I received the booklet containing entries written in regard to Teetzmann's essay. It is as thorough as I had thought it would be and I will send it on to State Counsellor v. Keppen in exactly this form. My honest thanks go to you for the zeal you have demonstrated in rescuing our steppes from slander. With his superficial knowledge of agricultural management, Teetzmann falsely denied all the positive aspects of our work.

Brother David has accepted the seeds and sends his report in the enclosed letter. I passed the economics book on to Cornelius Wiens, and will not fail to take care of the letter to Gloekler.

With the greatest esteem I remain, constantly and without change, your most honest J.C.

581. Johann Cornies to Traugott Blueher. 20 March 1846. SAOR 89-1-1170/58.

Esteemed Mr. Blueher,

In answer to your valued letter of 1 March, I can report that absolutely no purchases of wool have been made in the surrounding region and no prices have therefore been established. Buyers reported that there was a little demand for sheep pelts, but prices at the last Kharkiv market were so poor that few were sold.

I await the arithmetic books you have sent.

---

3 Wilhelm Baumann had spent several weeks in the Molochnaia and wrote a complimentary article for the *Zhurnal Ministerstvo gosudarstvennykh imushchestv*: Wilhelm Bernhard Baumann, "Neskol'ko zemetok o khoziaistve iuzhnoi Rossii," *ZhMGI* 29 (1848): 3–14.

We had good winter weather and prospects for spring are equally good. Seeding began a week ago and grass is simply shooting up. On the whole, everything points to a blessed year.

That is my news for today.

I commend myself to your further friendship, send sincerest greetings to everyone, and remain your honest friend, Johann Cornies.

582. Molochnaia Mennonite Bible Society to Peter Neufeld. 26 March 1846. SAOR 89-1-1247/5.

To the Director of the Molochnaia Mennonite Section Committee of the Evangelical Bible Association, esteemed Peter Neufeld in Ohrloff,

On 12 January 1846, in item No.1, the Molochnaia Mennonite Section Committee presented you to the Main Committee of the Evangelical Bible Association as a replacement for the former Director, Peter Wedel. In communication No. 34 of 28 February 1846, on the basis of section fifteen of the statutes of the association, granted at the highest level, you were confirmed as future director of the Molochnaia Mennonite Section Committee of the Evangelical Bible Association. We wish you blessings for your work as we did for that of your worthy predecessor.

In so informing you, the local Section Committee expresses its confidence that you will work, in every way possible, to further the task before us.

583. Johann Cornies to Roslavets. 27 March 1846. SAOR 89-1-1170/66.

Yr. Excellency,

I have delivered your people to the Melitopol Judge Eshen in order that they might be sent along [to you]. This I regret. They were just starting to grasp the substances of good agricultural practices, but two years is too short for them to master the subject. Their behaviour has been very good and I am fully satisfied with them. Still, I think they should have, in their short apprenticeship, learned enough about good management to be of use in the many situations that they are likely encounter. Yr. Excellency will discover this yourself.

Commending myself to your valued benevolence, I remain, with respect, Yr. Excellency's obedient servant, Johann Cornies.

584. Johann Cornies to Peter Cornies, Cornelius Wiens, Johann Sukkau, and Heinrich Wiens. 28 March 1846. SAOR 89-1-1170/67.

Estimable Peter Cornies and Cornelius Wiens in Ohrloff and Johann Sukkau and Henrich Wiens in Blumenort,

In the fifth point of the terms concluded with the government, you have obligated yourselves to encourage your crown apprentices to learn practical agriculture while continuing their religious practices. They should, for example, be released from time to time to attend the nearest Orthodox Church.

Since I have learned that several agriculturalists are not too particular about this point and make their apprentices work even on the Russian Church feast days, I think it my duty to send you a serious reminder in this respect. Their fasts and feast days must be observed. Moreover, they should attend the nearest church, Terpenie, for example, several times a year and especially on major feast days.

I send you, for your information, a list of feast days on which the apprentices are not allowed to work. Each one of you should make a copy of this list and govern yourselves accordingly.

585. Johann Cornies to Guardianship Committee. 30 March 1846. SAOR 89-1-1172/5.

[Draft:] Your Excellency, Chairman of the Guardianship Committee for Foreign Settlers in Southern Russia,

Report from the Chairman of the Molochnaia Mennonite Society for the Advancement of Agriculture and Trades,

In carrying out Yr. Excellency's directive No. 1540 of 11 March 1846, I have the honour to obediently send you the following information regarding the youths from the Beresan Settlement District who will be sent to the Molochnaia Mennonite District. I must honestly admit that my estate offers the only opportunity to adequately teach them practical forest cultivation as desired. I am also not disinclined to accept them on my estate if this can be done on essentially the same terms as those for the crown apprentices already present for the same purpose.

Specifically:

1. The Beresan youths must be of good character, intelligent, completely healthy, i.e., physically strong, and no less than seventeen years old in every case.

2. The time of their apprenticeship must be fixed for at least four years.

3. When they begin, they should bring along the most necessary pieces of clothing from home.

4. In this exceptional case, I would request fifteen silver rubles annually for each apprentice because they cannot be boarded with their Russian comrades and must live separately. Somewhat more trouble must therefore be taken with them.

5. They will be supported according to their class in every other way.

6. Everyone must accept that their status will be provisional during the first year, so that if any one of them proves to be unsuitable during this probationary year, I would be able to send him back without further ado.

586. School Society Contract. 30 March 1846. SAOR 89-1-910/74.

[Draft:] Contract.

On 30 March 1846, the village community of Tiege agrees to lease the cottager site built up in 1822, to administrators of the Society School, Gerhard Enns, Altonau, and Gerhard Fast, Ohrloff, including the buildings and fences presently there, for the Society's unlimited use.

The conditions are as follows:

1. The individuals assuming the lease, Enns and Fast, will pay twenty-eight silver rubles, fifty-seven and one quarter kopeks in two instalments; fourteen rubles, twenty-eight kopeks on 1 May 1846, and fourteen silver rubles, twenty-nine kopeks on 1 May 1847, with no arrears.

2. The leaseholders will pay the Tiege village community fifty kopeks silver ground tax annually.

3. The leaseholders will maintain the buildings and fences in good order and do the obligatory plantings on this land according to the directives.

This contract, concluded with the agreement of the whole village community of Tiege, was personally signed by Village Mayor Isaak when the site was transferred to Enns and Fast, is attested to by the Village Mayor's Office, including signatures and the impression of the village seal.

587. Johann Cornies to Hermann Sudermann. 2 April 1846.
SAOR 89-1-1170/70.

To the supervisor of the Crown Model Plantation, Hermann Sudermann,

According to the enclosed directive about business office matters for the Crown Model Plantation, you should put the eight bound books included here to use immediately after they have been received. According to the rules and regulations, the applicable subjects should be entered clearly and with the requisite accuracy at all times during the current year, 1846. You should note that after the year has ended, these books will be subject to precise audit.

588. Johann Cornies to Andrei M. Fadeev. 3 April 1846.
SAOR 89-1-1170/82.

Yr. Excellency,

Your communication from Moscow of 11 March 1846 was an extraordinarily gratifying surprise. With these lines I discharge my sincere and heartfelt thanks for the enduring, trusting, and gracious support of your letter, as well as its sympathetic questions about the well-being of the Molochnaia Mennonite brotherhood. I feared that I had somehow earned your justified indignation for the long delay in my own communications. I can now, however, breathe more freely, take up correspondence in good conscience, and continue it frankly, openly, and with force. I, too, have encountered many troubled hours of the kind that a person must endure as part of his spiritual education and improvement. Granted, they do not equal those of someone like Yr. Excellency, who is of high position and whose activities encompass many people of varied qualities entrusted and subordinated to your direction and supervision. Without mentioning the many disagreeable situations I have encountered in introducing improved agricultural arrangements and community order, I have also had to suffer severe illness because of excessive exertions. The latter led to five weeks of confinement to bed late last summer. However, I praise God that I have recovered fully and feel no remaining weakness.

To his family's great sorrow, Wilhelm Martens, Halbstadt, ended his own life last June. In despair, he disappeared at a moment when he was not being carefully watched and was found only after he had already hanged himself. His children divided his wealth among themselves in equal parts. Widow Martens first received fifty thousand rubles as her widow's portion. She lives with her own son Willms in the beautiful, two-story house in Halbstadt Martens had built before his demise. Willms took it over for fifty thousand rubles and is carrying on the business there.

District Chairman Regehr has died. Gerhard Enns is living in Altonau as an active member of the Society. Abraham Wiebe, Rudnerweide, resigned, lives in Berdiansk, and is occupied in commerce with wheat and wool. In addition to Wiebe, another twenty-two Mennonite families live quietly in Berdiansk, well able to support themselves.

The first houses in the craftsman's settlement at Halbstadt were built two years ago according to plan. They are solid structures of fired brick with tile roofs. Several professionals reported for the same purpose this spring, and in this way, the settlement will become important for our local region as the population, in time, increases.

Scientific field cultivation has begun to develop and increase in the Mennonite villages and productivity is constantly on the rise. Livestock breeding is being carried on more carefully and barn feeding has become more popular. Tree planting is making rapid progress. The eighteen forest-tree plantations of the first division are completely planted and plantings are nearing completion in the others. Orchards are being extended at the same pace. A beginning has been made at planting trees along the roads between villages. Two years ago, to protect our cultivated fields from storms and snowstorms, Ohrloff villagers planted trees and mulberry hedges around one hundred desiatinas of their fields. This year this example is being followed by Altonau village. Silk production is increasing at an astonishing rate, and should the weather be only moderately favourable for silkworms, at least forty to fifty puds of raw silk will be harvested this year. A reeling facility for twenty reels is being projected for construction this year in the craftsman's village at Halbstadt.

As fireproof dwellings and agricultural buildings appropriate to their purpose are constructed with Dutch tile roofs the beautification of our villages is proceeding apace. Efforts at improvements are general and, because ground rules have been established for almost everything, a firm and enduring order is being established. Obstacles and disruptions are being cast aside and everyone is achieving much good for himself and his community, in accordance with his abilities and position.

You, State Counsellor, have laid the groundwork for this progress through your humane leadership at a time when we were still fortunate enough to have it. Your directives still serve as guidelines for the improved arrangement of our affairs.

As your noble feelings and positive attitudes continue and endure, along with your well-known diligence, the high authorities will not leave your fate without direction and consideration. You would surely not be content without a wide-ranging field of endeavour. May Yr. Excellency's providence spread its blessing over many. May God grant Yr. Excellency a long life, to the joy of your worthy family and the blessing of many.

These are the wishes of your honestly loving and most respectful friend, who may call himself Yr. Excellency's most respectful servant, Johann Cornies.

589. Johann Cornies to Fedor F. Rosen. 2 April 1846.
SAOR 89-1-1170/70.

Director Baron v. Rosen,

In response to Yr. Honour's inquiry No. 271 of 28 March 1846, I have the honour to report the receipt of two apprentices from Berdiansk District, three from Melitopol, and two from Dneprov. They are all suitable for the Crown Model Plantation and are now working.

590. Johann Cornies to Evgenii F. Hahn. 6 April 1846.
SAOR 89-1-1170/74.

Yr. Excellency,

In response to the esteemed commission received on 20 March 1846, I take the liberty of enclosing my honest opinion about the question of Jewish affairs which His Highness, the Minister, has raised.

I remain at all times Yr. Excellency's most respectful servant.

Opinion about re-educating Hebrews as agriculturalists:

His Highness, the Minister, is unquestionably correct when he says that in order to transform Hebrews into agriculturalists, experienced German landowners with some authority should be settled among them. However, I do not know where one could find persons to undertake such a role in distant regions. There are, in general, very few who simply out of love for their fellow man would willingly sacrifice all material and intellectual powers for any group. Separated from their own brethren, they could not possibly assure themselves and their descendants of an untroubled future even if designated as model agriculturalists and supervisors. While carrying out their purpose, one can assume that these German agriculturalists could only succeed in making progress and moving ahead themselves by marching in step with the Jews. Knowing nothing about agriculture, only this could prevent the Jews from becoming discouraged and in despair. Improvements could only be introduced in stages.

For instance, [one would think that] the Molochnaia Mennonite villages would have provided an example for their neighbours, the Russian villages close to them. [But this not the case.] The latter are prejudiced. They see the establishments of the former as too perfect and claim they are themselves too clumsy to ever achieve anything similar. Although the progress of the Russian village is barely perceptible, it is nevertheless true that with the passage of time, they have accepted much from the Mennonites without noticing this development themselves.

To the best of my knowledge, no one anywhere has thought through this problem seriously, to its conclusion, and devised the most appropriate methods to realistically re-educate Hebrews as agriculturalists. The attempt at settling Jews in Kherson Guberniia as agriculturalists cannot be cited as an example, since it was impossible to bring in effective inspectors such as those who had in the past worked under the direction of the Ekaterinoslav Bureau for Foreign Settlers. There were also no other people, either nearby or at some distance, who could serve as model agriculturalists for these settlers and influence their education in any way. Personally, I have recently become convinced that the present administration of those Jews is completely suffocating and sad. They have been forcibly fettered to their settlement near Bereslav without outside earnings as well as the encouragement or leadership to acquire even the most basic livelihoods.

In my opinion, it has not yet been demonstrated that the Jewish people are entirely incapable of field cultivation. Challenged by this subject, I presume to suggest to the high administration that a Jewish model colony of about thirty to forty householders be founded on three thousand desiatinas of crown land suitable for this purpose midway between the Molochnaia Mennonite settlements, the Berdiansk settlements, and the Nogais in Berdiansk District, specifically, between Pastwa and Rosenfeld villages and the Nogai village of Bescheul. In this neighbourhood, on land of the same quality, are examples of flourishing, poor, and poverty-stricken agriculture.

Special supervision combined with firm, step-by-step leadership in all aspects of agriculture is the main requirement. Because it is so close by, a dependable person to do this could be found more easily among the local Mennonites. He could be appointed as their immediate supervisor and also as a model agriculturalist. This person would also require a further cash salary, since he would only be able to carry on a small establishment of his own while he spends time at his second purpose, to act as a teacher. This German supervisor should be given an assistant from the Jewish community itself, and should also have a good secretary at his disposal. If this village were close by, I would be inclined to take it under my economic supervision from the very beginning. However, this settlement could not be carried out without overall administration by the president of the Guardianship Committee for Foreign Settlers in Southern Russia. The defined goal could not be conveniently achieved with District Supervisors.

The German supervisor would have to take up residence at the same time as the Jews since the process of settlement itself provides the best opportunity to learn. The necessary tradesmen, masons, carpenters, and roofers, would be hired from among the local Mennonites and could provide instruction in their trades at the same time. It is very necessary that agriculturalists should become able to do all of these trades themselves.

With the adequate establishment of this settlement, young Jews from the settlement will surely, over the years, be educated as agriculturalists. It would be primarily such young individuals who could best acquaint their brethren in faith in distant regions with the agricultural profession.

591. Journal of an inspection trip. 10 April 1846. SAOR 89-1-872/38.

[April 11] 533. Waldheim: Provide a certificate addressed to the District Office for Deputies Cornelius Unrau and Johann Schmidt in order that they might acquire the needed monthly passes for their journey to Ostroga.

[April 11] 534. Administrator of the crown-leased lands D. Cornies in Ohrloff: Investigate personally and immediately who, by name, is arranging the ploughing of the meadow on the crown land along the road from Margenau to Gnadenfeld. To be stopped without delay.

[April] 13. 535. Mariupol Mennonite District Office: Nothing can be settled in the matter between Johann Wiens from Schoenthal and Heinrich Wiebe from the Molochnaia village Pastwa about the disputed demand for ten rubles, twenty-six kopeks, although there is a written document in this matter. Order the District Office to direct Wiens to come to Pastwa during the slack period when, after spring seeding, there is no work, and reach an agreement with Wiebe in the above-mentioned matter. Should Wiens and Wiebe fail to reach such an agreement between themselves, they must visit me in Ohrloff to settle the dispute immediately without further ado. The Pastwa Village Office has also received a message in this regard.

April 15. 536. To the above. According to a written request from Johann [Dierks], Molochnaia inhabitant of Tiegerweide village, he is sick with the gout which I have seen myself, and is definitely in no condition to appear in Bergthal District to settle the accounts for which he has been called to task a number of times. This disputed matter must definitely be ended without further delay. I hereby order the District Office to indicate to the Bergthal inhabitants Jacob Martens and Wilhelm Rempel Jr., and also to Johann Funk and Peter Elias, Heubuden, that they must gather in Tiegerweide without delay, during the work-free period, to settle the disputed money demands with [Dierks]. Should they fail to reach a peaceful settlement, they must all, including [Dierks], come straight to see me in Ohrloff so that the matter can be settled without further written documents.

April 15. 537. To the above and also to the Society.

In accordance with an earlier order, fallow fields must be introduced in the appropriate way this year in all the villages in the Mariupol Mennonite District. I hereby again order the District Office and Society to pursue this matter for the benefit of district inhabitants. None of the fullholders may plant potatoes on fallow fields. They must keep them black and free of weeds at all times and plough them repeatedly. Only in this way, and in no other, can the recognized advantages of fallow fields ensure productive grain cultivation. The District Office and Society must pay special attention to this latter point, and will be called to account if they neglect their duties. This must be observed punctually.

April 15. 538. Pastwa.

Johann Wiens, Schoenthal, has orders to appear at the home of Heinrich Wiebe, Pastwa, to end the disputed money matter. If they cannot come to agreement, they must come to Ohrloff to have the matter settled. The Village Office should report any agreement to the Society.

[April 15] 539. Tiegerweide.

Previous contents about Joh. [Dierks] and also Jacob Martens, Wilhelm Rempel from Bergthal, and Johann Funk and Peter Elias from Heubuden.

592. Johann Cornies to Hermann Sudermann. 22 April 1846. SAOR 89-1-1170/88.

Overseer of the Crown Plantation,

Measurements should be taken of the outside borders of the plantation to prepare a sketch that must be sent in by noon tomorrow, Tuesday.

593. Agricultural Society authorization document for Heinrich Franz. 26 April 1846. SAOR 89-1-872/17.

No. 577 at the Society for the Advancement of Agriculture and Trades meeting on 26 April 1846.

Authorization Certificate:

The high authorities have proposed that Heinrich Franz, Mennonite from the Molochnaia village of Gnadenfeld, should become a teacher in the Khortitsa community school. Franz is hereby given written permission by the Molochnaia Mennonite Society for the Advancement of Agriculture and Trades to conclude a contract to take up a position as Khortitsa community schoolteacher for three years. Further submissions must be made to the Society at the end of this period.

594. Johann Cornies to Traugott Blueher. 1 May 1846. SAOR 89-1-1170/97.

Esteemed Mr. Blueher,

The time for sheep-shearing is quickly approaching and I would ask you to sell the wool for me on consignment as you have done before. Moreover, would you be inclined to do so again in future? Please, by return mail, let me know how this might be organized. Specifically, should the wool be sent to the washing facility or straight to you in the city?

There is little demand for wool here, except for a few Russian merchants who are starting to offer eighteen rubles per pud for sweaty wool. Please send me more specific information from Moscow. We were spoiled by things last year. It now appears that our producers will hold out to the end and not accept any advances for their wool.

Your letter of 15 February 1846 with the enclosed and honoured letter from Mr. v. Fadeev was received in good order, as were the indigo, sheep shears, and three hundred copies of Bible stories. We should soon know whether the sheep shears can be cleared out this spring. I will do what I can in this regard.

We have had an early, beautiful, and very fruitful spring that followed quickly after a very light winter. The grass came up wonderfully fast and all seeded fields fill villagers with high hopes for a good crop. After such favourable winter and spring weather, the fruit blossoms are simply beautiful.

I and my family commend ourselves to you and your worthy family, and send you our best greetings. Your honest, constant friend and servant, Johann Cornies.

595. Johann Cornies to *Unterhaltungsblatt für deutsche Ansiedler im südlichen Rußland*. 4 May 1846. SAOR 89-1-1161/27.

[Draft:] First correction

The Agricultural Calendar of the *Unterhaltungsblatt für deutsche Ansiedler im südlichen Rußland*, No. 1, indicates that it is possible to sow fallow fields with green fodder, such as [turnips], oats, buckwheat, barley, and peas. Although this procedure can be followed in other regions where green fallow is possible, it is not true on the Molochnaia and on the New Russia steppes generally. Because of a shortage of moisture, only clear or black fallow can be used in this area. Seeding them with the above-mentioned crops would rob them of moisture and prevent them from gaining the strength they would otherwise acquire from the atmosphere during fallow time.

Indeed, if fallow fields are to be useful, they must be spared planting with every variety of grain and plant. Ploughing them to a depth of four vershok several times each summer would not only clear the land of weeds but keep it sufficiently friable.

This tested, purposeful, and advantageous treatment of fallow fields has for the past number of years proved to be highly rewarding and useful for the agriculturalists in the Molochnaia Mennonite villages.

596. Johann Cornies to *Unterhaltungsblatt für deutsche Ansiedler im südlichen Rußland*. 4 May 1846. SAOR 89-1-1161/29.

[Draft:] Second correction:

Your directions for the cultivation of tobacco, remark No. 14 of item 8, issue No. 1 of the *Unterhaltungsblatt*, suggest that the cutting back of seeded plants and the breaking of their leaves should "only be done when they have ripened." This is incorrect. To grow good tobacco, attention must be paid to the plants and the quality of their leaves. Leaves that cannot maintain themselves well must be broken off immediately, without delay when the cutting-back is being done. This procedure allows for the remaining leaves to grow better and more vigorously. Rules for the cultivation of tobacco indicate that the strongest plants for all recommended varieties of tobacco should not have more than twelve leaves, even if twenty or more have set.

As for remark No. 16 about the ripening of tobacco leaves, experience teaches that if a high quality tobacco is to be harvested constant attention must be paid to preventing the leaves from mildewing or rotting.

597. Johann Cornies to *Unterhaltungsblatt für deutsche Ansiedler im südlichen Rußland*. 4 May 1846. SAOR 89-1-1161/24.

[Draft:] Explanation:

Remarks on page four of the *Unterhaltungsblatt* are a result of a lack of knowledge of our local conditions. Strict quarantine regulations against cattle plague exist among us. When the plague shows itself in even one head of livestock, the entire herd is immediately quartered in barns and all traffic between inhabitants is stopped lest the plague be transferred to other villages. For this same reason no herd, under these conditions, can be allowed to move about freely.

Following this rule, Mennonites were able to protect themselves from the plague in 1844. In 1845, however, our hay crop was extremely meagre and this shortage of fodder coupled with the need to make provisions for the coming winter made it impossible to barn-feed animals during the summer. Under these conditions, the quarantine of livestock in barns had to give way to a stern watch over our livestock on cattle pastures. The extraordinary watchfulness of the Mennonite herdsmen that followed made it possible to prevent the plague from spreading generally in our villages. This was in contrast to the incomprehensibly negligent policing of livestock that took place in the neighbouring Russian and Nogai villages.

598. Johann Cornies to the editor of the *Unterhaltungsblatt für deutsche Ansiedler im südlichen Rußland*. 5 May 1846. SAOR 89-1-1170/102.

Yr. Excellency,

Enclosed are my submissions, one, in regard to the cultivation of our fallow fields under the specific conditions of local climate and soils, and two, in regard to the purposeful cultivation of tobacco. I think it my duty to correct the inappropriate opinions expressed in the April issue of the *Unterhaltungsblatt*. Those opinions tend to mislead the less-skilled agriculturalists among our settlers.

In my third submission, I submit an explanation of why the strict quarantine regulations against cattle plague could not implemented because of a shortage of fodder in 1845.

I would therefore, Yr. Excellency, request that these corrections based on many years of experience appear in the *Unterhaltungsblatt*.

599. Johann Cornies to Guardianship Committee. 6 May 1846. SAOR 89-1-908/56.

To the very esteemed Guardianship Committee for Foreign Settlers in Southern Russia,

Report from the Molochnaia Mennonite Society for the Advancement of Agriculture and Trades,

In carrying out directive No. 2057 of 12 April sent by the highly esteemed Guardianship Committee regarding the establishment of a silk-reeling facility, the Molochnaia Mennonite Society for the Advancement of Agriculture and Trades has the honour to declare the following:

1. The Society prefers a solid, firm building for silk reeling over the light, open buildings used by the Italians. Such a structure seems better adapted to our local climate and superior in general. The Society thinks that a [closed] structure is better suited because, no matter how isolated the [Italian] building may be in its location, it would still be open to the dust widespread in our local region. It further seems more advantageous to have a solid building, built in the German style, where the entire length and breadth of the attic can be arranged to store cocoons, making another building for this purpose unnecessary.

Moreover, a light building constructed according to Mr. Raico's drawings and standing out in the open without protection and subject to frequent squalls, would not last for long and require many repairs. Indeed, work inside would probably have to be suspended during inclement weather. Finally, if private [silk-reeling] facilities were eventually established a solid building would have the advantage of being suitable for different uses.

2. As already stated, the warehouse for the storage of cocoons could be housed under the same roof and would be large enough. There might be a drying room as well, although this has not been taken into special consideration. The building would be handed over to the [Sericulture] Association overseeing this facility and organized according to its own specifications.

3. It is unlikely that a place to store water would be included in the projected facility.

4. An isolated location could be obtained anywhere without difficulty. It would naturally be necessary to prevent the spread of noxious emissions and this would be the first concern of the Sericulture Association under the supervision of the Society.

As is known, the Society for Agriculture and Trades has consulted with the Sericulture Association formed earlier, which found it quite impossible to accommodate Mr. Raico's proposals, even if simply because the suggested accommodations are too extravagant in light of our simple country existence. In fact we are not even in a position to provide a definite cost estimate for the proposed facility, or to anticipate the many problems likely to be involved in its establishment.

It is for these reasons that the Sericulture Association's activities have ceased, and it has withdrawn completely from this project. The Society, for its part, because it is not mandated to conduct such matters of business directly, regrets that it must consider the matter completely closed. The Society is in possession of the sum of three thousand silver rubles assigned for this purpose and will, at the end of the loan period, return it, with interest, to the District Office.

The Society must point out that the project for a silk-reeling facility has discouraged private reelers working in the district. The individuals in question have simply scaled back the improvements they had intended to make. To improve this useful and absolutely necessary branch of the economy, Society members have had ten new reeling devices bought at their own expense. They will be distributed and put to use in villages in order that work can continue actively. Further delays in this matter would inevitably give rise to fears that not all cocoons produced could be unreeled, to the inestimable disadvantage of producers. Now that sericulture has taken root and is making rapid progress, it would appear that a quite considerable quantity of silk might well be produced this year.

600. Johann Cornies Jr. to Johann and Aganetha Cornies. 7 May 1846. SAOR 89-1-1230/94.

With great joy, I report to you that my wife was confined with a completely healthy daughter at one o'clock this morning. Mother and child are both in the best of health.

With the sincerest greetings to you from me and also from my wife, I especially endeavour to be your honest son, Johann Cornies. Tashchenak, 7 May 1846.

601. Johann Cornies to District Office. 9 May 1846. SAOR 89-1-908/46.

[Draft:] From the Chairman of the Molochnaia Mennonite Society for the Advancement of Agriculture and Trades,

To the Molochnaia Mennonite District Office in Halbstadt,

On 5 May, Inspector v. Stempel from the Mariupol settlement travelled through Marienthal and Rosenfeld on matters of business, with instructions to expedite his trip as much as possible. A letter I have just received from Mr. v. Stempel, informed me that when Mr. v. Stempel travelled through Marienthal village, fullholder Jacob Dik addressed the Village Mayor in an exceptionally defiant manner and grievously insulted the Inspector. The latter cannot justifiably be satisfied with things as they are.

I enclose as evidence the above-mentioned letter from the Inspector, and humbly and urgently request that the District Office call Jacob Dik, fullholder in Marienthal village, to account without delay and have him strictly punished for his exceptionally rude and insulting behaviour towards the Inspector. This is a reflection of his malicious character. He has generally dishonoured the Mennonite name through his deportment.

If this situation is not treated severely as a warning to others, occurrences of this sort might well be repeated time and again. It would be to our own shame if all persons of distinction were to fear travelling through the Mennonite villages.

The District Office might kindly inform me of the results [of its intervention].

602. Johann Cornies to District Office. N.d. [May 1846?] SAOR 89-1-908/51v.

From Chairman, to the Molochnaia Mennonite District Office in Halbstadt,

The Mayor of Conteniusfeld and his deputy Kroeker appeared before me to complain that the Mayor's position had been made extremely difficult because of the actions of several local fullholders, principally Quiring, Block, and Bergen. The three had incited rebellion by accusing the Mayor of having cheated the coffers of the village community. Moreover, a growing number of villagers had accordingly been led into disobedient and refractory behaviour. The result is general disorder that might easily have evil consequences.

For these reasons, I would urgently propose to the District Office that, without having them face their Mayor at this time, the main instigators, Quiring, Block, and Bergen be severely punished for their rebellious inclinations and forced to show obedience. This would restore the Mayor to his former position and allow him to carry out his office and restore peace and good order generally. Action is absolutely necessary, because fullholdings are beginning to suffer, something the Society cannot tolerate.

To convince itself of the need for such measures, and to learn more about the above-mentioned matters, the District Office might call the Mayor and Deputy Kroeker to appear before it. It might also kindly inform me about the results of its actions.

603. Johann Cornies to Fedor F. Rosen. 10 May 1846.
SAOR 89-1-1170/104.

Director,

I have received in good order, with Yr. Honour's communication No. 335 of 23 April 1846, the total sum of 1,035 silver rubles, fifty kopeks, to cover salaries, the maintenance of apprentices, and other expenses at the Crown Model Plantation for the January and May terms.

604. Johann Cornies to Fedor F. Rosen. 10 May 1846.
SAOR 89-1-1170/104.

To the above,

Received in good order with Yr. Honour's communication No. 333 of 23 April 1846, a remittance of 592 silver rubles, the estimated sum needed for implements and for [the building of] a proposed livestock barn on the Crown Model Plantation.

605. Johann Cornies to Hermann Sudermann. 13 May 1846. SAOR 89-1-1170/104.

To the Overseer of the Crown Model Plantation, Hermann Sudermann,
Director Baron v. Rosen's communication No. 335 of 23 April 1846
included an extract from the official cost estimates for the Crown Plantation for 1846. You should note that the only allowed expenditures for
the current year must appear under the following heads:

a) payment of day labourers
b) purchase of trees
c) purchase of implements and their repairs
d) purchase of needed writing materials

An entry should be made in the monthly accounts for each item of
expenditure, specifying who bought the items and their exact purpose.
Since you are allowed no other expenditures absolutely none may be
included in the monthly accounts. Should you receive permission from
me for other types of expenditures, such as those needed for the buildings, etc., you must obtain the money for this especially from this Office.

606. Evgenii F. Hahn to Johann Cornies. 20 May 1846. SAOR 89-1-889/72.

I have received your three objections to the *Unterhaltungsblatt*. Since
the third issue has already been printed, they will appear in issue No. 4.
Many thanks for these communications. They were very welcome.

We do not expect a good crop year here. Grain is barely surviving
but the grass has been completely burned and there will be no hay. For
this reason, I would ask you to send me a very short submission for the
Unterhaltungsblatt about the cheapest way of keeping horses and livestock
[alive] when there is no hay or grazing available. When he was last here,
Toews told us how such things are done among the Mennonites and I
believe that this example should now be recommended to others as well.

I still do not know when time and circumstances this year will permit
me to visit the Molochnaia. I will certainly not neglect to make this visit,
since it gives me a rest. The best time may well be in July or August. If
your affairs permit, I would very much like to visit Khortitsa with you.
This could do no harm.

Yours truly, E. v. Hahn.

607. Johann Cornies to Fedor F. Rosen. 21 May 1846.
SAOR 89-1-1170/106.

Director Baron v. Rosen,

I respectfully report that I received one silver ruble with Yr. Honour's communication No. 406 of 3 May 1846 for the model threshing machine built in our villages for the Ministry of State Domains Bureau in the Caucasus.

608. Johann Cornies to Fedor F. Rosen. 30 May 1846.
SAOR 89-1-1170/110.

Director Baron v. Rosen,

Currently living on my estate to learn steppe forest-tree cultivation are the following: Stepan Shigun from the village of Berestova, Berdiansk District; Durmambet Opakov from the village of Kiltshik; Kupriian Ponkiratov from Malaia Lepeticha, Melitopol District; Nikolai Shatochin from Maiatchka village; and Trofim Saitchenko, from Liubimovka, the last two in Dneprov District. (Maksim Panasena of Andelflivna was released from service recently because of his stiff back.) The total number of apprentices included in this group is only five since no other apprentices arrived in place of either Gavril Kulinskii from Vadian, who was released, or Fedor Kiian from Bolshoi Tokmak, who is absent because of illness. I am pleased to respectfully report this to Yr. Honour for your gracious action.

609. Johann Cornies to Traugott Blueher. 30 May 1846.
SAOR 89-1-1170/112.

Esteemed Mr. Blueher,

The estate owned by the current Moscow police official, Aide-de-camp J. Lushin, has owed me 1,218 rubles since 1838. In the enclosed communication, I ask this gentleman to have this sum paid out to me in Moscow in return for a receipt. I enclose a special request that you kindly hand him the letter personally and inquire as to its resolution. I fear that he did not actually receive my earlier communications. I have personal knowledge about the better side of this gentleman's character which leaves me with the impression that he loves justice.

Please forgive my presumption, but I can think of no other way to proceed in this matter. Kindly write to me about the results, for which I will be much obliged.

With heartiest greetings to you and your valued family, Yr. honest respectful friend, J.C.

610. Johann Cornies to Carl Stempel. 4 June 1846. SAOR 89-1-1161/3.

From the Chairman of the Molochnaia Mennonite Society for the Advancement of Agriculture and Trades,

His Honour, Inspector of the Mariupol settlement, v. Stempel,

In response to your esteemed communication No. 615 of 19 March 1846, regarding Kronsdorf village inhabitant Friedrich Bengs's debts and demands, I am pleased to report the following. According to the contract concluded on 28 June 1843 between Bengs and Wilhelm Lange, Gnadenfeld village fullholder, the smithy and dwelling are not owned by Bengs, but are the property of fullholder Lange.

It is therefore essential that Bengs be ordered to go to Gnadenfeld village about this matter and also the matter that several persons do not agree with the demands he is making. An accurate accounting should be done between Lange and the other creditors and debtors in the Village Office. They must reach an agreement.

I respectfully request that Yr. Honour inform me about the agreement reached in this matter.

611. Johann Cornies to Fedor F. Rosen. 6 June 1846. SAOR 89-1-1170/116.

His Honour, Baron v. Rosen,

As you wished, I am honoured to report that I received the money owed me by Mr. Sherbina, amounting to 2,027 rubles.

I thank you, highly esteemed Baron, for your generous letter of sympathy sent to me in May.

I commend myself and my family to your further sympathy, which is of great value to us. With the most complete esteem, I will at all times remain Yr. Honour's truly respectful....

612. Johann Cornies to Traugott Blueher. 10 June 1846. SAOR 89-1-1170/117.

Esteemed Mr. Blueher,

I acknowledge receipt of your communications of 29 April and 17 May 1846. Your proposal [for the purchase of wool] and the prices you specify appear possible if the wool trade here continues at present prices. Sellers still hesitate [to put their wool up for sale] lest they receive more advantageous news in this regard from Kharkiv. In any case, I will spare no effort in seeking to realize your commission as best possible.

Of the sheep shears you sent for sale, thirty-one of the shears listed as No. 7 are still unsold as are fifteen of No. 3 1/2 and fifty-eight of No. 0. Please let me know what I should do with them. Put the sold ones on my account as twenty-eight rubles for a dozen of No. 7, twenty-six rubles for No. 3 1/2, and twenty-one rubles for No. 0.

613. Johann Wall to Johann Cornies. 10 June 1846. SAOR 89-1-1230/106.

To Mr. Johann Cornies in Ohrloff,

At your coachman's urging, I promised to report to you about Heinrich Wieb's daughter. I spoke with Wieb Sunday who insisted that he intends to hire out his daughter Margaretha, but would like to keep her at home until harvest time. He is presently working, but has not yet properly organized his fullholding. Wieb has seeded nine morgen [6.7 desiatinas] and is not able to work everything himself. He will arrange his fullholding so that his daughter can be let go.

614. District Office to Johann Cornies. 12 June 1846. SAOR 89-1-1230/108.

To the esteemed Johann Cornies,

Foreign artisans and citizens living in the village of Bolshoi Tokmak have submitted a petition requesting the establishment of a postal station to receive money and written correspondence. For this reason, the Governor directed the Berdiansk District Police Officer (*Ispravnik*) to gather information regarding the sum of money that would presumably be sent through Tokmak. Since they could easily send and receive money through Tokmak, the nearest Molochnaia villages are to be included in this assessment.

In notifying you about this matter, the District Office requests that you submit a careful estimate of the amount of money you have sent and received by mail during the year. District Deputy Braun.

District Office in Halbstadt

615. Johann Cornies to District Office. 17 June 1846.
SAOR 89-1-1170/118.

District Office at Halbstadt,

In regard to my own monetary and letter correspondence, the Melitopol post office is hardly any farther from me than would a proposed post office in the crown village of Bolshoi Tokmak. Indeed it is in many respects much more convenient and dependable for me. Because I am inclined to continue to use the old post office in future as well, the statement you demand regarding the monies I send and receive by mail during the course of one year will be unnecessary. This is even more true respecting my monetary correspondence on crown matters in which I am involved. That sum cannot be predicted, even were I to separate it out from my own monies.

In response to your communication No. 2819 of 12 June, I have the honour to report this matter with respect.

616. Johann Cornies to Traugott Blueher. 19 June 1846.
SAOR 89-1-1170/119.

Esteemed Mr. Blueher,

On 15 June my sheep's wool for this year was sent to you in Moscow, packed in 141 linen sacks, at a net weight of 1,343 puds, twenty-seven funt. It was loaded on forty-six carts. I am sending you a copy of the bill of lading and also the enclosed original of the contract according to which you are asked to pay the carter Mikhail Semenov and his assistants the remainder of 1,074 rubles, ninety-four kopeks upon proper delivery of the freight.

As in the past, the wool from Tashchenak is marked with a "T." I would be very pleased to again learn how it compares with the wool from Iushanle. This year's wool is generally clean, with the fodder washed out, but it is somewhat greasy.

Based on my knowledge, I have said what it is necessary to leave everything further to your best judgment.

Kindly notify me of the receipt of the wool.

I have already purchased about six hundred puds of wool on your account at the prices you specified and am at present involved in making a deposit for the rest. For this reason, I would be very pleased if you could send me the sum of about twenty thousand rubles by mail as soon as possible to complete this business transaction.

I send friendly greetings and remain your faithfully united friend and servant, J. Cornies.

617. Johann Cornies to Fedor F. Rosen. 22 June 1846.
SAOR 89-1-1170/122.

His Honour, Baron,

Having received urgent requests and applications from the Mennonites Franz Wiebe and Gustav Wilmsen, I venture to obediently repeat my submission of 17 January 1846 asking that Yr. Honour graciously make arrangements as soon as possible to ensure that Chernigov staff doctor Kvortzov finally pay the above-mentioned Mennonites the remainder of the money owing them. This comes to 266 rubles, fifty kopeks. Wiebe and Wilmsen, who are already in debt, find themselves in the most pressing situation. If they do not receive the above-mentioned sum of money from Mr. Kvortzov they face total ruin.

In the confident hope that I am not mistaken, I remain with honest esteem Yr. Honour's faithful servant.

Account for State Counsellor Baron v. Rosen in Simferopol:

Rye flour (twenty puds for forty rubles), wheat flour (ten puds for thirty-six rubles), barley (two puds for four rubles), all in sacks (for seven rubles) and with cartage fees paid to a Nogai (seventeen and a half rubles), two milk cows (at 120 rubles each), one of them for Mr. Lagori, ropes to lead them on the journey as well as oats and transport costs (fourteen rubles, ninety-three kopeks), for a total of 359 rubles, forty-three kopeks.

618. Johann Cornies to Hartwitz. 22 June 1846.
SAOR 89-1-1170/123.

Esteemed Mr. Hartwitz,

Responding to your commission sent to me on orders from Baron v. Rosen in Simferopol, I have sent the milk cow and three calves ordered from Wiebe, with the request that they be temporarily put under the care of Sultan Gerei. Costs of twelve puds of bagged rye flour are also included with this bill.

The cow has recently calved and today gave a total of nine [quarts] of milk. I am including short directions in the Russian language about the most effective care for the cow. I hope that you will be satisfied with this purchase.

Account for Mr. v. Hartwitz: flour, sacks, pay for messenger, cow with ropes and oats for journey for a total of 108 rubles.

619. Johann Cornies to Fedor F. Rosen. 22 June 1846. SAOR 89-1-1170/139.

Baron v. Rosen,

I am sending the two cows ordered for you and for Mr. Lagori with the carter Barakai Tulmisone. They are under the special supervision of crown apprentice Dusenbe Tiushchev. The red cow, No. 15 on its left horn, is for you. It calved a second time on 27 January 1846. On 3 May it gave twelve quarts of milk, its best performance to date, and ten and a half today. The red-spotted cow, marked No. 25 on its left horn, is for Mr. Lagori. It calved for the first time on 14 March 1846, and on 3 May, when the pasture was at its prime, gave ten quarts of milk. Today, after the onset of hot weather, it gave six and a half quarts of milk. Both cows are still young and should become primarily milk cows. I am completely convinced that they will be satisfactory. Because the one originally selected for Mr. Lagori has still not calved, I have had a different cow selected for him. This cow is smaller but also younger and not worse, I think.

In accordance with directions from Mr. v. Martniss, kindly have the cow and the three calves placed under the care of the Sultan until they are fetched along with the flour. The enclosed letter might graciously be forwarded by mail.

Enclosed, Yr. Honour will receive the account for the costs of the entire transport and short directions in the Russian language for handling these cows.

In order that he does not miss work during harvest time, please allow the apprentice Dusenbe to return with the peasant mail after he has taught your people how to milk.

To answer your last letter about cast iron railings, I must report that Mr. Baumann forgot to carry out your directions because he was forced to leave the local region in great haste and with a heavy heart.

620. Agricultural Society to Grossweide Village Office. 24 June 1846. SAOR 89-1-1334/31.

To the Village Office in Grossweide,

At a meeting on 21 June, the Mayor of Elisabeththal received verbal directions to respond to the petition of 9 May 1846 submitted to the

Society by Peter Schroeder, a Grossweide inhabitant. Schroeder will be allowed to build on the cottager lot in question, as he wishes to do, only if he is registered in the village. Otherwise he would have to deposit the money needed or provide dependable guarantors. The Elisabeththal village community cannot agree to the construction under any other conditions or without taking these precautions, since the Mayor's Office must obligate itself to ensure that the building is done in the prescribed manner.

The aforementioned Schroeder should be informed of this decision and directed to do his best to gain a better personal reputation by showing new zeal and activity. Otherwise he must certainly anticipate a miserable future.

Society at Ohrloff, 24 June 1846. Chairman

621. Johann Cornies to Evgenii F. Hahn. 26 June 1846. SAOR 89-1-1170/125.

Inspector for Agriculture in Southern Russia,

In response to Yr. Excellency's honoured inquiry of 21 June relating to improvements of the Graff silk-reeling machine, I have the honour to report that no improvements of this machine have yet been made.

Last autumn a careful, conclusive assessment was attempted locally to determine the advantages and disadvantages of the Graff machine over the simple reeling done here previously. However, this assessment could not be conducted because of several obstacles. First of all, the damp weather late in the season detrimentally affected the working of the machine. Moreover, there was a shortage of good cocoons. For these reasons, all further attempts last winter were suspended. A new start this year has been impossible because the worms have barely completed their spinning. These attempts, however, show that the machine can produce only one funt of organzine silk every eight summer days when working with three people. Were it to double that output of the finest silk, which the Graff machine can incontestably do, it would provide no advantage for our silk production since it demands high expenditures and a great deal of time.

The improvement that is deemed possible consists in increasing the present number of spools at least eightfold, while separating the reeling and twisting functions. In this way, only twice as many workers could produce eight times as much silk daily. This would cost only a quarter as much as at present.

These are the essential contents of my report to be made to the Guardianship Committee for Settlers in Southern Russia. I must remark that before the improvements believed to be possible with the machine are further pursued, one should await the second trial.

622. Agricultural Society to Marienthal Village Office.
27 June 1846. SAOR 89-1-1334/11.

To the Marienthal Village Office,

On 24 June, Marienthal inhabitant Giesbrecht's daughter Anganetha again ran away from service with her employer, Jacob Isaac, Margenau. On 26 June she appeared in the Margenau Village Office accompanied by her father. She behaved rudely towards the village officers and Isaac, her employer, thinking she owed them no attention.

The Society orders that the said girl be delivered back to her service in Margenau without delay. She should be reprimanded and warned that if she again runs away from her employer or refuses to pay due attention to him, a punishment will be imposed that would be disgraceful for her.

This should be observed strictly and a report that it has been carried out must be made to the Society without delay.

623. Agricultural Society to Village Offices. N.d. [June 1846.]
SAOR 89-1-1334/69.

To Village Offices,

A number of inhabitants of our district own Spanish sheep given over to the care of Nogais on contract for half the proceeds. Presently, there is no direct supervision over most of these arrangements and, as a result, several Nogais have acted unfairly. To prevent these evils and greater ones from occurring, the Society has decided to hire a dependable person to supervise the care of all such sheep among the Nogais.

Village Offices are required to publicize this matter thoroughly in their villages to ensure that anyone interested in such a position inform the Society Office by 1 July. A supervisor must be able to write German, as a minimum, and also to speak some Russian.

Furthermore, all inhabitants who now own sheep with the Nogais for half of the proceeds and would like to place them under supervision, should inform the Society accordingly by 1 July of this year, listing the total number of such Spanish sheep and lambs at the last shearing.

624. Johann & Kornelius Isaak to Agricultural Society. 27 June 1846. SAOR 89-1-1161/11.

To the Society for the Advancement of Agriculture at Ohrloff,

At the Society's request, we are submitting information about our sheep placed with Nogais on half shares.

On 23 May 1846 in the village of Tuluga, there were:

1. with Nogai Stamalee, sixty-eight old ewes, eighteen geldings, and one ram. He also has thirty-five ewe lambs, two rams, and twenty-two gelding lambs. Stamalee's total is 146 head.

2. with Nogai Sedambett, eighty-one old ewes, twenty-eight geldings, and one ram. He also has thirty-one ewe lambs, one ram, and twenty-two gelding lambs. Sedambett's total is 164 head.

The total number of sheep belonging to both of us, as brothers, in equal parts, is therefore 310 head. Johann Isaak and Kornelius Isaak.

625. Johann Cornies to Traugott Blueher. 28 June 1846. SAOR 89-1-1170/128.

Esteemed Mr. Blueher,

The esteemed Ministry of State Domains gave the local Mennonite community a silk-reeling machine as a gift. It was invented by Graff, a foreigner. Organzine silk as well as silk velvet can be produced on it and it is intended to encourage the cultivation of silk among us. Although this machine incontestably produces good silk, the manner of its construction makes it capable of producing only a small quantity of silk, thus wasting much time.

This circumstance compels me to ask you, valued friend, to have a knowledgeable person evaluate the enclosed two packages of organzine and velvet silk produced during our first attempts with the machine. Also, please have the silk sold as well as possible. Kindly, as soon as possible, notify me by mail about the information you receive regarding each variety of silk and also about its sale price. This would enable us to better evaluate the production of the above-mentioned machine and to make better decisions about it.

Without anything further for today, and with heartfelt greetings, your honestly respectful friend J.C.

626. Agricultural Society to Village Offices. N.d. [Before July 1846.] SAOR 89-1-1334/70.

To Village Offices,

We have received reports that buildings and fences in many villages could not be painted by the designated date because of rainy weather. The Society therefore repeats the directive in this regard and orders that the earlier directive be carried out punctually on all buildings and fences. The completion of painting should be reported by 1 July of this year.

627. Agricultural Society to Village Offices. N.d. [Before July 1846.] SAOR 89-1-1334/70.

To Village Offices,

Society member Jacob Martens has reported to the Society that he found many fallow fields to be in a most desolate condition, especially on land belonging to the villages above the Chumak road. Many fields have in fact not yet been turned over this year at a time when other agriculturalists are already busy doing this for the second time. This neglect by Village Offices who ignore all administrative directives on this matter works to the incalculable detriment of their inhabitants and will unfailingly lead to sanctions. The Society emphatically orders that where fallow fields remain untouched, arrangements be made to have this remedied without delay or exception. Absolutely no weeds are to be allowed to grow on fallow fields during the course of the summer.

A report must unfailingly be sent to the Society by 1 July of this year affirming that this order has been carried out and that every agriculturalist has thoroughly ploughed his fallow fields.

628. Johann Cornies to District Office. N.d. [June 1846?] SAOR 89-1-1224/19.

A poem written about the death of Wilhelm Martens has come to my attention and I cannot avoid the conclusion that its purpose is not to instruct others, as the writer suggests, but is mainly intended to insult the family he left behind. There are consequently no good intentions involved.

Since it must certainly be very sad for the family to know that this poem is circulating openly in our villages, I think the District Office should forbid it. I would therefore respectfully enjoin the District Office to find out who wrote the poem, and depending on its findings, provide correction and punish the wrongdoer.

629. Johann Cornies to Hermann Sudermann. N.d. [June 1846?] SAOR 89-1-1172.

Supervisor of the Crown Model Plantation:
Business office requirements:

1. Accounts, specified for all income and expenses, listing all money dispensed for the Crown Model Plantation
2. Catalogue of all implements obtained for the Crown Model Plantation and kept there, together with a notation of their value calculated on the basis of the price paid
3. Records of all plantings completed on the plantation, the different varieties of trees on site in each of the sections, which must be numbered
4. Records of the tree nurseries in the Crown Model Plantation, especially the names of trees in seedbeds and nurseries in each section
5. Records of crown apprentices, including their names and villages, listing also their ages and the date on which they arrived
6. Draft records of various notations, such as when planting began, etc.
7. Journal with a word-by-word record of reports sent to the Corresponding Member of the Learned Committee of the Ministry of State Domains, Mr. Johann Cornies, with their date and continuing number
8. Register of an abbreviated record of the contents of forwarded papers that make reference to the plantation

630. Agricultural Society to Landskrone Village Office. N.d. [June 1846?] SAOR 89-1-1232/7.

To the Landskrone Village Office,
The statements taken from local inhabitants, Franz Toews and his wife, about servant girl Anna Teichgrew, do not precisely satisfy the four points raised, particularly since no mention is made regarding the matter of what Franz Toews's wife is alleged to have said to Peter Born's wife. The Society therefore again orders that exact declarations be taken with respect to all four points, without accepting any refusals from Toews and his wife. These declarations should be sent to the

Society as soon as possible, thus completing the information previously submitted.

Society at Ohrloff.

631. Guardianship Committee to Khortitsa District Office. N.d. [June 1846?] SAOR 89-1-1190/1.

Notes of the Directive from the Guardianship Committee to the Khortitsa District Office and its Society, on the occasion of the transfer of supervision of the economic aspects of these villages to the Chairman of the Molochnaia Mennonite Society.

1. Raise the question of the general school system.

2. Improve community and private structures.

3. Regularize the working of cultivated fields.

4. Properly manage the natural forests.

5. Provide assistance for various crafts.

6. Assess Village and District Administrators before they are presented for confirmation.

7. Increase the community's income and thrifty housekeeping.

8. Secure funds created for villages renting out special village land so that this money is not wasted.

9. Examine cost estimates before they are submitted for approval to higher authorities.

10. [Improve] forest and orchard cultivation in the community plantation and in villages.

11. Regulate building sites in villages, taking future generations into account.

12. Supervise community assets such as sheepfarms, brickworks and roof-tile works, etc.

13. [Supervise] leadership for the new settlement in Kronsgarten.

14. Clearly publicize this directive to Village Offices, including that of Kronsgarten, in order that it might clearly publicize this directive to all inhabitants by word of mouth.

15. The Inspector should be informed of this directive in order that he might not interfere in these arrangements in any way and harmfully encroach on the subjects of this directive. The Inspector should, on the contrary, give all possible assistance and support in the realization of its objectives.

16. Encourage greater activity generally so that the more needy inhabitants are provided with means to better support themselves.

632. Johann Cornies to Halbstadt tradesmen. N.d. [June 1846?] SAOR 89-1-1161/70.

Announcement to the inhabitants of the tradesmen's settlement at Halbstadt:

1. As is known, each tradesman is required to build on the site he has accepted within two years. Since new settlers also need barn space with their original establishment, many have been setting up a type of nomadic structure for this purpose. These will not, in future, be tolerated. It is therefore specified that such shacks are only allowed for four years at the most, estimated from the time of the first settlement of each tradesman. After this time, every inhabitant needing an ordinary barn is obligated to build one roofed with tiles.

2. After the above-mentioned four-year term, no strawstacks or haystacks lacking fireproof coverings will be permitted in the tradesmen's settlement.

3. Agricultural land suitable for ploughing will now carry a tax of one silver ruble per desiatina, due on 1 February annually. Until further notice, the tax should be paid to Johann Neufeld, the current District Deputy in Halbstadt.

4. Land intended for a vegetable garden is part of the tradesmen's site. It should be enclosed and protected from the street. [One line illegible.] The vegetable garden must be in one spot and not cut up into little pieces. None of the tradesmen are permitted to make any special arrangements in this respect or to plant trees arbitrarily.

5. Residents at the community distillery, the inn, the District Office dwelling, etc. are allowed to graze their livestock on the community pastures until the tradesmen's settlement has paid its full two hundred rubles per inhabitant.

6. Fence enclosures should be done as follows:

a) Craftsmen living at the marketplace are obliged to establish fences of burned bricks with palisades, forming an even line with the houses. Accordingly, two sazhen of land will remain in front of the houses for the planting of a double row of trees. A railing will protect these trees from the marketplace.

b) Regular, neat, even dividing fences one arshin high will be built in a straight line on all side streets, so that one row of trees can be located in a straight line in front of the houses.

7. Tradesmen are obligated to build orderly, uniform, fireproof sheds for ashes immediately in their first year of settlement.

633. Johann Cornies to Evgenii F. Hahn. 4 July 1846.
SAOR 89-1-1170/131.

Yr. Excellency [v. Hahn],

Julius Wolf, a foreigner and a bookbinder by profession, arrived here with his family on a travel visa from Koenigsberg, East Prussia, last year. He is not a Mennonite but he intended to pursue his profession among the Molochnaia Mennonites. Because he could not find a sizeable house which would serve as a dwelling and also be suitable for the pursuit of his profession in the Molochnaia Mennonite settlement, necessity forced him to take temporary lodgings in small rooms in Prishib. To avoid living uselessly and without purpose, he began to heal various illnesses using cold water. It is obvious that he works carefully and sensibly in his manner of treatment, and that he is a principled man who understands hydrotherapy quite well. Also, he knows how to judge the origin of numerous illnesses and was therefore able to heal quite a few of them successfully. He earned the trust of many people in this way.

A few weeks ago, he sent me the article "about the application and effectiveness of cold water for different kinds of illness," which I have the honour to enclose. He requested that I send it to Yr. Excellency, presenting it as an article that might be generally useful for settlers and acceptable for the *Unterhaltungsblatt*. Among other things, he wrote to me:

"I know that weakness has also brought on many illnesses in your villages, and they can be removed in a desirable manner by the most natural means and at the least possible cost. This is not my only motivation in making my experience known in the villages, however. I would also like it to be a guide to alert my fellow human beings as to how they might maintain their health, which they should do in their own interests."

In case Yr. Excellency should not find this article suitable for the *Unterhaltungsblatt*, Wolf requests that you might kindly send it back to me. He has asked me to make inquiries as to how he can have it printed at his own costs and how he can best sell it.

With the greatest esteem, I remain Yr. Excellency's respectful servant –

634. Heinrich Wiens to Johann Cornies. 6 July 1846.
SAOR 89-1-1229/2.

To the Chairman of the Molochnaia Mennonite Society for the Advancement of Agriculture and Crafts,

Declaration from Master Blacksmith Heinrich Wiens, Mennonite in Blumenort village:

I was told that I was drunk when I received my payment from the Melitopol District Head for various smithing work. In response I can say that I have the honour to respectfully declare that no one can truthfully make this claim about me since I had consumed neither wine nor brandy before I completed my business with His Honour.

I feel myself to be completely innocent of this accusation, and am, indeed, insulted by it. The District Administrator was dissatisfied with me because of my delay in completing my work because I had to make unnecessary trips. He then caused me suffering by withholding the payment owed me. Finally, he now seeks to burden me with an offence of which I am not even remotely guilty.

Nevertheless, if I have indeed offended the required propriety and expressed myself improperly to someone, I must truthfully say that this happened because of excessive haste and vexation on my part when the payment I should have received created so many difficulties and caused me to neglect so much of my work. For this reason, I request kind consideration on your part, Heinrich Wiens.

635. Evgenii F. Hahn to Johann Cornies. 9 July 1846.
SAOR 89-1-889/73.

Your objections have been printed in the *Unterhaltungsblatt*. However, Mr. Jausch has commented further in regard to them. Do not allow this to irritate you. It is acceptable worldwide that responses to criticism may well be made. I read these annotations only after they had already been printed.

State Counsellor Fletsier, one of the Minister's officials, is travelling from here to Ekaterinoslav shortly and he wants to visit all of our settlements, including those in the Molochnaia. I am likewise making an excursion this month, specifically during the period when the moon shines most beautifully. My plan is to travel straight to Tashchenak and if I do not find you there, to visit the Hutterthal people and then to travel to Molochnaia. If your business affairs permit, I would like to travel with you to see not only the people in Mariupol and Berdiansk settlements but also those in Khortitsa, Josephsthal, Kronsgarten, and Schweden. This would be most useful, especially for the people in Khortitsa. But let me repeat that I would like to make this trip only on the condition that you are interested in accompanying me and that you have the time.

I made a report to the Minister that is identical to your opinion about the founding of a Jewish settlement and hope that His Excellency will agree completely with it. Still, we must at least take under consideration the possibility of finding several capable Mennonites who are prepared to settle elsewhere with the Jews. Kindly find such men so that I could have discussions with them when I arrive in the Molochnaia.

Yours truly, E. v. Hahn.

636. Johann Cornies to Evgenii F. Hahn. 11 July 1846.
SAOR 89-1-1170/136.

Yr. Excellency v. Hahn,

To carry out Yr. Excellency's honoured commission of 20 May 1846 to describe measures that might be taken to maintain livestock when hay or pasturage are not available, I asked our local District Chairman Toews to give me his written opinion regarding this matter. I received the results today. His article is based on his own practical experience and I hasten to respectfully enclose it for Yr. Excellency, with the remark that this procedure has already been widely introduced in the Molochnaia villages and that I give it my complete support. It also deserves to be recommended to other settlers.

I will gladly accompany Yr. Excellency on your journey to Khortitsa should you command it and believe that it could prove useful.

We thank God that our agriculturalists are taking pleasure in our splendid harvest of all varieties of grain. This is now keeping all hands busy.

With high esteem, I remain Yr. Excellency's most obedient servant.

637. David Fast to Johann Cornies. 16 July 1846.
SAOR 89-1-1230/226.

Mr. Johann Cornies,

We would gladly accept Johann Klaassen, the teacher you suggested to us, because we do not have anyone at this date. Kindly let us know whether Klaassen would come to visit us for this purpose, or whether we should go to see him. Where exactly can he be found?

Supervisor's office in Berdiansk, 16 July 1846. David Fast.

638. Johann Cornies to Evgenii F. Hahn. 18 July 1846.
SAOR 89-1-1170/140.

State Counsellor v. Hahn,

I cannot avoid disputing the editor's remarks appearing in the fourth issue of the *Unterhaltungsblatt*, but only to the extent that it is based on my own practical experience. Since this experience has been of great use for me and my fellow settlers, I believe I owe this [to the larger community]. I would therefore obediently request that my explanation be printed in the next issue of the *Unterhaltungsblatt* without any basic changes in its meaning.

With exceptional esteem, Yr. Excellency's most respectful J.C.

639. Johann Cornies to Village Offices. 19 July 1846.
SAOR 89-1-1229/14.

[Draft:] To Village Offices,

To my great astonishment, I find that a great deal of broomgrass is growing here and there in our orchards. You are most sternly ordered to have it completely removed immediately. Should unreported broomgrass be visible anywhere when the President of the Guardianship Committee makes his inspection tour, villages will be levied a fine of one silver ruble for the Mayor and fifty kopeks for each Deputy Mayor.

640. Andrei M. Fadeev to Johann Cornies. 21 July 1846.
SAOR 89-1-661/18.

You made me very happy, my dear, good Cornies, with your agreeable letter of 3 April. I am late in responding but wanted you to know something definite about my future which I can now report to you. As soon as Mr. Vorontsov learned that I had left the Saratov Governor's position, he suggested that I serve as his assistant in Georgia. I would much prefer to rest than take up a new job with all of its advantages at my age of fifty-five. However, worries about my children and the hope that I might still be useful prompted me to take up this proposal. In any case, I have been appointed as a member of the Prince's High Council.

During August I plan to visit Tiflis with my wife and unmarried daughter. It seems to me that specific duties await me, mainly colonization. The land is rich in God's gifts but poor in regard to industry and the presence of industrious inhabitants. I will inform you in greater detail when I reach Tiflis. Now I simply ask the Almighty to give me sufficient strength and good health to work in this new position conscientiously and satisfactorily for the good old prince.

I am grateful to you for your news about conditions in the villages. I very much regret the unhappy end of our good Martens. May God give his soul peace! I ask you to give his widow my greetings and also all good Mennonites who still remember me.

With feelings of the most sincere and hearty friendship, I remain forever your respectful A. Fadeev.

N.B. I will visit Sarepta on my journey to Tiflis. How very happy I would be to see your villages once more in my lifetime!

641. Johann Klaassen to Johann Cornies. 22 July 1846. SAOR 89-1-1230/227.

I received a communication through your local Village Office on 19 July and now take the liberty of providing you with this information. I reported to the Supervisor's office in Berdiansk on 19 July. By then someone named Foot, who speaks Russian, had accepted the position as teacher. While a majority of the local inhabitants would like to have a teacher in German only, a very few of them thought differently and so I could not get an absolutely certain answer. However, they will inform me about their intentions in writing within eight days.

With the greatest esteem, I sign myself as willing to be at your service, Johann Klaassen.

642. Evgenii F. Hahn to Johann Cornies. N.d. [Received 27 July 1846.] SAOR 889-1-889/76.

Best of friends,

As much as I would like to do as you wish, it cannot happen now since time is too precious for me. I have already inspected the villages from Halbstadt to Altonau this year, and since the Grand Duke himself took breakfast there, I know Isaac Loewen's fullholding in Lindenau well. I have probably visited it at least three times. I still intend to come to Iushanle this evening and to leave for Khortitsa at breakfast time tomorrow. If you cannot come along, which I understand very well, that trip can be left for another time. I hope that my honesty will please you and that you will be equally honest with me. As much as I would like to visit Khortitsa with you, I would sooner dispense with such a journey than create a burden for you.

Yours truly, E. v. Hahn.

643. Johann Cornies to Evgenii F. Hahn. 27 July 1846. SAOR 89-1-1333/25.

[Draft:] Notes for His Excellency, State Counsellor v. Hahn,

1. Kindly have confirmation certificates sent to me for the five young settlers who are supposed to learn agricultural practices.

2. The Guardianship Committee still owes fourteen rubles, fifty kopeks for the garden weeder it was sent.

3. With reference to Mr. Raico's booklet about sericulture sent to me, I am compelled to explain that, while I do have practical knowledge in sericulture, I would not dispute the improvements described by someone learned in the subject, although I myself believe and am convinced of something else.

This subject allows me to recommend to Yr. Excellency an article from the *Landwirtschaftliche Dorfzeitung* (Agricultural village newspaper) for the year 1846, "On the Treatment of Silkworms," by William Loebe. The simplicity of the article and its application to local conditions might well be generally instructive for our local settlers. Yr. Excellency will be able to convince yourself of this from the enclosed copy.

4. Applications for positions as director and as teacher in the Hebrew villages have come from the Blumenort Village Mayor, Peter Epp, and from Johann Klaassen at the community sheepfarm.

5. I am taking the liberty of respectfully enclosing the Russian directive from the Tavrida Guberniia Government. I request that Yr. Excellency might graciously inform me of the extent to which I should observe these orders on my own land on the Tashchenak.

644. Johann Cornies to Peter Regehr. 27 July 1846. SAOR 89-1-1170/142.

Valued friend,

Messages received from Moscow contain a commission to purchase a sizeable quantity of local silk for shipment to Moscow. This gives me honest pleasure because I have long made zealous efforts to provide good markets that might give our local silk production greater stability. Esteemed friend, I take this opportunity to prevail upon you most urgently, as is my duty and also in friendship, by asking you to obtain the silk for this order from the best reelers in the district, and do this in the best possible way, since a great deal could depend on good results in this matter. Please make every effort to help promote our interests and those of the merchant in this regard.

I know your realistic attitudes so well that they assure me that you will not misunderstand the wishes I have expressed.

With friendly greetings, I remain your honest friend, J.C.

645. Johann Cornies to Fedor F. Rosen. 29 July 1846. SAOR 89-1-1170/143.

Director Baron v. Rosen,

I have the honour to respectfully submit to Yr. Honour the enclosed sketch and precise cost estimates for the construction of the house intended for [the accommodation of] workers and apprentices on the model [forest] plantation. If you should approve this project after sufficient examination, I would ask you to make further arrangements to ensure that, if possible, the construction begin and be well underway this year. I would especially ask Yr. Honour to make arrangements to obtain the bricks from their source as soon as possible. This would spare villages already doing other work on the plantation the necessity of again providing carts for this purpose. I await an early resolution of these arrangements.

646. Johann Cornies to Heinrich Franz. August 1846. SAOR 89-1-1229/156.

[Draft:] To the honoured community schoolteacher in Khortitsa, Heinrich Franz,

After our local Society to Improve the School System had reviewed the proposal you prepared for the Khortitsa Community School and examined it carefully, the Society, guided by the principles on which its endeavours and work are based, found it necessary to give the following instructions:

1. Specifically, try to implement all instructions in notations the Society made on the proposal. Do as much of the teaching yourself as possible. Do not leave it to assistants.

2. In point three of your proposal, you extended the weekly instruction schedule to forty lessons. At the same time you attempted to prove that the number of subjects taught made this necessary. However, you paid absolutely no attention to the main purpose of this school, specifically the acquisition of a firm knowledge of the Russian language. At least one third of the total teaching time should be given over to the teaching of Russian, but you gave it only one-quarter of the time. In the Society's judgment, you should ensure that your school plan is changed in accordance with the following guidelines regarding the extent to which the following subjects should be taught in Russian:

a) for the third class: two Russian reading lessons, three of translation, two grammar, two speaking practice, two dictation, two Russian writing, for a total of thirteen lessons

b) for the second class: three lessons in Russian reading, three translation, two grammar, two speaking practice, two dictation, three Russian writing, for a total of fifteen lessons

c) for the third [*sic*] class, four reading lessons, three dictation, three speaking practice, two translation, three Russian writing, for a total of fifteen lessons

3. You are to alter the projected lesson plan according to the above, and to submit it as soon as possible to the Society for confirmation.

647. Johann Cornies to Peter Keppen. 3 August 1846.
     SAOR 89-1-1170/145.

His Honour, State Counsellor v. Keppen,

Ever since 1840, I have tried to ensure that the truth about the steppes in Southern Russia is well known and have, in this connection, commented on an essay about the administration of the Anhalt-Koethen settlement in Tavrida Guberniia. I had the honour to submit it to Mr. v. Radel, the former director of the Third Department, for his considered disposal.

I have now received the 1845 booklet published by Yr. Honour about various conditions on the land between the lower Dnieper and the Sea of Azov. It contains the essay by Mr. Teetzmann entitled, "About the South Russian Steppes, etc." I requested that the valued agronomist Mr. Baumann record his opinions in regard to this publication. Mr. Baumann has been in Tavrida Guberniia for the last two years and is an industrious and rare observer in his own profession. He cheerfully acceded to my request and provided me with a leaflet to correct Mr.

Teetzmann's assertions. When I examined it closely, I was quite surprised at the skill Mr. Baumann showed in successfully explaining my own thoughts clearly and understandably, faithfully and truthfully, in the fullest sense of those words.

For this reason, I think it my duty to respectfully send Mr. Baumann's leaflet to Yr. Honour, for whatever further action is deemed necessary. Also, in dealing with the doubts cast on the rational cultivation of the steppes, I find it necessary to include the most conclusive refutation from our own experience, a record of the yields on one acre of land that was regularly planted for forty years in succession, and worked appropriately following the rules of the four-field cultivation system followed during the last ten years. These results have been accurately and conscientiously noted year by year by Jacob Neumann, an agriculturalist in the local village of Muensterberg.

This year, Mennonites take great pleasure in a splendid harvest of all grain varieties. This harvest will guarantee large incomes attributable to the advantages offered us by the market close to us in Berdiansk. Our inhabitants are advancing their activities in all locations and this will result in the furtherance of new life [in all branches of our economy]. Tree plantations have progressed most favourably this year, growing and thriving with great success. Silk cultivation is advancing rapidly. It can be assumed that this year's reeled silk will approach fifty puds and it seems that we can be certain of an assured market for it, given the fact that orders for it have been received from Moscow where last year's silk was sold for 550 rubles per pud. The cultivation of tobacco will undoubtedly come to be accepted in our villages this year given the fact that successful examples on the Iushanle estate over several years seem to have conquered all prejudices against it. Many inhabitants already have tobacco plantations of varying sizes. This useful branch of industry will, in a few years, be epoch-making for our local region.

It has been reported that accurate and beautiful maps of each guberniia are available in St. Petersburg and that the villages presently in existence have been marked on them. Yr. Honour might be so kind as to graciously obtain for me the maps for the three guberniias of southern Russia. Please do not take this request amiss despite its disruption of your wide-ranging activities.

With feelings of the greatest esteem and the most honest thankfulness for the continuation of your graciousness, I remain Yr. Honour's most respectful servant, Johann Cornies.

648. Isaac Mathies to Johann Cornies. 7 August 1846.
SAOR 89-1-1230/252.

Most esteemed friend, Mr. Johann Cornies,

Yesterday, Tuesday, 6 August, I returned home safe and sound from my journey to Romen. I now hasten to ask whether you expect me to repay, at this time, part of the sum of money you lent me on 20 March 1846. Since the wool did not return the amount of money I had hoped it would, I would frankly ask you to permit me to use this money for a further period of time at the same rate of interest. I need it badly at the moment since we have already made many payments for wheat. Nevertheless, it is at your service and I would therefore ask you to inform me about the amount you would demand in payment and at what time. The longer the term, the better it would be for me.

With a hearty greeting, I remain your honest friend and servant, Isaac Mathies.

649. Agricultural Society to Village Offices. 7 August 1846.
SAOR 89-1-1244/2.

To Village Offices,

You are instructed to issue a general notification that instruction will begin again in the Ohrloff Society School on 21 August. For this purpose, all parents wishing to have their children attend this school should, when they pay the established school fee, obtain the prescribed entrance permissions from the school treasurer Gerhard Fast in Ohrloff.

Society at Ohrloff, 7 August 1846. The Chairman.

650. Friedrich Prinz to Johann Cornies. 9 August 1846.
SAOR 89-1-1230/253.

Most valued Mr. Cornies,

Abraham Janzen came to me immediately after His Excellency's departure and demanded that his garden should be staked. I responded that this could not be done now, since people are too busy at this time. I told him to clear his potatoes and other vegetables from the garden, since he has time until October, and that he will be informed about the specific date. He also asked me what the General had ordered to be staked. When I asked the General about this, he said that only the well-planted standing trees should be staked, the crippled and useless ones need not be staked, and that he could dig up and sell the young trees not planted in the right place, according to the rules. Janzen responded that he would not do this and would not touch another tree but would continue to look after them. He has spent this time travelling around to gather advice. He also visited Inspector Pelekh.

Since I am still unknowledgeable in such a matter, I respectfully request information. Kindly give me paternal advice in this situation. It is my heartfelt wish, and also the community's, that you might make it possible to come here about this matter.

With hearty greetings to you and your family, I remain your obedient servant, District Chairman Friedrich Prinz.

651. Johann Cornies to Evgenii F. Hahn. 13 August 1846. SAOR 89-1-1170/151.

Yr. Excellency,

In carrying out my promise, I have the honour to obediently submit the enclosed exact accounting from the financial record books of Jacob Neumann, Mennonite in Muensterberg village, detailing the seeding and the harvest results for all varieties of grain from 1806 to 1846. These could be printed in the *Unterhaltungsblatt* to encourage other settlers in southern Russia.

652. Evgenii F. Hahn to Johann Cornies. 19 August 1846. SAOR 89-1-889/77

Only after leaving Khortitsa did I remember that I had failed to give you the official permits I mentioned. I hope that you did not encounter any difficulties along the road. Kindly send me the accounts for your expenses so that, along with my many thanks for your efforts, I am able to repay them.

I have quarrelled badly with Mr. Jansch because he was so brazen about not wanting to include your objections in the sixth issue of the *Unterhaltungsblatt*. If we could only find another editor, this one could be discharged.

I do not consider it necessary to remind you again about the map on which Mr. v. Levshin requested that land divisions be indicated according to the number of fullholdings, or about the reeler that was also mentioned.

I am relying on you entirely in case His Excellency, the Minister, should visit the Molochnaia area. Yours truly, E. v. Hahn.

653. Johann Cornies to Peter Cornies. 23 August 1846. SAOR 89-1-1170/153.

Peter Cornies in Ohrloff,

When His Highness, the Minister of State Domains, responded to the 14 August report No. 697 from His Excellency, Inspector for Agriculture v. Steven, he graciously decided that taxes for the entire apprenticeship of Peter Negresko, the crown apprentice with you at present, should be paid for out of special capital funds. Arrangements have already been made in this regard, and the apprentice Peter Negresko informed accordingly.

654. Johann Cornies to Cornelius Wiens. August 1846. SAOR 89-1-1244.

To esteemed Cornelius Wiens in Ohrloff,

According to Point No. 5 of the conditions I concluded with the government governing the education of crown apprentices in agriculture, you have obligated yourself to most definitely encourage them to punctually fulfil their religious practices and to release them to attend the nearest Orthodox church from time to time.

For this reason and also because I have learned that several individuals are not being sufficiently careful in regard to this matter and are even making their apprentices work on Russian church holidays, I find myself compelled to bring this matter to your earnest attention, in order that both the fasts and the holidays might be observed. Moreover, the nearest church, such as the one in Terpenie, should be visited several times a year by the apprentices, especially on important holidays.

For your information, I am sending you a list of the holidays on which the apprentice is not allowed to work. You must govern yourself accordingly.

Ohrloff village, August 1846.

655. Agricultural Society to Hermann Janzen. September 1846. SAOR 89-1-1229/146.

Esteemed Hermann Janzen in Tiege,

On 15 August you submitted the standing silk-reeler you invented. It was tested by the Society and has received general approval. At its

6 September meeting, the Society for the Advancement of Agriculture and Crafts decided to assign you the right to construct these reelers for five years, until 6 September 1851. This will both reward your efforts and serve as encouragement to others.

Enclosed is a copy of the directive on this matter circulated to Village Offices, with the observation that your invention is also privileged in the Khortitsa settlement.

This Society hopes and feels that, given your obligations in this case, you will not fail to deliver reelers on order in the expected manner.

656. Agricultural Society to Village Offices. September 1846. SAOR 89-1-1229/168.

To Village Offices,

The standing silk-reeler invented by Abraham Janzen from Tiege village has already brought recognition to him from all sides. Because it is Janzen's own brainchild, it deserves a privileged position in order that he is rewarded for his efforts and to encourage others in our settlements.

Therefore, in its meeting on the sixth of the month, the Molochnaia Mennonite Society for the Advancement of Agriculture and Crafts decided that the production of these reelers is to be assigned to Abraham Janzen alone for five years. He has accepted the obligation that every reeler will be made of pinewood for a price of not more than seventeen rubles or of oak for not more than twenty silver rubles. At the same time, it should be delivered in a tin case and durable workmanship should be guaranteed.

All inhabitants of each village must therefore be informed that during the next five years, until 6 September 1851, no one is at liberty to build such a silk-reeler under any pretext whatsoever unless such a person makes an agreement each time with the inventor Janzen for one or more reelers and Janzen gives him written permission to do so.

Village Offices must supervise this strictly and if anyone, anywhere, proceeds with the construction of such a silk-reeler without written permission from the inventor, he should be censured with [a fine of] ten silver rubles for each reeler, to the advantage of the inventor.

657. Agricultural Society to Mayor of Waldheim. September 1846. SAOR 89-1-1229/148.

To the Waldheim Village Mayor,
    Secret directive:

Acting most secretly and without showing your hand, you should discover whether young Martens, your village inhabitant, actually has a violin in his possession and if he plays it. This has been reported to the Society and will absolutely not be tolerated. If such an instrument is discovered, it should immediately be sent to the Society.

658. Agricultural Society to Village Offices. September 1846. SAOR 89-1-1229/150.

To Village Offices,

The Society is completely in agreement with submission No. 54, dated the first of this month, from Orphans' Administrator Cornelius Wiens. At its meeting on the sixth of the month, it decided to send the following order to all Village Offices for their information and punctual observation:

1. No inhabitant of this district may hire young people of either gender who are still under guardianship without the knowledge and agreement of their guardians.

2. Guardians must personally visit their wards at their specific location at least once each year, whether they are in the care of parents or in service, in order to examine carefully and determine whether they are being provided with an appropriate upbringing for their best future success.

3. Guardians must, without exception, punctually submit a very careful annual report by the fifteenth of January, to the applicable guardianship overseer about the terms with whom, by name, the ward is located and also about the condition and behaviour of their wards. A prescribed outline should be used.

4. The Society itself also adds that from now on, absolutely no guardian has the freedom to take his ward into his own service or care. They must always be given to other people in the district in order to avoid offensive situations. Exceptions might be made for special reasons if special approval has been obtained from the applicable orphans' administrator and from the Society following a thorough examination.

All inhabitants and guardians in each village should be adequately informed about the above. It is assumed that all orphans' administrators are aware of these rules and will keep careful watch to ensure that they are followed.

659. Johann Cornies to Evgenii F. Hahn. 5 September 1846.
SAOR 89-1-1179/156.

Yr. Excellency,

I request that Yr. Excellency have the expenses I incurred to return from Schoenwiese to Halbstadt on 7 August 1846, amounting to four silver rubles, thirty-seven and a half kopeks, sent to the Khortitsa District Office with an order to give this money to the Schoenwiese Village Office for a receipt. Kindly have me notified that this was done.

I will obtain the map Mr. v. Levshin wanted with the land divisions indicated according to the number of fullholdings, as was desired, and I will also carry out punctually what we discussed about reeling machines.

From His Excellency, Director v. Levshin, I learned that His Highness, the Minister, would arrive in Orekhov on 16 August and would presumably summon me. For this reason, I went to Einlage village via Orekhov on 14 August and left behind a letter for the Minister with the Orekhov Mayor that I would await His Highness at the Dnieper and that I would be pleased to have the honour of attending upon him there. I then moved continually around the Khortitsa Mennonite sphere and this really gave me the opportunity to acquaint myself with the very basis of these settlements and with their internal life. I will express my opinions to Yr. Excellency in more detail later.

Finally, on 1 September, I had the great pleasure of greeting His Highness on the banks of the Dnieper. Although Director Gladkii objected, my submission bestowed on me the honour of being permitted to accompany the Minister in my own chaise through Einlage and Rosenthal villages, to the community plantation, and as far as Khortitsa. Here, His Highness chose to have breakfast and continued his journey via the community sheepfarm, Schoenhorst, and Neuhorst to the second station without touching Neuburg. District Chairman Bartsch and Chairman Siemens accompanied His Highness from Khortitsa to the community sheepfarm and, as a sign of special benevolence, the farm was given a ram from his own sheepfarm.

His Highness expressed his great satisfaction to us, and the more positively disposed Khortitsa Mennonites were honestly moved, which will likely result in new endeavours and greater activity. I cannot sufficiently express my surprise at Mr. Gladkii's really shameful behaviour during the journey through the Khortitsa villages but I am pleased that all his blows failed notably and entirely. In the end he himself had to praise the villages to the Minister.

With the most honest esteem, I remain respectfully, Yr. Excellency's most respectful servant, Johann Cornies.

660. Johann Cornies to Jacob Bartsch and Johann Siemens.
7 September 1846. SAOR 89-1-1170/158.

To Khortitsa District Chairman Bartsch and Society Chairman Siemens,

I have learned that on his most recent journey, His Highness, the Minister of State Domains, took the opportunity to judge the accomplishments of our Mennonites, considering them with reference to their Privilegium or of their special rights in Russia. His Highness's attention was drawn to the bad example set by many Mennonites who live elsewhere on leased land or among Russians. It would seem that this resulted in judgments and conclusions about our villages themselves.

The Minister travelled to the Khortitsa villages, partly aware of such prejudices. However, His Highness did not permit them to prevent him from convincing himself of something more positive. As you now know, His Highness referred to this matter when expressing his assurance to you that the Mennonite Privilegium would not be curtailed in the slightest.

With this motivation, I find that it is my duty to urgently draw to your attention, District Chairman Bartsch and Chairman Siemens, that the just demands of the high government should from now on be carried out specifically in the Khortitsa villages. More forceful progress must be made in every respect, if we wish to collectively ensure that our well-being is assured of an indestructible foundation. All secondary personal opinions and partisanship should recede into the background entirely. Noble motivations must direct and undertake regulations to establish the collective prosperity of our settlers. Only joint and united endeavours by the District Office and the Society can lead to this goal. On the other hand, evil results will follow if this principle is not accepted in all seriousness and supported by the endeavours of our leadership.

At present it is most necessary to carefully examine whether Khortitsa Mennonites living elsewhere could actually be useful among the Russians. All individuals not corresponding to this purpose should definitely return to their villages by spring or have themselves registered elsewhere. A number of good Mennonites could still establish fullholdings in Bergthal and many families could find an abundant livelihood in the Khortitsa villages themselves if general activity becomes more lively in all branches of agriculture and the trades.

In conclusion, I would express the hope that you will look at my honest statement of the situation from the appropriate viewpoint, since the weal and woe of our whole community in Russia depend on it. If you understand this sufficiently, you will make energetic, serious and forceful efforts wherever necessary.

661. Johann Cornies to Jacob Bartsch and Johann Siemens. 7 September 1846. SAOR 89-1-1170/161.

To the Khortitsa District Chairman Bartsch and Society Chairman Siemens. Valued friends,

I have learned from credible witnesses that Mr. Gladkii quite openly expressed doubts to the Minister as to whether the Mennonites are worthy of their Privilegium when judged against the very shocking behaviour of many Mennonites who live outside their settlements. Regrettably, Mr. Gladkii is not entirely mistaken and, as you know, the Minister very sternly indicated to me that this evil is to be stopped without further ado. As a result, a general meeting here decided that all Molochnaia Mennonites living elsewhere among the Russians and not specifically useful, should be called back without argument by 1 April 1847. Since the well-being of our entire community in Russia depends on this, there will not be the slightest deviation from this decision.

You are called upon to take like measures since, in this respect, one district cannot be permitted to lag behind the other in establishing the collective well-being of all Mennonites.

662. Johann Cornies to Village Offices. 7 September 1846. SAOR 89-1-906/44.

To Village Offices,

When he recently visited various areas of Ekaterinoslav Guberniia, the attention of His Excellency, the Minister of State Domains, was drawn to the life of many families belonging to the colonist class who live outside our settlements. They do not offer the desired example for their neighbouring Russian inhabitants, either in the manner in which they conduct their lives or, even less, by their various disorderly and bad economic arrangements. Left to themselves, they are becoming more harmful than useful.

As a result of this situation, His Excellency gave the Chairman of this Society a verbal order to sternly ensure that all such people living outside our settlements definitely be returned to them. Otherwise, they will be removed from the colonist class and banished from the country. The reason for this is that the government considers it to be an injustice if the great privileges granted our Mennonites generally are squandered on people who will not accommodate themselves to any order and reveal themselves as absolutely useless to their country.

For these reasons, and because it redounds greatly to the shame of the Mennonite community to be the recipients of such justified remarks from the highest levels of government, the Society for the Advancement of Agriculture and Trades together with the District Office reached the following decisions in their meeting on the sixth of the month. To ensure our community's future well-being in Russia, all families from this district who now live outside the district, with the exception of those in Berdiansk, should move back. Only such families will be permitted outside residence who in fact openly demonstrate a good example in the way they conduct their lives as well as with their exemplary economic arrangements. In all cases they must be true examples to Russian inhabitants and in this way redound to the honour of our community.

For this reason, Village Offices are ordered to ensure that all outside persons of every class return to the villages by 1 March 1847 at the latest. Using special messengers, all outside persons should be personally called back at their own expense, and this directive should be read to them clearly in Village Offices and made known to them. This will enable them to make their own arrangements in good time and to allow them no further exceptions. In the contrary case, legal measures will be taken to enforce their immediate return.

It also arises in this situation that Village Offices cannot give any such people permission to distance themselves from our villages.

663. Evgenii F. Hahn to Johann Cornies. 10 September 1846.
SAOR 89-1-889/80.

Best of friends, I am most thankful for your special attention recently, and that you were not inhibited by the time you were losing or by your expenditures in undertaking a second journey to Khortitsa. I also attribute the Minister's great satisfaction to your presence, which prevented him from succumbing to the intrigues of our enemies. His

Excellency departed from Odesa for Kyiv on 9 September. However, he first gave me orders whose execution will definitely need your cooperation.

I have now made arrangements to have the Khortitsa District Office send four silver rubles, thirty-seven and a half kopeks to the Schoenwiese Village Office. You will also receive the four silver rubles, twenty-five kopeks you are still owed for the garden weeder. I held up this money, expecting a bill for your travel expenditures. From the depths of my heart, entirely and truly your E. v. Hahn.

664. Johann Cornies to Fedor F. Rosen. 14 September 1846. SAOR 89-1-1170/164.

Director Baron v. Rosen,

Various tree and shrub seeds are very much needed for the Crown Model Plantation this autumn. Therefore Yr. Honour is requested to graciously have the seeds listed below and also various other seeds collected in the Crimea by the appropriate persons and have them sent to me as soon as this can be done, at least by this coming October, so that we can make use of the favourable autumn weather.

Seed varieties [not all varieties are clear on document]: 1. chestnut, 2. peach, 3. alder, *bitula alnus*, 4. catalpa, *bignonia* [?] *catalpa*, 5. small box tree, 6. ordinary hornbeam, *carpinus betulus*, 7. *celtis* [*Zuebelbaum*], 8. Judastree, *cersis*, 9. [*Schneefolkkenbaum*] *chionanthos*, 10. cornellian, *cornus*, 11. large hazelnut, *corylus*, 12. hornbeam, [including] *carathegus oria, carathegus uniflora, carathegus lucida, carathegus coccinea, carathegus alpina, carathegus osyacanthia flori-plena, carathegus xiridis*, 13. Crimean pine, 14. red beech, *fagus sylfatica*, 15. [*Zliditschia?*], 16. common black walnut, 17. several varieties of juniper, 18. *mispilus* [*Miszeln*], 19. [*Thiya?*], 20. quince, *pyrus sydonia*, 21. common buckthorn *rhumnus*, 22. tamarisk shrub, *tamarix*, 23. yew, *taxus*, 24. lime.

665. Johann Cornies to Evgenii F. Hahn. 14 September 1846. SAOR 89-1-1170/165.

Yr. Excellency,

When I spent almost two weeks in the Khortitsa District, I became acquainted with the main obstacle preventing many aspects of progress from advancing and improving the prosperity of the villages. Simply put, only prejudice motivates District Chairman Bartsch, causing him repeatedly to work in opposition to the Society, possibly not always intentionally. In my opinion the Khortitsa Society and its energetic members such as Chairman Siemens and Member Epp should definitely be given more independence. To achieve greater order and efficacy, all economic proposals should be subject to the Society's examination.

Under the present leadership, the District Office Chairman exercises an obviously constraining influence over the Society's growing activity. I would obediently request that if Bartsch is again selected as District Chairman, Yr. Excellency might take this interpretation of the situation into gracious consideration. Necessary arrangements could be made to ensure that the Khortitsa Society is not restricted or disturbed in the area of activity assigned to it, and even more, that it receive all possible help in this regard. I am, however, convinced that it would be better to allow Bartsch to be released from his service and a different District Chairman be selected to replace him. I will personally not fail to make enquiries and report what could be expected from a newly selected District Chairman and will make an effort to assist in having a useful selection made under present circumstances.

With the most honest esteem, I remain Yr. Excellency's most obedient servant, Johann Cornies.

666. Johann Cornies to Evgenii F. Hahn. 14 September 1846. SAOR 89-1-1170/167.

Yr. Excellency,

In April the local District Office made a submission to the Guardianship Committee on behalf of Mennonites Heinrich Cornelsen from Gnadenfeld and Peter Schmidt from Franzthal. They wished to obtain permission to return to Prussia on family matters and they have paid their three-year taxes accordingly. However, a definite decision has not yet been received.

Urgent requests from the above-mentioned Mennonites asking me to assist in expediting their matter and depart this autumn now move me to request that Yr. Excellency make the necessary arrangements, if possible. Please do not take amiss my application to Yr. Excellency for this reason.

With great esteem, I remain Yr. Excellency's most respectful servant, Johann Cornies.

667. Johann Cornies to Fedor F. Rosen. 15 September 1846. SAOR 89-1-1170/163.

Director Baron v. Rosen,

In accordance with a verbal order from His Highness, the Minister of State Domains, I am privileged to inform Yr. Honour that it is considered as appropriate to the purpose and absolutely essential that the apprentices learning practical agriculture be settled close together as soon as they are released from their apprenticeships. Apprentices from Ekaterinoslav Guberniia will also be included in this group if their parents give permission.

His Highness deigned to order me to write to Yr. Honour asking you to make a presentation in this case and to make the necessary arrangements to have the settlement in question established so that these apprentices are enabled to attain the usefulness for which they were intended.

Yr. Honour knows best what must now be done towards realizing this project.

668. Johann Cornies to Hermann Sudermann. 16 September 1846. SAOR 89-1-1170/168.

To the overseer of the Crown Model Plantation,

Cost estimates were confirmed and permission given to obtain a fire ladder and to finish the two water cisterns. The barrels should only be repaired with wooden hoops at this time, however, since it will eventually be necessary to obtain larger ones finished with iron. These must then also appear on the accounts.

669. Johann Cornies to Hermann Sudermann. 16 September 1846. SAOR 89-1-1170/168.

To the above,

On 18 September, eighty thousand bricks will arrive on the plantation from Novovasilievka on Nogai carts. Ten carters have been ordered to the site, each one to move eight thousand bricks on fifty carts. Also, the Elder himself will accompany each transport of fifty carts with a bill of lading from Novovasilievka. In dealing with this matter, you must take the following into consideration:

1. The bricks on each cart must be counted accurately and piled up in two varieties.

2. Bricks broken once into two pieces are to be considered as whole and are to be stacked onto that pile, while bricks broken into three pieces, etc. must be set aside.

3. The Elder should receive a receipt for the delivery of each transport, listing how many bricks were received whole and how many were broken in three or more pieces.

4. The road where the carts should drive in and out of the plantation must be indicated to them. They should not unharness in the plantation.

5. I should immediately receive a report when the entire quantity of bricks has arrived, including a list of the number of bricks delivered whole or in broken pieces by each *rasprava* by name.

6. The most careful attention and punctuality should be observed during the unloading to ensure that there no unnecessary problems.

670. Evgenii F. Hahn to Johann Cornies. 19 September 1846. SAOR 89-1-889/81.

In response to your communication of 14 September, I hasten to answer that, in accordance with our new regulations, emigrants cannot receive their completed release until the Domains Ministry has excluded them from the tax lists. Communications were sent to the Tavrida Domains Ministry on 20 May and 31 May about the release of the Mennonites Heinrich Cornelsen and Peter Schmidt, but no answer has yet been received.

As soon as the exclusion from the tax lists has occurred, I will not neglect whatever else must then be done.

Yours truly, E. v. Hahn.

671. Johann Cornies to Eiseler Company. 21 September 1846. SAOR 89-1-1170/171.

Messrs Eiseler and Comp. in Kharkiv,

To carry out my earlier assignment from Mr. Blueher, head of the Sarepta Trading Company in Moscow, I now take the liberty of sending to you in Kharkiv the washed Spanish sheep's wool purchased for him, packed into 104 linen sacks loaded on twenty oxcarts. My respectful request is that you take receipt of it from the carters according to the enclosed contract and bill of lading and pay them the applicable cartage charges of 440 rubles, thirty-one kopeks. You might graciously arrange to have this wool sent to the Sarepta Trading Company in Moscow according to your best insight, either through your own business or through the transport bureau. Please settle your accounts for these expenses with Mr. Blueher, and kindly inform me whether the wool was received in good order.

With all respect, I have the honour to be your....

672. Johann Cornies to Traugott Blueher. 21 September 1846. SAOR 89-1-1170/172.

Esteemed Mr. Blueher,

In accordance with your earlier instructions, I have now dispatched 865 puds, 344 and three-quarter funt net weight of washed wool purchased for you here, packed on twenty oxcarts in 104 linen sacks to Eiseler & Co. in Kharkiv. Cartage charges were agreed upon as seventy-three kopeks per pud, which amounts to 631 rubles, sixty-one kopeks. The carters received 170 rubles, thirty kopeks of this here on the spot and it was indicated to them that they will receive 440 rubles, thirty-one kopeks in Kharkiv. I have requested that Mr. Eiseler dispatch this wool to Moscow at his discretion, either through his own business or through the transport bureau, whatever seems most advantageous. He will settle costs with you.

According to the accompanying accounts, my credit with you is now 4,090 rubles after the twenty-one thousand (21/m) rubles you sent has been deducted, which money you might kindly remit to me.

The wool marked Litt. "A." is the third purchase made from that source while wool marked Litt. "H." is the second purchase from another source, and wool marked "#" is a quantity from one of the local villages. I hope that you will be satisfied with this purchase. May the Lord grant his further blessing. I did not find it advantageous to make further purchases, in part because the prices on the spot here continued to be fairly high and then also because I found that the wool stored here did not have the desired properties I sought.

In response to your letter of 12 August, I request that you sell the silk samples at as high a price as possible. Many thanks for your efforts involved in this business matter.

In conclusion, we send you and your dear family heartfelt greetings and remain your faithfully obligated friend and servant, J.C.

673. Johann Cornies to Madame Katte Ghery-Krim-Ghery. 5 October 1846. SAOR 89-1-1170/175.

Esteemed Madame Katte Ghery-Krim-Ghery,
It was necessary for me to wait some time before I could answer your communication of 12 July. Since capital funds are greatly in demand for the exchange of goods within the community of which I am a member, I cannot permit myself to do you this favour, esteemed Madame. With a few special exceptions, my money business is limited to my brethren and I have made it my specific task to use it for their well-being. This is also my duty. Under current circumstances, it would be detrimental for the whole community if I were to remove such a large sum.

With the greatest esteem, I have the honour to be your respectful servant, Johann Cornies.

674. Johann Cornies to Madame Hartwiss. 5 October 1846. SAOR 89-1-1107/176.

Esteemed Madame v. Hartwiss,
Your 30 July commission has been delayed by my almost constant absence from home and because I am overloaded with business matters. I now have the honour to report that no dependable man here wishes to undertake the desired purchase of the horned cattle mentioned. For this reason, my honest advice to you is that you inform Mr. Lamkii that it would, on the whole, be better and more secure for him to send someone from his own home to our settlements. The desired horned cattle should be chosen and bought on the spot. Also, kindly forgive me, esteemed Madame v. Hartwiss, that my answer took such a long time.

Be assured of my greatest esteem, with which I have the honour of calling myself your most respectful servant, Johann Cornies.

675. Johann Cornies to Johann Siemens. 8 October 1846. SAOR 89-1-1170/179.

Valued Friend Siemens,
A certain Major Potemkin wants to have a furrow plough manufactured here and sent to Feodosia. I request that you order it from the inventor, Dirk Dik, to ensure that it will be as precisely and strongly built as possible, with all of its parts answering perfectly to their purpose. Please let me know what this implement would cost and when it would be ready to be picked up. I would then notify Mr. Potemkin accordingly.

I will soon send you the winter barley and seed you ordered and have them shipped on the same cart.

With friendly greetings, your honest friend Johann Cornies.

676. Johann Cornies to Friesen. 10 October 1846. SAOR 89-1-1190/4.

To Schoolteacher Friesen, presently in Hutterthal,

I expressly ordered District Chairman Siemens to have you make your way to Hutterthal as soon as your wife recovers, and that you should stop off in Ohrloff on the way to see me about necessary matters.

You paid no attention to this request and travelled through Ohrloff without stopping off to see me. I am now travelling to Odesa, and am leaving you my directives that you should follow in detail.

In Hutterthal until at least Thursday or Friday of the coming week, you should train yourself in providing instruction with wall-primers, etc. You should then occupy yourself there for a whole week before you fetch the wall-primers from me in Ohrloff. These you should take along for the Bergthal District. You must follow this directive exactly. If not, you will have to make another trip to see me.

**677. Johann Cornies to Village Offices. October 1846.
      SAOR 89-1-1190/7.**

To Village Offices,

In many of the villages in our local district there are a number of single persons of both genders and perhaps also children still living with their parents whose better progress for the future necessitates that they be hired out to good managers. This prompts the Society to order Village Offices to make immediate arrangements to ensure that all local young people or children who should be hired out are put into service without fail by St. Martin's day [11 November] of this year. It is the duty of the Village Offices to take care of this. In the contrary case, these young persons or children will be hired out directly by the Society.

**678. Johann Cornies to Liebenau Village Office. October 1846.
      SAOR 89-1-1190/11.**

Liebenau,

According to report No. 45 of 26 June, the contentious matter involving Jacob Goossen's cottager site cannot be settled voluntarily within the village community itself. The Society is therefore forced to decide the matter on the basis of the wording of the contract and ignore any-thing else that is supposed to have been said about it.

This contract shows that the privileges agreed upon for this cottager site in 1826 were that it would be used as a mill site and to the benefit of the village community. In keeping with these original purposes, it must be assumed that the privileges assigned for this cottager site cannot be reduced in any way. This is especially the case because the contract included nothing about inherited privileges or non-inherited agreements.

As a result, the Society issues the following orders. While the mill continues to exist, the Village Office may not limit the original privileges given to it. Moreover they must remain in force when transferred to another person, unless that person agrees to other conditions.

The Village Office must govern itself accordingly for all time. The Society will never regard this matter in any other way.

679. Jacob Bartsch to Johann Cornies. 21 October 1846. SAOR 89-1-1230/153.

Honoured friend, Johann Cornies,

As requested, I am using a secure opportunity to send you the item that Peter Rempel of Rosenthal village discovered along the shore on the right side of Khortitsa Island last year. It consists of the remains of horns of an unusually large oxen, revealed by the very high water. Included also are the remains of a coat of mail householder Jacob Hoeppner found a short time ago on the Island on the left side of the river just below Einlage, on estate owner Marks's property. Except for some bare rocks, this island was destroyed by last year's high water.

No payment was requested for the latter item but I paid five rubles for the former, including the packing.

With a hearty greeting, your respectful Jacob Bartsch.

680. Jacob Bartsch to Johann Cornies. 21 October 1846. SAOR 89-1-1230/154.

Honoured friend, Johann Cornies,

I am sending you the promised report about the journey two local men, Peter Rempel and Johann Friesen, made to Kherson with a load of 320 puds of butter on a boat they had built. They left Rosenthal on 12 August and after they had been delayed for almost three days at

Bereslav because of the bridge, reached Kherson on 24 August. As they travelled opposite Nieder Khortitsa and again several verstas below the village, as well as at several spots between the estates of Bielenka and Tarasovka and opposite Iakovlev's island, they encountered flat water not more than three fut deep. It was three and a half fut deep at one spot twenty verstas below Nikopol and four fut deep at one spot between the villages of Karadovia and Olievka. However, from Bereslav to Kherson they had good, plentiful navigable water. They became stuck in shallow spots five times.

Rempel and Friesen encountered rocks in the river below Rasumovka, above Bienka, opposite Tarasovka, opposite Chernyshev, and finally below Nikopol. It is now possible to get around the rocks easily but they are likely to be well covered in spring.

The return journey began on 26 August and lasted sixteen days. They had to be towed most of the time because of adverse winds. The banks were suitable for towing because of the trees growing along the riverbank, but many large sunken trees uprooted by the water proved to be an especially great obstacle. In such spots their towering branches made towing impossible and caused many delays.

The men making this journey are of the opinion that it would be impossible to deepen the channel and keep it clear by dredging because the current constantly changes its riverbed, even at present low water levels.

With a hearty greeting, your respectful Jacob Bartsch.

681. Cornelius Janzen to Johann Cornies. 23 October 1846. SAOR 89-1-1230/157.

Greatly valued Mr. Cornies,

I can report that the new fruit orchards were surveyed on 9 October in the presence of Chairman Johann Siemens and 735 square sazhen were assigned to each fullholder. The projections for mulberry [trees] were subsequently surveyed and Schoenwiese fullholders felt compelled to ask the Society to reduce their number because the difficulties involved could be too much for them to handle. This was absolutely refused.

There has not yet been any mention of the accounts or of the tavern, but our householders appreciate the advances they received from you and also from the Committee.

I remain, with respect, your loving friend Cornelius Janzen.

682. Johann Cornies to Evgenii F. Hahn. 26 October 1846.
SAOR 89-1-1170/182.

His Excellency, Director of the Guardianship Committee, State Counsellor v. Hahn,

In 1838, I sold a number of Spanish sheep and rams to Alexei Kuteinikov, Captain of the Don Horde, then resident in Karikubasar. He still owes me 985 rubles, fifty kopeks for these sheep and also for training two of his apprentices in regular sheep breeding. Despite repeated requests, I have been unable to obtain anything from him and so I applied to the Ataman of the Don Horde. However, this petition was returned to me with a letter from the police assessor in Berdiansk District, stating that it could not be accepted because it was written on ordinary paper.

For this reason, I turn to Yr. Excellency with the respectful request to make the most gracious arrangements, so that Captain Kuteinikov is required to pay his debt to me as soon as possible.

683. Agricultural Society to Village Offices. November 1846.
SAOR 89-1-1174/11.

To Village Offices,

Punctually by 1 December, Village Offices should send the Society accurate, careful, and properly counted records, drawn up according to the accompanying formats:

1. Sale of butter and cheese during the year;
2. Production and sale of burned bricks and roof tiles;
3. Servants of both genders from outside who are at present working for village inhabitants;
4. Currently working spinning wheels, looms, etc.;
5. Current stock of wild pears and *Kruschki* planted by fullholders and cottagers
6. Forest trees, other than mulberry seedlings, growing in tree nurseries as of 1 January 1846;
7. Mulberry trees planted in hedges during the course of the year;
8. Forest trees found in orchards on 1 January 1846 and information about planting willows;
9. Beginning and completion of mulberry and enclosure hedges on 1 January 1846; Specifically, all fullholders and cottagers, by name, who

have just begun to do this and also who have finished this task and when;

10. The harvest of tobacco by individuals.

In addition, Village Offices are sternly reminded that they must send in two records by the fifteenth of this month detailing the following:

1. Forest trees planted this year, including notations as to who has completed this task;

2. Fruit trees transplanted this year in fruit tree nurseries, mulberry trees on their intended site, and mulberry seedlings in orchards.

This information should be given to the Society on the above-mentioned date, accurately and correctly. Added to this, Village Offices must punctually submit the record of replanting done in response to the recent audit. Numbers should be given according to varieties. This is to avoid any delay when the Society's office sends in its reports to the higher authorities.

Village Offices are further reminded about the records of setting trenches prepared this year in each of the plantations, including a report of their measurements, which should be sent to the Society no later than the above-mentioned 1 December of this year. Offices will note in the correct categories where preparations have been made, and which setting trenches have already been entered in the records. It must be noted whether this occurred following deep-ploughing to the regulation depth of three-quarter arshin.

May this serve as a reminder to Village Offices to carry out all of these tasks.

684. Johann Cornies to Ministry of State Domains. 6 November 1846. SAOR 89-1-1170/186.

To the Department of Agriculture in the Ministry of State Domains,

In response to the second communication of No. 2554 of 17 October, I am honoured to inform the Department of Agriculture that the report about results of tobacco seed sown here and the tests required can only be sent in in December. Because tobacco matures late, it is not yet ready to be bound into bunches and sent away.

685. Johann Cornies to Ministry of State Domains. 6 November 1846. SAOR 89-1-1170/186.

To the above,

The eight Italian maize kernels received with directive No. 3130 of 14 November 1845 were planted at my Tashchenak estate and yielded three funt, fifteen loth. I am enclosing a sample of it here, with the remark that these ears could not attain their full growth due to the prevailing drought, which limited the quality and production of the kernels considerably.

686. Johann Cornies to Fedor F. Rosen. 6 November 1846. SAOR 89-1-1170/187.

Director Baron v. Rosen,

The mulberry seed received with communication No. 154 of 20 February 1846 was sown in nurseries this spring at my Iushanle estate, at the Crown Model Plantation, and at other locations as well. They came up very well and the growing seedlings have been thriving into autumn, despite drought that lasted the entire summer. They promise the best results.

687. Johann Cornies to Christian Steven. 6 November 1846. SAOR 89-1-1170/188.

Inspector of Agriculture,

The four Italian maize kernels received with communication No. 837 of 13 December 1845 did not thrive when planted at my Iushanle estate. This may have been due to the summer drought. In contrast, the eight kernels received from the Agricultural Department planted at my Tashchenak estate yielded quite a good return of three funt, fifteen loth, although the ears had not developed fully.

688. Johann Cornies to Fedor F. Rosen. 7 November 1846. SAOR 89-1-1170/188.

Director Baron v. Rosen,

In response to Yr. Honour's communication No. 895 of 21 December 1845, I am honoured to report that, at this time, repeated seedings of American summer rye have not convinced me that its introduction would be worthwhile for agriculturalists in this region. This year, where all usual varieties of grain flourished exceptionally well, American summer rye yielded sparse returns, eightfold at the most. It has a nice, attractive kernel but cannot replace the usual rye and be used here because it produces less.

689. Johann Cornies to Christian Steven. 7 November 1846. SAOR 89-1-1170/189.

Inspector for Agriculture in Southern Russia,

In response to Yr. Excellency's communication No. 576 of 22 August 1845, I am honoured to report about the special wheat from Paris called Lammas. To test it, I had it sown in two places in autumn 1845 and in spring of this year, with the following results. The autumn seeding turned out quite well, especially at the Tashchenak estate where three puds, nine funt were harvested from the three funt seeded. The spring seedings all came up but dried out soon thereafter without having made any other progress.

690. Johann Cornies to Evgenii F. Hahn. 7 November 1846. SAOR 89-1-1170/189.

Yr. Excellency,

On 12 March 1846 I received a small amount of potato seed, which Yr. Excellency kindly asked me to test. I can now report that the two *zolotnik* of this potato seed were sown in a manured bed at the appropriate time in spring. After the small plants had grown to a height of one vershok, they were transplanted to well-dug garden land. Because of the early prevailing drought, they formed no potato tubers for a long time. Finally, towards autumn a fruitful rain promoted their growth beyond expectations. The above seed produced thirty-six funt of the nicest, tastiest potatoes. Some grew larger than a medium-sized apple, but the smallest were the size of only a hazelnut.

With great esteem, I remain Yr. Excellency's most obedient servant, Johann Cornies.

691. From Johann Cornies to District Physician [*Kreisphysikus*]. 7 November 1846. SAOR 89-1-1170/190.

Esteemed District Physician,

In response to your esteemed communication of 30 October, I am pleased to inform you that the local Mennonite administration has decided to employ its own doctor. Since this matter still requires some preparations, the construction of a suitable building in particular, it will not be possible to make more concrete decisions until next year.

I must add that I am honestly obliged to you for your offer, and will be pleased to make use of your availability as circumstances and more detailed information indicate.

With exceptional esteem, I have the honour to be your most respectful servant, Johann Cornies.

692. Johann Cornies to Traugott Blueher. 7 November 1846. SAOR 89-1-1170/191.

Esteemed Mr. Blueher,

Confirmation that the 4,090 rubles, eighty-five kopeks you sent me have been received will already have reached you.

You were keenly interested in Mr. Duborg's employment in our local region. He took a teaching position in the Sarata settlement, where a special, higher-level school has been built. State Counsellor v. Hahn, our Chief Guardian, assured me of this appointment during my last visit to Odesa. I had no opportunity to speak with Mr. Duborg in Odesa, but our conversation would not have resulted in anything better since I could suggest no more suitable position for him, despite my various efforts.

We honestly regret the sorrow you are suffering with the painful illness of your dear son-in-law. May the dear Lord direct everything for the best and stand graciously at your side in the worst case.

I can report to you, as an interested participant in all events within our family, that our dear daughter was married to the local Mennonite Phillip Wiebe in October. I have employed him for the past eleven years.

Commending myself further to your valuable friendship, and with heartfelt greetings to you and yours, I remain your faithfully respectful friend and servant, Johann Cornies.

693. Johann Cornies to District Office. 9 November 1846. SAOR 89-1-1170/194.

To the esteemed District Office in Halbstadt,

As a result of my earlier presentation and that of Johann Warkentin, Rosenort village, regarding debts assumed from Abraham Enns, Neukirch, only the following have yet appeared to pay these debts:

Peter Enns, Neukirch; Peter Fast and Widow Pauls, Prangenau; David Loewen, Fuerstenwerder; Heinrich Kasdorf, Jacob Kroeker, and Isaac Regier, Margenau. I would urgently and respectfully request that the other debtors on the enclosed list be strongly reminded to pay off their debts to us and end this matter.

694. Evgenii F. Hahn to Johann Cornies. 11 November 1846. SAOR 89-1-889/82.

The son of settler Kaiser in Alexanderhilf settlement is one of the youths sent to the Molochnaia. His father has in the meantime received absolutely no news from him and is very troubled. Enclosed is a letter from Kaiser that I would ask you to pass on to him. Tell the son to write a cheerful letter to his father that I would give him. The father wished to forward a silver ruble to the boy, but this I forbade as the latter hardly needs the money.

Yours truly, E. v. Hahn.

695. Johann Cornies to Fedor F. Rosen. 13 November 1846. SAOR 89-1-1170/194.

Director Baron v. Rosen,

After my presentation No. 196 of 7 November, I can further report that in Mikhailovka this year's American summer rye harvest yielded five puds, twenty funt from two puds, fourteen funt seed; in Kikulak, five puds, twenty funt from twenty-eight and a half funt seed; and in Andreevka, five puds, thirty funt from three and a half funt seed. The rye is stored in the Village Offices awaiting further direction.

696. Forestry Society to Village Offices. N.d. [Late 1846.] SAOR 89-1-1229/62.

To Village Offices,

It is known that nests of the feared "passion caterpillar" [*Passionsraupe*] can be found in large numbers in trees and shrubs and in village orchards and other tree plantations. If the worms are not destroyed in a timely fashion, they will rob us of fruit the following year and defoliate all trees. The caterpillar, in general, spares only mulberry and wild olive trees.

To prevent this great evil from occurring, the Society orders Village Offices to instruct their inhabitants immediately upon receipt of this order. During our current favourable weather, every nest of the harmful caterpillar should be destroyed in all orchards, other tree plantations, and individual bushes. The nests should not be buried but burned in piles on site.

Village Offices should offer leadership in carrying out this directive in all locations and should assure themselves on site that it has been carried out. The action should not be limited to the one-time removal of nests, but should involve repeated actions until all problems have been removed. Moreover, no exceptions should be made, for if caterpillars survive in even one orchard, all other orchards can be infested as the vermin migrate from orchard to orchard and even emigrate from distant regions.

697. Johann Cornies to Hutterthal Village Office. 13 November 1846. SAOR 89-1-1229/72.

To the Hutterthal Village Office,

Several children in the Hutterthal community have now passed the age at which school attendance is required and are being kept out of school. Since these children have had only one year of regular schooling, they could obviously not have established a firm educational foundation for themselves. I think it would therefore be of value to order the Village Office to summon the fathers or relatives of the children under discussion, as listed in the enclosed records, and order them to send their children to school on a regular basis this winter, specifically until seeding time in1847. Otherwise, the little they have learned in school will regrettably have been forgotten. Indeed, I hope that parents will realize that regular attendance is to their children's advantage and act accordingly, without my having to take further measures, as would otherwise be my duty.

A report of the results of this directive should be made to me by 18 November without fail, indicating whether the children have actually been enrolled in school.

698. Johann Cornies to Fedor F. Rosen. 14 November 1846. SAOR 89-1-1170/195.

Director Baron v. Rosen,

I would respectfully notify Yr. Honour that Pavel Stepanenko, a crown apprentice from Balok village, Melitopol District, who had completed his apprenticeship, fell ill with jaundice on 2 November. Although medications were used to cure him, he contracted a feverish illness that made such violent progress that his death followed on 3 November.

To ensure that the relatives of the deceased apprentice are notified, His Excellency, Inspector of Agriculture in southern Russia, is being informed about this matter, as is the Melitopol District Chief.

699. Johann Cornies to Evgenii F. Hahn. 25 November 1846. SAOR 89-1-1170/199.

His Excellency v. Hahn,

In Odesa Baron v. Mestmacher kindly permitted me to examine a small tobacco cutting machine from Tula and to acquaint myself with its advantages. I would now request that Yr. Excellency ask the Baron to permit the machine to be sent to me by mail. Since I am unable to adequately spell out the details of the machine's construction from memory, this would enable me to have a similar machine manufactured in our local villages. Once this information has been noted, I would send the machine back to you immediately without any damage. I would naturally assume all costs of packing and shipping, which I would ask you to kindly list for me.

Please forgive me for burdening you with this task and be assured that I remain in all honesty Yr. Excellency's most obedient servant.

700. Andreas Becker to Johann Cornies. 29 November 1846. SAOR 89-1-1229/83.

Most respectful request to the Chairman of the Molochnaia Mennonite Society at Ohrloff,

On 29 November 1846, the Nogai Takam Kadera from Akuyu came to see me here in Franzthal village. We concluded an agreement for the sale to the Nogai of ninety head of sheep at nine rubles, fifty kopeks apiece, one ruble to be paid when he receives the sheep, and three rubles, twenty-five kopeks a year from the above date for an additional two years. The Society Chairman is asked to complete the remaining arrangements on stamped paper.

701. Johann Cornies to Jacob Reimer. 3 December 1846.
SAOR 89-1-1170/201.

Dear friend Jacob Reimer,

I take the liberty of asking you for something that may well inconvenience you. However, the trust I cherish in you and in all residents of Felstenthal, gives me the confidence to take advantage of the love you have so often shown me.

Specifically, a young Fast family from Lichtfelde is serving with you this year. People wishing me well have suggested that this man, if you were willing to release him from your service, could become a suitable administrator for my Tashchenak estate, under the direction of my son. As you know, my son was widowed in spring and it is difficult for him to manage the estate by himself. He is tied down too much with this task and needs a dependable helper who would free him to think of matters other than the running of the estate. At present he has no one to rely on if he is away from this estate.

Several families have applied for the job but regrettably none have the required abilities I seek. Fast, who is now in service with you, was suggested to me as a most able administrator. What remains is your own view of this matter and whether Fast would be inclined to take up employment with me. Would you release him? I tell you openly that when Fast was suggested to me as a possible candidate, it seemed to me that another good family on your estate, where everything is well supervised, could possibly serve you in place of Fast. In my own situation, where matters run off in a number of directions, the people I employ are for the most part left entirely to themselves. This demands a man gifted with discretion and the ability to motivate himself.

Please examine my situation with goodwill. If it is possible for you to let him work for me, and if Fast agrees to do so, I would ask that you give my brother Heinrich Cornies, whom I have directed to deliver this letter, a firm answer, one way or the other.

I send you and your family my greetings, as your honestly sympathetic friend and well-wisher, Johann Cornies.

702. Johann Siemens to Johann Cornies. 4 December 1846.
SAOR 89-1-1230/184.

Esteemed friend,

You are hereby respectfully asked to have the following forest trees delivered to me with the carrier of this letter:

one hundred service trees, one hundred hornbeam trees, one hundred red beeches, one hundred maples. This makes a total of four hundred trees.

Please send me the bill and I will submit the applicable amount to you by mail.

I have failed to hire two girls for you in our villages. The probable reason is that girls in our area are usually hired in July or August.

I have received the plan for Schoenwiese village, confirmed by the Guardianship Committee. Otherwise, nothing worth mentioning has occurred in our area.

I remain, with a heartfelt greeting, your most respectful Johann Siemens.

703. Johann Cornies to Hermann Sudermann. 5 December 1846. SAOR 89-1-1170/203.

To H. Sudermann, Overseer of the Crown Model Plantation,

Enclosed is the payment of three rubles, thirty-six kopeks for expenditures made on behalf of Mikhailo, the watchman, and also eight rubles, twenty-four kopeks for construction in October and six rubles, eighty-seven kopeks for construction in November, for a total of eighteen rubles, forty-seven kopeks.

It is also noted that five windowpanes, one crossbar, and two bowls of milk have not been included as expenditures on this account. They should only be included in December, and cannot be considered as expenditures.

704. Johann Cornies to Martin Riediger. 7 December 1846. SAOR 89-1-1229/85.

To Martin Riediger, teacher in the Society School in Ohrloff,

I write in reply to your letter of 2 December 1846 in recognition of the fact that you are no longer able to perform the duties of a schoolteacher because of poor health. Since you are no longer able to discharge your duties, as you write, and since the school would suffer under these conditions, the school administration has decided to accept your proposal and release you completely and without obstacle from your position as of the New Year, 1847.

**705. Johann Cornies to Christian Steven. 7 December 1846.
SAOR 89-1-1170/203.**

Yr. Excellency, v. Steven,

I write to request that five copies of the previously mentioned Russian school books for crown apprentices be sent to me on my own account, and at the earliest possible time.

Because tobacco plants mature late, tobacco samples for the department are not yet ready to be sent out. They will follow, possibly even before the New Year.

**706. Johann Cornies to Christian Steven. 7 December 1846.
SAOR 89-1-1170/204.**

Inspector of Agriculture,

To correct Yr. esteemed communication No. 931 of 2 December, I submit that, as far as I know, the building of earthen dams to water haymeadows that abut on steppe rivers is unique in our local region. About 1,400 desiatinas in the Mennonite District are watered in this manner but no fields, gardens, or plantations, with the exception of a few vegetable gardens or plantations that are partly watered by spring flooding, the latter because of the rarity in our area of wells for this purpose.

**707. Johann Cornies to Hermann Sudermann. 11 December 1846.
SAOR 89-1-1170/207.**

To the Overseer of the Crown Model Plantation, H. Sudermann,

Osip Simarenko, an apprentice from the village of Bodian Vladiana who arrived on the Crown Plantation had, according to a communication from the District Chief, been selected for work in the orchard on my Tashchenak estate. Since he was mistakenly sent to the plantation, please deliver him to the Tashchenak estate as soon as possible and send me a detailed account of your expenses for his maintenance.

**708. Jacob Bartsch to Johann Cornies. 11 December 1846.
SAOR 89-1-1230/187.**

To the Chairman of the Molochnaia Mennonite Society for the Advancement of Agriculture and Trades, Mr. Johann Cornies in Ohrloff,

The Khortitsa District Office appointed the carrier of this letter, the Mennonite Jacob Knelsen, Rosenthal village, to work as a master in the local community roof-tile works. Since his understanding of this business is still imperfect, I would ask that you kindly have him shown your roof-tile works and familiarize him with its arrangements. This should help him acquire the necessary knowledge to pursue this occupation to the advantage of our community.

With esteem, I remain your respectful Jacob Bartsch, District Chairman.

709. Heinrich Goertz to Johann Cornies. 17 December 1846. SAOR 89-1-1230/188.

To the Chairman of the Molochnaia Mennonite Society in Ohrloff, J. Cornies,

You kindly sent along a reminder with the Sparrau Mennonite, Daniel Pauls, about the rebuilding of Sparrau village that is to be started soon. Aware now of your interest in this matter, I have the honour to submit a short report about its progress.

Once the plan had been confirmed in your presence by His Excellency, President of the Guardianship Committee, construction sites were marked off with furrows. Wells for the nine fullholders are to be rebuilt next year at a depth of thirty fut to the water. Also, trenches four fut wide and two and a half fut deep have been prepared for the planting of hawthorn hedges along the borders where estate lands abut the building area. Unless a sufficient number of hawthorn plants are available in the larger gardens of the Molochnaia District, we will not have enough to complete this phase of our rebuilding.

During the course of the summer, approximately 307,000 burned bricks were prepared for the construction of the first eight dwellings. The mason hired at six rubles per thousand has promised to begin work right after Easter.

With the cooperation of Colonial Inspector Biller, lots have been drawn for building sites in a way that will leave no gaps in the row except for the church site.

The Khortitsa District Office has directed that specific measurements be observed. Buildings should be at least fifty fut long and thirty fut wide. Rooms should have a height of nine fut. Windows should be three fut, ten *diumi* high and three fut, six and a half diumi wide. If these directives are observed householders can do carpentry work undisturbed throughout the winter.

Given your queries, I am encouraged to think that you will personally inspect our buildings and give us your opinion of the above directives.

To the limits of my ability and of my position, I will, with your help, do what I can to contribute to the beautification of the village.

I remain, with the appropriate respect, your respectful Heinrich Goertz, Village Mayor.

710. Heinrich Goertz to Johann Cornies. 17 December 1846. SAOR 89-1-1230/189.

To the Office of Chairman J. Cornies,

Kronsgarten village will need seven to eight thousand hawthorn saplings this coming spring or autumn. How much will they cost? If these should be available in your gardens, please let me know.

711. Johann Neufeld to Johann Cornies. 18 December 1846. SAOR 89-1-1230/197.

Esteemed brother-in-law,

Brother-in-law Boldt spoke with Zacharias on the Tashchenak. He agreed to accept the administrator's position on your estate, but cannot be available before March 1847, when his service at the Tashchenak ends. In the meantime I am able to suggest another individual, namely Abraham Driedger, son of Overseer Johann Driedger. Although he is single, he is twenty-five years old or even older, and in my opinion as capable for the above position as is Zacharias. Abraham is completely free and can begin at any time. I am told that he is also not disinclined to do so.

With a heartfelt greeting, your honest brother-in-law, Johann Neufeld.

712. Johann Cornies to Christian Steven. 20 December 1846. SAOR 89-1-1170/208.

Yr. Excellency,

Although the requested cows in good condition are always difficult to gather together, this in itself was not the greatest obstacle to my carrying out your esteemed commission. More importantly, I was afraid that the shipment would be endangered by the outbreak of pestilence that ran rampant among horned livestock in this region in autumn. I guarantee that the best possible milk cows will reach you next May.

Yr. Excellency is probably referring to the large earthen dam in Tashchenak that alone watered about three hundred desiatinas of haymeadows. Since it also flooded the post road and several agricultural buildings and could not continue to function usefully in this spot, it had to be lowered to the level at which it had been damaged by the stream because of the narrowness of the channel.

We had the first frost and snow the day before yesterday. This morning, the thermometer showed fourteen degrees. Until then, we had had such nice weather that our Mennonites continued to do their ploughing and to prepare the land for next spring's seeding. Snakes were still seen last week.

With exceptional esteem, I remain Yr. Excellency's most respectful servant.

713. Johann Cornies to Fedor F. Rosen. 20 December 1846. SAOR 89-1-1170/210.

Director Baron v. Rosen,

To carry out Yr. Honour's communication No. 899 of 3 December, you are respectfully requested to select another eight apprentices for the spring of 1847. They are to be added to the eight apprentices already present at the Crown Model Plantation (the ninth was mistakenly sent there by the District Chief, but he belonged in the orchard at Tashchenak to replace Gavriel Kalitchenko, who left). Could they be sent to me in Ohrloff for a preliminary testing? There will only be enough work to occupy sixteen apprentices in the coming year. With this number everything can proceed step by step and in the best order.

714. Johann Cornies Jr. to Johann Cornies. 24 December 1846. SAOR 89-1-1230/202.

Esteemed Father,

We only arrived in Odesa last Saturday and our journey was difficult. At the Inguletz the back axle of our conveyance broke, and having it welded caused a half-day's delay. Crossing the Bug over thin ice was very difficult. The wagon had to be completely disassembled, which again took considerable time. The road from Nikolaiev onwards was rough and we had to inch our way along at a walking pace for long stretches to keep the wagon from breaking apart. We are now ready and if it is God's will, we will depart tomorrow, 25 December. The road is not very good. Many sleds are already in use and this makes the snow slippery in spots.

His Excellency, Mr. Hahn, asks me to send you hearty greetings. His wife has completely recovered from the birth of a daughter.

On the insistence of Mr. Forestier, I exchanged the Danzig currency to Hamburg currency. Since Odesa had no direct trading connections with Danzig, he said it would be quite impossible to make a direct exchange.

We are quite healthy, thank God, and wish this for you as well from the bottom of our hearts.

I strive to remain your most respectful Johann Cornies.

715. Evgenii F. Hahn to Johann Cornies. 27 December 1846. SAOR 89-1-889/83.[4]

In response to your queries, I hasten to reply that former Church Elder Wiens cannot be treated as insane and hence cannot be lodged in an insane asylum. According to law, this can only be done after he has been thoroughly examined by the Guberniia Government.

If Wiens refuses to abide by the judgment pronounced against him by the other Church Elders, he naturally denies the leadership of his Mennonite colleagues and evades their influence. The spiritual leadership and the District Office should accordingly lodge a complaint against him. As soon as I have received such a complaint, I will approach His Excellency, the Minister, about sending him across the border. There will be no long wait for an answer since he must be exiled if your Church Elders cannot, by other means, gain the respect of Wiens.

Someone should explain to Wiens that the government keeps watch over such matters. The example of the Neuhoffnung settler Kraft will convince everyone that this is so. I had hardly reported to the Minister that the community no longer knew what to do with Kraft before a supreme order appeared, exiling him to Siberia. This has already occurred. Something similar could easily happen to Wiens if he does not remain peaceful and leave the country voluntarily.

---

4 Regarding the exile of Heinrich Wiens, see Heinrich Neufeld, "A Further Examination of the Molotschna Conflict," trans. Ben Hoeppner and Delbert Plett, *Preservings* 24 (December 2004), 24–8.

It seems as though the Mennonites are too privileged here in Russia and are getting restless. From this, evil consequences are sure to follow. Children will not be able to achieve as much as their fathers will lose through their own arrogance and stupidity. Yours truly, E. v. Hahn.

716. Johann Cornies to Village Offices. N.d. [1846.]
SAOR 89-1-1229/3.

To Village Offices,

According to a new directive regarding the Hebrews, it has been decided to take steps to settle them among the special settlements in the guberniias of Southern Russia.

Directing His Supreme attention to the Hebrews, His Majesty the Tsar has graciously expressed doubts that the Hebrews can be transformed into agriculturalists unless special measures are taken on their behalf.

An order has therefore been ordered to realize the government's intentions. His Highness, the Minister of State Domains, has decided that one or two of the most dependable householders in German villages, and especially in Mennonite villages, will be settled in every Jewish village. They are to serve not only as examples of good husbandry for the Hebrews, but should also provide leadership as superiors, as Elders, for example.

Such persons will, in the first place, be allotted special land with no payments. They will additionally receive monetary advantages for performing their services as Elders, and enjoy benefits for the successful introduction of agriculture.

In accordance with the wishes of His Excellency, President of the Guardianship Committee, it has been directed that Village Offices should be thoroughly and clearly informed immediately about His Highness, the Minister's suggestion. The directions indicate that if dependable people willing to settle among the Hebrews are found, they should report to the Chairman of this Society by the twenty-fifth of this month at the latest.

717. Johann Neufeld to Johann Cornies. N.d. [1846.]
SAOR 89-1-1229/98v.

Dear Brother-in-law,

Dirk Wiebe from Lichtfelde arrived here the day before yesterday. He was quite upset and wanted to find out more about the situation in which Russians were mistreated in Blumenort last spring. He accused Abraham Isaac from Tiege of not retracting his declaration, as David Warkentin did, and that someone's rib had been broken. Wiebe told me he would inform the District Office and the villages that he will give up his functions entirely because of Isaac.

This defiant declaration is the reason I am writing to you. If Wiebe really should appear at the District Office on this matter, he can be rebuffed, explaining that the District Office has not appointed him and does not therefore find it necessary to revoke anything. He may do whatever he wants.

Isaac's problem is not the business of the District Office or the Society. Local authorities have responded with a punishment appropriate for the mistreatment of these Russians. Whether the rib was broken or not does not matter to the District Office or the Society.

718. Agricultural Society to Landskrone. N.d. [1846.] SAOR 89-1-1229/150.

To Landskrone Village Office,

As soon as possible, the Village Mayor must send the Society a detailed report about the probable reasons for the Peters couple living together in such extreme disharmony, with suggestions about who is possibly at fault. The results are the neglect and ruin of their fullholding. Might there still be ways to try to restore peace between them? What could that be? This is the only way to keep the fullholding in an orderly condition. If the fullholding cannot be maintained, it must be taken from them.

719. Agricultural Society to Conteniusfeld. N.d. [1846.] SAOR 89-1-908/35.

To Conteniusfeld Village Office,

The administrator of the community sheepfarm reported that Abraham Koop, inhabitant of Conteniusfeld village, arrived there 11 April to perform the applicable punitive labour applying to him. However, Koop did not bring food with him and the manager sent him back. Koop promised to return by 15 April at the latest.

In the meantime Koop has ignored his promise and not yet reappeared. He has alleged to the Village Office that he lacks the provisions he is required to take along for his meals on the sheepfarm. The

Society orders the Village Office to ensure that Koop appears in the community sheepfarm without delay, by the seventh of this month, supplied with sufficient provisions for the required time of his compulsory labour.

Koop is also expected to repay the village community by working off the expenditure for these provisions. Because this matter reveals great weakness and negligence, the Village Office will be punished for every further delay.

This must be observed and a report in this regard required by the eighth of this month.

720. Agricultural Society to Ohrloff Village Office. N.d. [1846.] SAOR 89-1-1229/161.

To the Ohrloff Village Office,

According to a directive from His Excellency Director for Agriculture in the Ministry of State Domains and on the orders of the President of the Guardianship Committee, I am required to have an exact sketch prepared of Ohrloff village and of the land belonging to it, indicating especially the existing division of haymeadows and ploughed land. It should be marked according to number as to how the land is presently divided and how it is used by every fullholder in particular. This work will be completed by my son Johann Cornies as quickly as possible and sent to the Agricultural Department through the Guardianship Committee.

As a result, my son will arrive Wednesday, the twenty-fifth of this month, to start surveying and recording. For this reason, I hereby order the Village Office to have the workers required for surveying standing by, so that the land records may be made available under the Mayor's supervision and leadership. This must be observed.

721. Agricultural Society to Rueckenau Village Office. N.d. [1846.] SAOR 89-1-1229/166.

To Rueckenau Village Office,

Shepherd Martin Hamm knew that thefts had occurred but did not report them. He is therefore considered to be a participant in them. In response to Report No. 85 of the Village Office, the Society has decided to punish Hamm with three days of community work for this unacceptable situation. To carry out this work the Village Office should deliver him to administrator Jacob Wall at the community sheepfarm without delay. A report should be made to the Society that this has been done.

722. Agricultural Society to Heinrich Kroeker. N.d. [1846.]
    SAOR 89-1-1232/1.

To Heinrich Kroeker and associates, inhabitants of Ladekopp village,

The Society responds to the written request you submitted regarding the disputed matter with Peter Voth of Friedensdorf. You are hereby notified that, because a formal decision has already been made by the District Office, the Society is not empowered to pursue further discussions in regard to this matter. It can do nothing except to give the above-mentioned inhabitants of Ladekopp village the freedom to apply to higher authorities if they believe that they are in the right. Granted, it would be better if the matter in question could be settled here on the spot.

1847

723. Johann Siemens to Johann Cornies. 1 January 1847. SAOR 89-1-1271/56.

Esteemed friend,

According to information received today, all election documents for our District Elders were confirmed by the Guardianship Committee. I am convinced that the election document for Deputy Chairman Siemens should not be included. You might still wish to change it and I would respectfully ask that you do so. In my opinion, it would be better if someone else were chosen to replace Siemens, but, leaving this to your discretion, I remain hopeful that you will carry out your obligation in regard to this matter.

On 5 December, we received a directive from the Guardianship Committee confirming the transfer of our settlement's economic activity to you. The enemies of progress were clearly notified accordingly at the same time. The Inspector was also informed that he should desist from making any arrangements that might result in measures contrary to what you have suggested and directed. I do not know whether you have received a copy of this directive from the Guardianship Committee, but I can provide a copy for you at once. Kindly notify me about this matter.

With a heartfelt greeting, I remain Yr. respectful J. Siemens.

724. F. Fein to Johann Cornies. 1 January 1847. SAOR 89-1-1271/57.

Valued Mr. Cornies,

Please receive ten bottles of wine from Mr. Alexander Ivanovich Kaznachov in the Crimea. This is to remind you of his friendship. Your servant, F. Fein.

725. Evgenii F. Hahn to Johann Cornies. 3 January 1847. SAOR 89-1-889/92.

I thank you for plans for two hearth-sites and information about livestock.

Since His Highness, the Minister, has not yet informed us of his decisions I cannot yet be specific about the number of German families thought necessary to settle in each Jewish village, and whether these Germans can be granted sixty desiatinas of land per family. The Minister had hoped that about ten German families might be settled in each Jewish village. It is a number that can therefore be accepted as a norm. Since the rights and privileges of Germans will be observed, I also think that sixty desiatinas [of land] per family is likely.

Here in Kherson Guberniia, we have thirteen villages awaiting village officials and German settlers. I suggested to the Minister that an appropriate salary for each Village Mayor should be 250 to 300 silver rubles, but I have still to be informed of a concrete decision in this regard. Should this sum be approved, I have several outstanding men available for appointment. Our hopes for success depend on the appointment of men of this quality in every village.

I am writing nothing about your son's stay here, since he wrote to you himself when he left. Yours truly, E. v. Hahn.

726. Johann Cornies to Ministry of State Domains. 4 January 1847. SAOR 89-1-1260/2.

To the Ministry of State Domains, Economic Department,

In response to the Department's honoured communication No. 2338 of 22 September 1845, I can report that the varieties of tobacco seed sent at the time, specifically Virginia, Maryland, and Kentucky, were sown in spring 1846. They developed exceptionally well and produced the most excellent leaves. Two bunches of each variety, Virginia No.1, Maryland No. 2, and Kentucky No. 3, were sent to the offices of the Director of the Tavrida State Domains Bureau for examination. They show that the Department can be assured that this tobacco is of good quality. I also find it necessary to remark that all three tobacco varieties listed are high yielding and produce a large number of leaves from each plant. This, in particular, recommends them for cultivation.

727. Johann Cornies to Evgenii F. Hahn. 5 January 1847. SAOR 89-1-889/91.

Yr. Excellency,

I have another question about the settlement of German model householders among the Jews. Might it make sense to have all empty houses now found in Jewish villages made available to as many German settlers as necessary, that is, until their own dwellings have been established? The Jewish villages already in existence should account for all their empty houses. I saw some myself in the village near Bereslav. It would be desirable for the German settlers to repair these houses and move into them for the time being. Yr. Excellency might, as soon as possible, graciously send me a decision in this matter.

With the most honest esteem, I remain Yr. Excellency's most obedient servant, Johann Cornies.

728. Heinrich Cornies to Johann Cornies. 8 January 1847. SAOR 89-1-1271/59.[1]

Dear brother,

We arrived in Warsaw safely and in good health on 5 January. The journey went very well. The front axle of the wagon broke on the road from Odesa to the little town of Linten in Podolsk Guberniia, and the back wheel was damaged later on. On Monday, 6 January, we took a boat trip on the Vistula and on 7 January visited the city of Lowitz, eighty-four verstas from Warsaw by railroad, a journey that took six hours there and back. I will tell you personally about all of this.

We are getting ready to travel again and our passes have been approved by the authorities. We are all, thank God, healthy, and intend to have crossed the border into Prussia tomorrow by this time. There is little snow throughout Poland but the frost is quite sharp, about fifteen to eighteen degrees Réaumur.

Give my greetings to my wife and children. I think of them often. Also, I send greetings to all of you. Johann Cornies Jr. sends his greetings to you and your wife.

I remain the brother who loves you, Hein. Cornies.

---

1 Heinrich Cornies was accompanying Johann Cornies Jr., who was traveling to Prussia.

729. Evgenii F. Hahn to Johann Cornies. 9 January 1847.
SAOR 89-1-889/93.

I hasten to answer your inquiry of 2 January. In my opinion, Mennonites should preferably be settled in Jewish villages situated closest to the Mennonite District. This would be Novoberislav village, established between the town of Bereslav and the Swedish District. We estimate that there will be land for ninety-two families in this village, at forty desiatinas per family, for a total of 3,680 desiatinas. Ninety-two families are available to settle there, but they own a total of only thirty-four horses and seventy-eight oxen and hence pursue little field cultivation. Eight to ten Mennonite families could easily be settled here. They would find the village to their liking. It is situated on water, close to a town, and could, from time to time, be inspected by the Molochnaia Society. A second Jewish village is to be located on the Dnieper, beyond Bereslav towards Kherson. I do not have information about the village yet. There is, in any case, room for a total of about fifteen Mennonite families in both villages.

Your Mennonites might begin by inspecting these villages before they declare their further intentions. Permission for their inspection is not necessary, but I am enclosing an open order to the village offices in these villages. Use it as you see fit and then destroy it.

If you have people who would like to settle in these villages after inspection, we could conclude a twenty-year contract with them. Please give me your views about the details of this contract. The settlers would have to be able to manage well on their own, to construct buildings at their own expense, to serve as models for the Jews, and to desist from leasing any land from them. They should be content with the land assigned to them.

Yours truly, E. v. Hahn.

I just received an inquiry from the Saratov Bureau for Settlements asking whether it would be possible to send several young persons from Saratov to the Mennonite villages to learn agriculture. I replied that this was definitely possible, but decisions as to payment would first have to be negotiated, depending on the age and capabilities of the pupils.

730. Evgenii F. Hahn to Johann Cornies. 10 January 1847.
SAOR 89-1-889/91.

This can be done easily but the following must be observed: these houses were built at the cost of the crown and charged to the Jews as a debt.

German settlers could possess them only if they made the necessary payments for them. The German settlers might use the empty houses temporarily for low payments to the Jewish community, but could not demand compensation for improving them.

731. Johann Cornies to Fedor F. Rosen. 11 January 1847. SAOR 89-1-1260/3.

To the Director,

This is a brief report regarding the establishment of a crown model plantation approved for Berdiansk District and the progress made in this regard, including a list of operations already carried out.

Once the plantation had been measured off according to plan, and the length of its boundary ploughed, it was anticipated that progress would follow immediately that fall. In fact the construction of a forestry dwelling and the watchman's house is already well underway. The latter structure, built of dried clay bricks and roofed with roof tiles, was completed on 8 October 1845. The watchman has already moved in, but only the masonry walls of the forestry structure could be roofed before the onset of winter.

During fall, three and a half desiatinas of land were ploughed and prepared for the planting of an avenue of trees one versta long.

On 13 March 1846, two Mennonite families, those of the overseer and gardener, took up temporary quarters in the watchman's house. Land already ploughed was prepared for trees that were dug up in various places in our villages and transported to the location. The work of digging holes began immediately and another 2,350 square sazhen of land were ploughed to extend the avenue mentioned above as far as the post road.

A temporary well was dug in the hollow beside the hill at the beginning of April. Planting began on 4 April and the first tree was planted at 9:45 a.m. that morning. This spring a total of 1,846 trees were planted on permanent sites. Director Baron v. Rosen sent a total of 2,546 trees in nurseries from the Crimea, including five hundred mulberry trees.

One desiatina of the lowlands was prepared for seed nurseries. The first seeds were sown on 18 April, including mulberry seeds on eighteen square sazhen, American acacias on twelve square sazhen, and Siberian acacias on eighteen square sazhen.

On 25 April, the marking of boundary ditches began, and on 29 April another ten desiatinas of land were ploughed five vershok deep for further plantings.

On 3 May, compulsory labourers completed the boundary ditches around the plantation. They are 2,944 sazhen long and two arshins, nine vershok wide. However, to protect the lowlands from changes in water levels and to create a higher shoreline, a second ditch was dug, as wide as the above and 492 sazhen long. These two ditches form a dam two arshins high in the middle. The edges of the ditches were everywhere levelled to a width of two arshins, to be planted later with protective living hedges.

Four earthen dams were also constructed immediately in spring 1846 wherever sharp depressions cut through the boundary. Their measurements are:

No. 1: twenty-five sazhens long, three sazhen, two and a half vershok wide, and one sazhen, eight vershok high;

No. 2: thirty-three sazhen long, five sazhen, two and a half vershok wide, one sazhen, two vershok high;

No. 3: twenty-one sazhen long, three sazhen, one arshin wide, and one sazhen, one arshin high.

The fourth dam is intended as a convenient road out of the forestry yard into the lowland. It could not, however, be completed because dry earth was being ploughed out of the hill. It is twenty-five sazhen long, four sazhen wide, and one sazhen high.

On 15 May a well to water livestock was dug at a depth to the water level of two and a half sazhen. On 24 May, 108 square sazhen of land were sown with various kinds of elm. On 29 May, a semicircular area seven and a half sazhen deep was marked off for a well beside the hill, where the road at the same level as the dam leads down towards the lowlands.

In June, a ditch was excavated in an easterly direction to protect the plantings already in existence near the house. It is sixty arshins, ten vershok wide, and one arshin, four vershok deep.

The forestry building was completed on 6 June with the exception of a few small items, and the two Mennonite families then occupied it. A well was dug at the seed nurseries during the same month and a road through the plantation was marked off in the same direction as the avenue that is already planted. It was ploughed and levelled.

In July, 228 holes for fence posts were dug around the seed nurseries. The livestock barn was built in July and August, together with a cartwright's facility and rooms to store gardening tools. It is a total of eight sazhen, ten vershok long, three sazhen, two arshins high and nine and a half vershok wide. It is framed with wood, the partitions are built of fired brick, and the structure is roofed with Dutch tiles. In addition, gates were built and painted at three entrances into the plantation.

Construction of the house for apprentices was begun on 28 September. According to the floor plan, it will be twelve sazhen, one arshin in length, and four sazhen, two arshins in width. However when frost arrived the brick walls had been completed only up to the beams, and work had to be discontinued for 1846.

In October, an ash pit thirty-six sazhen square was built of wood with an overhang on the east side. This overhang will provide winter protection from cold winds for livestock. It is two sazhen long, one arshin wide, and is roofed with tiles. A well was also dug on the levelled area beside the hill but had to be closed because pressure from quicksand proved to be too strong.

Furthermore, 1,501 reeds for tying were used to create a dense fence around the seed nurseries. Also 2,773 forest trees were dug up at the Iushanle estate but had to be wrapped and kept moist for the winter when frost overtook the work.

Two and a half sazhen of the fence around the forestry yard were completed.

The land assigned for planting this autumn was harrowed towards the end of October. Then, because of a total lack of rain since 23 July, the soil dried out completely and further preparations had to be abandoned. Rain fell on 5 December, but penetrated the soil to a depth of only three vershok. As a result, planting was stopped and it became almost impossible to make preparations for the coming spring.

Despite these problems, efforts were made between 21 October and 3 December to work up an area of 297 square sazhen of land using spades. A variety of forest seeds were sown on this plot, making up for our futile efforts to plant trees because of poor weather conditions earlier.

732. Johann Cornies Jr. to Johann Cornies. 14 January 1847. SAOR 89-1-1271/63.

Esteemed Father,

We arrived safely in Elbing on 10 January 1847. Our journey did not proceed as quickly as we had wished because there was little snow and we had to stay in wagon tracks, especially in Poland, where we encountered almost no snow. Furthermore, since leaving Odesa the front axle and the rings on the back wheels cracked and had to be welded. This caused delays each time. As for the rest, we had to drive slowly, fearing more damage to the wagon on the bumpy, frozen roadway.

Here in Elbing I found our relatives quite well, except for Mr. Wiebe on the "Kichdenne" who has been a widower since fall. Aron Wiebe is living in the Wilke homestead at the Koenigsberger Gate. Agatha Wiebe has married someone in Frauenburg, while Gerhard Wiebe, who used to live in Oliva, is now in Danzig. Dick lives in Zeischendorf and his brother in Kaldova. The rest of their siblings are healthy, except for the Dicks in Zeischendorf who are getting steadily weaker and are often ill.

I am well and in good health, as is my uncle. We intend to depart for Freienbuden today, 14 January 1847. We will probably leave our wagon there, since sledding roads are good. We intend to travel to Danzig from Freienhuben, from there to Zeischendorf, then to Marienburg and back to Freienhuben by way of the Werder.

I expect news from you soon and with these hopes I remain, with heartfelt greetings, your son Johann Cornies.

733. Johann Siemens to Johann Cornies. 15 January 1847. SAOR 89-1-1271/60.

Esteemed friend, Johann Cornies,

With reference to the need to summon local Mennonites living outside of the district back to our villages, I must report that more than a hundred such families live outside our villages. Many have been living on leased land for extended periods of time. Since I assume that quite a few of your settlers live in similar circumstances, I would ask whether your locality is making exceptions for individuals with leases that have not yet ended. Have they been granted a delay to continue to live in their present places of residence until their leases have expired? I will naturally act in accordance with your decisions in this matter.

With heartfelt greetings, your respectful, Johann Siemens.

734. Johann Siemens to Johann Cornies. 15 January 1847. SAOR 89-1-1271/61.

Esteemed friend, Johann Cornies,

In accordance with our agreement, I went to see the craftsman in Ekatrinoslav and asked whether he might take over construction of a monument for the late Hoeppner.[2] He is prepared to do so and will construct it according to our design for a price of three silver rubles per pud. He estimates twenty puds for the monument itself. His price is the same for a fence if the area enclosed is one square faden. Actually, I have also asked my brother-in-law Dyck to look around in Kharkiv to see whether he can find monuments there like the model desired. However, I doubt whether such a design can be obtained there, and I believe it would be best to order it here in Ekaterinoslav. I am leaving for Bergthal tomorrow and intend to return in eight days' time.

With a heartfelt greeting, I remain your respectful Johann Siemens.

735. Martin Doehring to Johann Cornies. 17 January 1847. SAOR 89-1-1260/64.

Highly valued Mr. Cornies,

Based on the message you sent me and Johann Steinfeld, I would inform you that we think we have found two girls who will fill your needs. They would like to enter your service, but are willing to work only in Ohrloff or on the Iushanle estate, not on Tashchenak estate, and only until St. Martin's day [11 November]. They find the wages of 120 rubles acceptable, but ask for a hiring bonus and supplementary items of clothing. In addition, they want to be assured in advance that you will provide them with transportation at times of the year when it is most suitable for them to visit their homes. If you send a cart to fetch the girls, kindly tell the driver to come straight to me. I will take care of the rest.

In the meantime, I respectfully commend myself to you with a greeting from my wife and from Steinfeld and his wife, Martin Doehring.

736. Johann Cornies to Evgenii F. Hahn. 18 January 1847. SAOR 89-1-1260/6v.

Yr. Excellency,

I learned from my son about your esteemed wife's safe delivery of a healthy daughter, and could not do otherwise than to greet the child

---

2 Jacob Hoeppner was a delegate sent by the Prussian Mennonites to assess the original Mennonite land grant for the Khortitsa settlement in 1786. The monument is now located at the Mennonite Village Museum in Steinbach, Manitoba. On Hoeppner, see David H. Epp and Richard D. Thiessen, "Höppner, Jakob (1748–1826)," Global Anabaptist Mennonite Encyclopedia Online, January 2013, https://gameo.org/index .php?title=H%C3%B6ppner,_Jakob_(1748–1826)&oldid=145466.

with sincere and heartfelt interest. May the Almighty soon restore good health to the dear mother and increase your joys as parents of your heart's darling. And as the budding soul unfolds and blossoms, may both of you experience the most sincere joy in your beloved child entrusted to your tender care.

Convinced that no one more honestly wishes Yr. Excellency happiness in this safe delivery, I sign myself as Yr. Excellency's respectful servant, Johann Cornies.

737. Jacob Riediger to Johann Cornies. 19 January 1847. SAOR 89-1-1271/65.

Most esteemed Mr. Cornies,

I am sending you this tobacco cutting machine, to be delivered to you by Harder from Blumstein. His Excellency, General von Hahn, commissioned me to send it to you so that it can be duplicated on the Molochnaia. He expects that the machine will be returned, which you probably already know. There are also three packages numbered 210, 211, and 212, containing little packets of tobacco seeds numbered in the same way.

Mr. von Stempel's goods are still stored here. They had not been allowed through the customs office before you left and the stall where Mr. von Stempel bought them will not accept their return. We have no idea what to do with them. Should we keep the goods until Mr. von Stempel comes to get them himself? It is to be expected that this will take a long time, as he himself said the last time he was here. Alternately, should we send them along with the General when he goes to the Molochnaia this coming spring? The General said it might be reasonable for him to take them along when he travels in that direction but I assume that he has long forgotten about them and I do not know whether it would be proper to remind him.

Together with a hearty greeting from me and Bahnmann, I respectfully remain, your servant, Jacob Riediger.

738. Johann Cornies to Christian Steven. 23 January 1847. SAOR 89-1-1260/7.

Inspector for Agriculture in Southern Russia,

Along with the enclosed records about the crown apprentices who are presently here with me and other Mennonites, I repeat the following.

I am curious that no decision was sent to me in response to my presentation of 13 October 1845. The view I then expressed was that if the purpose of these crown apprentices is to be completely achieved, they must be:

1. settled together in one village, and
2. must receive remuneration of at least 250 silver rubles, instead of 200 rubles, when they establish themselves. Yr. Excellency might kindly make decisions in this regard.

At present, in addition to those listed earlier, a further three apprentices must be considered as qualified to leave their service, specifically those marked as numbers seven, eight, and nine in the record. I must give all three of these apprentices the best recommendation in every regard. They will, without doubt, justify my trust in them, including the one marked number seven, if they receive appropriate assistance from the government. A fourth apprentice, number six, is however being released from service because he shows absolutely no hope of ever becoming a real agriculturalist, able to stand on his own.

739. Johann Cornies to Alexander Ivanovich Kaznachov. 23 January 1847. SAOR 89-1-1260/7v.

Yr. Excellency,

Ten bottles of wine from you were forwarded to me through Mr. F. Fein as a reminder of your constant goodwill. Please receive my most obliging thanks for this mark of your heartfelt interest in my humble person. This gives me great joy. With my varied experiences, I will remain honestly thankful for all of your kindness.

Yr. Excellency's most dutiful servant, Johann Cornies.

740. Johann Cornies to Fedor F. Rosen. 23 January 1847. SAOR 89-1-1260/8.

Yr. Honour, Baron v. Rosen,

In accordance with your wishes, I send you the enclosed extract from my description of forest-tree cultivation of tree varieties common in this area, including a discussion of the manner in which it is practised here. This is intended for your own use. I hope these notes will provide you with adequate information.

741. Johann Cornies to Fedor F. Rosen. 24 January 1847.
SAOR 89-1-1260/8v.

Director,

An amount of 1,035 silver rubles, ninety-eight kopeks was provided for the support of the Crown Model Plantation in 1846. After the accounts were closed, however, it was revealed that expenditures equalled 1,352 rubles, ninety-two and three-quarter kopeks. Yr. Honour is respectfully requested to balance this account on the basis of the running account book, providing the 316 silver rubles, ninety-four and three-quarter kopeks which I spent. Please send it to me as soon as possible in order that the above-mentioned running account book and the records of the estimated money spent on construction can immediately be presented to the Domains Bureau.

742. Johann Cornies to Heinrich Cornies and Johann Cornies Jr.
25 January 1847. SAOR 89-1-1260/10.

Dear brother Heinrich and son Johann Cornies,

I got your letters describing your trip from here to Odesa and from there to Warsaw as having been safe and healthy, except for several mishaps en route with a broken wagon. This was no doubt annoying, but travellers must accept incidents of this kind, despite the waste of time that must have been irritating. Meanwhile, we are pleased that you are healthy and in good spirits, and hope that this might continue.

There is little here for me to write about. Thank God that everyone in our family is healthy and our various households and economies are moving ahead as usual. I assume that Wiebe and Hamm provided more details in their letters. Nothing much has happened since then except that the snow that fell at the time of your departure has melted completely in a warm rain. Since the meltwater penetrated the soil it did not reach the steppe rivers. This winter continues without change, with sixteen to twenty degrees of frost and no wind. The livestock is healthy. Wheat sells for twenty-two rubles per chetvert in Berdiansk and eighteen rubles in our villages and prices for ewes are nine to ten rubles. The prices for larger livestock have risen similarly. Reports from Moscow indicate that wool prices are low and our wool has not yet been sold. Yesterday gardener Reimer handed in his notice and will not, because of ill health, be able to serve this coming year.

I trust that you have been given a kind and friendly reception and managed to get around among relatives and acquaintances. Although I am far away, I enjoy these pleasures with you in spirit.

Busy with the Jewish settlements in Ekaterinoslav and Kherson Guberniias, I am persuading families from our villages to take up residence in them as model fullholders for twenty years, this under the most favourable terms. Last Monday a number of families left to inspect local conditions and land. The administration for all Jewish villages settled or still to be settled has been formally transferred to the Guardianship Committee for Foreign Settlers in Southern Russia.

The tides of unrest within the community have not yet settled down. They continue to roil, but here and there sensible people from the Wiens and Warkentin congregation are convincing themselves that all this ferment is nonsense and that a forceful decision is needed to restore lasting peace. Granted, a few individuals will be unhappy about this, but they can blame this on their own arrogance and stupidity.

In closing I would ask that you give my greetings to all our good acquaintances and especially to Mr. Johann Wiebe.

With this I commend myself to you, with a hearty greeting from all of us, as your loving brother and father, Johann Cornies.

743. Johann Cornies to Johann Cornies Jr. 25 January 1847. SAOR 89-1-1260/11v.

Dear son,

If your circumstances and affairs permit, please undertake a journey in May through Pomerania, Mecklenburg, and as far as the Holstein area in the following manner. On the way there, or back, travel to Stettin through Stolpe or Kanitz, and from Stettin through Mecklenburg, then to Hamburg by way of Schwerin and then as far as Friedrichstadt on the Eider by way of Glueckstadt in Holstein. Return to Hamburg by a different route, and from there also by a different route through Mecklenburg to Stettin. The purpose of this journey is to make yourself knowledgeable about agricultural practices in these regions, including details about practices that we might like to introduce here as well.

Visit the Mennonite community in Altona, also in Friedrichstadt, and greet my acquaintance Preacher Van der Smissen from me. Consult the consul in Danzig about obtaining a passport for this journey. He is undoubtedly empowered to provide you with such a document for the journey in a short period or could furnish you with a recommendation to the consulate in Hamburg. He can, at the very least, give you advice about these regions.

I have received eleven thousand silver rubles for you from brother-in-law Neufeld. Last week I sent them along with Mr. v. Stempel, who was traveling to Odesa, to be deposited in the Imperial Loan Bank to earn interest.

Mother is fairly well and sends you many greetings, as do your brother-in-law and your sister. Little Johann is cheerful and gives us great joy.

I send you greetings and commend you to God! May you fare well! Your loving father, Johann Cornies.

744. Johann Cornies to Peter Keppen. 25 January 1847. SAOR 89-1-1260/12.

Yr. Honour, State Counsellor v. Keppen,

You are quite justified in being angry at me for my negligence in making you wait for an answer for so long. I find this painful myself. I could mention many things that demand my attention, but I will remain silent, aware of my own failings. Please be indulgent with me and grant me forgiveness out of the goodness of your heart.

You have my sincerest thanks for graciously sending me six sheets of the Schubert special map of Russia, including some annotations that are particularly valuable for me.

From the very start, since the earliest settlements on the Moloch-naia, Jacob Neumann, a Mennonite from Muensterberg village, has been one of our best agriculturalists. Due to his faithful observation of the advantages and disadvantages of each undertaking, he has been of great service to us in improving agriculture in this region. Neumann is valued for his honest promotion of each benevolent undertaking and for his honest character. Should the decision be made to grant him recognition for his genuinely praiseworthy achievements, I am convinced, without asking him about it, that written thanks would be what he preferred.

As for mounds connected by paved footpaths, I have personally investigated two mounds of medium size, fifteen verstas west of Einlage village, on the land of estate owner Marks along the west bank of the Dnieper. I was unable, however, to find any clear trace of pavement. But on the heights of the Berda four to five verstas from the crown village of Nikolaievka, on Azov Cossack lands and along the [Cossack] host's old roadway from Mariupol to the Crimea, are two mounds of medium size beside this road, one versta along the banks of the Berda from the point at which the roadway goes through the Berda. Approximately forty sazhen apart, from east to west, they seem to show significant signs of having been connected by footpaths laid out with limestone squares. The squares have been hauled away but their impressions remain clearly marked in the soil among large numbers of small stones lying in the same direction. I can report that, economically, our local villages are thriving. Last year's harvest of various grains was blessed as never before, and the high price of wheat in Berdiansk moved agriculturalists as well as tradesmen to ever greater endeavours. Sericulture and tobacco cultivation are making equally rapid progress. Local tobacco won the prize at the Simferopol exhibition. A total of sixty puds of silk have been harvested, the largest portion of which was sold immediately on site for 480 to 520 rubles per pud. More than two million bricks and 140,700 roof tiles were fired locally. Used for various structures, they enhance the grandeur of our villages.

Winter began here when the first snow fell on 17 December. We have had constant frost since then with temperatures as low as twenty degrees with good sledding roads but without the huge snowstorms we are accustomed to having. At present, the snow has already thawed completely and the steppes have absorbed the moisture. There is absolutely no water in small rivers except for the Molochnaia River.

Gradually, our Nogai neighbours are occupying themselves a little more with field cultivation, although they pursue it quite irregularly. The introduction of Spanish sheep, on the other hand, has been completed and spread throughout all of their villages.

The Molokans have completely suspended their emigration to Georgia. As Yr. Honour predicted and wrote to me some time ago, most Molokans who had previously moved to Georgia have died out. This finally convinced [the remainder to stay].

I most urgently commend myself to Yr. further benevolence and remain, with honest esteem, Yr. Honour's most respectful servant, Johann Cornies.

745. Johann Cornies to Baumann. 25 January 1847.
SAOR 89-1-1260/14v.

Highly valued Mr. Baumann,

Your worthy lines of 11 December were a pleasant surprise for me. Your sincere friends here also send you their heartfelt wishes for a very happy New Year and for the best of success in all your endeavours that are rendered on behalf of our region.

Mr. v. Keppen wrote me that he had received your rebuttal to the Teetzmann essay. He regrets, however, that he does not have sufficient time to promote this interesting project further. For my part, there is nothing in your remarks to comment upon except to express my great surprise at your understanding of all aspects of this subject from the same viewpoint as mine.

As for my personal situation, I thank God that I am completely healthy and continue to be very busy in and outside our settlements. Recently the Khortitsa villages were assigned to me in order to improve their economic arrangements, as were several Nogai villages. This was done in accordance with the wishes that the Minister had personally expressed to me.

State Counsellor v. Hahn is progressing vigorously in his activities and all of the Jews have been put under his leadership, as you will know. At present, this places many demands on him as it also does on venturesome Mr. v. Stempel, who has been appointed as Guardian for the new Jewish villages in Aleksandrov District. At the same time he continues as Inspector for his dear settlers. Since one goal [of the Jewish villages] is to establish model German settlers in all Jewish villages, I am personally involved deeply in this whole matter.

Last year's harvest was particularly abundant for all grain varieties. Throughout the district there were average increases in the yields of wheat, rye, barley, and oats. Individual agriculturalists obtained yields of twenty-four-fold of seed sown for wheat and thirty-one-fold for barley. The high price of wheat on site, up to eighteen rubles per chetvert, produced particularly high incomes throughout our villages.

Only some of the flower seeds sent to us have flourished, but some of the flowers that grew to maturity were very pretty. At the same time, all tree seeds planted came up immediately and well without exception, and grew exceptionally tall throughout the summer. Brother David Cornies took special pleasure in them in his home garden.

To improve his health and provide distraction, my son departed for Prussia by stage on 17 December, accompanied by his uncle, Heinrich Cornies. They will also inspect local agricultural establishments along the way. On 3 October my daughter married my secretary Wiebe, with whom you are acquainted. David and Peter Cornies and their families are well and send you their heartfelt greetings. David Cornies anticipates a shipment of pine seeds with longing.

I have discussed with the Baron the plan prepared for Tokmak. Area administrators have expressed some objections and a community statement showed that the peasants were confused about the forest-tree plantations and wanted more cultivated than pasture land. I was nevertheless able to convince the Baron otherwise and therefore everything was left as you had projected it.

I used the journey of Mr. v. Levshin through our area to assure His Excellency that it would be very useful to have you return to this region. He promised to speak to you. I am very curious as to what might have transpired in the meanwhile or even if you encountered Mr. v. Levshin.

At the present time, I would suggest that you take over a position as guardian for the Jews in Kherson Guberniia. This is an open field where you would be able to establish something worthwhile and find the best opportunity for your endeavours in assisting and promoting human well-being. I have already spoken with State Counsellor v. Hahn and he would find this most desirable. The salary for this position is approximately seven hundred silver rubles.

Kindly write to me about these matters, worthy Mr. Baumann, and also what your honest opinion might be. I await it most eagerly because I feel sorry for the poor Jews.

In closing, I commend myself to your further loving remembrance and am, with honest respect, your faithfully obligated friend, Johann Cornies.

746. Johann Cornies to Witte. 29 January 1847. SAOR 89-1-1260/16v.

Esteemed Mr. Witte,

In response to His Excellency, Director v. Levshin's commission, the German wagon is ready now with all attachments, seat, and ladders complete. For this reason, you might arrange to have it fetched from Isaak Braun, the master craftsman in the local village of Lindenau as soon as possible. How the wagon should be put together will be explained to the person commissioned, as will its various uses.

The wagon is completely equipped with all accessories and costs 362 rubles, eighty kopeks. I would request that you send the payment to Braun, the master craftsman, by mail via Melitopol or, if desired, or through your own people.

With exceptional esteem, your respectful servant, Johann Cornies.

747. Johann Cornies to Gersdorff. 29 January 1847.
SAOR 89-1-1260/17.

Esteemed Baron v. Gersdorff,

In response to your offer of items that I or local acquaintances might purchase or lease, I hereby respectfully notify you that I personally possess sufficient land and also a stock of sheep and livestock to be kept on it. I have no intentions of enlarging my establishment. At the moment I am also not acquainted with any other eventual bidders whom I could recommend to you. Should anything occur in either case later and purchasers or bidders for a lease appear, I will be happy to remember you and inform all of them in accordance with your commission.

With exceptional esteem, I remain your respectful servant, Johann Cornies.

748. Johann Klaassen to Johann Cornies. 1 February 1847.
SAOR 89-1-1271/79.

Mr. Cornies,

Prokofii, the head shepherd, has given me his word that on 24 January 1847 he hired Zimen Szerbin, a local inhabitant of the crown village of Balke, Melitopol District, as shepherd's servant for one year for 140 rubles. He then gave him an advance of thirteen rubles, two kopeks. Their agreement was that Szerbin would acquire a one-year visa and then report for service. However, yesterday, 31 January, Zimen Szerbin notified Prokofii that he cannot enter service because his brother will not permit him to acquire a visa.

Prokofii says that Zimen's brother was not present at the hiring but was informed on the evening of the same day that Prokofii had hired Zimen. Zimen's brother was at home and Zimen himself actually said at that time that his brother was opposed to providing him with a visa. However, he did not say he would not get the visa or express any doubts to Prokofii. Zimen has been in service here on Tashchenak in the past, last year in particular when he did not get his brother's permission. Therefore Prokofii believes that this allegation is not true and he requests that application should be made to the appropriate authorities so that the above-mentioned Zimen Szerbin enters service according to the agreement as soon as possible. Johann Klaassen.

749. Evgenii F. Hahn to Johann Cornies. 4 February 1847.
  SAOR 89-1-889/96.

There are many reports in the newspapers about an oxen brought to St. Petersburg from Ekaterinoslav Guberniia. However, I am of the opinion that this oxen is a dwarf in comparison to your large bull. Please be so kind, dear friend, as to inform me how high, how long, and what the girth of your bull is and, if possible, how much it weighs. A comparison could be interesting.

Yours truly, E. v. Hahn.

750. Johann Cornies to Fedor F. Rosen. 8 February 1847.
  SAOR 89-1-1260/18v.

To the Director,

In my absence, on 14 October 1846 you were sent a response to Yr. Honour's communication No. 219 of 14 March 1846. It was a detailed record of the potato harvest in Perekop District, and included a recommendation that the third variety be sold without delay.

I would now respectfully request that Yr. Honour send me the remuneration earned by Kokoi Frembetov from Mashkir who was hired as overseer for Perekop District. It totals sixty silver rubles, the same as last year. He spent almost the whole summer working in that district or on travels in it over great distances.

751. Johann Cornies to Fedor F. Rosen. 8 February 1847.
  SAOR 89-1-1260/19.

To the Director,

In response to Yr. Honour's communication No. 23 of 17 January 1847, I have the honour to point out that it is impossible to determine how many obligatory workers from the villages might be needed in the model plantation during the course of the present year since this will depend on the weather. More workers will be necessary if the weather is favourable, while fewer workers if the opposite is true.

In my opinion, the village communities of Mikhailovka, Timoshovka, Troizkoi, Terpenie, Sembinovka, Efremovka, Novovasilievka, Astrakhanka, Burkut, Edinokhta, and Nevkuss should be made available to me for general purposes. The Molokans would be employed building dams, the Burkut Nogais as drivers for the area and other smaller jobs, and the other villages to dig ditches still needed or for manual work.

I await Yr. Honour's early resolution of the decision in this matter.

752. Johann Cornies to Fedor F. Rosen. 8 February 1847.
SAOR 89-1-1260/19v.

To the Director,

In carrying out Yr. Honour's communication No. 245 of 21 March 1846, I have selected overseers to encourage the planting of potatoes and maize by inhabitants of all villages in Berdiansk, Melitopol, and Dneprov Districts. Much more could have been done in this respect if there had not been a shortage of seed potatoes because of last year's crop failures. Nevertheless, there are quite a number of potato and maize plantings in all three districts, and especially in Berdiansk District. Although they had not been planted as instructed, they had still been properly tilled.

753. Johann Cornies to Christian Steven. 8 February 1847.
SAOR 89-1-1260/21v.

To the Inspector of Agriculture in Southern Russia,

In response to Yr. Excellency's inquiry No. 73 of 27 January regarding the decision about the crown apprentices, I repeat the wishes His Highness, the Minister, made to me verbally in Einlage on 1 September 1846, namely that all apprentices be settled in one place in this vicinity, including those from Ekaterinoslav Guberniia and Lugansk, if their parents agree.

His Highness directed me to write to Baron v. Rosen in this regard and arrange for the creation of such a settlement for the benefit of these apprentices. On 15 September 1846, I advised Baron v. Rosen accordingly, but have not received a decision through him or from St. Petersburg. Yr. Excellency will know what it is best to do to realize this project.

754. Johann Cornies to Fedor F. Rosen. 8 February 1847.
SAOR 89-1-1260/23.

Right Honourable Baron,

I lack grafting shoots for several good varieties of peaches for my orchard, and also shoots or cuttings for box trees (*Buxus sempervirens,*

Zwengbuxus). Please obtain such grafting shoots and cuttings for me from recognized, dependable gardens in the Crimea. I will gladly repay the costs and am obligated for your kindness.

You should also know that I can give you the requested loan we discussed. This you can definitely count on.

With exceptional respect and devotion, Yr. Honour's honest servant, Johann Cornies.

755. Johann Siemens to Johann Cornies. 9 February 1847. SAOR 89-1-1271/81.

Esteemed friend,

I think it necessary to report that several days ago, Peter Siemens, Kronsgarten, informed me that a decision on Inspector Biller's recommendation had been made to the Committee. Siemens's forebear, Wilhelm Plenert, died without heirs. Since women cannot inherit a fullholding, Plenert's property does not belong to Peter Siemens but should be given to a young Kronsgarten Mennonite unless the community declares itself in Siemens's favour. I fear that Mayor Goertz's jealousy of Siemens could adversely affect the outcome.

With a heartfelt greeting, I remain your respectful Johann Siemens.

Khortitsa village, 9 February 1847.

N.B. The mouldboard attachment ordered for Major Potemkin is ready and can be fetched.

756. Johann Cornies to Fedor F. Rosen. 9 February 1847. SAOR 89-1-1260/24.

Right Honourable Baron,

Immediately after I received your communication of 1 February, I summoned the Molokan Golubov to give me an accounting. A few hours before he arrived, Voroshchev, from the same locality, came storming in. He had, by chance, heard about the matter and wanted to pay a half ruble more per chetvert for the rye. This could naturally not be considered since the prices have not risen. Extreme jealously is involved here. I nevertheless feel compelled to notify Yr. Honour about this matter and respectfully request that the confirmation for Golubov be sent to me as soon as possible. This would let me deliver the grain as it should be. I have received the entire sum of 4,260 rubles from Golubov for 551 chetvert of rye at the price of seven rubles, and one hundred chetvert, six chetveriki barley at the price of four rubles, and will await any further measures you agree to.

With the most complete esteem, Yr. Honour's respectful servant, J. Cornies.

757. Johann Cornies to Fedor F. Rosen. 13 February 1847. SAOR 89-1-1260/25.

To the Director,

I have released the peasant youth Prokhor Chervina from the village of Berestova, Berdiansk District [from his apprenticeship] because of his stupidity and complete inability to learn about practical agriculture and have asked the District Administration to allow a different, more competent youth to take his place.

758. Johann Cornies to Christian Steven. 15 February 1847. SAOR 89-1-1260/15v.

Inspector for Agriculture,

The apprentice Peter Negresko from the Ananiev area, Kherson Guberniia, has written to me. He is disconsolate about the condition of his relatives at home. His mother has died, his father has become blind, and his siblings are suffering want.

Might Yr. Excellency graciously make arrangements to have apprentice Negresko's father and siblings relieved of their crushing situation? Otherwise the son will become discouraged and fail to make the progress we would like him to. I would ask, at your convenience, for news about how this situation might be improved.

759. Evgenii F. Hahn to Johann Cornies. 26 February 1847. SAOR 89-1-889/88.

I just received a letter from Mr. Baumann offering me his services as Guardian of the Jewish settlements. I responded that I would very much like such an arrangement but could not say anything definite until the budget had been confirmed.

I have let Jansch go on your account. He first filled your composition about living hedges with question marks and then printed his own composition about the same subject. I also dismissed him because I would like to make the paper [*Unterhaltungsblatt für deutsche Ansiedler im südlichen Rußland*] more popular. As editor of the second yearly volume, I have appointed settler and District Secretary Sonderegger. He has command of the German language. I hope the paper will lose nothing because of this change, especially if you continue to support it by sending in as many articles as you possibly can.

I am overwhelmed beyond all measure by business matters and things to be written.

I have provided the Minister with a detailed report about Wiens and hope that there will soon be a decision that would banish him from the country. In the meantime, please let us keep this matter to ourselves.

Yours truly, E. v. Hahn.

760. F[ranz] Martens to Johann Cornies. 1 March 1847.
   SAOR 89-1-1271/88.

Mr. J. Cornies in Ohrloff,

It has been rumoured that old teacher Heese, Einlage, finds himself in a worrisome and difficult situation. Judging from appearances, he can barely subsist.

I have been assured that he would very much like to return to his old position in the Molochnaia and would accept that position thankfully. [F.] Martens.

761. Johann Cornies to Johann Cornies Jr. 2 March 1847.
   SAOR 89-1-1260/28.

Dear Son,

I gather from your letter that you and your uncle arrived safely in Elbing on 10 January. Your uncle wrote me from Freienhuben on 29 January reporting that you are both well and had already travelled through much of the Werder.

As for us, we are, thank God, healthy, although Mother still suffers from the cough she had at the time of your departure. However, she refuses to take to her bed.

Your uncle will likely be on his journey home by the time you receive this. He described an extreme shortage of food in Prussia that was forcing the lower classes into the greatest poverty. Please keep this in mind wherever you stay. Do not become a burden to anyone, pay well for everything, and do not give the appearance of stinginess. Tip coachmen and servants well, as was previously the fashion. This is even more necessary now. Get Mr. Wiebe to take payment for every service or item he provides. I know of his generosity and goodness of heart that he would extend to you without any thought of recompense. Nevertheless, try to return his friendship, kindness, and benevolence by deeds of your own. Should this journey cost us several hundred rubles more than otherwise and, even if some of it were to be wasted on an unthankful person, I and you will be left with the memory of having responded to every friendly and benevolent deed.

In the last letter, I wrote that I would like you to travel to the Holstein area. I repeat this now, but only on the assumption that this is also your wish and that circumstances permit. I therefore leave your journey to your own best judgment.

Winter continues in full force and there is much snow here and there. Three days ago I came back from Aleksandrov District where I had been commissioned to inspect the houses Gladkii is having built for the Jews. They are being constructed in winter, in fifteen to twenty degrees of frost and with knee-deep snow. The journey took ten days in deep snow, with snowstorms, and without the sight of a roadway or track on the barren steppe. I had difficulty getting anywhere.

Yesterday, Wiebe, his wife, and your son Johann travelled to Tashchenak by sleigh. Your little one is healthy, cheerful, and very obedient. Agnes is making an effort with a good, intelligent, and open approach. He sings, jumps about, and often speaks about Papa. I have heard that Justinchen, too, is completely healthy.[3]

Brother-in-law Neufeld writes that I should accept twenty thousand rubles from him on your behalf. Perhaps brother-in-law Wiebe has already let you know that Dirk Boldt and two others drowned in the Dnieper near Schoenwiese in a "Blenka" and have yet to be found. He is supposed to have had 1,500 rubles on his person. Yesterday, Neufeld's son Johann and Schoolteacher Voth from Halbstadt dropped by and asked me for a submission on their behalf for a permit to travel to Prussia. Rempel from Halbstadt, old Friesen from Altona, and Braun from Muensterberg have all received permission to visit Prussia.

Farewell and give many greetings to all of our good friends, Mr. Wiebe, Mr. David Epp, and the Wiebe family. Mother and all your relatives send their greetings. Write soon. I send you my own special greetings and remain your loving father, Johann Cornies.

---

3 Johann Jr.'s daughter Justina, who lived with his maternal grandmother.

N.B. I think it might be worthwhile for you find a good children's nurse who could also give the children a good education, especially in regard to behaviour and decency, someone willing to travel back with you and take over the supervision of your children. I assume that she would be a Mennonite, well brought up, virtuous, without reproach, and of gentle character.

762. David Hamm to Johann Cornies. 4 March 1847. SOAR 89-1-1271/101.

On 22 February 1847, the Bolshoi Tokmak crown peasant Ivan Mirin was hired, with his family, to work on the Iushanle estate for a year and for a salary of 190 rubles. He received an advance of three rubles, fifty kopeks. In accordance with the agreement, he would obtain his pass when fetched from Tokmak a week later.

After going to Tokmak on 28 February to obtain the pass, the above-mentioned Mirin refused to assume his service. Although I had him called to account by the Elder, the latter explained that he had accepted Mirin's excuse that he had failed to find accommodation for his few head of livestock. The Elder also claimed that, because of the inconsequential amount of the advance, he lacked the authority to force Mirin to accept service and had decided to take back the advance given him. I was not satisfied with this decision and returned without the advance.

If Mirin is still supposed to assume the service he accepted, I would ask that the necessary action be taken in the appropriate way. David Hamm.

763. Cornelius Froese to Johann Cornies. 9 March 1847. SAOR 89-1-1271/124.

His Honour, Mr. Johann Cornies in Ohrloff, Molochnaia Mennonite Settlement in Southern Russia,

Please accept my apologies for imposing upon you in this way. The bearer of this letter, Herrmann Froese, his wife, and four children, are members of the Elbing Mennonite community. After receiving a travel visa, they travelled to your local Mennonite villages. Let me report briefly on this man's conduct. Froese is an irreproachable, thoroughly energetic worker and father, completely capable of furthering himself through vigorous work. I can unreservedly give our good Froese this testimonial in the name of all who know him.

I feel that I can direct this brief message to Yr. Honour because of our acquaintance that goes back to 1827, when I met you in Elbing in the home of my brother-in-law, Aron Wiebe of Muehlendam, and also when you stayed with our relatives, the Wiebe family in Klakkendorff. Time will surely have erased me from your memory, but we still think of you often. My wife in particular remembers Mrs. Cornies, a friend from her youth.

Please permit me to also report that your esteemed son, Mr. Johann Cornies, has demonstrated his friendship and love by honouring us with a visit that gave my wife and me much pleasure.

Again expressing the hope that my small effort will be well accepted, I send my greetings to Yr. Honour and your wife, as well as to Mr. Heinrich Cornies, and greetings as well from my wife and daughter.

With esteem and love, Cornelius Froese, Oberherbswald, West Prussia.

764. Elisabeth Hartwiss to Johann Cornies. 9 March 1847. SAOR 89-1-1271/98.

Mr. Cornies

You will remember that you sent me some bagged rye flour in 1846. I would ask that you provide us with a further sixteen puds of the best bagged rye flour. Send it along with the carters when they move along in summer. I will pay promptly through Baron Rosen, or my husband will send along the money. Last year it came to three rubles per pud, with transportation.

With complete esteem, I sign myself as Elisabeth von Hartwiss.

765. Johann Cornies to Friedrich Wilhelm Lange. 10 March 1847. SAOR 89-1-1260/30v.

Honoured Elder,

It is my considered opinion that this madness will soon have reached its uttermost. Further hesitation on the part of our spiritual leadership could have tragic consequences for our leadership and all Mennonites. At the very least, the government would have to abandon its previous good impression of the Mennonites and see them through different, less favourable eyes. For this reason, I would ask that you take action on behalf of the Gnadenfeld Church Assembly by submitting a formal complaint about Wiens to the District Office. It should state that Wiens does not respect the judgment passed against him, that admonitions have borne no results, and that he disrupts spiritual influences within the community, etc. There seems to be no alternative but to present him to the District Office for further action by forcing him to respect the judgment passed against him, etc.

With a friendly greeting, I remain, as always, your honest friend and servant, Johann Cornies.

766. Johann Cornies to Fedor F. Rosen. 12 March 1847. SAOR 89-1-1260/32.

The Director,

The enclosed communication No. 27 of 25 February 1847 shows that the Iugartamgaeli village administration does not intend to return the original taxes paid for crown apprentice Salakai Shamanov by his father, although the village administration itself admits that it has been acquainted with the relevant regulations since 1842. I am therefore approaching Yr. Honour with the respectful request that you graciously order that the village administration repay the apprentice's father, Chamann Roshaliev, the taxes he was unjustly assessed. Kindly inform me about the decision in this matter.

767. Hermann Witte to Johann Cornies. 13 March 1847. SAOR 89-1-1271/99.

Highly valued Mr. Cornies,

I have received your letter of 29 January 1847 reporting that the German wagon ordered by His Excellency v. Levshin has been completely finished. I would send someone for the wagon immediately, as you wish, but the roads are presently very bad. I would accordingly request that you, kind Mr. Cornies, inform master craftsman Braun that I will send someone to fetch the wagon as soon as the roads are passable, and that the messenger will bring along the money.

With exceptional esteem, I have the honour to be your respectful servant, Hermann Witte.

768. Johann Siemens to Johann Cornies. 18 March 1847. SAOR 89-1-1271/102.

Esteemed Friend,

In accordance with your commission, I would inform you that Brother P. Siemens has already tried to find genuine angora goats, but without success. He found goats on the estates of Count Vorontsov in Pavlograd District, but they are no longer pure angora. And because the head administrator of the estate was absent he also failed to get a price for them. Siemens has now learned that estate owner Braslov in the same district supposedly has pure-breds. He will go there as soon as possible to make closer inquiries. I will report their results as soon as I can.

With hearty greetings, your most respectful, Johann Siemens.

769. Johann Neufeld to Johann Cornies. 22 March 1847. SAOR 89-1-1271/103.

Esteemed Brother-in-law,

In sending you the enclosed letter from Heinrich Zimmermann, from Praust, I can respond to your letter of 19 March by saying that in my opinion the above-mentioned Zimmermann cannot be employed in our brewery. The District Office would refuse to change the local brewery to the Prussian method, I do not know Zimmermann personally, and I have heard negative things about his character.

With friendly greetings and respect, your honest brother-in-law, Johann Neufeld.

770. Johann Cornies to Carl Stempel. 24 March 1847. SAOR 89-1-1260/35.

Most esteemed Mr. v. Stempel,

The unexpectedly rapid arrival of spring has suddenly given new life to agriculture that leaves no time for reflection. This moves me to ask that, for the moment, all attention in matters relating to Jewish settlement be directed towards planting grain and potatoes. I agree completely with Wedel that this can be done most quickly and advantageously by hiring Russians to do the ploughing, even at seven rubles per desiatina. No delay is permitted in this matter and there is no longer any time to prepare the most important places. You will forgive my having already indicated to Wedel that he should begin. Well-grounded reasons have caused me to decide the matter in this way and I am convinced that you will support me in this decision.

It is essential to call together the Jewish Mayors to establish how many spans they can themselves provide for ploughing. They can surely bring together some draught animals by now. Wedel has purchased five ploughs. This number can be increased with time, depending on the number of draught animals available for work. It would be best for now to hire Russians who would use their own ploughs under the supervision of experienced Germans to ensure that the ploughing is deep and well done. Wedel should immediately purchase potatoes and arrange to have them transported as cheaply as possible. You yourself know how to provide good seed grain at the appropriate time.

In my opinion, the Jews need German cows, specifically one cow per family. These cows give more milk and are presently not expensive. The other matters you mention must not occupy us at the moment. To enable a new settlement to prosper, everything can be done only step by step. Otherwise, settlers will become confused, nothing will develop as it should, and harm will eventually result everywhere. For this reason, I would also request that you indicate to Wedel that he should give the Mayors written directions on all points that have been decided. He should follow these punctually and give his further directions on their basis.

The choice of land for grain growing should show promise for future cultivation and be located in a way that minimizes the distance Jews would need to haul their grain.

I think that one, perhaps two, ploughs should be hired for every six to ten Jewish families, as circumstances suggest, and that these families should transport their seed grain and do their ploughing under the supervision of a knowledgeable person. They should learn all of these matters through practice. Efforts should be made to use the Jews in all tasks and take advantage of the little they can do with their own livestock and using their own energies.

Honest thanks for your remarks regarding the confusion sown by the two Waldheim Mennonite families that have decided to return to Volhynia. They are trying to spread information among their associates that is ill-founded and consists mostly of rumour.

Your honest servant, Johann Cornies.

771. Johann Cornies to Fedor F. Rosen. 26 March 1847.
   SAOR 89-1-1260/36v.

Director of the Tavrida State Domains Bureau,

Received in good order, with Yr. Honour's communication No. 97 of February 1847, one silver ruble, twenty kopeks for postage incurred in connection with the cultivation of potatoes and maize.

To the above,

In accordance with Yr. Honour's communication No. 93 of 22 February 1847, I have the honour to submit the enclosed receipt for my payment of sixty silver rubles to the Nogai Kokei Trembetov from Mashkir for his accomplishments, in 1846, in the cultivation of potatoes and maize in Perekop District.

To the above,

In accordance with Yr. Honour's communication No. 91 of 22 February 1847, I have the honour to respectfully submit the receipts for the correct payment of forty silver rubles to state peasants Trofim Klimenko from Kaikulak, and to Ivan Beloi, Terpenie, for their achievements in the cultivation of potatoes and maize in the districts of Berdiansk and Melitopol in 1846.

772. Johann Siemens to Johann Cornies. 26 March 1847.
SAOR 89-1-1271/115.

Esteemed Friend,

In accordance with your commission, I spoke with schoolteacher Abram Klassen who is prepared to take on service as District Secretary in Bergthal settlement, specifically for the amount of money you previously offered him. Granted, he is still obligated to teach his school until Pentecost, but should the transports provided for him arrive earlier, he would willingly go along with them. This is to inform District Chairman Siemens in this regard.

With hearty greetings, your most respectful Johann Siemens.

773. Hermann Witte to Johann Cornies. 4 April 1847.
SAOR 89-1-1271/108.

Highly valued Mr. Cornies,

In response to your communication, I send a total of 362 rubles, seventy kopeks as payment for the wagon ordered by His Excellency von Levshin. It is to be delivered by my messenger. I respectfully ask that he be shown how the wagon is to be assembled for its various uses.

At this moment I have received a commission from His Excellency, Baron von Frank, asking that you, kind Mr. Cornies, send someone along with my messenger to look up a potter from whom he is to purchase two hundred milk bowls that would be used as beehive covers. The craftsman is requested to pack these covers into the box of the wagon that is being delivered. The bowls must be at least eight vershok wide. It does not matter if they are wider, which I would really prefer. My messenger should pay for the bowls.

With the most complete esteem, I have the honour to be your respectful servant, Hermann Witte.

774. Johann Cornies to Johann Cornies Jr. 5 April 1847.
SAOR 89-1-1260/39.

My beloved son,

Your dear Mother caught a severe cold on Wednesday immediately after Easter and became ill. It was an illness that included severe diarrhoea that quickly weakened her to such a degree that the doctor, who had been called immediately, could only provide a little relief but do nothing to cure her. She grew weaker and weaker and, to our great sorrow, departed for a better life at two o'clock in the afternoon of the fifth day of her illness, 30 March. She was buried in the Ohrloff community cemetery on 2 April.

As painful as the passing of our beloved Mother is, we must remember, to our own great comfort, that the departed had experienced long years of repeated illness and prepared herself for this release with a steadfast Christian belief and that she went to sleep with peace in her soul.

I write to you out of fatherly love to give you support and consolation, but in the certain hope that you will accept God's unfathomable wisdom and not give yourself up to continuing, irrational sorrow and grief. "What God does is always well done." You know that Mother wanted you to make the journey to Prussia as much as I did. She encouraged me to write to you and grant you permission to travel even farther than Prussia. So do not despair. Carry out the purpose of your journey. May God grant you a quiet, peaceful heart and cheerful contentment! Time will lessen your pain little by little. This is the advice and the simple wish of your father who loves you with all his heart. Amen!

Your uncle and Klaassen, his travelling companion, arrived safely and in good health during the Easter holidays. All of us were pleased to hear that your health is good and that you were happy and in good spirits. He arrived just when spring seeding was beginning.

Your son continues to be healthy and well and is already wearing pants. This gives him a great deal of pleasure. Mrs. Martens, who was here for Mother's funeral, told me that Justina is well but did not want to bring her along because of the raw weather. I repeat, and cannot press it upon you sufficiently, that a good governess is absolutely essential for you, especially for little Johann. Very good qualities are revealing themselves in the boy. He is an eager child who understands his aunt quickly. She is giving him good direction. Almost all of the people who had known his great-grandfather say that your son resembles him entirely in regard to his features, characteristics, and behaviour.

In conclusion, I ask you to give many hearty and sincere greetings to my beloved friend Johann Wiebe and his dear wife, and also to all the relatives and acquaintances who remember me with love. Your brother-in-law, sister, and Uncle Klassen send greetings to you. Keep God in your sight and in your heart. This is the wish of your loving father, Johann Cornies.

775. Johann Cornies to Hermann Sudermann. 5 April 1847. SAOR 89-1-1260/40.

Overseer Sudermann,

The cost estimates presented with report No. 5 of 30 March 1847 cannot be accepted because of the unwarranted sum estimated for daily wages, 150 kopeks per day per labourer, including maintenance. Even if thirty kopeks are deducted for meals, one ruble, twenty kopeks is still much too expensive. As is known, the most recent market price was only seventy kopeks, eighty at most. By arriving late on the market, you may well have driven up the market price by 120 kopeks and attracted workers already hired elsewhere in the plantation. Some private employers are complaining about this increase and are very surprised. The plantation may not be disadvantaged in this way. You are permitted to pay a daily wage of one ruble per day, at most, and the additional twenty kopeks will come out of your own pocket. The latter sum cannot be listed in the accounts.

For this reason, I am returning the estimates with a request that you submit them again after deliberation and on the basis of the directions I have given you. These estimates should then be sent to me for my examination and confirmation.

776. Johann Cornies to Carl Stempel. 9 April 1847. SAOR 89-1-1260/41.

Most esteemed Mr. v. Stempel,

Enclosed, I am sending a copy of the Directive from His Excellency, President of the Guardianship Committee, in accordance with his honoured wishes. I must at the same time add that my objections to this Directive were sent with today's mail. I find it impossible for a settlement of German model agriculturalists to take place under the specified circumstances. I would therefore ask you, esteemed Mr. v. Stempel, not to allow anything respecting this directive to slip out. That would work to the disadvantage of the whole matter by making people hesitant. I have been assured that changes will be made once the General has finally had an opportunity to consider everything in greater detail.

With unchanging and exceptional esteem, Yr. Honour's most respectful servant, Johann Cornies.

777. Johann Cornies to Evgenii F. Hahn. 9 April 1847. SAOR 89-1-1260/42.

Yr. Excellency,

Yr. Excellency's special favour for me and Yr. kind sympathy for the circumstances of my family compel me to let you know, worthy Sir, that our loving God was pleased to take my wife from my side. She died in the fifty-sixth year of her life on 30 March after a five-day illness. Sickly for many years, she had resolutely prepared herself for this release. I am nevertheless deeply troubled by this separation forever from my friend, with whom I had lived for almost thirty-six years and with whom I had shared joy and sorrow. I must openly admit that at my advanced and considerable age, I feel terribly isolated and downcast. Still, I have found the strength to control my feelings in the conviction that I can accomplish nothing through faint-heartedness and frightened concern about a dark future. On the contrary, much that is positive and demanding in my duty would be disturbed in this way. Time, the quiet and gentle source of consolation, heals even the deepest wounds and lessens the most stifling grief with the soothing balm of forgetfulness.

With the most perfect esteem, I will always consider it to be the joy of my life to continue to see myself as Yr. Excellency's most obedient servant, Johann Cornies.

778. Johann Cornies to [unknown]. 19 April 1847. SAOR 89-1-1260/46.

Esteemed Sir,

On 14 March 1847 I received your valued letter of 18 February, and the cigars of your own manufacture. Much to my regret, the cigars were so damaged during transport that they were unrecognizable. I return my honest thanks for your kindness and courtesy.

It is quite natural that the tobacco in your region does not equal the quality we can obtain locally. This is also true of cigars made of leaves from my own plantation that have been improving in appearance as well as in flavour and aroma. I will shortly take the liberty of sending you some samples.

If I could be useful to you otherwise, I would gladly do so. I enclose a small description regarding the raising, care, and preparation of tobacco, in the manner undertaken on my estate and found to be useful.

With the most complete esteem, your respectful servant.

779. Johann Cornies to Baumann. 21 April 1847. SAOR 89-1-1260/47.

Highly valued Mr. Baumann,

Since I am honestly sympathetic to the further progress of poor Jewish settlers, I must return my most obliging thanks to you. In agreeing to cooperate on this important reform for Russia and for a not inconsiderable part of the Jewish population, you have not worked for your own advantage. As you know from State Counsellor v. Hahn, the act has not yet been confirmed, and there is no rush in transferring the position of Guardian. You should have enough time to visit the eastern provinces and deal with your own family affairs. I will do everything I can to draw you into this proposed sphere of activity because I honestly believe that this is the only way to achieve real success.

The fourteen Jewish villages in Kherson Guberniia have been settled and are at no greater distance from one another than sixty verstas. I do not know anything about the situation regarding schools and little about the condition of the villages. The current director lives in the village of Nagaslav, but his successor will presumably not live in a city that would distance him physically from observing the Jews and be detrimental to his activities. There will surely be no shortage of land for gardening and other useful activities.

Heartfelt thanks for your offer of seeds. You will forgive me if I do not include a list of those available here. Bring along only a small number of rare varieties, provided this does not cause you any inconvenience.

We had much snow this winter that covered the soil at great depth for some time. Spring could not have been better. The snow vanished slowly, permitting the soil to soak up much of its winter moisture. Rivers filled up only later on. Seeding was done as we would have wished and the seeds are coming up with great promise. The grass is up equally well and, with God's blessing, we expect the best of futures.

This week three Mennonite families left for the Jewish colony of Novoberislav on the Dnieper and the Mennonite Mayor appointed for the village will leave soon. My brother David Cornies has received the package of seeds and is grateful for your kindness.

With most exceptional esteem, your constantly honest servant, Johann Cornies.

780. Johann Cornies to Hermann Sudermann. 23 April 1847.
   SAOR 89-1-1260/48v.

To the overseer of the Crown Model Plantation,
   Since we cannot find a good tile roofer at this time, I would direct you to sort out the tiles yourself, separating the hollow from the flat ones. All tiles should then be put in the hands of Master Stobbe. Stobbe should do all the laying himself to make sure that it is well done. The tiles, hollow and flat, should be closely laid to prevent the rain from penetrating. The best tiles should be used for the yard side. The actual roofing can be finished later. Stobbe should get the apprentices on the plantation to help. They can do their own work later.

You should keep water carts on hand to ensure that no trees die because of their lack. Keep watch that these carters bring along as much water as do our own and that nobody lazes about.

781. Johann Cornies to Hermann Sudermann. 3 May 1847.
   SAOR 89-1-1260/49v.

Overseer of the Crown Plantation,
   The master mason has been told to let you know when you should go to Terpenie to receive sixteen thousand bricks and have them loaded on carts. No bricks broken into three pieces are acceptable. To avoid further problems, you must supervise all of this and receive the bricks correctly, in the required quantity and quality.

782. Johann Cornies to Hermann Sudermann. 3 May 1847.
   SAOR 89-1-1260/49v.

To the above,
   To dig the boundary ditches you have asked for 140 men to work on Wednesday, 7 May. These ditches should first be carefully marked off.

This has not yet happened and cannot be done without Gardener Fast who must ensure that no mistakes are made. I would, for these reasons, instruct you to prepare everything well before moving ahead. When preparations are made you should time your request for the above-mentioned workers so that the gardener is not unnecessarily disturbed at planting time and workers do not encounter delays.

In this case and in several others, I have noticed that you and Gardener Fast are not in agreement about various projects and you simply act on your own. This must now stop categorically. Everything is to be discussed with Fast. As far as orders for workers are concerned, no submissions of this kind will in future be accepted until you and the gardener have both signed them.

This must be observed punctually.

783. Johann Cornies to Christian Steven. 10 May 1847.
   SAOR 89-1-1260/52.

The upright silk-reeler Yr. Excellency ordered from the local Mennonite Abram Janzen is now ready to be picked up. Please let me know by return mail whether the destination is Simferopol. If so, I will send it by the first available transport.

After a beautiful warm April, May has been rainy and cool. The grain has come up well and we hope that the moisture will better root the grass intended for hay. All of our plantings, orchards, and forest-tree plantations have been infested by numberless passion caterpillar and spindle worm nests. They would have caused great damage had they not been destroyed in spring. Nearby Russian villages pay little attention to these vermin and their gardens have lost their leaves as though scorched by fire. The feared passion caterpillar is also found in great numbers on the steppe and mainly in haymeadows where they have eaten away many plants. Our blossoming fruit trees have been a delight to see and look promising, except for apricots, which winter frosts seem to have damaged. Silkworms should not lack good and sufficient fodder for the year.

I will send you the desired two milk cows this month. With respect.

784. Johann Siemens to Johann Cornies. 10 May 1847.
   SAOR 89-1-1271/125.

Esteemed Friend Cornies,

I can report that local Elder Jacob Dyck approached me for the third time to seek reconciliation. This happened on 3 May when he promised not to interfere again in worldly matters. As a sign of his honest friendship, he paid me a personal visit the following Sunday. I hope he will be faithful to his promise.

We have been very busy painting buildings and fences, and I await your arrival almost daily.

With hearty greetings, I remain your respectful servant, Johann Siemens.

785. Johann Cornies to Heinrich Zimmermann. 10 May 1847. SAOR 89-1-1260/53.

Esteemed Mr. Zimmermann,

I have received your valued letters of 3 March and 30 April. I did not respond to the first because I was grieving the death of my wife. Moreover, I could not give you a definite answer about the brandy lease before first reaching an agreement with my partner. [As you know], my brother-in-law Neufeld in Halbstadt and I hold the lease for the production of brandy in partnership. Even now I am unable to give you an answer one way or the other. I should tell you that I find Jewish methods of distilling dirty and lacking in order. My brother-in-law understands the problem but still hesitates to hire you as I would like. I hope that once the Jew has been let go when his contract expires a month from now, I can talk my brother-in-law into accepting my proposal. He objects out of fear that if we hire a new distiller in the distillery built and outfitted with community funds, costly new arrangements would have to be made that would cost a lot and have to be covered by us.

As you can tell, my good Mr. Zimmermann, even with the best of intentions, I have failed to accomplish anything in response to your proposal. But do not give up hope. I will soon discuss the subject of your appointment thoroughly with my brother-in-law and inform you accordingly.

My brother-in-law's son Johann Neufeld travelled to Prussia in spring and has already arrived. Perhaps you will see him and could show him a well-run distillery. When he left, I suggested he get to know you and inspect your arrangements. He could then tell his father how important it is that we arrange and manage everything better here.

Should you catch sight of my son, greet him from me and tell him that everyone in our household is well. And should you have the

opportunity, give my friendly greetings also to Mr. v. Steen in Langefuhr and Mr. Wiebe and his siblings in Elbing.

With exceptional greetings, I commend myself especially to you
and your dear family and remain, with respect, your obedient friend,
Johann Cornies.

786. Fr. Gavel to Johann Cornies. 22 May 1847.
SAOR 89-1-1271/127v.[4]

Highly valued Mr. Cornies,

The good tobacco I smoked last summer while visiting your esteemed
brother in Iushanle prompts me to make the same request of you as did
Mr. Fedorovich. Please send me a pud of your best tobacco to Odesa,
with information regarding its price. I will, by return mail, pay you with
thanks. You should have no problem sending it to Odesa. My address is
as follows: "To be delivered to Professor Fr. Gavel, in General Schnell's
house on Rissellaux Street."

I hope to see you again in Odesa sometime soon. I am heartily glad
to have left my former despot in Ekaterinoslav. What a pleasure to
have a superior such as General Hahn. I forgot to say that the Guardianship Committee has also given me command over the Jewish settlements. It is my genuine desire to deal with everything according to
your wishes.

787. Johann Cornies to Peters. 27 May 1847. SAOR 89-1-1260/56.

Esteemed Mr. Peters,

I honestly thank you for your offer to transfer your monopoly on
"Cammeral" sheep to me for a reasonable price. My business affairs
on behalf of the common good of the inhabitants of this region give
me too little time to devote to my own business. It is for this reason
that I must forego your offer. I have not replied to you for such a
long a time because of my failure to find other buyers for these
sheep.

With honest esteem, I remain your respectful servant.

---

4 Gavel was a Ministry of State Domains agronomist and the author of a biographical
  essay about Cornies, published in the *Journal of the Ministry of State Domains* after his
  death.

788. Johann Cornies to Jacob Klaassen. 28 May 1847.
SAOR 89-1-1260/57v.

Master Carpenter Jac. Klaassen in Halbstadt,

The foundation for the forestry building on the Crown Plantation should have been laid and the structural work undertaken according to our agreement. You are to appear at the plantation next Monday, 9 June to prevent any further delays, the costs of which would have to be added to your accounts.

789. District Office to Johann Cornies. 31 May 1847.
SAOR 89-1-1271/141.

Death certificate No. 2849 sent to the esteemed Johann Cornies in Ohrloff,

In response to your application of 26 May, the District Office has prepared a death certificate for the deceased Dietrich Claassen, its format in accordance with the law for foreigners. It, and its supplements, are being sent to you for your attention.

The District Office further notes that in accordance with directive No. 767 of 15 October 1839 from the Director of the Ministry of the Interior, death certificates for foreigners who have died in Russia, together with an inventory of their estates and any testaments, are to be submitted to the Police Assessor [for the division of the estate] and for forwarding to the guberniia director.

District Chairman Toews, District Secretary Reimer.

790. Johann Klaassen to Johann Cornies. 31 May 1847.
SAOR 89-1-1271/139.

Chairman in Ohrloff,

I respectfully request that you not be angry with me for not attending Communion, the Lord's Supper, at Ohrloff. First of all, I had not asked for your permission to do so before you left Tashchenak and, secondly, I would sincerely like to partake of the Lord's Supper with my children. I would therefore request that I be permitted to visit my children in Ladekopp in autumn, if roads and circumstances permit, to partake of the Lord's Supper with them in Petershagen, should God will and you kindly agree.

On 28 May, Peters listed the beams he transported from the brickworks on 28 April....

With the greatest esteem, I commend myself to you as your respectful
Johann Klaassen.

791. From Agricultural Society to Village Offices. June 1847. SAOR 89-1-1268/60.[5]

This village was founded in 1803 and presently consists of twenty
agricultural fullholders, twenty professional craftsmen, ten others
pursuing various crafts, and eight day-labourers. The total is thus
fifty-eight families, or 210 persons of both genders who are healthy
and well off.

In this village there are eighty dwelling houses, one church, one
District Office building, one building for the office of the Agricultural
Society, one village school, one district school, one society school [pri-
vate school], one storage warehouse, eighty livestock barns, thirty grain
storage sheds, seven granaries. There is, in addition, one cloth factory,
one drying mill, one silk-reeling facility, one beer brewery, one vinegar brewery, one brandy distillery, one dye-works, two windmills, one
watermill, one corn mill powered by horses, one building for oil-pressing,
one barley mill, one groats mill, one inn, one smithy, six approved bak-
ing ovens, one bathhouse, one laundry house, one building for silkworms, one house for the livestock herder, etc. This makes a total of
[blank] buildings, of which ten are solidly laid out in fired brick, four
are built of stone, and five are roofed with Dutch roof tiles, one with
planking.

In addition to this, one brick-firing kiln, one Dutch roof-tile kiln,
one pottery and one lime kiln are located in special places close to the
village.

No contagious disease is rampant among the livestock. The grass on
the haymeadows is growing well and the appearance of grain on fields
as well as of fruit in orchards promises an abundant harvest.

Twelve fullholders are keeping orderly accounts of their income and
expenditures, thirteen families are occupied with sericulture, and eight
with cultivating tobacco.

---

5 The same letter was sent to all of the villages in the Molochnaia, apparently as a
   template for the villages to follow in their own reports. This example is the one sent
   to Halbstadt.

792. Summary of the duties of Village Offices. N.d. [June 1847 documents.] SAOR 89-1-1268/94.

In accordance with the "Instruction" for the internal administration of New Russian settlements for foreigners, the duties of the Village Offices are:

1. To teach inhabitants subordinate to them and explain to them that it is everyone's duty to live decently and in peace with others, and that everyone acquire the knowledge necessary for a husbandman. They should strive to earn the respect of young people and their Elders, enjoy their obedience, and provide the young with models of deportment.

2. Inhabitants subject to each Village Mayor and Assistant Mayor owe them the requisite respect and esteem.

3. Village Offices are required to promote everything that is of advantage to village inhabitants and to prevent everything inimical from happening.

4. In carrying out the duties of their position, [Village Offices] should insist in a stern and orderly fashion that whatever ordered is carried out punctually.

5. Village Offices must act in an affable and agreeable manner towards their inhabitants, listen to all their requests, pay attention to their concerns, and become their honest advocates.

6. As soon as the Mayor calls for the inhabitants to assemble, they must appear at the assembly point quickly, hear all orders quietly, and fulfil them punctually. When an assembly is called, the penalty is fifty kopeks for someone absent or disobedient, and two rubles for persons who conduct themselves loudly and in a disorderly manner.

7. Everyone who appears in the Village Office or in a community assembly must wear a head covering.

8. It is the duty of the Village Offices to ensure that poor or infirm persons are not permitted to loiter, whatever their excuse, ask for charity, or especially beg. All persons who cannot earn their livelihood by their own efforts must be supported by the community.

9. Moreover, the Hutterthal community is especially obligated to ensure that none of their members borrow money or make outside debts, except with their brethren in faith, the Molochnaia Mennonites. Anyone who does otherwise without the community's advance knowledge must be punished.

793. Johann Cornies to Christian Steven. 5 June 1847.
SAOR 89-1-1260/60.

Yr. Excellency [v. Steven],

The two milk cows bought for you left yesterday, 4 June. My honest wishes are that they arrive in good condition and thrive. The purchase price is seventy-five rubles for one, eighty rubles for the other, for a total of 155 rubles. Local expenses were six rubles, transport to Simferopol nine rubles, forty-five kopeks. The transport of a reeling machine will cost ten rubles, seventy-five kopeks, for a total of 181.20 rubles. Please remit this sum to me at Yr. convenience. Since there is no butter on hand at present it will follow at a later date.

Summer grain and potatoes are growing very well. Rye, however, was only mediocre and grass for hay is sparse on the meadows. Foot-and-mouth disease has broken out here and there among horned cattle in our villages. Still, we have means to quickly counter and cure this illness which no longer has the dire consequences it did in times past. There is little demand for wool.

With exceptional esteem, I remain Yr. Excellency's most respectful servant, Johann Cornies.

794. Johann Cornies to Novoberislav Overseer. 5 June 1847.
SAOR 89-1-1260/60v.

To the Village Overseer of the Hebrew village of Novoberislav,

In response to your communication of 29 May, let me say that extensive inquiries about land leasing for Jews and about the contract in question must be taken to the Director, or *Upravlaiushchii*. I have heard it said that no definite boundaries were indicated to the leaseholder. If this is really the case, and if livestock belonging to Jews suffer as a result, it is your first obligation to investigate the matter thoroughly. Then, brief and plausible inquiries should immediately be made of the Guardianship Committee, to discover what might be done in circumstances of this kind in order that inhabitants of Novoberislav not suffer.

You should not wait for any further papers from the Committee. The Directive you have in hand makes it your duty to keep your eye on all circumstances that might be useful to Jewish settlers. You should not allow yourself to be distracted from this obligation. Any long delays in stepping in where necessary can only have unacceptable consequences.

You should act with real deliberation, steadfastly, justly, and without delay in cases of anything that might promote the economic well-being of the community.

By law, the Jews cannot keep a Russian shepherd unless the German settlers hire one for themselves and he is then given care also of the Jewish livestock. This is the only way in which Jews can take part in the hiring. Otherwise, the local police would have to investigate, resulting in much trouble and fines.

I have discussed everything about accommodations for German settlers with Peter Loewen, and he will inform you verbally about this. I repeat again that you should be prudent, steadfast, just, and constantly active in your work, and not submit anything to the Committee unless you have good reason to do so. In this way you will gain the respect and trust of the community and the administration under your oversight.

795. Johann Cornies Jr. to Johann Cornies. 19 June 1847. SAOR 89-1-1271/149.

Esteemed Father,

My journey has been very slow until now. Several delays have occurred, especially in Mecklenburg where there was always something worthwhile to investigate that prompted me to leave the carriage every time. There are, along the way, very fine sheepfarms with sheep that produce a great deal of wool. I have seen good, large, horned cattle bred here, partly for milk and partly to fatten for sale, and as well as especially large, heavy horses that are not very quick on their feet. I visited Baron v. Hahn's stud farm, considered the best in Mecklenburg, but the horses there were all English breeds. The breeding of horned cattle is highly important in Holstein where marshes provide especially nutritious pasture. In contrast, there is more field cultivation pursued towards Jutland, but not as good as it is in Mecklenburg. The livestock destined for England is fattened in western Holstein.

I have been well received among our brethren in faith who are most kind-hearted. I have made the acquaintance of almost all members of the small congregation in Friedrichstadt who exhibited a sincere interest in our well- being. The Van der Smissen brothers, sons of the deceased pastor, asked me to send you their heartfelt greeting.

My journey seems to have reached its farthest point. I know that if I had not taken it, I would always have been sorry for not doing so when I was so close by. I take pleasure in being completely healthy. At times I almost feel homesick, especially for my little ones who are often in my thoughts, although I know they are in the best of hands.

With filial greetings, I strive to remain your son, Johann Cornies.

796. Abraham Driedger to Johann Cornies. 22 June 1847.
SAOR 89-1-1271/150.

Chairman Johann Cornies, Ohrloff,

We finished cutting hay by noon yesterday but the harvest at Tashchenak is very sparse. Since it rained almost every day this week we will probably be busy bringing it in for another week. Heinrich Cornies told us we would haul hay up from the Molochnaia next week. We had already arranged to have all of our wagons in place by then. There are 2,060 haystacks at the Molochnaia and I estimate that four of them will make up one cartload.

Rain and hail have damaged the rye a lot and it is just lying there, quite flattened. Our summer grain has also been battered in places but wheat is showing hardly any signs of damage. We expect only a small yield of rye but quite a lot of summer grain. [During the rain and hailstorms] about twenty-five windowpanes were broken in the yard, thirty in the granary, and another thirty in the cow and ox barns.

Nothing unusual has happened on the estate. Everyone on the yard is quite healthy.

Since I am now in need of money, I respectfully request that, if possible, you send me approximately thirty-five silver rubles with this messenger.

Your most respectful Abraham Driedger.

797. Johann Cornies to District Office. 24 June 1847.
SAOR 89-1-1260/62.

To the worthy Molochnaia Mennonite District Office in Halbstadt,

In the fall of 1846, I bought a covered wagon from miller Isaak Braun in Lindenau to use on a trip to Odesa. I put my trust in him, but later discovered that he had cheated me. An axle had broken on my return trip from Odesa and the Khortitsa master blacksmith had welded it using inferior iron.

Since the axle had been shortened a little, I took the wagon to Braun for repairs and had other work done by Franz Klaassen, Rosenort, our local master blacksmith. With renewed confidence I now entrusted the wagon to my brother and son for a journey to Prussia. En route they encountered great difficulty when the axle in back and then the axle in front broke and had to be repaired. They also lost several wheel casings that had split apart, suggesting the kind of iron Klaassen must have used. Now my son has returned the wagon to me from Prussia with a certain Buran, again with a broken axle.

All this prompts me to make a formal complaint against Klaassen who pursues his own advantage by buying cheaper iron of lower quality than other blacksmiths. He deceives people from both inside and outside the district.

The District Office should force blacksmith Klaassen to pick up the wagon, replace the axles, and put new casings of high quality on all four wheels. His work must satisfy me completely. Finally it should force Klaassen to abandon his self-interest and conduct his trade more conscientiously.

798. Johann Cornies to Peter Froese. 24 June 1847. SAOR 89-1-1260/63.

Mr. Peter Froese in Tiegerweide, West Prussia.

Treasured Friend,

I have received your valued communication of 1 May together with a request from several brethren in faith about a [new] settlement near Vitebsk and Mogilev. You propose that further reports for those approved for settlement be sent directly to them. I think this is inadvisable. The government knows that I have been conducting these negotiations for some time and will deal with only one person designated for this purpose, not with many, or one after another. I must therefore keep you, my valued friend, as my only correspondent until this matter is concluded.

At the present time and in accordance with my honoured commission, I can have no direct dealings through letters received both from you and others wishing to emigrate. I took the occasion of the Director of the Tavrida State Domains Bureau's departure for St. Petersburg to have this entire matter raised again. He kindly promised to send me information from St. Petersburg privately because the Russian government had earlier already reached a decision to buy [other] private lands purchased for the settlement of Prussian Mennonites. His Highness, the Minister of State Domains, whom I had the honour to accompany through the Khortitsa villages last fall mentioned this settlement without prompting and asked me how far it had progressed from our side.

Meanwhile all this prompts me to ask you to prepare a list, by name, of everyone who wishes to emigrate, including the size of each family, the ages of its members, the value of their property, and the cash they would bring along to Russia. This would help me to work more effectively with our high authorities. Please send me this information as soon as you can. There is no sense in sending a deputation of emigrants before the land has been assigned.

I will, without delay, notify you about every development in this matter. I do this work gladly, with pleasure and to the limits of my ability, in order that I might, in every respect, be useful to my brethren in faith.

With honest intentions, I commend myself to you and our valued brethren there and remain, with respect, your faithful friend.

799. Johann Cornies to Johann Wall. 25 June 1847.
SAOR 89-1-1260/65.

Beloved Friend Johann Wall in Schoensee near Tiegenhoff,

I am only now in a position to answer your letter of 14 May that I received with great pleasure. I was away from home and could not do so earlier.

I still have vivid memories of your friendship and love that I enjoyed in your house twenty years ago. Were it not for the great distances and pressure of work, I would have come to Prussia long ago to renew our old friendship.

I can, for now, send you only a few details about the projected settlement of Prussian Mennonites in the guberniias of Mogilev and Vitebsk. I have been told by the Ministry that land must first be purchased in these guberniias.

When I was privileged to accompany His Highness, the Minister, through the Khortitsa villages in September last year, he asked me without prompting about the situation of the Prussian Mennonites and whether they wanted to settle in these guberniias. He planned to settle two hundred families there. I told him that, according to reports from my correspondent, Mennonites in Prussia had declared themselves willing to do so. First, however, they wanted to inspect the land and familiarize themselves with the conditions attached to it. The Department of Agriculture, for its part, had told me that the lands for settlement by Mennonites needed first to be bought, otherwise nothing further could be done. For this reason, I can do nothing more in this matter and await a decision.

Two days after receiving your letter and one from Peter Froese, Baron v. Rosen, Director of the Tavrida Domains Bureau, visited me on his journey to St. Petersburg. I took this opportunity to show him the letters from Prussia. Since I am not permitted to approach the Ministry directly before a decision is made in this matter, I asked the Director to take along a note from me to St. Petersburg and submit it to the Minister on what he thought was a favourable occasion. The Baron promised he would and notify me from St. Petersburg accordingly. Should I hear anything further from Baron v. Rosen in this connection, I will not neglect to send correspondent Peter Froese news for those interested in emigration.

A few days ago I received a letter from the Crimea, asking me to find bidders for land purchases on the peninsula. The land in question, located on a level part of the peninsula, is said to be very large. I know nothing about its quality, only that it is twenty-five verstas from the city of Karasubasar, on the Karasu River.

We anticipate a splendid grain harvest, just like last year, but grass is sparse. Indeed, the crop of hay will be too small to meet our needs. Should you meet my son, please give him my greetings and tell him that everyone at home is healthy, praise God.

With sincere, heartfelt greetings to you and your dear family, I will continue to remember you with esteem, your true friend Johann Cornies.

800. Johann Cornies to Traugott Blueher. 29 June 1847.
SAOR 89-1-1260/67.

Esteemed Mr. Blueher,

I write this letter at the same time as the dispatch of my wool, some 1,364 puds and fourteen funt net weight. It is packed in 145 linen sacks and transported on forty-seven carts. I enclose the original of the contract concluded with the carter, Mikhail Semenov and his associates, as well as a copy of the bill of lading. Please accept this wool on consignment, as in the past, and kindly pay the carters what remains of the freight charges of 1,423 rubles, seventy-six and three-quarter kopeks.

For the rest, I count on your many years of experience in the business to carry out this matter as you find best. May the Lord grant his blessing. The wool is quite clean of fodder, and I have had the sweat washed out as well as I can. Please do not have it washed again, only for this year, but sell it as it is. As in the past, the balls from Tashchenak are marked with a "T." All balls containing lambswool are marked "#."

I was unable to make any wool purchases on your account at the price you set. The wool for which you said we might bid up to twenty-one rubles was sold for twenty-nine and one-quarter rubles. Very ordinary washed wool sold for twenty-two rubles per pud at the start. By now buyers are paying twenty-seven rubles. Purchasers of this wool are largely Russians. Foreigners seem to be more hesitant and have concluded fewer large transactions in our locality. The largest proportion of wool, especially from our settlements, is shipped to Romen where it is sold on consignment.

Your remittance of two thousand silver rubles arrived in good order on 26 June. Many thanks for your kindness in carrying out last year's wool business. I am entirely satisfied. I will not delay in sending you the receipt for the remainder of the money owing.

The harvesting of grain in our villages has already begun and is very promising, but the hay crop is mediocre. An unusually powerful hailstorm with heavy showers damaged the fields and gardens throughout our area, although not too much in our villages. Quite a few head of livestock in several Russian villages were killed and many houses and mills were knocked over.

I earnestly commend myself to you and your family and greet all of you in friendship, as your constant and faithful friend and servant, Johann Cornies.

P.S. I received your communication of 13 June just now, after this letter was completed. I must repeat that, despite our best efforts, we were unable to conclude the purchase of wool for you because, as mentioned, the prices for this kind of wool far exceeded the maximum you were willing to pay.

Esteemed Friend, the loss of my life's partner, with whom I was united for many years, has shattered me. I feel bowed down by the resulting emptiness and at my advanced age. Still, it was God's will and I do not want to complain. Yesterday, I received a letter from my son in Hamburg. He still wants to visit the Rhine before returning back home by way of West Prussia. The few of us left at home are in the best of health, God be praised. May the Lord grant you and your dear ones equally good health.

Again commending myself with an honest heart, the above.

801. Johann Cornies to Jacob Klaassen. 2 July 1847.
SAOR 89-1-1260/68v.

Master carpenter Klaassen,
The following are necessary to complete the dwelling house on the Crown Model Plantation:

1. Fittings to be attached around two gable windows;
2. Appropriate hinges for both house doors;
3. Four sash windows, with shutters and mountings;
4. Quarter rounds to be nailed to six window frames;
5. Screws for ten sets of shutters;
6. Attachments, specifically clasps and storm hooks, for all window frames on the house and gable;
7. Bolts for the shutters to be bolted from the outside;
8. Four latches trimmed on the four inside doors that open outwards;
9. Latches are still missing on several doors;
10. Improvements to one inside door, one window shutter, and the fittings around several windows.

Please see to it that these items are available and then make arrangements to have the painting done.

802. Johann Cornies to Fletnitzer. 6 July 1847. SAOR 89-1-1260/69v.

Mr. Provost Fletnitzer in Odesa,
I write as someone who supports the general improvement of our school system, to ask that you send us a further eighteen copies of the earlier edition of the wall-primers you received earlier, by August if possible. We will naturally pay promptly once we hear from you.
With honest esteem, I remain your most respectful servant, Johann Cornies.

803. Evgenii F. Hahn to Johann Cornies. 8 July 1847.
SAOR 89-1-889/101.

I plan to leave for the Molochnaia sometime this week and should reach you by Sunday at the latest. Unless I hear otherwise from you en route, I will probably go to Prishib and decide on my further route from there. Although I will spend little time in the Molochnaia villages this time, there are many matters I need to discuss with you before making my way to visit Mr. von Stempel's Jews.

I will also visit the Swedish settlers at Bereslav, but only on my return journey once I have conferred with you. Perhaps you will even accompany me there.

Yours truly, E. v. Hahn.

804. Guardianship Committee to the Molochnaia Mennonite District Office. 12 July 1847. SAOR 89-1-1271/173.

This is in response to the grievance of Johann Cornies, Mennonite in Ohrloff village, against Colonel Kuteinikov for refusing to pay him the 985 rubles owing him for Spanish sheep he bought to teach two youths sheep breeding. The Guardianship Committee has informed the general administration of the Don Host regarding this matter and asked it to collect this sum from Colonel Kuteinikov.

The army administration has provided the Guardianship Committee with Major General Kuteinikov's declaration, in which he declares:

1. His two boys really did learn sheep breeding from the Mennonite Cornies for 480 rubles. The Don estate paid Cornies 230 rubles. In October 1841, Kuteinikov himself paid the remaining 250 rubles to the secretary, surname unknown, whom Cornies had sent for this purpose. After this payment, Kuteinikov owes Cornies absolutely nothing, and believes, on the contrary, that he could well make demands of Cornies because the two boys, who had learned sheep breeding there, worked in Cornies's institutions for a further one and one-half years.

2. In 1838, Kuteinikoff bought sheep from the Mennonite Cornies, and sent Corporal Sulin to fetch them. At the time he paid Cornies the entire sum agreed upon. When Sulin fetched the sheep, Cornies persuaded him to buy a further number of sheep for 452 rubles. For these sheep, Kuteinikov paid forty half Imperials at twenty-one rubles for these sheep, sent through Sulin. In sum, he declares that he owes Cornies nothing more and finds the latter's demands completely unfounded.

The Guardianship Committee informs the District Office that it should make this declaration known to the Mennonite Johann Cornies. It should then report Cornies's answer to the Committee, in order that the matter might be pursued further here, or discontinued.

The original was signed by Committee member Evdokimov, Secretary Loginov.

Identical to the original, Assistant District Secretary Neufeld.

805. Evgenii F. Hahn to Johann Cornies. N.d. [July 1847.] SAOR 89-1-889/97.

I arrived in Prishib today, where I intend to stay until Sunday noon. Then, after the morning church service, I will come to see you. Please let me know where we can meet.

After completing my other business, I can stay with you until I leave for Odesa. You very well know what pleasure this will give me.

We will probably inspect the Berdiansk and Mariupol people together. Yours truly, E. v. Hahn.

806. Johann Siemens to Johann Cornies. 16 July 1847. SAOR 89-1-1271/169.

Valued Friend,

In response to your esteemed communication of 7 July, I hasten to report that the Forester, Staff Captain Graff, arrived here last Saturday, 12 July, on his return trip from Ekaterinoslav. At his request Society member Epp and I accompanied him to Khortitsa Island where we inspected the forests by moonlight. The forester continued his journey from here. He was in a great rush because of news in Ekaterinoslav that General Levshin would arrive at Forester Graff's home in [Novotroitzk] on 15 July. Much to my regret, the forester, because his visit was short and badly timed, gave us few instructions about the management of natural forests. He promised to come back for several days in August. On that occasion, he will instruct us about how to tidy up the woods and prune the trees. We have already cut off branches close to the trunks.

I can further report that His Excellency Fabre, the recently appointed Governor of Ekaterinoslav, was kind enough to make his way through our settlement on his inspection tour of the guberniia. Towards evening on Saturday, 5 July, I welcomed His Excellency in Einlage. From there we drove to Khortitsa, where the Governor spent the night at my house. He explained that during his last visit to St. Petersburg, His Highness, the Minister of State Domains Kiselev, had directed him to inspect the settlements in the vicinity after his appointment.

We inspected Khortitsa Island in great detail on Sunday, from early morning until noon, driving around its entire circumference as the governor wished. At his request, I am having a detailed map of the island prepared to give to him. On the trip to the island, the governor also visited the community plantation. After the midday meal at my home, we viewed the community sheepfarms in Gruenfeld and Schönfeld before moving on to the posting station at Neuenburg. The governor expressed his great satisfaction about everything he had seen in our area.

With a friendly greeting, I remain your respectful friend, Johann Siemens.

807. Johann Siemens to Johann Cornies. 16 July 1847. SAOR 89-1-1271/170.

Esteemed Friend,

The former secretary Gerhard Penner has sold his house in Einlage, and is now shelterless and in a very difficult situation in other ways. In my opinion it would be advisable to declare the sale invalid and reverse it. I would respectfully request that you kindly advise me in this regard as soon possible.

With esteem, I remain your respectful friend, Johann Siemens.

808. Johann Cornies to Tavrida State Domains Bureau. 19 July 1847. SAOR 89-1-1260/71.

To the Tavrida Bureau of State Domains,

I obediently enclose the four records the Bureau required by 1 July for the crown apprentices located here, specifically for 1. practical agriculture, 2. tree culture, 3. the Crown Model Plantation, and 4. to learn the professional trades.

Let me add that apprentices number seven, eight, and fifteen on the Crown Plantation and apprentice number two working with master blacksmith Heinrich Wiens in Blumenort were returned to their villages because of their complete lack of common sense and interest. Every effort to help them has been in vain. The Berdiansk District Chief has been informed accordingly and asked to select others in their place.

809. Jacob Bartsch to Johann Cornies. 23 July 1847.
SAOR 89-1-1271/174.

Esteemed Friend, Johann Cornies,

I received your valued communication of 24 June with the enclosed twenty-eight silver rubles from Wiebe only on 21 July because the District Office had received notice of it from the Post Office only on 17 July.

My respectful thanks for the enclosed information.

Our local community sheep wool has not yet been sold. The price offered me casually at the wool market in Ekaterinoslav was identical to the price you received for your wool, thirty-five rubles per pud. I would have agreed to this price had the merchant not immediately expressed second thoughts about it, insisting on first inspecting the wool within a time period that has long since passed. As a result, the District Office is in financial trouble. Necessary expenditures have to be made, but there is no money in the treasury.

I would respectfully request your advice. Should the District Office secure a loan to cover expenses that are absolutely necessary, or sell the wool at the first opportunity, even if the price is low?

Anticipating your judgment, I remain, with esteem, your respectful Jacob Bartsch.

810. Johann Siemens to Johann Cornies. 23 July 1847.
SAOR 89-1-1271/175.

Esteemed Friend,

We do not have any firm regulations in this district regarding the hiring of servants. They have always been hired as needed. The Society has now decided to introduce rules regulating such appointments that are identical to those existing in the Molochnaia Mennonite District.

I would therefore respectfully ask you inform me in detail about such rules in your district.

With a hearty greeting, your honest friend, Johann Siemens.

P.S. Let me also inform you about church teachers [preachers] who have been disciplined. After his punishment, Jacob Dyck, Neuosterwick, has officiated at a marriage ceremony and preached one sermon. Jacob Wienz, Kronsthal, has not put in an appearance in church since that time. Franz Wiens, Rosenthal, on the other hand, still takes his place as preacher in church every Sunday but has not preached.

811. District Office to Johann Cornies. 23 July 1847.
SAOR 89-1-1271/172.

To the esteemed Johann Cornies in Ohrloff,

The District Office sends you the enclosed copy of the Guardianship Committee for Foreign Settlers' Directive No. 4194, dated 12 July 1847. It is in reference to your demands of Colonel, now Major General, Kuteinikov. The District Office has been instructed to provide an answer in the form of a report on this matter to the Guardianship Committee as soon as possible.

812. K. Fletnitzer to Johann Cornies. 29 July 1847.
SAOR 89-1-1271/209.

Mr. Johann Cornies, Esquire, Ohrloff.
Highly valued Sir,

On 6 of July you did me the honour of sending me a friendly communication, expressing a wish to purchase another eighteen complete copies of the same wall-primer that you purchased from me earlier. The wall-primers were to reach you, if possible, with a secure opportunity by this coming August.

It gives me great pleasure to fulfil your wishes. I have today applied to Consistorial Counsellor Foell, Hochstadt, in this regard. He will look after this matter.

The price is what it was before, ten rubles per copy. I would ask you, very esteemed Mr. Cornies, to send notice of the receipt of these copies directly to the Consistorial Counsellor, but to have the money of 180 rubles sent to me.

How are you managing in the midst of your extremely busy life? I would so much like to spend several weeks with you on the Molochnaia again.

My wife and I send you and your dear spouse hearty greetings. I would also ask you to extend my greetings to all of my treasured friends, Brother Leonhardt Fast, Klassen, and everyone who remembers me with love, including Riediger, Wiebe, etc. May the Lord keep you and your whole house well and bless you richly in body and in soul. May Jesus bless you and all of us.

With honest love and respect, I have the honour to remain your most respectful servant, K. Fletnitzer.

[Note added in another hand]

The office keys are missing from ten copies of the wall-primer. There are only forty-eight tablets in one copy, although there should be fifty-seven, and one tablet is unusable. On another copy, the tablets are damaged along the edges.

813. Johann Cornies to Jacob Klaassen. 31 July 1847. SAOR 89-1-1260/72.

To Master Carpenter J. Klaassen in the tradesmen's village of Halbstadt,

According to Plantation Overseer Sudermann's report of 23 July, the following items are needed to complete the construction:

1. Fittings for two pairs of gable windows;
2. Ten sliding bars for ten pairs of windows;
3. Four basement windows with shutters, together with the required hardware;
4. The press bar shortened on four door latches;
5. Attachments to fasten ten pairs of window shutters from outside;
6. One inside door and one window fitting to be improved;
7. Painting.

814. Johann Cornies to District Office. 4 August 1847. SAOR 89-1-1260/73.

To the highly esteemed Molochnaia Mennonite District Office in Halbstadt,

In response to your communication No. 3499 of 23 July 1847, including a copy of directive No. 4194 from the Guardianship Committee regarding my demands of Major General Kuteinikov, I have the honour to submit this declaration together with four copies of the covering documents. [Documents not extent.]

815. Contract between Johann Cornies and Jacob Stobbe. 6 August 1847. SAOR 89-1-1295/1.

On 6 August 1847, the Society Chairman for the local district made the following agreement with master carpenter Jacob Stobbe, Blumenort:

Stobbe undertakes to manufacture fifty ploughs of the same construction as the Witte model plough he has been given, on the following conditions:

a) The ploughs will be of good, durable, well-dried young oak wood. Wherever necessary, these ploughs should be worked better and made stronger [than the model plough], especially the ploughing beam itself.

b) The same applies to the iron. Careful attention must be given to the source from which this is bought.

c) Every plough must have an appropriate ordinary blade, a tongue to which horses will be harnessed, a setting device, and a brake.

d) Instead of the customary chain on a German plough, Stobbe is obligated to provide good, strong double straps of well-turned leather.

e) It is not considered necessary to have the ploughs painted, but Stobbe is obligated to brush tar once over all parts in an orderly fashion.

f) Each time Stobbe has ten ploughs ready, he will give notice and they will be tested on the spot in Blumenort in the presence of several Jews. Stobbe will provide the harnessed team for this procedure. If they pass muster, the ploughs will be picked up after the issuance of a receipt.

g) Ploughs found to be unacceptable in any regard will be returned to Stobbe for improvement, especially if the wood or iron work is not up to standard or the ploughs do not plough well.

h) The fifty ploughs must be ready by 15 September 1847, or by 20 September at the latest.

2. Payment for each of these ploughs has been agreed upon with master Stobbe at ten silver rubles apiece. He has received 250 silver rubles of this sum at the time of the signing of the contract and the final 250 silver rubles when the ploughs are delivered.

816. Contract between Johann Sukkau and Johann Cornies. N.d. [August 1847.] SAOR 89-1-1295/3.

I, Johann Sukkau, the undersigned inhabitant of the Molochnaia Mennonite village of Blumenort, hereby attest that I have been called upon by the Molochnaia Mennonite Society Chairman to test, on a cultivated field, all fifty of the Witte crown model ploughs manufactured by the master carpenter, Mennonite Jacob Stobbe for the use of Jewish settlements in Aleksandrov District. I can, in truth, testify that all of these implements plough sufficiently easily and well and will answer entirely to their purpose if those handling them know how to use the plough and how to set a Little Russian plough properly.

817. Heinrich Cornies to Johann Cornies. 7 August 1847. SAOR 89-1-1271/191.

On Tuesday, 5 August, I was returning from Novomoskovsk with a herd of twenty horses, when the local Elder stopped me up in Bolshoi Tokmak and demanded that I pay for damage supposedly done to the Tokmak grain fields by our herd the previous night. I am personally completely convinced that we did no damage. The herd spent the night at the town of Orekhov and, even after I explained this to the Elder, he demanded a silver ruble as passage money. He told me that a Chumak had informed him that he had been charged one silver ruble of passage money on our steppe.

This assertion by the Elder is entirely without foundation, since we have never demanded passage money from travelling Chumaks. I would therefore request that the Elder be required to declare which Chumaks were charged passage money on our steppe and who, by name, made the demand. Only in this way might we punish this person. In the contrary case, the Elder should be legally punished for such a false accusation. Administrator Heinrich Cornies, Iushanle estate.

818. Johann Cornies to Jacob Wiebe. 9 August 1847. SAOR 89-1-1260/73v.

Dear friend,

I received your letter of 30 July informing me that you would like to buy a well-situated plot, with houses, near the market, and were requesting a loan of two thousand silver rubles for this purpose. As lucrative as this advantageous offer might be for you, and as heartily as I wish you and others good progress in this undertaking on behalf of our brethren in Berdiansk, I still cannot be of service to you in this way. As almost everyone knows, in order to support professional tradesmen in our district, I make loans of money to no one outside of our district, but restrict them to persons in our own district and then not for years, but only for three months, possibly four. Duty and principle demand this. I trust you will not think ill of me and do justice to my principles which I feel obligated to uphold.

With a friendly greeting, I remain your willing friend, Johann Cornies.

P.S. Please give my greetings to Mr. Wolf. Tell him that I have received his letter but regret that I cannot support the introduction of something positive, even desirable, were it to damage a firm regulation of a different nature.

819. Johann Cornies to Friedrich Werner. 12 August 1847. SAOR 89-1-1260/75.

Dear Werner,

Recently I had another opportunity to become acquainted with the business matters the District Secretary for the Swedish District has been dealing with. I have concluded that this is not a suitable position for you if you wish to have a wider range of duties. In my opinion, it is of even less consequence than the position you presently occupy in Neuhoffnung. I can therefore not advise you to take it.

I would like to help you in other ways should a suitable position become open for you.

Constantly wishing you the best, Johann Cornies.

820. Evgenii F. Hahn to Johann Cornies. 17 August 1847. SAOR 89-1-889/102.

Best of friends,

It would like to get the secure prizes from the Imperial Agricultural Association for Claassen and the Grunau gardener. They would consist of a hundred silver rubles for the first and fifty silver rubles for the second. I cannot make such a submission myself as Vice-President of the Association and as a colonial administrator. You, however, as a member of the Learned Committee and as Chairman of the Molochnaia Mennonite Society, could make such an application, outlining the conditions that earlier prevailed in the Grunau Community Garden and the improvements since made by Claassen and the gardener, whose name escapes me. This submission could be written in German, addressed to the Imperial Agricultural Association, and sent to me. Describe the nurseries as they were earlier and as they are now in order that one might justifiably conclude that they have developed into a model plantation, which is certainly true.

I would also urgently ask you to let me know whether you might have a Mennonite like Goertz in mind for the Lviv settlement. A request in this regard has been made by a local but I would in all cases prefer a Mennonite like Goertz, and will await your answer.

Yours truly, E. v. Hahn.

821. Alexander Voth to Johann Cornies. 18 August 1847. SAOR 89-1-1271/194.

Esteemed Mr. Cornies,

In my present critical situation, I take the liberty to saddle you with a request in the firm conviction that it will not arouse your anger. Although I have no father and no one else to support me with advice, I am aware of your great influence. You alone can help me in working towards my goal. Specifically, I would like to be entirely released from our settlements. This would put me in a position to remove all of my mother's worries and debts.

Since I am leaving behind a family in difficult circumstances, you would show me great benevolence by carrying out this request for a man you called to Russia. At this moment, I urgently need a valid pass until the time when I would be granted my release. This would enable me to overcome some of my worries.

By fulfilling this request, you, esteemed Mr. Cornies, would fill me with unending thankfulness, which I express in advance and sign myself as your most respectful Alexander Voth. Kharkiv, 18 August 1847.

[Marked] Answered by District Chairman, 27 August 1847: "He will not receive a pass."

822. Johann Cornies to Evgenii F. Hahn. 20 August 1847. SAOR 89-1-1260/77.

Yr. Excellency,

I respectfully ask that five copies of the first year's issues of the *Unterhaltungsblatt* be sent to me as well as the same number of copies published for the second year, up to the present time. These copies are intended for the Community of Brethren in Sarepta. With my encouragement, a number of its inhabitants there have started to occupy themselves with agriculture. I will, upon receipt of an invoice, happily cover the costs.

With exceptional esteem I remain with respect, your Excellency's most devoted servant, Johann Cornies.

823. District Office to Johann Cornies. 20 August 1847. SAOR 89-1-1271/195.

To honourable Johann Cornies in Ohrloff,

In response to your report regarding the poor craftsmanship evidenced in his work for you, Rosenort master blacksmith Franz Klaassen was required to appear in the District Office on 5 July. He was there confronted with the mediocre quality of his work and told to conduct his profession with greater care and without selfish interests. Specifically, he was ordered to fetch your damaged wagon from you and return it to you in good condition by 12 August.

In response to repeated orders from the District Office, the Mayor's Office in Rosenort village reported that the master blacksmith in question had not yet kept his promise. He claims that he possesses no good iron with which to repair your wagon or, indeed, to complete any blacksmith work. He intends, for this reason, to travel to the city of Rostov to purchase good iron. Thereupon he will immediately repair your wagon.

The local District Office informs you of this matter and directs you, at the appropriate time, to send in a report as to whether the above-mentioned master blacksmith has carried out his promise. District Chairman Toews.

824. Johann Cornies to Hermann Sudermann and Peter Fast. 20 August 1847. SAOR 89-1-1260/77v.

To Overseer Sudermann and Gardener Fast at the Crown Model Plantation,

Given the commission granted me by our highest administration, the confidence it has placed in me, and the government's humane intentions, I am obligated to do everything in my power to remedy the wrongs committed when the government's good intentions and interests appear to have been prejudiced or endangered.

On my recent inspection trip through the Crown Model Plantation, I found that crown apprentices lived under extremely oppressive conditions. The food they were required to cook was so badly prepared and filthy as to endanger their health. Their clothes were extremely shabby, infrequently provided, and dirty. Nor did they have boots. Not wanting to show themselves to me in this state, I found several of them slinking shyly away into the corners of their rooms, barefoot, discouraged and reluctant to show themselves to me. I concluded that they had not been encouraged to maintain themselves in decency and order, but had simply been left to themselves.

This attitude does not simply deny the government's intentions, but causes the apprentices to develop into flawed human beings. With my responsibility as Head Overseer, I must now deal with this situation. Until now, I have cherished the view that both of you, as overseer and as gardener of the plantation, were enlivened by better, more just, and philanthropic intentions. I am now convinced of your excessive arrogance, lack of consideration and efforts to enrich yourselves at the expense of the apprentices' food and clothing.

You have, after all, been granted considerable and sufficient sums for good food and clothing. I can scarcely avoid feeling mistrust of you as overseer and gardener. How can such greed exist in people who belong to the brotherhood of the Christian community? Even if you do not fear God, you should be clever enough to comprehend that, when government officials visit, your positions as overseer or gardener will eventually end or even that wrongs of this kind will be revealed, shortly or over a longer period of time. Such behaviour would redound to the shame of our whole Mennonite community and especially to my own administration.

To improve every apprentice's existence with respect to food and clothing as quickly as possible, I demand information about what pieces of clothing, from head to foot, is possessed by every apprentice by name. I further demand that this information be the absolute truth. Also, why are the apprentices required to prepare their own meals and do their own cooking? What foods and means of nutrition do they receive each week? Do they get exactly the same bread, which is the main concern, that the overseer and gardener have on their own tables? Also, who bakes it?

I expect an answer to these demands by Saturday, 23 August.

825. Molochnaia Agricultural Society Journal Entries. 20 August 1847. SAOR 89-1-1250/3-11v.[6]

• Khortitsa Society to report by 15 October whether all number posts have been securely erected in all plantations in Khortitsa District.

---

6 Most entries in the personal correspondence journal are copies of letters sent and received. However, for 1847–8 there are also a series of abbreviated journal entries, beginning with this document. A selection of these abbreviated entries is reproduced in the following pages.

• Guardianship Committee: The Committee might send the expense money for travelling back and forth to the Swedish settlements, estimated for two horses covering 462 verstas from the local village of Muensterberg to Schlangendorf village.

• To the District Office in Halbstadt, request to have inquiries made whether the Alexanderwohl village community agrees with Benjamin Unruh's wishes to be transported to the Bessarabian village of Hoffnungsthal and whether or not they are prepared to release him. In the latter case, a submission should be made to the Guardianship Committee and the Society informed of the results.

• Tiegenhagen: Orders are to report immediately whether the Gross Tokmak crown apprentice Konstantin Smechka, who was released by Gerhard Giesbrecht, is back in service with Giesbrecht.

826. Daniel Janzen to Johann Cornies. 24 August 1847. SAOR 89-1-1271/203.

Report to Mr. Chairman in Ohrloff,

I intend to open the school again shortly. However, since you will presumably have some new rules of conduct for us, I would like to know what they are. I had originally intended to open the daily school on 1 September, but it seems almost impossible to me that people would be able to manage without the help of their children by then. I think we should wait at least another week before opening the school. Still, I leave it to you and to the Mayor, who intends to visit you, to determine how I might deal with this matter. Schoolteacher Daniel Janzen, Hutterthal.

827. Molochnaia Agricultural Society Journal Entries. 25 August 1847. SAOR 89-1-1250/3-11v.

• Schoensee: The 23 August report about applications for passes for Russian servants by this Mayor's Office should be made to the required authority and this Society also notified of the results.

• Fischau: The sample outline, noting conditions in village "N" sent on 12 August by the Chairman of this Society should be remitted without delay.

• Guardianship Committee: Inquiry whether the Committee can approve the Josephsthal settler Johann Schroeder for a lease to sell beer in Kronsgarten village for ten years at an annual fee of one hundred silver rubles.

• Guardianship Committee: Submission for examination of the contract concluded between the Khortitsa District Office and Kronsgarten resident Heinrich Plenert to take over the lease to sell brandy between 1 September 1847 and 1 January 1849 is hereby submitted for examination, with the request that, after examination, it should be sent to the Khortitsa District Office as a directive and also that I am notified about the decision and resolution.

• Tiegenhagen: Records must be completed and sent back to this Society about keeping of accounts, about ploughing of topsoil, and of threshing tests. Householder Jacob Martens was not included.

828. Johann Cornies to Christian Klaassen. 27 August 1847. SAOR 89-1-1260/79v.

To Christian Klaassen, Grunau village, member of the Society for the Advancement of Forest-Tree and Orchard Cultivation, Sericulture, and Viticulture in Mariupol Colonist District,

In reply to a directive that I have received, I find it necessary to request that, as soon as it is possible, you send me detailed information about the following questions:

1. What size, in desiatinas, is the community plantation located at Grunau and in what year was the plantation founded?
2. For how long did it stumble along without making any progress? Since when has purposeful and speedier progress been made?
3. How many standing fruit trees of all varieties does it have and how many forest trees?
4. How many improved fruit saplings are there in nurseries, how many unimproved ones, and how many seedlings?
5. How many forest trees were transplanted into nurseries and how many seedlings are there in seedbeds?
6. How many hedges, bushes, and shrubs of all varieties are there?
7. How much of the land, in desiatinas, has been planted and how much is still unused, waiting for planting?
8. How many trees were sold and given away to settlers in the last two years? What number of trees are needed for dispersal from the plantation this year?

9. How many forest-tree plantations are there at the individual villages and how many forest trees and mulberry trees are there in each of these?

10. When were these forest-tree plantations founded and how well are the trees generally growing in them?

11. How many forest-tree plantations will still be laid out at villages and how soon is this to be carried out?

12. For how many years has the current gardener overseen the Grunau community plantation? What is his name, to what class does he belong, and where is he registered?

13. For how many years have you overseen and provided leadership for the community plantation and the forest-tree plantations in individual villages?

I would like to receive the most accurate information you can give me regarding all of these points as soon as possible. Please include your own remarks. Johann Cornies.

829. Molochnaia Agricultural Society Journal Entries. 27 August 1847. SAOR 89-1-1250/3-11v.

• Tiegerweide: The Mayor's Office is required to send the local householder Gerhard Rempel to the community sheepfarm because he was negligent when he forwarded the Society's directive about receiving His Excellency, the President of the Guardianship Committee, on 1 September. He must complete one day of punitive work on the sheepfarm. The Society should be notified when this work has been completed.

• Overseer Wall, on the community sheepfarm, must report whether Rempel from Tiegerweide completed the punitive work assigned to him.

830. Molochnaia Agricultural Society Journal Entries. 6 September 1847. SAOR 89-1-1250/3-11v.

• Mennonite Administrative Office in Berdiansk: Two petitions from Fuerstenau villager Peter Regehr, now resident in Berdiansk, are enclosed, one about his neighbour, Khortitsa Mennonite Johann Eidzen, the other about another Khortitsa Mennonite Bahnmann, now resident in Berdiansk. Regehr complains that they are not paying him the money he is owed. The Office is ordered to take up Regehr's complaints as it is obligated to do, to investigate them according to the law, and to report the results in detail to this Society.

• Hutterthal: Money still owing on fences must be collected from all inhabitants of this village and sent to me without fail by 15 October.

831. Cornelius Wedel to Johann Cornies. 8 September 1847. SAOR 89-1-1271/204.

Esteemed Sir,

I received your letter of 6 August with questions in regard to a grave monument and railings. I can report that no monuments of the shape and measurements you mentioned are available at the present time. They must be ordered.

I have spoken with the administrator of the local ironworks about this matter. He told me that since moulds of the format desired do not exist, they will first have to be created. Moreover the above work cannot proceed until an advance payment is made and a drawing for the design received. Should the monument be made the way poured monuments are usually fabricated here, fired from the bottom using a moulding-box, or should it be done otherwise? The price on site is six rubles per pud.

At present, we have no grave railings in stock and they too must be ordered. The most popular railings are similar to those shown on the enclosed drawing [not extant]. They cost from sixty to sixty-five silver rubles. Should you, however, desire to have railings of a different format, drawings would likewise have to be made.

I enclose my old pass, with the respectful request that you obtain a new one for me. I had intended to come by myself, but since pressing business did not permit, I cherish the hope that you would not refuse me your help. I also request that my two children, namely Heinrich and Cornelius, who attend school locally and are missing their pass, be written into the new pass.

The cholera that ran rampant here and has killed many local people, is now rarer.

Together with a greeting, your servant, Cornelius Wedel. Lugansk Foundry.

832. Peter Keppen to Johann Cornies. Sent St. Petersburg, 8 September 1847. SAOR 89-1-1294/2.

Beloved friend, I received your valued communication of 11 August and will submit it to the Scientific Academy, as you request, and send you its conclusions.

Permit me only to tell you that sometime this autumn, a Mr. Riesenkampf will approach you with a few lines from me. I commend this man to you since he is the brother of the very respected local Doctor v. Rauch, Imperial Physician who manages the doctor's estate in Kherson Guberniia. It is Mr. v. Rauch's intention to buy five hundred ewes directly from you or on your recommendation. I would be much obliged to you for help in this matter. I'm very grateful for any help you can give Riesenkampf in this connection. Please keep me fully informed.

With honest devotion, your Keppen.

833. Evgenii F. Hahn to Johann Cornies. 8 September 1847. SAOR 89-1-889/103.

Best of friends, you asked me for five copies of our newspaper for Sarepta. The supply of last year's issues is almost gone, but I can send you two copies free of charge. I also enclose five copies for the current year, likewise gratis from Dr. Sonderegger for your Sarepta friends. The latter encloses a communication commending himself to the Sarepta community that you might forward with the newspapers. If you wish, we could in future send along five copies of the newspapers directly to Sarepta.

It is admirable and a pleasant surprise that the Sarepta German settlers assume they will want 143 copies. Settlers in this area are hardly interested in the newspaper. No one has subscribed and the government refuses further expenditures to cover costs. Starting this year, I therefore intend to charge every community one and a half silver rubles for the three copies provided to it.

Yours truly, E. v. Hahn.

834. Molochnaia Agricultural Society Journal Entries. 9 September 1847. SAOR 89-1-1250/3-11v.

• Gnadenfeld: You should question your local householder, W. Lange, about the kind of witnesses Lange can cite to confirm that two Nogais from Argakle, Mambedali Deberdijev and Tukei Dyberdijev, still owe him twenty-eight rubles, two and a half kopeks that were not registered as well as the properly registered sheep debt. Lange's declaration should be reported to the Society immediately.

835. Phillip Wiebe to Doehring. 10 September 1847.
SAOR 89-1-1260/81.

Highly valued Mr. Doehring,

According to inquiries made by my father-in-law to Messrs. Blueher and Niederstaedter, the former thinks that winter wheat as well as winter barley should grow well at Sarepta. For this reason, I enclose two packages, one of winter wheat marked Litt. "A," and one of winter barley marked Litt. "B." They should be distributed to your brethren in your community who are most interested in agriculture. You might, as a test, sow this seed on cleared and well-prepared soil immediately upon its receipt, provided the weather allows. A like quantity of each variety, for the same purpose, will follow with the next mail. Father will be very interested in the results and requests information in this regard.

Along with the above, my father-in-law sends you some mulberry seed, and requests that half of it be sown now, in autumn, and the other half next spring. You have some of the instructions, and Mr. Blueher will give you the rest. This dear friend requested that these shipments, in particular, be made.

As your people departed yesterday to stay with master tradesmen on the Molochnaia they seemed to be healthy and of good cheer. More next time.

With hearty greetings from Father to you and all dear brethren of his acquaintance, I remain, most honestly, your respectful friend, Phillip Wiebe.

836. Molochnaia Agricultural Society Journal Entries. 11 September 1847. SAOR 89-1-1250/3-11v.

• To the esteemed church teacher in the Margenau congregation: The esteemed church leadership is requested to exercise its spiritual influence with the Poetker couple in Landskrone and to seriously seek to bring about a reconciliation between this married couple. An early circumstantial report to the Society is requested soon.

837. Molochnaia Agricultural Society Journal Entries. 12 September 1847. SAOR 89-1-1250/3-11v

• Pastwa: The Mayor's Office should inform local householder No. 13 that it cannot pay attention to his complaints in connection with his actions towards the servant girl Efrosinia Raikova and the way he treated her. Instead, he must definitely be forbidden to keep any Russian servants and he should be ordered to appear in the Mayor's Office at the same time as the servant girl, so that they can be admonished immediately. The results should be reported by the Mayor's Office.

838. Molochnaia Agricultural Society Journal Entries. 13 September 1847. SAOR 89-1-1250/3-11v.

• Khortitsa District Office: You are hereby commissioned to report to the Society about the three former church teachers who were sentenced to community work because they opposed community order. Have they been made responsible for obligations to perform travel service and were they put on an equal footing with the other householders?

839. Johann Cornies to Carl Stempel. 15 September 1847. SAOR 89-1-1260/82.

Most esteemed Mr. v. Stempel,

A payment of 250 silver rubles is needed as a down payment for the ploughs which I contracted to have built here. They were supposed to be ready by 20 September. This I reported to Yr. Honour in my communication No. 1161 of 6 August, with a request that the down payment be sent to me as soon as possible. Since there was no response, I have given the master tradesman a temporary advance from my own money to buy the necessary wood. The most unfortunate part is that, despite great efforts that have been made in completing these ploughs, not all will be finished by 20 September. I have encouraged the master tradesman to do what he can to complete the ploughs quickly. I have assured him that, if need be, he will get the full payment for the ploughs from me as well. I would therefore respectfully ask, esteemed Inspector, that you send me the down payment as soon as possible. I will notify you promptly when the ploughs are ready.

With exceptional esteem and constant respect, your honest servant, Johann Cornies.

840. Molochnaia Agricultural Society Journal Entries. 16 September 1847. SAOR 89-1-1250/3-11v.

• All Village Offices: By 4 October 1847 at the latest, all offices should send in their records about community potatoes and cleaned flax for the year 1847, completed as accurately as possible.

• Pastwa: you are ordered to send the Society your record book of forest-tree plantings as soon as possible.

• Pordenau likewise.

841. Carl Stempel to Johann Cornies. 18 September 1847. SAOR 89-1-1271/212.

Most esteemed Mr. Cornies,

My heartfelt thanks to you for paying down 250 silver rubles to the master craftsman who has been manufacturing the ploughs. I wanted to send all the money at one time and, for this reason, did not send you the 250 silver rubles you asked for in your valued request of 6 August. I have not yet, however, received the money I still need to pay for the ploughs of the Jews. I had only 250 silver rubles to send you at the beginning, esteemed Mr. Cornies, but with a promise that I would not neglect to send you the last 250 silver rubles as soon as the ploughs were completed.

When you were last here, you kindly mentioned that you would advance money to these people, should that be necessary. This is the reason why I did not hurry with this matter.

With exceptional esteem and constant respect, your honest servant Carl Stempel.

Grunau settlement, 18 September 1847.

842. Molochnaia Agricultural Society Journal Entries. 18 September 1847. SAOR 89-1-1250/3-11v.

• Ladekopp: In response to his request, Ladekopp blacksmith, Jakob Klaassen, has been given approval to rebuild his smithy by 1 August 1848, doing this in accordance with the established order. The Mayor's Office has the duty to keep this under observation so that Klaassen fulfils his promise completely and in accordance with the established order. At the appropriate time, the Mayor's Office should report to the Society about the way this was done.

• Elisabeththal: You are ordered to report by 30 September about the method by which your local cottager lot No. 4 was surveyed and divided.

843. Johann Cornies to Boettlingk. 20 September 1847. SAOR 89-1-1260/83v.

Most esteemed Mr. Boettlingk,

Your letter of 6 June 1847 about land being offered for sale by the Society for Sheep Breeding in Southern Russia has not yet induced the appearance of any bidders among my acquaintances or from other agricultural people in our local region. The greatest obstacle to finding a purchaser is the well-known shortage of workmen in those regions. It simply scares buyers away. It is a huge challenge to work land without sufficient workmen. German agriculturalists, who have no intention of occupying themselves exclusively with sheep breeding, are particularly concerned with field cultivation that requires a sufficient supply of workmen at all times.

I will continue to keep this subject in mind in future, and gladly dedicate my services to you in this way.

With exceptional esteem, your respectful servant, Johann Cornies.

844. Johann Cornies to Wedel. 20 September 1847. SAOR 89-1-1260/84.

Dear Wedel,

In reply to your letter of 8 September, let me say that I like the sketch of grave railings which you sent, but would ask that all the knobs on the top be properly gilded in the forge. Therefore, order two such railings for two graves to be manufactured by the appropriate person and make the enclosed down payment of twenty-five silver rubles. The work could perhaps be expedited so that it might be picked up by a cart I would send along in good, dry weather expressly for this purpose. Please, by return mail, let me know how many puds such a railing would weigh and when both would be ready.

I would further like to know what kind of grave urns are manufactured in Lugansk. Perhaps you could send me sketches of several, again by return mail. I could then choose from among them and let you know accordingly. Do not, however, forget to list their size. The urns or grave markers need a design [and space] on which to inscribe words appropriate to their subject.

Because it is entirely too late, orders for iron stoves have been cancelled for this year.

Enclosed, you will find a three-month pass for both of your sons that cost me seventy silver kopeks.

845. Johann Cornies to Evgenii F. Hahn. 20 September 1847. SAOR 89-1-1260/85.

Yr. Excellency,

Let me respond to Yr. Honour's honoured request. I will send you a report about the condition of the Grunau community gardens, etc., once I have received the information needed to put together a thorough presentation.

I have not yet found an overseer to work with Goertz at the Lviv settlement. Since everyone is presently busy it is quite possible that this might not be decided until wintertime. Since finding a capable man willing to take this position is close to my heart, I will do what I can to help. I will, at the appropriate time, send you a report about this matter.

I received copies of the *Unterhaltungsblatt* for Sarepta and thank Yr. Excellency for his kindness to me and the community of brethren. I accept your offer to send the newspaper straight to Sarepta, and I will inform my friends about this. The communication from Editor Sonderegger enclosed with your letter will be included with the newspapers and properly dispatched.

Encouraged and delighted by the luxuriant growth of the plane trees raised from seeds that Yr. Excellency graciously sent me, I would ask that, if possible, another ten funt of this seed be sent to me for seeding during this autumn. It could be sent by mail, at my cost, but I do ask that the seed be fresh. Please forgive me for this imposition.

With the most complete esteem and faithful respect, I humbly remain Yr. Excellency's most obedient servant, Johann Cornies.

846. Johann Cornies to Sarepta Community Chairman. 20 September 1847. SAOR 89-1-1260/86.

To the Chairman of the Evangelical Brethren Community in Sarepta,

During his stay here, my treasured friend Mr. Blueher, Moscow, became acquainted with many things, including a newspaper published for foreign settlers in Southern Russia. After discussing it in detail he was of the view that the newspaper might well be of great interest to your community. This induced me to ask the esteemed Chief Guardian for the Colonists in Odesa, von Hahn, for five copies of the *Unterhaltungsblatt* for Sarepta from last year, 1846, and for this year, 1847. I was pleased with the response, although last year's issues were almost gone and I only managed to get two of them. As an act of friendship, the editor, Sonderregger, provided the community with the paper at no cost. I enclose his communication, in which he commends himself to the Sarepta Brethren Community. By special arrangements made by State Counsellor v.

Hahn, further issues of the *Unterhaltungsblatt* will be sent to Sarepta directly from Odesa.

I send you these copies with an honest heart, hoping that they will be of great interest to you as an agriculturalist.

I commend myself to you and to all dear friends and remain, with respect, your most obedient, Johann Cornies.

847. Molochnaia Agricultural Society Journal Entries. 20 September 1847. SAOR 89-1-1250/3-11v.

• To the Swedish District Office and its Society: The enclosed sketch is of the cultivated land beside Schlangendorf village, divided for thirty-five householders. Your orders are to complete the sketch immediately with particulars for each householder and to determine who the users will be. A detailed, specific report of the results is expected.

• Altonau: the Mayor's Office should report whether Altonau householder Dirk Janzen actually responded to the report of the Popov village council's judgment and whether he dismissed Danilo Famoilenko and Evdokia Sidorenkova who are in his service.

848. Johann Cornies to Carl Stempel. 23 September 1847. SAOR 89-1-1260/87.

Highly esteemed Mr. v. Stempel,

I know you are heavily burdened with business affairs, and that you and the General may well have forgotten that you asked me to have only fifty ploughs manufactured locally here. The reason, conveyed through Mayor Wedel, was that you were having a large number of ploughs manufactured there. As a result, I concluded that you might need no more than twenty-five or thirty ploughs from here. In that case, I thought I might be able to do what the government asks of me and buy up some of the Witte model ploughs from here.

Please send me a messenger with a reply and I will give you a definite answer.

With complete esteem, I have the honour to be Yr. Honour's respectful servant, Johann Cornies.

849. Molochnaia Agricultural Society Journal Entries. 25 September 1847. SAOR 89-1-1250/3-11v.

• District Office in Halbstadt: The Hutterthal Mennonites have requested a year's delay, until autumn 1848, in completing their required restitution of the rye they received from various supply storehouses in our local district when they arrived from Radishchev. The District Office is requested to submit this request the Hutterthal Mennonites have made to the [Guardianship] Committee and to notify me about the decision.

• Fuerstenwerder and Alexanderwohl: A report is required by 1 November 1847 about the completion of preparations for setting trenches along the road between Fuerstenwerder and Alexanderwohl.

• Ohrloff, Tiege, Blumenort, and Rosenort: Measures to regulate tree planting along the roads between these villages should be taken by this autumn, removing dry or damaged trees and replacing them with others. Fencing should be repaired wherever this is necessary. A report must be sent to the Society by 1 November 1847 about the completion of all of the above.

• Lichtfelde and Rueckenau: Report similar to the above by 1 November.

• Neukirch: Report similar to the above by 1 November, including also information about whether the last setting trenches prepared in spring this year have been evenly planted with trees of the required size and appearance.

• Tiegerweide: Report about the same required by 1 November.

850. Carl Stempel to Johann Cornies. 26 September 1847. SAOR 89-1-1271/215.

Highly valued Mr. Cornies,

The information Wedel gave you about the order for ploughs is definitely incorrect. I instructed him to inform you that we had ordered up to thirty additional German ploughs to complement the fifty ploughs already ordered from you. We did this because the Jews are paying half of the money needed to buy the ploughs, and also because a German plough costs only ten silver rubles. My purpose in asking Wedel to inform you about this matter was to provide you with an overview of the means available to us locally to take care of the winter seeding.

I am surprised that Wedel interpreted the information I gave him entirely in the opposite sense. I expressly told him not to report that we would not need all fifty ploughs on order because we had decided to assign one plough for every three families, instead of one plough for every six families. Were we now unable to count on fifty ploughs from you, we would have to apportion the ploughs among families differently. This would slow down the speedy completion of the winter seeding. Since all of the German ploughs will now not be ready on time, in any case, the Jews have undertaken to manage their winter seeding by renting ploughs themselves.

Even with the fifty ploughs under construction we would still be short of ploughs for the number of families needing them in future. In other words, we will have to take advantage of your kindness and order a larger number of ploughs during the winter months.

You have been so kind as to send me the money for the sale of my horse that was in your care for several years. Many thanks, even though I would have preferred that you apply this sum to a reduction of the debt I owe you. I will now try to repay the latter as soon as possible, with many thanks.

I have the honour to remain, with constant esteem, your most respectful servant, C. Stempel.

851. Molochnaia Agricultural Society Journal Entries. 26 September 1847. SAOR 89-1-1250/3-11v.

• Schoensee: Ordered to report without delay the number of trees crown peasant Kovun from Sladkobolev broke off in the local plantation and what the estimate of damage is.

852. E. Lagori to Johann Cornies. 27 September 1847. SAOR 89-1-1271/214.

Highly valued Mr. Cornies,

I have been waiting here for three days and have heard nothing but unpleasant stories that annoy me so much that I would happily run away from the whole business. The story involving the yearly market annoys me in particular because one of my assistants seems to have become entangled in the mess in a most shameless way. I hope that he will not be able to repeat this too easily again.

Tokmak is truly a nest of muddles and drunkards. The Elder is completely useless and it is unfortunate that he has no other candidate to take his place. I have had new candidates selected, and will now present them to the Board. Since I know very few of the local peasants, I don't really know if the men selected are any good, but I hope they will be better than the present Elder.

The Volost Secretary died, leaving behind much disorder. It is obvious that he must have been a great rascal.

I fined the Elder today, but could not punish him more at the time, because he is ill. I fear that he is coming down with the cholera.

Early tomorrow I intend to go to Orekhov to inspect that volost with the Mayor. I will come back here on Friday or Saturday and, if nothing detains me, I will go from here to visit you on the assumption that you will be at home and willing to accommodate me. Could you kindly let me know with this messenger whether you will be at home this coming Sunday?

Kindly accept my respect, E. Lagori.

853. Johann Cornies to Foell. 27 September 1847. SAOR 89-1-1260/88v.

Most esteemed Consistorial Counsellor,

Twenty copies of the wall-primer were received in good condition, together with your valued letter of 19 September. I hope to put the two special copies to use at the appropriate time. I return my respectful thanks, esteemed Consistorial Counsellor, for kindly obtaining them.

I will not neglect to forward the two hundred rubles owing to Mr. Provost Fletnitzer and to order the tablets still missing from Odesa.

With exceptional respect, I have the pleasure to be your respectful servant, Johann Cornies.

854. From *Unterhaltungsblatt* to the Molochnaia District Office. 27 September 1847. SAOR 89-1-1268/105.

To the Molochnaia Mennonite District Office,

Included among the enclosed copies of the first issue of the *Unterhaltungsblatt* are ten copies for Chairman Cornies of the Agricultural Society. According to the last clause of No. 6, the publisher has reserved two to ten copies for every contributor of an essay.

855. Molochnaia Agricultural Society Journal Entries. 27 September 1847. SAOR 89-1-1250/3-11v.

• Khortitsa District Office: The sons of Khortitsa Mennonite Andreas Wollman have become resident in Hutterthal village and refuse to subjugate themselves to any general orders. Therefore, the Khortitsa

District Office is commissioned to demand that the Hutterthal Mayor's Office return the above-mentioned Wollmann brothers. They should be brought back so that they can be hired out to good agriculturalists in the Khortitsa District by this year's St. Martin's Day [November 11]. The District Office is requested to attend to the execution of this order and then notify me.

856. Molochnaia Agricultural Society Journal Entries. 29 September 1847. SAOR 89-1-1250/3-11v.

• Altonau: The Mayor's Office is directed to report to me whether or not the crown peasant Peter Kirilshenko from Bolshoi Tokmak has returned to service with his householder.

• To all Village Mayors' Offices: These orders are for all villages who at present have trees planted along the roads across their lands. Immediately after this is received, a suitable ploughed furrow should be drawn along both sides. After this rule has been publicized, no one will be permitted to cross this border with his own plough during regular ploughing. Reports that this has been completed should be sent to the Society by 25 October 1847.

• Rudnerweide: Report to be made by 25 October 1847 whether local inhabitant Johann Regier has paid his debt of 114 rubles to Widow Quiring, previously resident in Grossweide.

857. Johann Cornies to Fletnitzer. 30 September 1847. SAOR 89-1-1260/88.

Most esteemed Mr. Provost,

Accompanying your esteemed communication of 29 July, eighteen copies of the desired wall-primers arrived on 19 September from Consistorial Counsellor Foell as well as two further special copies which Mr. Foell offered me and which I also hope to put to use. However the first tablet of one copy is torn and it is missing nine tablets, numbers forty-nine to fifty seven. Therefore, I urgently request that this copy be completed.

Hoping that you will assist me with this, I am sending the entire sum of two hundred rubles with this letter. I respectfully thank you for your efforts to obtain the tablets mentioned.

Mr. Consistorial Counsellor Foell has been notified and he was sent a receipt that the shipment has been received.

I must inform you that in the spring of this year, it was God's will to call my dear wife from this world to our heavenly home. Thank God, our family is otherwise well. Brothers Bernhard Fast and Klassen are also enjoying the best of health. Although my business affairs on behalf of the well-being of my brethren and fellow man are almost overwhelming, these efforts provide me with rich rewards. I am conscious of my ability to actively make a generally beneficial contribution.

With the most honest esteem, I remain your most respectful servant, J. Cornies.

858. Johann Cornies to Traugott Blueher. 30 September 1847. SAOR 89-1-1260/89v.

Most esteemed Mr. Blueher,

I honestly thank you that the business affairs involved with my wool shipment of 1846 have been concluded to my complete satisfaction. Enclosed is the applicable receipt.

Yesterday, I received your valued communication of 11 September informing me of your safe arrival in Moscow. Thank God that I and my children find ourselves very well.

With nothing further for today, we all send our most urgent greetings. I remain your faithfully respectful friend, J. Cornies.

859. Molochnaia Agricultural Society Journal Entries. 30 September 1847. SAOR 89-1-1250/3-11v.

• Hutterthal: The local Mayor's Office should call in master mill-builder Bock and question him about the amount Heinrich Thiessen from Kronsweide, who is Bock's assistant, will presumably still earn this autumn. Bock must be warned that he should not give his assistant Thiessen any more money this autumn, and the Mayor's Office should report without delay how much money Bock declares Thiessen has already earned.

• Gnadenfeld: Gnadenfeld inhabitant Theodor Voth brought the Society sufficient money to satisfy his creditors in Kherson and it has been forwarded to them. However, the postal charges of thirty silver kopeks were not included. Therefore, the Mayor's Office should collect this amount and send it to the Society as soon as possible.

860. Martin Riediger to Johann Cornies. 3 October 1847. SAOR 89-1-1271/230.

Esteemed Chairman,

I have just received the letter of esteemed Peter Neufeld's of 27 September, in which he responded to your valued suggestion that I take over the Mullah's sheep myself, in order to prevent complications and difficulties. I must appeal to your kindness in this matter, especially because I am, at this time, the only one here with my wife and can hardly leave her at home alone with two little ones. It would take me at least ten days to clear up the whole matter regarding these sheep since the road from Berdiansk through Ohrloff to Tulga is about two hundred verstas. The Nogais would also not release the sheep to me without a concrete order.

I would respectfully ask that you, Mr. Chairman, kindly send an order to Mr. Peter Neufeld in this regard that would enable him to take care of the matter for me, since I still do not feel very well. I am also writing to him at this time.

Hoping for your benevolence, your servant Martin Riediger, Berdiansk.

861. Isaac Mathies to Johann Cornies. 3 October 1847. SAOR 89-1-1271/231.

Most esteemed friend, Mr. Johann Cornies,

I send the enclosed four thousand silver rubles to reduce my debt. Forgive me that this has taken so long and that the amount is so small. It really seems almost impossible to do more right now. Trusting in your consideration, I request more patience. I will repay the remainder as soon as I can.

With a hearty greeting, and wishing you good health, I respectfully remain your most obedient Isaac Mathies.

862. Johann Cornies to Imperial Agricultural Association. 4 October 1847. SAOR 89-1-1260/90v.

To the Imperial Agricultural Association of Southern Russia in Odesa,

Respectful submission from the Corresponding Member of the Learned Committee in the Ministry of State Domains and the Chairman of the Molochnaia Mennonite Agricultural Society,

I am gratified that my endeavours to foster the improvement of agricultural practices and to increase tree planting have been everywhere rewarded in our local, treeless region, particularly in the German settlements. The most recent living advance is the establishment of the Mariupol settlement's community plantation at Grunau that has been brought about through the energetic efforts of a local inhabitant, Christian Klaassen, the immediate supervisor of the plantation.

The plantation was founded on an enclosed area of eleven desiatinas in 1827. For nine long years the project slumbered, completely forgotten through a lack of interest and inadequate administration. In 1835, this situation was brought to the attention of Administrative Counsellor Fadeev, then a member of the Guardianship Committee, who made arrangements to have direct authority over this project given to Christian Klaassen, inhabitant of Grunau village. Mr. Klaassen has been awarded the small silver medal and is at present a member of the local Society for the Dissemination of Plantings. This man who had the ability to provide insight and intelligent leadership was immediately chosen as a deputy by settlers when they first immigrated to the area. At the beginning, Klaassen had to suffer much annoyance whenever he introduced improvements to the community plantation. However, he overcame such opposition with great courage and the help of a good gardener and later also through forceful actions of the local Inspector for Settlements, Mr. v. Stempel. At present, the plantation has reached a level worthy of praise in every respect and deserving of every attention.

Stock of trees in the plantation:

Fruit trees:
1. Fruit trees of different varieties on site – 1,427;
2. Improved fruit trees in nurseries – 14,615;
3. Trees to be improved and ready to transplant from seedbeds to nurseries – 7,392;
4. Trees still growing in seedbeds – 9,838.

Forest trees:
1. Trees of different varieties on site – 1,768;
2. Transplanted in nurseries – 25,000;
3. Mulberry trees in seedbeds – 18,372;
4. Forest trees of different varieties in seedbeds – 159,400;
5. Bushes and hedges – 5,132.
Total: 242,944

Improved fruit trees sold to settlers in the district and elsewhere in the past two years – 11,262;
   Mulberry trees sold to settlers – 11,422;
   Improved trees ready to be sold this year – 8,350;
   Mulberry trees to be given to settlers of district – 10,000
   Forest trees to be given to settlers of district – 25,000.

When efforts followed to establish forest-tree plantations at villages in the Mariupol District, Christian Klaassen was again the only man who assiduously dedicated himself to the project and oversaw its advancement. Since 1844, forest-tree plantations have been laid out at twenty-three villages. At present they contain the following numbers of healthy trees:
   Listed are the numbers for the following twenty-three villages:
   Kirschwald, Tiegenhof, Rosengart, Schoenbrun, Kronsdorf, Grunau, Rosenberg, Wikkerau, Reichenberg, Wimpern, Mieran, Goettland, Neuhoff, Eichenwald, Tiegenort, Thiergart, Ludwigsthal, Elisabethdorf, Beloniescha, Kaltschinowa, Rundewiese, Kleinwerder, Groswerder
   Totals for the entire group are:
   Forest trees on site – 80,663;
   Mulberry trees on site – 40,455;
   Mulberry trees in hedges – 94,810.

These results, produced through the efforts of settler Christian Klaassen, can be described as unusual and worthy of attention. Aware of the value of this achievement, which has been amply demonstrated, I humbly propose this man be given an award by the Imperial Agricultural Association, confident that his useful efforts will be thus encouraged and recognized.

Specifically, I would propose that Klaassen be awarded one hundred silver rubles and the community plantation's Gardener, Johann Roshinskii, Eichwald, fifty silver rubles. The latter has likewise, since 1836, made zealous efforts to assist in promoting this good work under the leadership of Society member Klaassen.

863. Molochnaia Agricultural Society Journal Entries. 7 October 1847. SAOR 89-1-1250/3-11v.

• Muensterberg: Acting immediately, during this month of October, you are ordered to set aside an area of at least a hundred desiatinas of cultivated land, survey it accurately, and divide it to plant elm trees and mulberry hedges. The required sketch and estimates should be presented to this Society by 1 November 1847.

864. Molochnaia Agricultural Society Journal Entries. 8 October 1847. SAOR 89-1-1250/3-11v.

- Fuerstenau: Without delay, the Mayor's Office should provide warm accommodations for the wife of Fuerstenau inhabitant Abraham Tiessen, who is in custody. A report that this has been carried out is required by 20 October.

865. Johann Cornies to Hermann Sudermann. 10 October 1847. SAOR 89-1-1260/94.

To the Crown Model Plantation Administration,

I have been informed that Mikhail Kobka, the apprentice who ran away from his work on 7 October, seems to possess absolutely no ability to undertake the training of an apprenticeship, something I had noticed as well. For this reason, the administration of the Crown Model Plantation should submit a different report that does not conclude with a request for the return of this apprentice. Your report of 7 October is thus being returned for revision.

866. Johann Cornies to Baumann. 10 October 1847. SAOR 89-1-1260/95.

Valued Mr. Baumann,

I have, with genuine pleasure, read your faithful discussion of field cultivation and agricultural arrangements in Southern Russia and extend to you my heartfelt thanks for this valuable work. It is surely the first significant depiction of the south and its various deficiencies in regard to agriculture. Your discussion contains valuable suggestions on how to improve these conditions and insights that might enable our humane government to undertake measures that might help it to realize its goals. Since your essay, in my opinion, must be positively accepted, I have forwarded a copy to acting State Counsellor v. Hahn. I know that he will be pleased to receive it and apply many of the useful proposals it contains.

I would argue with your suggestions relating to the ideal size of villages. In my opinion and based on my experience, I think that villages should contain no fewer than forty houses, but not many more than sixty. Villages possessing only twenty properties, on the other hand, are called upon to shoulder community burdens that are far too heavy for them to manage and may well put their very existence in question. I would further suggest that the agricultural implement you suggest for the maintenance of black fallowed fields is not suited to that purpose. It would stir up the soil but not cut down, and hence destroy, the weeds. The latter is much to be desired.

I was pleased to learn from your welcome letter of 27 June that Director v. Levshin was so appreciative of your efforts and that he would appreciate receiving your notes relating to steppe cultivation. He is surely the man who would best know how to apply them.

Your letter of 4 August arrived on 18 August, together with your discussion of steppe cultivation and my observations about the Doukhobors. For various reasons I have been unable to set aside enough time to answer them. Kindly forgive me.

To return to your request for my conscientious opinion, I cannot do more than to repeat that there is nothing that I can add to what you have to say about steppe agriculture. Your little work is completely, word for word, identical with my own thoughts and much that you describe is what I have myself often pondered. I have often thought that these needed to be publicized more broadly. This you have done. I am therefore not in a position, nor do I have the right to criticize you, nor does anyone else.

Let me also inform you, valued Mr. Baumann, that my dear wife died on 31 March 1847. A brief and violent illness put an end to her years of physical suffering. May her ashes rest in peace. My son is still abroad. Recently he returned to West Prussia from the Rhine and, if I am not mistaken, will soon come home. I would gather from his letters that the change in climate has much improved his health.

On the Molochnaia and in the surrounding region, this has been another year of rich blessings. Day in, day out, carts loaded down with wheat creak and groan on their way to Berdiansk where the grain is sold at prices up to twenty rubles per chetvert, and even slightly more. An exceptional number of ships lie at anchor in port and the city has become a swarming throng. New structures are springing up everywhere with the result that shockingly high prices have to be paid for everything, workmen, food, lodgings, etc.

Our villages are thriving and everything is making rapid progress. As I have long wished, our economy is now based on field cultivation that promotes brisk activity among all of our people. The autumn weather has been ideal for the preparation of our fields for seeding. Not to be ignored, Mennonites this year will harvest about seventy-five puds of raw silk.

Everything in the Crimea is terribly expensive and there is a real scarcity of hay. Although in early summer it seemed that the Kherson Guberniia would have a crop failure, later rains provided some relief and the harvest did not turn out too badly.

There is much talk about cholera that has claimed many lives in Rostov, Taganrog, Kerch, and Kharkiv. The countryside has had many fewer deaths although, even here, cholera has taken its share of victims from here and there, especially among the Nogais.

We had our first frost of two degrees on 23 September and seven degrees on the 27th, but yesterday was warm with ten degrees and the weather has been beautiful for several days.

Friendly greetings to you, and with the most complete respect, I remain your unchanging and honestly devoted friend, Johann Cornies.

867. Peter Bahnmann and Dietrich Wiebe to Johann Cornies. 10 October 1847. SAOR 89-1-1271/234.

Esteemed Mr. Cornies,

During your visit to Odesa last autumn, His Excellency, the General, promised to find books for Mennonites working with the Committee. This he did by directing Mr. Kuk, the Committee Treasurer, to provide some left behind by General Inzov. Finally, however, Mr. Kuk cancelled the deliveries, claiming that Madame Evdokimova was reading them.

At present we have nothing with which to occupy ourselves during the long winter evenings and are totally bored. We therefore come respectfully to ask whether you might help us in this regard, either through a request to His Excellency or by some other means. Your fatherly care gives us hope that we have not been mistaken in our request.

With the most filial respect, your thankful Peter Bahnmann, Dietrich Wiebe.

868. Molochnaia Agricultural Society Journal Entries. 13 October 1847. SAOR 89-1-1250/3-11v.

• To all Village Mayors' Offices: The following should be sent to the Society by 1 November:

1. Records of new buildings constructed of fired brick and other building materials which were built this year.

2. Records of new buildings constructed of fired bricks and other materials during this year on new sites where no house or other structures existed previously.

3. Records of this year's sales of fresh fruit from orchards.

• To all Village Mayors' Offices: You are ordered to make immediate careful and punctual general inspections to discover if it is necessary for any householders to take action so that they bring about the required order for their trees and especially for the mulberry fencing hedges in plantations. Should more be planted? Results of this directive must be reported to the Society by 1 November, including reports about whether it was followed punctually in every respect.

869. Peter Keppen to Johann Cornies. 14 October 1847.
   SAOR 89-1-1294/3.

Esteemed Friend,

The Academy of Sciences has gratefully accepted your communication as proof of your willingness to promote the purposes of our program. Regrettably, however, the items found in the grave mound at Melitopol arrived in such a poor condition that nothing could be concluded from them. Granted, the value of the metal was assessed and found to be worth about nine rubles. To keep this honourable effort from failing entirely, the Academy is prepared to send you ten to fifteen silver rubles if these peasants are prepared to accept such a small sum. This should not, however, encourage similar investigations. These should be discontinued entirely and left for the future. Some grave mounds should remain for posterity.

In letting you know of the Academy's conclusions, I would ask you to accept my special thanks for your participation in our purposes.

A publication by Freiherr von Haxthausen, who was your guest some time ago, has just appeared. Its title is: *Studien ueber die inneren Zustaende, das Volksleben und insbesondere die laendlichen Einrichtungen Russlands* (Studies of the interior conditions in the Russian Empire, the life of its people, and particularly of its rural institutions), Hannover, 1847, in two volumes. I had intended to obtain this work for you (since you are often mentioned in it) and to send it along with Baron v. Rosen who plans to pass through your villages on his return to Simferopol. However, I would first like to know if you wish to spend eight silver rubles on it. Let me know what I should do.

With honest respect, your friend and servant, Keppen.

870. Molochnaia Agricultural Society Journal Entries. 16 October 1847. SAOR 89-1-1250/3-11v.

• To the Mariupol Mennonite District Office: You are ordered to make arrangements to have the money cottager Jacob Dik from Schoenthal owes, according to a signed note, paid to Franz Quiring from Conteniusfeld. The total of 124 rubles should be paid from the estate of Jacob Dik. When this has been completed, it should be reported to this Society.

• Khortitsa District Office: You are informed that the Guardianship Committee has reported no objections to the intended lease of beer sales in Kronsgarten village to Josephsthal villager Johann Schroeder, if the Kronsgarten community issues a community statement that it agrees to this. At the same time, the District Office is required to publicize in Khortitsa and Molochnaia Mennonite District villages the terms under which the beer sales will be granted to Schroeder and to specify the date by which bidders might possibly be prepared to bid and to pay an even greater sum than the one Schroeder is paying. The results should be reported.

• To the District Office in Halbstadt: You are requested to commission Margenau inhabitant Abram Reimer to go to Hutterthal without delay in order to properly vaccinate children for smallpox. Results should be reported.

• Mariupol Mennonite District Office: David Teichgrew, of Rueckenau village, has notified the Society that his son David Teichgrew is seriously ill in Schoenthal village in the house of his father-in-law, Heinrich Quiring. Quiring gives him no attention and little care, showing him no mercy. The father wants to have him removed from this house and the District Office is therefore required to investigate the situation in Schoenthal village. If what Teichgrew has reported actually proves to be true, the Office should require Quiring to give the invalid good care and accommodation in his house. Results must be reported.

871. Johann Cornies to Hermann Sudermann. 18 October 1847. SAOR 89-1-1260/98.

Overseer of plantation,

Because of a shortage of time, workers ordered to dig the canal on the 20th and 23rd of this month could not come. Instead, twenty-seven men from Timoshovka have been ordered to begin three days of work on Tuesday, 21 October, and twenty-seven men from Mikhailovka for three days on 27 October.

872. Johann Cornies to Traugott Blueher. 18 October 1847. SAOR 89-1-1260/98v.

Most esteemed Mr. Blueher,

In reply to your communication of 2 October, I hasten to report that a remittance of three thousand silver rubles, in payment for this year's wool, has arrived in good order by mail. I am completely satisfied with the selling price, and am most grateful to you.

My partners and I will discuss sending Iakovlev's silk to Moscow, and, if you permit, will take advantage of your kindness in this matter.

There is little more that we can do this year regarding your desire to purchase silk. Almost all of the silk has been sold or forwarded on consignment. In addition, your offer of three silver rubles per funt is too low, given the way silk is sold here. Nevertheless, acting on your instructions, I will see that offers are made for good silk at three silver rubles per funt and will try to have a minimum of four hundred funt bought for you. Success, however, is doubtful.

As you expected, we failed to buy any pears. I will pay friend Johann Siemens in Khortitsa the forty-two silver rubles as soon as possible. As for the sheep shears I have had on consignment from you, it arises that you must still enter into my accounts a balance of two dozen and seven at twenty-eight rubles, one dozen and three at twenty-six rubles, and four dozen and ten at twenty-one rubles.

My son is still not back from his trip, and since I have not heard from him directly I do not know when he will arrive. Otherwise, praise God, all of us are healthy and well. Knobloch is back in my house. The trade he tried to undertake is not for him. It is far too hard, and working under wet conditions is harmful. Niederstaedter, on the other hand, can do it all. He is sprightly and well and will learn the trade very quickly. He is our guest every Sunday. Both of them send their most hearty greetings.

After having had much rain and cold weather, it seems as though spring is back with cheerful and warm days.

Commending myself sincerely and with friendly greetings, I remain your honestly loving Johann Cornies.

873. Molochnaia Agricultural Society Journal Entries. 18 October 1847. SAOR 89-1-1250/3-11v.

• Franzthal: Report is required by 25 October about householder Richert's runaway Russian servant, the crown peasant Kondrat Vasilenko from Soltishchina. Has he returned to service?

• Waldheim: The supervision of the Waldheim widow Woerbel is inappropriate, with no action by the curator, and this leaves her in danger of squandering her property and become a burden to the community. Therefore, the Mayor's Office is ordered to assign other, more careful men as curators in place of the undependable curators, Peter Wedel and Johann Ewert. This matter should be reported to the Society.

• Tiegenhagen: You should carefully question your local inhabitant Johann Wiebe, guardian for the children of Dirk Boldt's widow, and report the following as soon as possible to the Society:

1. Where is his ward, Susanna, daughter of the above-mentioned widow D. Boldt at present?

2. How is she being brought up?

3. Has she been sent to school properly during the past three years? And,

4. What kind of further education to assist her future progress does the guardian Johann Wiebe together with the other guardian intend to grant his ward Susanna in the coming year?

874. Johann Cornies to District Office. 20 October 1847. SAOR 89-1-1260/99v.

District Office in Halbstadt,

The badly built wagon of master blacksmith Franz Klaassen in Rosenort has now been fitted with new rims and axles. I would therefore ask the District Office to respectfully invite three impartial master blacksmiths from the vicinity to inspect the work done according to my instructions. They are to check if it is reliable and report the results of their inspection in writing.

875. Molochnaia Agricultural Society Journal Entries. 20 October 1847. SAOR 89-1-1292/7-13.

• Fuerstenau: The Mayor's Office should find accommodations for the wife of Abraham Tiessen without delay. By 25 October it is required to report to the Society where accommodations for Mrs. Tiessen can be obtained.

876. Molochnaia Agricultural Society Journal Entries. 21 October 1847. SAOR 89-1-1292/7-13.

• Tiegenhagen: Report required whether Konstantin Chveshka, the Russian servant who ran away from Gerhard Giesbrecht, is working for Giesbrecht again.

• Tiegenhagen: The Mayor's Office should, without delay, submit the cost estimates and the sketch for the new school to be built in this village so that they can be examined.

877. Johann Cornies to Evgenii F. Hahn. 22 October 1847. SAOR 89-1-1260/100v.

Your Excellency,

When I was in Odesa with Mr. v. Stempel in October of last year, Yr. Excellency kindly promised to ensure that the young Mennonites working within the Committee would be provided with books to read for entertainment and instruction, as I requested. Many thanks for this benevolent deed, which was carried out by Mr. Kuk, who made a number of books available on Yr. orders. They now report that Mr. Kuk has put an end to this practice with the excuse that Madame Evdokimova was reading the books. The young Mennonites urgently ask for my assistance.

Because I fear that they have absolutely nothing with which to occupy themselves during long evenings and are plagued by boredom, I take the liberty to request that books be graciously provided in one way or another, even if payment is needed.

In the hope that I have not made a mistaken request, I sign myself with great esteem as Yr. Excellency's thankful servant, Johann Cornies.

878. Johann Cornies to Evgenii F. Hahn. 22 October 1847. SAOR 89-1-1260/101.

Your Excellency,

Mr. Baumann, an agronomist whom Yr. Excellency will recognize, at least by name, has sent me a composition to examine. It consists of observations about the steppes of Southern Russia in relation to the development of field cultivation. I find it very interesting and most appropriate because it truthfully expresses the thoughts I have developed over the course of many years. This prompts me to send Yr. Excellency a copy of the work, in the hope that you might be inclined to read it. Mr. Baumann was encouraged to undertake this task by His Excellency, Mr. v. Levshin. One can therefore hope that it will, with time, actually become useful for the crown peasants.

With the most exceptional esteem, I have the honour to be Yr. Excellency's most respectful servant, Johann Cornies.

879. Johann Cornies to D. Janzen in Hutterthal. 22 October 1847. SAOR 89-1-1260/101.

Treasured friend,

I have ordered the Khortitsa people to send you two of their most energetic local teachers, Penner and Teichgrew, and to instruct them in the use of a wall-primer to teach the alphabet to small children. Do not be offended that I have arranged this matter directly without first asking for your agreement. I know that, because of the great usefulness of such instruction, you would not likely have denied me your agreement. Still, I should personally have been more polite and courteous. One should not burden anyone, especially not good friends, without first asking them for their agreement. Whatever you wish to have people do unto you, you should do likewise to them! I could of course have excused myself, as is generally the fashion, saying that I had forgotten to ask your agreement when we had last met. That might, however, have made it seem that the Khortitsa schools were not close to my heart, which is really not so. I am therefore coming to you after the fact to ask that you undertake the effort involved in teaching two Khortitsa schoolteachers the practical use of the wall-primer in your own school. Would it be possible for intelligent minds to learn such methods in two or three days? I will look forward to your kind response as soon as possible.

I commend myself, with the friendliest of greetings, as your true friend, Johann Cornies.

880. Wilhelm Remy to Johann Cornies. 24 October 1847. SAOR 89-1-1271/251.

His Honour, Mr. Johann Cornies in Ohrloff,

Encouraged by His Reverence, the St. Petersburg General Superintendent, and trusting in Yr. Honour's very well known sympathetic willingness to support whatever is generally useful and to promote noble undertakings, I have the honour to send you three copies of an "Invitation to contribute to the construction of a German St. Michael's Church and Institution for the Poor" in the St. Petersburg settlement. My respectful request is that Yr. Honour use your well-disposed qualifications to obtain several contributions to the above-mentioned cause from your community.

Most respectfully, Pastor Wilhelm Remy at Molochnaia.

881. Johann Wiebe to Johann Cornies. 24 October 1847.
SAOR 89-1-1271/264.

Esteemed Friend,

Your honourable son is today celebrating his engagement to Therese Thiessen in Elbing. The Wiebe gentleman who suggested this individual hopes that it will be a happy choice. According to inquiries made to my Elbing friends and other acquaintances, this lady has an especially good reputation, is most respectable, and well educated. Outwardly, she is engaging, yes, she could be called beautiful. If I am not mistaken, she is about twenty-eight years old. Her father's bankruptcy and retirement a few years ago may have contributed to her failure to marry thus far, as he is supposed to be in difficult circumstances.

I am also pleased to be able to report to you that I spoke with an acquaintance in Danzig yesterday. He is related to the Thiessen family and he praised them. It seems that your future daughter-in-law is reputed to be very good natured and to have a gentle, noble temperament. As for the main question, mutual attraction was said to be the reason for this connection. When Cornies was refused on the occasion of his first approach to her, he was left deeply unhappy and could not calm down. When he received the same answer again on 28 September, he was inconsolable and deeply hurt, having lost this hope for happiness.

He quickly planned his departure and, on 14 October, I accompanied him as far as Marienburg. There he learned that the lady who possessed his heart was also inconsolable and, to all appearances, shared the same longings. This moved him to travel to Elbing one more time and yesterday I received a few lines from him, inviting me to the engagement, which I could not accept because of prior business.

May Heaven grant that his happiness is equal to my good wishes and that he can bring home a faithful, loving wife and a good mother for his two dear little children.

I close with this wish, and commend myself to you at all times, with friendship and respect, Johann Wiebe, Freienhuben, Prussia.

882. District Office to Johann Cornies. 25 October 1847. SAOR 89-1-1271/265.

To the esteemed Johann Cornies in Ohrloff,

The Ohrloff village master blacksmith Abraham Kroeger and Heinrich Wiens from Blumenort were today directed by the applicable village offices to appear at your residence at 10:00 a.m. this coming Monday, 27 October, to inspect the wagon repaired by Franz Klaassen, Rosenort, and to judge the quality of the work done. The District Office is hereby informing you about this matter. District Chairman Toews.

883. Johann Cornies to Carl Stempel. 28 October 1847. SAOR 89-1-1260/103v.

Esteemed Mr. v. Stempel,

On 17 October, His Excellency, Chairman of the Guardianship Committee, Acting State Counsellor v. Hahn, wrote suggesting that I use the occasion of your trip to Odesa to have twenty funt of mulberry seeds shipped to him. Should I send the seed for this purpose to Grunau, or wait for you to come by on your journey to Odesa? In the latter case I could keep twenty funt of mulberry seed on hand until then.

Awaiting your gracious answer, I have the honour to be Yr. Honour's respectful servant, Johann Cornies.

884. Molochnaia Agricultural Society Journal Entries. 28 October 1847. SAOR 89-1-1292/7-13.

• Fuerstenwerder: You are ordered to have the ward Friesen, about whom his guardians Johann Reimer and Isaak Friesen have quarrelled, put into service with householder Gerhard Fast in Ohrloff village by the coming St. Martin's Day, 11 November. A report to the Society is required as soon as this has been carried out.

• Fuerstenwerder: You are ordered to have Peter, the son of your local inhabitant Dirk Thun, put into service with householder Cornelius Wall in Ohrloff punctually by St. Martin's Day, 11 November, and to report to the Society when this has been carried out.

• Peter Stobbe in Schardau: By 5 November 1847, you should not fail to submit exact accounts to the Society, listing the number of wethers you sold for Jacob Klaassen, Halbstadt, the prices at which they were sold, the buyers, by name, and the year in which they were sold. You must also not fail to produce the money you presumably received.

• Chairman of Khortitsa Agricultural Society: You are commissioned to attend the examination of Kronsgarten schoolteacher Wieler by the medical doctors Glokhovskii and Shirovskii in company with Inspector Riller, and to report the results.

885. Contract confirmed by Johann Cornies. 31 October 1847. SAOR 89-1-1273/1.

Apprenticeship contract:

31 October 1847, the following agreement was made between Ph[illipp] Wiebe, inhabitant of Ohrloff village, and the master carpenter Cornelius Fast in Tiege:

1. Ph. Wiebe puts his seventeen-year-old brother Cornelius into the charge of master carpenter Fast for three years, from St. Martin's Day 1847 to St. Martin's Day 1850 to thoroughly learn the carpentry trade.

2. During the period of this apprenticeship, Ph. Wiebe obligates himself to supply his brother Cornelius with all necessary pieces of clothing and their repair, washing, and cleaning. The master carpenter, on the other hand, will provide him with bedding and board without compensation.

3. Master carpenter Fast obligates himself to hold the apprentice, Cornelius Wiebe, to good order and punctual activity, to provide him with a good example, and to keep his deportment under special observation. Generally and in particular he will ensure that this youth becomes not only a skilled master carpenter but also a useful and respectable member of the community.

To this end, both parts have signed, in their own hand, Ph. Wiebe; Master carpenter Cornelius Fast.

Confirmation that this apprenticeship contract is to be carried out in the declared manner comes from the Molochnaia Mennonite Society for Agriculture and Trades.

886. Molochnaia Agricultural Society Journal Entries. 31 October 1847. SAOR 89-1-1292/7-13.

• To the esteemed Margenau Church Assembly: You are requested to inform the Society by 6 November at the latest about your response to its 11 September 1847 communication. What has the Church Assembly done to reconcile the Poetkers, a married couple in Landskrone, and what has come to pass?

887. Johann Cornies to Jacob Neumann. 1 November 1847. SAOR 89-1-1260/105.

Dear Friend,

If your relative in Prussia seeks your advice, simply advise him to come here, look around, and discover for himself the nature of our local circumstances. Should our life and local establishments please him, advise him to buy an ordinary piece of land anywhere in the villages. In this way, without troubling your own conscience, you would have provided your relative with the best, most assured advice that would allow him to establish a safe asylum for himself and find peaceful prosperity with God's blessing.

With greetings, your faithful friend, Johann Cornies.

888. Molochnaia Agricultural Society Journal Entries. 1 November 1847. SAOR 89-1-1292/7-13.

• Blumstein: Where, with whom by name, and on what conditions are the late inhabitant Johann Harder's children and stepchildren at the present time? A report to the Society is required from the Mayor's Office as soon as possible.

889. Johann Cornies to Johann Cornies Jr. 2 November 1847. SAOR 89-1-1260/105v.

Sincerely beloved son,

For a long time I waited painfully for a letter from you, experiencing great anxiety as well as hope and fear from early September until last night. You can well imagine the surprise and pleasure I felt when yesterday I broke open your letter of 21 October. Its contents have set my mind completely at rest, especially since divine guidance has led you to find your heart's desire, your life's companion. Your choice gives me great pleasure. May God grant you and your dear bride His blessing. It is my hope that, by the time this letter reaches you, she will have been publicly entrusted to you with religious blessings. May He keep both of you in good cheer and well-being, in good health, strength, and spiritual serenity to the end of your life. This would also give me true joy and great tranquillity. As your father, I embrace both of you and include you in my prayers and in my heart. Genuinely and sincerely, I have always felt gratitude for your love and obedience that are the greatest joys of my life, but I feel this even more sincerely now that you are not here with me or close by. So much greater will that joy be next spring when, should it be God's will, I am able to rejoice at your return and at the sight of your dear wife, my sincerely beloved daughter-in-law.

Dear son, tell your dear wife many affectionate and sympathetic things about me and assure her of my sincere love and appreciation. You should both know that no one more honestly wishes you heartfelt happiness in your union, which gives me such great joy. No one can more sympathetically take pleasure in your happiness, than your loving father, who sends heartfelt greetings to you and commends you to God.

Although I do not know him, I ask that you give your loving father-in-law many greetings, and assure him that here, far away, I will take his place as his daughter's father, and that her happiness and well-being will be as close to my heart as is my own.

On my order from Odesa, I have commissioned your brother-in-law Wiebe to send you a bill of exchange to Elbing for about two thousand silver rubles. You will probably not be able to sell it advantageously anywhere other than in Danzig.

Also give my hearty thanks to my brothers-in-law Wiebe and Dik and also Mr. Wiebe in Freienhuben and Mr. v. Steen in Langefuhr.

Your brother-in-law Wiebe will shortly report to you about our household and business affairs. Everyone in our family is healthy and cheerful. Write soon and often.

With honest love, I am and remain your and your wife's faithfully loving father, Johann Cornies.

890. Johann Cornies to Ferestivo. 2 November 1847.
   SAOR 89-1-1260/106.

Esteemed Mr. v. Ferestivo,

Circumstances make it necessary for me to provide my son, presently in West Prussia, with a bill of exchange in the value of two thousand silver rubles. Might it be possible for you in Odesa to prepare a bill of exchange for Hamburg that could then be turned into silver in Danzig (since Odesa has no direct connections with Danzig). Since I am aware that you are connected with Mr. Abraham Wiebe in Berdiansk, you might specify that this money is being deducted from me through Mr. Wiebe. If it is not possible to proceed in this manner, I would request advice, by return mail, on how this amount might be transferred from here, if necessary in cash.

I would be much obligated to you for your efforts, and will gratefully pay your costs. Please pardon my frankness and accept my assurance of the great esteem with which I remain your honestly respectful friend and servant.

891. Molochnaia Agricultural Society Journal Entries. 3 November 1847. SAOR 89-1-1292/7-13.

• Khortitsa Agricultural Society: The Society is ordered to report where each of the deceased Andreas Wollmann's sons, Franz and Jacob by name, are to go into service.

• Altonau: Report required by 15 November about completion of autumn planting on its cultivated fields.

• Schardau: Report to the Society required as soon as possible about the following:

1. Does your local inhabitant Harms, who has learned the shoemaker's craft, own a horse?

2. If he does own one, what does he use it for? and,

3. Does he need this horse? Couldn't he look after himself without it?

892. Johann Cornies to Johann Wiebe of Freienhuben, West Prussia. 5 November 1847. SAOR 89-1-1260/107.

Very valued friend,

Only forty-eight hours before I received your agreeable letter of 24 October, my son wrote to me that he intended to celebrate his engagement to the Thiessen daughter in Elbing on 24 October. He also shared some of the anxieties and internal struggles he had experienced when Therese, whom he loved sincerely and with whom he had hoped to have a happy life, had turned down his proposal. Your letter was full of love and I have difficulty in expressing my feelings. How will I ever repay you for the great sympathy you have shown for my son's happiness, and for mine. May God, the giver of all good gifts, reward you richly, giving you and your beloved family many happy and cheerful days for years to come.

When I confided in you in confidence, dear friend, and gave my son permission to travel abroad, you were my support. You will now remain this in future as well despite the fact, which I gather from your letter, that you do not wish to be considered a collaborator in my son's marriage. It is nevertheless true that you are the first, best, and most sympathetic promoter of my son's marriage and happiness. In fact, if I had not enjoyed your faithfulness and friendship over many years and known your noble attitudes, I would have doubted the wisdom of granting my son permission to marry in Prussia. Faithfulness and honesty vouch for the fact that I treasure you, especially now with the marriage of my son. What I say is not the flattery of a worldly attitude.

The qualities you describe in my son's bride indicate that she will become a good wife, an attentive housewife, and a loving mother. Grounded in mutual love and delicate feelings, this union will make a genuinely blessed marriage. There is nothing to fear if one loves and is loved. I am filled with joy to know that you approve the choice and think it will be a happy one. This, in my eyes, is of the greatest value to me! Should you meet the engaged couple, please give them my heart-felt greetings. Also let my son know that my brother Peter Cornies has departed this world and that the latter's son Peter will celebrate his marriage to the daughter of teacher Johann Dik this coming Thursday. Otherwise everyone is healthy and well.

We hear very little about cholera here. It was rampant in only a few Nogai villages and resulted in the death of very few. As far as I know, only Johann Penner, Pastwa, died of cholera in our district.

Together with my family, I commend myself to you and your loving family in friendship and with honest thoughts, and remain your friend, who is indebted to you, Johann Cornies.

893. Johann Cornies to Jacob Wiebe. 5 November 1847. SAOR 89-1-1260/108v.

Greatly loved brother-in-law Jacob Wiebe, Elbing, West Prussia,

I received two letters in a row, one from my son, the second from my old friend, Mr. Johann Wiebe in Freienhuben. Both let me know that my son had become engaged to a certain Miss Thiessen in Elbing. It is a happy event and I thank you sincerely for your fatherly support and sympathy. I feel truly honoured that my son enjoyed your friendship and love throughout and that, as a faithful advisor, you supported him in his decision to take this important step.

Mr. Johann Wiebe's investigation suggests that my future daughter-in-law is a most lovable and decent person. He hopes that the marriage will be a happy one. Surely it will if it is grounded in mutual inclination and mutual love. I am deeply grateful to you and your family for overwhelming my son with kindness during his stay with you.

Also please give my greetings and heartfelt thanks to your relatives for their friendly reception of my son. I would be delighted to receive a few lines about their well-being. Kindly give my best wishes to the betrothed pair, and let them know I am well, as is everyone in my house.

Commend me to your worthy wife and treasured family and may I continue in your love. It is my greatest joy to call myself your thankfully respectful brother-in-law, Johann Cornies.

894. Molochnaia Agricultural Society Journal Entries. 6 November 1847. SAOR 89-1-1292/7-13.

• Tiegerweide: A report to the Society is required by 10 November whether your local householders Schoenke and Hildebrandt have been called into the Mayor's Office to receive definite punishment for their wanton rioting. Has the District Office ordered them to appear?

• District Office at Halbstadt: Should send notification to the Society whether the punishment of householders Hildebrandt & Schoenke has been carried out.

• To the above: Should send notification to the Society that the two householders from Ladekopp village, Fast & Walde, have been punished for their malicious, rebellious behaviour at the time that persons inhabiting earthen huts in Waldheim were transferred.

• Blumenort: The village is directed to decide which piece of ploughed land should be planted with elms and mulberry hedges, and to survey and divide it neatly, submitting a sketch of this work together with the estimates to the Society by 20 November.

895. Johann Cornies to Johann Cornies Jr. 8 November 1847. SAOR 89-1-1260/110v.

Dear son,

I approve your wish to stay in Prussia until next spring. I forgot to include this in my letter amid the joyful surprise of your engagement,

Do you plan to travel in this area and use your own horses or post horses? I leave this decision entirely to you, but think it would be more relaxing and pleasant to undertake the journey with your own horses. I know this would involve several more weeks of your time, but I don't think this would really matter since I assume you would be coming on at least two wagons and with people useful to your domestic economy here. I have also heard that Mr. Janzen, Neuteicher Unterfeld, has told you about his plan to visit us here next spring. You might well travel in company with him. Please, give me your views about these matters, even if you have not yet reached a decision yourself.

With the most sincere greetings to you and your bride, I remain your loving father.

896. Johann Cornies to Christian Steven. 8 November 1847. SAOR 89-1-1260/111.

Yr. Excellency, Inspector of Agriculture in Southern Russia,

In pursuance of Yr. Excellency's communication No. 397, I write to let you know that the fifty Witte ploughs ordered for the Hebrew settlement this fall are ready. They have been tested by knowledgeable people in my presence. On average, despite the usual discrepancies, they work easily and are quite suitable for their purpose. Anyone who knows how to plough or even how to set a Little Russian plough will find the Witte plough to his liking. This is doubly true given the fact that the plough is cheap, only ten silver rubles with all accessories. All of its parts can be used somewhat more vigorously than those of the model.

897. Johann Cornies to Tavrida Bureau of State Domains. 8 November 1847. SAOR 89-1-1260/111.

To the Tavrida Bureau of State Domains,

In pursuance of communication No. 20,077 of 31 December 1846, I have the honour to report that we have repeated the experiment with American summer rye and the results are again negative. In the village of Kaikulak, twenty-seven puds, sixteen funt were harvested from the five puds, thirty-five funt of seed. In Andreevka thirty-five funt were harvested from twenty-seven funt seed. The best result was a fivefold yield, seed to harvest. Since we sowed the original seed three years ago, the grain harvested has dropped so much in quality that there is no purpose in repeating these trials. The drought we experience here in summer precludes a harvest of this summer rye at the level of its customary quality. My own seedings have produced similar results.

Please let me know if the harvested seeds are the possession of the peasants involved as their own property.

898. Johann Cornies to Peter Keppen. 8 November 1847. SAOR 89-1-1260/111v.

His Honour, Mr. State Counsellor,

I respectfully thank Yr. Honour for your communications of 5 September and 16 October 1847. In following your wishes, I have arranged to select five hundred good, young ewes from my own herds that are now available for Doctor v. Rauch's estate, in readiness and waiting for Mr. v. Riesenkampf's judgment. I am assured that he will be completely satisfied with this selection. I am also convinced that there is no small herd here or anywhere that can equal it in quality and uniformity. I will inform you about the further progress of this matter.

I was pleased to read in your second letter that the Imperial Academy recognized the excavations of peasants that were made here with my permission, sending them a reward of ten to fifteen silver rubles. They will be much satisfied. Respectfully, I ask permission to make these payments to them. In keeping with the Academy's decision, I will not approve any further excavations.

I would be much in your debt if Yr. Honour would provide me with a copy of Freiherr v. Haxthausen's publication. Its price is reasonable. Reading it will give me much pleasure, especially since it will include much discussion of agriculture. Please send me the bill.

Thanking you for all your kindness and with the greatest esteem, I have the honour to remain, forever, Yr. Honour's most respectful servant, Johann Cornies.

899. Johann Cornies to Jacob Klaassen. 8 November 1847. SAOR 89-1-1260/112.

Master carpenter Jacob Klaassen in Halbstadt,

To complete the forestry building on the Crown Model Plantation, the work still needs:

1. a framework for two pairs of gable windows;
2. four cellar windows and their shutters with necessary mountings;

3. door locks for two rooms;
4. improvements for an interior door and its casing.

These items should definitely be completed during the month of November. You are required to make final arrangements to complete them in order that the Crown's account might be closed.

900. Molochnaia Agricultural Society Journal Entries. 8 November 1847. SAOR 89-1-1292/7-13.

• Tiege: A report is required whether cottager Isaak Neufeld has fetched the remainder of the hay he purchased from the Nogai Oterbei in Akkerman. Has he paid the thirty-seven rubles, ninety-two kopeks still owing?

• Mariupol Mennonite District Office: The Office is required to investigate the reasons why Jacob Wall from Schönfeld forwarded deceitful news to his father-in-law, David Teichgrew in Rueckenau, suggesting that Teichgrew's son David, who is confined by illness in the home of his parents-in-law in Schoenthal, is receiving little care and nursing attention. Results should be reported.

• Jacob Klaassen, at the Halbstadt tradesmen's settlement [Neu-Halbstadt]: A report to the Society is required about a gelding sale. How much more money did Klaassen receive from the Nogai in addition to the thirty-five rubles Stobbe from Schardau gave him.

901. Johann Cornies to Christian Steven. 11 November 1847. SAOR 89-1-1260/113.

Yr. Excellency,

To answer your communication of 23 October, I write to inform you that you are still in arrears by a total of seventeen rubles, sixty-four kopeks. Your full account consists of money owing in the sum of: seventy rubles for a silk-reeler plus another ten rubles, seventy-five kopeks to transport it. I have added a further eleven rubles, ninety kopeks for twenty-nine and three-quarter funt of cheese that I have today sent along to you with Mr. Lagori. Previously, the balance in your favour totalled seventy-five rubles, fifteen kopeks. Yr. Excellency will kindly refer to your own records and let me know how we might reconcile our reciprocal accounts.

Heavy frost began today, with seven degrees of frost this morning. We have until now had the best possible weather and agriculturalists have made great progress in the cultivation and planting of their fields. Our granaries are full because the last ships have left [our port of Berdiansk].

902. Phillip Wiebe to Deubner. 12 November 1847. SAOR 89-1-1260/113v.

Esteemed Mr. Deubner,
Starting with the New Year of 1848, we ask that fifteen copies of the *Dorfzeitung* (Village newspaper) be mailed to us instead of the thirteen copies we have been receiving, as well one copy of the *Wochenblatt* (Weekly newspaper). If you can, please send us the bill for the current year at the beginning of December.
With exceptional esteem, Phillip Wiebe.

903. Johann Cornies to Hermann Sudermann. 12 November 1847. SAOR 89-1-1260/114.

To the Overseer of the Crown Model Plantation,
As a result of report No. 58 of 26 October, I have today sent an order to the Mikhailov Starschina to have crown peasant Vassily Rodenko from Mikhailovka returned to the plantation. He had started as a worker at the plantation on 15 October and was then assigned work as overseer. He arbitrarily released the workers under his supervision and must therefore complete the work left behind as punishment for his action. Since the weather is presently unfavourable for the completion of the assigned work mentioned above, please estimate the time needed to accomplish it and add that sum to the days normally assigned the Overseer Rodenko for other necessary work. In this way we would ensure that Rodenko completes as much work as should have been performed by the workers assigned to him. The results are to be reported to me after the work is completed.

904. Molochnaia Agricultural Society Journal Entries. 13 November 1847. SAOR 89-1-1292/7-13.

• Khortitsa [Agricultural] Society: Payment for the ten copies of wall-primers commissioned and received there should be sent as soon as possible. The account enclosed was for the 470 rubles, forty-four and a half kopeks owed.

• Society member Martens in Tiegenhagen: You are commissioned to obtain accurate records of silk reeling done in this district. How many chetveriki of cocoons for reeling were obtained from producers, listed by name and village, and how much silk has been harvested from each of them. These records should be sent to the Society by 1 December 1847 at the latest.

• Pordenau: The enclosed sketch shows which sections of fullholdings two, three, four, and five are not suitable for fruit trees, especially for apple trees, and also shows where pear trees, mulberry trees, and hedges should be planted. A report should be made to the Society when this has been carried out.

• Khortitsa [Agricultural] Society: The fourteen rubles, seven kopeks enclosed with this communication are being sent for the wife of the Kronsweide Mennonite Heinrich Thiessen. The Society should report whether this money was given to Mrs. Thiessen and whether she also received fourteen rubles at some previous time.

905. Molochnaia Agricultural Society Journal Entries. 14 November 1847. SAOR 89-1-1292/7-13.

• Chairman's Office in Berdiansk: Should report without delay if Jacob Sudermann, the youth about whom teacher Johann Voth had complained, is now attending school, as he did in the past.

• Chairman's Office in Berdiansk: A report is required without delay whether the matter of the complaints made by the Fuerstenau Mennonite Peter Rempel, who now resides there, has been expedited.

906. Molochnaia Agricultural Society Journal Entries. 15 November 1847. SAOR 89-1-1292/7-13.

• v. Stempel: Please make arrangements to ensure that settler Buettner's daughter, who was hired by Mennonite Erdmann Nikkel for shopkeeper Peters in Gnadenheim, and who is now refusing to enter service, is delivered to service for Peters without difficulties.

• Rudnerweide: You are ordered to report whether your local inhabitant Johann Teek has received satisfaction from crown peasant Smail Tascherbanov.

• Schardau: Arrangements should be made to ensure that both horses and also the wagon belonging to the unmarried son of local inhabitant Harms are sold without delay. His debts should be covered with the proceeds. Harms's son should be directed to hire himself to a good master craftsman and that he must show no opposition. Failing this, the Society will employ means to place him under supervision. A report that this directive has been carried out is required as soon as possible.

907. Johann Cornies to Hermann Sudermann. 18 November 1847. SAOR 89-1-1260/116.

Overseer Sudermann,

If Vassily Rodenko, the Mikhailovka peasant who acted without orders in sending away workers before the completion of their work, has now engaged other workers to substitute for him in completing this task, this should be approved in order that this disagreeable matter might be concluded.

908. Johann Cornies to Hermann Sudermann. 18 November 1847. SAOR 89-1-1260/116v.

Overseer of the Crown Plantation Sudermann,

In response to your report No. 68 of 15 November, I hereby inform you that the Mikhailovka Elder has been sternly ordered to return to the plantation the five men from Mikhailovka who had only worked a day and a half instead of the three days needed to complete the work assigned them at the plantation.

As soon as these five men arrive at the plantation, you will direct them to work for the time period assigned to them.

909. Molochnaia Agricultural Society Journal Entries. 18 November 1847. SAOR 89-1-1292/7-13.

• To the Orphans' Administrator Janzen in Petershagen: Claas Wiebe in Halbstadt and Johann Wiebe, Tiegenhagen, the guardians of the ward [Justina] Boldt, are not taking care of her physical and spiritual well-being, as they are in duty bound to do. Therefore, Orphans' Administrator Janzen is commissioned to remove them from their office and to select dependable guardians to replace them. Also, he should take this ward away from Martens in Schoensee, where she is at present, and find shelter for her with better people, who obligate themselves to send her to school. A report that this has been carried out should be made to the Society with all possible speed.

910. Molochnaia Agricultural Society Journal Entries. 19 November 1847. SAOR 89-1-1292/7-13.

• Lichtfelde: Has the daughter of your local resident Abram Wall, whom he listed as being superfluous in his home and without useful occupation there, been voluntarily hired to Abram Warkentin, Tiege householder? The village office should report about this.

911. Molochnaia Agricultural Society Journal Entries. 22 November 1847. SAOR 89-1-1292/7-13.

• Rudnerweide: You are ordered to take care that local resident Johann Regehr pays Widow Quiring the 114 rubles he owes her. It should be indicated to him that he is definitely not permitted to appear at the Society to explain this matter. The results should be reported to the Society.

912. Johann Cornies to Hermann Sudermann. 24 November 1847. SAOR 89-1-1260/117.

Overseer of Crown Plantation,

Accompanying this communication is another crown apprentice by the name of Demian from Novogrigorievka. He is to replace the runaway Mikhail Kobka, who was considered incompetent in his work.

In response to your report No. 72 of 23 November, I would serve notice that you were mistaken in your view, referred to in your earlier report of 2 August, that the previously discharged Demian Vavk had not been replaced. Indeed, on 30 September, Mikhail Kobka had already been delivered to the plantation in place of Vavk. On 13 October you reported that Kobka had run away and was not wanted back because of his stupidity. In this case, you should have followed proper procedures by referring to the latter in your report No. 50. Not Vavk but Kobka has still not been replaced.

913. Johann Cornies to Anton Schellenberg. 25 November 1847. SAOR 89-1-1260/117v.

Dear Friend,

You did me a very great favour by notifying me on 13 November about Mr. Akim Kolossov's sale of land and about the money involved. I am most thankful to you for doing this. Immediately upon receiving your letter, I sent someone to see him in Aleksandrovka. Although I have not been repaid all of his debt to me, I did receive a large part of it. He wrote to me that he will remain in possession of only four hundred silver rubles of the entire sum of money he received for his land. Personally, I think he will be ruined by his disorderly life.

With a friendly greeting, I sign myself as your thankful friend, Johann Cornies.

914. Molochnaia Agricultural Society Journal Entries. 25 November 1847. SAOR 89-1-1292/7-13.

• To all village offices: You are required to search all villages to find whether the [Prussian] citizen Growahl, a foreigner, might be in one of the villages. If he is found, he should be ordered to appear at the Society without delay. In any case, however, a report to the Society that this search was carried out should be made by 10 December 1847.

• Ohrloff: You are ordered to carefully investigate the matter between Treksel and the Jewish woman Isaaksohn from Novoberislav settlement. Either the items taken from Mrs. Isaaksohn or the money owed for them, a total of thirteen rubles, seventy-nine kopeks must be collected from Treksel. The Society should receive a report about this matter.

915. Johann Cornies to Peter Bahnmann. 28 November 1847. SAOR 89-1-1260/118v.

To Peter Bahnmann in Berdiansk,

Franz Doerksen, the foreign resident at present in my service, gave you his document of safe conduct in order to obtain a pass from the Governor of the Crimea. Doerksen is in possession of a receipt from the Berdiansk post office showing that these papers were sent in February. However, despite the passage of time, Doerksen still does not have this pass. Since it presumably should have been received long ago, you are requested to send it to me in Ohrloff. This would enable us to accomplish whatever must still be done in this matter. In any case, I expect a detailed answer very shortly.

With greetings, your friend J. Cornies.

916. Peter Keppen to Johann Cornies. 28 November 1847. SAOR 89-1-1294/4.

Esteemed Friend,

Please accept my profuse thanks for your welcome communication of 8 November. The permanent secretary of the Academy of Sciences will send you the fifteen silver rubles mentioned for the peasants who opened the grave mound. Along with the money, you will receive the Haxthausen work, which I could not purchase for less than seven silver rubles, twenty kopeks. Today, I heard from Haxthausen that the third volume will consist of individual studies. I will also obtain it for you when it appears, although this may well not be very soon, because he is still requesting a contribution to the volume from me. On the whole, the work seems to have been favourably received.

Since you owed me eight rubles, sixty-six and five-sevenths kopeks, I now owe you only one ruble, twenty-six and five-sevenths kopeks. Several issues of the Baer-Helmersen contributions should appear again shortly, and I will send them to you at that time.

With honest respect, your friend and servant, Keppen.

P.S. Many thanks for your willingness to carry out Mr. v. Rauch's wishes. I have communicated your lines to him. He visited me afterwards, although he came when I was not at home. You will probably have heard the details of this matter from the administrator of his estate.

917. Molochnaia Agricultural Society Journal Entries. 28 November 1847. SAOR 89-1-1292/7-13.

• To the Mariupol Mennonite District Office: This repeats the commission and follows the 16 October 1847 communication that action should be taken to ensure that the debt owed by the deceased Schoenthal inhabitant Jacob Dik to the Mennonite Franz Quiring of Conteniusfeld is discharged from Dik's estate. A report that this was carried out is required.

918. Johann Cornies to Johann Neufeld. 28 November 1847. SAOR 89-1-1260/119.

Esteemed Johann Neufeldt in Halbstadt,

Dear Brother-in-law,

I have been invited to appear at the District Office on 10 December to receive a part of the amount I am claiming from Peter Regier, who is in Berdiansk at the present time. Should my business affairs keep me from appearing personally, please be so kind as to receive the money for me and send it to me at your convenience.

With friendly greetings, your honest brother-in-law, Johann Cornies.

919. Phillip Wiebe [for Johann Cornies] to Voth. 28 November 1847. SAOR 89-1-1260/119.

Dear Friend Voth,

The Society that supervises the school system will always favour any-thing useful that promotes the education of our young children. There-fore, if you wish to occupy yourself with the preparation of a book for primary teaching, your essential and most important assignment will be to arrange it in such a way that it is easily understood, simple, and planned only with our schools in mind. Such a publication would in no case be permitted without an approved prior review by the Society. Once the book has been completed, it must be submitted to the Society for this purpose. The Society assumes that you will not neglect your responsibilities at your own school because of work on this publica-tion. Should the contrary be the case, the Society would be in its rights in forbidding you to become involved in the preparation of this book.

With a greeting, Wiebe.

920. Johann Cornies to [unidentified]. 29 November 1847. SAOR 89-1-1260/118v.

Valued friend,

With respect to your inquiry of 21 November asking what to do with the money that has already come in from Enns, I hereby request that you do the calculations and kindly deliver the account to me, as well as the specific portion of the money I am owed. This might also be an opportunity to discuss further what could be done about Jacob Fehdrau so that his debts can be arranged in a similar manner.

In order to be sure to find me at home, you might perhaps not come until next Monday.

I was pleased that you were well received on my Tashchenak estate, since this corresponds to my wishes. That is the way it should be.

With friendly greetings, your friend Johann Cornies.

921. Molochnaia Agricultural Society Journal Entries. 29 November 1847. SAOR 89-1-1292/7-13.

• To village offices in the seventh *revier*: During the course of the winter, you must arrange to have numbered markers prepared for the forest-tree plantations in all villages within the seventh revier and to ensure they are securely erected at the plantations by 1 March 1848. A report to the Society is required after this has been carried out.

922. Johann Cornies to Agricultural Department, Ministry of State Domains. 3 December 1847. SAOR 89-1-1260/120.

To the Agricultural Department of the Ministry of State Domains,

Enclosed with directive No. 3470 of 30 November 1846 was a quantity of the best Havanna tobacco seed that I had planted and tended on my Iushanle estate. The plants had been transplanted into soil that had just been loosened after having been meadowland the previous fall. They reached a height of two and a half arshins and put out up to fifteen leaves that were only very moderate in size. However, the tobacco ripened very quickly, which is highly desirable for tobacco in this region where frost occurs early in fall. It seems that the soil was well suited for the cultivation of this variety of tobacco. The tobacco, however, is considerably different from other varieties in that it produces only a few small leaves. This reduces its returns. For testing, I enclose one bunch of leaves of this tobacco.

923. Isaac Mathies to Johann Cornies. 3 December 1847. SAOR 89-1-1271/289.

Most esteemed friend Mr. Johann Cornies,

Recently Heinrich Siebert, the Supervisor of Orphans' Affairs in Sparrau, asked me to report to you and to request permission to continue my care for one of the children who was left behind by the deceased Johann Fast of Berdiansk. The person in question is Johann Fast, whom I have been supporting for the past four years. This has permitted him to attend school in Steinbach, where he is at present. As the appointed guardian, I have never thought that I would not be permitted to continue in this role. This possibility occurred to Siebert only now. He has urgently requested that I submit this matter to you and negotiate an arrangement that would permit me to continue in the role of guardian of Johann Fast in future as well.

Secondly, I would ask you to kindly write to the Beranli and Schesklen administrators to help me collect the money still outstanding. Several amounts have been outstanding for three to four years.

Thirdly, I would repeat my request that you continue to have patience with me for the repayment of my debt. Once I am able to sell wheat again, I will repay everything with thanks. This I would already have done had my wife's illness not kept me at home. At the present time I think that I still have three thousand chetverts of wheat lying unsold in Berdiansk, although it may already have marketed. I expect, in any case, that I will receive the proceeds of the sale of another 1,100 chetvert of wheat already sold before the New Year. Kindly forgive me for what I have overlooked. I will strive to put this matter in order again.

Your honest friend, Isaac Mathies.

924. Johann Cornies to Johann Heinrich Sonderegger, Editor of *Unterhaltungsblatt für deutsche Ansiedler im südlichen Rußland*. 3 December 1847. SAOR 89-1-1260/120v.

Mr. Johann Heinrich Sonderegger in Grosliebenthal,

I take pleasure in providing you with the enclosed answer from Mr. F.W. Schulz-Roechling, Chairman of the Sarepta Brethren Congregation regarding mailings of the *Unterhaltungsblatt*. He asks Acting State Counsellor v. Hahn to kindly ensure that the paper is sent to him directly from Odesa.

Please ensure that this request is appropriately acted upon.

With exceptional esteem, your respectful Johann Cornies.

925. Johann Cornies to Remy. 3 December 1847. SAOR 89-1-1260/120v.

Mr. Pastor Remy,

Because my position as Chairman [of the Agricultural Society] is a secular one, I cannot carry out the collection you propose from our local congregations. I have only been able to discuss the matter under consideration with my good, closest friends and acquaintances. As a result, only a small contribution of ten silver rubles has been raised. This I have the pleasure to enclose with a request that you accept this small gift with love.

With exceptional esteem, your most respectful Johann Cornies.

926. Molochnaia Agricultural Society Journal Entries. 3 December 1847. SAOR 89-1-1292/7-13.

• To the Kronsgarten Mayor's Office: In order to ensure that all children eligible to attend school are able to benefit from instruction in your village school, the Mayor's Office should send in an accurate record by 25 December showing the names of all inhabitants' children six to fourteen years old.

• To Heinrich Goertz, Overseer of the Hebrew settlement Novo-berislav: The Jewish woman Isaaksohn dwelling with Jacob Treksel from Ohrloff should be investigated most carefully. A report about the results of the investigation is required without delay.

927. Johann Cornies to Martin Kroeker. 5 December 1847. SAOR 89-1-1260/122.

To Martin Kroeker in Margenau,

The wood merchant who is your creditor appeared in my office to complain about the small amount of money he has been able to get from you, since he knows that the amount of the debt the Nogai repaid to you was more. Your actions surprised me as well. I had given the merchant hope because you promised that you would direct the entire amount of the Nogai money to the merchant's claims.

You have put me into a doubtful light by doing this and I demand that you immediately bring me the remaining money to be forwarded to the appropriate place.

928. Molochnaia Agricultural Society Journal Entries. 6 December 1847. SAOR 89-1-1292/7-13.

• Waldheim: This is an order to use the first occurrence of favourable weather during a time when [other] work is light, to raise a dam in the Kurushan river along the road from Waldheim to Gnadenfeld. At the appropriate time, a report is required to the Society showing that this has been done.

929. Johann Cornies to Philipp Matthias. 9 December 1847. SAOR 89-1-1260/122v.

Mr. Philipp Matthias in Berdiansk,

Several years have elapsed and I am still waiting for your payment of interest on the capital sum I lent you. I have not troubled you about this, although you have been letting me know from time to time that you would pay the interest as soon as possible. Each time the term for your payment passed without it being produced, I thought that it was perhaps because your circumstances did not allow you to pay. Now I have heard that your business matters have, thank God, turned out so that you are able you to pay this interest without creating a burden for yourself. Also, an opportunity to send the money has presented itself in the person of my neighbour, Johann Neufeld. I ask you to send me the remainder of the interest with Neufeld and to obtain a receipt from him, showing that the money was paid.

With the firm hope that you, dear friend, will settle this request of mine which is my just demand, I greet you as your friend Johann Cornies.

930. Phillip Wiebe [for Johann Cornies] to Reimer. 9 December 1847. SAOR 89-1-1260/123.

Valued Friend Reimer,

I presume that a variety of improvements and new features have taken place on the Felstenthal estate since 1846. It would therefore be most desirable to include these in the description previously submitted since it has, for particular reasons, not been used to date. Therefore, I come to you with the request that you go over the enclosed description one more time and make additions wherever they are necessary, even if the subjects are of little importance. After this has been completed, I request in the Chairman's name that you send the description to us again to enable us to make the desired use of it.

With esteem, greeting you heartily, your friend Wiebe.

931. Phillip Wiebe [for Johann Cornies] to unidentified. 9 December 1847. SAOR 89-1-1260/123v.

Valued Friend,

You are asked to peruse the enclosed imperfect comparison of production on two agricultural establishments, one in Prussia, the other here, and then, with reference to your own experiences, prepare more specific comparative accounts to the extent that you can. You need not keep to this format. Please bring forward whatever you find useful or necessary.

Once you have completed this task, which might be of great importance for our agriculture, please send it to the Chairman.

With the greatest respect, and with polite greetings, your honest friend, Wiebe.

932. Johann Cornies to Johann Cornies Jr. 13 December 1847. SAOR 89-1-1260/124.

Dear son,

How could I respond differently than with heartfelt pleasure when I read your letters and those of your dear bride. I have great and loving sympathy for the touching, sensitive, and sincere words of your bride, my beloved and treasured daughter-in-law. If I could only avoid the total stagnation of my business matters while away, I would come to Elbing and accompany you back home together with Agnes and her dear husband. For the moment, however, I must suppress my desires and desist.

As you requested, I immediately paid the money you asked me to to Franz Klaassen, Neukirch, and Elizabeth Toews, Tiegerweide. Fourteen days ago, Lukovich appeared before me to pay down 1,200 rubles of his debt and asked for the deferral of the rest of his debt until June 1848. He told me that he still owes you 1,070 silver rubles. Since the 1,200 rubles he brought with him would be lying around uselessly and are secure with him, I did not accept the money and gave him time to pay off the entire capital sum in June.

Matters in Tashchenak are a little jumbled with respect to St. Martin's Day. Since I expected your imminent arrival I paid no attention to the need to hire yearly people at the appropriate time to care for the upkeep of your household. When I learned about the change in your plans and that you could not come, I was in a rush to find people to look after matters for you. However, it so happens that there are fewer people available this year than ever before. The administrator Driedger could not wait to hear from me, while housekeeper Martens got married. Maria did not want to stay on any longer, nor did Hofer's Anna or the coachman Andres. Elis, on the other hand, had been accepted for an apprenticeship to a tradesman. Of the entire group only the business secretary Klaassen and Swedish Anna stayed on.

All household positions are thus emptied of people while we have enough to fill all of the positions in our economic establishment. Jacob Dik and his family turned up, having just arrived from Prussia and in search of a position. There was one waiting for him in Tashchenak and he accepted it with the greatest of pleasure. I have hired a sensible girl from Hutterthal and a recently arrived Mennonite took the place of Andres. Although I handed the administration of the establishment over to young Hoemsen, who had worked as Driedger's assistant in summer, I had to dismiss him from this position within two weeks because of his disorderly behaviour. I have transferred that position to Pauls until Dik has become better accustomed to the country. He already speaks quite a bit of Russian. Things are now going quite well, in an orderly fashion, and I am no longer so concerned.

I nevertheless wish that you would hire yourself at least two decent Mennonite girls in Prussia, who could help in serving your wife and provide her with companionship and help on the road and here, even if you have to promise that they can return home at our expense after several years of service and when an opportunity arises. Also, hire on coachmen and anyone else you think might be needed. By now, people for yearly service are almost impossible to find and any individuals still available are generally useless.

When I think about your homeward journey, which in my opinion could be done most comfortably with your own horses and wagons, I doubt that the two thousand silver rubles I forwarded to you from Odesa to Hamburg will be enough to equip yourself fully and to make the journey. I assume you will be travelling with three wagons, each harnessed with two strong horses. All three of the wagons, or at least two of them, should have springs. We could use the wagons here. If necessary, find someone to lend you as much as you need. Alternatively, report to me immediately about how much extra money you would need in order that I might send you another bill of exchange to Hamburg from Odesa.

In sending you many greetings from me and Agnes and your brother-in-law, I also ask you not to forget to pass on my most genuine greetings to your dear bride and thank her for her letter. This is something I consider to be very important. Please commend me most urgently to your father-in-law and his relatives. May you and your dear bride enjoy life in good cheer and joy.

This is wished by one who loves you from the bottom of his soul, and calls himself your father, Johann Cornies.

933. Molochnaia Agricultural Society Journal Entries. 17 December 1847. SAOR 89-1-1292/7-13.

• Hutterthal: A report is required as to what decision has been made about the situation between Christian Wurz and Melitopol merchant Karobot and about its results.

• Khortitsa [Agricultural] Society Chairman: You are commissioned to take the necessary measures to ensure that the old school is rebuilt as planned, to the obvious advantage of the Khortitsa village community, instead of simply having it repaired. Results are to be reported.

• Ohrloff: Money for the Novoberislav Jewish woman's various belongings that disappeared from Treksel's wagon must be collected from Treksel. It should be submitted to the Society for further action.

934. Phillip Wiebe [for Johann Cornies] to Traugott Blueher. 20 December 1847. SAOR 89-1-1260/126v.

Esteemed Mr. Blueher,

On 9 December, four crates of raw silk and three balls of silk cocoons were dispatched to you via Kharkiv, to be sold on merchant Aleksandr Iakovlev's account.

The crates marked "A" contain, in crate No. 1: four puds, seven funt, seventeen lot; in crate No. 1/5: four puds, seven funt, six loth; in crate No. 2/6: three puds, eighteen funt, sixteen lot; and in crate No. 3/7: two puds, thirty-seven funt, nine lot, for a total of fourteen puds, twenty-seven funt, sixteen lot. Iakovlev priced most of this silk at 520 rubles per pud on his own accounts here.

The balls marked "A.J." contain cocoons weighing seventeen chetverik in No. 2, and cocoons weighing eleven chetverik in Nos. 3 & 4. The latter quantity of cocoons are mostly double or emptied cocoons, unsuitable for reeling. Iakovlev bought these on speculation, wanting to experiment if they might possibly be usable in some manner or if some application might be found for them. They were bought at the relatively expensive price of six rubles per chetverik.

My father-in-law will send you the desired authorization and the accounts for Iakovlev's retrospective debts as soon as possible so that this business can be completed.

The recently sent four thousand silver rubles were received correctly on 15 December.

Whenever a transport opportunity occurs before next autumn, you might forward to us a shipment of up to three hundred copies of Bible stories of the known edition.

We send all of you our most sincere greetings and wish you pleasant holidays and a very blessed New Year.

With honest love, I commend myself as your respectful Phillip Wiebe

**935. Johann Cornies to Cornelius Wiens. 29 December 1847.
SAOR 89-1-1260/127v.**

Honourable Cornelius Wiens in Ohrloff,

On the enclosed report for each of the crown apprentices in your care, you should enter: 1. his age, 2. the progress he is making, and 3. his behaviour. You should also include your own comments, if necessary. This report must then be sent back to me by 5 January 1848, without fail, to enable me to prepare the semi-annual list required by the General Inspector. For this reason, I would also stipulate that this should be confirmed conscientiously, not superficially.

SAOR 89-1-1260/128: [same content also to seven other Molochnaia residents] Heinrich Wiens, Blumenort; Heinrich Epp, Muntau; Johann Sukkau, Blumenort; Peter Cornies, Ohrloff; Jacob Neumann, Muensterberg; Isaac Wiens, Altona; Jacob Wiebe, Liebenau.

**936. Jacob Neumann to Johann Cornies. 29 December 1847.
SAOR 89-1-1243/2.**

To Mr. Johann Cornies, Chairman of the Agricultural Society in Ohrloff,

This is my response to a commission received from the Society's worthy secretary, Mr. Phillip Wiebe, asking me to compare two agricultural establishments, one in the Grosser Werder in West Prussia with fifteen and a half desiatinas of land, and the other on the Molochnaia in Southern Russia, assuming that the two are in good, average condition. (However, because I am not sufficiently acquainted with the former strip of land and also because the grain prices in West Prussia are so very different from those in Southern Russia, I have used average prices.)

Upon deep reflection, I decided to compare two agricultural establishments, one with twenty desiatinas of ploughed land and the other with twenty-five desiatinas of ploughed or cultivated land. If both are well managed, there would be a great difference in the amount of grain produced by each. In my opinion, it is better not to keep too many sheep in an establishment because they take the best pastures away from the other livestock while, on the other hand, their yield is much lower. The other livestock can be better maintained if more land is ploughed.

Here is my overview of the grain I harvested per desiatina this year, by variety and by income. The costs are calculated on the basis of the kind of work involved, each one listed separately (seeding, ploughing, harvesting, threshing). The costs are totalled as is the clear profit.

• Purchased seven and a half chetvert of Hirka wheat, six of rye, twenty-two of barley, twelve of oats, and sixty of small and large potatoes.

• Price of a chetvert of grain this year: sixteen rubles for Hirka wheat, eight rubles for rye, five and a half rubles for barley, six rubles for oats, and an average of five rubles for potatoes.

• Cost of seed [per desiatina]: eight rubles for Hirka wheat, four for rye, five and a half for barley, six and three quarters for oats, and thirty rubles for potatoes.

• Ploughing, seeding, and harrowing: eight rubles for each grain, forty for potatoes.

• Harvesting and transporting grain home: twelve rubles for Hirka wheat, ten rubles for rye, twelve rubles for barley, ten rubles for oats, and thirty-six rubles for potatoes.

• Threshing of grain: ten and a half rubles for Hirka wheat, nine rubles for each of the other grains.

• Entire income for one desiatina: 120 rubles for Hirka wheat, forty-eight rubles for rye, 121 rubles for barley, seventy-two rubles for oats, and three hundred rubles for potatoes.

• Total cost of working one desiatina: thirty-eight and a half rubles for Hirka wheat, thirty-one rubles for rye, thirty-four and a half rubles for barley, thirty-three and three-quarter rubles for oats, and 111 rubles for potatoes.

• Clear profit on one desiatina: eighty-one and a half rubles for Hirka wheat, seventeen for rye, eighty-six and a half for barley, thirty-eight and a quarter rubles for oats, and 184 rubles for potatoes.

Here I have given an overview [of a fullholding] with twenty-five desiatinas of ploughed land and the returns from it. Such a fullholding returns much more than one with twenty desiatinas because more grain is necessary for working horses.

• Land use: twenty-five desiatinas ploughland, two and a half desiatinas plantations [*Anlagen*], eight desiatinas haymeadows, twenty-nine and a half uncultivated land.

• Stock of animals: six horses, four young horses, eight cows, four young cows, seventy-five sheep, five pigs.

• The twenty-five desiatinas ploughland are divided:

  • five desiatinas left fallow, with fallow land being manured or sometimes also used for other purposes;

  • one desiatina of oats produced fifteen chetvert so that three desiatinas of oats produced forty-five chetvert;

• one desiatina of barley produced eighteen chetvert so that three desiatinas produced fifty-four chetvert;

• one desiatina of rye produced nine chetvert so that three desiatinas rye produced twenty-seven chetvert;

• one desiatina of wheat produced eight chetvert so that eleven desiatinas wheat produce eighty-eight chetvert;

• Total produced on twenty desiatinas is 216 chetvert [of grain].

Grain used:

• thirty-five chetvert of oats used as fodder and as seed, leaving ten chetvert to be sold at six rubles for a total of sixty rubles;

• thirty-five chetvert of barley used [to feed] pigs and for seed, leaving twenty-nine chetvert for sale at five and a half rubles for a total of 159.50 rubles;

• twelve chetvert of rye used for bread and seed, leaving fifteen chetvert to be sold at eight rubles, for a total of 120 rubles;

• twelve chetvert of wheat used for seed and for flour, leaving seventy-six chetvert to be sold at fifteen and three-quarter rubles, for a total of 1,197 rubles;

• Total [income for grain] was 1,536.50 rubles.

Livestock:

• eight cows can bring in 220 rubles;

• shearing seventy-five sheep produced six puds of wool, bringing in 150 rubles;

• ten inferior sheep sold at three rubles each, yielding thirty rubles;

• eight geldings sold at five rubles each, yielding forty rubles;

• ten lambs sold at two and a half rubles each, yielding twenty-five rubles;

• fruit and trees sold from the gardens and woods yielded seventy-five rubles;

• fifteen funt spun silk for sale for 150 rubles;

Total income [from all above sources] 2,226.50 rubles.

Expenses: land tax for the piece of land: eleven rubles, ninety-four kopeks; pay for workers employed: 510 rubles;

Total expenses are therefore 521.94 rubles to be deducted from above income.

Final total income is 1,704.56 rubles, which is what remains in a good, average year.

A comparison of what two fullholdings, one in West Prussia and one here in Southern Russian on the Molochnaia, can yield in a good, average harvest:

In the first years of the current century, a Mennonite in the Grosser Werder near Marienburg in West Prussia sold a fifteen and a half desiatina piece of land, clay soil mixed with sand, for 16,050 gulden.

• The fifteen and a half desiatinas were divided as follows: three desiatinas of fallow, one and a half desiatinas of meadows, and eleven desiatinas of ploughland.

• The eleven desiatinas of ploughland were divided: three desiatinas for oats, one and a half for barley, three and a quarter for rye, and three and a quarter for wheat.

• Stock of animals was four horses, one foal, three cows, one calf, five pigs.

• one desiatina of oats produced twenty-four chetverts and three desiatinas produced seventy-two chetverts;

• one desiatina of barley produced twenty chetverts and one and a half desiatinas produced thirty chetverts;

• one desiatina of rye produced fourteen chetverts and three and a quarter desiatinas produced forty-five and a half chetverts;

• one desiatina of wheat produced ten chetverts and three and a quarter desiatinas produced thirty-two and a half chetverts;

• Total of eleven desiatinas produced 180 chetverts [of grains].

[Grain used:]

• twenty-four chetvert of oats required as fodder and seed so that forty-eight chetvert oats remain to be sold;

• eighteen chetvert of barley required to feed pigs and as seed so that twelve chetvert barley remain to be sold;

• fourteen chetvert of rye required for bread and as seed so that twenty-eight and a half chetvert rye remain to be sold;

• seven chetvert of wheat used for flour and as seed so that twenty-six and a half chetvert wheat remain to be sold;

Total of 115 chetvert [of grain] remain to be sold.

• forty-eight chetvert of oats were sold at six gulden per chetvert, yielding 288 gulden;

• twelve chetvert of barley were sold at ten gulden per chetvert, yielding 120 gulden;

• twenty-eight and half chetvert of rye were sold at sixteen gulden per chetvert, yielding 456 gulden;

• twenty-six and a half chetvert of wheat were sold at twenty gulden per chetvert, yielding 530 gulden;

Total amount of grain sold produced 1,394 gulden.

• Three cows can bring in 225 gulden

Therefore, the total income would be 1,619 gulden.

Expenses totalled 300 gulden, including 150 gulden land taxes and 150 gulden to work the land.

Final income in a good, average year amounts to 1,319 gulden.

A fullholding of sixty-five desiatinas of land on the Molochnaia in Southern Russia, all properly worked in an ordinary fashion, with barn and orchards, the land maintained adequately, and with livestock, wagons, and implements, and assuming that such a fullholding is supplied with sufficient workers, the results in a good average year will be:

• Sixty-five desiatinas of land, including twenty desiatinas of ploughed land, two and a half desiatinas of plantings, eight desiatinas of haymeadows, and thirty-four and a half desiatinas of grazing land.

• Livestock : six horses, three young horses, eight cows, four young cattle, seventy-five sheep, four pigs.

Crops produced on twenty desiatinas of ploughed land, divided as follows, after five desiatinas of fallow were set aside:

• oats produced fifteen chetvert per desiatina so that thirty-seven and a half chetvert of oats were produced on two and a half desiatinas;

• barley produced eighteen chetvert per desiatina, so that forty-five chetvert were produced on two and a half desiatinas;

• rye produced nine chetvert per desiatina, so that twenty-two and a half chetvert were produced on two and a half desiatinas;

• wheat produced eight chetvert per desiatina, so that sixty chetvert were produced on seven and a half desiatinas.

Total of grain produced: 165 chetvert.

On such a fullholding, grain is used:

• thirty chetvert of oats (fodder and seed). Seven and a half chetvert oats remain to be sold;
• twelve chetvert barley (pig feed, seed, and porridge). Fifteen chetvert barley remain for sale;
• twelve chetvert rye (bread and seed). Ten and a half chetvert rye remain for sale;
• eight chetvert wheat (seed and household use). Fifty-two chetvert wheat remain for sale;
Total amount of grain for sale: eighty-five chetvert.

[Income from above]:

• Seven and a half chetvert oats at six rubles per chetvert: forty-five rubles;
• fifteen chetvert barley at five rubles, fifty kopeks per chetvert: eighty-two rubles, fifty kopeks;
• ten and a half chetvert rye at eight rubles per chetvert: eighty-four [sic] rubles;
• fifty-two chetvert wheat at fifteen rubles, seventy-five kopeks per chetvert:

814 rubles;
Total [of income for grain]: 1,030 rubles, fifty kopeks.

• eight cows can bring in: 220 rubles;
• wool from seventy-five sheep: 150 rubles;
• ten inferior sheep to be sold at three rubles each: thirty rubles;
• eight geldings to be sold at five rubles each: forty rubles;
• ten lambs to be sold at two rubles, fifty kopeks each: twenty-five rubles;
• fruit from orchard and young trees from woods: seventy-five rubles;
• fifteen funt of harvested silk sold: 150 rubles;

Combined total of all of the above: 1,720 rubles, fifty kopeks.
Land tax for this piece of land: eleven rubles, ninety-four kopeks.
Cost of working this piece of land: 490 rubles.
Total costs to be deducted: 501 rubles, ninety-four kopeks.
Therefore, in a Molochnaia village, 1,218 rubles, fifty-six kopeks remain.

937. Molochnaia Agricultural Society Journal Entries. 30 December 1847. SAOR 89-1-1292/7-13.

• Lichtenau: The foreigner Groswahl resided with Cornelius Heidebrecht in Lichtenau when he was in service there. He has died in the Khortitsa village of Rosenthal and you are ordered to put his possessions into storage. As soon as there is a secure opportunity, they should be sent to the Rosenthal Mayor's Office for a decision. Results should be reported to the Society.

• Sparrau: A Sparrau Mennonite took a rifle from Chernigov District Chairman Chlepetko to repair it and it has definitely not been returned. You should present a receipt by 5 January 1848, showing that the [above-mentioned] District Chairman has received satisfaction.

• Friedensdorf: You should collect three silver rubles, thirty-six kopeks from householders number twenty-eight and twenty-nine for trees they did not plant in the plantation and submit this money to the Society by 5 January 1848 at the latest.

• Fuerstenwerder: fifty-four kopeks silver [should be collected from] householder number three.

• Gnadenheim: a total of three silver rubles, thirty-three kopeks [should be collected from] householders number twenty-one, twenty-three, and twenty-four.

• Liebenau: a total of three silver rubles, sixty kopeks [should be collected from] householders number eight, ten, eleven, and sixteen.

• Lichtfelde: Your local householder number twenty has not completed planting trees or hedges in his section of the forest-tree plantation and the Society orders a fine of two silver rubles for his negligence. The money should be sent to the Society immediately, by 5 January 1848, at the latest.

938. Johann Cornies to Hermann Sudermann. 31 December 1847. SAOR 89-1-1260/128.

Overseer of the Crown Plantation,

Using exactly the same method as you did this past July, you should send me a careful report about the Crown apprentices on the plantation, including: 1. their age, 2. the progress they are making, 3. their behaviour, and 4. what can presumably be expected from them in future. Also, include anything else that is noteworthy. I should receive this by 10 January 1848 to enable me to send my reports to the Tavrida State Domains Bureau.

939. Molochnaia Agricultural Society Journal Entries. N.d. [1847.] SAOR 89-1-1292/7-13.

Agricultural Society record: Society punishments during the course of the year 1847:
Fines were levied:

• one Mayor for serving as a bad example to the people subordinate to him during the most recent selection of a District Chairman,
• five householders for neglecting forest-tree plantations,
• one householder for his raillery and his behaviour on the public road,
• one householder for cultivating the fallow badly,
• one cottager for irresponsibly undertaking to build on a cottager lot.

Work penalties were issued:

• two householders for their defiant behaviour towards their local administrator,
• one householder for malicious lies that disturbed the peace of his village community,
• two householders for neglecting Society directives,
• two householders for outrageous behaviour in the village office.

Work penalties issued and arrests by the District Office:

• two householders for their malicious behaviour towards the District Chairman,
• four householders for their dissolute behaviour at the weddings of their Lutheran servants,
• one cottager and his daughter for breaking the seal on a Society package containing money,
• four servants and one carpentry apprentice who participated in the forced entry into a house and the disturbance created there.

Arrests by the Village Offices:

• one householder for insulting the Village Mayor,
• one cottager for theft,
• one householder's wife who secretly abducted her daughter from foster care.

Strokes using a rod were levied:

• one cottager's son and two servants for instigating a forced break-in at a house and for the uproar created.

1848

940. Annual Report. 1 January 1848. SAOR 89-1-1296/1.

I. Tree Planting

a) At present the total of all varieties of trees growing in the district is:

- In plantations: 636,579 forest trees and 367,128 mulberry trees, totalling 1,003,707 trees in plantations.
- In orchards: 335,924 fruit trees, 14,074 forest trees, and 10,988 mulberry trees, totalling 360,986 trees in orchards.
- Along streets and in various other locations: 16,615 wild pear trees and *Kruschki*, 73,096 willows in all plantings, and 1,237,179 mulberry trees in hedges, in plantations and orchards.
- In nurseries: 69,433 improved fruit trees, 279,707 unimproved fruit trees, 752,248 forest trees, and 691,828 mulberry trees, totalling 1,793,216 trees in nurseries.
- With the exception of hedges and wild olive trees and hawthorns, which were not counted, the total number of existing trees is 4,484,799 trees.

b) Trees specifically planted during the year 1847:

- In plantations: 57,893 forest trees and 41,636 mulberry trees, for a total of 99,529 trees.
- In orchards: 8,003 apple trees, 4,900 pear trees, 7,936 plum trees, 5,251 cherry trees, and 1,460 apricot trees for a total of 27,550 trees.
- 94,701 mulberry trees in hedges.
- 1,742 wild pear trees.

c) By 1845, exactly 373 quartals were completely planted in the eighteen plantations of the first revier.

In 1847, the three plantations of the second revier finished planting fifty-eight quartals.

In the plantations of the third revier, 109 quartals were completely planted, specifically, three in Fischau, thirty in Alexanderwohl, seventeen in Alexanderthal, five in Schardau, seventeen in Rudnerweide, thirteen in Grossweide, and twenty-four in Franzthal.

In the fourth revier, planting was completed in eighty-one quartals, specifically thirteen in Liebenau, fourteen in Gnadenheim, nineteen in Fuerstenwerder, eleven in Margenau, fourteen in Neukirch, and ten in Marienthal.

In the fifth revier, forty-seven quartals were completely planted, five in Friedensdorf, twenty-three in Tiegerweide, eleven in Prangenau, and eight in Elisabeththal, [three?] in Wernersdorf.

In the sixth revier, Sparrau completed four quartals.

[No number] for the seventh revier, including Gnadenfeld, Conteniusfeld, and Waldheim.

The total number of quartals [already planted], each with an area of a half-desiatina, is 572 quartals.

d) The largest nurseries that contain all the different varieties of forest trees, other than nurseries on estates, are:

- Martin Schierling, fullholder in Blumstein village with twelve thousand trees,
- Stephan Kerber, cottager in Alexanderthal village with nine thousand trees,
- Isaak Braun, cottager in Lindenau village with 9,675 trees, and
- Abraham Friesen, fullholder in Rueckenau village with five thousand trees.

Mulberry trees growing in individual nurseries:

- Cottager Jacob Isaac in Rudnerweide, twenty thousand trees,
- Cottager Abrah[am] Huebert in Neukirch, fifteen thousand trees, and
- Cottager Jacob Barkmann in Rueckenau, 11,540 trees.

e) Villages distinguishing themselves in planting fruit trees were Gnadenfeld with 2,423 trees, Sparrau with 1,804 trees, and Blumstein with 1,431 trees.

• Individual inhabitants who have distinguished themselves by planting more than two hundred fruit trees are the following full-holders: Gnadenfeld villagers Salomon Ediger with 328, Heinrich Goertz with 275, Gerhard Voth with 270, and Abraham Bekker with 242. Fullholder Peter Hoge in Blumstein village planted 227 fruit trees. Also, the following cottagers, Gerhard Giesbrecht, Blumstein, planted 140 fruit trees; Gerhard Thomsen, Neukirch, planted eighty-two fruit trees; and Jacob Pankratz, Gnadenfeld, planted seventy-four fruit trees.

f) Most notable in raising fruit trees from seed and improving them were cottager Isaak Braun in Lindenau with 4,134 improved trees and 485 unimproved trees; fullholder Isaac Wiens in Altonau with 1,605 improved trees and 1,510 unimproved trees; and fullholder Peter Penner in Prangenau with 1,105 improved trees and 2,100 unimproved trees.

g) Planting of wild olive trees for enclosures and to protect the plantations was completed by 692 fullholders and started by eighty-two individuals for a total of 774 fullholders.

Mulberry hedges around the quartals were completed by 646 fullholders and started by 275 for a total of 921 fullholders.

h) Hedges for enclosures and to protect fruit in orchards were completed by 826 fullholders and cottagers and started by 126, for a total of 988 individuals.

Mulberry hedges to form the boundary between yard areas occupied by fullholders and cottagers were completed by 937 individuals and started by 495, for a total of 1,432 individuals.

i) Sales from the tree nurseries in the district during the course of this year totalled: – 19,646 fruit trees for 880 silver rubles, ninety-seven kopeks – 212,853 forest trees for 2,792 silver rubles, fifty-five kopeks.

These total sales are approximately thirty thousand nursery trees higher than the sales of 1846 but the returns are lower. Prices increasingly indicate that there is a surplus of trees, despite the fact that the market for them is wider.

Fresh fruit income was lower during the year just elapsed. It totalled only 3,564 rubles, fifty-nine and a half kopeks. Sales prices were as high as sixty kopeks per chetverik for summer fruit and as high as one silver ruble, twenty kopeks for winter fruit. The largest income for fresh fruit, thirty-one silver rubles, thirty-nine kopeks, was earned by Franz Krueger, Blumstein fullholder.

Despite all efforts in May to eliminate various caterpillars, *Passionsraupen und Spindelraupen* (passion caterpillar and spindle worm) caused a great deal of damage. The former increased so quickly that during the course of one week all tree plantations and even meadows and pastures were swarming with them. Then, unusually heavy hail in June knocked a great deal of fruit from the trees in several villages and lacerated the rest so that it could not reach the necessary firmness.

j) The usual variety of vegetables generally thrived very well this year.

II. Sericulture

A total of 513 inhabitants (410 fullholders and 103 cottagers) in thirty-nine villages harvested 3,041 and seven-eighths chetverik of cocoons. These figures show an increase of 231 inhabitants and two villages over those involved last year. Twenty-three local silk-reelers unwound 2,799 and seven-eights chetverik of this total. The unwound silk weighed an average of thirty-three and one-ninth loth per chetverik, for a total of seventy-two puds, sixteen funt, ten loth. Due to a shortage of reeling machines, 242 chetverik of cocoons were not unwound. Assuming that the average weight per chetverik was thirty-three loth, it can be accepted that about seventy-nine puds of silk were produced during 1847.

Producers who distinguished themselves were Peter Loewen, Gnadenheim, with twenty-six funt, five loth; Peter Neufeld, Petershagen, with twenty-one funt, seventeen loth; Peter Renpenning, Lindenau, with twenty-one funt; Peter Toews, Tiege, with twenty funt, eighteen loth; and Johann Dik, Muensterberg, with twenty funt, two loth.

Since this considerable upswing in sericulture is not sufficiently served by the imperfect unwinding methods for cocoons used previously, the Society is giving serious thought to remedying the problem by suitable means and it has already made suggestions to the government so that future silk production can be ensured.

III. Planting along streets

The villages of Ohrloff, Tiege, Blumenort, Rosenort, and the community sheepfarm are connected by streets along which trees have been planted at intervals of eight sazhen on both sides, all properly fenced as well. Tiegerweide is also connected with Rueckenau and Fuerstenwerder and Lichtfelde is connected with Neukirch. For the coming year, 1848, setting trenches have been prepared for plantings along the street between Fuerstenwerder and Alexanderwohl.

IV. Plantings to protect cultivated fields

In order to provide protection from storms and to enable the soil to retain more moisture, the villages of Ohrloff and Altonau are being used as examples since their plantings are already growing very well. This year, 1847, the villages of Muensterberg and Blumenort have each assigned about one hundred desiatinas of cultivated land to be planted systematically with trees and mulberry hedges.

V. Tobacco cultivation

The tobacco harvest by inhabitants of twenty-seven villages was only a total of 283 puds, twenty-eight funt this year. Distinguishing themselves in tobacco cultivation this year were cottager Aron Peters in Rueckenau with ten puds of tobacco and fullholder Johann Reimer in Waldheim with ten puds.

More specific expert knowledge is needed before tobacco cultivation can make progress here, including the ability to choose varieties that are able to defy storms. In addition, the fields must be protected for this purpose. Every year, winds take away tobacco fields to some extent. This year hail ruined the leaves on the plants in several areas.

VI. Field cultivation (wheat cultivation):

Total amount of land sown with wheat was 153 desiatinas and 900 faden for Arnautka, and 12,192 desiatinas and 2,300 faden for Hirka. These totals are approximately 180 desiatinas less for Arnautka and 490 desiatinas more for Hirka than in 1846.

In all forty-five villages, yields of the wheat harvest were: in Halbstadt twenty-two-fold [of amount sown]; Muntau thirteenfold; Schoenau twelvefold; Fischau thirteenfold; Lindenau elevenfold; Lichtenau thirteenfold; Blumstein thirteenfold; Muensterberg twelvefold; Altonau eightfold; Ohrloff elevenfold; Tiege thirteenfold; Blumenort twelvefold; Rosenort twelvefold; Fuerstenau fourteenfold; Rueckenau elevenfold;

Margenau tenfold; Lichtfelde tenfold; Neukirch elevenfold; Alexanderthal tenfold; Schardau elevenfold; Pordenau thirteenfold; Marienthal fourteenfold; Rudnerweide twelvefold; Grossweide thirteenfold; Franzthal fifteenfold; Pastwa twelvefold; Sparrau twelvefold; Conteniusfeld twelvefold; Gnadenfeld seventeenfold; Waldheim elevenfold; Landskrone twenty-five-fold; Friedensdorf twelvefold; Gnadenheim twelvefold; Alexanderwohl tenfold; Fuerstenwerder ninefold; Wernersdorf twenty-four-fold; Liebenau twelvefold; Schoenau tenfold; Petershagen fourteenfold; Ladekopp tenfold; Tiegenhagen thirteenfold; Elisabeththal fourteenfold; Prangenau thirteenfold; Tiegerweide ninefold; Hutterthal sevenfold.

Average yields [of grain sown] in the entire district were: rye harvest, six and five-sixths fold; wheat harvest, thirteen and a third fold; barley harvest, fifteen and a half fold; oat harvest, eight and a half fold; and potato harvest, seven and a half fold.

Potato cultivation:

A total of 18,569 and a half chetvert of potatoes were harvested from the 2,484 chetvert that were seeded, an average increase of almost seven and a half fold. The upper villages obtained a return as high as sixteenfold, and individual fullholders a great deal more and these potatoes were tasty and healthy as well. In contrast, potatoes in the lower villages rot very easily and generally have little value.

The highest potato yields were gained in Rudnerweide with 1,469 chetvert, Marienthal with 1,187 chetvert, Pordenau with 970 chetvert, and Grossweide with 825 chetvert. The lowest yields occurred in Fischau with 139 chetvert, Schoenau with 145 chetvert, Tiege with 152 chetvert, Lichtenau with 187 chetvert, and Fuerstenau with 191 chetvert.

Fullholders who distinguished themselves in potato cultivation were Abraham Klassen, Rudnerweide, with eighty-five chetvert; Johann Regier, Rudnerweide, with eighty chetvert; Peter Schroeder, Marienthal, with seventy-five chetvert; Johann Wiebe, Rudnerweide, with seventy chetvert; Abraham Klassen, Grossweide, with seventy chetvert; and Heinrich Toews, Pordenau, with sixty-seven chetvert.

Flax cultivation:

Flax generally succeeded only very moderately this year. The entire harvest of 648 pud, eight funt in the entire district does not even cover half of our own needs. Gnadenfeld village distinguished itself with eighty-seven puds and householder Johann Janzen in Ladekopp village with seven puds.

Muntau, Wernersdorf, Friedensdorf, Gnadenheim, Lichtfelde, Schardau, Pastwa, and Sparrau villages harvested no flax. The Mayor's Offices in these villages must therefore encourage their inhabitants to cultivate flax to cover their own needs, especially the villages Wernersdorf, Friedensdorf, Schardau, and Sparrau who have harvested no flax for two years in succession.

This winter, 2,253 persons are occupied with spinning flax and ninety-five people are weaving yarn.

IX. Domestic economy:

The total quantity of butter sold was 8,526 puds, two funt, bringing in 82,093 rubles, twenty-eight kopeks. A quantity of 376 puds, eighteen funt of cheese was sold for 3,756 rubles, forty-six kopeks.

Villages with the most important income from butter were Alexanderwohl, with 3,755 rubles, twenty-nine kopeks; Rueckenau with 2,978 rubles, thirty-nine kopeks; Lichtenau with 2,764 rubles, twenty-seven kopeks; and Rosenort with 2,732 rubles, forty-five kopeks. Conteniusfeld had the lowest income from butter, with 915 rubles.

Individuals taking precedence for butter sales are Johann Sukkau, Blumenort, who earned 324 rubles, forty-eight kopeks; Johann Warkentin, Blumstein, 280 rubles; Peter Toews, Tiege, 275 rubles, forty-eight kopeks; Dietrich Loewen, Fuerstenau, 260 rubles; and Johann Loewen, Rueckenau, 240 rubles. Those who earned most with cheese sales were Peter Epp, Blumenort, with three hundred rubles, twenty-eight kopeks; Heinrich Schmidt, Alexanderwohl, with 189 rubles; and Widow Wiens, Ohrloff, with 182 rubles.

Sparse grazing was experienced almost everywhere early in the summer and this limited milk production considerably. Also, foot-and-mouth disease removed a great number of livestock in some areas.

Servants hired annually from outside of the Molochnaia villages included 306 Russian males and 125 Russian females, for a total of 431 Russians, and also 108 male colonists and eighty-one female colonists, totalling 189 colonists. Local Mennonites of both genders hired totalled 810. The combined total of hired servants was thus 1,430. One hundred and ten more individuals were hired from outside the local villages while seventy fewer local inhabitants were hired than last year. It can thus be concluded that the collective wealth of our own inhabitants is increasing.

Orderly accounts of income and expenditures within their own economy were kept by 364 householders in this district. This number is twelve individuals fewer than in the past year, which is surprising. Inhabitants are strongly encouraged to see this as the first necessity of a properly regulated economy and not to neglect it as wealth increases.

X. Trades and construction.

Brick and roof-tile kilns: a total of 3,172,280 bricks were fired in fifteen brickworks during the course of 1847, while 2,967,299 bricks were used the same year. A total of 109,540 roof tiles were fired in two works in 1847 and 107,117 were used. Bricks kept on hand from this year and previous years totalled 607,272. The total number of tiles on hand was 8,423.

There were 107 threshing machines in operation [in 1847], nine more than during the past year. Also in operation were one chaff cutter powered by a machine and 120 powered with horses.

The number of chaff cutters was twenty-seven more than last year, proof that barn feeding is taking a firmer direction due to the frequent shortages of hay.

New constructions included six cylindrical treadmills built in a newer, more advantageous manner and twenty-two treadmills with disks. New structures built during the year 1847 are listed as sixty-five dwelling houses, thirty-four of them built with fired brick and thirty-one with other materials. Two schoolhouses [were built] of fired brick. A total of five granaries and four regular blacksmith works were constructed, one granary and three regular blacksmith works of fired brick, the others of other materials.

Constructed of wood were a total of 182 buildings, fifty-one barns, thirty-two sheds, and twenty-three other buildings for the use of craftsmen. This respectable number of structures would have been higher if an exceptional shortage of wood for construction had not been felt as it never has before.

In 1847, thirty-one structures were roofed with Dutch roof tiles. Thus the total number of buildings with Dutch roof tiles is now 118, including two churches, forty-four dwellings, seven schools, twelve granaries, one storage warehouse, four factory buildings, one paint work, three vinegar distilleries, two beer breweries, two brandy distilleries, twenty blacksmith works, and seventeen other buildings.

XI. Estimates of incomes in Molochnaia Mennonite District

Inhabitants of the villages in this district had a total income of 325,390 silver rubles, fifty-three and a half kopeks from various agricultural products and 64,442 silver rubles, twenty and a half kopeks for wool, for a total of 389,832 silver rubles, seventy-three kopeks. This total is 56,066 silver rubles, seventy-four kopeks more that during 1846.

The average income for each of 7,273 souls of both genders between the ages of sixteen and sixty and capable of working was fifty-three rubles, sixty kopeks. Alternately, it was six rubles, ninety kopeks for each soul [in the Molochnaia Mennonite District].

Excluding wool, the highest incomes for all other agricultural products were in the villages of:

Gnadenfeld: with 241 souls of both genders capable of working, its total was 15,590 [silver] rubles, fifty kopeks, or sixty-four [silver] rubles, sixty-nine kopeks per soul.

Ohrloff: with 118 souls of both genders capable of working, the total was 7,273 [silver] rubles, forty-six kopeks, or sixty-one silver rubles, sixty-four kopeks per soul.

When the above was recorded, Gnadenfeld still had 654 chetvert wheat waiting to be sold and Ohrloff had 677.

XII. Principal income of district consists of:

1. 58,346 chetvert wheat, at an average of four rubles, forty-seven kopeks, totalling 261,163 silver rubles, fifty-seven kopeks.

2. 614 horses, at the average of twenty-five rubles, eighteen kopeks, totalling 15,465 silver rubles, twenty-one kopeks.

3. 625 head of horned cattle, young and old, at an average of twelve rubles, thirty kopeks, totalling 10,150 silver rubles, fifty-six kopeks.

4. 15,315 sheep of all types at the average price of one ruble, sixty kopeks each, totalling 24,413 silver rubles, ten kopeks.

5. 8,717 puds, eleven funt of wool were shorn from 98,524 sheep. On the average, each head produced sixty-five kopeks, for a total of 64,442 silver rubles, twenty kopeks.

6. Cheese and butter income totalled 24,528 silver rubles, thirty-five kopeks.

During the course of 1847 the punishments handed out by the Society were:

Fines:

• one Village Mayor for the bad example he provided to those under his control during the most recent selection of a District Chairman;
  • five fullholders for neglected forest-tree plantings;
  • one fullholder for instigating raillery on the public streets;
  • one fullholder for working his fallow fields badly;
  • one cottager for his irresponsible undertaking of building on a cottager allotment.

Work penalties:

• two fullholders for their defiant behaviour towards local authorities;
  • one fullholder for maliciously bringing up lies and thus disturbing the peace in his village community;
  • two fullholders for neglecting [Agricultural] Society directives;
  • two fullholders for wanton rioting at their Village Mayor's Office. They were arrested at the District Office;
  • two fullholders for malicious behaviour towards the District Chairman. They were also arrested at the District Office;
  • Four fullholders for their dissolute behaviour at the weddings of their Lutheran servants;
  • one cottager and his daughter for breaking the seal of a Society package containing money;
  • four servants and one carpentry apprentice for forcibly entering a house and creating a disturbance there.

Penalties of arrest in Village Mayors' Offices:

• one fullholder for insulting the Village Mayor;
  • one cottager for theft;
  • one woman fullholder for secretly abducting her daughter from foster care.

Caning penalties:
• one cottager's son and two servants for instigating a forcible break-in of a house and the uproar created.
  [apparent signature]: Chairman Joh. Cornies.

941. Johann Cornies to [unknown]. 2 January 1848.
    SAOR 89-1-1331/2.

Yr. Excellency,

Before I can carry out your honoured commission of 20 December, I must first ask about your plans for the use of the threshing roller. Will the threshing be done with oxen or with horses? This matters because its size must be appropriately adjusted. Moreover, how is your description of the implement you plan to use on the fallow land to be understood?

Once I receive this information, I will comply with your wishes as best I can. The stone roller [threshing stone] has been willingly accepted in our villages and later also in the surrounding region. This clearly testifies to its usefulness. In dry weather, this method greatly speeds up the grain harvest.

With the greatest respect, I remain Yr. Excellency's most humble servant, Johann Cornies.

942. Johann Cornies to Sarepta Community Chairman. 3 January 1848. SAOR 89-1-1331/3v.

Chairman of the Sarepta Brethren community,

Following my earlier shipment to you of wheat and barley, and in keeping with a request of Mr. Blueher, my friend in Moscow, I enclose a parcel of the so-called golden oats that were first grown on my estates and have since spread widely everywhere in our villages. The oats grow more abundantly and are of a better quality than the varieties we have previously grown. For this reason, friends of field cultivation in Sarepta might like to subject them to further trials themselves. I would suggest that the oats be distributed among your most experienced landowners for the next seeding. Please let me know the results each of these test seedings. Kindly notify me about the receipt of this shipment and the earlier ones.

With exceptional respect, I send heartfelt greetings to you and to all my old acquaintances and wish you a blessed New Year. Your most humble servant, J. Cornies.

943. Agricultural Society to Jacob Martens. 5 January 1848. SAOR 89-1-1292/12v.

Society Member Jacob Martens,

I would direct you to find the location of the Society's deep ploughs. What kind are they and what accessories do they have? In what condition do they seem to be? I expect a report in due course.

944. Johann Cornies to Klassen. 5 January 1848. SAOR 89-1-1331/4v.

Dear friend Klassen,

The period for which I hired my servant Katharina Luetke, Rosengart, in your [Khortitsa] district, ended on 31 December 1847. Since she has agreed to work for me for a further period, I enclose her pass with the urgent request that you obtain a renewed yearly pass for her and have it sent to me by mail. When I receive the pass, I will reimburse you for your expenses. I am much obligated to you for your cooperation.

With a friendly greeting, your friend Johann Cornies.

945. Anna [Bieky or Benky] to Johann Cornies. 11 January 1848. SAOR 89-1-1322/75.

Most esteemed Mr. Cornies,

My cousin, Mr. Benjamin Hempel, Marienburg, recently informed me that my uncle, G. Ludwigs, Danzig, had departed this world. He died leaving a will in which he is said to have remembered me with a bequest of four hundred or five hundred thalers.

Enclosed is the original of this communication for your inspection, with the respectful request that you provide me with good advice that would permit me to proceed appropriately in obtaining the said capital amount. Should I send authorization and my deceased husband's death certificate to Mr. Hempel or wait for an inquiry by the Russian consulate in Danzig? Should you think it best to do the former, without further ado, then I would ask you to make the required forms available to the local District Office, specifically for the authorization and for a death certificate. You might, on the other hand, think it much preferable to have these papers prepared immediately and sent to me, accompanied by an order for the needed signatures. I will reimburse you for your expenses with the greatest thanks.

In the hope you will advise me on how best to proceed, I have the honour to sign myself as your very respectful servant,

P.S. I would much prefer to have your esteemed son, J. Cornies, bring along the money this spring, if it is not too much of an imposition.

946. Johann Cornies to Johann Cornies Jr. 18 January 1848. SAOR 89-1-1331/5.

Dear Son,

I write to let you know that I received your letters of 6 and 24 December 1847 and read them with the greatest of pleasure. I agree that you should make the journey back home with a wagon and posting horses. I would, at the same time, ask you to hire two good coachmen from the Werder countryside who know how to cut chaff and do the feeding. Also hire four good girls for housekeeping, or at least two. We can no longer find such people here. Let them travel on hired carts, by all means, but sign a contract with them regarding their service. Otherwise, someone will hire them out from under your nose in Halbstadt where there are always recruiters from the villages on the lookout.

We have had terrible weather. A storm, or *buran*, of the first magnitude, like nothing we have experienced before, raged here for about twenty days, starting on 25 December. It threatened death to our livestock and the destruction of buildings. Many thousands of livestock of every kind have lost their lives and many buildings have been crushed under the drifting snow. I took a chance and travelled to Tashchenak on 8 January where I found the Verigin and Berg sheep barns crushed by the snow. Except for sixty to seventy head of livestock, however, the sheep had been saved. Because of the interrupted communications and dangerous driving, I had to remain there for nine days. So far, everything at Tashchenak is in the best of order and doing well, taking our circumstances into account. However, the woods in front and back are buried under fifteen to twenty fut of snow. Only the tops of trees peek out a foot or two above the snow line. I enclose a drawing of the yard to give you an idea of how things are. The view is from the middle of the yard. Because of the cold and stormy weather the barn and granary are not pictured along the yard as they actually are.

When I arrived home from Tashchenak last night, I found that the mountains of snow were reportedly much higher at Iushanle and that the loss of livestock was much greater. I will try to get there tomorrow to put things back together as best I can. Messengers of Job are starting to come from every direction with their shockingly sad news of what the disastrous weather has caused.

To everybody's pleasure, your little Johann is healthy, strong, and growing well. He is a very obedient boy who loves the mountains of snow, riding down them – always under supervision – on a small sled and then entertaining us with long tales about his adventure. During my absence in Tashchenak, the wife of Gardener Wilke died and will have to be buried in Darmstadt because there is no place that is not under the deepest snow. The Northern Lights were seen here on 5 December.

In closing, I wish you and your dear Therese a happy and prosperous New Year. Your father, who loves you dearly sends you a thousand greetings. Johann Cornies.

**947. Johann Cornies to Feodor F. Rosen. 25 January 1848.
SAOR 89-1-1331/6v.**

Director Baron Rosen,

According to the accounts, we spent a total of 741 silver rubles, eighty-one and a quarter kopeks more than what we received. The money was spent on maintaining the Crown Model Plantation during 1847. To balance the books I would ask you, Yr. Honour, to kindly arrange that this sum of money is sent to me as soon as possible.

I have the honour of submitting to Yr. Honour the enclosed records regarding the crown apprentices under my direction on the plantation and with craftsmen. [Records not extant.]

948. Johann Cornies to Werner. 27 January 1848. SAOR 89-1-1331/7.

Dear Werner,

In response to your letter of 15 January, I have approached His Excellency, the Chairman of the Guardianship Committee, with a suggestion that you should be transferred to the Swedish District as its District Secretary. District Office business in the Swedish District has, to a large extent, been carried out by Russians. They have created much disorder as drunkards and good-for-nothings. This transfer would put you into a different position, working under my direct supervision and protection. You could, at the same time, restore order to the advantage of the community and assist in alleviating the shortage of German secretaries in the Swedish District. You would earn the trust I have placed in you by carrying out your obligations conscientiously and filling the position faithfully and honestly.

Although I am unfamiliar with the salary, I do know that your further existence could be guaranteed, especially under conditions and circumstances unrelated to the reasons that have now forced you to leave your present position. You will receive notification confirming all of this as soon as His Excellency's decision in this regard arrives.

With best wishes for your further well-being, your well-disposed Johann Cornies.

**949. Andrei M. Fadeev to Johann Cornies. 27 January 1848.
SAOR 89-1-661/21.**

My good friend, I have had no news from you for almost two years. Whatever the reasons may be, I know of your noble intentions and that you will not have wanted someone to disappear from your memory whose love for you has been unceasing for thirty years and who has stood in a continuing friendship with you. Therefore, send me news about your health. How is your family and all the Molochnaia Mennonites? ...

[Several illegible paragraphs.]

As for me, my situation in Tiflis includes much that is good and much that is bad, as everywhere. My real difficulty is that my health and weakness due to my age are taking their toll and my desire for repose becomes ever more powerful. However, I can truthfully say that my current position is not as burdensome and unpleasant as was that in Saratov. I can perhaps still do something useful for the country, even if it is not that much. This is the case with the high [illegible] and willingness of my worthy superior, Vorontsov (who remembers you and not long ago told me a lot about you and your achievements on behalf of the general well-being). This obligates me to dedicate a few more years to these matters, should this be God's will.

It is true, is it not, that your settlements are thriving? The prices paid for your crops have been much to your benefit. I hear that your harvest was not bad either. Also, how are the plantations doing? The breeding of Spanish sheep? Please send me news about all of these subjects.

Here we have had a great shortage of food. The winter is exceptionally severe. A large proportion of the working cattle is dying. The lot of the German settlers is probably the worst of any in Russia. [illegible]

I wish you the best of health and I again ask you not to forget me. My sick wife sends her heartfelt greetings. Your respectful A. Fadeev.

950. Johann Cornies to Feodor F. Rosen. 27 January 1848.
   SAOR 89-1-1331/8v.

Director Baron Rosen,

I am honoured to respectfully submit the enclosed report to Yr. Honour:

Short report about the progress that was made in operations at the Crown Model Plantation in Berdiansk District during 1847.

During the winter of 1846 to 1847, apprentices were taught to bind straw matting. Some two hundred bundles of straw were used to make twenty-one mats as coverings for the seedbeds.

Operations began on 25 March with the harrowing and preparation of about three desiatinas of land for planting. To lengthen the main laneway towards the southern boundary, a further two desiatinas were ploughed, harrowed, and levelled. On 28 March, after setting trenches had been measured and marked off, steps were taken to dig 5,653 setting trenches and 155 sazhen of channels for living hedges were dug along the post road.

During the month of March, transportation to the plantation was arranged for 2,773 trees buried in earth at Iushanle over the winter and for another 3,871 trees. A further 2,120 trees purchased in various villages were moved at the same time. At the beginning of April, 730 square sazhen of low-lying land was dug to a depth of six vershok for a poplar nursery. Seedbeds were uncovered and trees already on site were freed of their straw.

Planting began on 12 April and lasted until 10 May: 5,653 trees were planted on their intended sites and 1,108 in hedges. The remainder were transplanted to nurseries. The 131 trees that had died on site were replaced. The entire yard was completely enclosed with a good strong fence.

Construction of the house for apprentices was resumed.

During the course of the summer, twelve desiatinas of land were twice ploughed for the next planting and the area that had already been planted was cleared of weeds three times this summer, using both horse-drawn and hand implements.

In spring, twenty square sazhen of tree nurseries were seeded with various forest seeds. Another 115 and a half square sazhen were seeded in autumn, and 1,429 sazhen of channels were dug to protect plantings inside this area.

Because spring water had damaged it, the earthen dam through the hollow at the southwestern corner of the plantation needed improvement. This was done by increasing its height by one arshin and its width by two arshin. The still uncompleted dam on the road to the lowlands was likewise raised by three-quarters of an arshin and widened by one arshin.

Two wells were dug higher up on the plain in June. The first was six sazhen deep to the water. At this depth, where two sazhen of sand were already causing difficulty, an investigation of the soil with a drill revealed quicksand below. This made it necessary to abandon this well and dig another one. This well was dug to a depth of only three sazhen this summer.

Preparations have proceeded to plant a lane of chestnut trees in the lowland.

June saw completion of the forestry dwelling except for a few small items, and it was also painted. Arbours were erected in front of both doors. The barn was also painted.

In August, workmen began to build a reed fence around the entire seed nursery. Some 228 sazhen long, its construction is progressing well.

October demanded that new preparations be made for plantings: 112 setting trenches were dug for a lane of chestnut trees, another 767 trenches were dug along roads in the interior of the plantation, and trenches were dug for a hedge of olive trees on top of the mounds of earth that had been thrown up by the digging of 5,871 sazhen of channels. Six hundred fifty-two trees were planted on their intended sites in October and 1,700 olive trees for hedges were transported to the plantation.

Fall planting proceeded from 18 October to 25 November. Fall was generally auspicious for all operations. Trees already on site were bound with straw for the winter. Trees set out in nurseries were entirely covered with earth. With this operation work ended for the year.

Planted during 1846:

- 208 oaks in setting trenches and 326 in nurseries, total 534
- 309 ash trees in setting trenches and 316 in nurseries, total 625
- 934 elms in setting trenches and 256 in nurseries, total 1,190
- 353 maples in setting trenches and twenty in nurseries, total 373
- thirty-one acacias in setting trenches
- eleven aspens in setting trenches and six in nurseries, total seventeen
- 1,622 mulberries

Making a total of 1,846 trees in setting trenches and 2,546 in nurseries

Trees planted in 1847:

- twenty-four oaks
- 1,492 ashes in setting trenches and 639 in nurseries, total 2,131
- 886 elms in setting trenches, 51,680 in nurseries, total 52,566
- 1,936 maples in setting trenches, 34,440 in nurseries, total 36,374
- 887 acacias in setting trenches
- ninety-one chestnuts in setting trenches
- forty-two olive trees in setting trenches, 2,808 in hedges, total 2,850
- eight mountain ashes in setting trenches
- four hundred pseudoplatanus trees in setting trenches

• 458 barberry plants in setting trenches, 102 in nurseries, total 560
• ninety-five wild rose bushes in setting trenches, eleven in nurseries, total 106

Making a total number of 95,997 trees in 1847: 6,317 in setting trenches; 86,872 in nurseries; 2,808 in hedges

In stock 1 January 1848:

• 232 oaks in setting trenches, 326 in nurseries, total 558
• 1,801 ashes in setting trenches, 955 in nurseries, total 2,756
• 1,820 elms in setting trenches, 51,936 in nurseries, total 53,756
• 2,287 maples in setting trenches, 34,460 in nurseries, total 36,747
• 918 acacias in setting trenches
• ninety-one chestnut trees in setting trenches
• forty-two olive trees in setting trenches, 2,808 in hedges, total 2,850
• eight mountain ashes in setting trenches
• eleven aspens in setting trenches, six in nurseries, total seventeen
• four hundred pseudoplatanus in setting trenches
• 1,633 mulberries in nurseries
• 458 barberries in setting trenches, 102 in nurseries, total 560
• ninety-five roses in setting trenches, eleven in nurseries, total 106

Making a total of 100,389 trees on hand on 1 January 1848: 8,163 in setting trenches; 89,418 in nurseries; 2,808 in hedges.

951. Johann Cornies to Johann Cornies Jr. 28 January 1848.
  SAOR 89-1-1331/11.

Dear Son,

Yesterday, when your brother-in-law and my son-in-law Wiebe came to my room, he told me that he had just received your letter of 13 January, and asked me whether I would like to have it read to me. Its entire contents gave me great pleasure. Although your dear bride wishes to receive a letter from your sister Agnes, this is no longer needed because your brother-in-law, your sister, and your son Johann will be leaving by post this coming Monday to attend your wedding celebration in Elbing. Everything has already been prepared and put in order for their journey.

I had battled with this matter privately for many weeks. How should I decide? Should I make this journey myself or have my children go? I felt much relieved once the decision was made that some would go. But who? On 21 January, this past Wednesday, I conveyed my irrevocable resolve to my children that they should be the ones and that they should depart within fourteen days. They have my permission to return as late as 15 May or even 25 May of this year, that is, shortly before harvest time.

This decision filled me with great and spirited joy. Your son hopped about, hugging and kissing me. What else can I do to increase the joy of my children, what more can I sacrifice? The happiness of my children is my happiness, their joys are my joys. They are going out into the world and I am leaving it.

The journey will start here, and proceed through Tashchenak, Odesa, and Warsaw. I have already notified the General. Their passes and all else will be ready and waiting for them in Odesa on their arrival. It is not for me to give advice and commendations. After all, you are siblings. One heart speaks to another. I have nothing further to say than to send you and your bride my most affectionate greetings.

Commending all of you to the care of our Heavenly Father, your loving father, Johann Cornies.

P.S. Give my most obliging thanks to my brother-in-law Wiebe for the friendly letter he and his relatives sent me. Also, give my greetings to your father-in-law.

Your son Johann is a solid boy, who will survive this journey well, even at twenty degrees of frost. Also, Agnes will not leave anything undone to keep him healthy and in good cheer. Since he is eating fewer sweets on doctor's orders, he has become much more active. You will be surprised how he has grown and how broad his shoulders are. I will miss him very much. He has raised the spirits of our entire household. Adieu. The same.

952. Johann Cornies to Bernhard Doerksen. 28 January 1848. SAOR 89-1-1331/11v.

To the carpentry journeyman, foreigner Bernhard Doerksen living with his uncle Johann Rempel in Berdiansk city,

Since I am much in need of a good carpenter who can work with a journeyman or apprentice to do two years of carpentry work on my properties at Iushanle, Ohrloff, and Tashchenak, your brother Franz, in service with me at Tashchenak, told me about you. He thinks you might well take up this position. I have a spacious room at Tashchenak that could easily accommodate two carpentry benches.

It would please me greatly if you would consider taking up this position. I would ask you to let me know as soon as possible. We can reach an agreement to pay you by the day, week, or year, as you prefer. I do not think that a piecework agreement would work, however. It would require too much detail. Matters arise, such as small repairs that would demand little real work on your part but take a very long time. In the meantime, as mentioned, I am agreeable to whatever your wishes in this regard might be.

With a greeting, your friend Johann Cornies.

My mailing address should be directed by way of Melitopol.

953. Johann Cornies to Enns. 28 January 1848. SAOR 89-1-1331/12.

To the Family Enns in the Mennonite Church at Pordenau in West Prussia,

Most valued brothers and sisters,

Your brother Jacob Enns, my cousin, ended his long journey by living in the Molochnaia settlement for years. He registered as a Russian citizen, joined the local Mennonite community, and lived most of the time with an old family, the Abraham Konrads in Blumenort, where he occupied himself as a day labourer for agriculturalists. He declined over the last few years, as old age weighed him down, but remained active and earned as much as he needed for anything essential to his maintenance. Since he managed everything he possessed parsimoniously, spending no kopek to excess and limiting his clothing to what he needed most, he had saved a considerable, actually a remarkable, amount of money, especially for his position.

In December, he visited my brother, David Cornies in Ohrloff, where he had often stopped by in the past, staying there for several days and weeks at a time. He arrived healthy and quite active for his age. However, on the fourth day, he fell ill. He thought the illness would pass easily and for this reason did not want to accept the attention and care he was most willingly given in my brother's house. They paid no attention to his wishes and looked after him, giving him the best care that they possibly could. As soon as his illness began, they could see that his recovery was in doubt. He retained his intelligence and consciousness to the end although he did not believe that he was about to die.

After an illness of ten days, he died on the morning of 22 December 1847, falling into a final sleep without making any confession, although we hope that he passed into a better life. His body was consigned to the earth here in Ohrloff on 24 December.

Cash found with him amounts to 669 rubles, forty-seven kopeks. The estimated value of his clothes is fifty-two rubles, fifty kopeks for a total of 721 rubles, ninety-seven kopeks.

Expenditures were sixteen rubles for a coffin, eight rubles, fifteen kopeks to dig a grave in three feet of frozen ground, and six rubles, fifty kopeks for his funeral procession. Total expenditures were thirty rubles, sixty-five kopeks. My brother covered the costs of a fairly large funeral meal.

What remains for distribution among the heirs is 691 rubles, thirty-two kopeks. This equals 197 silver rubles, fifty-nine kopeks according to current exchange rates.

Agnetha Friesen, née Bartsch, who resides in Muntau village, lays claim to ten thalers of the legacy, maintaining that when Widow Penner left for Prussia she owed Agnetha Friesen ten thalers in wages for weaving. Since Widow Penner is the deceased Jacob Enns's sister and thus one of his inheritors, Mrs. Friesen wishes to receive this sum out of the accounts for Widow Penner in the Enns legacy. I am therefore required to give these claims a just hearing, and am keeping back ten thalers from the entire amount, which amounts to nine silver rubles, eleven and a half kopeks. This will be until such time as I have been informed whether such a claim by Mrs. Friesen is justified and whether the money should be paid out to her, or if it should be sent to Prussia to add to the total. I request that you inform me about this matter as soon as possible.

Not including these ten thaler, the entire amount of 188 silver rubles, nineteen kopeks remaining will be paid out by my son-in-law Wiebe during his visit to Prussia. I request that he be given a receipt for the money.

Now, my dear relatives, I send you many greetings and wishes from the bottom of my heart. May you all be healthy and contented, may God give you his blessings, and protect and keep you until the last days of your life.

This is the sincere wish of your loving cousin, Johann Cornies.

**954. Agricultural Society to Village Mayors. 1 February 1848.
SAOR 89-1-1296.**

To the Village Mayors' Offices,

You are hereby being sent a short overview of all the existing tree plantations together with various remarks about the cultivation of forest trees and orchards, about sericulture and tobacco, as well as the progress in agriculture and trades in the local district.

You are ordered to make a copy of all of these communications in every Village Mayor's Office and to acquaint the village's inhabitants with it. However, after the copy has been made, this overview should be forwarded, without delay and unsoiled, to the next address. From Ladekopp it must be sent back to the Society by 20 March 1848, in a clean condition.

Society at Ohrloff, 1 February 1848. Chairman Jn. Cornies.

955. Johann Cornies to Bernhard Thiessen. 5 February 1848. SAOR 89-1-1331/15v.

Highly Valued Friend,

You have given me the greatest pleasure by sending me an invitation to the wedding of your mademoiselle daughter with my son. I only regret that I am unable to accept this invitation that is so very pleasing for me. My urgent business affairs are of such a nature that it is utterly impossible for me to distance myself from them at such a long distance from my home and for several months. I must therefore deny myself this pleasure and grant it to my children instead. They will depart for Elbing today. It is also my hope that as your daughter gets to know my daughter Agnes better, this familiarity will help ease the anguish of your dear daughter Therese as she takes leave of her father's house. Furthermore, they will provide more companionship on the journey and make it more pleasant than would my presence.

I must admit that I found the first letter I received from my son's bride utterly captivating. It gave me such pleasant feelings that I asked myself whether I might be able to arrange my affairs in a manner that would permit me to fulfil the wishes of my dear daughter-in-law in one way or another. I thought about this matter for weeks, although I did not permit my children to notice that I was doing so. Neither the great distance nor the hardships of the journey frightened me. The road from here is not so far nor as cumbersome, especially with post horses, as one might well think in Elbing. This your dear daughter will confirm in a few years' time when she comes to visit you, especially if she chooses the best time of year. No, this decision is due simply and alone to the excessive business matters involved with our settlement's economic affairs. I have succeeded in arranging them in so favourable a way as to permit my son-in-law to travel calmly to Elbing without being disturbed.

My children will tell you of my feelings about this happy event, something my pen is incapable of expressing properly at this time. The tumult of preparing for this journey and visits from friends bidding my children farewell have disturbed my calm composure. For this reason, I ask you to kindly give my heartfelt greetings to all of your children, and dear Therese in particular.

I commend myself to your further friendship, remaining, with respect, your friend, Johann C.

956. Johann Cornies to Learned Committee of the Ministry of State Domains. 7 February 1848. SAOR 89-1-1331/17.

To the Learned Committee of the Ministry of State Domains,

I read the three leaflets entitled, "Thriving Agriculture Is Our Fatherland's Wealth," attentively and several times. I think they are admirable and really apply to Southern Russia.

I have only a few objections:

1. Forty years of practical experience show that fallowing must became the main basis of field cultivation. This practice alone can provide an enduring foundation for ploughland agriculture in the region.

2. Harrowing oats after they have sprouted can only be harmful in our region. It might be useful a decade from now, but this should not be assumed as a rule.

3. I gather from my extensive experience that all planted trees should be as thoroughly watered as are seedlings in nurseries.

Otherwise, I am much impressed by the concise, knowledgeable, and easily understood manner in which the author has expressed himself. The publications are of great value in every way, fully in keeping with the government's purpose, and much better than every other one that I have read. The author has undoubtedly earned the first prize and the publication should appear also in German. There is much here that German settlements could learn.

I have the honour to obediently return the above-mentioned three leaflets to the Learned Committee.

957. Molochnaia Agricultural Society Journal Entries. 7 February 1848. SAOR 89-1-1292.

• Gnadenfeld: The Society should send the Gnadenfeld village community and Village Office an inquiry regarding their local inhabitant, Alexander Voth. He has been staying elsewhere for some time. Should he be approved for another yearly pass until such time as he can be enumerated elsewhere?

• Fuerstenwerder: You are informed that your local inhabitant Erdmann Nikkel is absolutely not permitted to move to the Russian village of Polova. When he gives up his service with Peters, he must return to the Molochnaia Mennonite District without delay. Once Nikkel returns, the Village Office must immediately report this to the Society.

• Orphans' Administrator Johann Friesen, Friedensdorf: In response to wishes expressed by Johann Reimer, Fuerstenwerder Village Mayor, you are ordered to remove the guardianship he has over eight wards, the children of Jacob Friesen. Another dependable man should be confirmed as guardian to replace him and the Society should be informed as soon as possible that this has been done.

958. Johann Cornies to Traugott Blueher. 11 February 1848. SAOR 89-1-1331/18v.

Most esteemed Mr. Blueher,

You will receive four crates and three balls of silk, weighing twenty-two puds, twenty funt, according to the enclosed freight bill. It is being shipped with the Kharkiv Transport Company. Mr. Iakovlev bought the silk here in the Molochnaia villages in 1846. As you will see from the documents signed by me and other inhabitants, we were promised an advance of 1,389 silver rubles, fifty kopeks, to be paid in May 1847 when the silk was to change hands. However, because Mr. Iakovlev did not keep his promise, the parties involved have agreed to send you the silk, along with the monetary claims we make against Mr. Iakovlev. We request that you summon Mr. Iakovlev to pay you the entire sum of the money owing for the silk, which is 1,429 silver rubles, forty-three kopeks, as per the enclosed accounts, including freight charges and other costs. After reviewing and settling all accounts with Mr. Iakovlev, and when the monetary payment has been made in full, you may permit him to take delivery of the silk.

I authorize you, in my name and that of my partners, to settle this account with Mr. Iakovlev. I assure you that I and my partners will be completely satisfied with whatever you think appropriate. We obligate ourselves to compensate you for all costs and delays, as per your records. Once you have received the money from Mr. Iakovlev, please send us the accounts and money.

With the most exceptional esteem, I have the honour to be your honestly loving Johann Cornies.

959. Traugott Blueher to Johann Cornies. 13 February 1848. SAOR 89-1-1322/17.

Mr. Johann Cornies, Ohrloff village,

Sincerely Beloved Friend,

I have heard nothing from you for some time. The last favourable news was from your dear son-in-law, reporting that you are healthy and well. May our dear Heavenly Father, with His great and inestimable kindness, keep you during all of this year.

One crate and two sacks of silk cocoons from Kharkiv arrived in good condition on 5 February. I hope that you have sent along the expense accounts. The owner, Aleksander [Iakovlev] has visited me often to take receipt of this shipment, but I cannot handle it because I do not know the amount involved in this matter.

Please let me know as soon as you receive dependable information about future wool prices. The Khortitsa wool is still in storage because bids for the wool have been too low.

Commending myself to your further loving memory, I greet you in friendship, Traugott Blueher.

Moscow, 13 February 1848.

960. Johann Cornies to Evgenii F. Hahn. 13 February 1848. SAOR 89-1-1331/20.

His Honour, Director of the Tavrida Bureau of State Domains,

According to reports that I have received, the forest-tree seeds listed as ready for distribution through the Domains Bureau are mostly for trees whose seeds should be sown in autumn, as they require. This would allow them to come up in spring, as winter's moisture permits. It is thus desirable for foresters to collect such seeds in good time and send them immediately to the Domains Bureau. They should then be distributed for October seeding.

There is no point in seeding these varieties in spring. Nothing could make them sprout. For this reason, I list below the nine varieties included in the above-mentioned report and ask that you kindly direct that an appropriate quantity of these seeds be sent to me as soon as possible for seeding at the Crown Model Plantation.

961. Johann Cornies to Feodor F. Rosen. 13 February 1848.
  SAOR 89-1-1331/20.

Honoured Baron,

During your most recent visit to the Crown Model Plantation, you were pleased to mention that you would send a shipment of mulberry trees from the Crimea for planting here in the plantation. Kindly permit me, Honoured Baron, to give you my opinion about this matter.

Although mulberry trees have frequently been sent to our villages, most recently to this plantation on your orders, these shipments have never had the desired results. The mulberry trees were generally heavily damaged in shipment. Most arrived with dried-out roots and even with the best of treatment, only a very small proportion were able to establish themselves, and their progress was weak and miserable. The work and effort were not worthwhile.

At present, the plantation already has several thousand young, two-year-old mulberry trees that were raised from seed and are flourishing. Indeed, they are large and strong enough to be planted in hedges this coming spring. Should another several thousand four- to five-year-old, high-stemmed mulberry trees be needed for planting along the inside of the quartals, they could easily be bought nearby at five silver kopeks each. I doubt, however, that mulberry trees from the Crimea would develop sufficiently in three or four years' time to permit their transplantation to permanent sites, even with the best care and attention. In the meantime, the plantation would already have raised more than a thousand trees in its nurseries for distribution to the peasantry.

Should Yr. Honour respectfully share my opinion, which is based on experience, I would request that you cancel the further shipment of young mulberry trees from the Crimea to the Crown Plantation.

With exceptional esteem, I have the honour to remain Yr. Honour's most respectful servant, Johann Cornies.

962. Johann Cornies to Phillip Wiebe. 13 February 1848. SAOR 89-1-1331/21v.

Dear Son,

After escorting you as far as Akimovka, my brothers said that your dear wife felt weak when you left Tashchenak and that she was still weak but cheerful when you reached Akimovka. I therefore awaited your first letter with much anxiety and it arrived today, 13 February, from Artsina. It was dated 6 February. I gathered that Agnes was quite exhausted, but otherwise cheerful. I was greatly pleased to hear that little Johann keeps you amused with his singing. I strongly encourage you in your plan to buy a new and more comfortable wagon in Odesa for the remainder of your trip. With longing, I now await your news from Odesa. Were you able to buy a good wagon, as planned and as I hope? How has your dear wife survived the trip? I expect the best but not without worries, especially with the start of the spring breakup. But I console myself, knowing that you are an experienced traveller and will know how to keep everybody safe. May God keep you well until you reach home safely and in good health.

I thank God that I am still vigorous and strong, and have enough to do from morning until ten at night. Everything is still in the best of order. The District Chairman seems to be recovering from his illness. I had two meetings with Braun in Ohrloff. The two of us were able to finish off an agenda of more than thirty items. I have not left the home since your departure, except to visit Brother David today for a couple of hours. Even there people would not give me peace.

I am thinking of leaving for Khortitsa and Kronsgarten in fourteen days' time. This coming Monday, Brother Heinrich is off to Ekaterinoslav Guberniia to hire people. Local roads are quite impassable at the moment, but people say they are beginning to dry up. Songbirds are said to be swarming on the Molochnaia Estuary and the peewit has put in its appearance, announcing the arrival of spring. But the sheer disaster of the buran, that terrible storm, can be seen everywhere throughout the Nogai lands. Thousands of dead livestock, camels, horses, sheep, and horned cattle were driven by the storm and now lie stretched out on the ice.

The little old woman from Peitzmerdorf was picked up yesterday. They were testing me to see if I really wanted her to stay. These good people are really quite mistaken. I was happy that they got her, since I had already decided to send her away this week. Granted, she was not a hindrance, like the fifth wheel of a wagon, but still much like an old piece of furniture, out of style and useless. Without my doing, good friends are now trying to find me a household administrator. I do not object. I will thank them if they manage to find me a person with whom I can be content.

I did not keep my word to send you a letter to Elbing last Wednesday. I have been so busy these last few days that I had no time. I also wanted to first read a letter from Anhalt-Koethen and know how dear Agnes was feeling. You will receive this letter only when you reach Elbing. By then you may well have talked to your brother-in-law and gotten to know his dear bride. Give them both a thousand heartfelt greetings and let them know my deepest sentiment and love for them, as I asked you and Agnes to do. Commend me to Mr. Bernhard Thiessen with the greatest and most heartfelt friendship and to his family and to the brothers Jacob and Aron Wiebe. I wish you the best of health and happiness and may you have the most joyous days in the company of your friends. Write to me as I have already asked you to.

With this, I commend you to God, send greetings to you, Agnes, and little Johann, and remain, with heartfelt love, your father Johann Cornies.

963. Peter Keppen to Johann Cornies. Sent St. Petersburg, 16 February 1848. SAOR 89-1-1294/5.

Highly esteemed friend,

Recently volume twelve of the *Beitraege zur Kenntnis Russland* (Contributions to knowledge about Russia) appeared and I will send you a copy herewith. It costs one and a half silver rubles. This cancels my debt to you. I will send you further volumes only if you ask me to. The same holds true for the [third] part of Haxthausen's work that will probably appear this year.

Sometime, please let me know how the Doukhobor and Molokan villages are faring. I would gladly visit your regions again, but hardly think that will be possible this year.

You will probably have received the fifteen silver rubles you were supposed to have been sent from the Academy.

With honest devotion, your most willing friend Keppen.

964. Johann Cornies to Traugott Blueher. 18 February 1848. SAOR 89-1-1331/24v.

Most esteemed Mr. Blueher,

I write in response to your valued communication of 26 January 1848 that I received in good order, as well as the money for my last year's wool. Enclosed is the receipt. It completes this transaction. Many thanks for your efforts in regard to my wool business that turned out to be in my favour. I would ask you to take on the sale of my wool on consignment again as you have in the past.

I received ten copies of Russian regulations and five copies of Memorsky's grammar, as you notified me. I also received in good condition, via Kharkiv, a crate for Ferd. Niederstaedter; a crate, marked "J.C.," listed as No. 276, that contained a small box of publications for Tobias Gaier; a packet for Ferd. Niederstaedter; and nine dozen No. 7 English sheep shears and three dozen No. 3 1/2 [shears], everything packed in mats.

To reply to your communication of 19 December 1847, I withdrew the price offered to District Chairman Toews because of his overly long delay in sending me the wool. Also, I have given the Khortitsa District Chairman preliminary notification that if the sample sent in advance did not agree with the findings of the first inspection of all the wool as to cleanliness, you will have the right to suggest a change in terms.

My children left here on 5 February for Elbing, Prussia. I am now deprived of all of my children but look forward to the return of at least some of them in May. Luckily I am overwhelmed with work in regard to my business affairs, otherwise the time of my current loneliness would seem far too long. As it is, time passes quickly. Our young friends Niederstaedter and Knobloch are both healthy and in good spirits. The former is making good and speedy progress and visits me almost every Sunday. The latter is lodging here with me in my house and takes care of several small household affairs.

Spring seems to have arrived, with warm temperatures of ten degrees. Sunshine and rain are constantly alternating. April days. Within five or six days the man on the land will be preparing to move out onto his fields with his plough, if the weather holds.

Winter caused astonishing damage. A buran [snowstorm] of the first magnitude raged for twenty days and killed a large number of

sheep. This did not happen in our villages, but many sheepfarm owners on the steppe were totally ruined, as were the sheep farms of
many Nogais.

I send heartfelt greetings to you, your dear wife, and children, and
commend myself to your continued friendship, which I will never forget. I remain, with feelings of thankfulness and love, your friend and
servant, Johann Cornies.

Receipt.

On 26 January 1848, I received 53,295 rubles banco, or 15,226 silver rubles, eighty kopeks for 145 balls of washed Spanish wool sent
on consignment in 1847. This was to settle my final accounts with
the Sarepta Trading Company of Sorenson and Company and is here
receipted.

965. Johann Cornies to Jacob Dik. 18 February 1848.
   SAOR 89-1-1331/26v.

Dear Friend,

For a long period of time I have received no information about what
is happening on the Tashchenak estate or regarding its welfare. How
could this have happened? The business secretary knows full well that
I must periodically receive a report about every aspect of the business.
Why has this been neglected? I fear that things may well have been
done without soliciting my advice and orders. There may have been
instances, large or small, that have created intolerable situations that
have disrupted agricultural operations. Seeding is at hand about which
I know nothing. Are you making preparations to get farm implements
in order that the seeding of various grains can be done according to the
orders left behind by my son?

I would therefore ask you to send Pavlo, with whom my son left
instructions and directions. I will require him to explain to me what
my son wanted and what orders he left about the total quantity of seed
of each variety that was to be sown on specific fields. Pavlo should
be directed to come here with Doerksen, using two wagons harnessed
with horses as soon as the road has dried out and is passable. Pavlo
can then explain matters that would enable me to make appropriate
arrangements and send orders. This is my firm principle from which
I will not deviate in the slightest. Should orders have been neglected,
they must be carried out even if a quick overview shows me that something better could have been introduced.

The above-mentioned wagons could then pick up linen from here for the fabrication of sacks there or in Hutterthal. I would also like to know whether the millet for gruel has been transported to Iushanle and what quantity of oats has been used as feed during the past two months. How many horses are being fed gruel?

With a greeting, I remain your friend Johann Cornies.

966. Johann Cornies to Evgenii F. Hahn. 18 February 1848. SAOR 89-1-1331/27v.

Yr. Excellency [v. Hahn],

In response to Yr. Excellency's honoured directive of 1 February 1846, I have finally received the description of the Felstenthal estate from its inhabitants. As Yr. Excellency wished, I had commissioned it immediately at the time it was requested. I take the honour of obediently enclosing it for Yr. Excellency. However, I doubt that this description will satisfy your wishes. In my opinion, it lacks a description of the estate's specific situation.

Respectfully, I have the honour to remain Yr. Excellency's most devoted servant, Johann Cornies.

967. Johann Cornies to Berdiansk District Secretary Werner. 18 February 1848. SAOR 89-1-1331/28v.

Valued Mr. Werner,

In response to my submissions of 7 February, the General has notified me that His Excellency is prepared to accept my recommendation that you be appointed District Secretary in the Swedish District, provided your knowledge of the Russian language is adequate for this purpose. His Excellency has informed him about this. The General adds that the Swedish District Secretary's salary is only eighty-five silver rubles and that this can be increased only slightly.

I therefore ask you about your command of the Russian language and whether you would be satisfied with the salary that is naturally small, but could perhaps be increased to a full one hundred silver rubles. Nevertheless, I believe that a much wider field of activity would be available to you there and that your endeavours would soon lead to an increase in your salary.

Expecting the information needed, I remain your friend, Johann Cornies

968. Johann Cornies to Siemens. 18 February 1848.
   SAOR 89-1-1331/29.

Dear friend, District Chairman Siemens in Bergthal,

Dirk Guenther, presently in the town of Berdiansk, has applied to me for permission to establish a retail shop in the Bergthal settlement. I advised him that, should the Bergthal District Office and the local village community be agreeable, I would myself have no objections to this development. On the contrary, I think it would be to Bergthal's advantage if a large general store were established there by a wealthy man. According to the rules, the contract with Guenther cannot be concluded for more than twenty years but, as you can see, I believe it would be good for your local villages if such a larger general store were established there.

With a greeting, your friend Johann Cornies.

969. Johann Cornies to Bernhard Doerksen. 19 February 1848.
   SAOR 89-1-1331/28.

Dear Friend,

Your letter tells me of your willingness to do carpentry work for me. I would prefer that you start work for me immediately. My children will be returning from Prussia by 25 May. I would, by that time, like to have completed certain improvements in the Tashchenak house. For the time being, I will wait hoping that you might come several weeks earlier than what you specified. In any case, let me know in lots of time, even eighteen days in advance. I have to make plans to have you picked up well in advance, because I am not always able on short notice to change directives I have already given. It should also be noted that Tashchenak is a fully forty verstas away from here. This means that an entire day is needed to transmit orders.

I hope that you will try to carry out my wishes as soon as possible and remain, with appreciation, your friend, Johann Cornies.

970. Johann Cornies to Jacob Dik. 21 February 1848.
   SAOR 89-1-1331/29v.

Dear Friend,

I have had Pavlo explain to me the directives my son left for spring cultivation and seeding on specific cultivated fields. Pavlo could not, however, give me any definite information about spring planting this spring, since my son had only provided orders for last spring as to the seeds to be planted and the specific cultivated fields on which each was to be sown. For this spring, he could only put me in a position where I could decide some detailed directives myself.

I would therefore ask you to personally inspect the cultivated fields at each location with Pavlo and have him explain the extent to which he knows my son's intentions about them. However, at places where he does not know which crop should be sown, you and Pavlo must discuss the variety of grain most suitable and advantageous to that site, taking into account the composition of the soil. Then you should make a rough sketch of all cultivated fields, their location, and the total number of desiatinas each main section contains. Finally, when this has been completed you should, if possible, see me on Tuesday with this sketch and explain the details to me. I need also to reach an agreement with you about other agricultural details. For the moment, I cannot come to Tashchenak yet. I am so loaded down with business that I have to stay inside and work like a Capuchin monk in his cell.

With a greeting, your friend Johann Cornies.

971. Molochnaia Agricultural Society Journal Entries. 21 February 1848. SAOR 89-1-1336.

• Muensterberg: There must be evidence of tree plantings on ploughed fields by the spring of 1849.

• To the Berdiansk Administrative Office: Johann Penner from Prangenau supposedly ruined the treadmill he built for Jacob Wiebe, and the latter is demanding compensation. On the other hand, Penner is demanding that he be repaid for his expenditures on various materials. Because these two individuals are arguing, the administrative office should inspect the construction and report in detail about the validity of the demands on each side.

972. From Johann Cornies to Hermann Sudermann. 24 February 1848. SAOR 89-1-1331/30v.

Overseer of the Crown Model Plantations,

I have been informed that the Director of the Tavrida State Domains Bureau has assigned fourteen crown apprentices chosen by various village authorities to be educated at the Crown Plantation. Along with this directive, the Tavrida Domains Bureau also ordered the selection of other apprentices at the appropriate locations to replace everyone released as unfit. They will be sent along without delay. This is your notification.

973. Johann Cornies to Benjamin Unruh. 24 February 1848. SAOR 89-1-1331/31.

Dear Friend, Benjamin Unruh in Hoffnungsthal,

Your monetary assets in Alexanderwohl have been sent to me by the District Office. Mennonites Christian Dofko and Benjamin Unruh lay claim to sixty rubles of this capital sum for a horse. For this reason, you should report to me by mail whether the claims of the above-mentioned Mennonites are justified so that this claim can be settled here immediately, after which I can send the remaining money to Hoffnungsthal, together with the accounts.

Your letter of 15 December 1847 requested that I arrange to have certificates of baptism sent to you. I will pass them on to your brother and have him forward them to you.

With a greeting, your friend Johann Cornies.

974. Johann Cornies to Khortitsa District Chairman Jacob Bartsch. 27 February 1848. SAOR 89-1-1331/31v.

Dear Chairman,

A communication of 18 February 1848 from Odesa informed me that a sad incident has taken place with Johann Peters, the young man from Khortitsa District who was sent to the Committee to learn Russian secretarial practices.

The landlady at Peters's lodgings suddenly missed two pair of white tricot trousers and various other things. After she found one pair of these trousers in Peters's trunk and removed them, she demanded the other pair as well. Although he stubbornly denied the theft, he paid her twenty rubles for the trousers to satisfy her. Similarly, Peters pilfered money several times from the German living in the same room with him. After the theft was discovered, he gave this person a little more than a silver ruble, insisting that he had only taken that amount. The German claimed he was satisfied with this although he had insisted that he lost more than three silver rubles. When Peters was called to account, he admitted to pilfering only one pair of trousers from the landlady and only a bit more than one silver ruble from the German. He expressed remorse and politely asked that he might not be put into an unfortunate position over it.

However, this matter could not be kept secret and the story spread. It was to be feared that it could reach the members of the Committee and the General, where such secrecy would be interpreted very negatively. All the circumstances of this sad situation with Peters were therefore disclosed to one member, Mr. Pelekh, who advised that the matter be kept secret from the General while he would personally make an effort to suppress it. Mr. Pelekh did, however, admonish Peters severely.

I have received a report that Peters is displaying an attitude that suggests every good teaching can be arrogantly rejected. At the present time he is an object of contempt on the Committee, and with anyone who knows about his deeds. For this reason, it is most essential that he should be removed from Odesa shortly without drawing much attention. This would be best for him and for all of us generally as Mennonites.

I therefore commission the District Chairman to approach the General with a request to have Peters released from the Committee for a period of two months and to send him home on essential family matters. Transport should be sent at the same time to fetch him from Odesa. In the meantime, efforts should be made to find another young person in the district who has a good, faithful character and the necessary qualifications and to have him sent to Odesa with an introduction to replace Peters.

With a greeting, your friend Johann Cornies.

975. Evgenii F. Hahn to Johann Cornies. 27 February 1848. SAOR 89-1-889/109.

After Wiebe and his dear family had departed cheerfully from Odesa, I was surprised to receive a letter from him on 24 February. He notified me that, because the roads were bad and because his wife was indisposed, he was obliged to stop in Balta, about two hundreds verstas from Odesa. Since he would be short of money, he asked me to send him 150 silver rubles and I did this on the same day. My outlay, together with postage and insurance charges, amounts to 151 rubles silver, sixty-three kopeks.

I hope that your daughter has recovered completely and that their journey has continued, since the roads here have improved greatly in the meantime.

Yours truly, E. v. Hahn.

976. F.W. Schulz-Roechling to Johann Cornies. 11 March 1848.
SAOR 89-1-1322/113.

Mr. J. Cornies at Ohrloff village,

Your valued lines sent 3 January 1848, as well as the sample of golden oats you kindly included, arrived here in good time. Also, your earlier shipments to Mr. Doering reached him as desired and I have cause to express my special thanks for everything.

The samples have been distributed among dependable agriculturalists and I will allow myself the pleasure later of advising you carefully about the results.

On the whole, please receive our heartiest thanks for your friendship which we value so highly. Please continue to grant it to us in future.

You would give us great joy if it were possible for you to permit us the pleasure of a visit from you. Your invitation to do so remains constant.

Please accept these assurances, with special esteem, of your respectful F.W. Schulz-Roechling.

Sarepta 11 March 1848.

P.S. We have beautiful spring weather here, as high as ten degrees, but dry, which causes the agriculturalists to worry.

In the next few days, the settlement's herd of horned cattle will be driven out for the first time this year. Foot-and-mouth disease raged among the cows all winter long, although it was not virulent. Several calves were also infected with it and did die. The same.

977. David Cornies to Evgenii F. Hahn. 14 March 1848.
SAOR 89-1-1331/33v.

Yr. Excellency [v. Hahn],

I hasten to respectfully report to Yr. Excellency that my brother Johann Cornies died yesterday, 13 March 1848, at 4:45 p.m. after an illness of fourteen days. On Sunday, 29 February 1848, he fell ill with a cold, as the doctor asserted. Until Monday, 8 March, his illness was up and down, but it always seemed serious. During this time, the patient was able to leave his bed and walk around in his room. Monday his illness increased somewhat and Tuesday, a feverish swelling was found at his jawbone on both sides of his head. The swelling increased so much during the course of the day that the patient found it difficult to speak. The following day speaking was almost impossible. Despite this, he was still strong enough to lift himself upright in bed with almost no help.

Friday, he improved somewhat and until nine on Saturday morning. However, after this, his strength waned very quickly and the doctor had given up hope by twelve noon, although he continued to apply all possible means to save the sick man. Regrettably, these were in vain, and at forty-five minutes after four that afternoon, he very gently slipped away without a battle and without convulsions.

The deceased was still able to read Yr. Excellency's esteemed communication of 27 February 1848 and expressed his thanks for your kindness, but he was no longer capable of remitting your expenditures or of expressing his thanks in writing. For this reason, I now have the honour of respectfully sending Yr. Excellency the sum of 151 silver rubles, sixty-three kopeks advanced for Phillip Wiebe.

With deep respect, I remain Yr. Excellency's obedient servant, David Cornies.

978. Note in Correspondence Journal. 18 March 1848. SAOR 89-1-1331/34v.

Riediger sent very short reports to Baron v. Rosen and Mr. v. Stempel, specifically that Johann Cornies died 13 March 1848 after a fourteen-day illness, and was to be buried on 17 March. Doerksen wrote the same thing to Chairman Siemens in Khortitsa.

979. Evgenii F. Hahn to David Cornies. 19 March 1848. SAOR 89-1-889/110.

I received the news of your worthy, estimable, and noble-minded brother's death with heartfelt sadness. It is an irreparable loss for all of us who knew and loved him. It seems to me that the Molochnaia Mennonite District has been orphaned and that we will constantly miss the chief promoter of all things positive and useful. I have lost a true friend.

I received correctly the 151 silver rubles, sixty-three kopeks enclosed with your letter. I am sorry that you had to trouble yourself with this small thing in such an important situation. E. v. Hahn.

980. David Cornies to Traugott Blueher. 18 April 1848. SAOR 89-1-1331/35.

Mr. Blueher in Moscow,

Please accept my honest thanks for the sincere sympathy you expressed in your letter of 29 March 1848 about the painful loss of my beloved brother, Johann Cornies. Although the death has burdened me deeply, I would still like to honour God's unfathomable act prayerfully and without complaint, with humility and devotion: "Lord, thy will be done, for what you do is always well done."

On Saturday, 28 February, my brother was still hale and hearty, and worked at his business from morning until late at night. Sunday morning, around four, he developed a fever and had a headache. He slept all day, but by noon of the following day he again turned to his affairs. That Monday, however, through until the following Sunday, he kept to his bed. Sometimes he seemed better, then worse, but still always without danger. Sunday he seemed much better, dressed, and walked about indoors, although not entirely without support. On Monday, he again stayed in bed, but his illness did not seem acute, dangerous, nor deadly.

Tuesday, around three or four in the morning, a feverish swelling appeared at his cheekbones, on both sides of his head. This made his breathing very difficult and speech almost impossible. Called in, the doctor said that the illness had lifted, the crisis had been overcome and there no cause for further concern. Yet despite diagnosis and remedies, the illness worsened and by noon, Saturday, 13 March, the doctor abandoned hope. He did what he could to save his beloved patient, but to no avail. That afternoon, at forty-five minutes past four, my brother slipped into a gentle sleep and his spirit left his mortal body.

On 17 March 1848, the day of the burial, a large crowd gathered, consisting of Germans, Russians, Tatars, and Jews who wished to say their final goodbyes to the beloved remains. At three in the afternoon, the procession proceeded to the burial place. Uncovered for the last time, the body was lowered into the grave. The thudding of the first clods on the coffin lid seemed to utter a muted, "Good Night."

May our gracious God send rays of tender consolation into the hearts of his children who were denied the satisfaction of sweetening the last hours of their beloved father's life with devoted love and filial care.

The wool trade is at present entirely quiet and we have heard nothing in regard to prices. The community wool has not yet been sold.

Commending myself to you and your valued family, I remain your respectful friend and servant, David Cornies.

981. Phillip Wiebe to Traugott Blueher. 5 June 1848.
SAOR 89-1-1331/41v.

Most valued Mr. Blueher,

A sincere heart like yours can well fathom the sentiments that I express from my homeland, treasured friend of my father, but I cannot find words to express them. The journey to Prussia, from start to finish, was a journey of painful detachment, especially the illness of my dear Agnes from which she suffered so much. Then, at a great distance, we learned about the death of her unforgettably good father. More difficult, upon our return, was our entry into the desolate house of our father where we were welcomed by the stream of tears of many sympathetic and painfully grieving relatives and friends. This tore at our hearts and especially that of my dear wife who has, since then, kept mainly to her bed, and is only slowly regaining her strength. Only the Lord can and will comfort us and help us to bear what cannot be changed. May his will remain holy for us.

The last days of our father passed calmly and solemnly. No complaints crossed his lips, nor did he, as he prepared for his imminent release, ask for human assistance. Instead, his glance was upwards where he sought his physician, from whom alone help could come. Uncle D[avid] Cornies stayed at his side and shortly before the final departure of our father he touchingly grasped Uncle's hand, rested his tired head on his arm and repeatedly said, "You will do everything." Our dear father went to his rest gently and entered the joys of the Lord.

The last service for the treasured body was on 16 March. On this day, many, very many people from near and far took their final leave of their lost benefactor and protector. Many a quiet tear flowed into his coffin as clear evidence of the sincere love and attachment they had borne him during his lifetime. The scene must have been a beautiful one, yet also painful, as Molochnaia Germans, Russians, Nogais, and Hebrew colonists from distant places thronged past the coffin to say their final farewells. Many a person's most beloved wishes were buried with him. After the Church Elder's final words, and since the church could naturally not accommodate everyone, the body was displayed in the churchyard. The gathered crowd then joined in the procession to the cemetery. The most beautiful weather blessed the celebration of this burial. Death had not changed the facial features of the deceased in any way. The serious features we remembered from the past had come back fully. Only the now closed but once lively eyes betrayed the fact that his soul had departed its mortal frame. May his ashes rest gently.

982. Phillip Wiebe to Daniel Schlatter. 22 October 1848. SAOR 89-1-1331/106v.

Valued Mr. Schlatter,

Sympathetically and with sorrow, I would like to inform you that our much beloved father, my treasured benefactor and your dear friend, Johann Cornies has left us forever. He departed this world in March of this year. It pleased the Lord to call him away quite unexpectedly in the still vigorous prime of his life and at a time when none of his loving family were around to support him. This has afflicted all of us deeply. It was especially difficult for my beloved wife to accept this hard fate. Still, the dear Lord has given us strength to bear what cannot be changed. His Will shall remain holy for us forever. Enclosed, you will find the life story of the immortalized.

My beloved wife still frequently remembers you, esteemed friend, and by coincidence I learned from her that you are in possession of an excellent portrait of my dear father-in-law. This moves me to earnestly request that you provide the family with a copy of this portrait that we regrettably do not have. Nor do we know where to find one. Please, if possible, do us this especially great favour. This all of us request, believing longingly that you will not refuse us.

I enclose a survey of the blossoming condition of the villages, for which we can principally thank the relentless activity of my blessed father-in-law.

Peter Cornies died a year ago. David and Heinrich are still alive and in good spirits. The latter administers Iushanle. Manufacturer Klassen died recently. Brother-in-law Cornies is resident at Tashchenak, forty verstas from here. Peter Neufeld is the local church teacher. Peter Schmidt, senior and junior, are both healthy.

We all send you our heartfelt greetings, your honest friend and servant, Phillip Wiebe.

Appendix I:
Genealogy of Johann Cornies's Immediate Family

Johann Martin Cornies (1741–1823), father of Johann Cornies

Maria Klassen (1760–1833), mother of Johann Cornies

Johann Cornies (1789–1848)

Anganetha Klassen Cornies (1792–1847), wife of Johann Cornies

Peter Cornies (1791–1847), brother of Johann Cornies

David Cornies (1794–1873), brother of Johann Cornies

Heinrich Cornies (1806–?), brother of Johann Cornies

Johann Cornies Jr. (1812–82), son of Johann Cornies

Agnes Cornies (1819–59), daughter of Johann Cornies and wife of Philip Wiebe, secretary of Johann Cornies. After Johann Cornies's death in 1848, Wiebe succeeded him as Chairman of the Forestry Society.

Appendix II:
List of Correspondents

Barth, Johann Ambrosius, bookseller, No. 681 Grimmaischestrasse, Leipzig
Bartsch, Jacob, District Chairman of the Khortitsa settlement in the 1840s
Bartram, Johann, Viborg, Finland, sometime visitor to Molochnaia
    Mennonite District
Baumann, Wilhelm, agronomist employed by the Ministry of State
    Domains
Biess, Senior Magistrate, Petersdorf, Saxony
Biller, Colonial Inspector
Blueher, Traugott, Director of the Sarepta Merchandising Firm in Moscow
Bradke, Georg von, senior official in the Ministry of State Domains
Contenius, Samuel, Curator of Guardianship Committee in Ekaterinoslav
Cornies, Agnes, daughter of Johann Cornies
Cornies, David, brother of Johann Cornies
Cornies, Heinrich, brother of Johann Cornies, with business in Ekateri-
    noslav in the 1820s and 1830s
Cornies, Johann, Jr., son of Johann Cornies
Dik, Jacob, manager of Johann Cornies's Tashchenak estate while
    Johann Jr. travelled in Prussia in 1846–8
Dmitriev, Larion, master mason living in Gremelsteva village near
    Peremishl
Doering, Daniel, member of the Moravian Brethren
Dohna, Count G., Herrnhut (also Hermsdorf, near Dresden), grandson
    of Count Zinzendorf, who was the founder of the Pietist Moravian
    Brethren
Draisma, Peter Orens, Grunau village in Molochnaia Colonist District
Driedger, Deputy District Chairman in 1835
Duebner, a book merchant in Prussia

Dyck, Klaas, a brother-in-law of Johann Cornies

Dyck, Gerhard, Molochnaia resident who designed and constructed various farm machines

Dyck, Johann, debtor

Enns, Gerhard, Forestry Society member and Director of the Ohrloff School Society in the 1840s

Ennz, Gerhard, employee of Johann Cornies

Epp, David, Heubuden near Marienberg, West Prussia

Epp, David, Khortitsa Mennonite District

Fadeev, Andrei Michaelovich, senior member of Guardianship Committee

Fast, Bernhard, Halbstadt, Church Elder in Molochnaia

Fast, Peter, head gardener (forester) at the Berdiansk model forest plantation in the 1840s

Fein, a wealthy German colonist; owner of the Faltz-Fein estate

Flaming, Andreas, Schardau inhabitant

Fletnitzer, Karl, pastor of St. Paul's Lutheran Church in Odesa and director of the church's school

Franz, Heinrich, schoolteacher in Ekaterinoslav and then in Khortitsa settlement

Frank, Wilhelm, employed as translator, clerk, etc., with Guardianship Committee

Friesen, Peter, described as his foster son by Johann Cornies

Gavel, Fr., Ministry of State Domains agronomist and author of biographical essay about Cornies

Goerz, Franz, Church Elder in Molochnaia

Graf, bookseller

Guardianship Committee, originally in Ekaterinoslav, later in Odesa

Guildenschanz, Georg, senior judge on Odesa Guardianship Committee

Hahn, Evgenii von, Deputy Director of the Guardianship Committee from 1842–5 and Director from 1845–8

Hahn, Peter von, son-in-law of Andrei M. Fadeev

Harder, Deputy District Chairman of Molochnaia Mennonite settlement in 1835

Hausknecht, Caspar Adrian, teacher in Mennonite village schools

Heese, Heinrich, teacher in Mennonite village schools

Horwitz, Theodor E.

Inzov, Ivan Nikitich, Head Curator of Guardianship Committee

Janz, Benjamin, teacher in a Molochnaia village school

Janzen, Cornelius, resident in Schoenwiese village

Keppen, Peter, statistician, archaeologist, and Director of the Learned
  Committee of the Ministry of State Domains
Khortitsa Mennonite District Office
Kirilovskii, translator for the Guardianship Committee in Ekaterino-
  slav and tutor for Johann Cornies Jr.
Kiselev, Pavel, the Minister of State Domains
Klaassen, Christian, Grunau village in Molochnaia Colonist District
Klaassen, Johann, cloth manufacturer in Molochnaia Mennonite
  District
Klassen, Johann, Molochnaia Mennonite District Chairman
Kliewer, Gerhard, Schardau village inhabitant
Koshani, manager at Tsarskoe Selo sheepfarm
Lange, Friedrich Wilhelm, Elder of the Gnadenfeld congregation from
  1842–8
Lange, Wilhem, Gnadenfeld fullholder
Lemke, Abram, inhabitant in Molochnaia Mennonite District
Levshin, Aleksei, Director of the Third Department of the Ministry of
  State Domains
Loewen, David, debtor
Mark, Major
Martens, Gerhard, employed by Molochnaia Mennonite District Office
Martens, Jacob, son of Wilhelm Martens and Wilhelm's replacement
  on the Agricultural Committee
Martens, Jacob, Tiegenhagen village inhabitant
Martens, Wilhelm, wealthy Mennonite settler, one of wealthiest Men-
  nonite estate owners in the Molochnaia area, and business partner
  of Johann Cornies
Mathias, Karl, Hochstadt village in Molochnaia Colonist District,
  debtor
Neufeld, D., Molochnaia inhabitant
Neufeld, Johann, Halbstadt resident, Johann Cornies's brother-and-
  law, and partner in their brandy distillery
Neufeld, Peter, Ohrloff resident and director of the Molochnaia Men-
  nonite branch of the Russian Evangelical Bible Association
Neufeld, Peter, Ladekopp village inhabitant
Pelekh, Khariton Trokhimovich, Inspector of Colonies
Penner, Gerhard, Mennonite from Khortitsa settlement
Penner, Jacob, Khortitsa District Chairman who later moved to
  Molochnaia District
Prinz, Friedrich, Chair of the Württemberg Pietist settlement

Ratzlaff, Benjamin, Elder of the Rudnerweide congregation
Regier, J., Schoensee village inhabitant
Regier, Regina, Molochnaia inhabitant
Reimer, David, owner of the Felstenthal estate
Reimer, Heinrich, employed as manager of Iushanle estate in 1834
Reimer, Peter, employed by Radishchev Mennonites (Hutterites)
Reuss, Prince Heinrich von, Klipphausen near Wilsdorf, Saxony
Riedel, Herman, merchant in Odesa
Riediger, Martin, teacher in the Ohrloff school
Rosen, Fedor F., head of the Tavride Ministry of State Domains
Roslavets, Viktor, Civil Governor of Tavrida Guberniia
Schlatter, Daniel (1791–1870), independent Swiss missionary to
    Nogais, author of 1830 book on Nogais
Schubert, State Counsellor in St. Petersburg, involved with Bible
    Society
Semenov, Member of Guardianship Committee
Siemens, Johann, Chair of the Khortitsa Agricultural Society
Sieter, Colonial Inspector for Molochnaia settlements
Smissen, van der, Jacob, Danzig minister
Steen, Heinrich van, Danzig
Stempel, Carl, Colonial Inspector for the Württemberg and Bergthal
    settlements
Steven, Christian, Minister of State Domains, Director of Agriculture
    for South Russia
Sudermann, Hermann, Supervisor of the Berdiansk Crown Forestry
    Plantation
Sukkau, Johann, Mennonite resident in Rothenbude on the Vistula,
    West Prussia
Sukkau, Johann, employed by Cornies
Thiessen, Bernhard, father of Johann Cornies Jr.'s second wife, Theresa
    Thiessen
Tihlmann, Johann, Mennonite settler
Voht, Frantz, Rueckenau village inhabitant
Voth [or Voht], David, Molochnaia inhabitant
Voth, Tobias, teacher at Ohrloff Society School
Wall, Cornelius, Molochnaia community sheepfarm manager
Walther, Ernst
Warkentin, Dietrich, Elder of the Petershagen congregation
Warkentin, Dirk, Forestry Society member
Warkentin, P., Molochnaia inhabitant

Wedel, Peter, Elder of the Alexanderwohl congregation
Werner, Rosenthal village inhabitant in Molochnaia Colonist District
Wiebe, Abraham, Forestry Society member
Wiebe, Abram, Rudnerweide village inhabitant
Wiebe, Jacob, a friend of Cornies from Elbing, Prussia
Wiebe, Johann, Tiege, later Neuteich, West Prussia
Wiebe, Johann, a friend of Cornies's from Freienhuben, Prussia
Wiebe, Phillip, husband of Agnes Cornies and Johann Cornies's
 secretary
Wiens, Dirk, assistant manager at Iushanle in 1834
Wiens, Heinrich, Elder of the Gnadenheim congregation
Wilke, August, gardener on Cornies's sheepfarm
Wollmann, Christian, Kirschwald village in Molochnaia Colonist
 District
Zamero, an expert on silk reeling
Zille, Inspector at Raeubersdorf near Zittau, Saxony

Appendix III:
Glossary

Arshin: measure of length equal to 71 cm or 28 inches

Chetverik: dry measure, also called mirka, equal to one-eighth of a chetvert

Chetvert: dry measure equal to 2.099 hectolitres or 5.95 bushels

Cottager or *Anwohner:* a landless village inhabitant with a house on a half-desiatina garden and orchard plot

Desiatina: land measure equal to 1.092 hectares or 2.7 acres

District Office or *Gebietsamt:* headed by elected Chairman, or *Ober-schulz,* and two assistants

Fullholding *or Wirtschaft:* Mennonite family farm, normally with sixty-five desiatinas of land, consisting of house and farm buildings on a one-and-a-half-desiatina home and garden plot in a village, a half-desiatina woodlot, and plough, hay, and pasturelands in common fields around the village

Funt: weight equal to 0.41 kilograms or 0.9 pounds

Fut: English foot

German mile: equal to 7,420 metres

Guberniia: major administrative division, a province of the Russian Empire

Khutor: an owned or leased individual farm or group of farms outside of a village

Orphans' administration *or Waisenamt:* a district body with executive authority to administer and enforce Mennonite inheritance practices

Pud: weight equal to 40 *funt,* 16.38 kilograms, or 36 pounds

Renter or Einwohner: a landless village inhabitant, often young and recently married, who occupies rented rooms in a village

Ruble: monetary unit, equal to one hundred kopeks; in 1839, the value of one silver ruble was fixed at 3.6 paper rubles

Sazhen: length equal to 2.134 metres or 7 feet

Uezd: administrative district

Versta: length equal to 1.065 kilometres or 0.633 miles

Village Office or Schulzenamt: village administration headed by elected Village Mayor, or *Schulz,* and two assistants, or *Beisitzer*

Volost: administrative subdivision of the peasantry comprising a number of villages; the equivalent of a Mennonite District before 1871

Bibliography

Antonov, Sergei. *Bankrupts and Usurers of Imperial Russia: Debt, Property, and the Law in the Age of Dostoevsky and Tolstoy*. Cambridge, MA: Harvard University Press, 2016. https://doi.org/10.4159/9780674972599.

Balzer, Heinrich. "Faith and Reason: The Principles of Mennonitism Reconsidered in a Treatise of 1833." Edited and translated by Robert Friedman. *The Mennonite Quarterly Review* 22 (April 1948): 75–93.

Bartlett, Roger P. *Human Capital: The Settlement of Foreigners in Russia 1762–1804*. Cambridge: Cambridge University Press, 1979. https://doi.org/10.1017/CBO9780511561030.

Batalden, Stephen. "The BFBS Petersburg Agency and Russian Biblical Translation, 1856–1875." In Batalden, Cann, and Dean, *Sowing the Word*, 169–96.

Batalden, Stephen. "Musul'manskii i evreiskii voprosy v Rossii epokhi Aleksandra i glazami shotlandskogo bibleista i puteshestvennika." *Voprosy istorii* 5 (2004): 46–63.

Batalden, Stephen. "Printing the Bible in the Reign of Alexander I: Toward a Reinterpretation of the Russian Bible Society." In *Church, Nation and State in Russia and Ukraine*, edited by Geoffrey A. Hosking, 65–78. London: Macmillan, 1991. https://doi.org/10.1007/978-1-349-21566-9_5.

Batalden, Stephen, Kathleen Cann, and John Dean, eds. *Sowing the Word: The Cultural Impact of the British and Foreign Bible Society, 1804–2004*. Sheffield: Sheffield Phoenix Press, 2004.

Baur, Susan. *Hypochondria: Woeful Imaginings*. Berkeley: University of California Press, 1989. https://doi.org/10.1525/9780520351943.

Beznosova, Oksana. "A Foreign Faith, but of What Sort? The Mennonite Church and the Russian Empire, 1789–1917." In Friesen, *Minority Report*, 110–41. https://doi.org/10.3138/9781487514266-007.

Brandes, Detlef. *Von den Zaren adoptiert: die deutschen Kolonisten und die Balkansiedler in Neurussland und Bessarabien 1751–1914*. Munich: R. Oldenbourg Verlag, 1993.

Brown, George. *The History of the British and Foreign Bible Society, from its Institution in 1804, to the Close of its Jubilee in 1854*. London: W.M. Watts, 1859.

Center For Volga German Studies Gazetteer, s.v. "Karass." Retrieved 11 June 2014. https://www.volgagermans.org/who-are-volga-germans /settlements/resettlement-within-russia/caucasus/karras-north-caucasus.

Cherkazianova, Irina. "Mennonite Schools and the Russian Empire: The Transformation of Church-State Relations in Education, 1789–1917." In Friesen, *Minority Report*, 85–109. https://doi.org/10.3138/9781487514266 -006.

Cooper, Frederick, and Ann Laura Stoler. "Between Metropole and Colony: Rethinking a Research Agenda." In *Tensions of Empire: Colonial Cultures in a Bourgeois World*, edited by Frederick Cooper and Ann Laura Stoler, 1–56. Berkeley: University of California Press, 1997. https://doi.org/10.1525 /9780520918085.

Deppermann, Klaus. *Der hallesche Pietismus und der preussische Staat unter Friedrich III*. Göttingen: Vandenhoeck & Ruprecht, 1961.

Druzhinin, N.M. *Gosudarstvennye krest'iane i reforma P.D. Kiseleva*. 2 vols. Moscow: Izdatelstvo Akademii nauk SSSR, 1946.

Dyck, Harvey L., ed. "Agronomist Gavel's Biography of Johann Cornies (1789–1848)." *Journal of Mennonite Studies* 2 (1984): 29–41.

Dyck, Harvey L. "Introduction and Analysis." In Dyck, *A Mennonite in Russia*, 3–74.

Dyck, Harvey L. "Landlessness in the Old Colony: The Judenplan Experiment 1850–1880." In John Friesen, *Mennonites in Russia*, 183–202.

Dyck, Harvey L., ed. *A Mennonite in Russia: The Diaries of Jacob D. Epp, 1851–1880*. Toronto: University of Toronto Press, 1991.

Dyck, Harvey L. "Russian Servitor and Mennonite Hero: Light and Shadow in Images of Johann Cornies." *Journal of Mennonite Studies* 2 (1984): 9–28.

Dyck, Harvey L., John R. Staples, and Ingrid I. Epp, eds. *Transformation on the South Ukrainian Steppe: Letters and Papers of Johann Cornies, Volume I: 1812–1835*. Translated by Ingrid I. Epp. Toronto: University of Toronto Press, 2015. https://doi.org/10.3138/9781442622371.

Dyck, Harvey L., John R. Staples, and Ingrid I. Epp, eds. *Transformation on the Southern Ukrainian Steppe: Letters and Papers of Johann Cornies, Volume II: 1836–1842*. Translated by Ingrid I. Epp. Toronto: University of Toronto Press, 2020. https://doi.org/10.3138/9781487530280.

Eisfeld, Alfred. "Introduction." *Samuil Khristianovich Kontenius ob inostrannoi kolonizatsii IUzhnoi Rossii*. Edited by Olga Eisfeld. Odesa: Astroprint, 2003.

Epp, David H. *Johann Cornies*. Translated by Peter Pauls. Winnipeg: CMBC Publications and Manitoba Mennonite Historical Society, 1995.

Epp, David H., and Richard D. Thiessen. "Höppner, Jakob (1748–1826)." Global Anabaptist Mennonite Encyclopedia Online. January 2013. https://gameo .org/index.php?title=H%C3%B6ppner,_Jakob_(1748–1826)&oldid=145466.

Fadeev, Andrei Mikhailovich. *Vospominaniia Andreia Mikhailovich Fadeeva, 1790–1867 gg*. Odesa: IUzhno-Russkogo Obshchestva Pechatnago Dela, 1897.

Foote, Paul. "Introduction." In Lermontov, *A Hero of Our Time*.

Friedmann. Robert. "Anabaptism and Pietism." *The Mennonite Quarterly Review* 14 (April 1940): 90–128.

Friedmann, Robert. *Mennonite Piety Through the Centuries: Its Genius and Its Literature*. Scottsdale, PA: Herald Press, 1998.

Friesen, John. "Education, Pietism and Change among Mennonites in Nineteenth-Century Prussia." *The Mennonite Quarterly Review* 66 (April 1982): 155–66.

Friesen, John, ed. *Mennonites in Russia, 1788–1988: Essays in Honour of Gerhard Lohrenz*. Winnipeg: CMBC Publications, 1989.

Friesen, Leonard G. *Mennonites in the Russian Empire and the Soviet Union: Through Much Tribulation*. Toronto: University of Toronto Press, 2022. https://doi.org/10.3138/9781487505677.

Friesen, Leonard G., ed. *Minority Report: Mennonite Identities in Imperial Russia and Soviet Ukraine Reconsidered, 1789–1945*. Toronto: University of Toronto Press, 2018. https://doi.org/10.3138/9781487514266.

Friesen, Peter M. *The Mennonite Brotherhood in Russia, 1789–1910*. Rev. ed. Translated by John B. Toews et al. Fresno, CA: General Conference of Mennonite Brethren Churches, 1980.

Fry, Gary Dean. "Doukhobors 1801–1855: The Origins of a Successful Dissident Sect." PhD diss., Washington University, 1976.

Goerz, H. *The Molotschna Settlement*. Winnipeg: CMBC Publications, 1993.

Goossen, Benjamin W. "Mennonites in Latin America: A Review of the Literature." *The Conrad Grebel Review* 34, no. 3 (Fall 2016): 236–65.

Haralampieva, Tsvetelina. "Scottish Missionaries in Karass and Their Role in the Russian Colonization of the North Caucasus in the First Quarter of the XIX Century." *Via Evrasia* 2 (2013).

Haxthausen, August von. *Studien über die innern Zustände, das Volksleben und insbesondere die ländlichen Einrichtungen Russlands*. Vol. 1–2: Hanover, 1847; Vol. 3: Berlin, 1852.

Haxthausen, August von. *Studies on the Interior of Russia.* Translated by
Eleanore L.M. Schmidt. Chicago: University of Chicago Press, 1972.

Heafford, Michael R. *Pestalozzi: His Thought and Its Relevance Today.* London:
Routledge, 1967.

Heese, Heinrich. "Autobiography." Translated by Cornelius Krahn. *Mennonite
Life* 24, no. 2 (April 1969): 73–7.

Herlihy, Patricia. *Odessa: A History, 1794–1914.* Cambridge, MA: Harvard
University Press, 1986.

Hilton, Boyd. *The Age of Atonement: The Influence of Evangelicalism on Social and
Economic Thought, 1785–1865.* Oxford: Clarendon Press, 1992. https://
doi.org/10.1093/oso/9780198202950.001.0001.

Huebert, Helmut T. *Molotschna Historical Atlas.* Winnipeg: Springfield
Publishers, 2003.

Isaac, Franz. *Die Molotschnaer Mennoniten. Ein Beitrag zur Geschichte derselben.
Aus Akten älterer und neuerer Zeit, wie auch auf Grund eigener Erlebnisse und
Erfahrungen dargestellt.* Halbstadt: H.J. Braun, 1908.

Jantz, Harold. "Pietism's Gift to Russian Mennonites." *Direction* 36, no. 1
(Spring 2007): 58–73.

Jantz, Harold. "A Pietist Pastor and the Russian Mennonites: The Legacy of
Eduard Wuest." *Direction* 36, no. 2 (Fall 2007): 232–46.

Janzen, Tim, trans. "Molotschna Mennonite Settlement Census for October
1806." http://www.mennonitegenealogy.com/russia/Molotschna
_Mennonite_Settlement_Census_27_October_1806.pdf.

Jehle, Marianne. *Anna Schlatter-Bernet, 1773–1826: eine weltoffene St. Galler
Christin.* Zürich: Theologischer Verlag Zürich, 2003.

Karev, V.M., A. Eisfeld, S. Bobyleva, D. Brandies, A. Engel-Braunschmidt, A.
Hermann, W. Mathies, I. Petrivnaia, Iu. Petrov, I. Pleve, and O. Sukhareva,
eds. *Nemtsy Rossii Entsiklopediia.* Moscow, 1999–2006.

Keppen, Petr. *Deviataia reviziia: izsledovanie o chisle zhitelei v Rossii v 1851 g.* St.
Petersburg: Tipografiia Imperatorskoi Akademii Nauk, 1857.

Keppen, Petr. "Spisok izvestneishim kurganam v Rossii." Part 1, *Severnaia
Pchela* (2 January 1837): 3–4; part 2, *Severnaia Pchela* (3 January 1837): 7–8;
part 3, *Severnaia Pchela* (4 January 1837): 10–12.

Kivelson, Valerie A., and Ronald Grigor Suny. *Russia's Empires.* Oxford: Oxford
University Press, 2017.

Klassen, Peter J. "Faith and Culture in Conflict: Mennonites in the Vistula
Delta." *The Mennonite Quarterly Review* 57 (July 1983): 194–205.

Klassen, Peter J. *Mennonites in Early Modern Poland and Prussia.* Baltimore:
Johns Hopkins University Press, 2009. https://doi.org/10.1353/book
.3461.

Klier, John D. "State Policies and the Conversion of Jews in Imperial Russia." In *Of Religion and Empire: Missions, Conversion, and Tolerance in Tsarist Russia*, edited by Robert P. Geraci and Michael Khodarkovsky, 92–112. Ithaca, NY: Cornell University Press, 2001. https://doi.org/10.7591/9781501724305 -005.

Krahn, Cornelius. "Bergthal Mennonite Settlement (Zaporizhia Oblast, Ukraine)." Global Anabaptist Mennonite Encyclopedia Online. 1953. http://gameo.org/index.php?title=Bergthal_Mennonite_Settlement _(Zaporizhia_Oblast,_Ukraine)&oldid=144812.

Lavater, Johann Casper. *Essays on Physiognomy Designed to Promote the Knowledge and the Love of Mankind*. Translated by Thomas Holcroft. London: B. Blake, 1840.

LeDonne, John P. *Forging a Unitary State: Russia's Management of the Eurasian Space, 1650–1850*. Toronto: University of Toronto Press, 2020. https:// doi.org/10.3138/9781487533311.

Leonard, Carol S. *Agrarian Reform in Russia: The Road from Serfdom*. Cambridge: Cambridge University Press, 2010. https://doi.org/10.1017 /CBO9780511780639.

Lermontov, M. *A Hero of Our Time*. Translated by Paul Foote. Baltimore: Penguin, 1966.

Lincoln, W. Bruce. *In the Vanguard of Reform: Russia's Enlightened Bureaucrats, 1825–1861*. DeKalb: Northern Illinois University Press, 1982.

Loewen, Jacob A., and Wesley J. Prieb. "The Abuse of Power among Mennonites in South Russia, 1789–1919." In Redekop and Redekop, *Power, Authority, and the Anabaptist Tradition*, 95–114.

Loewen, Royden. *Family, Church, and Market: A Mennonite Community in the Old and the New Worlds, 1850–1930*. Toronto: University of Toronto Press, 1993.

Lothe, Jean. "La 'British and Foreign Bible Society' en Russie (1812–1826)." *Revue des pays de l'est* 30, no. 2 (1989): 70–81.

Madariaga, Isabel de. *Russia in the Age of Catherine the Great*. New Haven, CT: Yale University Press, 1981.

Marmont, Auguste Frédéric Louis Viesse de. *Voyage de M. le maréchal duc de Raguse en Hongrie, en Transylvanie, dans la Russie méridionale, en Crimée, et sur le bords de la mer d'Azoff, à Constantinople et sur quelques parties de l'Asie-Mineure, en Syrie, en Palestine et en Égypte*. 4 vols. Brussels: Société typographique Belge, 1837.

Martin, Alexander M. *From the Holy Roman Empire to the Land of the Tsars: One Family's Odyssey, 1768–1870*. Oxford: Oxford University Press, 2022. https:// doi.org/10.1093/oso/9780192844378.001.0001.

McGrew, Roderick Erle. *Russia and the Cholera, 1823–1832*. Madison: University of Wisconsin Press, 1965.

Menger, Phillipp. *Die Heilige Allianz: Religion und Politik bei Alexander I. (1801–1825)*. Stuttgart: Franz Steiner Verlag, 2014. https://doi.org /10.25162/9783515108218.

Meshkov, D.Iu. "K istorii sukonnoi fabriki Ioganna Klassena." *Voprosy Germanskoi Istorii* (2001): 156–64.

Moon, David. *The Abolition of Serfdom in Russia, 1762–1907*. Abingdon: Routledge, 2002.

Moon, David. "Agriculture and the Environment on the Steppes in the Nineteenth Century." In *Peopling the Russian Periphery: Borderland Colonization in Eurasian History*, edited by Nicholas Breyfogle, Abby Schrader, and Willard Sunderland, 81–105. London: Routledge, 2007.

Moon, David. *The Plough that Broke the Steppes: Agriculture and Environment on Russia's Grasslands, 1700–1914*. Oxford: Oxford University Press, 2013. https://doi.org/10.1093/acprof:oso/9780199556434.001.0001.

Myeshkov, Dmytro. *Die Schwarzmeerdeutschen und ihre Welten, 1781–1871*. Essen: Klartext, 2008.

Neufeld, Heinrich. "The Dismissal of Aeltester Jakob Warkentin, 1842." Translated by Ben Hoeppner and Delbert Plett. *Preservings* 24 (December 2004): 19–21.

Neufeld, Heinrich. "A Further Examination of the Molotschna Conflict." Translated by Ben Hoeppner and Delbert Plett. *Preservings* 24 (December 2004): 23–8.

O'Neill, Kelly. *Claiming Crimea: A History of Catherine the Great's Southern Empire*. New Haven, CT: Yale University Press, 2017. https://doi.org /10.12987/yale/9780300218299.001.0001.

Pallas, Peter Simon. *Travels through the Southern Provinces of the Russian Empire in the Years 1793 and 1794*. 2nd ed. 2 vols. London: John Stockdale, 1812.

Penner, Glenn, and Steve Fast. "Waldheim, Molotschna and Heinrichsdorf, Volhynia, 1833–1851." Russian Mennonite Genealogical Resource Page. Mennonite Genealogy. 25 June 2016. https://www.mennonitegenealogy .com/russia/Waldheim_and_Heinrichsdorf.pdf.

Plesskaia-Zebold, E.G. *Odesskie nemtsy, 1803–1920*. Odesa: Institut germanskikh i vostochnoevropeiskikh issledovanii Gettingen, 1999.

Plett, Delbert F. *The Golden Years: The Mennonite Kleine Gemeinde in Russia, 1812–1849*. Steinbach, MB: DFP Publications, 1985.

Postnikov, V.E. *IUzhno-russkoe krest'ianskoe khoziaistvo*. Moscow, 1891.

Raeff, Marc. *The Decembrist Movement*. Upper Saddle River, NJ: Prentice-Hall, 1966.

Redekop, Benjamin W., and Calvin Redekop, eds. *Power, Authority, and the Anabaptist Tradition.* Baltimore: Johns Hopkins University Press, 2005.

Redekop, Calvin W., Victor A. Krahn, and Samuel J. Steiner, eds. *Anabaptist/ Mennonite Faith and Economics.* Lanham, MD: University Press of America, 1994.

Reimer, Johannes. *Johann Cornies: der Sozialreformer aus den Steppen Südrusslands.* Nürnberg: VTR Publications, 2015.

Reimer, Klaas. "Ein Kleines Aufsatz." In Plett, *The Golden Years,* 163–6.

Rempel, David G. "From Danzig to Russia: The First Mennonite Migration." *Mennonite Life* (January 1969): 8–28.

Rempel, Peter. *Mennonite Migration to Russia, 1788–1828.* Rev. ed. Edited by Alfred H. Redekopp and Richard D. Thiessen. Winnipeg: Manitoba Mennonite Historical Society, 2007.

Riasanovsky, Nicholas V. *Nicholas I and Official Nationality in Russia, 1825–1855.* Berkeley: University of California Press, 1969.

Richmond, Walter. *The Circassian Genocide.* New Brunswick, NJ: Rutgers University Press, 2013.

Schlachta, Astrid von. *From the Tyrol to North America: The Hutterite Story through the Centuries.* Translated by Werner O. Packull and Karin Packull. Waterloo, ON: Pandora Press, 2008.

Schlachta, Astrid von. "The Hutterian Brethren in the Molochna, 1842–74." *Preservings* 24 (December 2004), 38–40.

Schrader, Abby M. *Languages of the Lash: Corporal Punishment and Identity in Imperial Russia.* Dekalb: Northern Illinois University Press, 2002.

Schroeder, William. *The Bergthal Colony.* Rev. ed. Winnipeg: CMBC Publications, 1986.

Schroeder, William. *Mennonite Historical Atlas.* Winnipeg: Kindred Productions, 1996.

Slocum, John W. "Who, and When, Were the Inorodtsy? The Evolution of the Category of 'Aliens' in Imperial Russia." *The Russian Review* 57, no. 2 (April 1998): 173–90. https://doi.org/10.1111/0036-0341.00017.

Smith-Peter, Susan. *Imagining Russian Regions: Subnational Identity and Civil Society in Nineteenth-Century Russia.* Leiden: Brill, 2018. https://doi.org /10.1163/9789004353510.

Stanley, Brian. "Christian Missions and the Enlightenment." In *Christian Missions and the Enlightenment,* edited by Brian Stanley, 1–21. Grand Rapids, MI: Wm.B. Eerdmans, 2001.

Staples, John R. *Cross-Cultural Encounters on the Ukrainian Steppe: Settling the Molochna Basin, 1783–1861.* Toronto: University of Toronto Press, 2003. https://doi.org/10.3138/9781442673625.

Staples, John R. "Iogann Kornis i osnovanie Berdianskogo Lesnichestvo." *Voprosy Germanskoi Istorii* (2017): 18–21.

Staples, John R. "Johann Cornies, Money-Lending, and Modernization in the Molochna Mennonite Settlement, 1820s–1840s." *Journal of Mennonite Studies* 27 (2009): 109–27.

Staples, John R. *Johann Cornies, the Mennonites, and Russian Colonialism in Southern Ukraine*. Toronto: University of Toronto Press, 2023. https://doi.org/10.3138/9781487549183.

Staples, John R. "The Mennonite Commonwealth Paradigm and the Dnepropetrovsk School of Ukrainian Mennonite Historiography." *Voprosy Germanskoi Istorii* (2007): 58–68.

Staples, John R. "'On Civilizing the Nogais': Mennonite-Nogai Economic Relations, 1825–1860." *The Mennonite Quarterly Review* 74, no. 2 (April 2000): 229–56.

Staples, John R. "Religion, Politics, and the Mennonite Privilegium: Reconsidering the Warkentin Affair." *Journal of Mennonite Studies* 21 (2003): 71–88.

Staples, John R. "Romance, Marriage, Sex and the Status of Women in Nineteenth-Century Tsarist Russian Mennonite Society." In van Veen, Visser, and Waite, *Sisters*, 302–18.

Starr, S. Frederick. "Introduction." In *August von Haxthausen, Studies on the Interior of Russia*, translated by Eleanore L.M. Schmidt. Chicago: University of Chicago Press, 1972.

Sunderland, Willard. "The Ministry of Asiatic Russia: The Colonial Office that Never Was but Might Have Been." *Slavic Review* 69, no. 1 (Spring 2010): 120–50. https://doi.org/10.1017/S0037677900016727.

Sunderland, Willard. *Taming the Wild Field: Colonization and Empire on the Russian Steppe*. Ithaca, NY: Cornell University Press, 2004.

Thaden, Edward C. *Russia's Western Borderlands, 1710–1870*. Princeton, NJ: Princeton University Press, 1985. https://doi.org/10.1515/9781400854950.

Toews, John B. *Czars, Soviets & Mennonites*. Harrisonburg, VA: Faith and Life Press, 1981.

Toews, John B. *Perilous Journey: The Mennonite Brethren in Russia, 1860–1910*. Winnipeg: Kindred Press, 1988.

Unruh, Benjamin Heinrich. *Die niederländisch-niederdeutschen Hintergründe der mennonitischen Ostwanderungen im 16., 18. und 19. Jahrhundert*. Karlsruhe: Selbstverlag, 1955.

Urry, James. "The Mennonite Commonwealth Revisited." *The Mennonite Quarterly Review* 84, no. 2 (April 2010): 229–47.

Urry, James. *Mennonites, Politics, and Peoplehood: Europe – Russia – Canada, 1525 to 1980*. Winnipeg: University of Manitoba Press, 2006. https://doi .org/10.1515/9780887553448.

Urry, James. *None but Saints: The Transformation of Mennonite Life in Russia, 1789–1889*. Winnipeg: Hyperion Press, 1990.

Urry, James. "Ohm Heinrich Balzer 1800–46, Tiege." *Preservings* 24 (December 2004): 12–15.

Urry, James. "'Servants from far': Mennonites and the Pan-evangelical Impulse in Early Nineteenth Century Russia." *The Mennonite Quarterly Review* 61, no. 2 (1987): 213–27.

Urry, James. "The Social Background to the Emergence of the Mennonite Brethren in Nineteenth-Century Russia." *Journal of Mennonite Studies* 6 (1988): 8–35.

Veen, Mirjam van, Piet Visser, and Gary K. Waite, eds. *Sisters: Myth and Reality of Anabaptist, Mennonite, and Doopsgezinde Women, ca 1525–1900*. Leiden: Brill, 2014.

Venger, N.V. *Mennonitskoe predprinimatel'stvo v usloviiakh modernizatsii IUga Rossii: Mezhdu kongregatsiei, klanom i rossiiskim obshchestvom (1789–1920)*. Dnipro: Dnipropetrovsk National University, 2009.

Wardin, Albert W. *On the Edge: Baptists and Other Free Church Evangelicals in Tsarist Russia, 1855–1917*. Eugene, OR: Wipf & Stock, 2013.

Werth, Paul W. *The Tsar's Foreign Faiths: Toleration and the Fate of Religious Freedom in Imperial Russia*. Oxford: Oxford University Press, 2014. https:// doi.org/10.1093/acprof:oso/9780199591770.001.0001.

Woodcock, George, and Ivan Avakumović. *The Doukhobors*. London: Faber and Faber, 1968.

Young, Robert J.C. *Empire, Colony, Postcolony*. New York: Wiley, 2015. https:// doi.org/10.1002/9781394261178.

Zhuk, Sergei I. *Russia's Lost Reformation: Peasants, Millennialism, and Radical Sects in Southern Russia and Ukraine, 1830–1917*. Baltimore: Johns Hopkins University Press, 2004.

Index

Notes: Johann Cornies's correspondence does not appear in the index under "Cornies, Johann," but under the names of senders and recipients, respectively.

Numbers in **bold** represent dates.
"**JC**" indicates items of Johann Cornies's correspondence.

Abitochna River: viticulture along, 227; watermill on, 50
"About the South Russian Steppes, etc." (Teetzmann), 340, 348, 386–7
Abramovich (report to Mariupol District Chairman), 174
Academy of Sciences, 508, 529–30
accounts books, 130, 147
administrative system: district (*volost*) system, l–li n17; *Gebiet*, li n15; *Gebietsamt*, li n17; Mennonites in, xxv; Nogai village administration selections, 31–2; Village Mayors, l–li n17
afforestation. *See* forestry
Agricultural Society: Annual Report (1848), 547–56; creation of, xxvii, xxix; and crop agriculture, xxxii; Directive about Prussian Mennonites, 125–6; durability of reforms, xlvi; and education, xxi, 69, 70; Forestry Society compared to, xxix; to Guardianship Committee, 75–6; Hahn's departure and, xlvi; JC and, xxi–xxii, xxv, xxix, xxxvii; JC's death and, xlvi; journal entries, **1847**: 485–7, 488–9, 490, 491–3, 496–7, 498, 499–500, 501, 505, 507–8, 509, 511–12, 515–17, 519, 521, 524, 525–7, 528, 529, 530, 531–2, 533–4, 537–8, 545, 546, **1848**: 570, 579; on living outside settlements, 396; and modernization, xxxiv; postal service for, 18; power of, xxix; and Reading Association Library, 277; and reforms, xxxvii; and schools, xli, 9; to Village Offices, 149; waning of power, xlvi; and Warkentin-JC relationship, xxv; and Württemberg settlement, xl

Agricultural Society, correspondence:
to Altenau Village Office, 314;
authorization for Heinrich
Franz, 358; to Berdiansk
Mennonite Village Office, 104;
to Blumenort Village Office,
148; to Church Elders, 118–20;
to Conteniusfeld Village Office,
422–3; Conteniusfeld Village Office
to, 322–3; to Cornelius Wall, 20; to
District Office, 19–20; to G. Enns,
266; to Franzthal Village Office,
107–8; to Fuerstenau Village Office,
29; to Fuerstenwerder Village
Office, 321; to Guardianship
Committee, 266, 268, 300–1; to
Halbstadt District Office, 146–7; J.
and K. Isaak to, 374; to Hermann
Janzen (in Tiege), 390–1; **JC's**
notes for business of, 297–8; to
H. Kroeker, 424; to Landskrone
Village Office, 376–7, 422; to
Margenau Village Office, 148–9; to
Marienthal Village Office, 373; to
J. Martens, 277; to Jacob Martens,
557; to Mennonites in Berdiansk,
105; notes of inspection tour, 30; to
Ohrloff Village Office, 237, 423; to
Rueckenau Village Office, 423–4;
to Schardau Village Office, 100; to
schoolteachers, 313–15; to Village
Mayors, 567–8; to Village Offices,
147, 182, 268, 284, 294–5, 309–10,
373, 375, 388, 391, 392, 406–7, 464;
to A. Voth, 237–8; to Waldheim
Mayor, 391–2; to D. Warkentin, 300
agriculture: agricultural societies,
xxv; apprentices/apprenticeships
in, 95, 164, 167, 173, 175, 224, 349,
350, 399, 428, 476; Hahn and,
xxxiv; machinery manufacture,
xxxvi; Mennonites and, xxiv,
xxxii, xxxiii, xlvii; progress in,
276; Prussian vs. Molochnaia
establishments compared, 535,
539–44. *See also* crops; field
cultivation; livestock
Agriculture Department, Ministry of
State Domains: **JC to**, 302–3, 532
Akkerman: JC and, xliv; mosque in,
23; mulberry trees in, 154; *Starosta*
of, 288; trees in, 213
Akmambetov, Abdir, 262
Albrecht (agreement with Kroeker of
Margenau), 148–9
Aleksandria Crown Model Farm, 86,
155, 168; **JC to**, 86
Aleksandrov: Jewish settlements in,
439, 447, 480; plantations in, 228
Aleksandrov Model Establishment,
149; **JC to**, 168
Alexander, Crown Prince, xxii
Alexander I, Tsar, xxii, xxvi, xlvi
Alexanderwohl: congregation, 101,
118, 221, 222, 279; Kerber plantation
in, 111; Unruh leaving, 486
Altonau: bricks in, 181; Hahn in,
280, 383; plantings in, 550; post
road setting trenches, 146; school,
314; sericulture in, 353; windbreak
in, 301
Altonau/Altona, 437
Amangelov, Begal, 232
Andreev/Andreevka: Crown Prince
Konstantin travelling through,
286; potatoes in, 131; runaway
settlers, 21; rye in, 218; summer
rye in, 522
Andreevskii (re. Franz/Zokurinkova
matter), 236

Andreevskii (potato inspector), 7, 27, 31–2, 36
Andres (Tashchenak coachman), 536
apple trees, 192, 346, 526, 547
apprentices/apprenticeships: for agriculture, 164, 167, 173, 175, 349, 350, 399, 428, 476; appeal for, 13–14; awards for, 302; for carpentry, 516; for cattle care/dairying, 107, 118, 122, 371; clothing for, 211, 484–5, 516; to craftsmen, 253; for Crown Model Plantation, 178, 354, 364, 419, 528, 545, 579–80; deceased, 412–13; and education, 14; family situation, 446; at Felstenthal estate, 190; female, 295, 307–8; for forest-tree cultivation, 84, 168–9, 178, 188, 190, 209, 271, 285, 291, 316, 350–1; guidelines, 84–5; house construction for, 302, 385, 431; for household management, 107, 295; implements for, 302; on Iushanle estate, 205, 224; JC and, 11, 38, 50, 59, 84–5, 95, 205, 271, 295, 301–2, 307–8, 316, 366; for landkeeping, 107, 118, 122; living conditions, 484–5, 516; maintenance expenses, 320; Ministry of State Domains and, xxi–xxii; monetary rewards/ remuneration for, 295, 435; Nogais as, 209, 262, 285, 301, 302; for orchards, 253, 291, 416; peasants and, xxii, 168–9, 175, 178, 205, 209, 291; for potato cultivation, 262; records of, 376; release of, 301–2, 307–8, 366, 399, 446; religious practices, 350, 390; reports for each, 539; requirements/criteria for, 58, 188; runaway, 505, 528; Russian-language learning, 234; Russian

school books for, 416; for sheep breeding, 263, 474; for silk, 262; on Tashchenak estate, 122, 320, 416, 419; and taxes, 291, 390, 451; terms of, 167; village for, 301–2, 435, 444
apricots, 346, 460, 547
ashes, sheds for, 379
Assanov, Begitir, 288
assemblies, community, 465

Baerg, Franz (Halbstadt), 133
Bahnmann, Peter: to JC, 507; JC to, 529
Balin, Vassily, 308
Balmann, Peter, 104
Balzer (Waldheim), 102
Balzer, Heinrich, xxxv
Bamasanov, Mrak, 322
baptismal certificates, 580
Bargen (Conteniusfeld), 30
Barkmann, Jacob, 548
barley, 192, 277; Hamalei, 219; prices, 121, 339, 446; seed, 403; winter, 191, 339, 403, 491
Bartsch, Jacob, 93, 393, 397–8; to JC, 404–5, 416–17, 477; JC to, 394–5, 580–1
Batichkovskii, Matvei (apprentice), 95
Batirov, Bekube, 341
Bauer (Neuhoffnungsthal), 220
Bauer, Peter (Landskrone), 297
Bauerdak village administration selection, 32
Baum, Bernhardt: to JC, 103
Baumann (forced to leave region), 371
Baumann (Guardian of Jewish settlements), 446
Baumann, Wilhelm (agronomist), 348n3, 386–7, 512–13; JC to, 348, 439–41, 458–9, 505–7

Becker, Andreas: **to JC**, 413
beech trees, 292, 397, 415
beehive covers, 454–5
beer lease, 486–7, 509
Beindorf, C., 47
Beitraege zur Kenntnis des russischen Reiches (Contributions to the knowledge of the Russian Empire), 276, 340
Beitraege zur Kenntnis Russland (Contributions to knowledge about Russia), 574
Bekbulatov, 93
Bekker, Abraham, 549
Beloi, Ivan, 341, 454
Bengs, Friedrich (Kronsdorf), 367
Bengs brothers, 278–9
Berdiansk/Berdiansk District: craftsmen in, 252–3; dissension in, 77, 92; District Chairman, 138, 142–3, 152–3; forestry plantations at, 14–15; guidelines for director in, 76; implements in, 219; JC visiting, 36; maize in, 444; Nogais and sheep in, 273; Pietists in, 113–14, 120, 141, 154; port at, xxxii, 506; potatoes in, 183, 218, 264, 341, 444; salary of District Chairman, 143; schoolteachers in, 105; tree planting in, 268; village officials election, 104; villages under Stempel's supervision, 232
Berdiansk District Office: **JC to**, 57, 299
Berdiansk Mennonite Village Office: Agricultural Society to, 104
Berdiansk model forestry plantation. *See* Crown Model Plantation
Berdibolotov, Ali, 139
Berdilatov, Ali, 31, 242, 255–6

Bereslav: Jewish settlement in, 355, 428; resistance to survey, 31; Swedish settlers in, 474
Berg (Prussian Mennonite), 304–5
Bergen (Conteniusfeld rebellion inciter), 364
Bergen, Gerhard, 260
Bergen, Heinrich (Schoenthal), 168
Bergthal, xxxix; brandy sales in, 85; District Secretary for, 454; general store in, 578; Hahn visiting, 43; house construction, 51; JC as supervisor, xxii; plantations, 51, 115–17, 190; Stempel as Inspector, 32; tree plantation in, 115; villages comprising, xxxix
Bestvater (Ladekopp), 30
beverages: leases to Jews in Mariupol, 9; tavern lease, 85; trade, 87–8. *See also* beer lease; brandy
Bible: geographies, 342; natural histories, 215; New Testament, 117, 324; sales, 324; stories, 59, 81, 163, 215, 247, 297, 324, 538
Bible Society: to G. Fast, 324; to Main Evangelical Bible Committee, 323–4; to I. Mathies, 324; to P. Neufeld, 349; New Testament sales, 324; Secretary, 323, 324
Bieky/Benky, Anna: **to JC**, 558
Bigsev (merchant), 144
Biller (Colonial Inspector), 417
Birkhan (Crimea), 265; **JC to**, 196
birthplace certificates, 332
Bishtek, Marfa, 295, 308
blacksmithing, 253, 468–9, 476, 484, 493, 511, 515
Blavatskaya, Helena, li n20
Block (Conteniusfeld), 364

Blueher, Joseph (son of Traugott):
T. Blueher on, 180–1; cost to JC,
283; to Crimea, 270, 272; in JC
household, 240, 247, 272; in JC
office, 180–1, 185; with I. Mathias
in Rudnerweide, 185, 189, 194; and
Mathies, 272, 283; return home,
257, 283; travel to Moscow, 270
Blueher, Traugott: and mulberry
seed, 491; and sale of Steven's
estate, 286; son-in-law's illness,
410; wife, 45; and winter wheat/
barley at Sarepta, 491
Blueher, Traugott, correspondence:
D. Cornies to, 583–4; **to JC, 1843:**
5, 36, 44–5, 47–8, 67–9, 143–4, **1844:**
171–2, 180–1, **1845:** 246–7, 257,
259, 261, 265–6, **1846:** 342; **JC to,**
1843: 22, 33–4, 67, 80–2, 133, 134–5,
1844: 162–4, 178, 182–3, 184–5,
188–9, 193–4, 203, 215, 234–5, **1845:**
238–40, 269–70, 272, 280–1, 282–3,
312, **1846:** 348–9, 358–9, 366–8,
369–70, 374, 401, 410, **1847:** 471–2,
501, 510, **1848:** 570–1, 575–6; P.
Wiebe to, **1843:** 58–9, **1846:** 324,
1847: 538, **1848:** 585–6
Blumenort: Crown Prince
Konstantin travelling through,
286; plantings along roads,
497, 550–1; planting with elms
and mulberry hedges, 521, 551;
Russians mistreated in, 422;
school, 314; schoolteachers,
314–15; teachers in, 314–15
Blumenort Village Office:
Agricultural Society to, 148
Bock (Kronsweide), 501
Boettlingk: **JC to**, 493–4
Bogosov (tobacco manufacturer), 338

Bokushiliev, Esale, 288
Bold, Johann, 30
Boldt (J. Neufeld's brother-in-law),
418
Boldt, Dirk, 448, 511; widow of, 511
Boldt, Justina, 527
Boldt, Susanna, 511
Bolshoi Tokmak: damage to grain
fields, 481; peasant on Iushanle
estate, 449; postal station at, 368,
369; potatoes in, 154; runaway girl
from, 236
Boman (seller of stallion to D.
Cornies), 269
Bonellas (messenger), 46
books, 36–7, 228, 507, 512;
arithmetic, 342, 348; Bible
geographies, 342; Bible sales,
324; Bible stories, 59, 68, 81, 163,
215, 247, 324, 538; Biblical natural
histories, 215; church histories, 59,
68, 215, 324, 342; geographies, 59,
68, 215, 254, 324, 335; on Hutterite
Brethren, 248, 249; Memorsky's
grammar, 575; natural histories,
59, 68, 324, 342; New Testaments,
117, 324; for primary teaching, 531;
Reading Association Library, 277;
Russian regulations, 575; Tappe's
grammar, 117
Born, Peter, wife of, 376
box trees, 444–5
Bradke, Georg von, 61n18; **JC to**, 61
Brailko (re. cartage charges), 265
brandy: distilleries, 87–8;
distribution in Bergthal, 85;
JC sales monopoly, 87n21;
JC-Martens partnership in, xxiv;
lease, 461, 487; smuggling, 303–4
Branndler, D.: **to JC**, 145

Braslov (estate owner), 452
Braun (Deputy), 88, 300
Braun (re. lease of tavern), 85
Braun (master craftsman), 451
Braun (Muensterberg), travel to
 Prussia, 448
Braun (son-in-law of A. Wilke), 77–8
Braun, David, 76
Braun, Isaak (Lindenau tree planter),
 548, 549
Braun, Isaak (master craftsman), 441
Braun, Isaak (miller), 468–9
Braun, Peter J., xi
brick(s), 399–400; for apprentices'
 house, 385; burned, 417;
 construction, 51, 60, 65–6;
 counting numbers of, 319; for
 Crown Model Plantation, 345–6,
 459; firing/fired, 204, 230, 319,
 353, 439, 507–8; for houses, 65–6;
 kiln, 51, 60, 65, 71, 78, 83; makers,
 60, 78; Mariupol brickworks, 64,
 66–7; at Tashchenak, 319
bridges, 8, 9, 30, 87, 405
broomgrass, 382
Brüdergemeinde Colony. *See*
 Württemberg settlement
Buettner, daughter of, 526
buildings: painting of, 182, 375;
 records of new, 507–8. *See also*
 churches; houses
Bultrak (Elder), 66
Bulutmek: seed potatoes bought for,
 271
buran (storm), 469, 559, 575–6
Bureau of State Domains: **JC to**, 49–50
Burkut: and Crown Model Plantation,
 331; village administration
 selection, 31–2
butter, 339, 340, 553

cabbages, 121
canal digging, 509–10
carpenters/carpentry, 319, 516,
 565–6, 578
carrot seed, 316
carters/cartage, 59; of bricks,
 399–400; missing crate, 133–4, 143,
 151; Nogais as, 399; and passage
 money, 481; requirements, 79;
 silk, 311; transportation charges,
 278; of wool, 188, 369, 400–1; wool
 transportation, 184, 185
caterpillars, 192; "passion"
 [*Passionsraupe*], 411–12, 460, 550
Catherine the Great, ix
cattle: breeding bulls, 344; buying,
 284–5; counting, 319; cows and
 calves, 370–1, 418–19; cows for
 Jewish settlement, 453; diseases,
 45; fences for, 111; foot-and-mouth
 disease, 80, 192, 194, 196, 466, 582;
 in Hutterthal village pasture, 52;
 milk cows, 466; milk quantity,
 370–1; pestilence, 418–19; plague,
 136, 192, 194, 196, 201–2, 205–6,
 231, 284–5, 360, 361; purchase, 402.
 See also dairying
cemeteries, 297
Chaikbaiev, Bolat, 341
cheeses, 39, 41, 158, 231, 339, 346, 524
Chelebi, Absaut, 241–2, 255–6
Chenaleev, Kuvadik, 322
Chenkashchin, Nikita, 188, 280–1
Chernigov/Chernigovka: Archduke
 Konstantin's visit, 286; Crown
 Prince Konstantin travelling
 through, 286; Hutterites from, 61,
 62, 170; potatoes in, 131; potato
 mounders, 21–2
cherry trees, 24, 25, 192, 297–8, 547

Chervina, Prokhor, 446
children: hiring out, 403. *See also* education; schools
Chlepetko (of Sparrau; Chernigov District Chairman), 548
cholera, 489, 499, 507, 520
Christian School Society, xxiv–xxv, xxxiii
Chumak roads, 8, 28
churches: building, 37; Communion (Lord's Supper) attendance, 463; congregational authority, xxxiii; construction, 51, 114, 120, 155; exclusion from, 177; in Grunau, 33; Neuhoffnung, 155, 161; reacceptance into, 190; tree planting along walkways to, 108; worship practices, 212; worship services in houses vs., 114
church leaders/Elders: Agricultural Society to, 118–20; discipline of, 477; insanity of, 420; **JC to**, 90–1, 149–50; and schools, 70; sentenced to community work, 492
Chveshka, Konstantin, 512
cigars. *See under* tobacco
Claassen, Dietrich, 463, 482
cloth: dying, 6, 22; prices, 48, 259; samples, 6
clover seed, 124–5
coat of mail, remains of, 404
community sheepfarm, punishment on, 422–4
Conrad, Isaac: **to JC**, 144–5; son, 144–5; wife, 144
Conteniusfeld: accused Mayor of, 364; neglectful fullholders in, 16; rebellion incitement against, 364; transfer of fullholdings in, 16

Conteniusfeld Village Office: to Agricultural Society, 322–3; Agricultural Society to, 422–3
Contributions to the Knowledge of the Russian Empire, 196
Cornelsen, Abraham, 16
Cornelsen, Heinrich (Gnadenfeld), 398, 400
Cornies, Aganetha (mother of JC), xxiii
Cornies, Aganetha (wife of JC), 195; death, xlv, 455, 457, 472, 501, 506; health, 34, 45, 80, 144, 195, 447, 457; JC Jr. to, 363; medications for, 163, 171, 183, 185
Cornies, Agnes (daughter of JC), 45; Blueher and, 45; and JC Jr.'s son, 448, 456; marriage to Wiebe, 410, 440; and mother, 81; in Prussia for JC Jr.'s wedding, 537; and Therese Thiessen, 568; travelling to JC Jr.'s wedding, 536, 564, 565, 573, 574, 581, 585; and M. Vogel, 174
Cornies, David (brother of JC), 348, 356, 440, 459, 586; to Blueher, 583–4; and F. Doerksen, 566, 567; to Hahn, 582–3; health, 586; immigration, xxiii; **to JC**, 264–5; on JC's death, 582–4, 585; JC visiting, 573; lease of land, 270; limits on ploughed fields, 75; purchase of stallion, 269; wife, 265; and Wollmann, 242
Cornies, Heinrich (brother of JC), 50; and administrator for Tashchenak estate, 414; birth, xxiii; and damage in Bolshoi Tokmak grain fields, 481; and hay, 468; health, 586; hiring in Ekaterinoslav, 573; **to JC**, 281, 346, 427, 481; **JC to**, 436–7;

travel to Prussia, 427, 432, 436–7, 440, 447–8, 455; watermill, 50

Cornies, Johann (JC): achievements, xxi–xxii; and afforestation, xlvi–xlvii; as agent of state, xxii, xxxiv; and Agricultural Society, xxxvii; and Bergthal settlement, xxxix; bill of exchange to JC Jr., 518–19, 537; brandy/spirits distribution, xxiv; and crop agriculture, xxxi, xxxvi; death, xxii, xlv–xlvi, 582–3; and doctors, 89, 92; and economic reforms, xlvi, xlviii; economic success, xxiv; and education, xxxi, xl–xlii, 10–11; employment, xxiv; and *Gebietsamt*, xxv; and *Gebietsamt* elections, xxx; gold medal awarded to, 275, 317; and Guardianship Committee, xxiv, xxxv, xxxvi–xxxvii; Hahn, relationship with, xxxvii; health/illness, xxii, xxv–xxvi, xlv, 294, 303, 312, 313, 582–3, 584; and Hutterites, xxxvii–xxxix; immigration, xxiii; and *Judenplan*, xliii–xlv; and Khortitsa Central School, xlii; and Kuteinikov, 474, 479; legacy, xxii, xlvi–xlvii; and Mennonites as supervisors vs. models, xlviii; and Mennonite settlement as laboratory for modernity, xxiii; and Ministry of State Domains, xxxv, xxxvi–xxxvii; and modernization, xlvii; and Nogais, xxxv, xliv, 27–8; note in correspondence journal, 583; obituary, xlvi; partnership with W. Martens, xxiv; personality, xlvii; possession/inheritance rights for leased land, 28; and potatoes, xxxv; and Privilegium, xxx–xxxi; records, xxiii; Saxony sheep-buying trip, xxv; and secularity, xlvii; and sheep raising, xxxii, 227, 228, 234; as surveyor, xxiv, xxv; and trades/crafts, xxxii; travel journal (1844), 189–90; waning public role, xlii–xliii; and Warkentin Affair, xxxiii–xxxiv; and Württemberg settlement, xl

Cornies, Johann (son of JC Jr.), 448, 455–6, 559, 564, 565; with JC while JC Jr. in Prussia, 438, 448, 455–6; travelling to JC Jr.'s wedding, 573

Cornies, Johann, Jr. (son of JC): bill of exchange from JC to, 518–19, 537; Blueher and, 45; drawings, 45; engagement to Therese Thiessen, 514, 517–18, 519–21; and Fast family, 414; and C. Froese, 450; hiring Prussian Mennonite girls, 537; and horses, 522; illness, 163; instructions re. Tashchenak estate during absence, 576, 578–9; nurse/governess for children, 449, 456; sketch of Ohrloff village, 423; in Tashchenak, 81; travel home from Prussia, 467–8, 472, 506, 510, 537, 558–9; travel to Odesa, 419–20; travel to Prussia, 427, 431–2, 436–8, 440, 447–8, 455–6, 506, 519–21, 564–5; as widower, 414; to P. Wiebe, 54

Cornies, Johann, Jr. (son of JC), correspondence: **to JC, 1843:** 112–13, 121, **1846:** 363, 419–20, **1847:** 431–2, 467–8; **JC to, 1847:** 436–8, 447–9, 455–6, 517–18, 521–2, 536–7, **1848:** 558–9, 564–5

Cornies, Justina (daughter of JC Jr. and Justina), xlv, 448, 455–6

Cornies, Justina (wife of JC Jr.), xlv, 363

Cornies, Katherina (sister of JC), xxiii

Cornies, Peter (brother of JC), xxiii, 13, 58, 95, 167, 440; and apprentices, 175, 211, 224; death, xlv, 520, 586; **JC to**, 350, 390, 539

Cornies, Peter (son of Peter), 520

Cornies, Theresa (née Thiessen; JC Jr.'s wife), 514, 517–18, 519–21, 536, 537, 565, 568

couch grass, 71

cows. *See* cattle

crafts. *See* trades/crafts

Crefeld/Crefeldt, silk manufacturing in, 17, 71–2, 76, 77

crimes/misdemeanours, 153, 155–6, 289, 364, 521, 524. *See also* punishments

crops: and agricultural machinery, xxxvi; agricultural transformation to, xxxi, xxxii; experimentation with range of, xxii, xxxvi; failures, 137; four-field system, 253; rotation, xxxii; spring seeding, 48; variety of, xxxi. *See also* field cultivation; grain(s); grass(es); harvests; potatoes

crown land boundaries, 8

Crown Model Plantation, xxxv, 178, 178n2, 273, 290, 292, 305, 429–31; accounts/account book, 436; allowed expenditures, 365; annual report (1847), 561–4; apprentices for, 354, 364, 419, 484–5, 528, 545, 579–80; bricks for, 345–6, 399–400; Burkut and, 331; business office, 352, 376; forestry building, 463, 523–4; gardening position on, 290; house construction on, 293, 332, 345–6, 385, 429, 473, 479; implements on, 364; livestock barn, 364; maintenance spending (1847), 560; mulberry trees, 408, 572; Nogais and, 331; overseer position in, 290; progress report, 429–31; release of workers, 525, 527; road for, 331; roof tiles, 459; salaries, 338; storage building for, 332; surveyor marking out, 292; wages on, 456; watchman for, 296, 429; water cistern for, 399; workmen hiring on, 344–5

cultivators, garden, 154

Dahlke, Ludwig, 16

dairying, 39, 107, 118, 122. *See also* cattle

dams: along Kurushan river, 534; assignment to communities, 30; earthen, 12, 416, 419, 430

death certificates, 463

Deberdijev, Mambedali, 490

debtors: Bahnmann to Regehr, 488–9; Bengs, 367; Dierks, 357; Dik to Quiring, 530; Eidzen to Regehr, 488–9; Harms's son, 526–7; in Hutterthal, 465; Kroeker to wood merchant, 534; Kvortzov to Wiebe/Wilmsen, 370; Nogais to Lange, 490; Nogai to Eytzen, 179; Regehr to Quiring, 528; Regier to Milinovich, 4, 6–7, 23; Regier to Quiring, 500; Treksel to Isaaksohn, 529; T. Voth, 501

debtors to JC: Aleksandria Crown Model Farm, 86; Braun, 77–8;

Enns, 531; A. Enns, 290–1, 300, 410; P. Enns, 411; Esau, 24; P. Fast, 411; Fehdrau, 531; Gerhard Klaassen, 4; Jantzen, 137–8; E. Janzen, 290–1; Kasdorf, 411; Kolossov, 528–9; Kroeker, 411; Kuteinikov, 406; J. Lange, 151–2; D. Loewen, 411; Lukovich, 536; Lushin, 262–3, 366–7; W. Martens, 101; I. Mathies, 388, 502, 532–3; P. Matthias, 89, 534–5; Widow Pauls, 411; G. Penner, 298; I. Regier, 411; P. Regier, 530; Rosen, 45; Rueckel, 325; Schmidt, 49; Sherbina, 367; Steven, 524; Tessmann, 261; Waldner, 145; C. Wedel, Jr., 290–1; Abram Wiebe, 43–4, 171, 257–8; Jacob Wiebe, 481; D. Voth, 132

Decembrist Revolt, xxvi

Deriaven, Pavel, 318

Derksen (interested in sale of Guenter's half-holding), 14

Deubner: **JC to**, 273–4, 335, 345; P. Wiebe to, 525

Dick (Zeischendorf, Prussia), 432

Dick, Aron, 190

Dick, Jacob, 226

Didenko, Ivan, 205, 224

Dierks, Johann, 357

Dik (Prussian Mennonite), 304–5

Dik, Dirk, 402

Dik, Jacob (Marienthal), 363

Dik, Jacob (Schoenthal), 509

Dik, Jacob (Tashchenak), 530, 536, 537; **JC to**, 576–7, 578–9

Dik, Johann (Muensterberg), 550

Dik, Johann (teacher), daughter of, 520

Dik, Peter, 16

Dionditz, Nikolai, 205, 224

District Chairman: **JC to**, 14; release from position, 138, 142–3, 152–3; salary, 143, 152

District Office: Agricultural Society to, 19–20, 146–7; and brandy distillery, 88; to Guardianship Committee, 75–6; inspections of gardens/yards, 57; **to JC, 1843:** 7–10, 87–8, **1844:** 183–4, **1845:** 287, 288–9, 291, 300, **1846:** 368, **1847:** 463, 478, 484, 515; **JC to, 1843:** 24, 91–2, **1844:** 208, **1845:** 261, **1846:** 363–4, 369, 375–6, 410–11, **1847:** 468–9, 479, 511; to W. Martens, 87–8; *Unterhaltungsblatt für deutsche Ansiedler im südlichen Rußland* to, 499

District Offices: **JC to**, 57

District Physician [*Kreisphysikus*]: **JC to**, 409–10

ditches: around hearth-sites, 130; around plantings, 345; boundary, 430, 459–60; enclosing plantations, 200

Dmitriev, Larion, 50, 345–6

Dneprov District: implements in, 219; maize in, 444; potatoes in, 24–5, 29, 33, 38, 183, 218, 264, 309, 444

Dnieper River flooding, 282, 288–9

doctors/medicos, 370, 516; building for, 409–10; employment by local administration, 409–10; exams for medical papers, 204; and hydrotherapy, 337

Doehring, Martin, 34, 45, 80, 87, 582; **to JC**, 433; P. Wiebe to, 491

Doering, Daniel F.: **to JC**, 72–3; **JC to**, 194–5

Doerksen (in Fischau, interested in Guenther's fullholding), 19–20

Doerksen (Schoenfeld Mayor), 187
Doerksen, Bernhard: **JC to**, 565–6, 578
Doerksen, Franz, 529, 565, 576, 583
Doerksen, Jacob, 287
Doerksen, Johann, 165, 168
Dofko, Christian, 580
Dolbinskaia, Anna, 308
Dorfzeitung (Village newspaper), 525
Doukhobors, xxxi, 82, 115, 197, 198,
    267, 277, 506, 574
drawings, 97–8
Driedger, Abraham, 418, 536, 537; **to
    JC**, 468
Driedger, Gerhard, xxxi
droughts, 81, 299, 308, 365, 408;
    Great Drought of 1833–4, xxvii,
    xxviii, xxxii
Dsenko, Stepan, 318
Duborg (teacher in Sarata), 410
Dudkina, Evdokia (apprentice),
    295, 308
Dueck, Franz: **to JC**, 287
Duek, Abraham, 303
Dyberdijev, Tukei, 490
Dyck (Elder in Khortitsa District), 93
Dyck (Kharkiv), 433
Dyck, Gerhard: **to JC**, 181–2
Dyck, Harvey, xlvi
Dyck, Jacob, 461, 477

earth-sledges, 12
Ediger, Peter, 38, 169, 309
Ediger, Salomon, 549
Edinokhta: apprentice village in,
    301; cattle plague in, 136
education: Agricultural Society and,
    xxi, 69, 70; apprentices and, 14;
    and economic development, xli;
    JC and, xl–xlii, 10–11; Molochnaia
    Mennonite as model, 69; Pietism

and, ln15; professionalization of,
    xl–xlii; quality of, 69; religion and,
    69, 70. *See also* schools
Eidzen, Johann (Khortitsa), 488
Eiseler, C.S. (company), 238, 246,
    401; **to JC**, 243; **JC to**, 284–5, 400–1
Ekaterinoslav: apprentices from,
    291; cattle plague in, 201; flooding
    in, 275; Jewish settlements
    in, 347; *Judenplan* villages in,
    xliii; Mennonite school, xlii;
    schoolteachers in, 306
elections: **1838**: xxv, xxx, xxxi,
    1841–2: xxxiii–xxxiv; for Berdiansk
    director, 76; Berdiansk village
    officials, 104; District Elders, 425;
    in Hutterthal, 297; landowning
    and, xxviii; in Shuet, 341
Elias, Peter, 357
Elis (Tashchenak), 536
Elisabeththal: building on cottager
    lots, 371–2
elm trees, 108, 301, 521
Enns (silk-reeler), 20
Enns, Abraham (Gerlitzke estate),
    177
Enns, Abraham (Neukirch), 291,
    410–11, 531
Enns, David, 16
Enns, Gerhard, 76; Agricultural
    Society to, 266; **JC to**, 207–8;
    Ohrloff School Society to, 315–16;
    to Zamero, 217–18
Enns, Gerhard (Altonau), 353; and
    lease of cottager site, 351
Enns, Jacob, 566–7
Enns, Peter, 411
Enns family (Pordenau): **JC to**, 566–7
Ensz, G. (Altonau), 182
Epp, Bernhard, 73; **to JC**, 40–1

Epp, David (Heubuden), 103; **to JC**, 46–7; **JC to**, 16–17, 34–5; P. Wiebe for JC to, 74–5
Epp, David (Khortitsa), 398
Epp, Heinrich: **JC to**, 539
Epp, Johann, 16
Epp, Peter, 384, 553
Esau, Dirk, 24
Esau, Jacob, 64
Eshen (Judge), 255–6, 349
Evangelical Lutheran Church: pastor as Pietist spiritual leader, 92, 96–7, 99–100, 113–14; Pietists joining, 72
Evdokimova, Madame, 507, 512
Ewert, Johann (Waldheim), 511
Eytzen, Cornelius: **to JC**, 179–80

Fabre (Governor of Ekaterinoslav), 475–6
Fadeev, Andrei M.: about, xxvi, li n20; and afforestation initiative, xxvi; daughter, 330; family, li n20; and Forestry Society, xlvi; and Grunau community plantation, 503; and Guardianship Committee, xxvi, xxxvi; and JC, xxvi; **to JC**, 26–7, 103–4, 173, 330, 382–3, 560–1; JC and, xxvii, xxix; **JC to**, 170–1, 352–4; and Kalmyk Tatars, xxxi; Keppen as replacement for, xxx; resignation as Governor of Saratov, 330; success of Mennonites and, xxvii; transfer of, xxix; travel to St. Petersburg, 27; and tree planting, xxviii; and Warkentin, xxvii; wife, 26, 330, 561
fallow fields, 297, 357, 359, 375, 569
Famoilenko, Danilo, 496
Farlarov, Romahan, 123

Fast (Ladekopp householder), 521
Fast (son-in-law of Heinrich Heese), 63
Fast, Abraham, 140
Fast, Bernhard, 90, 247, 501; **to JC**, 95–6, 99
Fast, Cornelius, 516
Fast, David, 76, 104; **to JC**, 381–2
Fast, Gerhard, 139–40, 315–16, 351, 388, 515; Molochnaia Mennonite Bible Society to, 324; wife of, 140
Fast, Isaak: **to JC**, 36–7
Fast, Jacob, 16, 298
Fast, Johann (Berdiansk, deceased), 532; son of, 532
Fast, Johann (Petershagen school teacher): **to JC**, 10–11
Fast, Leonhardt, 478
Fast, Peter (gardener), 290, 338, 460, 482; **JC to**, 484–5
Fast, Peter (Penner building mill for), 210
Fast, Peter (Prangenau), 411
Fast family (Lichtfelde), 414
Fedorovich (re. salt locations), 160
Fedorovich (surveyor), 200, 201
Fehdrau, Jacob, 531
Fein, F.: **to JC**, 425
Felstenthal estate, 110, 183–4, 190, 535, 577
fences: around hearth-sites, 43; around Kerber's plantation, 111–12; around tree plantations, 117; money owing for in Hutterthal, 489; mulberry, 508; painting, 149, 182, 200, 375; in tradesmen's settlement, 378; for tree planting along roads, 497
Ferestivo: **JC to**, 518–19
Fidler Apothecary (Kharkiv), 79
Fiedler (brother-in-law of Keppen), 136

field cultivation, 126; annual report
(1847), 551–2; as basis of economy,
506; Baumann composition on,
512–13; fallowing in, 569; four-
field system, 387; Jewish settlers
and, 355; workers for, 494. *See also*
agriculture; crops; grain(s)
Fifth Department of the Tsar's Own
Chancellery, xxix. *See* Ministry of
State Domains
fires: ladders, 399; prevention, 206
First Department, Ministry of State
Domains, xlvi
Fischau: conditions in village "N,"
486; fullholding lease in, 19–20;
sale of half-holding in, 14; schools
in, 300
flax, 492, 552–3
Flemish congregation, xxv
Fletnitzer, Karl, 26n10, 499; **to JC**,
258–9, 478–9; **JC to**, 230, 252, 473,
500–1
Fletsier (State Counsellor), 380
flooding, 162, 210, 275, 282, 288–9,
291, 336, 419
flower seeds, 37, 440
fodder, 339, 359, 361
Foell (Consistorial Counsellor
[Hochstadt]), 478, 500; **JC to**, 499
Forchhammer, 184; **JC to**, 185
Forestier (Odesa), 153–4; **JC to**, 157
forestry: afforestation project, xxvi,
xlvi; apprentices for, 350–1; on
Bergthal settlement, xxxix; and
Nogais, xxxv; and peasants, xxxv;
school, xxxv; supervisors, xliv. *See
also* trees
Forestry Department, Ministry
of State Domains: and forestry
apprentices, 169; **JC to**, 84–5, 106–7

Forestry Society: account books,
321–2; Agricultural Society
compared to, xxix; creation of,
xxvi; expenditure estimates,
322; Fadeev and, xxvi, xlvi;
and *Gebietsamt*, xxvi, xxviii; to
Guardianship Committee, 321–2;
to Hahn, 109–12; JC and, xxv,
xxvi, xxviii; to Jacob Martens, 147;
postal service for, 18; and sale
of fullholdings, xxvii–xxviii; to
Sparrau Village Office, 109; and
tree planting, xxviii; and village
offices, xxviii; to Village Offices,
108–9, 411–12; to Village Offices
from Altonau to Ladekopp, 146;
and Warkentin-JC relationship,
xxv; to Heinrich Wiens, 32
forest-tree plantations, 6; at
Berdiansk, 14–15; at Bergthal,
51, 115–17; ditches enclosing,
200; fences surrounding, 117;
fruit trees in, 116; at Grunau, 43,
487–8; increase in, 13; inspection
by Graff, 475; Kerber's in
Alexanderwohl as exemplary,
111; at Mariupol, 14–15; markers
for, 531–2; near Berdiansk, xxxv;
numbers of trees in, 547–8;
peasants and, 229; potatoes in, 117;
potential, 229; progress, 229, 387;
soil preparation for, 109, 116–17;
Sparrau, 109; Stempel's, 39; tree
planting in, 115–17; trees broken,
498; trenches in, 117
forest trees: along post road, 147;
apprentices for, 84, 168–9, 209; on
D. Cornies's leased land, 270; on
Felstenthal estate, 110; growth,
72; in Grunau plantation, 503–4;

Nogais and, 213; numbers in Stempel's community plantation, 39; numbers of, 547; numbers sold at Tashchenak, 320; nurseries, 110, 376, 547, 548; ordered by Siemens from JC, 414–15; planting, xxviii, 80, 268; planting along walkways to churches, 108; seeds, 34, 87, 192–3, 195, 235, 292, 397, 440, 571–2; setting trenches between, 146; staking, 388–9; at Tashchenak, 319, 320; windbreaks, 301. *See also* fruit trees

Frank, Baron von, 454–5

Franz, Heinrich, xlii, xlvii–xlix n1, 36, 150, 236, 306, 358; **to JC**, 288; **JC to**, 274, 385–6

Frembetov, Kokoi, 443

Friedrichstal, xxxix

Friesen (Elder of Kleine Gemeinde), 46–7

Friesen ("old Friesen" [Altona]), 448

Friesen (preacher from Halbstadt), 140

Friesen (schoolteacher in Hutterthal): **JC to**, 403

Friesen (ward), 515

Friesen, Abraham (Rueckenau), 548

Friesen, Abram (Elder in Blumstein), 90

Friesen, Agnetha (née Bartsch), 567

Friesen, Bernhard, 190

Friesen, David, xlvi

Friesen, Heinrich, 128

Friesen, Isaak, 515

Friesen, Isbrand, 260

Friesen, Jacob, children of, 570

Friesen, Johann (Friedensdorf), 570

Friesen, Johann (Rosenthal?), 404–5

Froese, Cornelius: **to JC**, 449–50

Froese, Herrmann, 449

Froese, Peter, 73, 103; **to JC**, 243–5; **JC to**, 164, 216–17, 249–50, 304–5, 469–70

fruit trees, 111, 195–6, 460, 526, 548–9; blossoms, 359; dried fruit, 285; frost and, 285; grafting shoots from, 25; in Grunau plantation, 503–4; harvests, 81, 192, 194, 199, 285; on Iushanle estate, 346; numbers of, 547; quantity of fruit, 276; sale of, 24; from seed, 549; in Stempel's community plantation, 39; transplanting, 407; in tree plantations, 116. *See also* orchards; *and names of specific fruit trees*

Fuerstenau: Agricultural Society inspection tour, 30; Agricultural Society to Village Office, 29; boundary with Tokmak land, 30; fullholding No. 17, 29; roads, 30

Fuerstenwerder: Agricultural Society to Village Office, 321; orchard fencing in, 30; plantings along road, 551; setting trenches along road, 497; ward Friesen in, 515

fullholdings: accounts books, 130, 147; division of, 129–30, 146; improvements to, 48; inheritance of, 445; leasing, 19–20; neglected, 16, 18, 328; obedience to heads of, 129–30; release, 328; removal of owner, 328; sales/transfers of, xxvii–xxix, 16, 18, 107–8, 126, 142, 190, 220; second families on, 146

Funk, Abraham, 100

Funk, Johann, 357

Funk, Peter, 100

furrow scrapers, 181–2

Gaier, 575
Gakstaeter (Bauer's Neuhoffnungsthal fullholding given to), 220
Gan, Elena Andreevna, li n20
Gavel, Fr. (agronomist), 462n4; **to JC**, 462
Gebietsamt, l–li n17; elections, xxv, xxviii, xxx, xxxi; Forestry Society and, xxvi, xxviii; and Saxony sheep-buying trip, xxv
"General Rules on the Instruction and Treatment of School Children," xli–xlii
Georgia: emigration to, 187; Fadeev in, 382–3; Molokan emigration to, 197, 439
Gerasimov, Ivan, 133, 134
Gerei (Sultan), 370, 371
Gerlitzke estate, 177
German model agriculturalists' settlement directive, 457
Gersdorff, Baron v.: **JC to**, 442
Geyer, Tobias, 171, 273–4; **to JC**, 151; **JC to**, 191
Ghery-Krim-Ghery, Katte: **JC to**, 402
Giesbrecht (father of Anganetha), 373
Giesbrecht, Anganetha, 373
Giesbrecht, Gerhard, 486, 512, 549
Gladkii, 393–4, 395, 448
Glanzen, Samuel, 128
Gloekler, 348
Glokhovskii (inspector), 516
Gnadenfeld: Agricultural Society to Village Mayor, 268; Church Assembly, 118–20; complaint re. Wiens, 450–1; Forestry Society to Village Office, 108; fruit trees in, 548, 549; investigation in, 95–6; *Landwirtschaftliche Dorfzeitung* in, 268; Langes situation, 118–20, 221–2, 224–5, 233; Pankratz and, 279; protective planting at, 9; schoolteachers in, 306; tree planting along walkway to church, 108; wall-primers in, 298
goats, 174, 274, 303, 451–2
Goertz (Lviv settlement), 482–3, 495
Goertz, Heinrich, 445, 534, 549; **to JC**, 417–18
Golubov (Molokan), 445–6
Goossen, Jacob, 403–4
Gordenenko, Demian (apprentice), 38
gout, 357
Graff (forester), 85, 229, 475
grain(s), 365; cost/profit, 539–40; drought and, 81; exports, xxxix; fallow fields and, 357; fertilization of, 3, 253; four-field system, 253; frosts and, 81; growth, 192, 195–6; harvests, 72, 80, 194, 199, 201, 381, 387, 439, 440, 472; at Jewish settlement, 452–3; in land use, 540–1; Neumann's record books regarding, 389; planting, 130; prices, 27, 121, 339, 506; rollers, 161; seeding, 276–7, 319, 323; seeds, 124; at Tashchenak, 319; uses of, 541; A. Wiebe and, 43n14; winter, 339. *See also* harvests; *names of specific grains*
grass(es), 3; growth, 192, 194, 195–6, 349, 359; seeds, 124
grave mounds, 12, 13, 80, 340, 438–9, 508; excavations, 121, 135–6, 195, 198; money for peasants opening, 529–30
graves: monument for Hoeppner, 433; monuments/railings, 489; railings, 494; urns, 494

Great Comet of 1843, 48
Great Tokmak: Crown Prince Konstantin travelling through, 286; potatoes in, 131
Gross, F.: **to JC**, 97–8, 112, 138–9; **JC to**, 122
Grossweide: Agricultural Society to Village Mayor, 267; *Landwirtschaftliche Dorfzeitung* in, 268; protective planting at, 9
Grossweide Village Office: **JC to**, 371–2
Groswahl (Lichtenau), 545
Growahl (Prussian citizen), 529
Grunau: brick kiln in, 71; church construction, 33; community gardens, 482, 494–5; community plantation, 43, 487–8, 502–3
guardianship: of Boldt children by Wiebes, 511, 527; of children of Johann Fast, 532; by Johann Friesen over Jacob Friesen's children, 570; young people under, 392
Guardianship Committee, 249; and 1838 elections, xxxi; about, xlviii n1; Agricultural Society to, 266, 268, 300–1; and Bergthal settlement, xxii; declining power of, xxix; and economic reforms, xlvi; end of colonization and, xxix; Fadeev and, xxvi, xxxiv, xxxvi; and Forestry Society, xxvi; Forestry Society to, 321–2; Hahn and, xxxiv, xlvi; JC and, xxiv, xxxv, xxxvi–xxxvii; **JC to**, 14–16, 17–19, 350–1, 361–2; to Khortitsa District Office, 377; Ministry of State Domains and, xxxiv–xxxv; Molochnaia Agricultural Society to, 75–6; to Molochnaia District Office, 474–5; Molochnaia District Office to, 75–6; and schools, xli
Guenter/Guenther (half-holding for sale), 14, 19–20
Gulich, Peter, 21

Hahn, Evgenii F., von, xxxiv, xxxv, xxxvi–xxxvii, xliii; and agriculture, xxxiv; appointment to Guardianship Committee, xxxiv; at Bergthal, 43; and Bergthal settlement, xxxix; and brick-firing kiln, 60, 78; and D. Cornies, 264; daughter's birth, 420, 433–4; as First Department director, xlvi; Gavel regarding, 462; Haxthausen and, 115; and Hutterites/ Hutterthal, xxxix, 62, 292; and Jewish settlements/*Judenplan*, xliv, 381, 440; in Khortitsa, 282, 365, 383–4; and Khortitsa Central School, xlii; and Khortitsa schoolteachers, 305–6; and Langes, 221–2, 224–5, 233; leaving Guardianship Committee, xlvi; Mecklenburg farm, 467; in Molochnaia, xxxiv, 43; and monetary advance to Hutterthal, 292; and mulberry seed, 515; and Nogais, xliv; observations on appearance of properties, 149; Prinz and, 132; progress in settlements under, 12–13; rumours regarding, 289; and Schoenthal mayoralty, 166, 168; and sericulture, 207–8; son's death, 159; and staking of trees, 388–9; and Stempel, 329; at Tashchenak, 184, 186, 187, 199, 200, 275; and tobacco cutting machine, 434; 1843 tour, 57, 64, 149; 1844 tour, 168, 176, 184, 186, 189, 200; 1845 tour, 268–9, 275, 279, 280; 1846 tour, 365, 380–1, 383–4; 1847 tour, 473–4; and *Unterhaltungsblatt*, 389, 495–6, 533; villager decorum during visits, 57; and Warkentin Affair, xxxiv, xlviii, 150; wife of, 159, 420; and Württemberg settlement, xl

Hahn, Evgenii F., von, correspondence: to Agricultural Society, 69–70, 305–6; to church leaders, 70; to D. Cornies, 583; D. Cornies to, 582–3; Forestry Society to, 109–12; **to JC, 1843**: 76–7, 92–3, 120, 125–6, 138, **1844**: 152, 159, 164, 168, 176, 184, 186, 199, 204, 207, 209–10, 223–4, 233, **1845**: 245–6, 254–5, 275, 306–7, 311, **1846**: 333, 335–6, 340, 343–4, 347–8, 365, 380–1, 383–4, 389–90, 396–7, 400, 411, 420–1, **1847**: 426, 428–9, 443, 446–7, 473–4, 475, 490; **JC to, 1843**: 5–6, 25–6, 28, 42–3, 48–9, 71–2, 113–15, 137, 142–3, **1844**: 152, 154–6, 165, 166–7, 173, 175, 176, 199–200, 214–15, 219–21, 224–7, **1845**: 241, 242–3, 248, 250–1, 252, 256–7, 262–3, 268–9, 280, 285–6, 305–6, 310–11, 312–13, **1846**: 326–7, 332–3, 334–5, 336–7, 342–3, 354–6, 372–3, 379, 381, 382, 384, 389, 393–4, 397–8, 406, 409, 413, **1847**: 427, 433–4, 457, 482–3, 494–5, 512–13, **1848**: 571–2, 577, 581; to Prinz, **1844**: 152–3

hail, 468, 472, 550; insurance, 266

Halbstadt: brandy distillery, 88; craftsman's village beside, xxxii, 8, 353, 378; furnace facility, 8, 9; Hahn in, 280, 383; manufacturing village, 8; medical establishment, 335; schoolteachers, 331. *See also* District Office

Ham (secretary in Molochnaia), 94

Hamm, David, 436; **to JC**, 449

Hamm, Martin, 423–4

Handelszeitung (Commercial newspaper), 173

Harder (Gnadenfeld), 181–2

Harder, Johann (Blumstein), 434; children/stepchildren of, 517

Harms (Schardau): and horse, 519; son of, 526–7

harrows, 160, 211

Hartwiss, Elisabeth: **to JC**, 450; **JC to**, 402

Hartwitz: **JC to**, 370–1

harvests, 104, 136–7; grain, 201, 381, 387, 439, 440, 472; hay, 360, 472; potatoes, 295–6; rye, 411; yield comparisons from Prussian vs. Molochnaia establishments, 542–4

Haubt (money lender to Braun), 78

hawthorn trees, 417, 418

Haxthausen, August von, xxii, 82n20; and copying of Hutterite Brethren chronicles, 249; and Hahn, 115; and JC, xxii; **to JC**, 82, 115, 248–9; **JC to**, 283–4; *Studien ueber die inneren Zustaende, das Volksleben und insbesondere die laendlichen Einrichtungen Russlands* (Studies of the interior conditions in the Russian Empire, the life of its people, and particularly of its rural institutions), 508, 523, 530, 574; visit to Molochnaia, 248, 283

hay: harvest, 192, 199, 339, 360, 472;
Hutterites and, 72; meadows, 3,
71, 111, 416, 419, 423, 460, 466;
scarcity, 365, 381, 464, 468, 507; at
Tashchenak, 319
hearth-sites, arrangement of, 50–1
hedge mustard (*erysimum*), 71
hedges, 116, 301, 406–7, 417, 526, 549;
mulberry, 353, 521, 547, 549
Heese, Heinrich, xlii, 226, 305–6, 447;
to JC, 63; son of, 63
Heidebrecht, Cornelius (Lichtenau),
548
Heidelberg Roman Catholic Church,
145
Hekel (preacher), 64
Hempel, Benjamin (Marienburg), 558
Henke (Pastor), 99, 113, 120, 155, 157
Herr (Doctor), 137; **JC to**, 35
Hesse-Darmstadt, immigrants from,
228
Heubuden, xxxix; congregation,
34n13, 35; teachers [preachers]
sending letters to elders, 149–50.
See also Epp, David (Heubuden)
Heufeld, Dirk, 67
Hiebert (Heubuden), 46
Hildebrand (Altonau schoolteacher),
314
Hildebrand, Heinrich
(Muensterberg), 243
Hildebrandt (Tiegerweide
householder), 521
Hoelbling (on field cultivation), 126
Hoemsen (Tashchenak estate), 536–7
Hoeppner, Jacob, 404, 432–3, 433n2
Hofer, Anna (Tashchenak estate), 536
Hofer, David (Preacher), 90
Hofer, Johann, 128
Hofer, P. (Hutterthal Deputy), 297

Hofer, Paul, 52
Hoffer, Johann (Hutterite), 146–7
Hoge, Peter (Blumstein), 549
Holtfretter (Pastor), 120, 161
Hooge, Heinrich, 107
Horn (tree buyer), 346
horses: breeding station, 93;
counting, 319; demand for, 339;
gelding for sale, 524; Harms and,
519; Hutterite, 56, 57, 90; JC Jr.
and, 522; missing, 208; prices, 192,
194; purchases, 128, 231; sales, 196,
498; stallions, 161, 187, 264, 269; at
Tashchenak, 319; thefts, 260
hospital, 311, 313, 335
house construction, 80; for
apprentices, 302, 385, 431; cost,
293; for Crown Model Plantation,
332, 345–6, 429; fired bricks for,
204; in Halbstadt craftsman's
settlement, 353; for Hutterites, 56,
62, 65–6, 72, 90; in Hutterthal, 206,
293; for Jewish settlement, 448;
for poor, 9; in Sparrau rebuilding,
417–18
household management/skills:
apprentices for, 224; apprentices/
apprenticeships for, 295
houses: beside Bergthal plantation,
51; on Bergthal settlement, xxxix;
bricks for, 65–6; building, 12–13;
chimney frames, 189; design, 260;
gable windows, 206–7; holes in
roofs, 189; inspectors', 166, 260;
in Mariupol, 189; painted gables,
200; plans/estimates/sketches,
60, 83; and side buildings, 42; sod
huts, 128; windows, 148; window
shutters, 189; wood for, 90;
worship services in, 114

Huebert (Heubuden?), 35
Huebert, Abraham (former potato
   supervisor), 49, 141–2
Huebert, Abrah[am] (Neukirch), 548
Huebner (cheese buyer), 265
Huebner: **JC to**, 24, 36, 93
hurricanes, 229
Huter, Jakob, xxxvii
Hutterite Brethren, 81–2; books on,
   248, 249, 283–4
Hutterites, Radishchev community,
   xxxi; about, xxxvii–xxxviii;
   community well for, 8; credit for,
   62; donations for, 54, 55, 56–7,
   90–1, 99, 100; economic conditions,
   15, 16; exemption from taxes, 15;
   harvest, 72; horses, 56, 90; house
   construction, 56, 62, 72, 90, 121–2; JC
   and, xxxvii–xxxix, 15–16; land for,
   209–10; livestock, 91; in Melitopol,
   209–10; poverty, 61, 62; qualities, 61;
   tax exemption for, 61, 62, 167
Hutterthal, xxxviii; cattle in village
   pasture, 52; cattle plague and,
   205–6; elections in, 297; grain
   growth at, 199; hay at, 199; hiring
   out of children/siblings/wards
   in, 235; house construction in,
   65–6, 90, 121–2, 206, 293; land
   lease in, 242; monetary advance
   to, 292; money owing on fences
   in, 489; nightwatchmen in,
   128–9; Pelekh and, 311; rules/
   methods for founding, 170; rye
   in, 496–7; school attendance in,
   412; schoolhouse, 159, 167; school
   reopening, 486; sod huts in, 128;
   travel restrictions in, 129; village
   construction, 62; well digging, 159;
   wheat harvest, 292; wheat in, 294

Hutterthal Village Office: **JC to**,
   1843: 52, 65–6, 128–30, **1844**: 204,
   205–7, 235–6, **1845**: 292, 293, 294,
   297, **1846**: 412
hydrotherapy, 198, 337, 347, 379

Iakovlev, Aleksandr, 538, 570–1
Iamberkekli Elder election, 322
Iamen (friend of Meinecke), 86–7
Imperial Academy, 523
Imperial Agricultural Society, 482;
   and agricultural trainees, 164, 173;
   JC to, 502–4
imperial project, Russian, xxii–xxiii
implements, 160, 161, 294, 309;
   catalogues, 376; on Crown Model
   Plantation, 364; inventory, 319;
   for Kherson, 203; for Kursk,
   211; potato, 219; purchase for
   apprentices, 302; at Tashchenak,
   319. *See also names of specific
   implements*
incomes, annual report (1847), 555
inheritance, 93–4, 96, 445, 558
"Invitation to contribute to the
   construction of a German S.
   Michael's Church and Institution
   for the Poor," 514, 533
Inzov, I.N., xxix, xxxi, xxxiv, 110, 507
Isaac, Abraham (Tiege), 422
Isaac, Franz (Marienthal), 30
Isaac, Jacob, 548; **to JC**, 287
Isaac, Peter, 207
Isaak (Mayor of Tiege), 351
Isaak, Johann, to Agricultural
   Society, 374
Isaak, Kornelius, to Agricultural
   Society, 374
Isaaksohn, Mrs. (Novoberislav),
   529, 538

Iushanle estate, xxiv, xliv;
apprentices on, 205, 224; Birkhan
at, 196; *buran* and, 559; cheese
making at, 41; drawings/views of,
98, 112, 122, 138; Forestry Society
headquartered on, xxvi; fruit trees,
346; Hahn visiting, 383; maize
at, 408; Mirin in service on, 449;
missing horses, 208; mulberry
planted at, 408; nursery, 346; ox
carts from, 208; rye on, 218–19;
tobacco at, 123, 387, 532; wool
from, 163, 188, 281

Jansch (editor of *Unterhaltungsblatt*),
380, 389, 446–7
Jantzen, Abram: **to JC**, 137–8
Jantzen, Mikhail, 318–19
Janz, Jakob, 101, 102
Janzen (Neuteicher Unterfeld), 522
Janzen (Orphans' Administrator in
Petershagen), 527
Janzen, Abraham (Berdiansk), 253
Janzen, Abraham (Tiege silk-reeler
inventor), 391
Janzen, Abraham (re. tree staking),
388–9
Janzen, Cornelius, 41; **to JC**, 405; **JC
to**, 39
Janzen, Daniel, 55; **to JC**, 54, 254,
486; **JC to**, 56–7, 513
Janzen, Dirk (Altonau), 496
Janzen, Eduard, 291
Janzen, Hermann, Agricultural
Society to, 390–1
Janzen, Johann, 553
Jewish settlements/*Judenplan*, xxii,
xliii–xlv, 458; as agriculturalists,
354–5, 421; applications for
director and teacher, 384; cows
for, 453; founding of, 347–8; Gavel
and, 462; German/Mennonites
settled among, 347–8, 354–6,
381, 421, 426, 427, 428, 437, 440,
459; Guardian, 441, 446, 458;
houses for, 428–9, 448; and land
leases, 466; livestock, 466; in
Novoberislav, 428; planting grain
and potatoes, 452–3; ploughs for,
480–1, 493, 497–8, 522; Russian
shepherds, 467; supervision/
leadership and, 355–6
Jews: Nicholas I and, xliii; and
peasants, xliii
Journal of an inspection trip (**JC**),
1846: 356–7

Kadera, Takam, 413
Kaikulak, rye in, 218, 522
Kaiser (Alexanderhilf), son of, 411
Kalitchenko, Gavriel, 419
Kalmyk Tatars, xxix, xxxi
Kalonichenko (assistant to
Gnadenfeld District Chief), 21
Kaloshin (Acting State Counsellor),
187
Kaltschmidt, J.H., 345
Karobot (Melitopol merchant), 537
Kasdorf, Heinrich, 411
Kaznachov, Alexander Ivanovich,
425; **JC to**, 435
Keppen, Peter, xxx; and cattle
plague, 201; and excavations, 121;
and JC, xxx; and JC on Teetzmann
essay, 440; **to JC**, **1847**: 489–90,
508, 529–30, **1848**: 574; **JC to**,
1843: 12–13, 79–80, 135–7, **1844**:
195–6, 198–9, **1845**: 276–7, **1846**:
340, 386–7, **1847**: 438–9, 523; and
Teetzmann's essay, 348

Kerber, Stephan, 111–12, 548

Kerch: stolen wagons in, 133

Kherson: apprentices for, 205; apprentices from, 291; implements for, 203; Jewish settlements in, xliii, xliv, xlv, 347, 355, 426; Village Mayors, 426

Kholodnoi, Ivan, 341

Khortitsa: and Bergthal settlement, xxii; church teachers sentenced to community work, 492; Dnieper flooding, 288–9; Fabre's tour of, 475–6; flooding in, 275; Hahn visiting, 282, 365, 381, 383–4; horse-breeding station in, 93; Mennonites living outside settlements, 394–5; number posts in plantations, 485; obstacles to progress in, 397–8; poverty in, 289; rebuilding of old school, 538; schools/schoolteachers, xlii–xliii, 305–6, 358, 385–6, 513; transfer of supervision to Molochnaia, 377; villages assigned to JC, 440

Khortitsa Agricultural Society, xxi, xlii; **JC to** Chairman, 263

Khortitsa District Office: **JC to**, 298; and settlers in Mariupol, 42

Khortitsa Orphans' Administration, 189–90

Khortitsa School District: JC and, xlviii–xlix

Kichkin, Samoilo, 205

Kiltshik: potato growing in, 27; rotten potatoes in, 49–50, 141–2

Kirilshenko, Peter, 500

Kirschner (Inspector), 245

Kiselev, Pavel D., xxvii, xxxii, xlii, 75, 475; and angora goats, 274; and Fabre's tour of Khortitsa, 475; and Hutterites, xxxviii; and JC, xxii; **JC to**, 61–3; and Jewish settlement/*Judenplan*, xliii, 354–6, 381; in Khortitsa, xlii; and Neu-Halbstadt, xxxii; and Prussian Mennonite immigration, 469–70; and Secret Committee on Peasant Affairs, xxvii; visit to Khortitsa area, 393–4, 396–7; visit to Saratov, 104

Klaasen, Isaac, 30

Klaassen (blacksmith), 471

Klaassen (Tashchenak business secretary), 536

Klaassen, Christian, 9, 10, 503, 504

Klaassen, Christian (Grunau): **JC to**, 487–8

Klaassen, Franz (master blacksmith in Rosenort), 484, 511, 515

Klaassen, Franz (Neukirch), 536

Klaassen, Gerhard (Lindenau): **to JC**, 4

Klaassen, Hermann (Prishib): **JC to**, 212

Klaassen, Jacob (Halbstadt, re. sheep sales), 516

Klaassen, Jacob (master carpenter in Halbstadt): **to JC**, 463; **JC to**, 473, 479, 523–4

Klaassen, Jacob (Neu-Halbstadt), 524

Klaassen, Jakob (master blacksmith in Ladekopp), 493

Klaassen, Johann (Halbstadt cloth manufacturer): on Chinese oil radish, 163; re. crate delivery, 133; death, 586; **to JC**, 6

Klaassen, Johann (re. Lord's Supper non-attendance): **to JC**, 463–4

Klaassen, Johann (re. sheepfarming), 384; **to JC**, 442

Klaassen, Johann (teacher), 381–2, 384; **to JC**, 383
Klassen (Brother), 501
Klassen (Khortitsa): **JC to**, 558
Klassen (tailor of Gnadenfeld), 303
Klassen, Abraham (Grossweide), 552
Klassen, Abraham (Rudnerweide), 552
Klassen, Abram (District Secretary in Bergthal), 454
Kleine Gemeinde, 46–7, 113–14, 120
Klimenko, Trofim, 341, 454
Kliuchko (watchman in Crown Model Plantation), 338
Knelsen, Jacob, 417
Knobloch (employee of JC), 510, 575
Knoerzer (re. wool prices): **JC to**, 275–6
Kobka, Mikhail, 505, 528
Koloshin (accompanying Hahn on travel), 200
Kolossov, Akim, 528–9
Komalenko, Pavel, 329–30
Konrad, Abraham, family, 566
Konshegale watermill, 50
Konstantin Nikolaivich, Archduke, 285–6, 299
Koop, Abraham, 322–3, 422–3
Koshuchar, Samoilo (apprentice), 205
Kovalev (Staff-Doctor), 202
Kovtun, Anton, 205
Kovun (Sladkobolev peasant), 498
Kraft, exile of, 420
Krefeld. *See* Crefeld/Crefeldt
Krei (District Secretary), 85
Kritsch (re. silk), 134–5, 143–4, 158, 163
Krivoruchenko, Hordli, 321
Kroeger, Abraham (master blacksmith), 515

Kroecker, Peter (Deputy, West Prussian Mennonites), 73
Kroeker (re. agreement with Albrecht), 148–9
Kroeker (Mayor of Conteniusfeld), 364
Kroeker, Abram (Tiege), 297
Kroeker, Franz (Conteniusfeld), 303–4
Kroeker, Heinrich, Agricultural Society to, 424
Kroeker, Jacob (Margenau), 411
Kroeker, Jacob (son of Peter), 148
Kroeker, Martin: **JC to**, 534
Kroeker, Peter (Rueckenau), 148
Kronsgarten: beer lease, 486–7, 509; hawthorn in, 418; school, 533–4
Krueger (preacher), 140
Krueger, Franz (Blumstein), 550
Kruschki, 297, 406, 547
Kuk (re. books), 512
Kulinskii, Gavril (apprentice), 316
Kursk: implements for, 159, 211; ploughs, 296
Kurushan Community Sheepfarm, 206
Kurushan river dam, 534
Kuteinikov, Alexei, 406, 474, 478, 479
Kvortzov (Chernigov staff doctor), 370

Labodasho, Anisim, 59
Ladekopp: boundary with Tolmak land, 30; Kroeker-Voth dispute, 424; post road setting trenches, 146; smithy, 493; Village Office, Forestry Society to, 146
Lagori, E., 265, 371, 524; **to JC**, 498–9
Laleoglu, Labit, 79

land: apprentices for landholding/
landkeeping, 107, 118, 122;
importance of landowning,
xxvii–xxviii; landlessness, xxviii,
xxxii, xxxvi, xliii; for Melitopol
Hutterites, 209–10; for Prussian
Mennonites, 210–11, 215–16; for
Reimer's sons, 110–11
Landskrone: Agricultural Society
to Village Office, 376–7, 422;
allotments near, 111; Poetkers in,
491, 517
Landwirtschaftliche Dorfzeitung
(Agricultural village newspaper),
143, 266, 268, 312, 384
Lange (Gnadenfeld), 86
Lange, Friedrich Wilhelm, 90, 101–2,
105–6, 118–19, 221–2, 224–5, 233;
JC to, 450–1
Lange, Henrietta, 101–2, 105–6,
118–19, 221–2, 224–5, 233
Lange, Julius: **to JC**, 151–2
Lange, W. (Gnadenfeld; re. Nogai
debts), 490
Lange, Wilhelm: contract with
Bengs, 367; **to JC**, 101–2, 105–6
Large Flemish Congregation, xxv
Larion (Master Mason), 200, 228
latticework, 93
Learned Committee, Ministry of
State Domains, xxx; **JC to**, 569
LeDonne, John, xxiii
Lehmann (cloth dyer), 6
Leidlitz (re. lattice railings), 75
Leonard (re. rapeseed), 144
Leshinskaia, Anna, 122
Letvinenko, Joseph, 95
Levchenko (re. sheep buying), 202–3
Levshin, Aleksei: and Baumann, 506,
513; **JC to**, 210–11, 215–16, 250, 317;

journey through Molochnaia, 191,
441; and map of land divisions,
389, 393; and Molokans, 197; and
Prussian Mennonite settlement
near St. Petersburg, 216–17; and
reeler, 389, 393; and sericulture,
246; travel through Stempel's
settlements, 191, 200; visit to Graff,
475; wagon ordered, 451, 454
Lichtenau: broken trees in, 147;
teachers [preachers] sending
letters to Heubuden Elders, 149–50
Lichtfelde, teachers in, 314–15
Liebenau Village Office: **JC to**, 403–4
lifters, 160, 161, 211, 219, 309
Lindenau: Hahn in, 383; trees in, 147
linseed, 44, 162
Lisovik, Naum A., 38–9
Liubenko, Ivan, 224
livestock: barn feeding, 353; barn
for Crown Model Plantation, 364;
breeding, 353; *buran* and, 559;
demand for, 339; expenses/profits
from, 541; fodder for, 253, 316,
365, 381; foot-and-mouth disease,
553; grazing on community
pastures, 378; hailstorms and, 472;
Hutterite, 91; Jewish settlers and,
466; losses, 91; Nogais and, 53;
potatoes for, 131; prices, 436.
See also cattle; goats; sheep
locusts, 72, 104, 136, 193, 196
Loebe, William: "On the Treatment
of Silkworms," 384
Loewen, Abram, 147
Loewen, David, 411
Loewen, Dietrich, 553
Loewen, Franz, 303
Loewen, Isaac, 383
Loewen, Johann, 553

Loewen, Peter (re. German settlers in Jewish settlements), 467
Loewen, Peter (Gnadenheim; re. sericulture), 550
Loewen, Wilhelm, 89, 91–2, 204
lucerne, 192
Ludwigs, G. (Danzig), 558
Luetke, Katharina, 558
Lukovich (debtor to JC Jr.), 536
Lushenko, Akim, 308
Lushin, J., 262–3, 366
Lutheran Church, xl, 1 n15; and Separatists, 329. *See also* Evangelical Lutheran Church
Lviv settlement, 482–3, 495

madder, 191; seed, 123–4
madia seed, 41
Main Evangelical Bible Committee: Molochnaia Mennonite Bible Society to, 323–4
maize, 121; in Berdiansk/Melitopol/ Dneprov districts, 218, 308; Italian, 317–18, 408; Nogais and, 232, 454; peasants and, 341; quality, 317–18, 408; quantity, 317–18, 408; supervisors for, 341, 342
Mambet (Nogai), 318–19
maple trees, 415, 563
maps, 387; of land divisions, 389, 393; of Russia, 438
Margenau: schoolteachers, 314–15; teachers in, 314–15; teachers [preachers] sending letters to Heubuden Elders, 149–50; Village Office, Agricultural Society to, 148–9; weedy plantations in, 298
Margenau congregation: Poetker couple, 491, 516–17; H. Wiens and, 177

Marienthal: Stempel insulted in, 363; Village Office, Agricultural Society to, 373
Mariupol: beverage leases to Jews in, 9; brickworks, 64, 66–7; forestry plantations at, 14–15; guarantors for Mennonites, 50; houses in, 189; JC visiting, 36; Khortitsa Mennonite settlers in, 42–3; land surveying in, 8; provision of wagon in, 83; Prussian foreign families in, 267; side buildings in, 42; Stempel and, 200; tree plantations in, 502–4
Mariupol District Office: **JC to**, 57, 115–17; Secretary, 94–5, 98–9
markers, 160, 161, 211, 219, 308–9, 531–2
Marks (estate owner), 404, 438
Martchenko, Karp, 154
Martenenko, Gavrilo (apprentice), 205
Martens (Schoensee), 527
Martens (Tashchenak housekeeper), 536
Martens (Village Office Deputy), 139–40
Martens, F. (son of Wilhelm): **to JC**, 153–4, 337
Martens, F[ranz]: **to JC**, 447
Martens, Jacob (Bergthal), 357
Martens, Jacob (re. Lindenau trees), Forestry Society to, 147
Martens, Jacob (son of Wilhelm), 76; Agricultural Society to, 557; on condition of fields, 375; **to JC**, 176–7; and silk reeling, 313, 327, 526; to Zamero, 217–18
Martens, Jacob (Tiegenhagen), 117, 487; **JC to**, 41
Martens, Johann, 303

Martens, Peter (Waldheim), 303
Martens, Mrs. Wilhelm, 352–3; **JC to**, 334
Martens, Wilhelm, 375–6; brandy distribution, xxiv; District Office to, 87–8; donation by heirs for hospital, 311; and Gerlitzke estate, 177; illness, 153–4, 153n1; **to JC**, 101; Milinovich and, 4; partnership with JC, xxiv; poem about, 375–6; and Presnitzer Baths, 153–4, 157; suicide, xlv, 279, 352–3, 375–6
Martens, Wilhelm, family/heirs, 334–5, 352–3; agreement with Peter Schmidt heirs, 334; donation for hospital, 311, 313, 334–5; donation for new school building, 335
Martens, Willms, 353
masons, 33, 51, 319, 356
Mathias/Mathies, Isaac: J. Blueher with, 185, 194, 272, 283; **to JC**, 388, 502, 532–3; Molochnaia Mennonite Bible Society to, 324; wife of, 533
Mathies, Abraham (Berdiansk), 240, 241
Mathies, Abraham (Rudnerweide), 86
Matthias, Philipp (Berdiansk): **to JC**, 89; **JC to**, 534–5
Mayors: and brandy distillery, 88; of Conteniusfeld, 364; duties, 465; *Gebiet*, l–li n15; incitement of rebellion against, 364; salaries, 426; in Schoenthal, 165, 166, 168, 187; and schools, 326
Meinecke, Friedrich A., 80, 194–5; **to JC**, 86–7, 173–4
Meinecke, Maria (née Vogel), 174

Melitopol: Archduke Konstantin's visit to, 286; Crown Prince Konstantin travelling to, 286; implements in, 219; maize in, 444; post office, 369; potatoes in, 24–5, 28–9, 33, 38, 183, 218, 264, 309, 341, 444; warehouse, 181
Membet (Nogai in JC's service), 35
Memorsky's grammar, 575
Mennonite Brethren, xl, 483, 490
Mennonites: and agricultural societies, xxv; and agriculture, xxiv; and education, xli; independence in state relationship, xlvii; *Judenplan* and, xliv–xlv (*see also under* Jewish settlements/*Judenplan*); living outside settlements/villages, 395–6, 432; and military service, xxiv; as model, xxiv, xxvi–xxvii, xxxv, xliii, xliv, xlviii, 354–5; and state, xxiv, xxv; and supervisors, xliv. *See also* Prussian Mennonite immigrants
Mestmacher, Baron von, 413
Meyerdorff, Baron von, 249
Mikhailo (watchman), 415
Mikhailov/Mikhailovka: Mikhailov Starschina, 525; potatoes in, 131; rye in, 218, 411
Milinovich, Dedato, 4, 6–7; **JC to**, 4, 23
Miliutin, Nikolai, xxii
millet, 137
mills, 50, 110, 179, 182, 210, 404
Ministry of Internal Affairs, xxvi, xlviii n1
Ministry of State Domains: and apprenticeships, xxi–xxii; crop experimentation by, xxii; and

economic reforms, xlvi; and
Guardianship Committee, xxxiv–
xxxv, xlviii n1; and Hutterites,
159; JC and, xxi–xxii, xxxv,
xxxvi–xxxvii; **JC to, 1843**: 79,
83–4, **1845**: 316, **1846**: 407, 408,
1847: 426; *Journal of the Ministry
of State Domains*, xlvi, 12; Kiselev
and, xxvii; potato promotion, xxii.
See also Agriculture Department,
Ministry of State Domains;
Forestry Department, Ministry of
State Domains; Kiselev, Pavel D.
Mirin, Ivan, 449
Mitridat (steamboat), 86
Modalov, Bultrak (Elder in Burkut),
31, 32
modernization: agricultural
machinery and, xxxvi; agricultural
societies and, xxv, xxxiv; JC and,
xlvii; Mennonite settlement and,
xxiii; privileges/Privilegium and,
xxii; Russian, xxv
Mogilev: new settlement in, 40;
Prussian Mennonites in, 53, 73,
103, 127, 164, 217, 244, 250, 305,
469, 470; Prussian settlers in, 70
Molenar, Rev., 47
Molochnaia District Office. *See*
District Office
Molochnaia Mennonite Bible Society.
See Bible Society
Molochnaia Mennonite settlement:
about, xxxii, xxxiii; and economic
development, xlvii; as model, 69,
355; Molochnaia region, xxiii; as
"oasis," xxiv, xxvii, xlvi; trees in,
xxvi. *See also* Mennonites
Molokans, xxxi, 82, 574; dam
building, 443–4; District

Supervisor, 197; emigration to
Georgia, 197, 277, 439
money disputes, 356–7. *See also*
debtors
Moravian Brethren, xxxi
Mory (Chairman in Sarepta), 87
mounders, 211, 219, 308–9
Muehlhausen (plantation owner),
25
Mueller, Justina, 128
Mueller, Zacharias (Hutterthal), 128
Muensterberg: Crown Prince
Konstantin travelling through,
286; trees/hedges planted in,
504, 550. *See also* Neumann, Jacob
(Muensterberg)
Mulbali (Burkut), 32
mulberry trees, 547, 548; at Bergthal,
116; from Crimea, 572; at Crown
Model Plantation, 408, 572; as
fencing, 508; hedges, 301, 353, 406,
521, 547, 549; at Iushanle estate,
408; Nogais and, 154; projections
for, 405; seedlings in orchards,
407; seeds, 121, 338–9, 491, 515; for
sericulture, 223, 276, 339

Nachtigal, David, 303
Nachtigal, Heinrich, 303
Nasargulov, Dschungase, 341
Negresko, Peter, 95, 390, 446
Nembetov, Kokoi, 261–2
Neufeld (Elder), 46–7
Neufeld, Dirk, 144
Neufeld, Gerhard: J. Doerksen as
stepson, 287; **to JC**, 54–5
Neufeld, Heinrich (Liebenau), 30
Neufeld, Isaak (Tiege), 524
Neufeld, Johann (brother-in-law
Johann's son), 448, 461

Neufeld, Johann (brother-in-law of JC), 76, 101, 325, 448; brandy lease, 461; **to JC**, 290–1, 303–4, 418, 421–2, 452; **JC to**, 530

Neufeld, Johann (District Officer in Halbstadt), 378

Neufeld, Johann (neighbour of JC), 535

Neufeld, Johann (Orekhov), 289

Neufeld, Johann (Rosenberg), daughter of, 263

Neufeld, Peter, 502; **to JC**, 59–60, 331; Molochnaia Mennonite Bible Society to, 349

Neufeld, Peter (church teacher), 586

Neufeld, Peter (Ohrloff; Director of Main Bible Committee), 323, 324

Neufeld, Peter (Petershagen), 550

Neufeldt (Prussian Mennonite), 35

Neufeldt, Gerhard (apprentice secretary), 8

Neu-Halbstadt, creation of, xxxii

Neuhoffnung: church, 155, 161; exile of Kraft, 420; foreign church leader for, 299; Hahn's visit to, 64; Pietists joining Evangelical Lutheran Church in, 72; preacher for church, 155, 157–8; spiritual leader in, 96–7, 99–100; tax payments in, 220–1

Neukirch: schoolteachers in, 314–15; setting trenches at, 496

Neumann, Jacob (Muensterberg), 167, 175, 387, 389, 438; and apprentices, 224; **to JC**, 539–44; **JC to**, 539

Neumann, Jacob (re. relative in Prussia): **JC to**, 517

Neumann, Peter (Muensterberg), 167, 175, 224

New Russian Steamboat Commission (Berdiansk), 86

new settlements: rules/methods for founding, 170

Nicholas I, Tsar, xlvi; death, xxvii; and Decembrist Revolt, xxvi; and Jews, xliii; and *Judenplan*, 421; and peasantry, xxii, xxvii, xxix, xxxi; and Privilegium, xxii, xxx–xxxi; tour of southern Russia, 201; and uniformity, xlvii

Niederstaedter, Ferd., 510, 575

nightwatchmen, 128–9

Nikkel, Erdmann, 526, 570

Nizhnii Novgorod market, 45

Nogai Tatars, xxiii; as apprentices, 285, 301, 302; and apprenticeship, 209, 262; Archduke Konstantin's visit and, 286; *buran* and, 576; as carters/drivers, 79, 399, 444; and cattle plague, 192, 194, 196, 201, 231, 360; and cholera, 520; "civilization" of, xxxi, xxxv; crimes among, 155; crop failures, 137; and Crown Model Plantation, 331; and excavations, 135; field cultivation, 439; and forestry, xxxv; JC and, xxxv, xliv, 27–8; and *Judenplan*, xliv; livestock, 53, 277; and maize, 232, 454; and Mennonite model, xxxv; and mosque in Akkerman, 23; move to Caucasus, 66; and potatoes, xliv, 27, 80, 122, 137, 261–2, 277, 454; and sheep, 273, 277, 373–4, 413, 439, 490, 502, 576; sheep buying, 11, 53–4, 123; sheep leasing, 63; and sheep plague, 318–19; and cholera, 507; tree cultivation, 285; and trees, 213; village

administration selections, 31–2;
and wheat, 277; and wheat theft,
241, 242; wool sales, 53–4
None but Saints (Urry), xlvii
Nordmann, Professor, 307, 313, 327
Norman (re. silkworms), 26
Novitzkii (cheesemaker), 39; **JC to**, 41
Novoaleksandrovka (later
Melitopol): post office, 18;
potatoes in, 131
Novoberislav: Jewish settlement in,
428, 459, 466–7; Overseer, **JC to**,
466–7
Novogrigorievka, maize at, 218
Novonikolaievka, cattle plague at,
205–6
nurseries: at Crown Model
Plantation, 429; at Iushanle, 346;
seed, 429; tree, 547, 548

oats, 121, 192, 277; golden, 557, 582;
harrowing, 569; prices, 339
Ohrloff: cemetery, xlv; contract
with JC, 180; Cornies family in,
xxiv; cottage plots for, 180; exact
sketch of, 423; plantings in, 550;
schoolteachers in, 314–15; tree
planting along roads, 497, 550–1;
windbreak in, 301
Ohrloff School, 388; Martens heirs'
donation to, 335; New Testaments
in, 117; Society, to Gerhard Enns,
315–16; teachers, 314–15
Ohrloff Village Office: Agricultural
Society to, 237, 423; **JC to**, 325–6
oil radish seed, 20, 163, 195
"On the Treatment of Silkworms"
(Loebe), 384
O'Neill, Kelly, xxiii
Onkianikova, Evdokia, 307–8

Opakov, Durmambet, 366
Oppenland (Rosenfeld), 86
orchards, 110; apprentices/
apprenticeships for, 253, 291, 416;
on Bergthal settlement, xxxix;
broomgrass in, 382; caterpillars
in, 411–12; fencing of, 30; growing
interest in cultivation of, 191;
harvests, 80; numbers of trees in,
547; progress, 353; surveying of,
405; at Terpenie, 198; weeder for,
159. *See also* fruit trees
Orekh District Chief, 202
Orlov-Denisov estate, 227
orphans. *See* guardianship
Orthodox Church fasts, 321
Oterbai (Nogai), 524
oxen, 443; herding, 281; ox carts, 208;
remains of horns, 404

painting: buildings, 182, 375; fences,
149, 182, 200, 375; house gables,
200; for preservation of wood, 182
Pale of Settlement, xliii
Palokay (at Tashchenak), 113
Panasena, Maksim, 366
Pankratz, Jacob, 549
Pankratz, Peter, 279
Papkov (seller of angora goats), 274
Parkani settlement, silk in, 238
Parttani, sericulture in, 77
passes, 332–3, 356, 486, 489, 529, 558
Pastwa: Agricultural Society to
Village Mayor, 267; householder's
treatment of servant girl in,
491–2; and Jewish settlement, 355;
Landwirtschaftliche Dorfzeitung
in, 268; protective planting at, 9;
schoolteachers, 331; tree-planting
record book, 493

Pauls (at Tashchenak), 537

Pauls, Daniel (Sparrau), 417

Pauls, Widow (Prangenau), 411

Pavlo (re. Tashchenak estate), 576, 578–9

peach grafting shoots, 444

pear trees, 109, 192, 406, 510, 526, 547

peasants, xxii; as apprentices, 168–9, 175, 178, 205, 209, 291; awards for, 317–18; and Baumann's composition on field cultivation, 513; and cattle plague, 201, 231, 360; excavations by, 523, 529–30; and forestry, xxxv; Jews and, xliii; and maize, 317–18, 341; Mennonite model and, xliv; Nicholas I and, xxvii; passes, 284; and potatoes, xxii, xxxv, xliv, 28–9, 33, 154, 169, 231–2, 317–18, 341; Prussian foreign families in Mariupol as, 267; reform of, xxvii, xxix, xxxi; and summer rye, 522; and threshing stones, 84; and tree cultivation, 178; and tree plantations, 229

Pefler (cloth dyer), 6

Peitzmerdorf, little old woman from, 573–4

Pelekh, Khariton (Inspector): and Bengs brothers' passes, 278–9; complaints against, 289, 311; and Hahn visit, 184; and Hutterthal, 311; Janzen visiting, 389; JC and, 220n3; lack of trust in, 220–1; and missing shipment, 14; J. Neufeld and, 289; new position vs. dismissal of, 333; and Pietists, 220, 232, 581; and Regier debt to Milinovich, 7; and Stempel administering Berdiansk villages,

232; Stempel compared with, 311; and tax payments, 221; transfer to Odesa, 220n3

Penner (building mill for P. Fast), 210

Penner (schoolteacher in Khortitsa), 513

Penner, Claas (Margenau), 207

Penner, Gerhard, 8, 213, 298, 476; **JC to**, 94–5, 98–9; wife of, 94

Penner, Jacob, xxxiii

Penner, Johann (Pastwa), 520

Penner, Johann (Prangenau), 579

Penner, Peter (Ohrloff), 325–6

Penner, Peter (Prangenau), 549

Penner, Widow (sister of Jacob Enns), 567

Penner, Wilhelm, 94, 98

Perekop District: harvest in, 271; maize in, 308, 454; potatoes in, 261–2, 308, 318, 344, 443, 454; seed potatoes bought for, 271

Pernitzky, Joseph (Neuhoff), 31

Peters: **JC to**, 462

Peters (preacher of Friedensdorf), 247

Peters (shopkeeper in Gnadenheim), 526

Peters, Aron (Altahir), 128

Peters, Aron (Rueckenau), 550

Peters, Johann (Khortitsa District), 580–1

Peters couple (Landskrone), 422

Petershagen: churches in, 46; school, 10, 139–40

Peterson: **JC to**, 228–9

Petrenko, Semen (apprentice), 11, 38

Petrov, Mikhail, 281

Pfifky (Berdiansk District Secretary), 141

Pietism: about, 1 n15; in Berdiansk, 141, 154; conservative Mennonites and, xxv; Evangelical Lutheran pastor as spiritual leader, 92, 96–7, 99–100, 113–14; Flemish congregation and, xxv; JC and, 219–20; Pelekh and, 220, 232; Pietists joining Evangelical Lutheran Church, 72; quietism vs., xxxiii; sensibility, xxiv; and Separatists, 329; spiritual leaders, 97, 99–100, 120, 141, 154, 298–9; Stempel and, 221; and Württemberg Colony, xl

pilfering, 580–1

pine seed, 234–5, 246, 440

plane trees, 495

plantations. *See* forest-tree plantations

Plenert, Heinrich, 487

Plenert, Wilhelm, 445

ploughing: in Bergthal plantation, 116–17; at Crown Model Plantation, 293–4; drought and, 293–4; fallow fields, 359; in four-field system, 252; at Jewish settlement, 452–3; for potato growing, 130

ploughs: for Aleksandria Crown Model Farm, 86; building by Stobbe, 479–80, 492; cost, 160; deep, 557; furrow, 402; German, 155, 159, 168; for Jewish settlers, 493, 497–8; for Kursk, 211, 296; Little Russian, 522; payment for, 493; potato, 162; prices, 522; requirements for, 479–80; ridging, 226; Witte, 479, 480–1, 496, 522

plum trees, 24, 192, 547

Poetker couple (Landskrone), 491, 517

Pommer (agricultural trainee), 164

Ponkiratov, Kupriian, 366

Ponrovskii (nobleman), 290

poplar trees, 116

Pordenau: fruit trees in, 526; teachers [preachers] sending letters to Heubuden Elders, 149–50

postal offices, 368, 369

potatoes/potato cultivation: abuses regarding, 27; annual report (1847), 552; apprentices/ apprenticeships for, 262; in Berdiansk District, 264, 444; crown, 32, 37, 122, 141, 218, 308; cultivation from seed, 343; in Dneprov, 33, 38, 264, 309; droughts and, 308; on fallow fields, 357; fertilization, 3; harvest, 193, 295–6, 443; implements, 24–5, 219; JC and, xxxv; at Jewish settlement, 452–3; for livestock, 131; in Melitopol, 33, 38, 264, 309, 444; ministerial, 131–2, 183; Ministry of State Domains and, xxii; mounders, 21–2; Nogais and, xliv, 27, 80, 122, 137, 261–2, 277, 454; outlay for hiring in cultivation of, 25; peasants and, xxii, xxxv, xliv, 28–9, 33, 154, 169, 317–18, 341; planting, 36, 169; ploughs, 162; prices, 121, 308; quantity, 80; records, 492; rotted, 27, 49–50, 56, 141–2; seed, 231, 262, 271, 345, 409, 444; seeding, 29, 345; storage, 7; supervisors for, xliv, 25, 230, 341, 342, 344; in tree plantations, 117; village records of seeded, 183; yields, 24–5

Potemkin, Major, 402, 445

poverty: community support, 465; flooding and, 289; of Hutterite Brethren, 82; of Hutterites, 61, 62;

of Prussian foreign families in
Mariupol, 267
Presnitzer Baths, Silesia, 153–4, 157
printer's ink, 191
Prinz, Friedrich: dismissal of,
142–3; and JC, xl; and Pietists,
72, 120, 142–3; request for release
from office, 138, 152; salary, 152,
172; and Separatists, 329; and
Württemberg settlement, xl
Prinz, Friedrich, correspondence:
Hahn's Directive to, 152–3; **to JC,
1843**: 64–5, 93–4, 99–100, 132, 141,
1844: 155, 161–2, 172, **1845**: 298–9,
1846: 388–9; **JC to, 1843**: 96–7,
1844: 157–8, 232–3
Pristupka (Melitopol peasant), 160
privileges/Privilegium, xxiv,
xxvi–xxvii, l n11; and direct
service vs. modelling, xlv;
JC and, xxx–xxxi; *Judenplan*
and, xliv–xlv; and leadership
vs. modelling, xliv, xlviii;
Mennonites as overprivileged,
421; and Mennonites living
outside settlements, 395; and
modernization, xxii; and religious
freedom, xxvii; uniformity vs.,
xxxi; Warkentin and, xxx–xxxi
Prokofii (shepherd), 442
Prussian Mennonite immigrants,
40; advice on immigration, 517;
directives for settlement, 137; on
Doukhobor land, 278; drawing
back from group settlement, 215;
flooding, and emigration of, 210;
land for, 127, 210–11, 215–16;
land purchases by, 470–1; list of
those wishing to emigrate from
Prussia, 469–70; in Mogilev, 53,
70, 73, 103, 127, 164, 217, 244, 250,
305, 469, 470; numbers interested
in emigration from Prussia, 244;
passes for, 332–3; professionals vs.
tradesmen as, 175; qualities of, 217;
regulations, 176; request for list
of, 470; settlement on farms vs. in
communities, 58; in St. Petersburg
area, 216–17, 244, 304–5; in
Tavrida, 278; in Vitebsk, 53, 70, 73,
103, 127, 164, 217, 244, 250, 305,
469, 470; in Warkentin Affair, 74–5
pseudoplatanus (tree), 26
punishments: administered by
Agricultural Society (1847), 546; in
Akhil Chodgiga, 66; annual report
(1847), 555–6; of church teachers
[preachers], 477; of Dik for insults
to Stempel, 363; for incitement of
rebellion against Conteniusfeld
Mayor, 364; for release of workers,
525; of Ruoff, 153, 161. *See also*
crimes/misdemeanours

quietism, xxvii, xxxiii, xl
Quiring (Conteniusfeld rebellion
incitement), 364
Quiring, Franz, ordered to Ohrloff,
322–3
Quiring, Franz (Conteniusfeld), Dik
as debtor to, 509, 530
Quiring, Heinrich (Schoenthal), 509
Quiring, Widow, 528; Regier as
debtor to, 500

Rabulo, Fedor, 205, 224
Radel (former Director of Third
Department), 386
Radi Kanakens (merchandizer),
153, 157

Radishchev Mennonites. *See*
Hutterites, Radishchev
community
Rahn, Johann, 73
Rahn, Peter, 73
Raico (sericulture), 361, 362, 384
Raikova, Efronsinia, 492
railings, cast iron, 371
Raiskii (Judge), 241, 255–6
Raiskii (Supervisor), 197
Ramahan (Elder in Akhil Chodgiga),
66
Ramakanov, Mrat, 318
rapeseed, 5, 144
Ratzlaff, Benjamin, 57, 90, 96, 101,
105, 118; **to JC**, 55; **JC to**, 6–7, 56,
190, 221–2
Rauch (Doctor in Kherson), 490, 523,
530
Rayko (silk producer), 77
Reading Association Library, 277
Regehr (District Chairman), 353
Regehr, Abram (Heubuden), 103
Regehr, Johann, 528
Regehr, Peter (formerly in
Fuerstenau, later in Berdiansk),
488–9
Regehr, Peter: **JC to**, 384–5
Regier (Elder in former Warkentin
congregation), 46, 74, 75
Regier, Abraham (Heubuden),
34n13, 35
Regier, Aron (Margenau), 207
Regier, B. (treadmill owner), 182
Regier, Elias (Sparrau), 303
Regier, Isaac, 411
Regier, Johann (District Mayor),
xxxi, xxxiii
Regier, Johann (Rudnerweide), 4,
6–7, 23, 500, 552

Regier, Mikh., 30
Regier, Peter (Berkiansk), 530
Regier, Peter (Deputy, West Prussian
Mennonites), 73
Regier, Peter (Elder in Tiegenhagen),
70
Reimer (Elder), 46
Reimer (re. Felstenthal estate): P.
Wiebe for **JC to**, 535
Reimer (gardener), 436
Reimer (re. Geyer), 273–4
Reimer (Kronsgarten): **JC to**, 202–3
Reimer (secretary in Molochnaia), 94
Reimer, Abraham (Wernersdorf), 303
Reimer, Abram (Margenau), 509
Reimer, David, 110–11, 112, 183–4, 190
Reimer, Jacob: **JC to**, 414
Reimer, Jacob, Jr., 318–19
Reimer, Johann (Fuerstenwerder
Village Mayor), 515, 570
Reimer, Johann (Waldheim), 550
Reimer, Peter (Secretary), 88, 184
Rempel (Halbstadt, re. travel to
Prussia), 448
Rempel (re. lease of tavern), 85
Rempel, Abram, 190
Rempel, Gerhard (Tiegerweide), 488
Rempel, Peter (Berdiansk), 104
Rempel, Peter (Rosenthal), 404–5
Rempel, Wilhelm, Jr. (Bergthal), 357
Remy, Wilhelm: **to JC**, 513–14; **JC to**,
533
Renpenning, Peter (Lindenau), 550
resident permits, 335
Reuoff (re. Berdiansk Pietists), 120
rice, 126
Richert (Franzthal), 511
Richert, Jacob, 303
Riediger (re. notifications of JC's
death), 583

Riediger, Jacob: **to JC**, 54–5, 434

Riediger, Martin (schoolteacher), 101, 207, 315–16; **to JC**, 502; **JC to**, 415; to School Society directors, 117

Riesen, M.: **to JC**, 52–3

Riesenkampf (brother of Rauch), 490, 523

Riller (Inspector), 516

Rodenko, Vassily (crown peasant), 525, 527

rollers, 160, 161, 289–90, 323

Rosen, Fedor F. von, 22, 34, 44, 121, 429, 444, 471; **to JC, 1843**: 50, 127, **1846**: 411; **JC to, 1843**: 7, 11, 14, 21–2, 23, 24–5, 27–9, 31–2, 33, 34, 38–9, 45, 53–4, 56, 58, 66, 75, 123–4, 131–2, 139, **1844**: 154, 160, 161, 165–6, 169, 178–9, 181, 183, 185–7, 188, 190, 197, 201–2, 203, 209, 211, 218–19, 229–30, 231–2, **1845**: 242, 243, 252–3, 261–2, 264, 265, 267, 270, 271, 273, 285, 288, 289–90, 292, 293–4, 295–6, 305, 308–9, 310, 316, 317–18, **1846**: 322, 323, 329–30, 331, 332, 337–8, 341, 342, 344–7, 354, 364, 366, 367, 370, 371, 385, 397, 399, 408–9, 412–13, 419, **1847**: 429–31, 435, 436, 443–6, 451, 453–4, **1848**: 560, 561–4, 572

Rosenort: blacksmithing in, 484; schoolteachers in, 314–15; tree planting along roads, 497, 550–1

Rosenstrauch (Prussian consul), 82

Roshaliev, Chamann, 451

Roshinskii, Johann, 504

Roslavets, Viktor: **to JC**, 118; **JC to**, 107, 122, 197–8, 349

Royko (sericulture), 343–4

Rudnerweide: Langes and, 222; potatoes in, 552; protective planting at, 9; retail shop in, 185; wall-primers in, 298

Rueckel, Johann Georg: **to JC**, 325

Rueckenau: schoolteachers in, 314–15; tree planting along roads, 497; Village Office, Agricultural Society to, 423–4

Ruoff, punishment of, 153, 161

Russian Bible Society, xxv, xxxiii

Russian language: German dictionary, 345; Prussian Mennonites and, 58; in schools, 238; for Secretary of Swedish District, 577

Russian language learning, 274; apprentices and, 234, 416; Franz and, 288, 306; P. Neufeld and, 60; in schools, 237–8, 386

Russification, xlviii

rye, 466, 468, 496–7; flour, 370, 450; harvest, 411; prices, 121, 339, 445; summer, 124, 218–19, 408–9, 522–3; winter, xxxviii

Saitchenko, Trofim, 366

salt locations, 160

Saratov: Bureau of Settlements, 428; Fadeev relinquishing position in, 300, 382, 560; Hutterthal as model for settlements in, 170; Kiselev in, 104; new settlements in, 170

Sarepta: barley at, 491; cattle disease in, 45; Community Chairman, **JC to**, 495–6, 557; finished products market in, 45; mulberries at, 491; *Unterhaltungsblatt* for, 483, 490, 495–6, 533; winter wheat at, 491

Savchenko, Fedor, 25, 141

Sawatzky (preacher of Friedensdorf), 247

Sawatzky, Franz, 51

Schapovakenko, Grigori, 154

Schellenberg, Anton: **JC to**, 528–9

Schellenberg, David (Tiege), 128

Schierling, Martin (Blumstein), 548

Schkurko, Pavel (apprentice), 307–8

Schlachta, Astrid von, xxxviii

Schlangendorf, sketch of cultivated land, 496

Schlatter, Daniel, Phillip Wiebe to, 586

Schmalchinskii, Jacob, 263

Schmidt, Heinrich, 553

Schmidt, Johann, 356

Schmidt, Nikolai: **JC to**, 49

Schmidt, Peter, 586; son, 586

Schmidt, Peter (Elder in Waldheim), 90

Schmidt, Peter (Franzthal), 398, 400

Schmidt, Peter, heirs of, 334

Schmit, R.: **to JC**, 139–40

Schoenke (Tiegerweide householder), 521

Schoensee: passes for Russian servants in, 486; roads, 30; trees broken in, 498

Schoenthal/Schönthal, xxxix; Strumer family in, 213; Village Mayor, 165, 166, 168, 187

Schönfeld, xxxix; community sheepfarm, 176; fullholding transfer in, 190; impregnation of J. Neufeld's daughter, 263

School Society: Contract, 351; JC and, xxvi

schools: "A," 266–7; ages of children, 295; Agricultural Society and, xli, 9; attendance, 294–5, 325, 326, 412, 511, 526, 533–4; Bible stories in, 297; book for primary teaching, 531; construction, 115; curricula, xli, 315; directives, 300; division into districts, xli; Doukhobor, 115; Elders and, 70; entrance permissions, 388; "General Rules in the Instruction and Treatment of School Children," xli–xlii; Guardianship Committee and, xli; in Hutterthal, 159, 167; JC and, 336; in Khortitsa, 358, 385–6, 538; mixed classes in, 314; new, at Tiegenhagen, 512; New Testaments in, 117; opening of new, xxxi; Petershagen, 10, 139–40; punishment in, 237; quality, 69, 70; rebuilding of old, 538; religion and, xli; Russian language in, 238, 386; six divisions, 315; under Society's direction, 9; Village Mayors and, 326; wall-primers in, 230, 252, 258–9, 298, 300, 403, 473, 478, 479, 499, 500, 513, 525. *See also* education

schoolteachers: accusations against, 139–40, 150, 315–16, 325; Agricultural Society to, 313–15; children's behaviour towards, 237; contracts, 207; and curricula, 315; dismissal of, 314; division into six school divisions, 315; in Ekaterinoslav, 306; Gnadenfeld, 306; Halbstadt School, 331; health, and release of, 415; hiring, 105; instruction in use of wall-primers, 513; instruction methods, 313–14, 315, 325; instructions for, 385–6; in Khortitsa, 305–6, 513; leadership, 313–15; Mayors and, 326; Pastwa, 331; qualities, 69, 70; and Russian language, 238; salaries, 207; in

Sarata settlement, 410; student, 54–5; Wiebe as substitute for Riediger, 26

Schroeder, Johann, 509

Schroeder, Peter (Grossweide), 372

Schroeder, Peter (Neutich), 128

Schroeder, Peter, et al.: **JC to**, 127–8

Schulz-Roechling, F.W., 533; **to JC**, 582

Schuneev, Ivan (apprentice), 38

Secret Committee on Peasant Affairs. *See* Ministry of State Domains

Seliutshka, Mikhail, 296

Semenov, Mikhail, 369, 471

Separatists, 299, 329

sericulture/silk: acceptance of, 276; annual report (1847), 550; apprentices/apprenticeships for, 262; Beindorf and, 47; butterfly eggs, 327; carters, 311; cocoons, 77, 199, 208, 212, 223, 231, 238, 327, 361, 362, 372, 538, 571; craftsman from Rhine, 9; demand, 510; doubling, 158, 163, 214; drying room, 362; facility, 246; increase in, 12–13, 17, 198–9, 215, 353, 387; Janzen's standing reeler, 390–1; from JC to Blueher, 570–1; Kritsch and, 134–5, 163; Levshin and, 246; Loebe's article on, 384; manufacturing of silk, 17, 71–2, 76, 77, 143–4; markets for, 384–5; mill, 143–4, 163; noxious emissions from, 362; organza, 143, 157, 327; in Parttani, 77; prices, 143, 158, 199, 203, 223, 231, 238, 306–7, 387, 401, 510; production rate, 163; progress in, 192, 276, 439; promotion, 339; purchases for Moscow, 384–5; quality, 158, 203, 214, 217, 223, 238, 306, 327; quantity, 212, 217, 276, 327, 372, 374, 507; Raico's booklet about, 384; reeler hiring costs, 310–11; reelers, 524; reeling, 20, 158, 163, 203, 208, 213–14, 238, 306–7; reeling facility, 214–15, 223–4, 231, 253, 310, 327, 343–4, 353, 361–2; reeling machines, 313, 327, 372–3, 374, 466; remuneration for reelers, 306–7; sales, 67, 134–5, 158, 243; samples for assessment, 156; sent to Blueher, 538; silkworm eggs, 26, 182, 212; silkworm fodder, 460; silkworm starvation, 276; silkworms, 212–13, 339, 353; spinning, 246; Tauchnitz and, 47; Terrier booklet on reeling, 20; twisting, 327; upright reeler, 460; weavers/weaving, 17, 72; A. Wiebe and, 43n14; Zamero and, 207–8, 223, 231, 246, 253, 262

Sericulture Association, 362

servants: annual numbers of hirings, 553–4; female, 433, 559; hiring regulations, 477; householders' treatment of, 491–2; passes, 284, 486; religious practices, 321; runaway, 236, 373, 511

Settlement Commission, xxiv

Shablikin, Emelian (driver from Veseloi), 133, 134

Shamanov, Salakai (apprentice), 451

Sharsto (master brickmaker), 64

Shatochin, Nikolai, 366

sheep: apprentices for breeding of, 263, 474; *buran* and, 559, 575–6; "Cammeral," 462; community farms, 8, 488; dispersal of rams, 8, 9; English, 239; ewes, 290, 436, 490, 523; farm supervisors, 247,

269; JC and, xxiv, xxxii, 227, 228, 234; lambs, 206, 227; leasing, 63; Nogai purchases, 11, 53–4, 123, 413, 490; Nogais and, 273, 277, 373–4, 439, 502, 576; numbers, 22; other livestock in competition for pasturage with, 539; pelts, 348; plague (*Raende*) and, 206, 239, 318–19; prices, 227, 231, 253, 339; rams, 202–3, 227, 290; sales, 234, 516; Saxony buying trip, xxv; shears, 247, 259, 282–3, 368, 575; shepherds, 442, 467; Stempel and, 227–8; supervision, 81, 206; wethers, 228, 516

Shelechina, Matrona, 308

Sherbakov (owner of goats), 174

Sherbina (debtor to JC), 367

Sheremetev (debtor to Hildebrand), 243

Shigun, Stepan, 366

Shirovskii (inspector), 516

Shkabinov, Fedor, 122

Shuet, elections in, 341

Shuiut Dzhuret, village administration selection, 31–2

Sidorenkova, Evdokia, 496

Siebert, Heinrich, 532

Siemens (District Chairman in Bergthal): **JC to**, 578

Siemens, Claas, 326

Siemens, Claas (son of Claas), 326

Siemens, Cornelius, son of, 237

Siemens, Franz (son of Martin), 189–90

Siemens, Johann (Khortitsa Agricultural Society Chairman), xlii, 225–6, 393, 398, 403, 405, 425; **to JC, 1845**: 282, 290, **1846**: 414–15, **1847**: 425, 432–3, 445, 451–2, 454,

460–1, 475–6, 477; **JC to, 1846**: 394–5, 402–3

Siemens, Martin (of Khortitsa), 189–90

Siemens, P. (re. angora goats), 451–2

Siemens, Peter (Kronsgarten), 445

Siemens, Peter (re. Prussian Mennonite settlements), 40; **to JC**, 70–1, 103

Silvander, Friedrich, 232–3; **JC to**, 245

Simarenko, Osip, 416

Sineib, Jacob: **to JC**, 31

single persons, hiring out, 403

Skelechina, Matrona (apprentice), 295

smallpox vaccination, 509

Smechka, Konstantin, 486

Smissen, Jacob van der, 437; sons of, 467

snakes, 419; cult, 195

snowstorms, 559, 575–6

Society for Sheep Breeding in Southern Russia, 493–4

Society to Improve the School System, instructions for Khortitsa Community School, 385–6

soil preparation: for plantations, 109; for tobacco, 256–7

Somarskii, Filon, 21

Sonderegger (District Secretary become editor of *Unterhaltungsblatt*), 447, 490, 495

Sparrau: fruit trees in, 548; plantation, 109; rebuilding of village, 417–18; Village Office, Forestry Society to, 109

spelt, 158

spindle worms, 460, 550

Spulenko, Ivan (apprentice), 205

Stahl, Dorius, 128, 204
Stahl, Mathias, 128
Stahl, Moses, 204
Stamalee (Nogai), 374
Steen (Langefuhr), 462
Steinfeld, Johann, 433
Stempel, Carl: about, 32n12; and
    Berdiansk Pietists, 120; goods
    stored with Riediger, 434; Hahn
    and, 329; health, 328; house, 328;
    and Hutterite settlers, 72; insulted
    in Marienthal, 363; and Jewish
    settlement/*Judenplan*, 440; and
    Pietism, 72, 221; and Prussian
    settlers in Mariupol, 200, 267; and
    Schoenthal mayoralty, 165, 166,
    168; visit to Ohrloff, 26; and wheat
    theft by Absaut, 241–2
Stempel, Carl, correspondence: **to
    JC, 1843:** 37, 39–40, 41–2, 43, 60,
    65, 71, 78–9, 85, **1847:** 493, 497–8;
    JC to, 32–3, **1843:** 50–2, 64, 66–7,
    83, **1844:** 166, 187, 191, 200–1, 213,
    227–8, 232, 234, **1845:** 240, 241–2,
    255–6, 260–1, 270–1, 278–9, 280,
    1846: 328–9, 367, **1847:** 452–3,
    456–7, 492, 496, 515
Stepanenko, Pavel, 412–13
Steven, Christian: Blueher and,
    286; estate for sale, 240, 247, 259,
    261, 269, 286; and grave mounds,
    12; silk sent to Kritsch, 134; and
    tobacco cultivation, 207; and C.
    Wiens's apprentices, 211
Steven, Christian, correspondence: **JC
    to, 1843:** 3, 11, 13–14, 20, 38, 58, 59,
    95, 121–2, 130–1, **1844:** 156, 158–9,
    162, 167, 168–9, 174–5, 191–3, 205,
    212–13, 224, 231, 234, **1845:** 253,
    262, 274, 275, 285, 286, 291, 295,

301–2, 307–8, 317, **1846:** 338–40,
    346, 408, 409, 416, 418–19, **1847:**
    434–5, 444, 446, 460, 466, 522, 524–5
Stobbe (curator for Heese), 63
Stobbe, Jacob (master carpenter),
    459; contract with JC, 479–80
Stobbe, Peter (Schardau), 516, 524
Stobbe, Peter (Tashchenak), 91–2; **to
    JC,** 89, 318–19
Strakhov, Semen (apprentice), 38
Striemer, Christoph (Schoenthal
    fullholder), 328
Strumer family, 213
*Studien ueber die inneren Zustaende,
    das Volksleben und insbesondere die
    laendlichen Einrichtungen Russlands*
    (Studies of the interior conditions
    in the Russian Empire, the life of
    its people, and particularly of its
    rural institutions) (Haxthausen),
    508, 523, 530, 574
Sudermann, Abraham: visit to
    Prussia, 250, 254–5, 263–4
Sudermann, Hermann: and
    Berdiansk plantation, 273;
    mother of, 263; as supervisor of
    Crown Model Plantation, 338;
    and Tambovka Model Crown
    Plantation, 290; visit to Prussia,
    250, 254–5, 263–4
Sudermann, Hermann,
    correspondence: **to JC, 1845:**
    263–4; **JC to, 1846:** 352, 358, 365,
    376, 399–400, 415, 416, **1847:** 456,
    459–60, 484–5, 505, 509–10, 525,
    527, 528, 545, **1848:** 579–80
Sudermann, Jacob, 526
Sukkau, Hermann, 52
Sukkau, Johann (Blumenort), 13, 58,
    95, 148, 167, 553; and apprentices,

175, 211, 224; contract with JC,
480–1; **JC to**, 350, 539
Sulin (Corporal), 474
Sunderland, Willard, xxii–xxiii
Sviridenko, Emelian, 260
Swedish settlers/settlements: at
Bereslav, 474; District Secretary,
482, 560, 577; Guardianship
Committee and, 486; Hahn to
visit, 474; JC commission with,
213; projected visit to, 336;
Silvander's visit to, 245; sketch of
cultivated land, 496
Szerbin, brother of Zimen, 442
Szerbin, Zimen, 442

Tappes Grammatik, 117
Tarasenko (Melitopol peasant), 160
Tarasenko, Semen, 205
Tascherbanov, Smail, 526
Tashchenak estate, 319; administrator
on, 414, 418; apprentices at, 122,
320, 416, 419; *buran* and, 559;
carpenters on, 319, 578; Fast as
administrator for, 414; Hahn at,
184, 186, 187, 199, 269, 275; hiring
of staff for JC Jr.'s absence, 536–7;
Hutterite Brethren near, 82; JC
Jr. on, 81; JC Jr.'s instructions for,
578–9; Lammas wheat at, 409;
maize on, 408; memorandum
to employees, 319–20; orchard
apprentice, 416; reports regarding,
576–7; rye on, 124, 218; spring
cultivation/seeding, 578–9; wool,
163, 188, 281, 369
Tauchnitz (Leipzig), 47
Tavrida: apprentices from, 291;
Jewish settlements in, 347;
Judenplan villages in, xliii; State

Domains Bureau, **JC to**, 141–2,
476, 522–3
Tchetter, Paul, 204
Teek, Johann, 526
Teetzmann, "About the South
Russian Steppes, etc.," 348, 386–7,
440
Tehrmann (Landskrone), 30–1
Teichgrew (schoolteacher in
Khortitsa), 513
Teichgrew, Anna, 376
Teichgrew, David (Rueckenau), 509,
524; son of, 509, 524
Teichgrew, Heinrich, 17–18, 207
Tenbaiev, Metalip, 154, 213
Tenbaiev, Temir, 288
Tenbine, Timev, 341
Terpenie: apprentice village in, 301;
bricks, 346, 459; hydrotherapy at,
198; springs at, 197, 198, 337, 347
Terrier: booklet on silk reeling, 20
Tessmann, Jacob, 261
Thiessen, Bernhard (father of
Therese): **JC to**, 568–9
Thiessen, Franz, 133
Thiessen, Heinrich, 501, 526; wife
of, 526
Thiessen, Theresa (later Cornies). *See*
Cornies, Theresa (née Thiessen; JC
Jr.'s wife)
Third Department, Ministry of State
Domains: **JC to**, 124–5
Thomsen, Gerhard, 549
threshing: machines, 186, 366;
rollers, 557; stones, 83–4, 160, 211
"Thriving Agriculture Is Our
Fatherland's Wealth," 569
throat illness, 89, 91–2
Thun, Dirk, xxxiv, 515
Thun, Peter, 515

Tiege: cottager site lease, 351; tree planting along roads, 497, 550–1

Tiege school: lease of cottager site, 351; schoolteachers, 314–15

Tiegenhagen: school, 512; silk reeling in, 526; wall-primers in, 298

Tiegerwand, teachers in, 314–15

Tiegerweide: rioting in, 521; schoolteachers in, 314–15

Tielov (works in Radi Kanakens), 153, 157

Tiessen (preacher), 140

Tiessen, Abraham (Fuerstenau), 505, 511–12; wife of, 511–12

tiles: makers, 112–13, 417; roof, 192, 353, 417, 439, 459

Timoshnichenko, Ivan (also Badak), 11

Tiushchev, Dusenbe, 371

tobacco: annual report (1847), 551; cigars, 457–8; cutting machine, 413, 434; directions for cultivation, 245, 252, 256–7; expert on, 340, 342–3; German directions for cultivation, 207; on Iushanle estate, 123, 242, 387, 532; markets, 338; prices, 338; quality, 130–1, 343, 439, 458; quantity, 338; report on, 407; samples, 416; spread of cultivation, 343, 387; Syrian seeds, 316; *Unterhaltungsblatt* on cultivation of, 333, 336, 359–60, 361; varieties, 123, 130–1, 242, 276, 336, 426, 532; wagon for trading, 79

Toews, Abram, xxxi, 10, 76, 88, 278, 381, 575; **to JC**, 159–60, 183–4, 288–9

Toews, Elizabeth, 536

Toews, Franz, 376

Toews, Heinrich, 90, 552; **to JC**, 100

Toews, Peter, xxxiii, xxxiv, 550, 553

Tokmak: Elder in, 498; Hahn travelling through, 275; situation in, 498–9; tree plantations in, 441

Tokmak River watermill, 110

Tolstoi (Count), 269

Tolstonog (Judge), 241–2, 255–6

Tovstanog (Judge from Berdiansk), 285–6

trades/crafts: annual report (1847), 554; craftsmen in Berdiansk, 252–3; **JC to** tradesmen of Halbstadt, 378–9; requirements for tradesmen of Halbstadt, 378–9; village at Halbstadt, xxxii, 8, 353, 378

treadmills, 579

tree cultivation: apprentices for, 84, 178, 188, 190, 205, 271, 285, 291, 316; Nogais and, 285; peasants and, 178. *See also* forest trees; fruit trees

tree plantations. *See* forest-tree plantations; orchards

tree planting(s): along roads, 353, 497, 500; along road to Crown Model Plantation, 331; along streets, 550–1; annual report (1847), 547–51; at community sheepfarms, 8; furrows along sides, 500; records/record books, 376, 493

Treksel (Ohrloff), 529, 538

Trembetov, Kokei/Kokoi, 25, 344, 454

trenches: setting, 146, 154, 301, 407, 497; in tree plantations, 117

Tulemishov (Burkut), 32

Tulemissov, Shrakai, 265

Tulmisone, Barakai, 371

turnip seed, 173–4

Tushchevskii (surveyor), 8, 159–60

Ulkanbeskele: Komalenko and, 329–30; seed potatoes bought for, 271

Ulkovits (inn owner in Odesa), 265

Unger (schoolteacher), 237, 325–6

Unrau, Cornelius (Deputy), 356

Unruh, Benjamin, 486, 580; **JC to**, 580

Unterhaltungsblatt für deutsche Ansiedler im südlichen Rußland, xlvi, 333, 336, 337, 359–61, 365, 379, 380, 389, 446–7, 483, 490, 495, 533; JC's obituary published in, xlvi; **JC to**, 359–61, 533; to Molochnaia District Office, 499; for Sarepta, 495–6

Urry, James, *None but Saints*, xlvii

Uslich, Prokofii (apprentice), 11

Varishkin (owner of stallion), 264

Vasilenko, Kondrat, 511

Vavk, Demian (apprentice), 528

vegetables, 193; harvest, 194; planting, 130. *See also* potatoes; *and names of other vegetables*

Venger, Natalia, xlvii

Verkhovskii, Trofim, 318

Village Mayors. *See* Mayors

Village Offices: building construction for, 7; Forestry Society and, xxviii; hiring out of children/single persons, 403; and Mennonites living outside settlements, 396; overviews, 57; records to be sent to Agricultural Society, 406–7; report template, 464; summary of duties, 465; year-end accounting sessions in, 309–10

Village Offices, correspondence: Agricultural Society to, **1843**: 147, 149, **1844**: 182, **1845**: 268, 284, 294–5, 309–10, **1846**: 373, 375, 388, 391, 392, 406–7, **1847**: 464; District Office to, 149; Forestry Society to, 146; **JC to**, **1843**: 123, 148, **1845**: 266–7, **1846**: 382, 395–6, 403, 421

villages: Archduke Konstantin's visit to, 286; inspection by Kaloshin, 187; size, 505–6

violins, 392

Vitebsk: new settlement in, 40; Prussian Mennonites in, 53, 70, 73, 103, 127, 164, 217, 244, 250, 305, 469, 470

viticulture, 226–7; grapevines, 103; wine, 425

Volhynia, Waldheim Mennonites from, 251, 251n2, 453

Vorontsov (Count), 81, 382, 452, 561

Voroshchev (re. Golubov), 445–6

Voroshchishev, Larion, 310

Voth, Alexander: **to JC**, 483

Voth, Andreas (assistant to Jacob Fast), 16

Voth, Andreas (Pastwa schoolteacher), 331; Agricultural Society to, 237–8; P. Wiebe [for JC] to, 531

Voth, David: **to JC**, 132

Voth, Gerhard, 549

Voth, Johann (schoolteacher), 526

Voth, Peter (Friedensdorf), 424

Voth, Theodor, 501

wagons, 454; broken axles, 419–20, 468–9; German, 441, 451; iron on, 469, 484; for JC Jr.'s travel home from Prussia, 537; loans of, 243; quality, 511; repair, 515; stolen, 133; for travel to Prussia, 573

Walde (Ladekopp householder), 521

Waldheim: about, 251n2; allotments near, 111; congregational acceptance of H. Lange, 118–20; disunity within congregation, 247; ditches around hearth-sites, 30; settlers from Volhynia in, 251, 253, 254

Waldheim Village Office Declaration, 289

Waldner, Christian (Hutterthal Mayor), 56, 57, 297

Waldner, Johann: **to JC**, 145

Waldner, Joseph, 128

Wall (overseer in Tiegerweide), 488

Wall (Prangenau), 298

Wall, Abram (Lichtfelde), daughter of, 528

Wall, Cornelius, 515; Agricultural Society to, 20

Wall, Franz (Alexanderthal), 303

Wall, Jacob (Rueckenau administrator), 423–4

Wall, Jacob (Schönfeld), 524

Wall, Johann (Deputy, West Prussian Mennonites), 73

Wall, Johann (Schoensee): **JC to**, 470–1

Wall, Johann (re. M. Wieb): **to JC**, 368

Walter, Jacob (re. pasturage), 52

Walther, Jacob (Elder), 90

Walther, Maria, 128

Walther, Tobias, 147

Walther, Zacharias, 128

Warkentin (Elder), and Schmit, 140

Warkentin, Abram (Tiege), 528

Warkentin, David, 422

Warkentin, Diedrich, Agricultural Society to, 300

Warkentin, Dirk (Elder in Petershagen), 90

Warkentin, Jacob: Fadeev and, xxvii; and *Gebietsamt*, xxv; and *Gebietsamt* elections, xxx; Hahn and, 150; JC and, xxv, xxvi; and Large Flemish Congregation, xxv; and Privilegium, xxx–xxxi; and punishment of members, 46; A. Regier on treatment of, 34n13, 35; removal from office, 74; and School Society, xxv; and Warkentin Affair, xxxiii–xxxiv

Warkentin, Jacob (Conteniusfeld, re. brandy smuggling), 303, 304

Warkentin, Johann (Blumstein), 553

Warkentin, Johann (Rosenort), 410–11

Warkentin Affair, xxi, xxxiii–xxxiv, xlviii, 46–7, 74–5

Warkentin congregation, 34n13, 35, 74, 437

Warkentin Party, xlvi

watchman: for Crown Model Plantation, 296; nightwatchmen, 128–9

water cisterns, 399

water springs at Terpenie, 197, 198, 337, 347

watermills, 50, 110

Wedel (re. plough purchasing), 452–3, 496, 497

Wedel, Cornelius (Lugansk Foundry): **to JC**, 489; **JC to**, 494

Wedel, Cornelius (son of Cornelius), 287, 291, 489

Wedel, Heinrich (son of Cornelius), 489

Wedel, Peter (Alexanderwohl Elder), 90, 323; **JC to**, 221–2, 279

Wedel, Peter (Waldheim Elder), 511; **to JC**, 247

weeders, garden, 196, 265, 310, 384, 397

wells, 294, 429, 430, 431

well thermometers, 79

Werner (Berdiansk District Secretary): **JC to**, 577

Werner, Friedrich (re. Swedish District Secretary): **JC to**, 482, 560

Wernersdorf: smuggled brandy in, 303, 304; watermill, 110

wheat, 468; Arnautka, 72, 136, 292, 294; Hirka, 292, 294; in Hutterthal, 292, 294; Lammas, 409; Nogais and, 277; prices, 121, 231, 253, 339, 436, 440; sales, 43, 44; theft, 241, 242, 255–6; threshing, 206; winter, 491

Wieb, Heinrich, 368

Wieb, Margaretha (daughter of Heinrich), 368

Wiebe (silk-reeler), 20, 306, 307

Wiebe, Abraham (Fuerstenwerder), 321

Wiebe, Abraham/Abram (of Rudnerweide, as Berdiansk merchant), xxxii, 25, 43n14, 353, 519; **to JC**, 43–4, 171, 257–8

Wiebe, Agatha (Elbing), 432

Wiebe, Aron (Elbing), 432, 574

Wiebe, Aron (Muehlendam), 450

Wiebe, Claas (Conteniusfeld), 107–8

Wiebe, Claas (Halbstadt, guardian of Justina Boldt), 527

Wiebe, Cornelius (brother of Phillip), 516

Wiebe, Dietrich: **to JC**, 507

Wiebe, Dirk (Lichtfelde), 421–2

Wiebe, Franz, 370

Wiebe, Gerhard (Danzig), 432

Wiebe, Heinrich (Pastwa), 356–7

Wiebe, Jacob (Elbing), 448, 574; **JC to**, 481–2, 520–1

Wiebe, Jacob (Liebenau): **JC to**, 539

Wiebe, Jacob (schoolteacher, substitute for Riediger), 26, 258

Wiebe, Jacob (re. treadmill), 579

Wiebe, Johann (church teacher, re. Gnadenfeld congregation), 222

Wiebe, Johann (Elbing), 437, 456

Wiebe, Johann (Freienhuben), 520, 521; **to JC**, 514–15; **JC to**, 519–20

Wiebe, Johann (Tiegenhagen, guardian of Boldt children), 511, 527

Wiebe, Peter (Andreev), 21

Wiebe, Peter (Conteniusfeld), 303–4

Wiebe, Phillip: to Blueher, 324, 585–6; and brother Cornelius, 516; and comparison of two agricultural establishments, 539; to Doehring, 491; JC Jr. to, 54; **JC to**, 573–4; on JC's death, 585, 586; on JC's funeral, 585–6; re. JC travelling to JC Jr.'s wedding, 564, 565; marriage, 410, 440; in Prussia for JC Jr.'s wedding, 537; repayment of money owing to Hahn, 583; to D. Schlatter, 586; travelling to JC Jr.'s wedding, 536, 581

Wiebe family (Klakkendorff), 450

Wiebe family (Lichtfelde), 103

Wieler (schoolteacher at Kronsgarten), 516

Wiens, Cornelius, 13, 58, 95, 348; **JC to**, 211, 390, 539

Wiens, Heinrich (Blumenort blacksmith), 476, 515; **to JC**, 380; **JC to**, 539

Wiens, Heinrich (Gnadenheim Elder), 74, 90, 177, 247, 420, 420n4, 450–1; Forestry Society to, 32

Wiens, Isaac (Altonau), 52, 167, 175, 224, 230, 549; **JC to**, 539
Wiens, Johann (Schoenfeld), 356–7
Wiens, Johann (son of Thomas), 315–16
Wiens, Thomas, 315–16
Wiens, Widow (Ohrloff), 553
Wiens congregation, 437
Wienz, Franz, 477
Wigand (re. Hutterite Brethren), 81
wild olive trees, 86, 411, 547, 549
Wilke (gardener), 24, 93; wife's death, 559
Wilke, August: **to JC**, 77–8
Willms, Heinrich, 101
Willms, Peter, 148
willow trees, 406, 547
Wilmsen, Gustav, 370
wine, 425, 435
Witte, Hermann: **to JC**, 451, 454–5; **JC to**, 441
Witte, Sergei, li n20
Wochenblatt (weekly newspaper), 525
Woelcke, Johann, 139
Woerbel (widow from Waldheim), 511
Wolf, Herman (re. hydropathy), 346–7
Wolf, Julius (re. bookbinding and water cures), 337, 379
Wollman/Wollmann, Andreas, 242, 297; sons of, 499–500, 519
Wollmann, Franz (son of Andreas), 519
Wollmann, Jacob (son of Andreas), 519
wood: demand for, 22; preservation by painting, 182; storage, 130
wool: advance payment for, 253; cartage/transportation of, 184, 185, 369, 400–1; on consignment, 59, 280–1, 358, 471–2; demand for, 188–9, 276, 312, 358, 466; from Iushanle estate, 281; long-haired, 239, 246, 265; from pelts, 163; quality, 163, 171, 178, 227, 239, 246, 259, 281, 312, 369; sales, 44–5, 53–4, 64, 81, 171, 172, 182, 188, 215; Spanish, 5, 33–4, 36, 44, 67–8; from Tashchenak, 281, 369; travelling speculators in, 312; washed, 5, 44, 67, 259, 358, 471–2; Zigay, 239
Wool Improvement Society/Sheep Society, xxv, xxvi
wool prices, xxxii, 60; **1843**: 5, 34, 44–5, 48, 121, **1844**: 163, 178, 188–9, 192, 193, 194, 196, **1845**: 259, 265, 269, 272, 275–6, 312, **1846**: 348, 367–8, **1847**: 436, 472, 477, **1848**: 571; deposits and, 239
wool purchases, 47–8, 67–8, 342, 367–8; by JC for Blueher, 22, 172, 178, 193–4, 269–70, 272, 281, 282, 369, 400–1, 472
Wurms, Herm., 22
Württemberg settlement, xxii, xl, 220n3
Wurz, Christian, 537
Wüst, Eduard Hugo Otto, xl, 299

Zacharias (potential Tashchenak administrator), 418
Zamero (expert on silk reeling), 207–8, 223, 246, 253, 262; **JC to**, 213–14; Society Members to, 217–18
Zimmerman, Heinrich, 452; **JC to**, 461–2
Zokurinkova, Marina, 236

TSARIST AND SOVIET MENNONITE STUDIES

General Editor: Harvey L. Dyck, Department of History, University of Toronto

A Mennonite in Russia: The Diaries of Jacob D. Epp, 1851–1880. Edited and translated by Harvey L. Dyck.

Ingrid I. Epp and Harvey L. Dyck, *The Peter J. Braun Russian Mennonite Archive, 1803–1920: A Research Guide.*

David G. Rempel with Cornelia Rempel Carlson, *A Mennonite Family in Tsarist Russia and the Soviet Union, 1789–1923.*

John R. Staples, *Cross-Cultural Encounters on the Ukrainian Steppe: Settling the Molochna Basin, 1783–1861.*

Anne Konrad, *Red Quarter Moon: A Search for Family in the Shadow of Stalin.*

Jacob A. Neufeld, *Path of Thorns: Soviet Mennonite Life under Communist and Nazi Rule.* Edited, with an introduction and analysis, by Harvey L. Dyck. Translated from the German by Harvey L. Dyck and Sarah Dyck.

Transformation on the Southern Ukrainian Steppe: The Letters and Papers of Johann Cornies, Volume 1: 1812–1835. Translated by Ingrid I. Epp and edited by Harvey L. Dyck, Ingrid I. Epp, and John R. Staples.

Leonard G. Friesen, ed., *Minority Report: Mennonite Identities in Imperial Russia and Soviet Ukraine Reconsidered, 1789–1945.*

Transformation on the Southern Ukrainian Steppe: The Letters and Papers of Johann Cornies, Volume 2: 1836–1842. Translated by Ingrid I. Epp and edited by Harvey L. Dyck, Ingrid I. Epp, and John R. Staples.

Leonard G. Friesen, *Mennonites in the Russian Empire and the Soviet Union: Through Much Tribulation.*

John R. Staples, *Johann Cornies, the Mennonites, and Russian Colonialism in Southern Ukraine.*
Transformation on the Southern Ukrainian Steppe: The Letters and Papers of Johann Cornies, Volume 3: 1843–1848. Translated by Ingrid I. Epp and edited by Harvey L. Dyck, Ingrid I. Epp, and John R. Staples.